Critical
Reading
and Writing
Across
the Disciplines

Critical
Reading
and Writing
Across
❧ the Disciplines ❧

Cyndia Susan Clegg

Pepperdine University

Holt, Rinehart and Winston, Inc.
New York   Chicago   San Francisco
Philadelphia   Montreal   Toronto
London   Sydney   Tokyo

Cover photograph by Michael Wilson

Library of Congress Cataloging-in-Publication Data

Clegg, Cyndia Susan.
  Critical reading and writing across the disciplines.

  Includes index.
  1. College readers.   2. English language—Rhetoric.
3. Interdisciplinary approach in education.   I. Title.
PE1417.C627   1988   808'.0427   87-8800

ISBN 0-03-006554-2

8 9 0 1   090   9 8 7 6 5 4 3 2

Holt, Rinehart and Winston, Inc.
The Dryden Press
Saunders College Publishing

ACKNOWLEDGMENTS

"Pornography and Censorship: The Argument Rages On, 25 Years After 'Tropic of
Cancer'" by Jack Smith. Copyright © 1986, *Los Angeles Times.* Reprinted by permission.
"Essays on Science and Education" by Thomas Henry Huxley.
"Attitudes and Science," from *The Game of Science,* 4th Edition by G. McCain and
E. Segal. Copyright © 1969, 1973, 1977, 1982 by Wadsworth, Inc. Reprinted by permission
of Brooks/Cole Publishing Company, Monterey, California 93940.
"The Sense of Human Dignity," from *Science and Human Values* by Jacob Bronowski. ©
1956 by Jacob Bronowski. Renewed 1984 by Rita Bronowski. Reprinted by permission of
Julian Messner.
"The Universe and Dr. Einstein," Chapter 5, including illustration from *The Universe and*

To my daughter
Caitlin Wheeler

PREFACE

Critical Reading and Writing Across the Disciplines grew out of my experiences teaching interdisciplinary human values and science and literature courses after teaching college composition for many years. In writing courses students often feel they have nothing to write about. In other courses writing topics grow naturally from the course material, but students encounter difficulty formulating arguments and strategies consistent with a discipline's conventions. These discoveries persuaded me that composition courses better prepare students for the college curriculum's writing demands when they introduce the writing approaches and subject matter from the various disciplines, and when they encourage students to think critically about the materials presented. A course like this gives students "something to say" and an approach to their topic. This book is designed for such a course.

Here you will find a combined text-anthology. The text presents chapters on process-centered writing and critical reading and a chapter on drawing upon reading for writing. The anthology contains essays by recognized authorities in a format encouraging students' critical responses. The readings provide models of informed thinking and effective writing, which study significant concerns in the natural and social sciences, history, and the arts and literature. The subject matter these essays address increases a student's understanding of the various disciplines' methods, at the same time that the essays stimulate a critical response. The essays appear in a format that

- informs readers of the assumptions governing a discipline's inquiry
- reflects important work within a discipline
- reveals dialogue and critical controversy.

Using This Book

The three chapters that compromise Part I prepare students for the demanding reading and writing required by the college curriculum. The first chapter, "Writing: An Introduction," opens with concrete suggestions for developing a positive attitude toward writing and overcoming writer's block. Then it takes students through each step of the writing process using timely illustrations and relevant exercises. The second chapter on critical reading shows first how to sharpen information-seeking reading and then how to read critically for an author's assumptions, arguments, tone, and persuasive devices. The final chapter indicates ways that reading informs and shapes writing: as information and topic source, as model, and as subject. These initial chapters enable students to work effectively with the essays and writing topics in the book's second part—the anthology.

The readings in the anthology are grouped in four sections, each representing a principal category of academic inquiry—the natural sciences, the social sciences, history, and the arts and literature. In each section the initial chapter introduces methodology, the second chapter presents actual studies in the discipline, and the final chapter contains essays that respond critically to the previous chapter's studies or the discipline's governing assumptions.

The disciplines appear in the text in an order indicating the increasing diversity of the governing assumptions. (The scientific method exists; *the* critical method in literary and art studies does not.) Consideration of a discipline's increasing reliance on other disciplines' governing assumptions also informs this order. For example, science's quest for objectivity and "fact" influences historical and literary inquiry. History and even psychology influence art studies. The collection begins with the natural sciences. This unit contains essays on physics and biology—clearly sciences—as well as psychobiology and anthropology, disciplines with affinities to the social sciences. A social science unit including essays on economics, sociology, psychology, and social anthropology follows the natural sciences. Some social science essays rely on scientific methodology, a few do not, and some disagree on their governing assumptions. Because some historians consider themselves social scientists and some consider themselves humanists, history stands alone as the third unit. In the last section on the arts and literature, essays define the critical task as objective study, interpretation, or evaluation. Other essays employ varying critical strategies to elucidate art, and the final essays query the relative merits of subjectivity and objectivity in art studies.

Three pedagogical aids accompany the essays. Preceding each essay is a detailed summary intended to make often difficult concepts more accessible. The questions following each essay focus on the three areas introduced in part one of the text: reading for information, recognizing writing strategies, and critical thinking and writing. Questions in the last section are intended as a stimulus both for class discussion and for writing. At the end of each discipline are topics for further research, synthesis, and writing.

The word "critical" in this book's title indicates the two principal criteria for selection of the readings. The essays are critical to a student's understanding of the different intellectual enterprises in the academic curriculum, and they reflect and encourage critical responses. They also meet the criteria most instructors use in evaluating writing: intelligence, clarity, completeness, conciseness, and vitality. The variety of the essays in style, length, and complexity meets the needs of diverse teaching approaches. Thematic and rhetorical tables of contents also address these concerns. Finally, the selections seek to engage students who represent social, ethnic, and intellectual diversity.

Of particular help were the comments and suggestions of the following individuals: Nancy Bent, Ithaca College; Shirley Ann Curtis, Polk Community College; Mary Dickson, Trinity College of Vermont; Julie Farrar, Purdue University; Steve Flaherty, De Vry Institute of Technology; Robert Forman, St. John's University; Lyle Morgan, Pittsburg State University; Jean Reynolds, Polk Community College; Mark Rollins, Ohio University; Susan Sharpe, Northern Virginia Community College; Keith Tandy, Moorhead State University; Robert Wess, Southern Tech; and Kate Morgan, Tracy O'Neill, Herman Makler, and Paula Cousin at Holt, Rinehart and Winston, Inc.

CONTENTS

Rhetorical
Table of Contents

Exposition by Analysis of Cause/Effect Relationships

Argument from Analysis

Argument from Evidence

Argument from Definition

Critical
Reading
and Writing
Across
⬊ the Disciplines ⬋

PART ONE

Critical
Writing
⬊and Reading⬋

Chapter *1*
Writing:
An Introduction

Whenever we write, we approach the task from the context of our prior writing experiences. This context is built upon the customary ways in which we use writing and the attitudes we have formed toward our limitations and our successes. Most of us use writing to communicate information to others—in letters to friends and family, in papers to colleagues, employers, and teachers. Some of us write to affect others—to change a Congressman's vote, to alter community opinion about a shelter for our city's homeless people, to persuade a prospective employer of our worth. Others write in journals and diaries or on miscellaneous scraps of paper to sort out personal feelings and responses to daily life. Writing allows some of us to express our creativity and unique perceptions about our experiences. For others, writing is a necessary evil—an assignment to complete, an expectation to meet, a job to be done.

How we feel about writing depends on the ease with which we write, the success our writing has met, and the criticism we anticipate—either from our readers or ourselves. Effective writers exert control over their writing contexts by recognizing their attitudes toward writing; by having an approach for writing—a time, a place, a purpose, and a process; by writing often; and by evaluating their own writing. This chapter's three sections—Attitudes and Writing, Preparing to Write, and The Writing Process—will help you master your writing contexts.

ATTITUDES AND WRITING

Being a Writer

If you responded today to a question on a census form or an application asking your occupation, you would very likely reply "student." At this point in your academic career, you know precisely what being a student requires—attending class, taking notes, reading texts, studying, participating in labs, and taking examinations. Your image alters little as you change from one student task to the next; you still see yourself as a student. If, however, you enroll in a dance class, an acting class, or a music performance class, you become a dancer, an actor, or a cellist. A writing class requires that you become a writer. All the lectures you hear about writing and all the materials you read telling you how to write mean nothing unless you regard yourself as a writer and do what writers do—write. To see yourself as a writer and to be able to write on a regular basis requires eliminating misconceptions about writing and replacing them with a clear picture of writers writing.

Misconceptions about Writing

Whenever I sit down to an empty pad of narrow-lined paper, black fountain pen in hand, I engage in what I call my "procrastination fantasy." Surely, if I wait a little longer, I will know precisely what to write. Words will flow magically from my pen, and the ten-page review I have due next week will be finished in two or three hours.

Admittedly, a few undeserved successes as an undergraduate English major fed this fantasy; I wrote papers entitled "Influences of Dostoyevsky's *Notes from Underground* on Ralph Ellison's *Underground Man*" and "Why All the Smutz, Mr. Roth?" the night before they were due and received "A's." Unfortunately, I tend to forget that such late night writing also earned me a few "D's." Remembering the "D's" pushes the fantasy aside, and I'm ready to struggle with covering those narrowly placed blue lines with my black scrawl.

This anecdote, related by a colleague who writes quite well, reveals three common misconceptions about writing:

- Inspiration directs writing.
- Writing progresses quickly.
- The first written draft is a finished piece.

Understanding these misconceptions can improve your attitude about writing.

Inspiration

In most writers' experience, inspiration is little more than what recent writing research identifies as pre-writing activity. It is the germ of an insight or idea that flowers into words, sentences, and paragraphs, having been fed by reflection, research, and rumination. Each writer establishes her own comfortable pre-writing activities and uses them whenever she writes. Suggestions for pre-writing activities appear later in the writing process discussion.

Rapid Progress

If writing requires reflection, research, and rumination, then clearly writing requires time—time from thought to hand to paper and time from conception to completion. Less experienced writers may ask how much time experienced writers allow. One novelist reports that she begins her day at 10:00 A.M. and writes four pages; this may take one hour or the entire day. The time required depends upon many factors—the nature of the writing task, the topic's complexity, the writer's comfort with the material, the amount of research required, and the writer's frame of mind. Few writers achieve the writer's three-hour, ten-page review in my colleague's procrastination fantasy on a regular basis. For every four-page hour a four-hour page lies in wait.

First Draft, Finished Piece

All too often, students (as opposed to writers) succumb to their schedules' inevitable rigors and submit first drafts as finished pieces, and sometimes, accustomed to saying how poorly students write, professors accept these pieces, read them for content, and put them aside mumbling their confirmed view that students do, indeed, write poorly. Experienced writers know that first drafts reflect a basic writing problem—people think faster than they write. In first drafts we inevitably omit a step in logic or a definition or explanation familiar to us but not to the reader. We use words imprecisely, and we make unconscious mechanical errors. When first we write, we are so close to the materials and so concerned about getting our ideas down, we care little about how a reader will read our writing. Experienced writers rely on the revision process to refine clarity, coherence, completeness of thought, and correctness.

Some Other Misconceptions

The procrastination fantasy touches three principal misconceptions about writing; a few others exist.

- Writers are born not made.
- Every writer works the same way—the right way.
- Some people simply cannot write.

These misconceptions derive from the idea that writers are different from you and me. They put writers into a category of "other" and suggest that all people in that category are similar. Probably the only generalization that can be made about writers is that writers differ. Each develops his or her own approach for writing and labors at a different rate and with different facility, and each encounters a different set of difficulties.

Writing and Mental Processes

To understand the varying levels of ease and difficulty different writers experience when they work, we can look at how the mind functions. Recent brain physiology studies explain that people process information differently. Studies of people who have lost the function of one brain side or the other show that the left brain processes information in a linear or conventionally "rational" manner and the right side processes information in patterns. Both brain sides have some language facility, but the dominant brain side affects the ease with which certain tasks are performed. The left-side dominant writer may construct plans, design outlines, and write logical arguments with ease. The right-side dominant person may use maps and diagrams to plan his or her writing and use language creatively, but may have difficulty ordering an essay's linear progress. Furthermore, other tests suggest that some people have greater verbal skills, while others possess greater computational abilities.

This research does not mean that only literary people write and mathematicians compute. (If it did, learning could not be communicated in all disciplines.) The research does help explain why each writer will work with ease at some aspect of writing and struggle with some other. As you recognize your strengths and limitations and allow for them, you will evolve your own approach to writing. This will be more helpful than holding on to those old misconceptions. When we put aside our misconceptions, we can begin to see ourselves as writers. Then, most likely, we will feel about writing as many writers do; we can dislike writing but like having written.

Writer's Block

Writing task in mind (or sketched on paper), many of us have sat down to write, only to find that those brilliant word strings that moments before flashed through our consciousness cannot find their way onto paper (or screen). We stare at the paper, at the wall, and out the window; we get up for another cup of coffee. Still the words elude us. Recognizing this as writer's block and knowing most writers experience it at one time or another offers little consolation, but perhaps understanding some of its causes and having some tricks to get past it will help.

Perfectionism and Writer's Block

While some writers experience serious writer's block that may require professional counseling, for most students the experience is temporary. When students discuss what they initially experience as panic, the panic becomes identifiable as fear of failure. Throughout the educational experience, writing receives criticism, judgment, and grades. Students learn to write with instructors as their audience, and pleasing the audience becomes as important as communicating. As a result, student writers find themselves writing in a voice not their own for an audience whose expectations they may not fully understand. This problem is particularly compounded by assuming that the first draft is the finished draft. An inner voice says, "This has to be perfect." Perfectionistic expectations create considerable pressure, and while some pressure may encourage a fine performance, the pressure for perfection usually interferes with truly excellent performance, particularly when it comes to writing.

Self-Esteem and Writer's Block

Not only do the perfectionistic demands we anticipate from others produce a writing block, but blocks develop when self-esteem becomes tied to writing. Writing is a personal act. Putting to paper personal experiences, observations, ideas, or emotions involves some personal risk, a risk which often makes writing more difficult. Writing becomes easier for writers who separate judgment of work from judgment of self. This sounds difficult to do, but consider what the world would be like if everyone thought the same thoughts and reacted to events in precisely the same way. Dull. When a writer records his personal perspective, he adds to the world's infinite variety. Writing would not be worth doing if everyone experienced the world in the same way. Anticipating our reader's different responses and hoping to share our special perceptions, we write with the knowledge that every reader may not agree with our ideas or share our insights. No writer seriously anticipates that every word or stylistic nuance will meet with every reader's approval and agreement; she anticipates debate and criticism. A reader's critical response neither lessens the written word's value nor diminishes the writer's worth.

Hints for Overcoming Writer's Block

However well a writer controls perfectionistic demands or separates self-esteem from the valuation of his work, writing blocks still occur. Here are ways some writers overcome blocking:

- I block at introductions so I move on to another section, usually one that interests me most or I understand best.
- I put the job I'm working on aside and write whatever comes to mind.
- If I'm writing a paper for a class, I try to envision an audience different from the professor. I can then write for a reason other than the grade.
- I consciously write without concern for style, even sometimes without concern for accuracy, so that I can get as much on the page as possible. This draft, barely a rough draft, demands extensive revision but allows me tremendous freedom.
- Brief written pieces rarely cause me difficulty; anything over 2,000 words intimidates me. When this happens, I envision a series of short papers, write them separately, then work them together at a later time, when I develop distance.
- I change my writing tool. If I block at the typewriter or computer, I pick up pen and paper; sometimes I go the other way—from pen to keys.
- I return to my research (either my notes or reading materials), because I am probably not yet ready to write.
- I stop writing and start talking, either to a tape recorder or a friend. I find working ideas through verbally focuses my writing.
- After I completed my doctoral dissertation (350 pages), I declared a six-month reprieve. Then when I tried writing again, I blocked. The ideas came, but I was unable to formulate them for an academic audience. To retain the ideas, I jotted them on paper scraps. Scraps changed to unlined standard paper sheets; cryptic notes became prose. The occasional notation turned into a daily routine, and I became a journal keeper—and a writer.
- I get up from the word processor, put on my athletic shoes, run or walk vigorously for an hour, shower, put on clean clothes, and begin again. If I still cannot write, I pledge myself to an early evening and an earlier start tomorrow.

These suggestions represent ways both professional and student writers cope with blocking. As you look through the above suggestions, you will notice that overcoming writer's block usually involves some change—an attitude change, a physical change in location or materials, or a shift of focus. If other writers' suggestions do not work for you, develop your own, but keep in mind both the necessity of seeing your first draft as tentative and the importance of allowing enough time between preliminary draft and due date to contend with possible blocks.

In the last few pages we have looked at the role attitude plays in becoming a writer. Learning to write requires seeing oneself as a writer and putting aside misconceptions that all writers write the same way and with the same ease. Writing requires developing a positive attitude toward both self and work, and finding escape routes when problems arise. The next section examines how writers prepare themselves for writing and what actually happens when they work.

Attitudes and Writing Exercises

1. List the most common reasons you write. For each reason rate the writing difficulty between 1 (very easy) and 5 (very hard). List three causes for your response. Looking over your responses, write a brief paragraph explaining what about writing is easy for you and what makes it difficult.

2. You have been asked to write a five-page essay for this class. Your instructor has given no guidelines except the topic—why you are attending college. Imagine yourself writing this assignment successfully. Write a brief description of your writing fantasy—what you write, what happens when you write, the teacher's response. When you read it over, how realistic is your fantasy? What misconceptions does it contain?

3. List the positive experiences you have had writing. How have these contributed to your attitude about writing?

4. List your negative writing experiences. How have these contributed to your attitude about writing? Do you have more positive or negative experiences?

5. Have you encountered writer's block? Write a description of what happened, how you felt, and how you overcame it.

PREPARING TO WRITE

Working writers recognize that writing takes time and discipline. Writing often in a comfortable place at a regular time helps many writers meet deadlines with greater ease. Some professional writers' practices can help you develop useful writing habits.

Writing Often

While professional writers often write for deadlines and write with certain tasks in mind—just as students do—most of them continue writing between tasks and deadlines. They write sketches for future articles or fragmentary descriptions of events, people, and places. They record their responses to personal and world affairs. Such writing often takes the form of a journal—literally a daybook—where a writer, unconcerned about audience, can test perceptions and ideas or experiment with style.

Keeping a Journal

While some writers discipline themselves to write daily, a journal is no mere calendar of daily events. Instead, it offers a qualitative response to experiences. Journals reflect a writer's individual interests and experiments with form and style. A journal entry might transcribe a conversation, describe a place, or work through angry feelings. For student writers, keeping a journal provides a good opportunity to become comfortable with putting ideas and experiences into writing.

While journal entries are necessarily individual, the following categories of experience often prove fruitful for journal writing:

- sensory details from a particularly vivid experience (pleasant or unpleasant)
- emotional self-examination (fears, preferences, prejudices, depression, elation, and their manifestations or causes
- investigations of personal belief (religion, politics, morality)
- responses to physical surroundings
- detailed descriptions of familiar places
- intellectual discourse (some newly acquired information and its impact)

Whether by keeping a journal or by attempting to write on some other regular basis, writing will become a more comfortable activity for you if you adopt the professional writer's practice of writing often.

A Comfortable Place

Walking through academic halls lined by professors' offices, I balk at the persistent clacking typewriters. I gaze in awe at students writing away, shoulder to shoulder, in the university library's typing room. While I do not resemble the Sunday supplement writer who confesses he writes better at the kitchen table than in his tidy office, I would find writing in the same place I teach, counsel students, and sit on committees impossible. I need to be able to focus my attention away from other career demands. On visiting my sun porch office, a friend asked how when writing I escape all the place's natural distractions—winter's draft, summer's heat, lounging sheep dogs, and all that glaring sunlight. However idiosyncratic, I cannot write without natural light, a window-framed view of something growing, and a place to sit cross-legged.

Students, particularly those confined to college dormitories, cannot always write in ideal circumstances, but they can usually find some compromise if they consider what might be ideal. For example, I work well at a fifth-floor desk looking out on the sculpture garden at UCLA's University Research Library. Recognizing a need for isolation, some students seek out empty classrooms. Other students write in dorm rooms, quiet after roommates have gone to class or to sleep. Many students find a library's quiet crowd reassuring, while others can work only when television or music fills the background void. Whatever conditions suit you, discover the place most comfortable for you, and write there. Write letters, write lecture and book summaries, write in your journal; then writing assignments there will be easier.

A Regular Time

Like the novelist who begins writing each morning at ten, find the time when you write best. Some writers rise with the sun, drink only coffee for breakfast, and work steadily until noon. Afternoons find them gazing at walls. Other people can only work when their coffee drinking begins at dinner and their writing at midnight. Studies indicate metabolic differences in "day people" and "night people" which account for performance variations. Even when a night person finds it necessary to be at work or class early, that person's peak performance still comes late in the day. The day person who stays up late several nights in a row will find concentration difficult and routine tasks exhausting. Schedules sometimes force students to disrupt regular sleep and work patterns, and when this happens demanding tasks like writing become even more difficult. Determine when you work best and regularly schedule writing for that time.

Once you have found the time and place conducive to writing and developed the practice of writing often for yourself, some understanding of what happens when writers write—the writing process—may simplify your writing.

Exercises for Preparing to Write

1. Buy a book or notebook to use as a journal. Find something comfortable for you. Set aside time each day for a week to write at least one page. Try writing by

- recording sensory details about an experience
- examining an emotion like anger, satisfaction, fear
- explaining a personal religious or political belief
- describing a special place you remember
- recording observations about your current physical surroundings
- record a new idea you learned through your reading or in class, and explain why it is important and what it means to your understanding of the subject

2. During the first week you keep your journal, investigate your writing comfort. Keep a log, recording the writing location, the instrument, the time of day, and your feelings about these. Based on this log, write a short paragraph describing your best writing time and place. Explain why your writing went best there.

THE WRITING PROCESS

Order and simplification are the first steps toward the mastery of a subject—the actual enemy is the unknown.

THOMAS MANN, *The Magic Mountain*

Identifying writing activities and ordering these tasks into a series of steps—a process—simplifies not only mastering the subject of writing but mastering the discipline of writing regularly as the professional writer must. While every writer does not work in precisely the same manner, enough similarities exist to allow us to identify a sequence of writing behaviors which include:

- *pre-writing activities*—identifying topics, collecting information, focusing, devising a preliminary plan
- *writing*—writing introductions, developing paragraphs, using specific language, and writing conclusions.
- *revising*—formulating criteria for self-evaluation, making and using a revision checklist

Reading this list from top to bottom suggests that the writing process is a linear, consecutive one. For some writers it is, but for some, paragraphs may take shape simultaneously with *focusing*. A writer may move from preliminary plan to developing paragraphs and move back to enlarging the preliminary plan before writing an introduction. While writers may move back and forth between tasks and perform some tasks simultaneously, some pre-writing activity must precede writing just as some writing must precede revision. You will find it easier to make the writing process your own when you better understand the separate writing activities described in the pages that follow.

Pre-Writing

Pre-writing resembles the phase in legal procedure known as "discovery." During discovery a lawyer questions both her own and the opponent's clients to determine the case's facts, before she brings these facts into "evidence" by presenting them in front of judge and jury. During pre-writing, a writer identifies a topic, finds his topic's limits, discovers what he already knows about the topic, researches what he does not know, and formulates a writing plan. Like the discovery phase in law, information at this stage is tentative; any new information may significantly alter the writer's plan. Perhaps because information is so tentative at this stage, pre-writing poses difficulties for student writers. Breaking pre-writing into its smaller activities makes it easier.

Identifying Topics

Students frequently write in response to an assignment. The easiest assignment defines the subject, relies on information presented in the course, and suggests an approach for organizing the writing. Here, the writer needs only to rely on discovery to determine what information has been presented in the course relevant to the topic assigned. More often, instructors suggest a general topic and allow students freedom to limit the topic, discover information about the topic, and organize their writing approach. While such freedom may ultimately afford the best learning experience from an instructor's viewpoint, the student usually responds that he knows nothing to write about and thus has nothing to say.

Recognizing What You Know—Brainstorming

If you identify with the student who thinks he knows nothing, you can benefit by beginning with an inventory of what you know. An effective technique for discovering what you know on a subject is called *brainstorming*. To brainstorm, you list rapidly any words or phrases that come to mind without evaluating each suggestion's feasibility until you have at least forty entries. Then you look back at the list for patterns and possibilities. Here is a brainstorm inventory developed by a student whose instructor asked for a paper on toys in American life.

A Brainstorm Inventory

Assigned Topic: Toys in American Life

G.I. Joe
Barbie
"He who has the most toys wins"
games
competition
Monopoly
poor craftsmanship
self-destruct
planned obsolescence
bicycle
roller skates
media creates toys
Star Wars, Rambo
computer games
new technology
individualistic toys
middle-class and sex-role stereotypes
importance of play fantasy "The Hurried Child"
too many toys
my nephew at Christmas
toys do everything
dolls with beds, strollers, high chairs
wardrobes
Cabbage Patch Kids
fads
advertising on cartoon shows
throwaway society

toys imitate adult activities
trucks, trains, planes
toys teach expectations
toys sold in toy department stores
bears as fad
dolls not to play with, but to collect

ASSESSING A BRAINSTORM INVENTORY.   A brainstorm inventory may merely be a list of potentially interesting topics, but usually in an inventory, groups and categories emerge. The writer reviewed the brainstorm list above looking for similarities and differences and discovered the following categories:

Kinds of Toys: G.I. Joe, Barbie, bicycles, roller skates, Star Wars, Rambo, dolls with beds, strollers, high chairs, trucks, trains, planes, bears, dolls not to play with but to collect

Kinds of Games: Monopoly, computer games

Characteristics of Toys: poor craftsmanship, self-destruct, planned obsolescence, imitate media, reflect new technology, sex-role identified, too many toys, faddish, fads created by advertising

Characteristics of Society: "He who has the most toys wins," competitive, planned obsolescence, media-oriented, technological, individualistic, faddish, throwaway society

What Toys Do: allow children to fantasize, overwhelm little children with abundance (my nephew at Christmas), replace a child's imagination by doing everything for him, allow kids to imitate adult activities, teach children about society's expectations (role models for male/female)

Miscellaneous: advertising on cartoon shows, toy department stores.

FINDING A PROSPECTIVE SUBJECT.   This brainstorming inventory and the student's analysis of it suggests several potential subjects for a paper on toys and American life:

Board Games and America's Competitive Spirit
Toys Related to Sex-Role Stereotypes
Toys and a Consumer Society's Bad Habits
Toys Rob Children of Imagination
Throwaway Toys in a Throwaway World

CRITERIA FOR GOOD SUBJECTS.   To determine if a subject will work well for a writing assignment, the subject should meet four criteria:

1. It should interest the writer.
2. It should come within the scope of the instructor's suggested assignment.
3. It should indicate a specific subject.
4. It should be manageable within the assignment's allotted time and length.

If I were going to write on one of the subjects developed from the brainstorming, my interests would direct me to sex-role stereotyping, consumerism, and imagination. On reconsidering the instructor's assignment, I find that only one topic, America's competitive spirit, truly meets the assignment's original limits. I could, however, emphasize American consumerism and, quite probably, American male and female roles, and still be able to use three of the other topics. Since imagination extends beyond the United States, that topic lies outside the assignment's original limits.

Concern for a specific topic poses the greatest problem. None of the topics is truly specific, though board games comes the closest. When I look back to the original inventory, I find specifics—Barbie, G.I. Joe, Cabbage Patch Kids, bicycles, roller skates. When these specific words replace "toys," the writing topics improve.

G.I. Joe and Barbie Related to Stereotyped Sex Roles
Cabbage Patch Kids and a Consumer Society's Principal Bad Habit: Spending on Created Needs
Today's Poorly Constructed Bicycles and Skates in Our Throwaway World

When we revise subjects to meet the criteria of specificity, we usually ensure they will be more manageable. Specificity allows a writer to focus an assignment and direct any research or reading which the assignment requires. Locating information about specific dolls like the Cabbage Patch Kids, Barbie, or G.I. Joe is a more clearly defined task than locating information on toys generally. Even without research, it is easier to discover our own ideas and responses to a specific, concrete object—one with clearly identifiable characteristics—than it is to a general category. More often than not, when preparing to write on a specific topic, so much information emerges that a writer must select from the information to limit the topic to meet particularly stringent length and time limits.

Identifying Topics Through Journals and Browsing

We have traced a writing topic's development beginning with brainstorming, through categorizing, and developing effective writing topics. But brainstorming is only one way to identify a writing subject. You might also want to consider your journal, periodical browsing, index browsing, or assigned course readings. If you have used your journal to respond to important ideas or emotions, you have recorded several subjects that compel your interest at the same time that they relate to course materials. Reading, assigned or not, can spur ideas for writing, particularly if you develop the habit of reading critically. (The next two chapters look in detail at the relationship between reading and writing.) Sometimes merely browsing in a magazine or journal reminds us of topics that interested us once or we wish to explore further.

While periodical browsing may limit us to the topics included in our choice of magazine or a particular issue, browsing in an index may suggest the broadest range of potential writing subjects, at the same time that it suggests specific topics. Depending on whether a writer is more interested in business or psychology, looking at the major index in each field (*Business Periodicals Index* or *The Social Science Index*, respectively) could have taken the paper on toys in American life in very different directions.

Whatever approach a writer uses to find a topic, testing the topic by the criteria of interest, original assignment specifications, specificity, and manageable limits will make the next steps in the writing process easier.

Collecting Information

Identifying a topic usually begins the process of collecting information. As the writer brings the writing subject into focus, he calls forth what he knows about the subject. An activity such as brainstorming allows the writer to see what information he already possesses on a topic before he begins gathering information from other sources. Sometimes a second brainstorming session related to the specific topic will provide greater focus and detail.

MAPPING.   Another useful technique for topic identification is *mapping*. Mapping resembles brainstorming in that you list ideas about the topic as they come to mind. But because mapping works spatially rather than linearly, it begins developing some pattern and order. Mapping begins with placing the specific topic at the center of a paper and adding phrases and words in different directions. Using this approach allows the mind to identify relationships between words and ideas, and to develop a topic's various aspects simultaneously. This concept will be more clear if you look carefully at the map on page 17 on G.I. Joe, Barbie, and sex-role stereotypes.

Using mapping, this writer discovered what she knew about G.I. Joe and Barbie; she also learned where she needed to strengthen the information. In the map's margins she identifies other resources she will use—a toy store and a library—to extend her collecting outward from what she already knows to information she must seek. This outward collecting (research) goes to two classes of sources— *primary* and *secondary*.

USING PRIMARY SOURCES.   Primary sources require that the writer obtain information directly. As a writer engages with a primary source, she observes, questions, and records responses as objectively as possible. Primary sources include:

- the writer's personal experience of an event. a place, a person, or an object
- an interview with another person
- an interview with several people, often in questionnaire form
- a controlled event or experiment

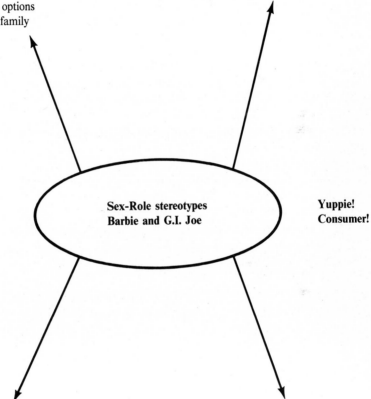

Sex Role Stereotypes
Theoretically changed in last
  twenty years
Stereotype—men must be strong,
  not show emotion, willing to
  stand up and fight
Supposedly replaced by view of
  nurturing gentle male
  even have boy dolls for little boys—
  not G.I.J.
Women have options
  career and family

G.I. Joe
Declined in popularity during
  Vietnam era
Brought back in '80s
Marketing campaign with cartoon
  show on TV
Doll complete with rifle, grenade,
  Army fatigues
Almost exclusively bought by boys—
  not like Ken

Sex-Role stereotypes
Barbie and G.I. Joe

Yuppie!
Consumer!

Nonsexist toys
Bicycles
Games

Needs research: Look up sales
  for Barbie and G.I. Joe
Go to toy store, check items

Barbie
Appearance
  Blond, blue eyes
  Voluptuous
  Tiny feet—if real could not
  support torso
Clothes: wedding, evening,
  leisure, Day to Night
Accessories: car, bed, spa
  condo, poodle

Pre-planned, clearly articulated questions get the best possible responses from primary sources. Minimally, the journalists' questions—who, what, where, when, why, and how—can uncover valuable information. If you wish to do more extensive primary research, consult books on interviewing, writing questionnaires, or designing scientific experiments.

USING SECONDARY SOURCES.   Secondary research takes us to other writers' work where they report their observations, investigative results, opinions, and conclusions. While we casually engage in secondary research each time we read the morning newspaper or pick up a magazine, such research best finds its home in a library, with such research tools as the card catalogue, subject bibliographies, newspaper and periodical indexes, and the librarians' invaluable ability to direct the research process. Familiar only with the card catalogue and *The Reader's Guide to Periodic Literature,* student writers usually restrict themselves to a small portion of a library's wealth. All the library could be theirs if they would approach a librarian and ask, "What index lists magazine and journal articles on . . . ?"

MAKING A RESEARCH PLAN.   Besides becoming familiar with a library's research tools, a good writer needs to have a research plan. The most common research problem is having too much rather than too little information. A good plan can direct the writer through the research maze to the relevant information. A workable plan contains:

- a specific topic
- a list of alternate terms identifying the topic to use in indexes and catalogues
- three or four questions that the research will seek to answer

For example, a research plan for the sex-role stereotypes, G.I. Joe, and Barbie topic would list other possible topics (toys and sex-role development, Mattel toy manufacturer, dolls and girls' sex identification, war toys) and include the questions:

- When was G.I. Joe reintroduced in the toy market?
- What have been the sales for Barbie? for G.I. Joe?
- How has Barbie changed in recent years?
- What responses have feminists had to Barbie? to G.I. Joe?

A writer familiar with the library would also list indexes where he would expect to find articles on his topic. A topic as narrow as Barbie would probably not appear in a card catalogue. Articles on sex roles would appear in both *The Social Science Index* and *The Readers' Guide to Periodic Literature* and articles on business in *The Business Periodicals' Index* and *The Wall Street Journal Index.* A writer armed with such a plan would make quick work of research.

Keeping Track of Information

Collecting information from self or a source refines a topic and stimulates a writer's thoughts about the writing subject. I usually find having two paper pads—one yellow, one white, one for collecting, one for writing—allows me to move back and forth between collecting and sorting information. As I read, selecting some information and discarding some, my final essay takes shape. Usually by the time my research has given my topic substance, a focus or plan has emerged. If not, I must move to focusing activities.

Focusing

Sometimes the information a writer collects does not conform to the research plan, or even sometimes to the original specific topic. Here the writer must review the collected information. In the same way he looked at the original brainstorm inventory or at the map, the writer must analyze his research. What things are alike? different? What categories emerge? What patterns appear? What relationships exist? How are causes and effects related? What pieces of information contradict each other? What information should be kept; what is irrelevant? Despite the time involved in research, writers need to be willing to discard information that does not really apply to the topic. Sometimes this may mean going back to find more information on what originally appeared to be an insignificant aspect of the subject.

USING A SUMMARY STATEMENT.   Sometimes formulating a summary statement helps focus collected information. Employing a simple formula can help. To focus, a writer needs to decide what precisely he thinks about his topic, and how the collected information relates to that informed opinion. The formula, "I believe . . . because . . . " can help. If a topic is complex, this summary statement can be cumbersome, but it requires the writer to identify a statement about the topic, and then select from the collected information the ideas important enough to finish this statement. For example, the student working on Barbie might decide that the doll teaches superficial values. This generalization lends little direction to an essay. If, however, she says, "I believe Barbie teaches superficial values because . . . ," she must formulate reasons that will focus her writing. The summary statement's "I believe" should not find its way into a finished paper, but it provides a starting point.

USING A THESIS STATEMENT.   Another way to focus information is to write a thesis statement that may actually find its way into the essay. A good thesis statement draws directly on a good writing topic by stating a specific topic and imposing limits on the topic. Such a statement also offers comment on the topic by taking the form of a sentence and adding a predicate to the topic's subject. Look at these topics:

- religious opposition to genetic engineering
- unlawful sports wagering in the NCAA
- the Gramm-Rudman Bill
- Barbie, the ultimate Yuppie

Each topic is fairly specific, although "genetic engineering" encompasses several different procedures. Two topics, the first and last, impose limits. The first will consider only religious opposition to genetic engineering; the last will consider only Barbie as a Yuppie. No topic makes a statement. But look what happens when we increase specificity, add further limits, and offer comments.

- Despite its potential for curing genetic disorders, some conservative Protestant groups oppose genetic engineering because they fear man is taking God's creative power into his own hands.
- To combat the team dishonesty that college football and basketball betting encourages, the NCAA has recently adopted a stiff set of regulations and penalties, which it hopes will deter future collegiate offenders.
- The Gramm-Rudman Bill offers better hope for eliminating the United States federal deficit than either raising taxes or asking Congress to cut popular programs.
- Barbie, the ultimate Yuppie, teaches little girls that a woman's most important role in American society is being a consumer.

These revised thesis statements focus the prospective paper by (1) *stating a specific topic*, (2) *limiting the discussion to one or two aspects of the topic*, and (3) *commenting on the topic*.

Additionally, these refined thesis statements indicate each paper's controlling approach. The first statement on genetic engineering suggests that the writer would first admit to genetic engineering's potential for curing genetic disorders before discussing conservative Protestant groups' religious reservations. The second will set out the NCAA regulations and penalties and suggest their effect on college football and basketball betting. The third will compare and contrast the relative effects of Gramm-Rudman, increased taxation, and congressional program-cutting on the federal deficit. The last will explain how Barbie as Yuppie teaches girls to be consumers. More than merely focusing a subject, formulating a good thesis statement can take a writer well into the next stage in the writing process—devising a plan.

Devising a Writing Plan

Before considering planning approaches, we need to review writing modes and development strategies. The writing modes (often called rhetorical modes) describe the writing task—they identify *what* the writer is doing: describing, narrating, explaining, or arguing. The development strategies suggest *how* the writing task proceeds—through classification, analysis, comparision and contrast, illustration, definition, and analogy. A single development strategy may shape an entire essay, or a writer may combine strategies.

Writing Modes

DESCRIPTION.   *Description* details the attributes of an event, a person, place, theory, or idea to create a dominant impression. These details, often identified by the strength of their sense impression, can be organized spatially, temporally, or analytically.

NARRATION.   While description may focus on a single event, *narration* relates a sequence of events—a story. We most readily identify story with fiction's plot, but narrative logic—the relationship between events and their causes—serves the journalist reporting on Supreme Court decisions as well as it serves the historian relating a war's progress or a scientist evolving a theory.

EXPLANATION.   While description identifies attributes and narration assigns sequence and causation, *explanation* (or exposition) offers a rationale. It considers the principles that control opinions, beliefs, practices, or events and examines its subject to inform an audience.

ARGUMENT.   An *argument* presents a position favoring or opposing a subject, which is neither a discernible fact nor a matter of personal taste but rather is "at issue"—subject to debate. A writer may choose to explain both sides of an issue, but explanation becomes argument when she favors one side over the other. Argument usually conforms to conventional deductive or inductive patterns. Induction proceeds from specific facts to a generalized conclusion—a pattern we most readily identify with the scientific method. Deduction employs formal logic's syllogism to identify an individual instance with a general class.

The deductive syllogism.   Because deduction can be easily misused, we need to consider the syllogism's pattern briefly. Three statements form a syllogism:

The *major premise,* which identifies an individual characteristic with a general group:

> All Americans possess constitutionally protected free speech.

A *minor premise,* which identifies an individual with the general group or category:

> David Brown is an American.

A *conclusion*, which assigns the individual the group's attributes:

Therefore, David Brown possesses constitutionally protected free speech.

Stated symbolically,

$$
\begin{array}{rl}
& A = B \\
\text{and} & C = A \\
\text{therefore,} & C = B
\end{array}
$$

where A is general category, B is category's attribute, and C is the individual instance.

For a syllogism to be valid, the terms and their places are not interchangeable. For example the syllogism

All Americans possess constitutionally protected free speech. (A = B)
David Brown possesses constitutionally protected free speech. (C = B)
Therefore, David Brown is an American. (C = A)

cannot be valid, even though the statement may or may not be true. David Brown may possess protected free speech, but from another country.

As long as a syllogism's terms remain in their places, the syllogism can also be expressed negatively,

$$
\begin{array}{rl}
\text{No} & A = B \\
& C = A \\
\text{therefore,} & C = B
\end{array}
$$

or as an if/then statement,

$$
\begin{array}{rl}
\text{If} & A = B \\
\text{and if} & C = A \\
\text{then,} & C \neq B
\end{array}
$$

Development Strategies

Whether writing inductive and deductive arguments, or description, narration, and exposition, writers use some of the same ordering strategies—classification, analysis, comparison and contrast, illustration, definition, and analogy.

CLASSIFICATION. *Classification* forms groups based on similarity. It is an essential ordering mechanism employed by writers in every discipline. Scientists classify experimental results, just as psychologists classify behavior, or critics classify literary forms. Classification enables the writer to explain the individual as well as the class. By classifying Claude Monet as an Impressionist painter, and by describing both Monet and Impressionism, a writer can educate the reader about both the man and artistic style.

ANALYSIS. While classification groups items together, *analysis* breaks a single entity apart. Classification establishes kinds of music (jazz or classical) and musical forms (ballad or symphony); analysis studies the musical elements of Beethoven's Ninth Symphony. Classification may look at kinds of men or forms of bravery; analysis breaks a human into mind and body, and a body into skin, bone, blood, muscle, and nerve. Analysis can enumerate effects or examine events as the product of causes. It may proceed spatially (right to left, top to bottom, outward to inward, small to large) or temporally (first to last or end to beginning). A writer can also present the components of analysis in order of their significance.

COMPARISON AND CONTRAST. *Comparison and contrast* studies two or more like entities' similarities and differences to understand the things themselves or to explain something else. For example, we might better understand the architect Frank Lloyd Wright's artistic achievement by comparing and contrasting his prairie-style houses around Chicago with his Los Angeles modern-style houses. Or by comparing and contrasting two patients' case histories, a psychiatrist might better understand the particular problems of each. Comparison and contrast proceeds by establishing categories and studying relationships within the categories. To compare and contrast architectural designs, for example, we might consider categories like floor plans, window placement, room sizes, internal ornamentation, external ornamentation, and materials. A writer could examine first one design in terms of these categories, and then the other, or proceed one category at a time, first one design, then the other.

ILLUSTRATION. We often express what we think and write as generalizations—as the conclusions we reach from experience and observations. *Illustration* justifies these generalizations by offering the specific, concrete experiences, observations, and instances that go along with them. While it might be of considerable value to have the historian Bruce Catton assert that post-Civil War Reconstruction would have been far less devastating for the American South if President Lincoln had lived, this assertion finds far more credence when Catton describes Lincoln's peace plans that were cast aside by the retribution-seeking faction who assumed power upon Lincoln's assassination.

DEFINITION.   *Definition* offers details about a particular term or phrase as a statement of equivalency. "A haiku is a Japanese verse form of three lines containing five, seven, and five syllables respectively." "A molecule is the smallest particle of a substance that retains the properties of the substance." Definitions appear brief, like the ones above, or they may be extended through examples, comparisons, or more extensive lists of attributes. Extended definitions thus rely on other development strategies.

ANALOGY.   *Analogy* identifies an unfamiliar concept, idea, event, or experience by comparing it with a known entity. We understand the unseen atom by analogizing it with the solar system. The great psychoanalyst C.G. Jung explained the relationship between the conscious and unconscious mind by using an analogy with land and sea: the sea of the unconscious flows and ebbs against the conscious shore. These examples illustrate that analogy as a developmental strategy combines definition with comparison.

Selecting a Development Strategy

Encountering all at once these means of developing your ideas can be bewildering. Choosing one or several of them when you are planning an essay poses less of a problem, when you recognize that these ways of ordering writing do not relate to writing alone. We constantly employ analysis, classification, definition, and comparison to think about our experiences. A good guide for choosing an organizational approach in writing is to consider how you are *already* thinking about a subject. Are you considering it in relation to similar knowledge? (comparison or analogy) Are you breaking it into smaller topics? (analysis) Are you assigning it attributes? (definition) Combine this awareness of your thought process with a consideration of what you want your essay to do—describe, narrate, explain, or argue—and you are well into formulating a plan for your writing.

The Written Plan

AN OUTLINE.   Most college students have learned elaborate outlining systems. A formal outline requires the writer to analyze his subject, breaking it into topics, subtopics, major points, and minor points, arranged in a system of letters and numbers which looks like this:

I. _____

    A. _____

        1. _____

            a. _____

            b. _____

        2. _____

            a. _____

            b. _____

    B. _____

II. _____

    A. _____

        1. _____

        2. _____

Each outline constituent represents a different aspect of the subject and may be expressed as either a phrase or sentence. Outlines are a valuable planning tool because they force writers to organize and become specific.

A SIMPLE PLAN.   Sometimes writers can become so concerned about outlining that they have difficulty moving from outlining to writing. In this case, using outlining principles in a simple plan may prove more useful. To do this, consider what outlining accomplishes. First, outlining breaks a subject into component parts, and second, it requires the writer to move from general topics to specific comments. An outline, however effective it proves in organizing information, may not actually suggest how a writer intends to approach his subject. A plan can do both. Here is a plan for a paper on preventing wagering on college sports.

Thesis: To combat the team dishonesty that college football and basketball betting encourages, the NCAA has recently adopted a stiff set of regulations and penalties, which it hopes will deter future collegiate offenders.

   I.   Introduction: Give background to problem
       Relate 1985 incident at Tulane
       Give Justice Department statistics on college sports betting
       State thesis
  II.   Explain the NCAA regulations
 III.   Explain penalties
 IV.   Implementation
       NCAA institutions self-monitor
       Clarification of each school's standards of conduct through required policy statement
  V.   Anticipated positive effects
       College administrators' responses to ruling
       Responses of coaches and alumni associations

VI.   Detrimental effects from NCAA policy's harshness
VII. Conclusion—weigh advantages against disadvantages and point out importance of integrity—use quotation from Tulane president

Like an outline, this plan breaks the subject into parts: the events leading to
NCAA regulations, the regulations, implementation, analysis of effects, and an
assessment of the NCAA action. The plan also suggests writing tasks—narrating
Tulane events, explaining regulations and penalties, describing implementation
process, and analyzing and weighing positive and negative effects. Clearly, this
plan does not have all the writer's information set out in detail. Instead it makes
almost cryptic reference to materials the writer has elsewhere (almost certainly in
his research notes).

However a writer formulates his plan, experienced writers recognize that plans
are tentative. As they write, new ideas and different approaches suggest themselves; what seemed important initially will yield to a new focus. The writing process's next stage—writing—builds on all pre-writing activities, but also may rein-
troduce them. At any point in the actual writing, you may find yourself revising
your plan, brainstorming, mapping, or returning to the library for more information.

Pre-Writing Exercises

1. Brainstorm on an event in your social life that altered your thinking about some
important social or political issue. Record every thought or word that comes to mind
until you have at least forty entries.

2. Browse in this book's essay collection to find a topic that interests you. Brainstorm
on this topic.

3. From brainstorm lists, identify at least three possible topics. Create a plan for gathering information on this topic.

4. Interview a person well informed about your topic. Prepare a list of questions—who, what, where, when, why, and how—before the interview. Be certain the
questions are specific so that you obtain good detailed information.

5. Ask your instructor or a librarian for appropriate current periodical indexes for your
topic. List at least ten possible sources. Check your library's periodical list or card
catalogue to find if the articles are available.

6. Prepare a preliminary writing plan for your writing topic using mapping or outlining, and including a thesis statement. Write a brief statement about your audience,
purpose, and organizational approach.

Writing

Attitudes adjusted, information collected, plan in hand, and strategies for overcoming writer's block reviewed, the only way to move toward a first draft is to write. Even though written pieces conventionally start with introductions, develop their purposes in the body, and end with conclusions, writing need not proceed the same way. I usually begin with the part of the project that excites me most; other writers might begin with the section they anticipate as the most difficult. Wherever you begin, realize that what you are writing need not be perfect. Work as rapidly as you can, settling for less than the perfect expression, even leaving out words and phrases if they prove elusive. *The first draft needs to be written with the full intention of revising.*

However you work, the first draft may proceed more easily if you consider that writing consists of (1) *making a commitment to the reader* and (2) *fulfilling that commitment.*

The Commitment

Before beginning writing, somewhere in the planning process, a writer decides what the writing should accomplish. This decision, whether or not the writer recognizes it, implies a reader. A reviewer recommending (or panning) a film or book writes for the specialized audience of the particular kind of film or book. The person responding with a letter to a newspaper editorial writes both for the editorial writer and the newspaper's circulation, whether a large city or a 2,500-student college. The college professor writing for a professional journal writes for colleagues who share her specialized knowledge. A student writing a research paper writes for the students in the class, his colleagues, as well as the instructor. A good writer forms a clear picture of the particular audience, and then writes to engage their interest. In doing this he makes a commitment to these readers. But commitment to the reader is only part of the writer's commitment. The rest is to his subject, and to his purpose, which mediates between the subject and reader. The relationship looks something like this:

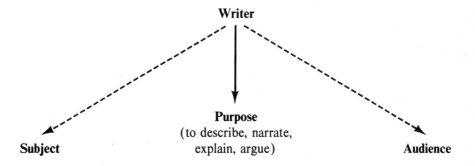

Writer

Purpose
(to describe, narrate,
explain, argue)

Subject   **Audience**

The writer commits to the reader to paint a word picture, tell a story, explain, or argue about the chosen subject. The beginning of a written piece—the introduction—engages the audience and offers the writer's promise. The remainder of the writing fulfills the commitment by presenting details.

The Introduction—Engaging the Reader

Effective introductions draw readers into the subject. They can engage human curiosity by presenting astonishing statistics or significant, surprising facts. They can identify a problem by creating a social or political context, or by telling a story where the problem touched individual human lives. An introduction may engage a specialized audience, like muscle physiologists, by surveying the literature and then stating directly the study's significance. On the other hand, an introduction that does not consider audience may alienate readers. If, for example, the muscle physiologist writes about his speciality for *Discover* magazine's popular audience, surveying the literature might discourage their interest. In its concern for engaging a specialized audience, a good introduction brings the audience to the subject.

The Introduction—the Writer's Promise

Besides engaging a specialized audience, an introduction offers the writer's promise to the reader, usually as a thesis statement. A good thesis statement presents a general statement about the written piece's specific subject—its comment on the topic commits the writer to both a subject and to a position. Thus, a thesis statement indicates what the writer is going to say about the subject, without saying "this paper will discuss . . ." In its presentation of the writer's commitment to the reader regarding his subject, the thesis statement brings the subject to the audience.

Consider what commitments the following thesis statements make.

It is no exaggeration to state that 19th century photographers ran as many risks in the dark as they did in the act of finding and taking pictures. (Bill Jay, *Death in the Darkroom*)

This thesis commits the writer to discussing the dangers a photographer developing film a century ago encountered in the darkroom.

The majority of these people [the elderly facing loneliness and isolation] are not seen by a psychiatrist. It is for them that I am trying to outline the changes that have taken place in the last few decades, changes that are ultimately responsible for the increased fear of death, the rising number of emotional problems, and the greater need for understanding of and coping with the problems of death and dying. (Elizabeth Kubler-Ross, *On Death and Dying*)

Here, Kubler-Ross not only identifies her subject, *changes*, she also commits to the writing task of analyzing how the changes affect the fear of death, rising numbers of emotional problems, and coping with death and dying. She also identifies her audience, the elderly, and suggests her purpose of helping her audience.

> I suspect that each sport contains a fundamental myth which it elaborates for its fans, and that our pleasure in watching such games derives in part from belonging briefly to the mythical world which the game and its players bring to life. I am especially interested in baseball and football because they are so popular and so uniquely *American*; they began here and unlike basketball they have not been widely exported. Thus, whatever can be said, mythically, about these games would seem to apply to our culture. (Murray Ross, *Football Red and Baseball Green*)

The writer here commits to explaining the myths embodied in football and baseball, and then to identifying these myths with American cultural myths.

In these thesis statements, Jay, Kubler-Ross, and Ross not only indicate their topic, but their comments make commitments about focus, purpose, approaches to writing, even audience. To do all this, Kubler-Ross and Ross use more than one sentence, whereas Jay uses only one but makes a specific statement. The number of sentences is not as important as making a statement about the topic which indicates the direction the writing will go.

The Body—Fulfilling Commitments

A writer fulfills the introduction's commitments by presenting specific details about the introduction's generalizations. Writers can improve specificity in both language and paragraph structure.

SPECIFIC PARAGRAPHS.   Paragraphs punctuate writing to let readers know that the writer is shifting focus. Conventions governing paragraphs are certainly familiar to college students. Even so, paragraph length sometimes proves a problem. Perhaps because we are so accustomed to seeing one-sentence newspaper paragraphs and advertizing copy, typed or handwritten paragraphs of more than three or four sentences seem unwieldy. Consequently, student writers often conclude paragraphs without adequate development—without adequate specificity.

Becoming aware of the relationship between general and specific sentences in a paragraph can help improve paragraph specificity. A well-developed paragraph usually has only one or two very general sentences; the rest of the sentences offer specific comment on these generalizations, and on each other. To better understand this, look at the following paragraph from Herbert J. Muller's essay "Education for the Future," which appeared in *The American Scholar*.

> Hence there is a wide field for courses on the future. Time and space do not permit a review of the many possibilities, but let us take a look at the already popular subject

of the environmental or biological crisis, aggavated by the population explosion. Ecologists tell us that if current trends continue we are headed for disaster, conceivably a world that will become uninhabitable. Together with the possibility of a thermonuclear war, these trends are faced with such immediate threats as the increasing pollution and the urban crisis, the steady deterioration of the central cities in the sprawling metropolitan areas. And behind all these problems is the accepted national goal of indefinite economic growth, even though Americans already consume many times their proportionate share of the world's dwindling natural resources. While one may doubt that such growth can continue indefinitely, neither business, government, nor the public is prepared to accept a program of national austerity, which scientists are insisting is necessary. Almost all economists have assumed that steady growth signifies a healthy economy; only of late have some begun to question it. I would welcome courses in economics for the future.

This paragraph offers specific considerations on future ecological projections to recommend a course on futurist economics. When we look at the relationship between sentences, the degree of specificity is more apparent. Look at this paragraph arranged this time by increased specificity. The most general sentences align at the left margin; each level of specificity is indented.

1   Hence there is a wide field for courses on the future.
2   Time and space do not permit a review of the many possibilties, but let us take a look at the already popular subject of the environmental or biological crisis, aggravated by the population explosion.
3   Ecologists tell us that if current trends continue we are headed for disaster, conceivably a world that will become uninhabitable.
4   Together with the possibility of a thermonuclear war, these trends are faced with such immediate threats as the increasing pollution and the urban crisis, the steady deterioration of the central cities in the sprawling metropolitan areas.
5   And behind all these problems is the accepted national goal of indefinite economic growth, even though Americans already consume many times their proportional share of the world's dwindling natural resources.
6   While one may doubt that such growth can continue indefinitely, neither business, government, nor the public is prepared to accept a program of national austerity, which scientists are insisting is necessary.
6   Almost all economists have assumed that steady growth signifies a healthy economy; only of late have some begun to question it.
1   I would welcome courses in economics of the future.

This paragraph begins and ends with very general topic statements on the desirability of college courses on the future. This particular paragraph is structured like a chain of paper clips with each sentence offering more specific information about the one before it until it gets to two responses to curtailing economic growth—one by the business, government, and the public sector; one by economists. At this point the two views are equally specific although they contain different information.

Few writers would write a paragraph intending to structure it like a chain of paper clips. However, seeing that a well-developed paragraph contains sentences at as many as six levels (from very general to very specific) tells you that adding sentences that comment more specifically on a previous sentence is a good way to develop an idea.

SPECIFIC LANGUAGE.   Specificity can be increased through the language as well as the paragraphs. Language communicates through a balance between abstract and concrete words and general and specific terms.

Abstract and Concrete Words.   Abstract words refer to intellectual conceptions—ideas like love, political responsibility, or sexism. Concrete language refers to something physically apprehensible.

love	a passionate embrace a statement like "I love you" listening to another person's concerns a sacrificial act as mundane as going to a film you do not care to see or as significant as risking your life to save another's
political responsibility	registering to vote reading voter information pamphlet following political debates contributing money to your cause voting writing letters to government officials
sexism	hiring a man instead of a more qualified woman awarding child custody to a mother less qualified than the father expecting girls to become wives and mothers, boys to become scientists or corporate managers

Concrete language communicates an object, a person, or an act which can be intellectually understood but which can also be perceived by the senses—seen, heard, touched, even smelled or tasted.

General and Specific Words.   General words may be either abstract or concrete, but they refer to broad categories—college students, colors, religious attitudes, intellectual disciplines.

Specific words refer to individual cases, but degrees of specificity exist for words as they do for sentences.

college students   UCLA students   UCLA undergraduate students   UCLA undergraduate history majors   students in UCLA's History 205

colored   pastel-colored   pale sky blue, faded rose pink, sweet-butter yellow

religious attitudes   Judeo-Christian attitudes   Christian attitudes   Roman Catholic attitudes   Roman Catholic liberation theology in Central and South America

intellectual disciplines   science   natural science   biology   biochemistry genetics   genetic engineering   recombinant DNA studies

Specific language communicates precisely. With it a writer can paint a vivid word picture for the reader. Without it, a writer can only hope that maybe, just maybe, the students, the colors, the religious viewpoints, or the intellectual disciplines the reader envisions are the same as the writer's intended ones.

The Conclusion

Having fulfilled the introduction's promises through specific language and developed paragraphs, the writer still has work left—writing a conclusion. Conclusions reverse introductions, but do some of the same things. While an introduction engages the audience's interest in the subject, a conclusion leads the audience away from specific information about the subject back to the audience's world. In this sense, introductions and conclusions are opposite. They are the same because they use some of the same writing devices: a relevant anecdote, startling facts, a generalization about the essay's most important points, a quotation from a recognized authority. It is equally as important for a writer to have her audience and purpose clearly in mind in a conclusion as in an introduction.

Look again at the muscle physiologist writing for different audiences. If he were writing for a professional audience, an anecdote or startling facts would be singularly inappropriate. Scientific writing conventions require a conclusion to state generalized theory derived from experimental data; a scientific conclusion summarizes how the experimental data verified or failed to verify the experimental hypothesis. The physiologist would not be bound by these same conventions in an article for *Discover*'s popular audience. Here he would have to decide whether he intends to educate the audience or to ask them to take some action based on his presented argument. In the first case, he might choose amazing facts, startling statistics, or even relate an anecdote that would emphasize the importance of what he has told his audience about how muscles work. If, on the other hand, he were appealing to his audience to follow a personal health routine, or to ask the government to increase funds for muscle research, the conclusion might restate the most important points and set out a course of action. In each situation, the conclusion's principal function is not just to end the writing, or summarize what has been said. A good conclusion leaves the audience with a clear idea of the importance of what the writer has said.

With an introduction, body, and conclusion, a writer has a complete first draft ready for the last stage of the writing process—revising. Writers know that this is the time to put the draft aside completely and catch up on the unread newspapers and unpaid bills or meet those needs for sleep, pizza, or the new Woody Allen film. A complete break between writing and revising makes revision easier and more productive.

Writing Exercises

1. Select three paragraphs from your journal and analyze the relationships between the sentences in terms of specificity.

2. Write a paragraph describing your favorite location on campus. Use at least eight sentences with one sentence reaching level six.

3. Rewrite the following sentences, changing general words to specific and abstract words to concrete.

A beautiful woman walked along the shore.
Sports are great entertainment.
Extinction is invisible, but by rebelling against it, we can make it visible.
People poorly understand arms control.
Bad weather makes me feel dreary.

4. Write a first draft for one of the papers you worked through in the last chapter. Do not revise it. If you prefer, generate your own topic from browsing or use one of the following topics. Be sure to work through the pre-writing steps.

Compare a place you remember from childhood with your recent revisit to it. What do the changes suggest about changes in society or changes in you?

Compare and contrast your expectation of an experience with the actual experience. What does this tell you about how you form judgments and opinions?

Find an editorial in your newspaper's opinion section on a controversial issue. Write a paper in which you assert your opinion on the topic. Give the reasons for your opinion, relying on personal experience, observations, and facts from newspapers or news magazines.

Revising

> What makes me happy is rewriting. In the first draft you get your ideas and your theme clear, if you are using some kind of metaphor you get that established, and certainly you have to know where you're coming out. But the next time through it's like cleaning house, getting rid of all the junk, getting things in the right order, tightening things up. I like the process of making writing neat. (Ellen Goodman, quoted in Donald Murray, *Write to Learn* [1984], p. 163)

Ellen Goodman's apt analogy between revising and cleaning house clarifies how first drafts and revising proceed, but also suggests a reviser's biggest problem—knowing what is junk and what is not. I do not share Goodman's enthusiasm for cleaning house perhaps because my mother cleaned house avidly. Every Friday when I was at elementary school, my mother swept into my room brandishing an oversized wastebasket and tossed away snapshots, school papers, art projects, and outgrown toys. Unlike my childhood room, my house is filled with every book I have ever read, first, second, and final drafts of everything I have written, photographs from every trip; only dirt and refuse find the trash can. I tell you this because one of the most difficult tasks student writers face is parting with anything they have written—even useless words. If your nature is more like mine than Goodman's, try my technique. I may not throw anything away, but I do put cast-off books and clothes in the basement. Prepare to revise by making a basement file or notebook where you can save your favorite "junk" for an appropriate occasion.

Revision Criteria

Experienced writers have little difficulty identifying junk. Experience has taught them to read their own writing as if it were a total stranger's. Objectivity is the first revising tool. The second is criteria for judgment. While writers may develop criteria for their special audiences and purposes, most readers expect writing to be *complete, coherent, clear,* and *correct.* These four C's of good writing provide a useful guide for revising. Writing that is read and rewritten four times, one for each C, succeeds.

COMPLETENESS.   In the first reading for completeness, the writer moves rapidly through the text, making sure that the writing covers all the topics in the original and revised plans. He concerns himself with whether or not the body has met the introduction's commitments. He looks at the paragraphs to determine if the information is specific. He makes large notes in the margins to indicate where information is missing, or where information does not relate to the introduction's commitment.

Questions for Completeness

- Does the introduction indicate the specific topic and make a commitment?
- Does the introduction interest the reader in the subject?
- Does the writing meet the introduction's commitments?
- Do the paragraphs have some sentences beyond level 3?
- Are generalizations and abstractions illustrated with concrete and specific detail?
- Do all the paragraphs relate to the topic and comment on that topic?

COHERENCE. Once a writer is satisfied that the writing is complete, the second reading for coherence begins. The word coherence embraces order, organization, movement through the writing, and logic, so the second reading will proceed more slowly, as the writer considers if paragraphs communicate ideas, if the writing moves from one paragraph and one idea to the next, and if the logic is valid.

Questions for Coherence

- Does the title reflect the topic and interest the reader?
- Do paragraphs have a topic sentence?
- Are all the sentences in a paragraph on that paragraph's topic?
- When the focus shifts from one aspect of the subject to another, does a new paragraph begin?
- When the focus shifts does the writer use transitional words? (*likewise, similarly, however, although, nevertheless, either, on the other hand, moreover, in addition, because, consequently, next,* and so forth)
- Do I link paragraphs through transitional devices like repeating key words and phrases or following organizational patterns like process, cause and effect, or comparison and contrast throughout the paper?
- Are any syllogisms both valid and true?
- If the writing uses inductive logic is there enough evidence to support the conclusion?
- Does the writing reach conclusions based on single experiences, that is, does it overgeneralize?
- Does the writing rely on solid evidence rather than emotion and prejudice?

CLARITY. "Clutter," according to journalist and professor William Zinsser, "is the disease of American writing. We are a society strangling in unnecessary words, circular constructions, pompous frills and meaningless jargon." The third reading and revision moves from ideas and structures to language. Here writers must mercilessly cut extraneous words, convert inaction to action, and revive personal responsibility. To revise for clarity, a writer must have a clear sense of what clear sentences should accomplish.

Clear sentences have concrete subjects and active verbs.

> *not* There were charges of bribery against the players, and they were arrested.
> *but* Tulane police arrested three basketball players for bribery.

They shun jargon, clichés, and unnecessary words.

not   The bilateral ethics committee composed of both students and faculty is in gear and ready to deal with all problems of cribbing and cheating.

but   The faculty-student ethics committee hears cheating cases.

They opt for simple English over bureaucratese.

not   Upon receiving input regarding the incursion of terrorist forces in the attack mode, non-military personnel were retired from embassy positions and Army personnel were deployed in their place.

but   Hearing of planned terrorist attacks, the Army replaced civilians at the embassy.

They eliminate unnecessary prepositional phrases.

not   The first wave of attack on the causes of this problem focused on the senior employees of the company.

but   The first attack on the problem's causes focused on the company's senior employees.

Revising for clarity makes demands on the writer to opt for simple language and direct statements. It requires him to write with an ear for spoken language and a desire to express ideas rather than impress readers.

Questions for Clarity

- Do sentences have concrete subjects?
- Do I use "I" rather than "one" when I am the subject?
- Where possible, do action verbs replace forms of "to be"?
- Does writing use active rather than passive verbs?
- Are there too many expletives (*it is...* and *there are...*)?
- Are there unnecessary words like *quite* and *very* or doublings like *peaceful and quiet, free and easy,* and so forth?
- Are there phrases frequently heard or seen in print (clichés)?
- Is there specialized language inappropriate to audience or subject (jargon)?
- Are sentences overloaded with prepositional phrases?

CORRECTNESS.   Finally, a writer reads for mechanical errors. Most writers discover many mechanical errors during the first three readings; the glaring sentence fragments, subject-verb agreement errors, and misspellings are usually corrected by the third reading. The remaining errors are the hardest to find because the writer may not recognize them as errors. Here are four things that can help: a friend, a handbook of standard English usage, a dictionary, and a small notebook. First, read the draft aloud to the friend. Often reading aloud forces a writer to see errors missed in silent reading, particularly sentence construction errors. Next, ask the friend to circle what she thinks are spelling, punctuation, grammar, and word use errors. One person's errors often differ from another's, so writer and friend will recognize different errors. Look up any potential error in the English handbook and dictionary.

Record the error and correction in the notebook, so that next time you read for correctness, you look for these particular errors. Also use this notebook to record any errors identified by instructors. After a while this notebook will become an invaluable editing tool.

Revising Exercises

1. Exchange essays with a classmate. Using the list of revising questions, mark the areas where the student needs to revise. Put necessary comments in the margins.
2. Using the revision questions, mark problems with clarity and clutter. Rewrite the following passage to improve specificity and remove clutter.

> Irony in film comedy can be defined as the difference between what is seen and said and what is actually meant. We, the audience, see the entirety of a film and know the truth. The audience can see everything happening in the film while the characters of the film see only what is going on around them. The satiric focus in *Dr. Strangelove* is directed toward the military and its attitudes, the arms race, Soviet and U.S. relations, nuclear war and the Doomsday device. In this film Slim Pickens, who is the protagonist, is sent with his men to bomb the Soviet Union. In *Dr. Strangelove* we, the audience, see that one bomber gets through the Soviet missiles. On their journey they encounter many different obstacles which they must overcome to achieve their goal of bombing the Soviet Union. The antagonists of the film are the President and Mandrake, both played by Peter Sellers. The reason these two are the antagonists is because they want to stop protagonist Pickens from accomplishing his goal, bombing Russia. The values of this film support the launching of a nuclear war. These values, by all means, are unreasonable and are contrary to what the audience feels to be reasonable. So the film's irony has the audience cheering Pickens and their crew on to their Russian target, which will set off the doomsday machine and nuclear war. This is achieved because the whole focus of the movie is to stop the one little bomber which has gone through radar and so many obstacles to get to its destiny. When the President tells the Soviet leader to shoot the plane down, not even caring about the men inside, we start to sympathize with Pickens and his men. The comedy is ironic because we want Slim and his crew to get through the Soviet missiles and bomb them, even though the result will be total destruction of the earth by the Soviet doomsday machine.

Chapter 2
Reading
Critically

In his book *Future Shock* (1970), Alvin Toffler brought to the world's attention the tremendous rate of change our technological society experiences. An information overload is part of this overwhelming change.

> Prior to 1500, by the most optimistic estimates, Europe was producing books at a rate of 1000 titles per year. This means, give or take a bit, that it would take a full century to produce a library of 100,000 titles. By 1950, four and a half centuries later, the rate had accelerated so sharply that Europe was producing 120,000 titles a year. What once took a century now took only ten months. By 1960, a single decade later, the rate had made another significant jump, so that a century's work could be completed in seven and a half months. And, by the mid-sixties, the output of books on a world scale, Europe included, approached the prodigious figure of 1000 titles per *day*. (pp. 30-31)

This information environment, combined with our lives' rapid pace, tempts us to read hastily, stuffing ourselves with mental fast food. Thus filled, but poorly nourished, we lack stamina for creatively solving intellectual, artistic, social, or scientific problems and writing convincingly about them. Becoming a good writer requires breaking the *fast read* habit and developing active reading skills.

FAST READ VERSUS ACTIVE READING

Written language uses a system of symbols (letters, spaces, punctuation marks) to represent words which in turn represent objects, events, relationships, and actions. When, as children, we learn to read, we learn to manipulate the code; we learn to move rapidly from symbol to concept and back to symbol. Our reading ability increases as we store more and more equivalencies in our memory. A child learns early that r-o-s-e equals a sweet-scented flower. Later she learns that a symbol's position in relation to other symbols—its context—also affects meaning. Following a noun or pronoun, r-o-s-e now signals the action *to rise* happened in the past. While children labor to learn this system of symbols, patterns, and relationships, adults use the system automatically. They assign meaning based on their knowledge of language, reading until a new word or unfamiliar context appears. The unfamiliar sends the reader to the dictionary to expand the code. Reading at this level resembles translation or transliteration.

Reading for Literal Meaning

To better understand this, compare the first four nonsense lines below with the first verse of Lewis Carroll's poem "Jabberwocky" following them.

Tsec brillig, te nie slithy toves
    Tiate gyre te gimble nad nie wabe;
Suot mimsy tneite nie borogoves,
    Te nie mome raths outgrabe.

'Twas brillig, and the slithy toves
    Did gyre and gimble in the wabe;
All mimsy were the borogoves,
    And the mome raths outgrabe.

The first four lines make no sense whatsoever, while Carroll's lines have enough English words to create a familiar context, suggesting meaning. An automatic reader can decode this to approximately, "It was sometime, and some slithy something did two actions in the somewhere; the something elses were all some condition (mimsy), and a third thing (mome) or class of things (raths) did something else. Assuming all these unfamiliar things, conditions, and actions could be found in a dictionary, a reader could "decode" the symbols.

At this decoding, we read for language's denotative meaning. Minimally, a reader must understand the denotative meanings of what he reads. Sometimes, however, readers become so habituated to "fast read," they satisfy themselves with basic sense rather than complete meaning. Let's return to Lewis Carroll for a moment. A reader might feel he knows what this stanza is about. After all, the relationship words are there, and words resemble familiar words. If an instructor asked that a student read this poem not for an exam but to get a sense about Lewis Carroll, and if he were also told that the only glossary Carroll provided for the rhyme was in another book on two-hour reserve in the library, the student might be tempted to go with a basic sense reading which might look like this:

'Twas brillig, and the slithy toves
'Twas summer, and the slimy toads
    Did gyre and gimble in the wabe;
    Did jump and gambol in the waves;
All mimsy were the borogoves,
All noisy were the crickets,
    And the mome raths outgrabe.
    And the silent rats ran away.

Almost certainly, the meanings the hypothetical student assigned to Carroll's nonsense words differed from the meanings you thought of as you puzzled over the strange words. In this case, the difference matters little; Carroll wrote his poem as part of Alice in Wonderland's looking glass world. If, however, an article on immunology mentioned *bacteriophage* or an art historian referred to *mannerism,* and a reader created meanings or relied on the passage's "general sense," the passage could not be decoded, even at its most basic literal level.

Identifying Important Ideas

Using a dictionary faithfully is the first step to becoming an active reader. The second step is to move from reading words and sentences for equivalent meanings to identifying important ideas and distinguishing them from less important ones. Here, remembering writing's structural conventions discussed in the last chapter's section "Writing," can suggest a way to read for important ideas. Most writing, remember, uses paragraphs to signal topic shifts. Further, good paragraphs contain both general and specific sentences, with the specific sentences offering comments on the more general ones. After learning the topic from the title, an active reader looks first for the general sentence (or sentences) which focuses the topic and makes a statement about the topic and then for the specific detail which fulfills the general statement's commitment. The active reader mentally restates the generalization and support in one or two summary sentences. Developing the habit of making mental sentence summaries especially helps when your reading is for a paper or an exam. (In this situation write the summaries in margins or notebooks.)

This paragraph from "The Dynamo and the Virgin" (1900) in an American historian's great autobiography, *The Education of Henry Adams,* and the comments following, illustrate using structural cues for active reading. Adams has earlier introduced scientist Langley as scholar Adams's guide to the technological displays at the 1889 Paris exposition, an early world's fair. (Adams writing about himself as though he were another person, refers to himself as the *scholar, he,* and *Adams.)*

> *Then he [Langley] showed his scholar the great hall of dynamos* [electric genera-
> tors], and explained how little he knew about electricity or force of any kind, even of
> his own special sun, which spouted heat in inconceivable volume, but which, as far as
> he knew, might spout less or more, at anytime, for all the certainty he felt in it. To
> him, the dynamo itself was but an ingenious channel for conveying somewhere the
> heat latent in a few tons of poor coal hidden in a dirty engine-house carefully kept out
> of sight; *but to Adams the dynamo became a symbol of infinity.* As he grew accus-
> tomed to the great gallery of machines, he began to feel the forty-foot dynamos as a
> moral force, much as the early Christians felt the Cross. The planet itself seemed less
> impressive, in its old-fashioned, deliberate, annual or daily revolution, than this huge
> wheel, revolving within arm's length at some vertiginous [dizzying] speed, and barely
> murmuring—scarcely humming an audible warning to stand a hair's-breadth further
> for respect of power—while it would not wake the baby lying close against its frame.
> Before the end, one began to pray to it; inherited instinct taught the natural expression
> of man before silent and infinite force. *Among the thousand symbols of ultimate
> energy, the dynamo was not so human as some, but it was the most expressive.*

Formulating a Summary Statement

In the preceding, the italicized sentences, the most general, establish the topic *dynamos,* and comment that they are, for Adams, symbols of *ultimate energy.*

- Then he [Langley] showed his scholar the great hall of dynamos.
- . . . but to Adams the dynamo became a symbol of infinity.
- Among the thousand symbols of ultimate energy, the dynamo was not so human as some, but it was the most expressive.

Other sentences offer details about the dynamo and the reverence it evokes.

- forty-foot dynamos as a moral force.
- force such as the early Christians felt the Cross.
- revolving within arm's length at some vertiginous [dizzying] speed, and barely murmuring
- The planet itself seemed less impressive

Combining specific detail with general statements gives the summary sentence:

The forty-foot dynamos, revolving silently at dizzying speeds—more impressive than
the earth—for Adams became a symbol of moral force, as impressive as the Cross to
early Christians.

Taken out of context, neither the paragraph nor its summary sentence give the full meaning of Adams's chapter. Since the dynamo is only half the chapter's focus, as the chapter's title "The Dynamo and the Virgin" indicates, an active reader would look for the other focus—the Virgin. The paragraph following contains part of the chapter's comparison. Adams here responds to a trip to the imposing French Gothic cathedral dedicated to the Virgin Mary at Chartres. Read the paragraph actively, underlining its most general sentences and noting the phrases and words offering specific details.

All the steam in the world could not, like the Virgin, build Chartres. Yet in mechanics, whatever the mechanicians might think, both energies acted as interchangeable forces on man, and by action on man all known force may be measured. Indeed few men of science measured force in any other way. After once admitting that a straight line was the shortest distance between two points, no serious mathematician cared to deny anything that suited his convenience, and rejected no symbol, unproved or unprovable, that helped him to accomplish work. The symbol was force, as a compass-needle or a triangle was force, as the mechanist might prove by losing it, and nothing could be gained by ignoring their value. Symbol or energy, the Virgin had acted as the greatest force the Western world ever felt, and had drawn man's activities to herself more strongly than any other power, natural or supernatural, had ever done; the historian's business was to follow the track of the energy; to find where it came from and where it went to; its complex source and shifting channels; its values, equivalents, conversions. It could scarcely be more complex than radium; it could hardly be deflected, diverted, polarized, absorbed more perplexingly than other radiant matter. Adams knew nothing about any of them, but as a mathematical problem of influence on human progress, though all were occult [concealed], all reacted on his mind, and he rather inclined to think the Virgin easiest to handle.

Although a difficult passage, particularly taken out of the entire chapter's context, a summary of it should look something like this.

While both the dynamo and the Virgin acted as interchangeable forces on man and both their energies were hidden to the historian Adams, that the Virgin had acted as the greatest force the Western world ever felt, inclined Adams to feel the Virgin the easiest to handle and hers the track of energy he would follow.

The difficult decision a reader makes about this passage is what he does with the materials about mechanicians and mathematicians and about radiant energy and the Virgin's energy. Seeing the balance between general and specific sentences should help a reader recognize that mentioning the mathematician's equating symbol and force allows Adams to equate Virgin as symbol with Virgin as force. Further, comparing the Virgin's energy with radiant energy, the historian admits his deficient knowledge of both and his need for study. While these are important parts of Adams's argument, this material is subordinate to the main idea—the great force exerted by the dynamo and the Virgin on Western man.

ACTIVE READING, THINKING READING

Uncovering denotative meanings and identifying main ideas and supporting detail takes active readers closer to a writer's meaning than the customary *fast read*. The written word, however, possesses the power to accomplish more than just express a writer's hobbyhorses; the written word is an encounter between a writer, her ideas and purposes, and an audience. Readers fully understand an article or a book when they know not just *what* it says, but how the writer presents herself and her ideas in relation to the audience, and what the writing seeks to accomplish. At this level a reader distinguishes between truth and distortion, information and propaganda, public policy and personal prejudice. Readers become thinkers. Becoming a thinking reader means learning to recognize audiences, writers' personas and purposes, and to evaluate arguments.

Recognizing Audiences

It is easier as a writer to choose an audience and identify its characteristics than it is for a reader to identify another writer's audience. A writer can determine his audience's likely education level, age, socio-economic group, even sex, when he decides where the writing will be submitted or published. Once a writer identifies his audience, the writing's assumptions, arguments, language, and syntax seek that particular audience's interests and abilities.

Consider how two different audiences—one, readers of a legal opinion journal published by a national association of women lawyers, the other, the readers of *Christian Century* (a mainstream Protestant magazine)—might affect an article favoring legal abortion. The audience of the women's law journal would be predominantly female, probably aged between 26 and 45, though some would be older, and unbound by traditional female sexual stereotypes. Most would have four years of undergraduate and three years of graduate education and be accustomed to logical argument. Because so many women have entered the legal profession in recent years, a writer cannot assume that all women lawyers are feminists, or that all favor abortion. He could assume their interest in abortion as women in their childbearing years. How would all this affect the article? If I were writing for this audience, I would assume a formal voice—a professional speaking to other professionals. I would present a balanced argument, considering and answering objections first, then advancing my position—that laws restricting abortion are laws instituting religious beliefs in violation of the Constitution—by referring to specific laws and religious canons.

Christian Century's audience is more diverse. The magazine's statement that it publishes articles of religious, social, and political interest indicates interest in wider issues than Biblical exegesis, but the title reflects the audience's shared interest in a Christian perspective. The audience includes all-aged men and women, some well-educated, some not, whose beliefs span the spectrum from fundamentalist to liberal. A writer here addresses a group separated from *Newsweek* or *Life*'s general readership only by their interest in Jesus's teachings. Since Jesus never spoke about abortion, the only safe assumption a writer can make about this audience's attitude toward the subject is they share a fundamental respect for human life, many to the point that they oppose abortion as a violation of God's commandment against killing. Writing for this audience, I would work to establish a relationship with them. The formal tone I used for the women's law journal would shift to the personal voice of an educated career woman, married with a child, the voice of a person, like other Christians and like Jesus, concerned about the quality of life for the poor and disenfranchised. The argument's focus would shift from legal justice to social justice, but the burden of reasoned argument and responsible evidence would stand for both audiences.

Surprisingly, if a writer opposing abortion wrote for these same two audiences the argument might shift but the writing approach would not. The women's law journal still would require a formal tone and a balanced argument based on legal precedents that laws allowing abortion violate the right to life. For *Christian Century*'s broad audience, a wife and mother's personal voice would argue from a social perspective for human life's dignity. Again, reasoned argument and responsible evidence would stand for both audiences.

The different ways a writer would approach these two audiences suggest what a reader must look for in a writing piece to find its audience: *diction, tone, argumentative assumptions,* and *evidence.*

Diction

DENOTATIVE LANGUAGE AND AUDIENCE.   The words a writer selects relate directly to the audience. At the denotative level, an audience understands only language that relates to its knowledge and experience. Familiar language speaks to everyone. Specialized words from medicine, law, theology, and literary criticism speak to doctors, lawyers, theologians, and critics. Precise language that shuns emotional colorations speaks to logical and reasonable people, regardless of profession.

CONNOTATIVE LANGUAGE AND AUDIENCE.   Language is not denotative only; it possesses the capacity to mean beyond the symbolic equivalency to object, action, idea, and relationship. As coin of the realm, words pass from hand to hand, acquiring their own patina. Not just ten cents; dime says cheap, like dime candy. "Give me a dime" asks for a handout. Language's connotative meaning refers to the patina, the social meaning words acquire through use. At the connotative level, language evokes the audience's emotional associations. When a writer uses highly connotative language he appeals more to his audience's emotion than to its reason. Think about the use of connotative language in the abortion controversy. *Abort* denotes to end prematurely, and even though *abortion* means the premature end of pregnancy, it also carries connotations of something hideous, a monstrosity. Those who favor abortion then not only favor ending pregnancy, they favor monstrosity. With this weight of connotative meaning, those who favor legal abortion refer to themselves as pro-choice. Even the anti-abortion groups avoid the word; they are not anti-*abortion* but *pro-life*.

Connotative language also reflects social, racial, political, or religious stereotypes. When a writer's language relies on these connotations, he expects his audience to share the beliefs at the stereotype's center. A writer referring to liberals as "bleeding hearts" or even "idealists" and conservatives as "hard-minded" communicates not only his own bias, but his expectation that the audience shares his bias.

Tone

FORMAL AND INFORMAL. Words combine with ideas to create the tone of a writing piece. Formal writing creates a distance between the writer and audience by removing most *I*'s and *you*'s, and by using elevated, specialized language. Formal tone suggests a serious, high-minded, probably well-educated audience. Informal tone introduces the personal. When a writer is informal, the kinds of stories she relates, the way she presents herself, even the words she uses suggest audience attributes by indicating what she expects them to accept.

IRONY, SARCASM, AND HUMOR. Few readers find identifying formality or informality as difficult as spotting irony, sarcasm, or humor. Irony and sarcasm point to discrepancies between what exists and what ought to be. Seeing the statement "students love exams," a casual reader might think, "Yes, I suppose they do." A more careful reader will look at the context and wonder if this is some extraordinary group of students, or if the writer is looking ironically at the educational system that employs as a central learning device so repellent a tactic. When a writer uses irony he anticipates a sophisticated audience of careful readers. Less subtle than irony, sarcasm (attacking something and saying the opposite) works for wider audiences. Humor reveals far more about audiences than irony and sarcasm because it plays on social group bias. When we laugh at something, we join with people who are of like minds to laugh at the other—the distorted, the unusual, or the exaggerated. When a reader can identify those who are aligned and those who are cast out in humor, the audience is clear.

The Importance of Argumentative Assumptions

An *assumption* supposes that something is so evident that it requires no explanation or proof. Writing for an American magazine or newspaper, a writer assumes her audience knows the major events of American history, the Judeo-Christian tradition, and the popular culture produced by television, film, and advertising. She cannot assume that the audience shares political views, religious beliefs, or moral values. The assumptions a writer and audience share are apparent more in what goes unexplained than in the position being argued. Writing for the women's legal journal, I would not explain to lawyers the value of legal precedent; I would have to argue that the right to choose abortion is just, or unjust.

Evidence and Audience

A few years ago, the magazine *Psychology Today* carried an article by a psychologist demonstrating that mass media eliminate the boundaries between children and adults because adults no longer share the exclusive store of privileged information about sex, violence, suffering, and the like that was theirs in a reading culture. Writing for an educated, but not necessarily professional audience, he related a few anecdotes and personal observations, but most of his evidence came from historical documents, other social scientists' reported research, and experimental data—all appropriate for the magazine's usual readership.

This psychologist later spoke to a women's group in my community. This time his entire evidence consisted of personal observations, anecdotes from television, and descriptions of mother-daughter look-alikes in supermarkets and shopping malls. The evidence selected for the women's group suggested an audience interested only in fashion, food, television soap operas, and gossip—an audience unable to comprehend difficult scientific or historical proof. The evidence a writer selects markedly illustrates a writing piece's audience—or, at least, what the writer believes about the audience.

RECOGNIZING A WRITER'S PERSONA

Diction, tone, assumptions, and evidence all point to a particular audience, but, as the discussion of these suggests, they also reveal the writer's relationship with the audience. The writer's presence in a written work is called a *persona*. One of the most important clues to persona can be found in the tone. In formal writing where the writer and audience are distant, persona is often unrecognizable. The writer, an expert on her topic, speaks as a scientist, critic, economist, or historian. If the scientist, critic, economist, or historian is defending a position, the formal expert becomes the reasoned voice of expertise. The closer a writer moves to his audience, the clearer the persona becomes. Repudiating any pretense of objectivity, the persona in personal writing may reveal preferences, prejudices, concerns, and doubts. The writer relies on personal experiences and familiar anecdotes as evidence. For writing in between formal and personal, evidence also identifies the persona. Here, persona emerges from the balance a writer strikes between hard evidence (like statistics, reported data, or historical record) and more human anecdotes and observations. Also, what a writer explains and assumes reveals persona in the same way assumptions reveal audience.

To better understand the difficult idea of persona, look at the next two passages by Joan Didion.

It was hard to surprise me in those years. It was hard to even get my attention. I was absorbed in my intellectualization, my obsessive-compulsive devices, my projection, my reaction-formation, my somatization, and the transcript of the Ferguson trial. (*The White Album*)

Some of us who live in arid parts of the world think about water with a reverence others might find excessive. The water I will draw tomorrow from my tap in Malibu is today crossing the Mojave Desert from the Colorado River, and I like to think about exactly where that water is. The water I will drink tonight in a restaurant in Hollywood is by now well down the Los Angeles Aqueduct from the Owens River, and I also think about exactly where that water is: I particularly like to imagine it as it cascades down the 45-degree stone steps that aerate Owens water after its airless passage through the mountain pipes and siphons. ("Holy Water," *The White Album*)

The *I* in both passages brings the writer into direct relationship with the audience, but the persona differs in each passage. The first passage states directly the writer's self-absorption. The evidence, a series of psychological buzzwords, reveals a neurotic persona hiding behind abstractions. This persona is remote from the reader. The second passage presents facts about the sources of Los Angeles water. The detail with which the writer traces the water's movement combined with the author's intrusion "I like to think" show a persona concerned about a local problem. She is a concerned citizen who lives in Malibu and dines at a Hollywood restaurant. Reading with sensitivity to language makes recognizing a persona far easier. Looking at Didion's diction in the first passage reveals a contrast between the direct statements' simple language and the abstract psychological jargon. This contrast shows a potentially reliable, honest persona distracted by over-intellectualization. In the second passage, the simple concrete language Didion uses to trace the water's path contrasts with words—*a reverence others might find excessive*—whose connotations establish the persona's emotional concern.

DETERMINING PURPOSE

From the last chapter you know that writers write to tell stories (narration), to re-create for their readers a sense impression of a person, place, or object (description), to explain an idea, an event, a procedure, or a phenomenon (exposition), or to argue a position. Since these purposes shape writing, recognizing description, narration, exposition, and argument is a fairly easy reading task discovered by asking, "*What* is this writing doing?" Thesis statements and other organizational and developmental strategies answer *how* writing proceeds. But the thinking reader needs to know more than *how* writing progresses; this reader's critical question begins with *why*.

To discover why something has been written, you need first to consider the circumstances surrounding its writing and then look more closely at the author in relation to his subject (point of view). A professor's history journal article on Thomas Jefferson would likely differ from a textbook study. Both would be expository, but the journal article should break new ground. The journal article would seek to change an accepted view; the textbook would advance widely accepted knowledge. A front-page newspaper story on nuclear power abuses, although it might cause readers to question the safety of nuclear power, has as its primary purpose informing the audience. An editorial page's article can ask the community to vote against a new nuclear power plant after detailing the same abuses as the front-page story. Both articles educate, but for different purposes. The description you write about yourself in a letter to a prospective employer seeks a different end than your bio-sketch for the management club newsletter. All these examples show that the place writing ends up—a professor's desk, a college newspaper, a letters-to-the-editor column, a professional journal, or a special interest magazine—gives the reader a clue about purpose.

Point of View and Purpose

After you find purposes related to the circumstances surrounding writing, look carefully at the writer in relation to his subject. A writer's point of view may be either objective or subjective. When a writer writes objectively, he removes himself from the written word and relates facts, events, and data. He assumes the reporter's pose and educational purpose, identifiable to a careful reader by concrete words uncolored by emotional bias. With a subjective point of view, a writer intrudes on his writing's factual content with interpretation, comments, and judgments. If the writer's reaction grows responsibly from his facts, and he argues logically, relying on concrete language appealing to a reader's intellect, such writing changes people's thinking and leads to action. Some subjective writing, however, appeals only to the reader's emotions through stereotypes, highly connotative language, and emotional situations. Such writing seeks to provoke action (or inaction) through positive feelings like compassion, moral virtue, and love and acceptance needs, but also through such negative ones as guilt, indignation, fear, or hatred. Thinking readers need to search subjective writing for emotional appeals to clearly see the writer's purpose.

Assessing Argument

Used loosely, argument refers to what a piece of writing says—its topic, main assertions, supporting evidence or development, and its organizational strategies. Used in this way *argument* refers to any writing. Assessing this kind of argument means making summary statements and describing evidence and organization.

Being an active, thinking reader means also identifying formal argument strategies—the kinds used to advance a position on a topic at issue—and recognizing the
argument's flaws.

Inductive Arguments and Valid Evidence

Inductive arguments, remember, reach generalized conclusions from observed
specifics. The logical flaws occur either in evidence or conclusion. First, evidence
must be valid. If the evidence consists of personal experience, personal observation, or expert testimony, the evidence source needs to be objective and reliable.

EVALUATING EXPERIMENTAL DATA. *A Representative Sample:* A reader also
needs to evaluate the validity of experimental data by considering study sample
and experiment design. A good study takes as its sample a representative population, or states directly that it is working with a limited population. For example,
the University of Michigan frequently inventories freshman students' attitudes on
politics, sex, religion, and morals. If it were to study only University of Michigan
students, the sample would not be nationally or socio-economically representative,
because the University of Michigan's student population is predominantly mid-
western.

An Adequate and Random Sample: If the study were confined just to University of Michigan students, describing only University of Michigan freshman students' attitudes, the sample could still have problems. To be valid the findings
must represent attitudes of 15 percent of the students selected randomly. That is,
the sample must be both large enough and wide enough. If 15 percent of the
freshman students were enrolled in History 101, the interviewer still would have a
poor sample if he inventories the attitudes of those students alone. Even though
they would make up a large enough sample, the sample would not be random.

An Unbiased Test: Suppose researchers establish a correct sample, will their
data necessarily be valid? This will depend on experiment design. Experiment design is a complex issue that students study in natural and social science courses.
Outside science courses, a good reader needs only to look for a description of the
experiment and indications that the researcher has tried to be honest and objective. He has not sought freshman attitudes on politics on the Young Republican's
or Young Democrat's letterhead or asked questions reflecting his own bias. Despite valid evidence, an inductive argument can have problems with conclusions.
Flawed inductive arguments overgeneralize from evidence, or sometimes, a
preconceived conclusion can cause a writer to select data which aligns the conclusion with the preconception. Look back to the University of Michigan freshman
inventory. Suppose a nationwide study found that 55 percent of freshman used
some dangerous drug (alcohol, marijuana, cocaine, uppers, and so forth) at least
once a month. An argument concluding from this that college freshman are drug
abusers would be a gross overgeneralization (particularly since alcohol is included). Another flawed conclusion might occur if a study began with the idea

that college students engage in promiscuous sexual behavior. An inventory could be designed to ask questions about sexual practices and frequency, but if it omitted questions regarding marital status, or lengths of relationships, the seemingly accurate evidence and the conclusion growing from it would be flawed.

Deductive Arguments

Deduction begins with a generalization and moves to the specific instance using the syllogism. The last chapter showed that for a syllogism to be valid, it must take the form:

$$
\begin{array}{ll}
 & A = B \\
\text{and} & C = A \\
\text{therefore} & C = B
\end{array}
$$

With this in mind you will recognize that the following is a valid deduction.

Men get hurt in relationships with career women.
John is a man.
John will get hurt in his relationship with Samantha, who is a career woman.

The number of married career women in good relationships suggests that the generalization forming this syllogism's first premise relies more on prejudice than fact. For deductive argument to succeed, the syllogism must be both valid and true. Just as the good reader must attend to the truth of the conclusions in inductive argument, she must be aware that deductive argument can proceed from false premises.

Other Argument Flaws

Although the most recognizable flaws occur in the larger deductive and inductive patterns, logical errors also appear in development strategies.

FLAWED ANALOGY.   An argument using analogy needs to establish more than one similarity between the things being compared to be a convincing analogy. Taken alone, the statement, "People should avoid caffeine because it produces cancer in experimental rats" appears to be a good basis for an argument against people using caffeine. The statement relies on the similarity between human metabolism and rat metabolism. This is only one similarity in the analogy. To be a strong argument, it would have to establish similarities in dosage, and some statistical indication that humans have problems with caffeine. The more similarities a writer establishes in an analogy, the more convincing the argument.

FLAWED CAUSAL ARGUMENTS.   Frequently an argument is structured to show causation—particularly in science and history. A strong argument for causation relies on causes which are necessary, sufficient, and contributory. Look at the relationship between the causes and the disease AIDS (Acquired Immune Deficiency Syndrome).

Exposure to the AIDS virus through blood transfusion or sexual contact causes AIDS.

- The virus and the means of transmission are *necessary* for a person to contract AIDS.
- The virus and sexual contact are *sufficient* to cause AIDS.
- The virus and sexual contact alone *contribute* to AIDS.

The incidence of AIDS is highest among hemophiliacs who receive potentially contaminated blood and among male homosexuals. A valid causal argument cannot be made here because being a hemophiliac or male homosexual is not a necessary, sufficient, or contributory cause of the disease.

Arguments from cause also run into problems when they assert cause when none exists. Until humans understood astronomy, they believed that such cosmic changes as comets caused political unrest. Similar to this, when one event precedes a second, the first is seen as the second's cause. How often have you assigned a cold's cause to a walk in the rain or intestinal flu to a bad meal. This reasoning error sometimes appears in historical writing. Darwin's theory on the survival of the fittest preceded late nineteenth-century laissez-faire economics and may even have influenced the theoreticians, but Darwin did not cause capitalism's vast expansion and abuses during this time—economic policy did.

A more subtle flaw in causal reasoning occurs when a contributory cause is seen as the only cause. A few years ago a teenager committed suicide after listening to rock music advocating suicide. The parents sued the rock group, saying the music caused the suicide. The court ruled that the music alone was not sufficient to cause the boy's suicide. An error in causal reasoning closely related to this occurs when one event is seen as the cause of the second, but actually they both proceed from a common cause. For example, some people argue that crime causes drug abuse, others that drug abuse causes crime. Rather than one causing the other, they may proceed from many complex socio-economic conditions.

FLAWED DEFINITION.   A good definition identifies a term as a member of a class and specifies its *essential, distinguishing* characteristics, using precise, denotative language. Poor definitions occur when writers use ambiguous language or define a thing using its own terms (circular definition). Stephen Jay Gould points out in "Evolution as Fact and Theory" (readings in chapter 3), that "scientific creationism" ambiguously defines itself by playing with "scientific." According to Gould, "Their brand of creationism, they claim, is 'scientific' because it follows the Popperian model in trying to demolish evolution." This relies on a misinterpretation of philosopher Karl Popper's argument that science's hallmark is the falsifiability of its theories; "science cannot prove absolutely but it can falsify." Gould demonstrates that their definition relies on ambiguous use of both *falsify* and *scientific*. Further, the statement that science is the branch of knowledge that studies nature scientifically defines science in its own terms. This is a flawed circular definition.

Definition's other abuses occur with the use of emotional language. In one case, a writer may use a highly connotative word to define a second word, and then use this as an argument's major premise. For example, when a writer argues against abortion from the premise that abortion is *murder*, she abuses definition as much as she would if she opposed capital punishment because it is *murder*. Further, writers may appeal to their readers' emotions by leaving terms undefined. An argument proceeding from terms like *true American, real men, true Christian,* or *concerned Democrat* may pretend definition but invokes stereotypes.

FALSE ARGUMENTS.   Sometimes writers seek to influence their audience by using approaches that appear to be arguments but actually appeal to their readers' emotions.

Argument to the person (ad hominem).   The first such argument avoids the issue and instead discusses the personal life or character of someone involved. Such an approach might ignore a Congresswoman's voting record and argue instead that she should not be re-elected because of her imminent divorce. Or someone might argue that Hemingway's novels and short stories should not be read by high school children because he committed suicide.

Argument to the people (ad populem).   The second kind of false argument might be structured soundly but its basic premises appeal to its audience's bias. Using this approach, Hitler's arguments for Aryan racial purity appealed to German nationalism.

False dilemma.   A writer also can bewilder his audience by presenting a false dilemma, where he presents only two alternatives, one desirable, the other distasteful. We have all heard the statement that unless the United States military intervenes in one country or another, the Communists will take over. Such an argument allows only black or white, and admits no possibility of gray.

Appeal to ignorance.   Finally, some arguments assert their own validity because no opposition exists. Such logic says that a university registration system works efficiently because no reliable complaints have been made against it, or that Jim Johns is a fine executive because he has done nothing wrong.

CRITICAL ANALYSIS

For a reader to keep in mind all writing's components as he reads may seem overwhelming. Active reading, like good writing, becomes easier the more you do it. At first, a checklist or set of questions might help you sharpen your critical reading. Some questions follow the essays in this book to guide you to important information and writing devices, but making your own questions will focus your critical abilities. Make sure that you have questions to help you identify

thesis
main supporting points
denotative and connotative language
tone
point of view
assumptions
audience
persona
purpose
argumentative approach
kind of evidence
validity of evidence
argument flaws

Once you have a checklist, read the following selection critically to discover what the writer is really doing. This selection, by columnist Jack Smith appeared in the *Los Angeles Times* "View" section (on community service and human interest). (Notice that it uses the conventional short newspaper paragraph.)

Pornography and Censorship: The Argument Rages On, 25 Years after "Tropic of Cancer"

Pornography seems to be in for it.

The people who make such decisions for the rest of us seem to have decided that photographs and descriptions of sexual debauchery cause rape and violence.

This time the moralists are a coalition of fundamentalist evangelists and radical feminists, abetted by the attorney general's commission on pornography.

Evidently the commission is about to conclude its inquiries with an opinion that pornography and sexual violence are related, though it has found no scientific evidence to support that conclusion, and neither has anyone else.

As Harvard Law School teacher Alan Dershowitz said the other day in this newspaper, "Rarely has so dangerous a conclusion been based on such flimsy evidence."

As always in inquiries that lead to censorship, the evidence seems to have been examined by men and women who are curiously immune to the pernicious effects they claim to have discovered in it.

Otherwise, having been exposed to the cause, shouldn't they naturally begin committing acts of sexual aggression against the innocents they encounter in general life?

Censors are people who decide that something is unfit for the rest of us to see, but are miraculously unharmed by it themselves.

As Dershowitz says, the trouble with pornography is that no one can define it. The notorious Roth decision held that pornography was any material which, taken as a whole, was utterly without social value.

Who can say whether a book, a movie, a painting, or a song has social value? Perhaps a pornographic movie might stir socially beneficial urgings in one person as well as evil in another.

The censorious mind is often the product of some such moral stronghold as religion or education. Some are censorious because of their righteousness; some are merely naive.

Incredibly, it was only 25 years ago that I covered a trial in which a jury found Henry Miller's "Tropic of Cancer" obscene under the Roth ruling, and convicted a young bookseller of selling it. Although it was more bawdy than pornographic, more comic than lubricious, it was banned for many years from this country, along with such works of marked literary value as "Lady Chatterley's Lover" and "Ulysses."

What I remember most about the trial is that a deputy city attorney read the book out loud in court, and the judge often was obliged to lean toward his court reporter as if giving him instructions, meanwhile hiding his face behind a manila folder to conceal his laughter, which made his shoulders shake, and the jurors often went through agonies of facial distortion in futile attempts at concealing *their* laughter.

And yet, that same jury solemnly returned a verdict of guilty and the judge solemnly sentenced the defendant to jail. Such is the result of censorship: hypocrisy and persecution.

More hilarious to me than Miller's book was the exposure of two highly placed educators as literary nincompoops, though they testified righteously for the prosecution. Under cross-examination, Donald S. McDonald, Ph.D., then president of Cal State Los Angeles, admitted he didn't have time to read novels.

"Have you ever read 'The Sun Also Rises,' by Ernest Hemingway?" he was asked.

"No, I haven't," he said.

"Have you ever heard of it?"

"I can't recall that I have."

McDonald had also never heard of "From the Terrace" or "Butterfield 8" by John O'Hara, "God's Little Acre," the perennial best-seller by Erskine Caldwell, or "By Love Possessed," a recent Pulitzer Prize novel on love and the law by James G. Cozzens.

"Are you familiar with the painter named Matisse?"

"I may have heard of him," McDonald answered. "At lectures and so forth."

"You can't say positively, yes or no?"

"No, I can't."

Here was a man who was not familiar with the most popular literature of his time, and one of the most famous artists of the century, yet he was the educational leader of 16,000 college students and had been enlisted in the cause of censorship.

Also a witness for the prosecution was Ellis A. Jarvis, who had recently retired as superintendent of Los Angeles city schools. Jarvis was also unfamiliar with the works of O'Hara and Hemingway, though he had "skimmed" "Lady Chatterley's Lover" (no doubt looking for the censorable passages).

"Have you ever heard of (Hemingway's) 'For Whom the Bell Tolls'?" he was asked.

"Yes."

"Do you know who wrote it?"

"No. I don't know for sure."

McDonald showed the censorious quality of his thinking when he was asked: "People should learn about life in the world to the extent that it is not morbid, is that right?"

"And filthy," he said.

"And if something is morbid and filthy, then they should not learn about it?"

"I'd say yes."

In the 1950's the sheriff's vice squad used to show blue movies they'd confiscated in raids on men's smokers. They were closed showings: just for cops and the press. I sometimes went, but I'd usually sneak out after about half an hour, because at first pornography is funny, but then it becomes boring.

Censors hold that whatever is prurient—that is, whatever excites lust, is pornographic and ought to be banned.

If that is so, then the fundamentalist Muslims are right, and women ought not to be allowed abroad unless shielded from the public eye from head to foot.

Nothing is more prurient than an ordinarily pretty young woman walking down the street on a summer day in a white cotton dress.

Even Jimmy Carter used to lust in his heart.

Developing your critical reading skills may take some practice, but, it is hoped, you recognized some of these elements in Smith's essay.

Thesis

Rather than provoking violence, at first pornography is funny; then it becomes boring.

Main Supporting Points

1. According to Harvard Law School teacher, Dershowitz, little evidence supports linking pornography and violence.
2. Henry Miller's *Tropic of Cancer* provoked laughter at a pornography trial twenty-five years ago.
3. Despite the laughter, the jury and judge reached a hypocritical decision in that pornography trial.
4. The expert witnesses lacked a general knowledge about literature in the trial of literary pornography.
5. The author found laughter and boredom at police vice squad showings of blue movies.
6. If whatever is prurient should be removed from public view, and an ordinarily pretty girl is prurient, then ordinarily pretty girls should be removed from public view.

Denotative and Connotative Language

Generally appealing to the audience's reason, most language, particularly in relating anecdotes, relies on denotation. Smith uses some connotations to discredit
the position of censorship and the censors themselves. The proponents of censorship are "moralists" ("fundamentalist evangelists" and "radical feminists") who
are censorious because of "righteousness" or are "merely naive." These words
carry negative connotations only to readers who disapprove of fundamentalist
evangelists and radical feminists. "Naive" is the greatest insult. Further, when
these moralists view pornography, they are "miraculously unharmed." Smith dis-
credits the trial witnesses by using "literary nincompoops." Denotatively, a fool or
simpleton, *nincompoop* connotes silliness.

Tone

The use of *I* and personal experience establishes an informal tone. The writer uses
irony in several places. First, he asks why censors are unharmed by the pornography they encounter:

> Otherwise, having been exposed to the cause, shouldn't they naturally begin commit-
> ting acts of sexual aggression against one another and against the innocents they en-
> counter in general life?

Second, the pornography trial of *Tropic of Cancer* is ironic because the book
today holds a place in the literary canon. Third, having the judge and jury laugh at
the damaging pornographic book being read aloud, and then finding the defendant
guilty of selling pornography is doubly ironic. Fourth, the educational experts
should know artist Matisse and major American writers. And finally, vice squads
should not show the blue movies they confiscated in raids.

Point of View

The writer, clearly present in the essay, approaches pornography and censorship
from a subjective point of view. His irony and his objective presentation of evidence, however, strengthen the essay's rational appeal.

Assumptions

Smith assumes his audience's familiarity with modern novels and their respect for
literature's value. He also assumes they prize life in a free society where women
dress as they choose and not as a religious government dictates. He also assumes
his audience's familiarity with President Jimmy Carter and his notorious *Playboy*
interview remark that even with his fundamentalist, born-again Christianity, he
lusted "in his heart."

Audience

Smith's assumptions and use of connotation suggest that he is writing for an educated audience old enough to remember Jimmy Carter, though not necessarily old enough to remember the *Tropic of Cancer* trial (he details this). The article's appearance in the *Los Angeles Times* indicates a general audience, perhaps an open-minded one if stereotypes about Los Angeles moral liberalism are true.

Persona

The writer constructs the professional newspaperman persona by mentioning he covered the pornography trial and went to vice squad blue movie showings for "cops and the press." The ironic tone and rational appeals present the persona as a reasonable man, and the assumptions about literary awareness and value mark him as cultured. His distaste for both conservative fundamentalist evangelists and radical feminists suggests that he is politically moderate. Finally, his own pleasure in an "ordinarily pretty young woman" juxtaposed with his pornography-provoked laughter and boredom, shows a benign (rather than violent) masculine interest in women.

Purpose

This article takes a position (opposition) to a subject (pornography and censorship) which is "at issue." Smith seeks to convince his audience that pornography is more laughable than dangerous and that censorship deserves ridicule.

Argumentative Approach

Primarily inductive, the writer follows his evidence (the trial and the blue movie showings) with the generalization "at first pornography is funny, but then it becomes boring." He follows his inductive argument with a deductive syllogism based on the censor's assertions and his own experience.

If:	whatever is prurient		should be removed from public view
	(A)	=	(B)
and:	a pretty girl		is prurient
	(C)	=	(A)
then:	a pretty girl		should be removed from public view
	(C)	=	(B)

This syllogism, clearly valid and clearly lacking truth, points out the censors' flawed arguments. The writer here demonstrates the flaws which, at the essay's beginning, only appeared as an assertion that the attorney general's commission on pornography will conclude with an opinion "that pornography and sexual violence are related, though it has found no scientific evidence to support that conclusion, and neither has anyone else."

Kind and Validity of Evidence

The author states facts about recent concern over pornography, Dershowitz's comments on the impossibility of a pornography definition, and the Roth decision. Testimony from the pornography is also factual, although the persona's position of "covering" the trial marks these facts as personal observation. Finally the writer relates personal experience in blue movie showings and his observations on a pretty girl. A reader has no way of knowing if the trial dialogue is accurate, but she may question the relevance of analogizing a pornography trial of Miller's *Tropic of Cancer* with current pornography not specified by the author.

Argument Flaws

The writer provides limited evidence to support the inductive generalization.

Critical Assessment

Active reading, as you just discovered, takes writing apart; assessment and evaluation put it back together. One valuable criterion by which to judge writing is what I will call "confluence," which means a gathering together. In a well-written article or book, the persona and argument will reach a specified audience to accomplish the writer's purpose. Nothing detracts from the purpose or strikes a discordant note. Thinking back to Smith's article, his rational arguments, irony, unemotional language, and factual evidence appeal to the moderate, literate audience who probably agree that pornography is more humorous than dangerous. His weak inductive pattern (too little evidence) and flawed analogy interfere with establishing an overwhelming argument against censorship, but then this was not the author's full purpose. In short, the various writing components work together fairly well.

Chapter 3
Writing
from Reading

From the previous two chapters you learned approaches for solving writing problems and for the sophisticated reading writers must do. You probably noticed the close link between reading and writing; reading serves as a writer's resource at every stage of the writing process. Reading suggests topics and provides information before you write. As you plan, write, and revise, seeing how other writers choose their purposes and shape their writing, serves as a model. Furthermore, the works you read can also be the subject of your writing.

READING AS SUGGESTION

When we read critically we find flawed argument strategies, unsupported assertions, overgeneralizations, and misinterpretations, which raise questions like:

- Is this true?
- Is there other evidence?
- Are there other interpretations?
- What is the other side's position?

Even when critical reading identifies solid writing strategies, we frequently ask if there is not more information about one point or another which commands our interest. Each question points to a potential research and writing topic.

Reading Jack Smith's essay on censorship and pornography in the last chapter raised a question about the validity of comparing a book, which twenty-five years ago was judged pornographic, with current pornography. Recently rock music has been criticized for being sexually explicit and advocating violence. Are the issues the same in the two cases? Is the rock music audience similar to the *Tropic of Cancer*'s audience? What about graphic visual pornography? Or pornography using children? Smith mentions three aspects of the censorship controversy which he does not develop—the difficulty in defining pornography, the source of the new wave of censorship, and the lack of evidence linking pornography with violence. Besides the Ross decision, what definitions of pornography exist? Are some definitions more useful than others? And regarding the censorship movement, what are the radical feminists' and the fundamental evangelists' positions? Are any moderate feminists criticizing pornography? What about religious groups besides fundamentalists? Finally, what evidence has been advanced linking pornography with violence?

Reading Smith's essay critically suggests several research and writing topics.

- Pornography then and now: a comparison between Miller's *Tropic of Cancer* and rock music (or rock music record jackets)
- A useful definition of pornography
- A recent history of censorship
- Pornography: comparing the definitions
- The radical feminists' (moderate feminists', Christian fundamentalists', liberal Christians', Roman Catholics', Jews') position on pornography
- A critique of the radical feminists' (et cetera) position on pornography
- The scientific case against pornography
- A critique of the scientific case against pornography
- Legal precedents for/against censorship

As this list shows, developing and using critical reading skills gives you a pre-writing edge.

READING AS SOURCE

Once critical reading raises questions that generate writing topics, you go on reading to answer the questions. Researching a topic requires you to read for information, recognizing thesis statements and supporting evidence, and making mental summary statements. Some special writing skills will help you make valuable use of sources in your writing. These are notetaking for quotations, paraphrasing, and summarizing. Before discussing these, you need to know a few things about research reading.

Start your research reading with a plan (like the one described in the first chapter) which has research questions and a list of appropriate bibliographies. Allow three or four hours in a block and go to the library with a package of index cards and a notebook. Make a separate index card noting author, title, publication information (publisher, city, and year for a book; periodical name, year, and month [full date if published more frequently] for an article), and library call number for each prospective source. (You will use the information on the bibliography cards later for documenting your sources.) Locate your sources, and skim the introductions for a thesis and the remainder for key supporting evidence to see if the sources are relevant. If so, begin writing reading notes on either index cards or notebook paper. Many writers use index cards (one card for each recorded note), but I prefer a yellow legal pad where I can make notes working consecutively through my source. I staple the bibliography card to the first page and leave a wide left-hand margin for recording the specific topic, page numbers, and brief comments.

Notetaking for Quotations

Writers quote directly from sources when they will respond to the source author's statement, when the source makes an important point that cannot be expressed in any other words, or when the quotation adds emphasis to the writer's own assertions. In these instances, since the exact words are so important, you have a responsibility to the original source to quote accurately. Write a few introductory notes indicating the context, and then copy carefully, being certain to preserve all punctuation. (Today, copying machines make this task easier. As a word of warning, though, copying a journal article may help when you intend to quote directly, but it can tempt you to feel that copying equals research.) To write well from sources, you need to paraphrase, summarize, and synthesize what you read. Writing that strings together a series of researched quotations really is not writing.

Paraphrasing

A paraphrase restates a passage's exact meaning, but in your own words. Writers use this as a research tool for taking reading notes and again when they refer to a source in their own writing. A good paraphrase, more concise than the original, clarifies a source's language and ideas for readers. To see how paraphrase works, read the following description of Chartres cathedral by Henry Adams and the paraphrase that follows.

Chartres was intended to hold ten thousand people easily, or fifteen thousand when crowded, and the decoration of this great space, though not a wholly new problem, had to be treated in a new way. Sancta Sofia was built by the Emperor Justinian, with all the resources of the Empire, in a single violent effort, in six years, and was decorated throughout with mosaics on a general scheme, with the unity that Empire and Church could give, when they acted together. The Norman Kings of Sicily, the richest princes of the twelfth century, were able to carry out a complete work of the most costly kind, in a single sustained effort from beginning to end, according to a given plan. Chartres was a local shrine, in an agricultural province, not even a part of the royal domain, and its cathedral was the work of society, without much more tie than the Virgin gave it. Socially Chartres, as far as its stonework goes, seems to have been mostly rural; its decoration, in the stone porches and transepts, is royal and feudal; in the nave and choir it is chiefly bourgeois. The want of unity is much less surprising than the unity, but it is still evident, especially in the glass. The mosaics of Monreale begin and end; they are a series; their connection is artistic and theological at once; they have unity. The windows of Chartres have no sequence, and their charm is in variety, in individuality, and sometimes even in downright hostility to each other, reflecting the picturesque society that gave them. They have, too, the charm that the world has made no attempt to popularize them for its modern uses, so that except for the useful little guide-book of the Abbé Clerval, one can see no clue to the legendary chaos; one has it to one's self . . . (*Mont St. Michel and Chartres*)

This is paraphrased as,

The great space of Chartres cathedral, built to hold ten thousand people easily or fifteen thousand when crowded, required a new approach for decoration than earlier cathedrals, particularly because it was built as an agricultural province's local shrine by a diverse society unified only by its faith in the Virgin Mary. Chartres was unlike either Sancta Sofia cathedral, built by the Byzantine emperor Justinian in just six years and decorated throughout with thematically consistent mosaics, or the twelfth-century cathedral at Monreale built by Sicily's rich Norman Kings and decorated with a theologically and artistically unified mosaic series. Local laborers did Chartres' stonework. Chartres' decoration in the transepts and porches came from the nobility, and in the nave and choir, from the middle class. Built by such a diverse society, Chartres has surprising unity, except in its windows, which charm by their variety, individuality, contrasts, and by their remoteness from modern popularization.

The paraphrase relies on the original passage's full meaning, rather than its sentence sequence, by drawing together references to Monreale, which were separated in the original, and by clarifying the contrast between Chartres and Sancta Sofia and the church at Monreale. Frequently, several sentences are combined into one with single words replacing phrases. This paraphrase, both simplifying and interpreting the original text, might find its way into a paper comparing architectural styles or one examining the relationship between great architecture's relation to the society which builds it. Used in this way, paraphrasing allows a writer to state the ideas of his source without the jarring shifts in tone and style that come from too frequent quoting. If, however, I were writing about historian Adams's particular vision linking Gothic architecture's artistic achievements with the cult of the Virgin, summarizing and emphasizing ideas through brief quotes might be more appropriate.

Writing Summaries

A written summary restates the source's main ideas and supporting detail. Unlike a paraphrase, a summary may select and emphasize certain parts of the original, but it does not offer interpretation and clarification. When a writer uses a summary as part of a longer essay, she usually identifies the source and tells what the passage is about, as in this summary of the Adams passage just paraphrased.

> At the beginning of the chapter, "The Court of the Queen of Heaven" in *Mont St. Michel and Chartres*, Henry Adams credits Chartres cathedral's architectural achievement to a diverse society brought together by their faith in the Virgin. Unlike such earlier cathedrals as Sancta Sofia and the one at Monreale, Sicily (built and decorated by the single efforts of rich and powerful rulers, the Emperor Justinian, and the Norman Kings, respectively), local laborers joined with nobility and the middle class to build Chartres. Although surprisingly unified, Chartres reveals the diverse society that built it in its stained glass windows.

This summary states the source, the main point or thesis, and two principal lines of evidence—the comparison with previous cathedrals and the diverse windows. Finding main points and supporting evidence uses the same skills you developed for reading critically—recognizing general sentences and distinguishing concrete detail that comments on the generalizations.

Writing summaries requires that you put these generalizations and concrete details into sentences much like the summary sentences you form as you read. A longer summary begins with the source's thesis statement followed by each paragraph's summary sentence and important supporting detail. For a long summary, you must be sure to give the reader links and transitions between diverse ideas or evidence.

The writing that comes from reading for source information—notetaking for quotation, paraphrasing, and summarizing—rarely serves as an end in itself. These are the building blocks of larger essays. As you argue or explain, you paraphrase another writer who has addressed the same topic. The summary you write of reported research becomes part of your evidence. You summarize a plot or an argument before you analyze or critique it. The larger writing task is still your own.

A Note on Documentation

Whenever you use a source in your writing, whether you quote directly, paraphrase, or summarize, you have an ethical (and in most cases, legal) responsibility to give credit to the source. This can be done by mentioning the author and title directly in your essay or by footnoting. Documentation style varies among the various disciplines, so you will want to consult an appropriate style manual. Some you may want to consider are the *Chicago Manual of Style*, the Modern Language Association's *MLA Style Sheet* or *MLA Handbook*, the *Council of Biology Editors Style Manual*, and the American Psychological Association's *Publication Manual*.

READING AS MODEL

When you read critically you become aware of how writers organize their materials. Although different essays or articles may appear very dissimilar, several patterns (or structures) recur in writing. These structures serve as models for your own writing. What this means is not that you will copy a writer's thesis and use his evidence, but that you will identify patterns—shapes—and fit your thesis and evidence on those bones.

To help you recognize these shapes, I will describe three essays from the Critical Readings section of this text: "Fail: Bright Woman" (chapter 5), "Evolution as Fact and Theory" (chapter 3), and "Underground Man" (chapter 11). (You may wish to look ahead at them.)

Finding a Model: The Scientific Report

In "Fail: Bright Woman" (pp. 231–237), Matina Horner presents her research on the differences between college men's and college women's motivation to achieve or avoid success. She begins by stating the problem—women and men seem to respond differently in competition with each other and in their reactions to achievement. She then summarizes the research on achievement motivation, where she finds the clue for her own research: women "get higher test-anxiety scores than do men." This leads to her hypotheses about the motive to avoid success: that it would be more characteristic of women than men, that it would be more characteristic of career-oriented than traditional women, and that anxiety over success would increase in a competitive environment. She goes on to describe her experiment—the sample and the test—and report her data, and the conclusion from her data. Horner's essay conforms to the scientific report's structure.

    inductive argument
    problem
    review of literature
    hypothesis
    experiment description
    data report
    data interpretation
    conclusion

Scientific report form is highly conventionalized, but patterns of other writings are less rigid.

Finding a Model: Critique and Rebuttal

In "Evolution as Fact and Theory" (pp. 148–155), Stephen Jay Gould criticizes the scientific creationists' position against evolution. He summarizes their views by explaining their definition of scientific creationism, and then attacks their definition on logical grounds. He then rebuts their view by demonstrating the relationship between scientific fact and scientific theory using evolution as evidence. The pattern

> position A summary
> position A critique
> rebuttal position (B) summary
> position B proof

is a model for an argumentative essay discrediting one position and advancing an alternative. Gould happens to build his argument from definition, but the kind of argument does not affect the pattern.

Finding a Model: Critical Analysis

A critique does not necessarily have to present an argument; it may, instead, analyze its object. In her essay "Underground Man" (pp. 548–551), Pauline Kael critiques Martin Scorsese's film *Taxi Driver*. The essay proceeds analytically, describing each of the film's features and evaluating its effectiveness. She begins by summarizing the plot, and then moves through director, characterization, theme, cast, music, and ties it together with an assessment of the film's violence. The pattern looks like this:

> summary
> description, component 1
> assessment, component 1
> description, component 2
> assessment, component 2
> description, component 3
> assessment, component 3
> description, component 4
> assessment, component 4
> description, component 5
> assessment, component 5
> conclusion

This structure could as well serve as a model for a critique of a poem, short story, novel, television series, or rock concert.

Developing Your Own Models

Developing a model from reading requires you to attend to a writer's purposes (argument, description, narration, explanation) and to distinguish developmental patterns. The patterns I have identified are only a few of the patterns your critical reading will find to serve as models for your writing.

WRITING ABOUT READING

College courses frequently require students to write about articles and books they have read. Typical assignments ask students to write an analysis, a comparative analysis, or a critique (review). With the critical reading you have been doing and your knowledge of the writing process, you should be able to write these kinds of papers well.

Analysis

Read Critically and Know Your Subject

An analysis, remember, looks at the parts of something. An assignment that asks you to analyze something you have read is basically asking you to explain *how* the object of analysis works. Your own purpose, then, is to educate your audience about the work. To do this you need to know your subject well, so you begin with careful critical reading. Once you feel you know the piece well, decide what kind of analysis you will write. You may choose to write an analysis based on your critical reading of purpose, audience, persona, and argument (a rhetorical analysis), or you may focus on only purpose or argument. Other components of writing that can serve as the object of analysis include style, imagery, tone, and language. If you are writing about literature, you may be asked to analyze a poem, short story, novel, or play or some component of these, like plot, character, theme, figurative language, meter, or tone.

To analyze some element of writing—for example, argument—a writer has to have a clear understanding of how argument operates in general. It would be quite difficult to analyze a character in a novel without knowing that writers reveal characters through what narrators say about the characters, through the characters' own actions, conversations, and thoughts, and through other characters' observations.

Establish Analytical Components

When you understand the object of analysis well (and this may require extra re-search), establish the analytical components you will examine. If I were writing a character analysis, I would look at the narrator's physical description of the character; the narrator's comments on the character's profession, ethical attitudes, and behavior; the character's actions, conscious thoughts, and conversations; and at other characters' responses to and statements about the character.

After you have established the analytical components and written them down, look for them as you read the piece you are analyzing. Make notes which record each example of the analytical component and quote specific passages which best illustrate it. These notes, representing your actual analysis, are the information on which you will base your essay.

At this point you need to focus your materials by asking what the various parts accomplish. Your answer will give you a beginning thesis statement to be revised for specificity and limits. The draft you write will present each analytical compo-nent, illustrate the component through direct quotation from the text, and relate the component to the thesis. The most important part of writing an analysis is presenting enough specific detail in the form of passage descriptions and quota-tions to enable your reader to see for herself that what you are saying is true. The pattern for an analysis looks like this:

introduction (including thesis)
brief summary
component 1
component 2
component 3
component 4, etc.
conclusion

Both the introduction and conclusion should reflect your consideration of the writer's purpose and how the analytical components accomplish that purpose. Also you may wish to include in the conclusion an evaluation of the writing's effective-ness, impact, or significance. A character analysis might conclude that the writer has thus created a complex image of a schizophrenic's personality to arouse the audience's compassion. The rhetorical analysis of Jack Smith's essay on censorship and pornography in the previous chapter led to an assessment of the essay's suc-cess. An analysis of Martin Luther King's "Letter from Birmingham Jail" (pp. 291–304) might state the letter's influence on the civil rights movement.

Comparative Analysis

A comparative analysis looks at the relationships between like parts of two or more similar writings. You might, for example, compare Smith's essay on pornography with Gloria Steinem's "Erotica and Pornography: A Clear and Present Difference" (pp. 286–290). When you write a comparative analysis, the essays require one common ground—the same author, the same genre, the same topic, and you must discuss the same analytical components of each essay. You could not, say, analyze Smith's tone and Steinem's arguments and reach any valid conclusions about their essays' relationships to their purposes. When you compare two or more pieces of writing, the comparison usually serves some purpose other than explaining to your audience how the two essays work. A comparative analysis usually clarifies the common ground of the essays. Thus, a comparative analysis of Smith's and Steinem's essays would clarify the pornography issue. A study of two critic's readings of Shakespeare's *Macbeth* would enlighten the reader about both the play and any critical controversy. After reading the two essays critically, you will be able to identify this common ground and use it to focus your own essay.

Preparing to write a comparative analysis is like preparing to write an analysis. You establish your analytical components, read each essay separately, and take notes and quotations for each. Focus your information, decide what the readings contribute to clarifying the common ground, and then write your draft.

Two organizational strategies can be used for comparative analyses. You can either analyze one completely, then the other, and follow the analyses with a discussion of the similarities and differences. Or, you can examine one analytical component after another, looking at both sources. The two patterns for a comparative analysis look like this

```
introduction (including thesis)
    brief summary A
        component 1-A
        component 2-A
        component 3-A
    component 4, etc. A
    brief summary B
        component 1-B
        component 2-B
        component 3-B
    component 4, etc. A
    similarities A & B
    differences A & B
conclusion

introduction (including thesis)
    brief summary A & B
        component 1 A & B
    similarities and differences
        component 2 A & B
    similarities and differences
        component 3 A & B
    similarities and differences
        component 4, etc. A & B
    similarities and differences
conclusion
```

Critique

A critique combines analysis with formal evaluation. When you evaluate something you have read, it is not enough to say "I like it" or "I didn't understand it." A critique explains *why* what you have read works or does not work. You need to bring to a critique all your analytical skills—a clear understanding of the analysis objective, specified analytical components, careful critical reading, and complete accurate reading notes focused on the analytical components. To this you will add standards by which you will judge the reading. These are called critical criteria.

Criteria and Evaluation

Understanding the criteria by which you judge a piece of writing requires you to determine what is important to you or relevant to the course for which you are writing a paper. The section on revising your own writing presented a revising checklist based on the criteria for good writing—coherence, completeness, clarity, and correctness. Writing teachers and textbook authors have established these criteria.

Developing Your Own Criteria

Sometimes an instructor will ask you to critique a book for his course and he will set up a textbook or another book as a model. In this case you will have to develop your critical criteria from a critical analysis of the book you have previously read. For example, in a history class you have discussed David M. Potter's book *People of Plenty*, which refines Frederick Jackson Turner's hypothesis that the frontier shaped the American character by replacing Turner's *the frontier* with Potter's *abundance*. The class discussion emphasized that the value of Potter's book lay in breaking new ground in social history by combining accurate historical observations with vital work done on national character by anthropologists, social psychologists, and psychoanalysts.

The book you are asked to critique argues that the privileges accorded white male landowners by the Constitution shaped the American character. Three criteria you should include in your critique would be "breaking new ground," "accurate historical observations," and the presence of "vital work done on national character by anthropologists, social psychologists, and psychoanalysts."

Sometimes you have no clue from the instructor or the course about what criteria should apply. In this case, you have to look to your own experiences with similar books on similar subjects and ask what you expect from them. These expectations should consider assumptions and issues that are important in the discipline in which a writing is categorized. Entertainment or humor may govern your choices when you pick up a magazine at the newsstand, but it would be unwise to use these as your principal criteria for evaluating a book on marriage for your introductory psychology course.

Using Analysis in a Critique

Once you have determined your criteria, you begin a critique the same way you began analysis—by establishing and understanding the analytical components and reading critically. The criteria you evolve and the analytical components will organize your critical reading and reading notes. Focus this information by stating your critical criteria and analytical components and ask *how* (not *if*) what you have read meets or fails to meet the criteria. When you go on to draft your essay, it should fit this pattern.

introduction stating criteria and thesis
summary
analysis
component 1
component 2
component 3
component 4, etc.
conclusion (which
measures the work by criteria
and states strengths and weaknesses)

The critical reading and process-centered writing skills you have been working with in this unit will help you as you read the selections in Part II and write about them. Study across the academic disciplines, whether you study the natural sciences, the social sciences, the humanities, or the arts—requires the same critical reading and clear, logical writing.

PART TWO

Critical ↘ Readings ↙

❦ THE NATURAL SCIENCES ❧

Chapter 1

The
Governing
Assumptions

Science is primarily an attitude toward problem solution.

—GARVIN MCCAIN AND ERWIN M. SEGAL

The essays in this chapter examine attitudes toward science. Before we look at these attitudes, we might best ask ourselves how we view science. Is science tedious memorization of accumulated facts about nature or the exploration of nature's unknown frontiers? Does science erect an edifice of knowledge or create technologies to destroy human existence? Is science an amoral or a self-regulated ethical community? How much does the nonscientist need to know about science? How much can he know? How important is this knowledge?

The following essays address these questions. Huxley's "The Method of Scientific Investigation" explains that science is "nothing but the necessary mode of working of the human mind." He would agree with McCain and Segal that science is principally an attitude, but he identifies the attitude as one which employs everyday patterns of induction and deduction. McCain and Segal help us further understand our attitudes toward science by dispelling common misunderstandings about science. Through organizing and explaining data, science accomplishes more than a mere accumulation of facts about less than an "ultimate explanation of natural processes." However close Huxley brings science to our everyday experience, McCain and Segal's essay seems to confirm the suspicion that science is a community's special property. Bronowski identifies the values of that select community in "The Sense of Human Dignity."

This chapter's essays make a strong case for science's importance. Besides helping us define science and suggesting how science conducts its business, these essays address the scientist's responsibility to society, and society's responsibility to understand and use wisely science's legacy—technology.

The Method of Scientific Investigation
Thomas Henry Huxley

Thomas Henry Huxley (1825–1895) served as "science's principal advocate in Victorian England"; he particularly championed Charles Darwin's theory of evolution. A scientist in his own right, Huxley studied medicine, held the natural history chair at the School of Mines for thirty-nine years, and engaged in tropical animal research. Through analyzing nonscientists' responses to ordinary experiences—indications of fruit's ripeness, evidence of a burglary—"The Method of Scientific Investigation" defines the scientific method while it demystifies science.

The method of scientific investigation is nothing but the expression of the necessary mode of working of the human mind. [By means of induction and deduction, scientists] wring from Nature certain other things, which are called natural laws and causes. [Out of these they build up hypotheses and theories.] To hear all these large words, you would think that the mind of a man of science must be constituted differently from that of his fellow men. You are quite wrong. All these terrible apparatus are being used by yourselves every day and every hour of your lives. [The example of choosing apples in a fruiterer's shop illustrates the principle of induction and deduction. In scientific inquiry a supposed law must be verified.] Our confidence in a law is in exact proportion to the absence of variation in the result of experimental verification. Let us turn to another matter: the method by which we prove that some [phenomena] stand in the position of causes toward the others. [The example of coming down one morning to missing teapot and spoons, an open window with a hand mark on the window-frame, and the hypothesis that someone has broken in illustrate this.] A hypothetical conclusion is only rendered highly probable by a series of inductive and deductive reasonings. [A hypothesis] based on sound scientific knowledge is sure to have a corresponding value; and that which is a mere hasty random guess is likely to have but little value. The value of the result depends on the patience and faithfulness with which the investigator applies to his hypothesis every possible kind of verification.

The method of scientific investigation is nothing but the expression of the necessary mode of working of the human mind. It is simply the mode at which all phenomena are reasoned about, rendered precise and exact. There is no more difference, but there is just the same kind of difference, between the mental operations of a man of science and those of an ordinary person, as there is between the operations and methods of a baker or of a butcher weighing out his goods in common scales, and the operations of a chemist in performing a difficult and complex analysis by means of his balance and finely graduated weights. It is not that the action of the scales in the one case, and the balance in the other, differ in the principles of their construction or manner of working; but the beam of one is set on an infinitely finer axis than the other, and of course turns by the addition of a much smaller weight.

You will understand this better, perhaps, if I give you some familiar example. You have all heard it repeated, I dare say, that men of science work by means of induction and deduction, and that by the help of these operations, they, in a sort of sense, wring from Nature certain other things, which are called natural laws, and causes, and that out of these, by some cunning skill of their own, they build up hypotheses and theories. And it is imagined by many, that the operations of the common mind can be by no means compared with these processes, and that they have to be acquired by a sort of special apprenticeship to the craft. To hear all these large words, you would think that the mind of a man of science must be constituted differently from that of his fellow men; but if you will not be frightened by terms, you will discover that you are quite wrong, and that all these terrible apparatus are being used by yourselves every day and every hour of your lives.

There is a well-known incident in one of Molière's[1] plays [*Le Bourgeois Gentilhomme*], where the author makes the hero express unbounded delight on being told that he had been talking prose during the whole of his life. In the same way, I trust, that you will take comfort, and be delighted with yourselves, on the discovery that you have been acting on the principles of inductive and deductive philosophy during the same period. Probably there is not one here who has not in the course of the day had occasion to set in motion a complex train of reasoning, of the very same kind, though differing of course in degree, as that which a scientific man goes through in tracing the causes of natural phenomena.

A very trivial circumstance will serve to exemplify this. Suppose you go into a fruiterer's shop, wanting an apple,—you take up one, and, on biting it, you find it is sour; you look at it, and see that it is hard and green. You take up another one, and that too is hard, green, and sour. The shopman offers you a third; but, before biting it, you examine it, and find that it is hard and green, and you immediately say that you will not have it, as it must be sour, like those that you have already tried.

Nothing can be more simple than that, you think; but if you will take the trouble to analyse and trace out into its logical elements what has been done by the mind, you will be greatly surprised. In the first place you have performed the operation of induction. You found that, in two experiences, hardness and greenness in apples went together with sourness. It was so in the first case, and it was confirmed by the second. True, it is a very small basis, but still it is enough to make an induction from; you generalise the facts, and you expect to find sourness in apples where you get hardness and greenness. You found upon that a general law that all hard and green apples are sour; and that, so far as it goes, is a perfect induction. Well, having got your natural law in this way, when you are offered another apple which you find is hard and green, you say, "All hard and green apples are sour; this apple is hard and green, therefore this apple is sour." That train of reasoning is what logicians call a syllogism, and has all its various parts and terms,—its major premiss, its minor premiss and its conclusion. And, by the help of further reasoning, which, if drawn out, would have to be exhibited in two or three other syllogisms, you arrive at your final determination, "I will not have that apple." So that, you see, you have, in the first place, established a law by induction, and upon that you have founded a deduction, and reasoned out the special particular case. Well now, suppose, having got your conclusion of the law, that at some time afterwards, you are discussing the qualities of apples with a friend: you will say to him, "It is a very curious thing,—but I find that all hard and green apples are sour!" Your friend says to you, "But how do you know that?" You at once reply, "Oh, because I have tried them over and over again, and have always found them to be so." Well, if we were talking science instead of common sense, we should call that an experimental verification. And, if still opposed, you go further, and say, "I have heard from the people in Somersetshire and Devonshire, where a large number of apples are grown, that they have observed the same thing. It is also found to be the case in Normandy, and in North America. In short, I find it to be the universal experience of mankind wherever attention has been directed to the subject." Whereupon, your friend, unless he is a very unreasonable man, agrees with you, and is convinced that you are quite right in the conclusion you have drawn. He believes, although perhaps he does not know he believes it, that the more extensive verifications are,—that the more frequently experiments have been made, and results of the same kind arrived at,—that the more varied the conditions under which the same results are attained, the more certain is the ultimate conclusion, and he disputes the question no further. He sees that the experiment has been tried under all sorts of conditions, as to time, place, and people, with the same result; and he says with you, therefore, that the law you have laid down must be a good one, and he must believe it.

In science we do the same thing;—the philosopher exercises precisely the same faculties, though in a much more delicate manner. In scientific inquiry it becomes a matter of duty to expose a supposed law to every possible kind of verification, and to take care, moreover, that this is done intentionally, and not left to a mere accident, as in the case of the apples. And in science, as in common life, our confidence in a law is in exact proportion to the absence of variation in the result of our experimental verifications. For instance, if you let go your grasp of an article you may have in your hand, it will immediately fall to the ground. That is a very common verification of one of the best established laws of nature—that of gravitation. The method by which men of science establish the existence of that law is exactly the same as that by which we have established the trivial proposition about the sourness of hard and green apples. But we believe it in such an extensive, thorough, and unhesitating manner because the universal experience of mankind verifies it, and we can verify it ourselves at any time; and that is the strongest possible foundation on which any natural law can rest.

So much, then, by way of proof that the method of establishing laws in science is exactly the same as that pursued in common life. Let us now turn to another matter (though really it is but another phase of the same question), and that is, the method by which, from the relations of certain phenomena, we prove that some stand in the position of causes towards the others.

I want to put the case clearly before you, and I will therefore show you what I mean by another familiar example. I will suppose that one of you, on coming down in the morning to the parlor of your house, finds that a tea-pot and some spoons which had been left in the room on the previous evening are gone,—the window is open, and you observe the mark of a dirty hand on the window-frame, and perhaps, in addition to that, you notice the impress of a hob-nailed shoe on the gravel outside. All these phenomena have struck your attention instantly, and before two seconds have passed you say, "Oh, somebody has broken open the window, entered the room, and run off with the spoons and the tea-pot!" That speech is out of your mouth in a moment. And you will probably add, "I know there has; I am quite sure of it!" You mean to say exactly what you know; but in reality you are giving expression to what is, in all essential particulars, an hypothesis. You do not *know* it at all; it is nothing but an hypothesis rapidly framed in your own mind. And it is an hypothesis founded on a long train of inductions and deductions.

What are those inductions and deductions, and how have you got at this hypothesis? You have observed in the first place, that the window is open; but by a train of reasoning involving many inductions and deductions, you have probably arrived long before at the general law—and a very good one it is—that windows do not open of themselves; and you therefore conclude that something has opened the window. A second general law that you have arrived at in the same way is, that tea-pots and spoons do not go out of a window spontaneously, and you are satisfied that, as they are not now where you left them, they have been removed. In the third place, you look at the marks on the window-sill, and the shoe-marks outside, and you say that in all previous experience the former kind of mark has never been produced by anything else but the hand of a human being; and the same experience shows that no other animal but man at present wears shoes with hob-nails in them such as would produce the marks in the gravel. I do not know, even if we could discover any of those "missing links" that are talked about, that they would help us to any other conclusion! At any rate the law which states our present experience is strong enough for my present purpose. You next reach the conclusion that, as these kind of marks have not been left by any other animal than man, or are liable to be formed in any other way than a man's hand and shoe, the marks in question have been formed by a man in that way. You have, further, a general law, founded on observation and experience, and that, too, is, I am sorry to say, a very universal and unimpeachable one,—that some men are thieves; and you assume at once from all these premises—and that is what constitutes your hypothesis—that the man who made the marks outside and on the window-sill, opened the window, got into the room, and stole your tea-pot and spoons. You have now arrived at a *vera causa;*—you have assumed a cause which, it is plain, is competent to produce all the phenomena you have observed. You can explain all these phenomena only by the hypothesis of a thief. But that is a hypothetical conclusion, of the justice of which you have no absolute proof at all; it is only rendered highly probable by a series of inductive and deductive reasonings.

I suppose your first action, assuming that you are a man of ordinary common sense, and that you have established this hypothesis to your own satisfaction, will very likely be to go off for the police, and set them on the track of the burglar, with the view to the recovery of your property. But just as you are starting with this object, some person comes in, and on learning what you are about, says, "My good friend, you are going on a great deal too fast. How do you know that the man who really made the marks took the spoons? It might have been a monkey that took them, and the man may have merely looked in afterwards." You would probably reply, "Well, that is all very well, but you see it is contrary to all experience of the way tea-pots and spoons are abstracted; so that, at any rate, your hypothesis is less probable than mine." While you are talking the thing over in this way, another friend arrives, one of the good kind of people that I was talking of a little while ago. And he might say, "Oh, my dear sir, you are certainly going on a great deal too fast. You are most presumptuous. You admit that all these occurrences took place when you were fast asleep, at a time when you could not possibly have known anything about what was taking place. How do you know that the laws of Nature are not suspended during the night? It may be that there has been some kind of supernatural interference in this case." In point of fact, he declares that your hypothesis is one of which you cannot at all demonstrate the truth, and that you are by no means sure that the laws of Nature are the same when you are asleep as when you are awake.

Well, now, you cannot at the moment answer that kind of reasoning. You feel that your worthy friend has you somewhat at a disadvantage. You will feel perfectly convinced in your own mind, however, that you are quite right, and you say to him, "My good friend, I can only be guided by the natural probabilities of the case, and if you will be kind enough to stand aside and permit me to pass, I will go and fetch the police." Well, we will suppose that your journey is successful, and that by good luck you meet with a policeman; that eventually the burglar is found with your property on his person, and the marks correspond to his hand and to his boots. Probably any jury would consider those facts a very good experimental verification of your hypothesis, touching the cause of the abnormal phenomena observed in your parlor, and would act accordingly.

Now, in this supposititious case, I have taken phenomena of a very common kind, in order that you might see what are the different steps in an ordinary process of reasoning, if you will only take the trouble to analyse it carefully. All the operations I have described, you will see, are involved in the mind of any man of sense in leading him to a conclusion as to the course he should take in order to make good a robbery and punish the offender. I say that you are led, in that case, to your conclusion by exactly the same train of reasoning as that which a man of science pursues when he is endeavouring to discover the origin and laws of the most occult phenomena. The process is, and always must be, the same; and precisely the same mode of reasoning was employed by Newton[2] and Laplace[3] in their endeavours to discover and define the causes of the movements of the heavenly bodies, as you, with your own common sense, would employ to detect a burglar. The only difference is, that the nature of the inquiry being more abstruse, every step has to be most carefully watched, so that there may not be a single crack or flaw in your hypothesis. A flaw or crack in many of the hypotheses of daily life may be of little or no moment as affecting the general correctness of the conclusions at which we may arrive; but, in a scientific inquiry, a fallacy, great or small, is always of importance, and is sure to be in the long run constantly productive of mischievous if not fatal results.

Do not allow yourselves to be misled by the common notion that an hypothesis is untrustworthy simply because it is an hypothesis. It is often urged, in respect to some scientific conclusion, that, after all, it is only an hypothesis. But what more have we to guide us in nine-tenths of the most important affairs of daily life than hypotheses, and often very ill-based ones? So that in science, where the evidence of an hypothesis is subjected to the most rigid examination, we may rightly pursue the same course. You may have hypotheses, and hypotheses. A man may say, if he likes, that the moon is made of green cheese: that is an hypothesis. But another man, who has devoted a great deal of time and attention to the subject, and availed himself of the most powerful telescopes and the results of the observations of others, declares that in his opinion it is probably composed of materials very similar to those of which our own earth is made up: and that is also only an hypothesis. But I need not tell you that there is an enormous difference in the value of the two hypotheses. That one which is based on sound scientific knowledge is sure to have a corresponding value; and that which is a mere hasty random guess is likely to have but little value. Every great step in our progress in discovering causes has been made in exactly the same way as that which I have detailed to you. A person observing the occurrence of certain facts and phenomena asks, naturally enough, what process, what kind of operation known to occur in Nature applied to the particular case, will unravel and explain the mystery? Hence you have the scientific hypothesis; and its value will be proportionate to the care and completeness with which its basis had been tested and verified. It is in these matters as in the commonest affairs of practical life: the guess of the fool will be folly, while the guess of the wise man will contain wisdom. In all cases, you see that the value of the result depends on the patience and faithfulness with which the investigator applies to his hypothesis every possible kind of verification.

Notes

[1] Molière (1622–1673), first a French actor and then a dramatist, wrote such classic comedies as *The Misanthrope* and *The Miser*.

[2] Sir Isaac Newton (1642–1724), an English natural philosopher and mathematician, formulated the idea of universal gravitation. This theory's proof established mechanical laws for physical phenomena within the earth's gravitational system.

[3] Pierre Laplace (1749–1827), a French astronomer and mathematician, wrote on celestial mechanics.

FOCUS: **READING REVIEW**

1. How does Huxley explain the logical patterns of deduction and induction? What role do these patterns play in the scientific method?
2. What is "verification"? What role does it play in science?
3. What is the relation between hypothesis and verification?

FOCUS: **AUTHOR'S STRATEGIES**

1. What in his language and examples suggests Huxley's audience and purpose?
2. Huxley uses extended examples to explain induction and deduction. Explain how these operate.

FOCUS: **DISCUSSION AND WRITING**

1. Construct a similar pattern of induction and deduction from your own daily experiences.
2. Explain the relationship between deduction and induction in some important decision you have made regarding your academic career, future professional goal, or your moral behavior.

Attitudes and Science

Garvin McCain and Erwin M. Segal

Garvin McCain (b. 1922) and Erwin M. Segal (b. 1936), respectively professors at the University of Texas at Arlington and the State University of New York at Buffalo, see science as the "dominant theme in our culture." Their book The Game of Science *(1977) addresses the educated person's need not so much to understand all science's findings, but to be familiar with science's structure and operation. "Attitudes and Science,"* taken from The Game of Science, *dispels common misunderstandings about science.*

Although science plays a dominant role in our society, only a small minority have any serious understanding of it. The popular conception of science emphasizes gadget production, mysterious midnight work in the laboratory, and data collection and storage. [Actually] science is primarily an attitude toward problem solution; as such, it often has implications far beyond the immediate data that may indeed profoundly influence beliefs. There are many common misunderstandings about science. We'll discuss each briefly. 1. *The accumulation of facts or data is the primary goal of science.* [In fact data does not lead to "scientific" understanding—explanatory and organizing concepts do.] 2. *Some sciences can be described as exact.* Statements in natural science have only probabilistic, not exact, confirmation. [Furthermore, scientific statements are incomplete.] 3. *Science is deficient because it cannot give any ultimate explanation of natural processes.* [Ultimate explanations are simply not part of the objective of science.] 4. *Science distorts reality and cannot do justice to the fullness of experience.* Limitation of the area of research is a vital tactic of science. [The expression of uniqueness and aesthetic qualities is worthwhile, but] it is just not a basic part of the scientific endeavor. 5. *Science is concerned primarily with man's practical and social needs.* [Unfortunately, these practical results of science are the most visible, but] for most scientists, science is a game played for understanding and not for practical solutions to existing problems.

THE IMPORTANCE OF ATTITUDES

At various places and times in the human struggle, there have been a variety of dominant attitudes or modes of thought. Nationalism, theology, the exquisite glories of war, business, and racism have each at one time or another functioned as the primary yardstick for human belief systems. Consider one of these yardsticks—theology. In the sixteenth century theology clearly dominated the thought of Western Europe. Of course not everyone was a theologian. For example, only a minute portion of the populace had even a foggy understanding of the ontological argument (an argument for the existence of God). But the dominant mode of thinking involved theology at some point. It is equally evident today that, although science plays a dominant role in our society, only a small minority have any serious understanding of it. We are all aware of the attempts to link science with such fascinating subjects as deodorants, gasoline additives, and false teeth. Whether or not these links are legitimate, they exemplify the advertisers' confidence that "science" has sufficient glamour and acceptance to be worth a few dollars' extra profit. Implied is the further assumption that the viewing, reading, or listening public does not understand science, so that an oblique reference to "science" will reduce them to helpless acquiescence. Whatever the effectiveness of this approach, it does reflect an assessment of popular views. Many people seem to believe that production of better monsters, tranquilizers, satellites, bunion pads, or more humane bombs is the aim of science and that the method by which these items are developed is through a collection and cataloging of facts. Such "practical" items may be necessary for late, late shows, employment in aerospace industries, comfort for aching feet, and the waging of wars, but their relation to science is rather remote. The popular conception of science thus emphasizes gadget production, mysterious midnight work in the laboratory, and data collection and storage. Our aim is to suggest a somewhat larger perspective regarding scientific attitudes and to present a more realistic view of what science is and what scientists do.

It needs to be emphasized that, although science affects belief, that is not its primary purpose. Science is primarily an attitude toward problem solution; as such, it often has implications far beyond the immediate data—implications that may indeed profoundly influence beliefs. For example, when Copernicus[1] and Galileo[2] shattered the earth's pretensions as the center of the physical universe, the impact was much greater than the astronomical consequences of accepting the sun as the center of the universe. Presumably, the Copernican concept of the universe did not change the productivity of the fields, turn wine to vinegar, or render martial and marital games less fascinating. And yet, when a long established and firmly held belief is shattered, life can never be the same. At least as menacing but more formless was the thought that, if one fundamental truth had to be discarded, it might prove to be the hole in the dike through which a flood of unknown and frightening consequences might follow.

Science is very much like other human endeavors in that attitudes are of extreme importance and reach far beyond the immediate effect. Consider the doctrine of the divine right of kings. At one time this idea was widely accepted, but by the latter 1600s it was seriously challenged or rejected through most of Europe. Although the initial change of attitude involved primarily the monarch, it foreshadowed curtailment of the privileges of the aristocracy. Later consequences of this shift in attitudes included the doctrine of equality of men and the questioning of hereditary property rights. It would be absurd to assume that all of these later developments in social structure resulted solely from the overthrow of the divine-right doctrine, but the change in attitude accompanying this overthrow did play a substantial part in their development. Today it is extremely difficult to understand, much less recreate, the attitudes and implications that accompanied acceptance of the divine-right doctrine.

In summary, when we change the way we view any important aspect of our world, our attitudes toward other aspects of the world also change, because attitudes are generally more important than specifics.

MISUNDERSTANDINGS ABOUT SCIENCE

There are a number of common misunderstandings about science. The following statements illustrate some of them. We'll discuss each of these misunderstandings briefly.

1. The accumulation of facts or data is the primary goal of science.
2. Some sciences can be described as *exact.*
3. Science is deficient because it cannot give any ultimate explanation of natural processes.
4. Science distorts reality and cannot do justice to the fullness of experience.
5. Science is concerned primarily with man's practical and social needs.

1. *The accumulation of facts or data is the primary goal of science.* An important part of the game is collecting data, but mere accumulation of facts does not necessarily give birth to science. All human groups collect data, but not all humans are scientists. Consider the following vignette. As in a dream, transport yourself to a gentle isle of the South Seas. Here frolic the happy children of nature, their golden skins glowing amid glittering sands, azure seas, and lush foliage. Dominating this spectacular beauty is a mountain from which a pale trickle of smoke arises. What do the people know about this object in their midst? Quite a bit! They have amassed a wide range of data. They recognize the rumbles that precede a shower of ashes; they know that the refuse of an earlier eruption is extremely fertile; they know that ashes and lava are hot and have a distinctive odor. Legends of the village tell of fireworks bursting high above the mountain.

We could continue to catalog their knowledge indefinitely, but a simple recital of data has not led to any "scientific" understanding. The missing ingredient is a set of general principles. The inhabitants' accumulation of data is extensive, but aside from the classic line "The gods are angry tonight," they make no sense of the welter of events.

To summarize the point of this illustration, data have been accumulated in all cultures, but science is recent and flourishes in only a few. The quality and character of explanatory or organizing concepts and the relation of concepts to data are critical additional ingredients in the game of science. The concept of angry gods doesn't lead to any reliable prediction of future events; nor does it integrate specific observations into an organized pattern. In addition, angry gods won't hold still for testing.

2. *Some sciences can be described as* exact. There are *no* "exact" sciences! And there is no prospect that there will be exact sciences in the future! It may occur to you that mathematics is "exact." Whether it is or not is beside the point, since mathematics, although vital to science, is not itself a science, as we define the term. Science must be related to observations, and mathematics is not derived

from nor dependent upon observations—it is simply based on the logical consequences of a set of postulates. Some people call observationally based sciences *natural* sciences and mathematics and logic *formal* sciences.

Statements made in natural science have only probabilistic, not exact, confirmation. Take as an example a long-established and repeatedly confirmed scientific law. Consider the distance (S) traveled by a falling body in its first two seconds of fall. The established law is presented as $S = \frac{1}{2} gt^2$ (g is a "constant" that varies with location and altitude; t is time in seconds). Actual measurement of distances (taken at St. Louis, Missouri), however, would generate a distribution of values [in which] repeated measures under the same conditions (as nearly identical as humanly possible) give different answers. The data conform to laws of probability that imply that one gets a particular range of results a certain percentage of the time. There is *no* way we can determine *exactly* how far a body will fall in a given amount of time under any specific condition. What we can do is state with a high degree of assurance that in this case 95% of the measures will fall within 0.0001 meters from the average.

In addition to their probabilistic nature, scientific statements are incomplete. Although it is generally unspoken, a qualification is implied in any scientific statement: "Based on the evidence available to me, interpreted to the best of my ability, I believe that . . . ." In other words, a scientific statement is inevitably incomplete in evidence and interpretation. "Evidence available to me" leaves the scientist's statement open to revision based on new evidence. Similarly, interpretation of existing evidence may change. For example, you may be walking down the street and suddenly hear an explosive sound. You fall to the ground out of fear for your life. But, as you lie there, on second thought you may decide that it was a car backfiring. Note that the evidence has not changed; it has just been reinterpreted. Changes in interpretation due to reanalysis of the prior evidence, adoption of new interpretations from external sources, and new interpretations derived from added evidence are all quite common. Sciences, whether as well developed as physics or as recent and incomplete as sociology, have at least one characteristic in common: pronouncements are tentative. If they were not, we would have to deny the importance and even the possibility of new evidence and new thought. Such denial is contrary to the way of a scientist.

3. *Science is deficient because it cannot give any ultimate explanation of natural processes.* This charge is often made by persons whose understanding of the methods and objectives of science can most charitably be characterized as limited. The charge is true but irrelevant. Ultimate explanations simply are not part of the objectives of science in the modern world. A quest for ultimate explanations dominated much prescientific thinking. Thousands of years of effort and thought did not lead to a resolution of any ultimate problems, such as "What is the essence of life?" or "What is the greatest good?" In contrast, the preoccupation of science with potentially solvable problems such as "Why didn't milkmaids contract smallpox?" has produced spectacular results.

As stated earlier, scientific statements are tentative. An attempt at ultimate explanations based on tentative statements could be handled only by Don Quixote[3] or Lewis Carroll's Red Queen.[4]

4. *Science distorts reality and cannot do justice to the fullness of experience.* If distorting reality means that scientists select only one small portion of phenomena for investigation at any time, then they happily plead guilty. In fact, this limitation of the area of research is a vital tactic of science. Otherwise the problems are simply beyond our capacities.

In any given situation, there are literally innumerable things scientists could measure or manipulate. Achievement of any reasonable answers requires them to focus on one or, at best, a few aspects of any given situation. At the same time they attempt to minimize, in some manner, other factors that might influence the result.

The limitation of a discussion to certain aspects of the total situation occurs in any endeavor. If you are describing a baseball game you may discuss the size of the stadium *or* the color of the uniforms *or* the eccentric motions made by the pitcher *or* the number of hits each team got *or* the team spirit exhibited *or* where the fans are from *or* the temperature at game time *or* . . . . Or you may compare any of these things with previous games. But *no one* can discuss everything. So the scientist, like anyone else, selects the aspects of the situation he wishes to discuss. He differs from the nonscientist in being aware of the fact that he is selecting and is systematically investigating those aspects he has selected, although he may not be aware of how arbitrary his selection is.

To aid his investigation, the scientist in many instances attempts to minimize the differential influence of aspects he is not currently investigating. He does so by manipulating the environment and performing experiments. Criticism that science distorts reality often focuses on the laboratory experiment. Experiments are alleged to distort "reality," since the situation is artificial. Of course the object of the scientist is not to distort reality but to find out how the real world works by temporarily controlling events related to those he is currently interested in measuring.

The importance of such controls can be illustrated in the field of genetics. Genetics remained a matter of rather vague statements about "blood" and "like begets like" until Mendel and those who followed him examined the situation in carefully controlled and limited conditions. Mendel succeeded where earlier hybridizers failed largely because he studied inheritance of single contrasting characters, carefully controlled other factors, and recorded the results in detail. As you may have suspected by this time, science becomes sophisticated when it is able to create and observe artificial situations in which only certain factors can have an influence. The success of science depends on the ability to screen out the booming, buzzing confusion that confounds orderly observation.

In addition to being charged with distorting reality, scientists are also charged with failing to do justice to the fullness of experience. This accusation is most often applied to psychology, and it usually takes the general form "People are too complicated and individually different to be studied through artificial laboratory situations." This argument is nonsense, of course. Scientists do in fact study humans from the standpoints of both underlying biological processes and observable behavior. From these standpoints they create theories attempting to account for all aspects of human character. Their knowledge is both extensive and incomplete, as might be expected.

Each person is unique. So what? Every snowflake is reputedly different, yet scientists can still make meaningful statements about moisture, size, temperature, or crystalline structure. It is also said that every single atom is different. This statement may or may not be true. It is irrelevant! We do study atomic structure, but science has little or no interest in the completely unique. Its primary goals are to understand how observed facts relate to each other, to formulate models that approximate the relations of these observations, and to extend predictions to new observations. Few would object if you chose to spend a career studying a single snowflake; however, the scientific gain would not seem to justify this devotion. Not that the expression of uniqueness and aesthetic qualities is not worthwhile—it is just not a basic part of the scientific endeavor.

5. *Science is concerned primarily with man's practical and social needs.* The last of our misunderstandings is the assertion that science is man's reply to his practical and social needs. It would be fruitless to deny that practical and social needs play a part in science, particularly applied science. But they play only a small part; they are not the game. Unfortunately, these practical results of science are the most visible, so they are often identified as the heart of science. We know that the desire for these by-products is responsible for some scientific work and that the financial backing of other work is motivated by hopes of practical gain. For most scientists, however, science is a game played for understanding, not for practical solutions to existing problems. There is no really good evidence that simple need produces scientific advancement. If the scientific groundwork has been laid, necessity may encourage solution. For those scientists who play the game for understanding rather than for practical advantage, it is a game whose chief delight is the addition of one neatly contrived stroke that helps give form to a picture; a game affording a glimpse of what no man has conceived before; a game from which may come the ecstasy of bringing order out of chaos.

A simple glance at a few of the more important figures in science reveals the absence of "practical" goals. Galileo, Newton, and Einstein would certainly make any all-world science team. What practical need could have driven Galileo to astronomy, where he was criticized, rebuked, and threatened, both by academics and by the church hierarchy? Where was the practical pay-off? Could Newton or Einstein have been motivated by the hopes of future space travel or weapons that would fry dull, uncomprehending masses as crisp as bacon? Utterly absurd. Nor does personal gain through either fame or money seem to have been their principal motivation. Both Newton and Einstein achieved fame at an early age but continued to work until their deaths. There is a story, which may be true, that Einstein, when invited to the Institute for Advanced Studies at Princeton, asked whether $3000 per year would be too large a salary to expect. Of course there *are* those in science whose aim is a better mousetrap or personal gain. They may achieve visibility, but rarely do they make serious contributions to the basic concepts in science.

Notes

¹ Nicolaus Copernicus (1478–1543), a Polish astronomer, in *De Revolutionibus Orbium Coelestium* (1543) advanced the theory that the earth rotates daily on its axis and the planets rotate around the sun.

² Galilei Galileo (1564–1642), an Italian astronomer and physicist, conceived laws describing the notion of falling objects, improved the telescope, and used it to discover that the moon's surface was mountainous and its shine was reflected light. For his writings which advanced the Copernican system, he was tried by the Inquisition and found guilty of heresy.

³ Don Quixote was the central character obsessed with romantic ideals in Miguel Cervante's seventeenth-century novel *Don Quixote*.

⁴ The Red Queen was the irrational queen in Lewis Carroll's *Alice in Wonderland.*

FOCUS: READING REVIEW

1. What is the distinction the writers make between collecting data and science?
2. In what ways are scientific pronouncements tentative?
3. What is the distinction between "potentially solvable problems" and "ultimate explanations"? What does this distinction suggest about science's ability to explain the universe?

FOCUS: AUTHOR'S STRATEGIES

1. What does the introduction suggest about the writers' assumptions about their audience?
2. What is this essay's purpose? What indicates this?

FOCUS: DISCUSSION AND WRITING

1. Read one of the selections in chapter 2 and identify where science is tentative.
2. After assessing the writer's responses to the misunderstandings about science, formulate a definition of science.

The Sense of Human Dignity
Jacob Bronowski

Jacob Bronowski (1908–1974), a distinguished mathematician who left academia to work for the war effort in England in 1942, became a historian and philosopher of science after World War II. He taught in England

and the United States. Most familiar to us for his work The Ascent of Man *(1973), Bronowski assumed a key role in trying to bridge the separation between science and the humanities made famous by C.P. Snow's* Two Cultures. *"The Sense of Human Dignity," taken from* Science and Human Values *(1965), asserts that the ethics which bind the scientific community differ little from the ethics of democratic societies.*

The values of science have grown out of the practice of science. Science is the creation of concepts and their exploration in the facts. Truth is the drive at the center of science. If truth is to be found, what conditions (and with them, what other values) grow [from science]? First comes independence, in observation and in thought. The byproduct of independence is originality. Dissent is essential to both. Dissent, however, is not an end in itself; it is the mark of freedom. [If] science is to become effective as a public practice, it must protect independence [with such safeguards as free inquiry, free thought, free speech, and tolerance]. The society of scientists must be a democracy. Science is not a mechanism but a human progress, and not a set of findings but the search for them. Science at last respects the scientist more than his theories; for by its nature it must prize the search above the discovery and the thinking (and with it the thinker) above the thought. In the society of scientists each man has earned a dignity more profound than his doctrine. The society of scientists has to solve the problem of every society, which is to find a compromise between man and men. The individual scientist must practice the community's values. The dilemma of today is not that the human values cannot control a mechanical science. It is the other way about: the scientific spirit is more human than the machinery of governments.

The values of science derive neither from the virtues of its members, nor from the finger-wagging codes of conduct by which every profession reminds itself to be good. They have grown out of the practice of science, because they are the inescapable conditions for its practice.

Science is the creation of concepts and their exploration in the facts. It has no other test of the concept than its empirical truth to fact. Truth is the drive at the center of science; it must have the habit of truth, not as a dogma but as a process. Consider then, step by step, what kind of society scientists have been compelled to form in this single pursuit. If truth is to be found, not given, and if therefore it is to be tested in action, what other conditions (and with them, what other values) grow of themselves from this?

First, of course, comes independence, in observation and thence in thought. I once told an audience of school-children that the world would never change if they did not contradict their elders. I was chagrined to find next morning that this axiom outraged their parents. Yet it is the basis of the scientific method. A man must see, do and think things for himself, in the face of those who are sure that they have already been over all that ground. In science, there is no substitute for independence.

It has been a byproduct of this that, by degrees, men have come to give a value to the new and the bold in all their work. It was not always so. European thought and art before the Renaissance were happy in the faith that there is nothing new under the sun. John Dryden[1] in the seventeenth century, and Jonathan Swift[2] as it turned into the eighteenth, were still fighting Battles of the Books to prove that no modern work could hope to rival the classics. They were not overpowered by argument or example (not even by their own examples), but by the mounting scientific tradition among their friends in the new Royal Society. Today we find it as natural to prize originality in a child's drawing and an arrangement of flowers as in an invention. Science has bred the love of originality as a mark of independence.

Independence, originality, and therefore dissent: these words show the progress, they stamp the character of our civilization as once they did that of Athens in flower. From Luther[3] in 1517 to Spinoza[4] grinding lenses, from Huguenot[5] weavers and Quaker ironmasters to the Puritans founding Harvard, and from Newton's religious heresies[6] to the calculated universe of Eddington[7], the profound movements of history have been begun by unconforming men. Dissent is the native activity of the scientist, and it has got him into a good deal of trouble in the last ten years. But if that is cut off, what is left will not be a scientist. And I doubt whether it will be a man. For dissent is also native in any society which is still growing. Has there ever been a society which has died of dissent? Several have died of conformity in our lifetime.

Dissent is not itself an end; it is the surface mark of a deeper value. Dissent is the mark of freedom, as originality is the mark of independence of mind. And as originality and independence are private needs for the existence of a science, so dissent and freedom are its public needs. No one can be a scientist, even in private, if he does not have independence of observation and of thought. But if in addition science is to become effective as a public practice, it must go further; it must protect independence. The safeguards which it must offer are patent: free inquiry, free thought, free speech, tolerance. These values are so familiar to us, yawning our way through political perorations, that they seem self-evident. But they are self-evident, that is, they are logical needs, only where men are committed to explore the truth: in a scientific society. These freedoms of tolerance have never been notable in a dogmatic society, even when the dogma was Christian. They have been granted only when scientific thought flourished once before, in the youth of Greece.

I have been developing an ethic for science which derives directly from its own activity. It might have seemed at the outset that this study could lead only to a set of technical rules: to elementary rules for using test tubes, or sophisticated rules for inductive reasoning. But the inquiry turns out quite otherwise. There are, oddly, no technical rules for success in science. There are no rules even for using test tubes which the brilliant experimenter does not flout; and alas, there are no rules at all for making successful general inductions. This is not where the study of scientific practice leads us. Instead, the conditions for the practice of science are found to be of another and an unexpected kind. Independence and originality, dissent and freedom and tolerance: such are the first needs of science; and these are the values which, of itself, it demands and forms.

The society of scientists must be a democracy.[8] It can keep alive and grow only by a constant tension between dissent and respect; between independence from the views of others, and tolerance for them. The crux of the ethical problem is to fuse these, the private and the public needs. Tolerance alone is not enough; this is why the bland, kindly civilizations of the East, where to contradict is a personal affront, developed no strong science. And independence is not enough either: the sad history of genetics, still torn today by the quarrels of sixty years ago, shows that.[9] Every scientist has to learn the hard lesson, to respect the views of the next man—even when the next man is tactless enough to express them.

Tolerance among scientists cannot be based on indifference, it must be based on respect. Respect as a personal value implies, in any society, the public acknowledgements of justice and of due honor. These are values which to the layman seem most remote from any abstract study. Justice, honor, the respect of man for man: What, he asks, have these human values to do with science? The question is a foolish survival of those nineteenth-century quarrels which always came back to equate ethics with the Book of Genesis. If critics in the past had ever looked practically to see how a science develops, they would not have asked such a question. Science confronts the work of one man with that of another, and grafts each on each; and it cannot survive without justice and honor and respect between man and man. Only by these means can science pursue its steadfast object, to explore truth. If these values did not exist, then the society of scientists would have to invent them to make the practice of science possible. In societies where these values did not exist, science has had to create them.

Science is not a mechanism but a human progress, and not a set of findings but the search for them. Those who think that science is ethically neutral confuse the findings of science, which are, with the activity of science, which is not. To the layman who is dominated by the fallacy of the comic strips, that science would all be done best by machines, the distinction is puzzling. But human search and research is a learning by steps of which none is final, and the mistakes of one generation are rungs in the ladder, no less than their correction by the next. This is why the values of science turn out to be recognizably the human values: because scientists must be men, must be fallible, and yet as men must be willing and as a society must be organized to correct their errors. William Blake said that 'to be an Error & to be Cast out is a part of God's design.'[10] It is certainly part of the design of science.

There never was a great scientist who did not make bold guesses, and there never was a bold man whose guesses were not sometimes wild. Newton was wrong, in the setting of his time, to think that light is made up of particles. Faraday was foolish when he looked, in his setting, for a link between electro-magnetism and gravitation. And such is the nature of science, their bad guesses may yet be brilliant by the work of our own day. We do not think any less of the profound concept of General Relativity in Einstein[11] because the details of his formulation at this moment seem doubtful. For in science, as in literature, the style of a great man is the stamp of his mind, and makes even his mistakes a challenge which is part of the march of its subject. Science at last respects the scientist more than his theories; for by its nature it must prize the search above the discovery, and the thinking (and with it the thinker) above the thought. In the society of scientists each man, by the process of exploring for the truth, has earned a dignity more profound than his doctrine. A true society is sustained by the sense of human dignity.

I take this phase from the life of the French naturalist Buffon who, like Galileo, was forced to recant his scientific findings.[12] Yet he preserved always, says his biographer, something deeper than the fine manners of the court of Louis XV; he kept *'le sentiment exquis de la dignite humaine.'* His biographer says that Buffon learned this during his stay in England, where it was impressed on him by the scientists he met. Since Buffon seems to have spent at most three months in England, this claim has been thought extravagant. But is it? Is history really so inhuman an arithmetic? Buffon in the short winter of 1738–9 met the grave men of the Royal Society, heirs to Newton, the last of a great generation. He found them neither a court nor a rabble, but a community of scientists seeking the truth together with dignity and humanity. It was, it is, a discovery to form a man's life.

The sense of human dignity that Buffon showed in his bearing is the cement of a society of equal men; for it expresses their knowledge that respect for others must be founded in self-respect. Theory and experiment alike become meaningless unless the scientist brings to them, and his fellows can assume in him, the respect of a lucid honesty with himself. The mathematician and philosopher W.K. Clifford said this forcibly at the end of his short life, nearly a hundred years ago.

> If I steal money from any person, there may be no harm done by the mere transfer of possession; he may not feel the loss, or it may even prevent him from using the money badly. But I cannot help doing this great wrong towards Man, that I make myself dishonest. What hurts society is not that it should lose its property, but that it should become a den of thieves; for then it must cease to be society. This is why we ought not to do evil that good may come; for at any rate this great evil has come, that we have done evil and are made wicked thereby.

This is the scientist's moral: that there is no distinction between ends and means. Clifford goes on to put this in terms of the scientist's practice:

> In like manner, if I let myself believe anything on insufficient evidence, there may be no great harm done by the mere belief; it may be true after all, or I may never have occasion to exhibit it in outward acts. But I cannot help doing this great wrong towards Man, that I make myself credulous. The danger to society is not merely that it should believe wrong things, though that is great enough; but that it should become credulous.

And the passion in Clifford's tone shows that to him the word credulous had the same emotional force as 'a den of thieves.'

The fulcrum of Clifford's ethic here, and mine, is the phrase 'it may be true after all.' Others may allow this to justify their conduct; the practice of science wholly rejects it. It does not admit that the word true can have this meaning. The test of truth is the known factual evidence, and no glib expediency nor reason of state can justify the smallest self-deception in that. Our work is of a piece, in the large and in detail; so that if we silence one scruple about our means, we infect ourselves and our ends together.

The scientist derives this ethic from his method, and every creative worker reaches it for himself. This is how Blake reached it from his practice as a poet and a painter.

He who would do good to another must do it in Minute Particulars:
General Good is the plea of the scoundrel, hypocrite & flatterer,
For Art & Science cannot exist but in minutely organized Particulars.

The Minute Particulars of art and the fine-structure of science alike make the grain of conscience.

The society of scientists is simple because it has a directing purpose: to explore the truth. Nevertheless, it has to solve the problem of every society, which is to find a compromise between man and men. It must encourage the single scientist to be independent, and the body of scientists to be tolerant. From these basic conditions, which form the prime values, there follows step by step a range of values: dissent, freedom of thought and speech, justice, honor, human dignity and self-respect.

Our values since the Renaissance have evolved by just such steps. There are of course casuists who, when they are not busy belittling these values, derive them from the Middle Ages. But that servile and bloody world upheld neither independence nor tolerance, and it is from these, as I have shown, that the human values are rationally derived. Those who crusade against the rational, and receive their values by mystic inspiration, have no claim to these values of the mind. I cannot put this better than in the words of Albert Schweitzer in which he, a religious man, protests that mysticism in religion is not enough.

Rationalism is more than a movement of thought which realized itself at the end of the eighteenth and the beginning of the nineteenth centuries. It is a necessary phenomenon in all normal spiritual life. All real progress in the world is in the last analysis produced by rationalism. The principle, which was then established, of basing our views of the universe on thought and thought alone is valid for all time.[13]

So proud men have thought, in all walks of life, since Giordano Bruno[14] was burned alive for his cosmology on the Campo de' Fiori in 1600. They have gone about their work simply enough. The scientists among them did not set out to be moralists or revolutionaries. William Harvey[15] and Huygens, Euler and Avogadro, Darwin and William Gibbs and Marie Curie, Planck and Pavlov, practised their crafts modestly and steadfastly. Yet the values they seldom spoke of shone out of their work and entered their ages, and slowly re-made the minds of men. Slavery ceased to be a matter of course. The princelings of Europe fled from the gaming table. The empires of the Bourbons and the Hapsburgs crumbled. Men asked for the rights of man and for government by consent. By the beginning of the nineteenth century, Napoleon did not find a scientist to elevate tyranny into a system; that was done by the philosopher Hegel. Hegel had written his university dissertation to prove philosophically that there could be no more than the seven planets he knew. It was unfortunate, and characteristic, that even as he wrote, on 1 January 1801, a working astronomer observed the eighth planet Ceres.[16]

I began this book with the question which has haunted me, as a scientist, since I heard it in the ruins of Nagasaki: 'Is You Is Or Is You Ain't Ma Baby?' Has science fastened upon our society a monstrous gift of destruction which we can neither undo nor master, and which, like a clockwork automaton in a nightmare, is set to break our necks? Is science an automaton, and has it lamed our sense of values?

These questions are not answered by holding a Sunday symposium of moralists. They are not even answered by the painstaking neutralism of the textbooks on scientific method. We must indeed begin from a study of what scientists do, when they are neither posed for photographs on the steps of spaceships nor bumbling professorially in the cartoons. But we must get to the heart of what they do. We must lay bare the conditions which make it possible for them to work at all.

When we do so we find, leaf by leaf, the organic values which I have been unfolding. And we find that they are not at odds with the values by which alone mankind can survive. On the contrary, like the other creative activities which grew from the Renaissance, science has humanized our values. Men have asked for freedom, justice and respect precisely as the scientific spirit has spread among them. The dilemma of today is not that the human values cannot control a mechanical science. It is the other way about: the scientific spirit is more human than the machinery of governments. We have not let either the tolerance or the empiricism of science enter the parochial rules by which we still try to prescribe the behavior of nations. Our conduct as states clings to a code of self-interest which science, like humanity, has long left behind.

The bond of technical science burdens and threatens us because we are trying to employ the body without the spirit; we are trying to buy the corpse of science. We are hag-ridden by the power of nature which we should command, because we think its command needs less devotion and understanding than its discovery. And because we know how gunpowder works, we sigh for the days before atomic bombs. But massacre is not prevented by sticking to gunpowder; the Thirty Years' War is proof of that. Massacre is prevented by the scientist's ethic, and the poet's, and every creator's: that the end for which we work exists and is judged only by the means which we use to reach it. This is the human sum of the values of science. It is the basis of a society which scrupulously seeks knowledge to match and govern its power. But it is not the scientist who can govern society; his duty is to teach it the implications and the values in his work. Sir Thomas More said this in 1516, that the single-minded man must not govern but teach; and nearly twenty years later went to the scaffold for neglecting his own counsel.

Notes

[1] John Dryden (1631–1700) was an English poet and playwright.

[2] Jonathan Swift (1667–1745) was an English political and social satirist, best known for *Gulliver's Travels*.

[3] Martin Luther (1483–1546), the German religious reformer, initiated the Reformation in Germany by his attack on the Catholic church's abuses.

[4] Baruch Spinoza (1632–1677), a Dutch philosopher, proposed the presence of God in all substance and derived a metaphysics from this proposition.

[5] Huguenots were Protestants in sixteenth-century France.

[6] Sir Isaac Newton's religious beliefs were anti-Trinitarian, a view contrary to orthodox Christianity.

[7] Arthur Stanley Eddington (1882–1944), an English astronomer, researched celestial motion, evolution, and internal constitution, and elucidated Einstein's theories of relativity.

[8] This limits the actions which the individual scientist thinks himself entitled to impose on others. He does not think himself entitled to play the benevolent despot, who can insist that he knows better than anyone what is good for everyone. By contrast, many non-scientists believe that the misuse of science can only be ended if individual scientists take away the responsibility of its proper use from the community, and decide to withhold from it the knowledge of discoveries which might be misused. On this view Einstein in 1939 should not have told the President of the United States that an atomic explosion might be produced—on the ground, presumably, that Einstein could be trusted to act with wisdom and humanity, and the man whom the United States had elected to act for them could not. In the event, however, the only scientist who aspired to dictate to the communal conscience in this way turned out to be Klaus Fuchs. I have discussed this issue at length in an essay on "Responsibilities of Scientist and Public" in the *Atomic Scientists' Journal* for September 1955. [Bronowski]

[9] The feud that was waged by Lysenko against the majority of geneticists in Russia in recent years had a parallel in a bitter quarrel that divided English geneticists about 1900. At that time, however, the roles were reversed: most biologists believed that heredity variation is continuous and it was the rebels who believed in the new Mendelian mechanism by which heritable characters are passed on as units. The rebels were led by William Bateson, who was (like Lysenko) a naturalist and a breeder, a man with green fingers. Like Lysenko, Bateson argued against what seemed to him the lifeless statistics of laboratory genetics; but the statistical studies he complained of were of continuous variations, and precisely opposite to those now attacked by Lysenko. Among those ranged against Bateson then was Karl

Pearson, a man as great and original, and as intransigent, who would not print Bateson's papers in *Biometrika*: for geneticists and statisticians seem always to have been (and remain) difficult and intemperate men. Yet at bottom (and this is the irony in their quarrel) Pearson's exact statistical methods were then as radically new, and as distasteful to academic biologists, as was Bateson's advocacy of Mendel—and indeed, Pearson and his friends had founded *Biometrika* because the Royal Society made difficulties about publishing their work. There was a fierce showdown between the two schools at the British Association in 1904, much like the showdown at the Academy of Agricultural sciences in Russia in 1948, with this difference: that at the British Association no one was humiliated, no one was silenced, and no one tried to change genetics on any other ground than the experimental evidence. [Bronowski]

[10] William Blake (1757–1817), an English Romantic poet, reflects a mistrust for science and rationalism in his poetry.

[11] Albert Einstein's theory of special relativity suggests the conditions which must be met by theories to be deemed laws of nature. According to this theory, measurements of space and time must correlate with the speed of light's constant velocity.

[12] These findings concerned, among other things, the origin of the earth. Buffon speculated intelligently on a number of related topics in biology and geology, and was probably the first scientist who clearly conceived a theory of evolution. [Bronowski]

[13] I quote from *The Philosophy of Civilization—Part I, Decay and Restoration* (London, 1932). I have discussed modern rationalism in my Conway Memorial Lecture "The Fulfillment of Man" (1954). [Bronowski]

[14] Giordano Bruno (1548–1600) was an Italian philosopher who championed Copernican cosmology.

[15] William Harvey (1578–1657), an English physician, discovered the circulation of blood. Christian Huygens (1629–1695), a Dutch mathematician, physicist, and astronomer, developed the wave theory of light. Leonhard Fuler (1707–1783), a Swiss mathematician and physicist, founded the calculus of variation. Amedeo Avogadro (1776–1856), an Italian chemist and physicist, authored the hypothesis that equal volumes of all gases at the same temperature and pressure contain equal numbers of molecules. Charles Darwin (1809–1882) was the English naturalist whose study of animal species' variations led to the theory of evolution by natural selection. Willard Gibbs (1839–1903) was a physicist whose investigations established the basis for physical chemistry. Marie Curie (1867–1934), a French physical chemist, discovered radium. Max Planck (1858–1947), a German physicist, originated and developed quantum theory, describing the behavior of light and energy. Ivan Pavlov (1849–1936), a Russian physiologist, conducted the famous experiment demonstrating conditioned reflexes in dogs.

[16] The working astronomer was Giuseppe Piazzi. I owe my knowledge of this bizarre incident to the most distinguished pioneer in the study of the history of science, the late George Sarton. The just comment on such speculations was made long before by Shakespeare:

Foole. The reason why the seven Starres are no more than seven is a pretty reason.
Lear. Because they are not eight?
Foole. Yes indeed. Thou would'st make a good Foole.

[Bronowski]

FOCUS: READING REVIEW

1. Bronowski seems to be answering a particular critic of science. What would you imagine his criticisms to be? What passages suggest this?
2. Bronowski assigns to science certain values. What are they?
3. What does the term "ethically neutral" mean in reference to science and Bronowski's argument?

FOCUS: AUTHOR'S STRATEGIES

1. What audience do Bronowski's language and evidence suggest? What is their principal attitude toward science?
2. Besides being critical of science, what other qualities does Bronowski's audience possess? In what assumptions about human endeavor does Bronowski seek a common ground to answer his audience's concerns?
3. The concluding section of this selection suggests Bronowski's purpose more clearly. What is it?

FOCUS: DISCUSSION AND WRITING

1. Are the values Bronowski identifies here what you would expect in a discussion of scientific values? Why or why not? Why does he choose to discuss these particular values in relation to his audience?
2. Can a scientist be ethically neutral? Use a contemporary issue such as genetic engineering or atomic weapons research to demonstrate your position.

Chapter 2
The
Natural Sciences
at Work

Science, we learned in the previous chapter, objectively gathers and interprets data about nature to formulate theories which explain natural phenomena. The essays in this chapter reflect the interplay between observation and interpretation, between fact and theory. Both Barnett's discussion of Einstein's Special Relativity Theory from *The Universe and Dr. Einstein* and the Beadles' essay "The Mendelian Laws" not only explain two fundamental scientific concepts but they also describe what spurred scientific investigation and how the discoveries proceeded. Darwin's essay "Coral Formations" focuses less on the discovery process than on data interpretation. The data—Darwin's nature observations recorded during his voyage on the H.M.S. *Beagle* beginning in 1827—did not become theory until years later when in 1839 he presented his findings to England's Royal Society. In "How Flowers Changed the World" Eiseley reconstructs what must have happened in the earth's slow growth to create an environment hospitable to animal life as we know it. In his essay we see scientific theory divorced from direct observation but still linked to verifiable data. Weintraub's essay, "The Brain: His and Hers," presents experimental data from anatomy, biochemistry, behavior, and neuropsychology studying differences between the brains of men and women, but arrives at any interpretation or theory very tentatively. As a whole, these essays reveal that science is indeed an attitude to a problem—a process of observation and interpretation—rather than a fixed body of knowledge.

from *The Universe and Dr. Einstein*
Lincoln Barnett

Lincoln Barnett (1909-1979), a reporter for the New York Herald Tribune *and an editor and writer for* Life *magazine, was best known for* The Universe and Dr. Einstein, *which sold more than a million copies, won a National Book Award special citation in 1949, and was translated into twenty-eight languages. In a foreword to Barnett's book, Albert Einstein comments that "main ideas of relativity are extremely well presented," which he observes is important because "restricting the body of knowledge to a small group deadens the philosophical spirit of a people and leads to spiritual poverty." This selection from* The Universe and Dr. Einstein *describes the scientific context for Einstein's work on relativity theory and explains some of its most fundamental concepts.*

[The Newtonian or Galilean Relativity Principle, formulated by Newton in 1687, states that] mechanical laws which are valid in one place are equally valid in any other place which moves uniformly relative to the first. The philosophical importance of this principle lies in what it says about the universe. It is essential to the scientist that he have confidence in the harmony of nature. He must believe that physical laws revealed to him on earth are in truth universal laws. For all ordinary purposes of science the earth can be regarded as a stationary system. But to the astrophysicist, the earth, far from being at rest, is whirling through space in a giddy and highly complicated fashion. Newton was troubled by the problem of distinguishing relative motion from true or "absolute" motion. [Newton] regarded space as a physical reality, stationary and immovable. [Newton's view prevailed for two centuries. When the wave theory of light was formulated, scientists endowed space with mechanical properties; they assumed that space was some kind of substance which they called "ether."] A universe permeated with an invisible medium in which the stars wandered and through which light traveled like vibrations in a bowl of jelly was the end product of Newtonian physics. It provided a mechanical model for all known phenomena of nature, and it provided the fixed frame of reference, the absolute and immovable space, which Newton's cosmology required. [In 1881 Michelson and Morley conducted an experiment to discover if ether really existed. They projected light rays into space. If the ether really existed then the velocity of the light would be affected. The result was that] there was no difference whatsoever in the velocity of the light beams regardless of their direction. [This presented scientists with an embarrassing alternative—scrap the ether theory or abandon the more venerable theory that the earth is in motion.] Among those who pondered the enigma of the Michelson-Morley experiment was Albert Einstein. [Einstein seized on the] indisputable fact established by the Michelson-Morley experiment that the velocity of light is unaffected by the motion of the earth. If the velocity of light is constant regardless of the earth's motion, [Einstein] reasoned, it must be constant regardless of the motion of any sun, moon, star, meteor, or other system moving anywhere in the universe.

From this he drew a broader generalization, and asserted that the laws of nature are the same for all uniformly moving systems. This is Einstein's Special Theory of Relativity. It simply reiterates the scientist's faith in natural law. All the stars, nebulae, galaxies, and all the vast gravitational systems of outer space are incessantly in motion. But their movements can be described only with respect to each other. [There is no absolute, stationary frame of reference in the universe.] Along with absolute space, Einstein discarded the concept of absolute time. Much of the obscurity that has surrounded the Theory of Relativity stems from man's reluctance to recognize that sense of time, like sense of color, is a form of perception. The Special Theory of Relativity proves by an unanswerable sequence of example and deduction that it is nonsense to think of events taking place simultaneously in unrelated systems.

In his great treatise *On Human Understanding,* philosopher John Locke wrote three hundreds years ago: "A company of chessmen standing on the same squares of the chessboard where we left them, we say, are all in the same place or unmoved: though perhaps the chessboard has been in the meantime carried out of one room into another.... The chessboard, we also say, is in the same place if it remains in the same part of the cabin, though perhaps the ship which it is in sails all the while; and the ship is said to be in the same place supposing it kept the same distance with the neighboring land, though perhaps the earth has turned around; and so chessmen and board and ship have every one changed place in respect to remoter bodies."

Embodied in this little picture of the moving but unmoved chessmen is one principle of relativity—relativity of position. But this suggests another idea—relativity of motion. Anyone who has ever ridden on a railroad train knows how rapidly another train flashes by when it is traveling in the opposite direction, and conversely how it may look almost motionless when it is moving in the same direction. A variation of this effect can be very deceptive in an enclosed station like Grand Central Terminal in New York. Once in a while a train gets under way so gently that passengers feel no recoil whatever. Then if they happen to look out the window and see another train slide past on the next track, they have no way of knowing which train is in motion and which is at rest; nor can they tell how fast either one is moving or in what direction. The only way they can judge their situation is by looking out the other side of the car for some fixed body of reference like the station platform or a signal light. Sir Isaac Newton was aware of these tricks of motion, only he thought in terms of ships. He knew that on a calm day at sea a sailor can shave himself or drink soup as comfortably as when his ship is lying motionless in harbor. The water in his basin, the soup in his bowl, will remain unruffled whether the ship is making five knots, 15 knots, or 25 knots. So unless he peers out at the sea it will be impossible for him to know how fast his ship is moving or indeed if it is moving at all. Of course if the sea should get rough or the ship change course abruptly, then he will sense his state of motion. But granted the idealized conditions of a glass-calm sea and a silent ship, nothing that happens below decks—no amount of observation or mechanical experiment performed *inside* the ship—will disclose its velocity through the sea. The physical principle suggested by these considerations was formulated by Newton in 1687. "The motions of bodies included in a given space," he wrote, "are the same among themselves, whether that space is at rest or moves uniformly forward in a straight line." This is known as the Newtonian or Galilean Relativity Principle. It can also be phrased in more general terms: mechanical laws which are valid in one place are equally valid in any other place which moves uniformly relative to the first.

The philosophical importance of this principle lies in what it says about the universe. Since the aim of science is to explain the world we live in, as a whole and in all its parts, it is essential to the scientist that he have confidence in the harmony of nature. He must believe that physical laws revealed to him on earth are in truth universal laws. Thus in relating the fall of an apple to the wheeling of the planets around the sun Newton hit upon a universal law. And although he illustrated his principle of relative motion by a ship at sea, the ship he actually had in mind was the earth. For all ordinary purposes of science the earth can be regarded as a stationary system. We may say if we choose that mountains, trees, houses, are at rest, and animals, automobiles, and airplanes move. But to the astrophysicist, the earth, far from being at rest, is whirling through space in a giddy and highly complicated fashion. In addition to its daily rotation about its axis at the rate of 1000 miles an hour, and its annual revolution about the sun at the rate of 20 miles a second, the earth is also involved in a number of other less familiar gyrations. Contrary to popular belief the moon does not revolve around the earth; they revolve around each other—or more precisely, around a common center of gravity. The entire solar system, moreover, is moving within the local star system at the rate of 13 miles a second; the local star system is moving within the Milky Way at the rate of 200 miles a second; and the whole Milky Way is drifting with respect to the remote external galaxies at the rate of 100 miles a second—and all in different directions!

Although he could not then know the full complexity of the earth's movements, Newton was nevertheless troubled by the problem of distinguishing relative motion from true or "absolute" motion in a confusingly busy universe. He suggested that "in the remote regions of the fixed stars or perhaps far beyond them, there may be some body absolutely at rest," but admitted there was no way of proving this by any celestial object within man's view. On the other hand it seemed to Newton that space itself might serve as a fixed frame of reference to which the wheeling of the stars and galaxies could be related in terms of absolute motion. He regarded space as a physical reality, stationary and immovable; and while he could not support this conviction by any scientific argument, he nevertheless clung to it on theological grounds. For to Newton space represented the divine omnipresence of God in nature.

In the next two centuries it appeared probable that Newton's view would prevail. For with the development of the wave theory of light scientists found it necessary to endow empty space with certain mechanical properties—to assume, indeed, that space was some kind of substance. Even before Newton's time the French philosopher, Descartes, had argued that the mere separation of bodies by distance proved the existence of a medium between them. And to eighteenth and nineteenth century physicists it was obvious that if light consisted of waves, there must be some medium to support them, just as water propagates the waves of the sea and air transmits the vibrations we call sound. Hence when experiments showed that light can travel in a vacuum, scientists evolved a hypothetical substance called "ether" which they decided must pervade all space and matter. Later on Faraday propounded another kind of ether as the carrier of electric and magnetic forces. When Maxwell finally identified light as an electromagnetic disturbance the case for the ether seemed assured.

A universe permeated with an invisible medium in which the stars wandered and through which light traveled like vibrations in a bowl of jelly was the end product of Newtonian physics. It provided a mechanical model for all known phenomena of nature, and it provided the fixed frame of reference, the absolute and immovable space, which Newton's cosmology required. Yet the ether presented certain problems, not the last of which was that its actual existence had never been proved. To discover once and for all whether there really was any such thing as ether, two American physicists, A.A. Michelson and E.W. Morley, performed a classic experiment in Cleveland in the year 1881.

The principle underlying their experiment was quite simple. They reasoned that if all space is simply a motionless sea of ether, then the earth's motion through the ether should be detectable and measurable in the same way that sailors measure the velocity of a ship through the sea. As Newton pointed out, it is impossible to detect the movement of a ship through calm waters by any mechanical experiment performed *inside* the ship. Sailors ascertain a ship's speed by throwing a log overboard and watching the unreeling of the knots on the log line. Hence to detect the earth's motion through the ether sea, Michelson and Morley threw a "log" overboard, and the log was a beam of light. For if light really is propagated through the ether, then its velocity should be affected by the ether stream arising from the earth's movement. Specifically a light ray projected in the direction of the earth's movement should be slightly retarded by the ether flow, just as a swimmer is retarded by a current when going upstream. The difference would be slight, for the velocity of light (which was accurately determined in 1849) is 186,284 miles a second, while the velocity of the earth in its orbit around the sun is only 20 miles a second. Hence a light ray sent *against* the ether stream should travel at the rate of 186,264 miles a second, while one sent *with* the ether stream should be clocked at 186,304 miles a second. With these ideas in mind Michelson and Morley constructed an instrument of such great delicacy that it could detect a

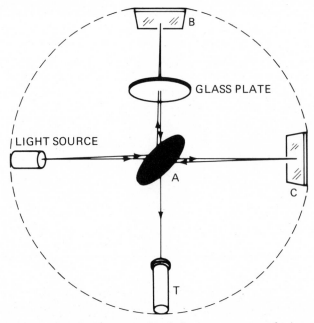

The Michelson-Morley interferometer consisted of an arrangement of mirrors, so designed that a beam transmitted from a light source (above left) was divided and sent in two directions at the same time. This was done by a mirror, A, the *face* of which was only thinly silvered, so that part of the beam was permitted to pass through to mirror C (right) and the remainder reflected at right angles toward mirror B. Mirrors B and C then reflected the rays back to mirror A where, reunited, they proceeded to an observing telescope T. Since the ACT has to pass three times through the thickness of glass behind the reflecting face of mirror A, a clear glass plate of equal thickness was placed between A and B to intercept beam ABT and compensate for this retardation. The whole apparatus was rotated in different directions so that the beams ABT and ACT could be sent with, against, and at right angles to the postulated ether stream. At first it might appear that a trip "downstream," for example from B to A, should compensate in time for an "upstream" trip from A to B. But this *is* not so. To row a boat one mile upstream and another mile downstream takes longer than rowing two miles in still water or across current, even with allowance for drift. Had there been any acceleration or retardation of either beam by the ether stream, the optical apparatus at T would have detected it.

variation of even a fraction of a mile per second in the enormous velocity of light. This instrument, which they called an "interferometer" consisted of a group of mirrors so arranged that a light beam could be split in two and flashed in different directions at the same time. The whole experiment was planned and executed with such painstaking precision that the result could not be doubted. And the result was simply this: there was no difference whatsoever in the velocity of the light beams regardless of their direction.

The Michelson-Morley experiment confronted scientists with an embarrassing alternative. On the one hand they could scrap the ether theory which had explained so many things about electricity, magnetism, and light. Or if they insisted on retaining the ether they had to abandon the still more venerable Copernican theory that the earth is in motion. To many physicists it seemed almost easier to believe that the earth stood still than that waves—light waves, electromagnetic waves—could exist without a medium to sustain them. It was a serious dilemma and one that split scientific thought for a quarter century. Many new hypotheses were advanced and rejected. The experiment was tried again by Morley and by others, with the same conclusion; the apparent velocity of the earth through the ether was zero.

Among those who pondered the enigma of the Michelson-Morley experiment was a young patent office examiner in Berne, named Albert Einstein. In 1905, when he was just twenty-six years old, he published a short paper suggesting an answer to the riddle in terms that opened up a new world of physical thought. He began by rejecting the ether theory and with it the whole idea of space as a fixed system or framework, absolutely at rest, within which it is possible to distinguish absolute from relative motion. The one indisputable fact established by the Michelson-Morley experiment was that the velocity of light is unaffected by the motion of the earth. Einstein seized on this as a revelation of universal law. If the velocity of light is constant regardless of the earth's motion, he reasoned, it must be constant regardless of the motion of any sun, moon, star, meteor, or other system moving anywhere in the universe. From this he drew a broader generalization, and asserted that the laws of nature are the same for all uniformly moving systems. This simple statement is the essence of Einstein's Special Theory of Relativity. It incorporates the Galilean Relativity Principle which stated that mechanical laws are the same for all uniformly moving systems. But its phrasing is more comprehensive; for Einstein was thinking not only of mechanical laws but of the laws governing light and other electromagnetic phenomena. So he lumped them together in one fundamental postulate: all the phenomena of nature, all the laws of nature, are the same for all systems that move uniformly relative to one another.

On the surface there is nothing very startling in this declaration. It simply reiterates the scientist's faith in the universal harmony of natural law. It also advises the scientist to stop looking for any absolute, stationary frame of reference in the universe. The universe is a restless place: stars, nebulae, galaxies, and all the vast gravitational systems of outer space are incessantly in motion. But their movements can be described only with respect to each other, for in space there are no directions and no boundaries. It is futile moreover for the scientist to try to discover the "true" velocity of any system by using light as a measuring rod, for the velocity of light is constant throughout the universe and is unaffected either by the motion of its source or the motion of the receiver. Nature offers no absolute standards of comparison; and space is—as another great German mathematician,

Leibnitz, clearly saw two centuries before Einstein—simply "the order or relation of things among themselves." Without things occupying it, it is nothing.

Along with absolute space, Einstein discarded the concept of absolute time—of a steady, unvarying, inexorable universal time flow, streaming from the infinite past to the infinite future. Much of the obscurity that has surrounded the Theory of Relativity stems from man's reluctance to recognize that sense of time, like sense of color, is a form of perception. Just as there is no such thing as color without an eye to discern it, so an instant or an hour or a day is nothing without an event to mark it. And just as space is simply a possible order of material objects, so time is simply a possible order of events. The subjectivity of time is best explained in Einstein's own words. "The experiences of an individual," he says, "appear to us arranged in a series of events; in this series the single events which we remember appear to be ordered according to the criterion of 'earlier' and 'later.' There exists, therefore, for the individual, an I-time, or subjective time. This in itself is not measurable. I can, indeed, associate numbers with the events, in such a way that a greater number is associated with the later event than with an earlier one. This association I can define by means of a clock by comparing the order of events furnished by the clock with the order of the given series of events. We understand by a clock something which provides a series of events which can be counted."

By referring our own experiences to a clock (or a calendar) we make time an objective concept. Yet the time intervals provided by a clock or a calendar are by no means absolute quantities imposed on the entire universe by divine edict. All the clocks ever used by man have been geared to our solar system. What we call an hour is actually a measurement in space—an arc of 15 degrees in the apparent daily rotation of the celestial sphere. And what we call a year is simply a measure of the earth's progress in its orbit around the sun. An inhabitant of Mercury, however, would have very different notions of time. For Mercury makes its trip around the sun in 88 of our days, and in that same period rotates just once on its axis. So on Mercury a year and a day amount to the same thing. But it is when science ranges beyond the neighborhood of the sun that all our terrestrial ideas of time become meaningless. For Relativity tells us there is no such thing as a fixed interval of time independent of the system to which it is referred. There is indeed no such thing as simultaneity, there is no such thing as "now," independent of a system of reference. For example a man in New York may telephone a friend in London, and although it is 7:00 P.M. in New York and midnight in London, we may say that they are talking "at the same time." But that is because they are both residents of the same planet, and their clocks are geared to the same astronomical system. A more complicated situation arises if we try to ascertain, for example, what is happening on the star Arcturus "right now." Arcturus is 38 light years away. A light year is the distance light travels in one year, or roughly six trillion miles. If we should try to communicate with Arcturus by radio "right now" it would take 38 years for our message to reach its destination and another 38 years for us to receive a reply.[1] And when we look at Arcturus and say that we see it "now," in 1957, we are actually seeing a ghost—an image projected on our optic nerves by light rays that left their source in 1919. Whether Arcturus even exists "now" nature forbids us to know until 1995.

Despite such reflections it is difficult for earthbound man to accept the idea that *this very instant* which he calls "now" cannot apply to the universe as a whole. Yet in the Special Theory of Relativity Einstein proves by an unanswerable sequence of example and deduction that it is nonsense to think of events taking place simultaneously in unrelated systems.

Notes

[1] Radio waves travel at the same speed as light waves. [Barnett]

FOCUS: **READING REVIEW**

1. What is the relevance of the Newtonian or Galilean Relativity Principle to Barnett's discussion of Einstein? What does this suggest about the purpose of this writing?
2. What was the Michelson-Morley experiment? Why did they perform it? What were its results?
3. What is Special Relativity? What does it mean for man's understanding of the universe?
4. In the Newtonian system what is absolute? How does this compare with Einstein's theory?

FOCUS: **AUTHOR'S STRATEGIES**

1. What does Barnett's inclusion of the discussion of the Galilean-Newtonian Relativity Principle suggest about the writer's purpose?
2. To explain Einstein's theory in nonmathematical language is the task Barnett has set out to accomplish. What features of language does he employ to accomplish this task?
3. Cite particular examples of his use of language that suggest the kind of audience for which Barnett is writing.
4. How does the author organize his argument? What does this kind of organization accomplish?

FOCUS: **DISCUSSION AND WRITING**

1. Einstein depicts a physical system where objects are relative to each other. What does relativity mean in this special case? Does this change our understanding of time and space in an earthbound system? Why or why not?
2. You have heard expressions like "justice is relative" or "truth is relative." How do these views relate to Einstein's Relativity Theory? In what ways does ethical relativism use and misuse Einstein?

Keeling Islands: Coral Formations

Charles Darwin

Charles Darwin (1809–1892), best known to us for his evolutionary theory set down in The Origin of Species *(1859), was a botanist, biologist, and geologist from a distinguished British scientific family. Though we often delight in biographers' comments that he showed no early promise and declined to become a physician because of his dislike for the operating room, Darwin did graduate from Cambridge University. Following his graduation, he took a post as naturalist on the scientific expedition of the H.M.S.* Beagle. *During the* Beagle's *voyage Darwin painstakingly recorded observations on the variations of geological formations, plants, and animal life, which years later, after careful thought and reconsideration, led to his evolutionary theory. "Keeling Islands: Coral Formations," taken from* The Voyage of the *Beagle, the 1839 publication of Darwin's edited journals, shows the rigorous adherence to scientific method which makes Darwin's ideas so convincing.*

I will now give a brief account of the three great classes of coral-reefs; namely, Atolls, Barrier, and Fringing-reefs, and will explain my views on their formation. The earlier voyagers fancied that the coral-building animals instinctively built up their great circles to afford themselves protection in the inner parts, [but the theory that has been most generally received is that] atolls are based on submarine craters. [A third and better theory says that as the corals growing more vigorously were exposed to the open sea, the outer edges would grow up from the general foundation before any other part.] Numerous soundings [measurements] were carefully taken by Captain Fitz Roy on the steep outside of Keeling atoll. [From this] it can be inferred that the utmost depths at which corals can construct reefs is between 20 and 30 fathoms. From the fact of the reef-building corals not living at great depths, it is absolutely certain that throughout these vast areas, wherever there is now an atoll, a foundation must have originally existed within a depth of from 20 to 30 fathoms from the surface. If then the foundations, whence the atoll-building corals sprang, were not formed of sediment, and if they were not lifted up to the required level, they must of necessity have subsided into it. As mountain after mountain, and island after island, slowly sank beneath the water, fresh bases would be successively afforded for the growth of corals. No theory on the formation of coral-reefs can be considered satisfactory which does not include the three great classes [atolls, barrier reefs and fringing reefs]. Let us take an island surrounded by fringing-reefs. As the island sinks down, living masses [of coral] bathed by the surf will soon regain the surface. The water, however, will encroach little by little on the shore, the island becoming lower and smaller, and the space between the inner edge of the reef and the beach proportionally broader. If, instead of an island, we had taken the store of a continent fringed with reefs, and had imagined it to have subsided, a great straight barrier would evidently have been the result. As the barrier-reef slowly sinks down, the corals will go on vigorously growing upwards; but as the island sinks, the water will gain inch by inch on the shore—the separate mountains first forming separate islands within one great reef—and finally, the last and highest pinnacle disappearing. The instant this takes places, a perfect atoll is formed. It may be asked whether I can offer any direct evidence of the subsidence of barrier-reefs or atolls. At Keeling atoll I observed on all sides of the lagoon old cocoa-nut trees undermined and falling; and in one place the foundation-posts of a shed, which the inhabitants asserted had stood seven years before just above high-water mark, but now was daily washed by the tide. It is evident, on our theory, that coasts merely fringed by reefs cannot have subsided to any perceptible amount; and therefore, they must, since the growth of their corals, either have remained stationary or have been upheaved.

I will now give a very brief account of the three great classes of coral-reefs; namely, Atolls, Barrier, and Fringing-reefs, and will explain my views[1] on their formation. Almost every voyager who has crossed the Pacific has expressed his unbounded astonishment at the lagoon-islands, or as I shall for the future call them by their Indian name of atolls, and has attempted some explanation. Even as long ago as the year 1605, Pyrard de Laval well exclaimed, "C'est une meruille de voir chacun de ces atollons, enuironné d'un grand banc de pierre tout autour, n'y ayant point d'artifice humain."[2] The accompanying sketch of Whitsunday Island in the Pacific, copied from Capt. Beechey's admirable Voyage, gives but a faint idea of the singular aspect of an atoll: it is one of the smallest size, and has its narrow islets united together in a ring. The immensity of the ocean, the fury of the breakers, contrasted with the lowness of the land and the smoothness of the bright green water within the lagoon, can hardly be imagined without having been seen.

The earlier voyagers fancied that the coral-building animals instinctively built up their great circles to afford themselves protection in the inner parts; but so far is this from the truth, that those massive kinds, to whose growth on the exposed outer shores the very existence of the reef depends, cannot live within the lagoon, where other delicately-branching kinds flourish. Moreover, on this view, many species of distinct genera and families are supposed to combine for one end; and of such a combination, not a single instance can be found in the whole of nature. The theory that has been most generally received is that atolls are based on submarine craters; but when we consider the form and size of some, the number, proximity, and relative positions of others, this idea loses its plausible character: thus, Suadiva atoll is 44 geographical miles in diameter in one line, by 34 miles in another line; Rimsky is 54 by 20 miles across, and it has a strangely sinuous margin; Bow atoll is 30 miles long, and on an average only 6 in width; Menchicoff atoll consists of three atolls united or tied together. This theory, moreover, is totally inapplicable to the northern Maldiva atolls in the Indian Ocean (one of which is 88 miles in length, and between 10 and 20 in breadth), for they are not bounded like ordinary atolls by narrow reefs, but by a vast number of separate little atolls; other little atolls rising out of the great central lagoon-like spaces. A third and better theory was advanced by Chamisso, who thought that from the corals growing more vigorously where exposed to the open sea, as undoubtedly is the case, the outer edges would grow up from the general foundation before any other part, and that this would account for the ring or cup-shaped structure. But we shall immediately see, that in this, as well as in the crater-theory, a most important consideration has been overlooked, namely, on what have the reef-building corals, which cannot live at a great depth, based their massive structures?

Numerous soundings were carefully taken by Captain Fitz Roy on the steep outside of Keeling atoll, and it was found that wihin ten fathoms, the prepared tallow at the bottom of the lead, invariably came up marked with the impressions of living corals, but as perfectly clean as if it had been dropped on a carpet of turf; as the depth increased, the impressions became less numerous, but the adhering particles of sand more and more numerous, until at last it was evident that the bottom consisted of a smooth sandy layer: to carry on the analogy of the turf, the blades of grass grew thinner and thinner, till at last the soil was so sterile, that nothing sprang from it. From these observations, confirmed by many others, it may be safely inferred that the utmost depth at which corals can construct reefs is between 20 and 30 fathoms. Now there are enormous areas in the Pacific and Indian Oceans, in which every single island is of coral formation, and is raised only to that height to which the waves can throw up fragments, and the winds pile up sand. Thus the Radack group of atolls is an irregular square, 520 miles long and 420 broad; the Low archipelago is elliptic-formed, 840 miles in its longer, and 420 in its shorter axis: there are other small groups and single low islands between these two archipelagoes, making a linear space of ocean actually more than 4000 miles in length, in which not one single island rises above the specified height. Again, in the Indian Ocean there is a space of ocean 1500 miles in length, including three archipelagoes, in which every island is low and of coral formation. From the fact of the reef-building corals not living at great depths, it is absolutely certain that throughout these vast areas, wherever there is now an atoll, a foundation must have originally existed within a depth of from 20 to 30 fathoms from the surface. It is improbable in the highest degree that broad, lofty, isolated, steep-sided banks of sediment, arranged in groups and lines hundreds of leagues in length, could have been deposited in the central and profoundest parts of the Pacific and Indian Oceans, at an immense distance from any continent, and where the water is perfectly limpid. It is equally improbable that the elevatory forces should have uplifted throughout the above vast areas, innumerable great rocky banks within 20 to 30 fathoms, or 120 to 180 feet, of the surface of the sea, and not one single point above that level; for where on the whole face of the globe can we find a single chain of mountains, even a few hundred miles in length, with their many summits rising within a few feet of a given level, and not one pinnacle above it? If then the foundations, whence the atoll-building corals sprang, were not formed of sediment, and if they were not lifted up to the required level, they must of necessity have subsided into it; and this at once solves the difficulty. For as mountain after mountain, and island after island, slowly sank beneath the water, fresh bases would be successively afforded for the growth of the corals. It is impossible here to enter into all the necessary details, but I venture to defy[2] any one to explain in any other manner, how it is possible that numerous islands should be distributed throughout vast areas—all the islands being low—all being built of corals, absolutely requiring a foundation within a limited depth from the surface.

Before explaining how atoll-formed reefs acquire their peculiar structure, we must turn to the second great class, namely, Barrier-reefs. These either extend in straight lines in front of the shores of a continent or of a large island, or they encircle smaller islands; in both cases, being separated from the land by a broad and rather deep channel of water, analogous to the lagoon within an atoll. It is remarkable how little attention has been paid to encircling barrier-reefs; yet they are truly wonderful structures. The illustration below represents part of the barrier encircling the island of Bolabola in the Pacific, as seen from one of the central peaks. In this instance the whole line of reef has been converted into land; but usually a snow-white line of great breakers, with only here and there a single low islet crowned with cocoa-nut trees, divides the dark heaving waters of the ocean from the light-green expanse of the lagoon-channel. And the quiet waters of this channel generally bathe a fringe of low alluvial soil, loaded with the most beautiful productions of the tropics, and lying at the foot of the wild, abrupt, central mountains.

Encircling barrier-reefs are of all sizes, from three miles to no less than forty-four miles in diameter; and that which fronts one side, and encircles both ends, of New Caledonia, is 400 miles long. Each reef includes one, two, or several rocky islands of various heights; and in one instance, even as many as twelve separate islands. The reef runs at a greater or less distance from the included land; in the Society archipelago generally from one to three or four miles; but at Hogoleu the reef is 20 miles on the southern side, and 14 miles on the opposite or northern side, from the included islands. The depth within the lagoon-channel also varies much; from 10 to 30 fathoms may be taken as an average; but at Vanikoro there are spaces no less than 56 fathoms or 336 feet deep. Internally the reef either slopes gently into the lagoon-channel, or ends in a perpendicular wall sometimes between two and three hundred feet under water in height: externally the reef rises, like an

atoll, with extreme abruptness out of the profound depths of the ocean. What can be more singular than these structures? We see an island, which may be compared to a castle situated on the summit of a lofty submarine mountain, protected by a great wall of coral-rock, always steep externally and sometimes internally, with a broad level summit, here and there breached by narrow gateways, through which the largest ships can enter the wide and deep encircling moat.

As far as the actual reef of coral is concerned, there is not the smallest difference, in general size, outline, grouping, and even in quite trifling details of structure, between a barrier and an atoll. The geographer Balbi has well remarked, that an encircled island is an atoll with high land rising out of its lagoon; remove the land from within, and a perfect atoll is left.

But what has caused these reefs to spring up at such great distances from the shores of the included islands? It cannot be that the corals will not grow close to the land; for the shores within the lagoon-channel, when not surrounded by alluvial soil, are often fringed by living reefs; and we shall presently see that there is a whole class, which I have called Fringing-reefs from their close attachment to the shores both of continents and of islands. Again, on what have the reef-building corals, which cannot live at great depths, based their encircling structures? This is a great apparent difficulty, analogous to that in the case of atolls, which has generally been overlooked. It will be perceived more clearly by inspecting the following sections, which are real ones, taken in north and south lines, through the islands with their barrier-reefs, of Vanikoro, Gambier, and Maurua; and they are laid down, both vertically and horizontally, on the same scale of a quarter of an inch to a mile.

It should be observed that the sections might have been taken in any direction through these islands, or through many other encircled islands, and the general features would have been the same. Now bearing in mind that reef-building coral cannot live at a greater depth than from 20 to 30 fathoms, and that the scale is so small that the plummets on the right hand show a depth of 200 fathoms, on what are these barrier-reefs based? Are we to suppose that each island is surrounded by a collar-like submarine ledge of rock, or by a great bank of sediment, ending abruptly where the reef ends? If the sea had formerly eaten deeply into the islands, before they were protected by the reefs, thus having left a shallow ledge round them under water, the present shores would have been invariably bounded by great precipices; but this is most rarely the case. Moreover, on this notion, it is not possible to explain why the corals should have sprung up, like a wall, from the extreme outer margin of the ledge, often leaving a broad space of water within, too deep for the growth of corals. The accumulation of a wide bank of sediment all round these islands, and generally widest where the included islands are smallest, is highly improbable, considering their exposed positions in the central and deepest parts of the ocean. In the case of the barrier-reef of New Caledonia, which extends for 150 miles beyond the northern point of the island, in the same straight line with which it fronts the west coast, it is hardly possible to believe, that a bank of sediment could thus have been straightly deposited in front of a lofty island,

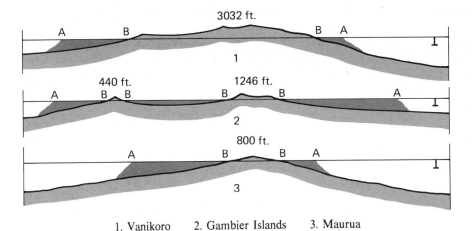

3032 ft.

A   B   B   A

1

440 ft.   1246 ft.

A   B B   B   B   A

2

800 ft.

A   B   B   A

3

1. Vanikoro   2. Gambier Islands   3. Maurua

The horizontal shading shows the barrier-reefs and lagoon-channels. The inclined shading above the level of the sea (AA) shows the actual form of the land; the inclined shading below this line shows its probable prolongation under water.

and so far beyond its termination in the open sea. Finally, if we look to other oceanic islands of about the same height and of similar geological constitution, but not encircled by coral-reefs, we may in vain search for so trifling a circumambient depth as 30 fathoms, except quite near to their shores; for usually land that rises abruptly out of water, as do most of the encircled and non-encircled oceanic islands, plunges abruptly under it. On what then, I repeat, are these barrier-reefs based? Why, with their wide and deep moat-like channels, do they stand so far from the included land? We shall soon see how easily these difficulties disappear.

We come now to our third class of Fringing-reefs, which will require a very short notice. Where the land slopes abruptly under water, these reefs are only a few yards in width, forming a mere ribbon or fringe round the shores: where the land slopes gently under the water the reef extends further, sometimes even as much as a mile from the land; but in such cases the soundings outside the reef always show that the submarine prolongation of the land is gently inclined. In fact the reefs extend only to that distance from the shore, at which a foundation within the requisite depth from 20 to 30 fathoms is found. As far as the actual reef is concerned, there is no essential difference between it and that forming a barrier or an atoll: it is, however, generally of less width, and consequently few islets have been formed on it. From the corals growing more vigorously on the outside, and from the noxious effect of the sediment washed inwards, the outer edge of the reef is the highest part, and between it and the land there is generally a shallow sandy channel a few feet in depth. Where banks of sediment have accumulated near to the surface, as in parts of the West Indies, they sometimes become fringed with corals, and hence in some degree resemble lagoon-islands or atolls; in the same manner as fringing-reefs, surrounding gently-sloping islands, in some degree resemble barrier-reefs.

No theory on the formation of coral-reefs can be considered satisfactory which does not include the three great classes. We have seen that we are driven to believe in the subsidence of these vast areas, interspersed with low islands, of which not one rises above the height to which the wind and waves can throw up matter, and yet are constructed by animals requiring a foundation, and that foundation to lie at no great depth. Let us then take an island surrounded by fringing-reefs, which offer no difficulty in their structure; and let this island with its reef, represented by the unbroken lines in the [illustration above] slowly subside. Now as the island sinks down, either a few feet at a time or quite insensibly, we may safely infer, from what is known of the conditions favourable to the growth of coral, that the living masses, bathed by the surf on the margin of the reef, will soon regain the surface. The water, however, will encroach little by little on the shore, the island becoming lower and smaller, and the space between the inner edge of the reef and the beach proportionally broader. A section of the reef and island in this state, after a subsidence of several hundred feet, is given by the dotted lines. Coral islets are supposed to have been formed on the reef; and a ship is anchored in the lagoon-channel. This channel will be more or less deep, according to the rate of subsidence, to the amount of sediment accumulated in it, and to the growth of the delicately branched corals which can live there. The section in this state resembles in every respect one drawn through an encircled island: in fact, it is a real section (on the scale of .517 of an inch to a mile) through Bolabola in the Pacific. We can now at once see why encircling barrier-reefs stand so far from the shores which they front. We can also perceive, that a line drawn perpendicularly down from the outer edge of the new reef, to the foundation of solid rock beneath the old fringing-reef, will exceed by as many feet as there have been feet of subsidence, that small limit of depth at which the effective corals can live:—the little architects having built up their great wall-like mass, as the whole sank down, upon a basis formed of other corals and their consolidated fragments. Thus the difficulty on this head, which appeared so great, disappears.

If, instead of an island, we had taken the shore of a continent fringed with reefs, and had imagined it to have subsided, a great straight barrier, like that of Australia or New Caledonia, separated from the land by a wide and deep channel, would evidently have been the result.

Let us take our new encircling barrier-reef, of which the section is now represented by unbroken lines, and which, as I have said, is a real section through Bolabola, and let it go on subsiding. As the barrier-reef slowly sinks down, the corals will go on vigorously growing upwards; but as the island sinks, the water will gain inch by inch on the shore—the separate mountains first forming separate islands within one great reef—and finally, the last and highest pinnacle disappearing. The instant this takes place, a perfect atoll is formed: I have said, remove the high land from within an encircling barrier-reef, and an atoll is left, and the land has been removed. We can now perceive how it comes that atolls, having sprung from encircling barrier-reefs, resemble them in general size, form, in the

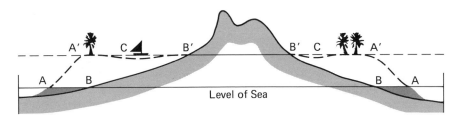

AA. Outer edges of the fringing-reef, at the level of the sea. BB. The shores of the fringed island.

A'A'. Outer edges of the reef, after its upward growth during a period of subsidence, now converted into a barrier, with islets on it. B'B'. The shores of the now encircled island. CC. Lagoon-channel.

N.B. In this and the following illustration, the subsidence of the land could be represented only by an apparent rise in the level of the sea.

manner in which they are grouped together, and in their arrangement in single or double lines; for they may be called rude outline charts of the sunken islands over which they stand. We can further see how it arises that the atolls in the Pacific and Indian oceans extend in lines parallel to the generally prevailing strike of the high islands and the great coast-lines of those oceans. I venture, therefore, to affirm, that on the theory of the upward growth of the corals during the sinking of the land,[3] all the leading features in those wonderful structures, the lagoon-islands or atolls, which have so long excited the attention of voyagers, as well as in the no less wonderful barrier-reefs, whether encircling small islands or stretching for hundreds of miles along the shore of a continent, are simply explained.

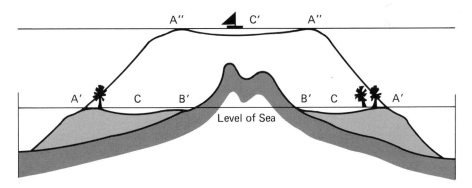

A'A'. Outer edges of the barrier-reef at the level of the sea, with islets on it. B'B'. The shores of the included island. CC. The lagoon-channel.

A"A". Outer edges of the reef, now converted into an atoll. C'. The lagoon of the new atoll.

N.B. According to the true scale, the depths of the lagoon-channel and lagoon are much exaggerated.

It may be asked whether I can offer any direct evidence of the subsidence of barrier-reefs or atolls; but it must be borne in mind how difficult it must ever be to detect a movement, the tendency of which is to hide under water the part affected. Nevertheless, at Keeling atoll I observed on all sides of the lagoon old cocoa-nut trees undermined and falling; and in one place the foundation-posts of a shed, which the inhabitants asserted had stood seven years before just above high-water mark, but now was daily washed by every tide: on inquiry I found that three earthquakes, one of them severe, had been felt here during the last ten years. At Vanikoro, the lagoon-channel is remarkably deep, scarcely any alluvial soil has accumulated at the foot of the lofty included mountains, and remarkably few islets have been formed by the heaping of fragments and sand on the wall-like barrier-reef; these facts, and some analogous ones, led me to believe that this island must lately have subsided and the reef grown upwards: here again earthquakes are frequent and very severe. In the Society archipelago, on the other hand, where the lagoon-channels are almost choked up, where much low alluvial land has accumulated, and where in some cases long islets have been formed on the barrier-reefs—facts all showing that the islands have not very lately subsided—only feeble shocks are most rarely felt. In these coral formations, where the land and water seem struggling for mastery, it must be ever difficult to decide between the effects of a change in the set of the tides and of a slight subsidence: that many of these reefs and atolls are subject to changes of some kind is certain; on some atolls the islets appear to have increased greatly within a late period; on others they have been partially or wholly washed away. The inhabitants of parts of the Maldiva archipelago know the date of the first formation of some islets; in other parts, the corals are now flourishing on water-washed reefs, where holes made for graves attest the former existence of inhabited land. It is difficult to believe in frequent changes in the tidal currents of an open ocean; whereas, we have in the earthquakes recorded by the natives on some atolls, and in the great fissures observed on other atolls, plain evidence of changes and disturbances in progress in the subterranean regions.

It is evident, on our theory, that coasts merely fringed by reefs cannot have subsided to any perceptible amount; and therefore they must, since the growth of their corals, either have remained stationary or have been upheaved. Now it is remarkable how generally it can be shown, by the presence of upraised organic remains, that the fringed islands have been elevated: and so far, this is indirect evidence in favour of our theory. I was particularly struck with this fact, when I found to my surprise, that the descriptions given by M.M. Quoy and Gaimard were applicable, not to reefs in general as implied by them, but only to those of the fringing-class; my surprise, however, ceased when I afterwards found that, by a strange chance, all the several islands visited by these eminent naturalists, could be shown by their own statements to have been elevated within a recent geological era.

Not only the grand features in the structure of barrier-reefs and of atolls, and of their likeness to each other in form, size, and other characters, are explained on the theory of subsidence—which theory we are independently forced to admit in the very areas in question, from the necessity of finding bases for the corals within the requisite depth—but many details in structure and exceptional cases can thus also be simply explained. I will give only a few instances. In barrier-reefs it has long been remarked with surprise, that the passages through the reef exactly face valleys in the included land, even in cases where the reef is separated from the land by a lagoon-channel so wide and so much deeper than the actual passage itself, that it seems hardly possible that the very small quantity of water or sediment brought down could injure the corals on the reef. Now, every reef of the fringing-class is breached by a narrow gateway in front of the smallest rivulet, even if dry during the greater part of the year, for the mud, sand, or gravel, occasionally washed down, kills the corals on which it is deposited. Consequently, when an island thus fringed subsides, though most of the narrow gateways will probably become closed by the outward and upward growth of the corals, yet any that are not closed (and some must always be kept open by the sediment and impure water flowing out of the lagoon-channel) will still continue to front exactly the upper parts of those valleys, at the mouths of which the original basal fringing-reef was breached.

We can easily see how an island fronted only on one side, or on one side with one end or both ends encircled by barrier-reefs, might after long-continued subsidence be converted either into a single wall-like reef, or into an atoll with a great straight spur projecting from it, or into two or three atolls tied together by straight reefs—all of which exceptional cases actually occur. As the reef-building corals require food, are preyed upon by other animals, are killed by sediment, cannot adhere to a loose bottom, and may be easily carried down to a depth whence they cannot spring up again, we need feel no surprise at the reefs both of atolls and barriers becoming in parts imperfect. The great barrier of New Caledonia is thus imperfect and broken in many parts; hence, after long subsidence, this great reef would not produce one great atoll 400 miles in length, but a chain or archipelago of atolls, of very nearly the same dimensions with those in the Maldiva archipelago. Moreover, in an atoll once breached on opposite sides, from the likelihood of the oceanic and tidal currents passing straight through the breaches, it is extremely improbable that the corals, especially during continued subsidence, would ever be able again to unite the rim; if they did not, as the whole sank downwards, one atoll would be divided into two or more. In the Maldiva archipelago there are distinct atolls so related to each other in position, and separated by channels either unfathomable or very deep (the channel between Ross and Ari atolls is 150 fathoms, and that between the north and south Nillamdoo atolls is 200 fathoms in depth), that it is impossible to look at a map of them without believing that they were once more intimately related. And in this same archipelago, Mahlos-Mahdoo atoll is divided by a bifurcating channel from 100 to 132 fathoms in depth, in such a manner, that it is scarcely possible to say whether it ought strictly to be called three separate atolls, or one great atoll not yet finally divided.

I will not enter on many more details; but I must remark that the curious structure of the northern Maldiva atolls receives (taking into consideration the free entrance of the sea through their broken margins) a simple explanation in the upward and outward growth of the corals, originally based both on small detached reefs in their lagoons, such as occur in common atolls, and on broken portions of the linear marginal reef, such as bounds every atoll of the ordinary form. I cannot refrain from once again remarking on the singularity of these complex structures—a great sandy and generally concave disk rises abruptly from the unfathomable ocean, with its central expanse studded, and its edge symmetrically bordered with oval basins of coral-rock just lipping the surface of the sea, sometimes clothed with vegetation, and each containing a lake of clear water!

One more point in detail: as in two neighbouring archipelagoes corals flourish in one and not in the other, and as so many conditions before enumerated must affect their existence, it would be an inexplicable fact if, during the changes to which earth, air, and water are subjected, the reef-building corals were to keep alive for perpetuity on any one spot or area. And as by our theory the areas including atolls and barrier-reefs are subsiding, we ought occasionally to find reefs both dead and submerged. In all reefs, owing to the sediment being washed out of the lagoon or lagoon-channel to leeward, that side is least favourable to the long-continued vigorous growth of the corals; hence dead portions of reef not unfrequently occur on the leeward side; and these, though still retaining their proper wall-like form, are now in several instances sunk several fathoms beneath the surface. The Chagos group appears from some cause, possibly from the subsidence having been too rapid, at present to be much less favourably circumstanced for the growth of reefs than formerly: one atoll has a portion of its marginal reef, nine miles in length, dead and submerged; a second has only a few quite small living points which rise to the surface; a third and fourth are entirely dead and submerged; a fifth is a mere wreck, with its structure almost obliterated. It is remarkable that in all these cases, the dead reefs and portions of reef lie at nearly the same depth, namely, from six to eight fathoms beneath the surface, as if they had been carried down by one uniform movement. One of these "half-drowned atolls," so called by Capt. Moresby (to whom I am indebted for much invaluable information), is of vast size, namely, ninety nautical miles across in one direction, and seventy miles in another line; and is in many respects eminently curious. As by our theory it follows that new atolls will generally be formed in each new area of subsidence, two weighty objections might have been raised, namely, that atolls must be increasing indefinitely in number; and secondly, that in old areas of subsidence each separate atoll must be increasing indefinitely in thickness, if proofs of their occasional destruction could not have been adduced. Thus have we traced the history of these great rings of coral-rock, from their first origin through their normal changes, and through the occasional accidents of their existence, to their death and final obliteration.

Notes

[1] These were first read before the Geological Society in May, 1837, and have since been developed in a separate volume on the "Structure and Distribution of Coral Reefs." [Darwin]

² It is remarkable that Mr. Lyell, even in the first edition of his "Principles of Geology," inferred that the amount of subsidence in the Pacific must have exceeded that of elevation, from the area of land being very small relatively to the agents there tending to form it, namely, the growth of coral and volcanic action. [Darwin]

³ It has been highly satisfactory to me to find the following passage in a pamphlet by Mr. Couthouy, one of the naturalists in the great Antarctic Expedition of the United States:—"Having personally examined a large number of coral islands, and resided eight months among the volcanic class having shore and partially encircling reefs, I may be permitted to state that my own observations have impressed a conviction of correctness of the theory of Mr. Darwin."—The naturalists, however, of this expedition differ with me on some points respecting coral formations. [Darwin]

FOCUS: READING REVIEW

1. In the conventional pattern of scientific writing Darwin examines the theories of other naturalists regarding the formation of the atolls. What are these theories? How does he respond to them?
2. What is Darwin's theory to explain the atolls, barrier reefs, and fringing reefs?
3. What is the initial evidence from which Darwin constructs his theory?

FOCUS: AUTHOR'S STRATEGIES

1. Darwin's writing provides a model of scientific investigation described by Huxley in "The Method of Scientific Investigation." What is Darwin's hypothesis? Describe the pattern of induction and deduction he employs to reach this hypothesis. How does he verify his hypothesis?
2. *The Voyage of the Beagle,* originally written as a journal, was revised for a public audience. What can you surmise about that audience from clues in this selection?

FOCUS: DISCUSSION AND WRITING

Explain the relationship between fact and theory in Darwin's essay. Explain what this demonstrates about scientific method.

How Flowers Changed the World
Loren Eiseley

Loren Eiseley (1907–1977) in his role as a contemplative naturalist published several books on science, as well as poetry and short stories. Trained as an anthropologist and a member of the Morrill paleontological expedition from the University of Nebraska, Eiseley wrote on human evolution, paleoarcheology, early man, and floral and faunal problems related to the rise of man. In "How Flowers Changed the World," from The Immense

Journey, Eiseley leads his reader through the landscape of the Age of Reptiles and shows how a minute biological alteration changed the face of earth's natural history.

If it had been possible to observe the Earth from the far side of the solar system over the long course of geological epochs, the watchers might have been able to discern a subtle change in the light emanating from our planet. A new and greener light would, by degrees, have come to twinkle across those endless miles. That slowly growing green twinkle would have contained the epic march of life from the tidal oozes upward across the raw and unclothed continents. In those first ages plants clung of necessity to swamps and watercourses. Their reproductive processes demanded direct access to water. [Then,] a little while ago—about one hundred million years—flowers were not to be found anywhere on the five continents. Somewhere, just a short time before the close of the Age of Reptiles, there occurred a soundless, violent explosion. It lasted millions of years, but it was an explosion, nevertheless. It marked the emergence of angiosperms—the flowering plants. Flowers changed the face of the planet. The true flowering plants grew a seed in the heart of a flower. The seed is already a fully equipped embryonic plant packed in a little enclosed box stuffed full of nutritious food. [Moreover, it can travel—in the wind, on an animal's hide, or in a bird's digestive tract.] The ramifications of this biological invention were endless. [The old world changed into something that] glowed here and there with strange colors [and] put out unheard-of fruits and concentrated foods. Animals arose to feed on the plants. [Great herbivores like the mammoths, horses, and bisons appeared.] Flesh eaters were being sustained on nutritious grasses one step removed. On the edge of the forest, a strange old-fashioned animal still hesitated. One day a little band of these odd apes—for apes they were—shambled out upon the grass; the human story had begun. Without the gift of flowers and the infinite diversity of their fruits, man and bird, if they had continued to exist at all, would be today unrecognizable.

If it had been possible to observe the Earth from the far side of the solar system over the long course of geological epochs, the watchers might have been able to discern a subtle change in the light emanating from our planet. That world of long ago would, like the red deserts of Mars, have reflected light from vast drifts of stone and gravel, the sands of wandering wastes, the blackness of naked basalt, the yellow dust of endlessly moving storms. Only the ceaseless marching of the clouds and the intermittent flashes from the restless surface of the sea would have told a different story, but still essentially a barren one. Then, as the millennia rolled away and age followed age, a new and greener light would, by degrees, have come to twinkle across those endless miles.

This is the only difference those far watchers, by the use of subtle instruments, might have perceived in the whole history of the planet Earth. Yet that slowly growing green twinkle would have contained the epic march of life from the tidal oozes upward across the raw and unclothed continents. Out of the vast chemical bath of the sea—not from the deeps, but from the element-rich, light-exposed platforms of the continental shelves—wandering fingers of green had crept upward along the meanderings of river systems and fringed the gravels of forgotten lakes.

In those first ages plants clung of necessity to swamps and watercourses. Their reproductive processes demanded direct access to water. Beyond the primitive ferns and mosses that enclosed the borders of swamps and streams the rocks still lay vast and bare, the winds still swirled the dust of a naked planet. The grass cover that holds our world secure in place was still millions of years in the future. The green marchers had gained a soggy foothold upon the land, but that was all. They did not reproduce by seeds but by microscopic swimming sperm that had to wriggle their way through water to fertilize the female cell. Such plants in their higher forms had clever adaptations for the use of rain water in their sexual phases, and survived with increasing success in a wet land environment. They now seem part of man's normal environment. The truth is, however, that there is nothing very "normal" about nature. Once upon a time there were no flowers at all.

A little while ago—about one hundred million years, as the geologist estimates time in the history of our four-billion-year-old planet—flowers were not to be found anywhere on the five continents. Wherever one might have looked, from the poles to the equator, one would have seen only the cold dark monotonous green of a world whose plant life possessed no other color.

Somewhere, just a short time before the close of the Age of Reptiles, there occurred a soundless, violent explosion. It lasted millions of years, but it was an explosion, nevertheless. It marked the emergence of the angiosperms—the flowering plants. Even the great evolutionist, Charles Darwin, called them "an abominable mystery," because they appeared so suddenly and spread so fast.

Flowers changed the face of the planet. Without them, the world we know—even man himself—would never have existed. Francis Thompson, the English poet, once wrote that one could not pluck a flower without troubling a star. Intuitively he had sensed like a naturalist the enormous interlinked complexity of life. Today we know that the appearance of the flowers contained also the equally mystifying emergence of man.

If we were to go back into the Age of Reptiles, its drowned swamps and birdless forests would reveal to us a warmer but, on the whole, a sleepier world than that of today. Here and there, it is true, the serpent heads of bottom-feeding dinosaurs might be upreared in suspicion of their huge flesh-eating compatriots. Tyrannosaurs, enormous bipedal caricatures of men, would stalk mindlessly across the sites of future cities and go their slow way down into the dark of geologic time.

In all that world of living things nothing saw save with the intense concentration of the hunt, nothing moved except with the grave sleepwalking intentness of the instinct-driven brain. Judged by modern standards, it was a world in slow motion, a cold-blooded world whose occupants were most active at noonday but torpid on chill nights, their brains damped by a slower metabolism than any known to even the most primitive of warm-blooded animals today.

A high metabolic rate and the maintenance of a constant body temperature are supreme achievements in the evolution of life. They enable an animal to escape, within broad limits, from the overheating or the chilling of its immediate surroundings, and at the same time to maintain a peak mental efficiency. Creatures without a high metabolic rate are slaves to weather. Insects in the first frosts of autumn all run down like little clocks. Yet if you pick one up and breathe warmly upon it, it will begin to move about once more.

In a sheltered spot such creatures may sleep away the winter, but they are hopelessly immobolized. Though a few warm-blooded mammals, such as the woodchuck of our day, have evolved a way of reducing their metabolic rate in order to undergo winter hibernation, it is a survival mechanism with drawbacks, for it leaves the animal helplessly exposed if enemies discover him during his period of suspended animation. Thus bear or woodchuck, big animal or small, must seek, in this time of descending sleep, a safe refuge in some hidden den or burrow. Hibernation is, therefore, primarily a winter refuge of small, easily concealed animals rather than of large ones.

A high metabolic rate, however, means a heavy intake of energy in order to sustain body warmth and efficiency. It is for this reason that even some of these later warm-blooded mammals existing in our day have learned to descend into a slower, unconscious rate of living during the winter months when food may be difficult to obtain. On a slightly higher plane they are following the procedure of the cold-blooded frog sleeping in the mud at the bottom of a frozen pond.

The agile brain of the warm-blooded birds and mammals demands a high oxygen consumption and food in concentrated forms, or the creatures cannot long sustain themselves. It was the rise of the flowering plants that provided that energy and changed the nature of the living world. Their appearance parallels in a quite surprising manner the rise of the birds and mammals.

Slowly, toward the dawn of the Age of Reptiles, something over two hundred and fifty million years ago, the little naked sperm cells wriggling their way through dew and raindrops had given way to a kind of pollen carried by the wind. Our present-day pine forests represent plants of a pollen-disseminating variety. Once fertilization was no longer dependent on exterior water, the march over drier regions could be extended. Instead of spores simple primitive seeds carrying some nourishment for the young plant had developed, but true flowers were still scores of millions of years away. After a long period of hesitant evolutionary groping, they exploded upon the world with truly revolutionary violence.

The event occurred in Cretaceous times in the close of the Age of Reptiles. Before the coming of the flowering plants our own ancestral stock, the warm-blooded mammals, consisted of a few mousy little creatures hidden in trees and underbrush. A few lizard-like birds with carnivorous teeth flapped awkwardly on ill-aimed flights among archaic shrubbery. None of these insignificant creatures gave evidence of any remarkable talents. The mammals in particular had been around for some millions of years, but had remained well lost in the shadow of the mighty reptiles. Truth to tell, man was still, like the genie in the bottle, encased in the body of a creature about the size of a rat.

As for the birds, their reptilian cousins the Pterodactyls, flew farther and better. There was just one thing about the birds that paralleled the physiology of the mammals. They, too, had evolved warm blood and its accompanying temperature control. Nevertheless, if one had been seen stripped of his feathers, he would still have seemed a slightly uncanny and unsightly lizard.

Neither the birds nor the mammals, however, were quite what they seemed. They were waiting for the Age of Flowers. They were waiting for what flowers, and with them the true encased seed, would bring. Fish-eating, gigantic leather-winged reptiles, twenty-eight feet from wing tip to wing tip, hovered over the coasts that one day would be swarming with gulls.

Inland the monotonous green of the pine and spruce forests with their primitive wooden cone flowers stretched everywhere. No grass hindered the fall of the naked seeds to earth. Great sequoias towered to the skies. The world of that time has a certain appeal but it is a giant's world, a world moving slowly like the reptiles who stalked magnificently among the boles of its trees.

The trees themselves are ancient, slow-growing and immense, like the redwood groves that have survived to our day on the California coast. All is stiff, formal, upright and green, monotonously green. There is no grass as yet; here are no wide plains rolling in the sun, no tiny daisies dotting the meadows underfoot. There is little versatility about this scene; it is, in truth, a giant's world.

A few nights ago it was brought home vividly to me that the world has changed since that far epoch. I was awakened out of sleep by an unknown sound in my living room. Not a small sound—not a creaking timber or a mouse's scurry—but a sharp, rending explosion as though an unwary foot had been put down upon a wine glass. I had come instantly out of sleep and lay tense, unbreathing. I listened for another step. There was none.

Unable to stand the suspense any longer, I turned on the light and passed from room to room glancing uneasily behind chairs and into closets. Nothing seemed disturbed, and I stood puzzled in the center of the living room floor. Then a small button-shaped object upon the rug caught my eye. It was hard and polished and glistening. Scattered over the length of the room were several more shining up at me like wary little eyes. A pine cone that had been lying in a dish had been blown the length of the coffee table. The dish itself could hardly have been the source of the explosion. Beside it I found two ribbon-like strips of a velvety-green. I tried to place the two strips together to make a pod. They twisted resolutely away from each other and would no longer fit.

I relaxed in a chair, then, for I had reached a solution of the midnight disturbance. The twisted strips were wistaria pods that I had brought in a day or two previously and placed in the dish. They had chosen midnight to explode and distribute their multiplying fund of life down the length of the room. A plant, a fixed, rooted thing, immobilized in a single spot, had devised a way of propelling its offspring across open space. Immediately there passed before my eyes the million airy troopers of the milkweed pod and the clutching hooks of the sandburs. Seeds on the coyote's tail, seeds on the hunter's coat, thistledown mounting on the winds—all were somehow triumphing over life's limitations. Yet the ability to do this had not been with them at the beginning. It was the product of endless effort and experiment.

The seeds on my carpet were not going to lie stiffly where they had dropped like their antiquated cousins, the naked seeds on the pine-cone scales. They were travelers. Struck by the thought, I went out next day and collected several other varieties. I line them up now in a row on my desk—so many little capsules of life, winged, hooked or spiked. Every one is an angiosperm, a product of the true flowering plants. Contained in these little boxes is the secret of that far-off Cretaceous explosion of a hundred million years ago that changed the face of the planet. And somewhere in here, I think, as I poke seriously at one particularly resistant seedcase of a wild grass, was once man himself.

When the first simple flower bloomed on some raw upland late in the Dinosaur Age, it was wind pollinated, just like its early pine-cone relatives. It was a very inconspicuous flower because it had not yet evolved the idea of using the surer attraction of birds and insects to achieve the transportation of pollen. It sowed its own pollen and received the pollen of other flowers by the simple vagaries of the wind. Many plants in regions where insect life is scant still follow this principle today. Nevertheless, the true flower—and the seed that it produced—was a profound innovation in the world of life.

In a way, this event parallels, in the plant world, what happened among animals. Consider the relative chance for survival of the exteriorly deposited egg of a fish in contrast with the fertilized egg of a mammal, carefully retained for months in the mother's body until the young animal (or human being) is developed to a point where it may survive. The biological wastage is less—and so it is with the flowering plants. The primitive spore, a single cell fertilized in the beginning by a swimming sperm, did not promote rapid distribution, and the young plant, moreover, had to struggle up from nothing. No one had left it any food except what it could get by its own unaided efforts.

By contrast, the true flowering plants (angiosperm itself means "encased seed") grew a seed in the heart of a flower, a seed whose development was initiated by a fertilizing pollen grain independent of outside moisture. But the seed, unlike the developing spore, is already a fully equipped *embryonic plant* packed in a little enclosed box stuffed full of nutritious food. Moreover, by featherdown attachments, as in dandelion or milkweed seed, it can be wafted upward on gusts and ride the wind for miles; or with hooks it can cling to a bear's or a rabbit's hide; or like some of the berries, it can be covered with a juicy, attractive fruit to lure birds, pass undigested through their intestinal tracts and be voided miles away.

The ramifications of this biological invention were endless. Plants traveled as they had never traveled before. They got into strange environments heretofore never entered by the old spore plants or stiff pine-cone-seed plants. The well-fed, carefully cherished little embryos raised their heads everywhere. Many of the older plants with more primitive reproductive mechanisms began to fade away under this unequal contest. They contracted their range into secluded environments. Some, like the giant redwoods, lingered on as relics; many vanished entirely.

The world of the giants was a dying world. These fantastic little seeds skipping and hopping and flying about the woods and valleys brought with them an amazing adaptability. If our whole lives had not been spent in the midst of it, it would astound us. The old, stiff, sky-reaching wooden world had changed into something that glowed here and there with strange colors, put out queer, unheard-of fruits and little intricately carved seed cases, and, most important of all, produced concentrated foods in a way that the land had never seen before, or dreamed of back in the fish-eating, leaf-crunching days of the dinosaurs.

That food came from three sources, all produced by the reproductive system of the flowering plants. There were the tantalizing nectars and pollens intended to draw insects for pollenizing purposes, and which are responsible also for that wonderful jeweled creation, the hummingbird. There were the juicy and enticing fruits to attract larger animals, and in which tough-coated seeds were concealed, as in the tomato, for example. Then, as if this were not enough, there was the food in the actual seed itself, the food intended to nourish the embryo. All over the world, like hot corn in a popper, these incredible elaborations of the flowering plants kept exploding. In a movement that was almost instantaneous, geologically speaking, the angiosperms had taken over the world. Grass was beginning to cover the bare earth until, today, there are over six thousand species. All kinds of vines and bushes squirmed and writhed under new trees with flying seeds.

The explosion was having its effect on animal life also. Specialized groups of insects were arising to feed on the new sources of food and, incidentally and unknowingly, to pollinate the plant. The flowers bloomed and bloomed in even larger and more spectacular varieties. Some were pale unearthly night flowers intended to lure moths in the evening twilight, some among the orchids even took the shape of female spiders in order to attract wandering males, some flamed redly in the light of noon or twinkled modestly in the meadow grasses. Intricate mechanisms splashed pollen on the breasts of hummingbirds, or stamped it on the bellies of black, grumbling bees droning assiduously from blossom to blossom. Honey ran, insects multiplied, and even the descendants of that toothed and ancient lizard-bird had become strangely altered. Equipped with prodding beaks instead of biting teeth they pecked the seeds and gobbled the insects that were really converted nectar.

Across the planet grasslands were now spreading. A slow continental upthrust which had been a part of the early Age of Flowers had cooled the world's climates. The stalking reptiles and the leather-winged black imps of the seashore cliffs had vanished. Only birds roamed the air now, hot-blooded and high-speed metabolic machines.

The mammals, too, had survived and were venturing into new domains, staring about perhaps a bit bewildered at their sudden eminence now that the thunder lizards were gone. Many of them, beginning as small browsers upon leaves in the forest, began to venture out upon this new sunlit world of the grass. Grass has a high silica content and demands a new type of very tough and resistant tooth enamel, but the seeds taken incidentally in the cropping of the grass are highly nutritious. A new world had opened out for the warm-blooded mammals. Great herbivores like the mammoths, horses and bisons appeared. Skulking about them had arisen savage flesh-feeding carnivores like the now extinct dire wolves and the saber-toothed tiger.

Flesh eaters though these creatures were, they were being sustained on nutritious grasses one step removed. Their fierce energy was being maintained on a high, effective level, through hot days and frosty nights, by the concentrated energy of the angiosperms. That energy, thirty percent or more of the weight of the entire plant among some of the cereal grasses, was being accumulated and concentrated in the rich proteins and fats of the enormous game herds of the grasslands.

On the edge of the forest, a strange, old-fashioned animal still hesitated. His body was the body of a tree dweller, and though tough and knotty by human standards, he was, in terms of that world into which he gazed, a weakling. His teeth, though strong for chewing on the tough fruits of the forest, or for crunching an occasional unwary bird caught with his prehensile hands, were not the tearing sabers of the great cats. He had a passion for lifting himself up to see about, in his restless, roving curiosity. He would run a little stiffly and uncertainly, perhaps, on his hind legs, but only in those rare moments when he ventured out upon the ground. All this was the legacy of his climbing days; he had a hand with flexible fingers and no fine specialized hoofs upon which to gallop like the wind.

If he had any idea of competing in that new world, he had better forget it; teeth or hooves, he was much too late for either. He was a ne'er-do-well, an inbetweener. Nature had not done well by him. It was as if she had hesitated and never quite made up her mind. Perhaps as a consequence he had a malicious gleam in his eye, the gleam of an outcast who has been left nothing and knows he is going to have to take what he gets. One day a little band of these odd apes—for apes they were—shambled out upon the grass; the human story had begun.

Apes were to become men, in the inscrutable wisdom of nature, because flowers had produced seeds and fruits in such tremendous quantities that a new and totally different store of energy had become available in concentrated form. Impressive as the slow-moving, dim-brained dinosaurs had been, it is doubtful if their age had supported anything like the diversity of life that now rioted across the planet or flashed in and out among the trees. Down on the grass by a streamside, one of those apes with inquisitive fingers turned over a stone and hefted it vaguely. The group clucked together in a throaty tongue and moved off through the tall grass foraging for seeds and insects. The one still held, sniffed, and hefted the stone he had found. He liked the feel of it in his fingers. The attack on the animal world was about to begin.

If one could run the story of that first human group like a speeded-up motion picture through a million years of time, one might see the stone in the hand change to the flint ax and the torch. All that swarming grassland world with its giant bison and trumpeting mammoths would go down in ruin to feed the insatiable and growing numbers of a carnivore who, like the great cats before him, was taking his energy indirectly from the grass. Later he found fire and it altered the tough meats and drained their energy even faster into a stomach ill-adapted for the ferocious turn man's habits had taken.

His limbs grew longer, he strode more purposefully over the grass. The stolen energy that would take man across the continents would fail him at last. The great Ice Age herds were destined to vanish. When they did so, another hand like the hand that grasped the stone by the river long ago would pluck a handful of grass seed and hold it contemplatively.

In that moment, the golden towers of man, his swarming millions, his turning wheels, the vast learning of his packed libraries, would glimmer dimly there in the ancestor of wheat, a few seeds held in a muddy hand. Without the gift of flowers and the infinite diversity of their fruits, man and bird, if they had continued to exist at all, would be today unrecognizable. Archaeopteryx, the lizard-bird, might still be snapping at beetles on a sequoia limb; man might still be a nocturnal insectivore gnawing a roach in the dark. The weight of a petal has changed the face of the world and made it ours.

FOCUS: READING REVIEW

1. In what ways did flowers change the world? How did flowers differ from prior plant life?
2. What are the central events in geological and evolutionary history Eiseley describes?

FOCUS: AUTHOR'S STRATEGIES

1. In what ways does Eiseley's introduction establish the kind of audience for which he is writing?
2. What kinds of scientific evidence does Eiseley provide his reader? How does he use this evidence?
3. One of the principal ways in which scientists communicate theories is through analogy. Explain how Eiseley uses analogy.
4. Explain the relationship Eiseley finds between flowers and animal metabolism. How does he make this understandable to the nonscientist?

FOCUS: DISCUSSION AND WRITING

Eiseley has created a narrative—a story about natural processes—based on scientific evidence. Using such a narrative approach, tell the story of atoll formation relying on Darwin's evidence in the previous essay, or tell the story of Mendel's genetic discoveries relying on evidence in the following essay.

The Mendelian Laws

George Beadle and Muriel Beadle

George Beadle (b. 1903), who won the Nobel Prize in medicine and physiology in 1958 for his work in biochemistry, taught at Cornell, the California Institute of Technology, Harvard, and Stanford, and served as president of the University of Chicago. He provided the substance and Muriel Beadle (b. 1915) the form for The Language of Life, *from which "The Mendelian Laws" is taken. They chose to collaborate on the book because they felt that Muriel, a nonscientist, could better convey to a lay audience the exciting biological concepts George encountered in his work. In a clear and direct style, "The Mendelian Laws" informs us not only about the work of Gregor Mendel, which is fundamental to modern genetics, but also about the sometimes perverse manner in which scientific knowledge advances.*

[Scientists] are liable to error, subject to luck, and affected by the political or emotional climate of their times. The myth of infallibility evaporates when one thinks of the number of great ideas in science whose originators were correct only in general but wrong in detail. It may be no easier for a scientist to challenge the prevailing thought of his time than for any other man. It's even harder for a scientist to defend an opinion that is unpopular among other scientists. If the history of science is a very human document, then Gregor Mendel, the father of modern genetics, is a very human scientist. Mendel's basic (and original) idea was that there might be simple mathematical relationships among the characteristic forms of plants in different generations of hybrids. [Mendel noted varieties of peas and chose seven paired characteristics to monitor.] He cross-pollinated only to produce the first-generation hybrids. Thereafter they were allowed to self-pollinate. When the second-generation peas were produced on a hybrid plant, a strange thing happened. The "lost" traits began to show up. One trait had *not* absorbed or destroyed the other. One trait must simply have been more "forceful" than the other. The determinants of the two traits had kept their separate identities—except that the weaker one had been submerged, its effect masked. Mendel called the forceful trait the "dominant" one; the less forceful, the "recessive" one. [He then determined the ratio between the appearance of the traits in successive generations. When Mendel established the ratio, he repeated the experiments. He found that] inheritance *did* follow an orderly rule. Given a pair of separate and distinct particles to start with, the way in which they would be passed along was statistically predictable. He had grown and harvested peas for twelve years, had kept meticulous records, and now he thought he had something worth talking about. So, in 1865, he appeared before the Brünn Society for the Study of Natural Science, read a report of his research, and postulated what have since come to be called the Mendelian Laws. Mendel's assertion that separate and distinct "elements" of inheritance must exist, despite the fact that he couldn't produce any, was close to asking the Society to accept something on faith. Surely the gentlemen of the Brünn Society can be forgiven for failing to realize that their modest neighbor had made a brilliant discovery about the fundamental nature of life.

You've seen him in the movies: the scientist who is infallible, insensitive, and coldly objective—little more than an animated computer in a white lab coat. He takes measurements and records results as if the collection of data were his sole object in life; and if a meaningful pattern emerges it comes as a blinding surprise. The assumption is that if one gathers enough facts about something, the relationships between those facts will spontaneously reveal themselves.

Nonsense.

In the real world of science, the investigator almost always knows what he's looking for before he starts. His observations are usually undertaken to prove the validity of an idea, and his emotions are as deeply engaged as those of a businessman planning a sales campaign, a general mapping out strategy, or a hunter stalking big game.

It's true that scientists strive for objectivity; what's more, they achieve it more often than other men. But they are no more capable than other men of maintaining absolute neutrality toward the outcome of their work. Nor could *you,* if you were testing an original hypothesis that you believed to be both unique and imaginative. Who among us would not like to make a successful thrust into the unknown, to find a missing link, to break a code?

Scientists are more curious than most of their fellows, more intelligent than many, and the best of them are as creative as the best composers, poets, or painters. But they are equally human. Thus they are liable to error, subject to luck, and affected by the political or emotional climate of their times in much the same way as anyone else is.

The myth of infallibility evaporates when one thinks of the number of great ideas in science whose originators were correct only in general but wrong in detail. Dalton,[1] for example, gets credit for the atomic theory as we know it today—yet his formulas for figuring atomic weights were basically incorrect. Copernicus[2] was mistaken in the particulars of his sun-centered universe; it doesn't explain the movements of the planets any better than Ptolemy's[3] earth-centered universe did. Newton[4] amended Kepler;[5] and even Newton's laws of physics have been modified (although not in ways important to the layman) by Einstein.[6]

It may be no easier for a scientist to challenge the prevailing thought of his time than for any other man. Witness Darwin's excessive caution in avoiding mention of *human* evolution when he wrote *Origin of Species.* He realized the implications of his work, and anticipated the storm of public protest.

It's even harder for a scientist to defend an opinion that is unpopular among other scientists. The Swedish chemist Arrhenius,[7] for example, was almost denied his Ph.D. because of wild ideas expressed in his thesis about the existence of particles he called "ions"; and although there is a Cinderella twist to his story—nineteen years later, after electrons had been discovered, he was awarded a Nobel prize for the same research that had nearly lost him his degree—there are numerous examples of other scientists who went to their graves with *their* wild ideas unnoticed or unvalidated. One such was the English physician Garrod,[8] the forgotten man of biochemistry. He suggested that genes control chemical reactions by the use of enzymes, but his theories fitted neither into the context of scientific thought of his time nor into an established scientific discipline, and neither chemists nor biologists took proper note of them.

Luck, too, has played as much of a role in scientific discovery as in any other human endeavor. The German astronomer Kepler, for example, made two mistakes in simple arithmetic in calculating the orbit of Mars; but by a fantastic coincidence they canceled each other, and he got the right answer. Pasteur[9] demonstrated, by sterilizing organic cultures in sealed flasks, that life does not generate spontaneously from air; but it was lucky that he happened to use an easy-to-kill yeast and not the hay bacillus that another investigator had chosen for the same experiment. We know now that hay bacillus is heat-resistant and grows even after boiling. If Pasteur had used it, his "proof" would have been long a-coming, despite the correctness of his basic idea.

And if the history of science is a very good human document, then Gregor Mendel,[10] the father of modern genetics, is a very human scientist. Like Dalton, his conclusions were correct only in general, wrong in detail. Like Arrhenius, he postulated the existence of particles for which there was no experimental evidence—except his; indeed, scientists weren't even prepared for the idea that such particles might exist. Like Garrod, and for the same reasons, he was ignored in his own time. Like Pasteur, he was incredibly lucky in his choice of research material. And like many an investigator before and after his time, his observations reveal the very human tendency to weight the scales in one's own favor, if only subconsciously.

Mendel, an Augustinian monk, had had some training in mathematics and the natural sciences. In addition, he was the son of a farmer, knew the soil, and had a green thumb. Plant hybridization interested him, and he began to read the professional literature. There were many puzzling problems. Crosses between certain species regularly yielded many hybrids with identical traits, for instance; but look what happened when you crossed the hybrids—all kinds of strange new combinations of traits cropped up. The principle of inheritance, if there *was* one, was elusive.

Mendel's basic (and original) idea was that there might be simple mathematical relationships among the characteristic forms of plants in different generations of hybrids. He decided, therefore, to establish some experimental plots in the monastery garden at Brünn, and there raise a number of varieties of peas,[11] hybridize them, count and classify the offspring of each generation, and see whether any mathematical ratios were involved.

Animal and plant breeding had been practiced from the days of the ancient Egyptians, and it was so apparent that children "take after" their parents and that traits "run in families" that the *fact* of inheritance was indisputable. But nobody knew the mechanism. Discoveries identifying the cell as the fundamental unit of life had not been pulled together in any orderly way until the German scientists Schwann and Schleiden did it in 1839, and about all that anyone knew for sure in the early years of the nineteenth century was that sperm cells fertilized egg cells. No one knew what went on inside either.

The seventeenth-century idea that sperm contained a "manikin" (a complete but miniature human being) had gone by the boards; and in 1854, when Mendel began his study of inheritance, the prevailing theory was that an "essence" from each vital organ of the parents' bodies somehow blended to create a new individual. (The belief that a baby gets half its blood from its father and half from its mother is memorialized by such phrases as "blood will tell.") Although it had occurred to various scientists that discrete particles, each affecting different traits, might be passed on from generation to generation, there was no experimental proof. Nor had anyone taken the possibility seriously enough to attempt to prove it.

Mendel had noted that in some varieties of peas, the unripe pods were green while in others they were yellow. Some varieties grew tall, others were dwarf types. Still other pairs of clearly distinct characteristics in different varieties of peas had to do with position of flowers (distributed along the stem or clustered at the top), the form of ripe pods (puffed out or indented), the color of the seed coats (white or gray), the color of the ripe seeds (green or yellow), and the form of the ripe seeds (smooth or wrinkled). Mendel chose these seven paired characteristics to keep tabs on.

He began with seed that other growers had certified as "pure" (that is, plants grown from it, if self-fertilized, faithfully duplicated the traits of the parental stock)—but just to make sure, he raised plants from it and harvested a crop. Then, by artificial pollination, he crossed varieties in different combinations. The result, for each of the seven paired traits he had chosen to study, was the same: *all* individuals in the first generation took after one parent. It was as if the other parent had no influence whatever on the result.

Take the cross between smooth and wrinkled peas as an example. All the seeds (which are in reality first-generation plants) were smooth. Why? Why weren't there some wrinkled ones, too? Maybe the two traits combined in such a way that one lost its identity, was absorbed by the other; in effect was destroyed. That would certainly be a reasonable conclusion on the basis of this first-generation evidence. But Mendel intended to draw no conclusions until he had followed the various traits in peas through several generations.

He cross-pollinated only to produce the first-generation hybrids. Thereafter—for example, when the first-generation hybrid seeds became plants—they would be allowed to self-pollinate, as is natural for pea plants. In this process, the eggs of a given flower are fertilized by the sperm carried in the pollen of that same flower. And when the second-generation seeds were produced on hybrid plants in this way, Mendel observed that a strange thing had happened. The "lost" traits began to show up! (See Figure 1.) An occasional *wrinkled* pea lay alongside the prevailing smooth ones. When the original cross had been between varieties with

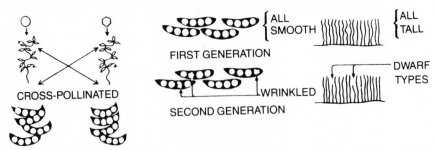

FIRST GENERATION
ALL SMOOTH
ALL TALL

SECOND GENERATION
WRINKLED
DWARF TYPES

CROSS-POLLINATED

Figure 1

yellow and green seeds, a few *green* pea seeds were now scattered among the prevailing yellow ones. For characters that show only in mature plants—such as height, position, or color of flowers—the second-generation seeds produced some plants like one of the original "pure" parents, some like the other parent.

Was there a mathematical ratio? Mendel harvested a large number of pods, and in the smooth/wrinkled group he found about 5400 smooth and about 1800 wrinkled seeds. Among those whose original ancestors had been yellow- and green-seeded, he found both types in the second generation in a ratio of about three yellow to one green—approximately 6000 to 2000 in one set of data he recorded. And in the five other paired characteristics he was studying, results were the same: in each case, about 25 per cent of the second-generation plants showed the traits that had appeared to "vanish" in the preceding generation.

Then one trait had *not* absorbed or destroyed the other. One trait must simply have been more "forceful" than the other. The determinants of the two traits had kept their separate identities—except that the weaker one had been submerged, its effect masked. Mendel called the more forceful trait the "dominant" one; the less forceful, the "recessive" one. He expressed the distinction by using capital letters to indicate dominants and lower-case letters to indicate recessives.

Here is the kind of exercise he must have done as he was figuring out the significance of what he had found:

In the cells that give rise to a sperm-carrying pollen and also in the cells that produce eggs, let A stand for the determinant for smoothness and a for its alternate, the determinant for wrinkledness. An egg cell has an equal chance of getting A or a, and the same is true for sperm cells. The primary ratio in such cells is therefore $1A$ to $1a$. One or the other will come together in each pairing that brings the next generation into being.

Consider next—as Mendel was having to consider—the possibility that each of the two determinants for a given pair of traits were present as discrete entities (even if invisible) in the cells of the first-generation plants. There would be four ways in which these traits could combine in producing the second-generation offspring. What has since Mendel's day come to be called a "checkerboard" diagram graphically indicates (see Figure 2) the four combinations.

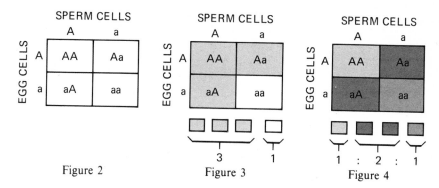

Figure 2

Figure 3

Figure 4

Figure 3 repeats the checkerboard, this time with shading overlying spaces holding dominant A's. All peas of this type would be smooth. Only peas of the aa type would be wrinkled. The second-generation ratio, then, would be $3A$ to $1a$—three-fourths of the progeny smooth, one-fourth wrinkled. This squared very nicely with Mendel's observations upon counting his second-generation crop of pea seeds, 75 per cent of which were smooth and 25 per cent wrinkled.

But 3:1 is not an accurate description of their *inherent constitution*; it is descriptive only of their outward appearance. As you see in Figure 4, one-fourth of the offspring would be pure for the dominant trait (*AA*—smoothness), one-fourth would be pure for the recessive trait (*aa*—wrinkledness), and one-half would be hybrid mixtures of A and a. The correct ratio, then, is $1AA$ to $2Aa$ to $1aa$.

The same principle is illustrated by tossing two coins simultaneously (see Figure 5). There is only one combination that will result in two heads, and only

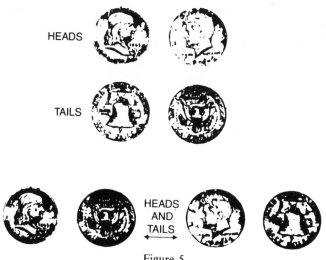

Figure 5

one combination that will result in two tails, but there are two combinations that will result in a heads-and-tails throw.

The ratio, here too, is 1:2:1.

Once Mendel had figured out these mathematical relationships in his first- and second-generation seeds, he knew what he was looking for in subsequent plantings.

He planted the second-generation seeds—the generation, remember, in which 25 per cent of the peas had made a wrinkled comeback; and in the third generation, these wrinkled peas, the "recessives," bred true to type. Furthermore, they did so in all the following years that Mendel planted their descendants.

Of those in the second generation that carried the "dominant" trait—the 75 per cent that looked smooth—only one in three (on the average) bred true to type, and continued thereafter to do so. The diagrams on the next page (Figure 6) show these "pure" lines.

And, on the average, two out of the three that looked smooth did *not* breed true to type, but repeated the pattern of the second generation (see Figure 6).

Indeed, inheritance *did* follow an orderly rule. Given a pair of separate and distinct particles to start with, the way in which they would be passed along was statistically predictable.

The logical next question was: Would the same results occur if *two* different traits were crossed? (Let *Aa* stand for smoothness-wrinkledness and *Bb* stand for yellowness-greenness.) The first-generation hybrid plants would then be symbolized as *Aa Bb*, and the eggs of such a plant would be of four kinds: *AB, Ab, aB,* and *ab.* All possible combinations would appear with equal frequency. Perhaps this is a good place to use the examples of coin tossing again, this time a half-dollar and a quarter, flipped at random. As you see in Figure 7 (p. 134), four combinations are possible.

Now, if eggs of the four kinds are fertilized at random by sperms of the same four kinds, the results can be shown by the checkerboard diagram of sixteen squares in Figure 8 (p. 134).

Count the squares that contain both *A*'s and *B*'s: there are nine of them, and the resultant peas should be smooth and yellow (dominant traits).

Count the squares that contain either *A*'s or *B*'s. There are three of each. Those with *A*'s should express themselves in the crop as smooth green peas; those with *B*'s as wrinkled and yellow.

There remains one square with no capital letters. Peas of this character should be wrinkled and green (recessive traits).

The ratio, as you see, is no longer 1:2:1 but

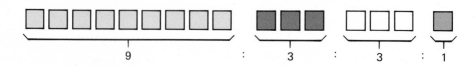

And how did this paperwork square with the results of a harvested pea crop when Mendel crossed smooth yellow peas with plants yielding wrinkled greens and then raised *their* offspring? Out of 556 ripe peas, he got

Smooth yellow	Smooth green	Wrinkled yellow	Wrinkled green
315	108	101	32

Approximately 9:3:3:1

The inevitable next question, of course, was: Would field tests confirm the statistical prediction of what would happen if one were to cross *three* characters? A first-generation hybrid *Aa Bb Cc* should produce a second-generation ratio of 27:9:9:3:9:3:3:1. We'll skip the checkerboard this time, because of its formidable

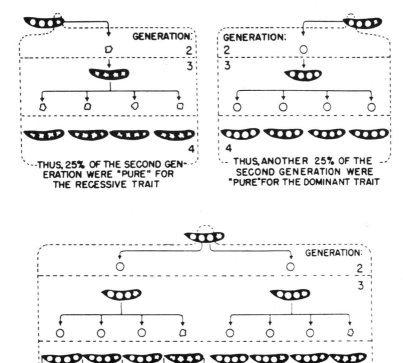

Figure 6

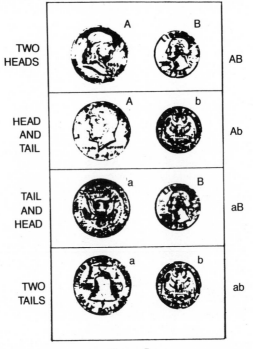

Figure 7

size and complexity[12] but when Mendel crossed hybrid peas that were smooth (*A*), yellow (*B*), and had grayish seed coats (*C*) with plants bearing peas that were wrinkled (*a*), green (*b*), and whose seed coats were white (*c*), his harvest tally of variations added up to a ratio of 27:9:9:3:9:3:3:1!

With these and other results that supported his hypothesis, his case was complete. He had grown and harvested peas for twelve years, had kept meticulous records, and now he thought he had something worth talking about. So, in 1865,

SPERM CELLS

	AB	Ab	aB	ab
AB	AABB	AABb	AaBB	AaBb
Ab	AABb	AAbb	AaBb	Aabb
aB	AaBB	AaBb	aaBB	aaBb
ab	AaBb	Aabb	aaBb	aabb

EGG CELLS

Figure 8

he appeared before the Brünn Society for the Study of Natural Science, read a report of his research, and postulated what have since come to be called the Mendelian laws:

1. Inheritance is based on pairs of particulate units, each of which determines specific traits. (He called them "elements"; we call them "genes.") Of each pair, offspring receive *one or the other* from each parent.

2. Of each pair of elements acquired by the offspring, one is dominant and the other is recessive. (Mendel called them "antagonistic factors"; we call the two versions of each trait its "alleles.") When both parents contribute a dominant element or when both parents contribute a recessive element (*AA* or *aa*), the individual will be "pure" for that trait. If the parent contributes one dominant and one recessive (*Aa* or *aA*), the individual will be hybrid, but will look the same as the pure dominant.

3. Since these paired elements, whether dominant or recessive, are capable of separating, reappearing in their original form, and pairing differently in later unions, they are obviously not contaminated or altered in any way in the course of their passage from individual to individual.

4. If two or more pairs of elements are hybrid in a single plant—*Aa* and *Bb*, say—they assort independently in the formation of eggs and sperm; that is, giving *AB, Ab, aB,* and *ab*. (This is the law of independent segregation.)

Members of the Society listened politely to Mendel, but insofar as anybody knows asked few questions and engaged in little discussion. It may even be that they sat in embarrassed silence as he proceeded, a suspicion slowly growing that a nice fellow had somehow gotten way off the track.

Mendel's assertion that separate and distinct "elements" of inheritance must exist, despite the fact that he couldn't produce any, was close to asking the Society to accept something on faith. Scientists resist accepting things on faith. There was no evidence for Mendel's hypothesis other than his computations; and his wildly unconventional application of algebra to botany made it difficult for his listeners to understand that those computations *were* the evidence.

Mendel was a careful worker, no doubt about that. And one certainly wouldn't presume to doubt the honesty of a monk. But he'd been raising those peas of his for a long time, and with such single-minded devotion that he might have developed some odd ideas about the implications of his work. Remember, too, that he was little more than a horticultural hobbyist, however dedicated. He lacked a degree, had no University connection, had no previously published research to give him a reputation. Now, if Pasteur had advanced the idea, or Darwin . . .

Anyway, who *really* expects the boy next door to grow up to be President? Surely the gentlemen of the Brünn Society can be forgiven for failing to realize that their modest neighbor had made a brilliant discovery about the fundamental nature of life. They printed his paper in their *Proceedings*—and remembered it as an oddity, if they remembered it at all.

Notes

[1] John Dalton (1766–1844), the English chemist and physicist, arranged the table of atomic weights in 1803 and gave the first clear statement of atomic theory between 1803 and 1807.

[2] Nicolaus Copernicus (1478–1543), Polish astronomer, advanced the theory *De Revolutionibus Orbium Coelestium* (1543) that the earth rotates daily on its axis and the planets rotate around the sun.

[3] Ptolemy, an astronomer, mathematician, and geographer in Alexandria in the second century A.D., proposed a system of astronomy and geography based on the theory that the sun, planets, and stars revolved around the earth.

[4] Sir Isaac Newton (1642–1724) formulated universal gravitation. This theory's proof established mechanical laws for physical phenomena within the earth's gravitational system.

[5] Johannes Kepler (1571–1630), a German astronomer, discovered the laws of planetary motion which supported Copernicus (see note 2).

[6] Albert Einstein (1879–1955), the eminent twentieth-century physicist, developed a theoretical model that describes movement of both the atom's infinitely small particles and space's vast bodies in his theories of general and special relativity.

[7] Svante August Arrhenius (1859–1927), a Swedish physicist and chemist, received the Nobel Prize in chemistry for his electrolytic dissociation theory.

[8] Archibald Garrod (1857–1936), professor of medicine, advanced theories of genetic causes for disease.

[9] Louis Pasteur (1822–1895) was a French chemist who discovered the role of bacteria and bacilli in disease.

[10] Gregor Mendel (1822–1884), an Austrian botanist, discovered the ratios of inherited characteristics.

[11] *Not* sweet peas, as is widely believed. The common garden pea, the kind you eat, was his research material. [Beadle and Beadle]

[12] If you want to check on Mendel's math and at the same time show yourself how many different individuals can result from just *three* paired traits, draw a checkerboard with 64 squares and place the following symbols for egg or sperm cell: *ABC, ABc, AbC, Abc, aBC, aBc, abC, abc.* One begins to see, with this exercise, why no human being—whose cells contain not three but thousands of traits—is ever like another human being (unless he has an identical twin). [Beadle and Beadle]

FOCUS: READING REVIEW

1. What view of the scientist do the Beadles present?
2. The Beadles retell Mendel's experimental method. Based on your knowledge of scientific methodology, determine his hypothesis. On what evidence did he build his inductive pattern? What was his method of verification?
3. Besides revealing how Mendel worked, this essay provides other insights about the scientific community. What are they?

FOCUS: AUTHOR'S STRATEGIES

1. The essay's title, "The Mendelian Laws," suggests one purpose—to inform. How does this relate to the purpose apparent in the introduction to the discission of the actual laws?
2. What do the essay's insights into the scientific community suggest about the Beadles' argument and purpose?
3. For what audience are the Beadles writing? What in the evidence and tone indicate this?

FOCUS: DISCUSSION AND WRITING

Compare and contrast the Beadles' view of the scientific community with the views of McCain and Segal and Bronowski.

The Brain: His and Hers
Pamela Weintraub

Pamela Weintraub, a free-lance writer, frequently writes for Discover, *a magazine popularizing science published by Time-Life publishers. "The Brain: His and Hers," which appeared in* Discover, *April 1981, examines scientific research in anatomy, biochemistry, animal behavior, and human behavior, suggesting that actual physiological differences in the brains of men and women may account for some observed sexual variations in thinking patterns.*

Are the brains of men and women different? Proof that behavioral and intellectual differences exist between the sexes are partly rooted in the structure of the brain. The evidence suggesting differences between male and female brains comes from research in behavior, biochemistry, anatomy, and neuropsychology. The finding [that men are superior in math] follows several recent studies proving that male and female brains, at least in animals, are physically different. [Scientists] think that the development of the brain parallels that of the genitals. Endocrinologist Imperato-McGinley studied an isolated group of men in the Dominican Republic who, because of a genetic disorder, started life as girls. [At puberty when their bodies were able to use the male hormone testosterone, they became males. Imperato-McGinley concluded that they adjusted because] their brains had been virilized by testosterone before birth. [Peterson believes that] cultural experiences can masculinize or feminize the brain. [Ehrhardt says that] certain types of sexual behavior are influenced by sex hormones. [She] cites cases of girls whose adrenal glands produced abnormally large amounts of androgens while they were still in the womb. "We find that they are extremely tomboyish," she says. "They are career oriented, and spend little time with dolls." [Researchers using hormones on animals conclude that hormones affect behavior in two ways. Before birth, hormones imprint a code on the brain.

Later other hormones activate the code. Goy has found that] masculinized monkeys display sexual behavior that ranges from female to male in direct proportion to the amount of testosterone they are given while in the womb and throughout life. [Other scientists have substantiated this evidence with hard biochemical data. In brain sections of rhesus monkeys, Pfaff saw that] the hypothalamus, a primitive structure at the base of the brain stem, [was the primary site for hormone action. McEwen found sex hormone receptors in the brain cortex. These receptors are hormone-specific. Once hormones pair up with receptors, they mold the structure of the brain.] Anatomical evidence that sex hormones change the structure of the brain came recently from Gorski, [who found different nerve cell clusters in the brains of male and female rats. These clusters responded to changes in male and female hormones.] Scientists studying mammals have also discovered anatomical differences between the sexes. [Diamond discovered that] in the male rat the right hemisphere of the cortex was thicker than the left—and that in the female the left was thicker than the right. Administering female hormones to males and male hormones to females affected the width of the cortex. [Levy finds strong anatomical support in Diamond's discoveries for her theory that] hormones early in life alter the organization of the brain's two hemispheres. The right hemisphere specializes in the perception of spatial relationships and the left in language and rote memory. [Levy has found that men excel in spatial reasoning and women do better with language. Levy thinks that] the estrogen that changes the size of the cortex in Diamond's rats may also change the size and organization of the human cortex. [These new findings promise to color the modern view of the world. But the implications can be misconstrued. One example of this is Dörner's desire to use testosterone as an antidote for homosexuality. Another example is a recent article citing the "latest" in brain research as an argument against equal rights for women.]

Are the brains of men and women different? If so, do men and women differ in abilities, talents, and deficiencies? A scientific answer to these questions could affect society and culture, and variously shock, intrigue, delight, depress, and reassure people of both sexes. Now an answer is coming into sight: Yes, male and female brains do differ.

That men and women think and behave differently is a widely held assumption. Generations of writers have lavished their attention on these differences, proclaiming, for example, that aggressiveness and promiscuity are natural to the male, that domesticity is the legacy of the female. Today's feminists acknowledge some differences, but hotly dispute the notion that they are innate. They stress that it is society, not nature, that gives men the drive to dominate and keeps women from achieving careers and power. But proof that behavioral and intellectual differences between the sexes are partly rooted in the structure of the brain, that women are inherently superior in some areas of endeavor and men in others would in no way undermine legitimate demands for social equality. Instead the result could be a better, more realistic relationship between the sexes.

The evidence suggesting differences between male and female brains comes from research in behavior, biochemistry, anatomy, and neuropsychology. The most recent study deals with the long-established fact that skill in mathematics is far more common among men than women. Feminists—and many scientists—blame sexual stereotyping. But psychologists Camilla Benbow and Julian Stanley, at Johns Hopkins University, challenged that interpretation after testing 9,927 seventh and eighth graders with high IQs. As Benbow told *Discover* reporter John Bucher, of the students who scored 500 or better on the math part of the Scholastic Aptitude Test, boys outnumbered girls by more than two to one. In other words, the psychologists argue, male superiority in math is so pronounced that, to some extent, it must be inborn.

This finding follows several recent studies proving that male and female brains, at least in animals, are physically different. From the hypothalamus, the center for sexual drive, to the cerebral cortex, the seat of thought, scientists have found consistent variations between the sexes. The causes of these differences, they say, are the sex hormones—the male androgens and female estrogens and progesterones that are secreted by the sex glands and carried through the blood stream to distant parts of the body, where they control everything from menstruation to the growth of facial hair.

Basic to all the studies of gender and the brain are the facts of sex determination. When a child is conceived, each parent contributes a sex chromosome, either an X or a Y (so-called for their shapes). When two X's combine, the fetus develops ovaries and becomes a girl. An X and a Y produce a boy; the Y chromosome makes a protein that coats the cells programmed to become ovaries, directing them to become testicles instead. The testicles then pump out two androgens, one that absorbs what would have become a uterus, and another, testosterone, that causes a penis to develop.

Though scientists have not yet been able to pinpoint any physiological differences between the brains of men and women, they think that the development of the brain parallels that of the genitals. If the fetus is a boy, they say, the testosterone that produces the penis also masculinizes tissue in the hypothalamus and other nearby structures deep within the brain. New data suggest that if the fetus is a girl, estrogen secreted by the ovaries feminizes brain tissue in the surrounding cerebral cortex. Scientists cannot dissect living human brains, but they have found ingenious ways to test their theories. The major approaches:

HUMAN BEHAVIOR

To shed light on the sexuality of the brain, endocrinologist Julianne Imperato-McGinley of Cornell Medical College in New York City studied 38 men in an isolated part of the Dominican Republic who, because of a genetic disorder, started life as girls. They stayed indoors playing with dolls and learning to cook while boys fought and shouted outside. At the age of eleven, when the breasts of normal girls began to enlarge, the children studied by Imperato-McGinley showed no change. But at twelve, most of them began to feel stirrings of sexual desire for girls. At puberty, their voices deepened, their testicles descended, and their clitorises enlarged to become penises.

These children came from a group of families carrying a rare mutant gene that deprived them of an enzyme needed to make testosterone work in the skin of their genitals. For this reason, their external genitals looked female at birth. But at puberty their bodies were able to use testosterone without the enzyme, and it became obvious that they were males—as chromosome tests confirmed. All but two are now living with women. They have male musculature and, although they cannot sire children, they can have sexual intercourse. They have assumed masculine roles in their society. "To the world," says Imperato-McGinley, "they looked like girls when they were younger. But their bodies were actually flooded with testosterone." She concludes that they were able to adjust easily because hidden in the girl's body was a male brain, virilized by testosterone before birth and activated by another rush of testosterone during adolescence.

Although Imperato-McGinley suggests that brain structure determines behavior, another scientist thinks that the reverse may also be true: Anne Petersen, director of the Adolescent Laboratory at the Michael Reese Hospital and Medical Center in Chicago, says that cultural experiences can masculinize or feminize the brain. In a recent study, Petersen found that boys who excel in athletics also excel in spatial reasoning—a skill controlled by the right hemisphere of the cerebral cortex, and defined as the ability to understand maps and mazes or objects rotating in space. Says Petersen, "An athlete must be constantly aware of his own body and a whole constellation of other bodies in space." A daily game of basketball might, through some still mysterious mechanism, stimulate the secretion of hormones that prime a player's brain for success in basketball. The same brain structures would be used to deal with spatial problems. "Women are far less athletic than men," says Petersen, "and also less adept at spatial reasoning. Part of the problem may be their lack of involvement in sports. Perhaps some women just never develop the area of the brain specialized for spatial control."

Like Petersen, endocrinologist Anke Ehrhardt thinks that society plays an important part in shaping gender behavior. Nevertheless, she says, "certain types of sexual behavior are influenced by the sex hormones." Leafing through the clutter of papers and books that cover her desk at New York City's Columbia Presbyterian Medical Center, Ehrhardt cites cases of girls whose adrenal glands, because of an enzyme defect, produced abnormally large amounts of androgens while they were still in the womb. "We find that they are extremely tomboyish," she says. "They are career oriented, and spend little time with dolls. And we've just learned that boys exposed before birth to drugs that contain high doses of feminizing hormones engage in less roughhousing than other boys."

ANIMAL BEHAVIOR

Ehrhardt admits that labeling the pursuit of a career masculine and playing with dolls feminine seems like stereotyping. To substantiate her evidence, she has compared her results with those obtained from studies of animals, whose gender behavior is rigid and easily defined.

Animal physiologists first made the connection between hormones and behavior in 1849, when the German scientist Arnold Berthold castrated roosters and found that they stopped fighting with other roosters and lost interest in attracting hens. When he transplanted the testicles into the abdominal cavities of the castrated birds, the roosters became aggressive again. Observing that the transplanted testicles did not develop connections with the rooster's nervous system but did develop connections with its circulatory system, he speculated that their influence on behavior came from a blood-borne substance, which was later identified as a hormone.

In 1916, Frank Lillie, a Canadian physiologist, noticed that the freemartin, a genetically female (X-X) cow that looks and acts like a male, always had a male twin. He speculated that the freemartin's gonads were masculinized in the womb by hormones secreted by the testicles of the twin.

Fascinated by this finding, scientists began using testosterone to make "freemartin" guinea pigs, rats, monkeys, and dogs. This set the stage for the landmark experiment conducted at the University of Kansas in 1959 by physiologists William Young and Robert Goy.

"We injected pregnant guinea pigs with huge amounts of testosterone," explains Goy. "This produced a brood of offspring in which those that were genetically female had male genitalia as well as ovaries." When the females were 90 days old, the researchers removed their ovaries and injected some of them with still more testosterone. The injected females began to act like males, mounting other females and trying to dominate the group. Says Goy, "We realized that we had changed the sex of the guinea pig's brain."

The researchers concluded that hormones affect behavior in two ways. Before birth, hormones imprint a code on the brain, "just as light can stamp an image on film," Goy says. "Later, throughout life, other hormones activate the code, much as a developer brings out an image on film. Whether the animal behaves like a male or a female depends on the code."

Goy has spent the past two decades proving that theory for a whole range of species, including the rhesus monkey. Now at the Primate Research Center at the University of Wisconsin in Madison, he has found that masculinized monkeys display sexual behavior that ranges from female to male in direct proportion to the amount of testosterone they are given while in the womb and throughout life. "It doesn't much matter whether it's rough-and-tumble play, mounting peers, or attempting to dominate the group," he says. "It's all related to the duration of treatment."

Perhaps more important, Goy has found that by varying the treatment he can produce monkeys that are physically female but behave like males. This is proof, he says, "that these animals behave like boys because of masculinizing hormones, not because of a male appearance that causes the other animals to treat them like boys."

Like the human brain, the brain of the rhesus monkey has a highly elaborate and convoluted cortex. But Goy believes that monkeys can be compared with people only up to a point. For while primitive drives may be similar, he says, human beings are guided by their culture to a greater degree than monkeys. "Nevertheless," he adds, "there are instances when people seem to be less bound by culture. Then they begin to look very much like our monkeys."

BIOCHEMISTRY

Other scientists have substantiated this evidence with hard biochemical data. To learn where sex hormones operate, neurobiologist Donald Pfaff of New York City's Rockefeller University injected various animals with radioactive hormones and removed their brains. He cut each brain into paper-thin sections, then placed each section on film sensitive to radioactivity. He thus made maps showing that the hormones collected at specific places, now called receptor sites, similarly located in the brains of species ranging from fish to rats to the rhesus monkey.

The primary site for hormone action, Pfaff saw, was the hypothalamus, a primitive structure at the base of the brain stem. That made sense, because the hypothalamus is the center for sex drive and copulatory behavior. "But the most intriguing thing," says Pfaff, "may be the receptors found in the amygdala [a part of the brain above each ear]. During the 1960s, surgeons found that when they destroyed the amygdala, patients with fits of aggression became completely passive. So we now suspect that sex hormones may control aggression, even fear." Neurologist Bruce McEwen, also of Rockefeller, recently found estrogen receptors in the cerebral cortex of the rat—receptors that disappear three weeks after birth. The cortex controls thought and cognition, but McEwen does not know the significance of these receptors.

The receptors are located at the same sites in both sexes, but because each sex has its own characteristic mix of hormones, male and female brains function differently. To unravel the secret of hormone operation, McEwen has been analyzing the chemistry of the rat brain. He has discovered that receptor sites are hormone-specific; a testosterone site, for example, is insensitive to estrogen. Perhaps more important, he has learned that once hormones pair up with receptors, they mold the structure of the brain by directing nerve cells to manufacture proteins. Early in life, the proteins build nerve cells, creating permanent structures that may exist in the brain of one sex but not the other. Later in life, the proteins produce the chemicals that enable one nerve cell to communicate with another, and precipitate various kinds of sexual behavior.

McEwen and Pfaff have not dissected human brains, but they feel justified in applying some of their findings to people. For, as Pfaff explains, evolution is a conservationist. "As new species evolved, nature didn't throw away old parts of the brain," he says. "Rather, new systems were added. Everyone has a fish brain deep inside. Outside the fish brain there is a reptilian brain, depressingly similar to the way it would look in a lizard. Wrapped around the reptilian brain there is a mammalian brain, and then, finally, the cerebral cortex in such animals as monkeys and human beings." McEwen thinks that the receptors in the hypothalamus probably have similar effects in people and rats. "The difference," he says, "is that human beings can override their primitive drives with nerve impulses from the powerful cerebral cortex."

ANATOMY

Anatomical evidence that sex hormones change the structure of the brain came recently from Roger Gorski, a neuroendocrinologist at the University of California at Los Angeles. Examining the hypothalamus in rats, he found a large cluster of nerve cells in the males and a small cluster in females. By giving a female testosterone shortly after birth, he created a large cluster of cells in her hypothalamus that resembled that in the male. If he castrated a male after birth, its cell cluster shrank. Gorski has no idea what the cell structure signifies, but he does know that it varies with changes in sexual behavior.

The anatomical differences do not stop there. Fernando Nottebohm, of Rockefeller, has discovered a large brain-cell cluster in the male canary and a small one in the female. These cells are not in the spinal cord or the hypothalamus but in the forebrain—the songbird equivalent of the cerebral cortex, the part that controls thought and cognition.

The function that Nottebohm studied was song. Only the male songbird can sing, and the more intricate the song the more females he attracts. That takes brainwork, says Nottebohm. "The canary puts songs together just as the artist creates. A large collection of syllables can be combined in infinite ways to form a repertoire in which each song is unique."

Until Nottebohm discovered the large cluster of male brain cells that control the muscles of the syrinx, the singing organ, he had assumed that male and female brains were anatomically identical. He found that if he gave female canaries testosterone before they hatched and again during adulthood, they could learn to sing. When he studied the brains of the singing females, he found that their cell clusters had grown. Says Nottebohm, "The intriguing thing is that the size of the repertoire was more or less proportional to the size of the cell clusters."

Scientists studying mammals have also discovered anatomical differences between the sexes in the thinking part of the brain—in this case, the cerebral cortex of the rat. Marian Diamond, of the University of California at Berkeley, discovered that in the male rat the right hemisphere of the cortex was thicker than the left—and that in the female the left was thicker than the right. But if she castrated the male rat at birth or removed the ovaries from the female, she could alter the pattern. Administering female hormones to males and male hormones to females also affected the width of the cortex. Says Diamond, "Hormones present during pregnancy, hormones present in the birth-control pill, all affect the dimensions of the cortex."

Jerre Levy, a neuropsychologist at the University of Chicago, is encouraged by Diamond's findings because they provide strong anatomical evidence for her theory: the cortex is different in men and women, largely because of hormones that early in life alter the organization of the two hemispheres.

Levy is responsible for much of what is known about the human brain's laterality—the separation of the roles performed by the right and left hemispheres. Levy began her work in this field in the 1960s, when she was studying "split brain" patients, epileptics whose hemispheres had been surgically separated as a means of controlling violent seizures. The researchers found that the hemispheres could operate independently of each other, somewhat like two minds in a single head. The right hemisphere specialized in the perception of spatial relationships, like those in mazes and solid geometry, and the left controlled language and rote memory.

Levy has found that these abilities vary with gender. In test after test, men excelled in spatial reasoning and women did better with language. Fascinated by the discrepancy, she decided to test laterality in normal people and based her experiments on a well known fact: light and sound perceived by the eye and ear on one side of the head travel to the hemisphere on the other side for processing.

She discovered that the right ear and eye are more sensitive in women, the left in men. She concluded that the right hemisphere dominates the masculine brain, and the left the feminine.

Levy points to the work of neuropsychologist Deborah Waber, of Harvard Medical School, who found that children reaching puberty earlier than normal have brains that are less lateralized—that is, their left and right hemispheres seem to share more tasks. Because girls generally reach puberty two years before boys, these findings have caused speculation that the bundle of nerve connections, the corpus callosum, between the two hemispheres of the female brain have less time to lateralize, or draw apart, during puberty. If that is true, says Levy, it could help to explain female intuition, as well as male superiority in mechanics and math. The two intimately connected hemispheres of the female brain would communicate more rapidly—an advantage in integrating all the detail and nuance in an intricate situation, but according to Levy a disadvantage "when it comes to homing in on just a few relevant details." With less interference from the left hemisphere, Levy says, a man could "use his right hemisphere more precisely in deciphering a map or finding a three-dimensional object in a two-dimensional representation."

All this brings Levy back to hormones. She thinks that the estrogen that changes the size of the cortex in Marian Diamond's rats may also change the size and organization of the human cortex. Her new tests are designed to study the organization of the cerebral cortex in people with hormonal abnormalities—girls who produce an excess of androgen and boys who are exposed to large amounts of estrogen before birth.

Levy has ambitious plans for future research, including scans of living brains and tests of babies whose mothers have undergone stress during pregnancy. Much remains to be done, for though the existence of physical differences between male and female brains now seems beyond dispute, the consequences are unclear. Talent in math, for example, is obviously not confined to men, nor talent in languages to women; the subtleties seem infinite. Already the new findings promise to color the modern view of the world. But the implications can easily be misconstrued.

Gunther Dörner, an East German hormone researcher, has claimed that he can put an end to male homosexuality by injecting pregnant women with testosterone. Dörner bases his theory on studies done by two American researchers, who subjected pregnant rats to stress by confining them in small cages under bright lights. They found that the rats' male offspring had low levels of testosterone during certain critical periods, and exhibited homosexual behavior. Dörner concluded that stress on pregnant females alters sexual preference patterns in the brains of their male offspring, and that this finding applies to human beings as well. His suggested antidote: testosterone.

His conclusions appall the American researchers, who agree that mothers under stress produce male offspring with abnormal behavior, but argue that Dörner has gone too far. Dörner's work is supported by the East German government, which is notorious in its aversion to homosexuality, and American scientists fear that he may get a chance to put his ideas into practice on human beings.

Another example of misinterpretation is the article that appeared in *Commentary* magazine in December, citing the "latest" in brain research as an argument against equal rights for women. This angers Anne Petersen. "A lot of people have been making a lot of political hoopla about our work," she says. "They've used it to say that the women's movement will fail, that women are inherently unequal. Our research shows nothing of this sort, of course. There are things that men do better, and things that women do better. It's very important to differentiate between the inferences and the scientific findings."

These findings could influence fields ranging from philosophy, psychiatry, and the arts to education, law, and medicine. If women are indeed at a disadvantage in mastering math, there could be different methods of teaching, or acceptance of the fact that math is not important for certain jobs. For example, tests of mathematical competence have been used as criteria for admission to law school, where math is barely used; tests of spatial ability have been used to screen people for all types of nontechnical pursuits. If scientists can prove that such tests discriminate unnecessarily against women, hiring policies could be changed. Eventually, psychiatrists and lawyers may have to assess their male and female clients in a new light. And brain surgeons may have to consider the sex of a patient before operating. For if the two hemispheres of the brain are more intimately connected in women than in men, then women may be able to control a function like speech with either hemisphere. Surgeons could feel confident that a woman would recover the ability to talk, even if her normal speech center were destroyed; they might proceed with an operation that they would hesitate to perform on a man.

Investigators have made amazing progress in their work on the sexes and the brain, but they have really just begun. They will have to link hundreds of findings from widely diverse areas of brain science before they can provide a complete explanation for the shared, but different, humanity of men and women.

FOCUS: READING REVIEW

1. Weintraub recognizes that the issue of differences in ability between men and women is controversial. How does she attempt to defuse the issue?
2. What kinds of evidence do scientists offer to support the masculinization/feminization of brain tissue? Do these examples exclude the possibility of socialization affecting male/female identification?
3. What categories of evidence besides human does this essay offer? In what ways do these substantiate the human evidence? In what ways do they seem inapplicable for humans?
4. Near the end of the essay Weintraub presents the misuses that have been made of findings on hormones and the brain, the work of Dörner, and the article in *Commentary*. In what ways do these instances differ from other evidence presented in this article?

FOCUS: AUTHOR'S STRATEGIES

1. How does the introduction engage the reader's interest? What does it indicate about the writer's purpose?
2. The author summarizes a significant body of research. Explain how she develops her argument using induction, deduction, and analogy.

FOCUS: DISCUSSION AND WRITING

1. Evaluate as a statement of scientific evidence the passage, "Ehrhardt cites cases of girls whose adrenal glands, because of an enzyme defect, produced abnormally large amounts of androgens while they were still in the womb. 'We find that they are extremely tomboyish,' she says. 'They are career oriented, and spend little time with dolls.' "
2. Explain why American researchers would be appalled by the East German research on stressed mothers and sexual preferences.

Chapter 3
Critical Responses
to the
Natural Sciences

Dissent and dialogue are as essential to the scientific enterprise as the scientific method and articulating scientific findings. In chapter 3 you will find essays that respond critically to science. In "Evolution as Fact and Theory," Gould counters scientific creationism's assertion that evolution is "only theory" by defining scientific "fact" and "theory" and by advancing the theory of evolution from evolutionary facts. Bodmer's essay, "Biomedical Advances: A Mixed Blessing?," explains recent biological advances that could eliminate such genetically transmitted diseases as Tay Sach's disease and sickle-cell anemia, and then points out that this knowledge places a tremendous ethical burden on society. In "Speculation and Concern," the eminent humanist Northrop Frye examines the scientific quest to objectify reality and separate the inquiring mind from the nature it observes. He contrasts this with the humanities' expression of "the nature of the human involvement with the human world." Although Frye does not respond directly to the writers in the other chapters on the natural sciences, he concerns himself with science's methods and their importance.

Evolution as Fact and Theory

Stephen Jay Gould

Stephen Jay Gould (b. 1941), well-known for his monthly column in the magazine Natural History, *is a teaching research biologist at Harvard University. Most widely recognized for his essays on evolutionary theory collected in* Ever Since Darwin *(1977) and* The Panda's Thumb *(1980), Gould has done specialized work on the evolution of the West Indian snail and authored* Ontogeny and Phylogeny. *"Evolution as Fact and Theory" from* Discover, *May 1981, sets out the debate between scientific creationism and science by defining the distinctions between fact and theory in light of natural evidence supporting evolution.*

The basic attack of the creationists falls apart on two general counts. First, they play upon a vernacular misunderstanding of the word "theory" [as "imperfect fact"] to convey the false impression that evolution is less than a fact and that scientists can't even make up their minds about it. Second, they misuse a popular philosophy of science—Popper's view that the primary criterion of science is the falsifiability of its theories—to argue that they are behaving scientifically in attacking evolution. Yet the same philosophy demonstrates that their own belief is not science and that "scientific creationism" is therefore meaningless and self-contradictory. In truth, evolution *is* a theory. It is also a fact. Facts are the world's data. Theories are structures of ideas that explain and interpret facts. Darwin continually emphasized the difference between his two great and separate accomplishments: establishing the fact of evolution, and proposing a theory—natural selection—to explain the mechanism of evolution. Our confidence that evolution occurred centers upon three general arguments. First we have abundant, direct, observational evidence of evolution in action, from both the field and the laboratory. The second and third arguments rest upon inference. The second argument is that the imperfection of nature reveals evolution. An engineer, starting from scratch, could design better limbs for rats, bats, porpoises and humans than the structures they all inherited from a common ancestor. The third argument is that transitions are often found in the fossil record.

Kirtley Mather, who died last year at age 89, was a pillar of both science and the Christian religion in America and one of my dearest friends. The difference of half a century in our ages evaporated before our common interests. The most curious thing we shared was a battle we each fought at the same age. For Kirtley had gone to Tennessee with Clarence Darrow to testify for evolution at the Scopes trial of 1925. When I think that we are enmeshed again in the same struggle for one of the best documented, most compelling and exciting concepts in all of science, I don't know whether to laugh or cry.

According to idealized principles of scientific discourse, the arousal of dormant issues should reflect fresh data that give renewed life to abandoned notions. Those outside the current debate may therefore be excused for suspecting that creationists have come up with something new, or that evolutionists have generated some serious internal trouble. But nothing has changed; the creationists have not a single new fact or argument. Darrow and Bryan were at least more entertaining than we lesser antagonists today. The rise of creationism is politics, pure and simple; it represents one issue (and by no means the major concern) of the resurgent evangelical right. Arguments that seemed kooky just a decade ago have re-entered the mainstream.

CREATIONISM IS NOT SCIENCE

The basic attack of the creationists falls apart on two general counts before we even reach the supposed factual details of their complaints against evolution. First, they play upon a vernacular misunderstanding of the word "theory" to convey the false impression that we evolutionists are covering up the rotten core of our edifice. Second, they misuse a popular philosophy of science to argue that they are behaving scientifically in attacking evolution. Yet the same philosophy demonstrates that their own belief is not science and that "scientific creationism" is therefore meaningless and self-contradictory, a superb example of what Orwell[1] called "newspeak."

In the American vernacular, "theory" often means "imperfect fact"—part of a hierarchy of confidence running downhill from fact to theory to hypothesis to guess. Thus the power of the creationist argument evolution is "only" a theory, and intense debate now rages about many aspects of the theory. If evolution is less than a fact, and scientists can't even make up their minds about the theory, then what confidence can we have in it? Indeed, President Reagan echoed this argument before an evangelical group in Dallas when he said (in what I devoutly hope was campaign rhetoric): "Well, it is a theory. It's a scientific theory only, and it has in recent years been challenged in the world of science—that is, not believed in the scientific community to be as infallible as it once was."

Well, evolution *is* a theory. It is also a fact. And facts and theories are different things, not rungs in a hierarchy of increasing certainty. Facts are the world's data. Theories are structures of ideas that explain and interpret facts. Facts do not go away when scientists debate rival theories to explain them. Einstein's theory of gravitation replaced Newton's, but apples did not suspend themselves in mid-air pending the outcome. And human beings evolved from apelike ancestors whether they did so by Darwin's proposed mechanism or by some other, yet to be discovered.

Moreover, "fact" does not mean "absolute certainty." The final proofs of logic and mathematics flow deductively from stated premises and achieve certainty only because they are *not* about the empirical world. Evolutionists make no claim for perpetual truth, though creationists often do (and then attack us for a style of argument that they themselves favor). In science, "fact" can only mean "confirmed to such a degree that it would be perverse to withhold provisional assent." I suppose that apples might start to rise tomorrow, but the possibility does not merit equal time in physics classrooms.

Evolutionists have been clear about this distinction between fact and theory from the very beginning, if only because we have always acknowledged how far we are from completely understanding the mechanisms (theory) by which evolution (fact) occurred. Darwin continually emphasized the difference between his two great and separate accomplishments: establishing the fact of evolution, and proposing a theory—natural selection—to explain the mechanism of evolution. He wrote in *The Descent of Man*: "I had two distinct objects in view; firstly, to show that species had not been separately created, and secondly, that natural selection had been the chief agent of change . . . Hence if I have erred in . . . having exaggerated its [natural selection's] power . . . I have at least, as I hope, done good service in aiding to overthrow the dogma of separate creations."

Thus Darwin acknowledged the provisional nature of natural selection while affirming the fact of evolution. The fruitful theoretical debate that Darwin initiated has never ceased. From the 1940s through the 1960s, Darwin's own theory of natural selection did achieve a temporary hegemony that it never enjoyed in his lifetime. But renewed debate characterizes our decade, and, while no biologist questions the importance of natural selection, many now doubt its ubiquity. In particular, many evolutionists argue that substantial amounts of genetic change may not be subject to natural selection and may spread through populations at random. Others are challenging Darwin's linking of natural selection with gradual, imperceptible change through all intermediary degrees; they are arguing that most evolutionary events may occur far more rapidly than Darwin envisioned.

Scientists regard debates on fundamental issues of theory as a sign of intellectual health and a source of excitement. Science is—and how else can I say it?—most fun when it plays with interesting ideas, examines their implications, and recognizes that old information may be explained in surprisingly new ways. Evolutionary theory is now enjoying this uncommon vigor. Yet amidst all this turmoil no biologist has been led to doubt the fact that evolution occurred; we are debating *how* it happened. We are all trying to explain the same thing: the tree of evolutionary descent linking all organisms by ties of genealogy. Creationists pervert and caricature this debate by conveniently neglecting the common conviction that underlies it, and by falsely suggesting that we now doubt the very phenomenon we are struggling to understand.

Using another invalid argument, creationists claim that "the dogma of separate creations," as Darwin characterized it a century ago, is a scientific theory meriting equal time with evolution in high school biology curricula. But a prevailing viewpoint among philosophers of science belies this creationist argument. Philosopher Karl Popper has argued for decades that the primary criterion of science is the falsifiability of its theories. We can never prove absolutely, but we can falsify. A set of ideas that cannot, in principle, be falsified is not science.

The entire creationist argument involves little more than a rhetorical attempt to falsify evolution by presenting supposed contradictions among its supporters. Their brand of creationism, they claim, is "scientific" because it follows the Popperian model in trying to demolish evolution. Yet Popper's argument must apply in both directions. One does not become a scientist by the simple act of trying to falsify another scientific system; one has to present an alternative system that also meets Popper's criterion—it too must be falsifiable in principle.

"Scientific creationism" is a self-contradictory, nonsense phrase precisely because it cannot be falsified. I can envision observations and experiments that would disprove any evolutionary theory I know, but I cannot imagine what potential data could lead creationists to abandon their beliefs. Unbeatable systems are dogma, not science. Lest I seem harsh or rhetorical, I quote creationism's leading intellectual, Duane Gish, Ph.D., from his recent (1978) book *Evolution? The Fossils Say No!* "By creation we mean the bringing into being by a supernatural Creator of the basic kinds of plants and animals by the process of sudden, or fiat, creation. We do not know how the Creator created, what processes He used, *for He used processes which are not now operating anywhere in the natural universe* [Gish's italics]. This is why we refer to creation as special creation. We cannot discover by scientific investigations anything about the creative processes used by the Creator." Pray tell, Dr. Gish, in the light of your last sentence, what then is "scientific" creationism?

THE FACT OF EVOLUTION

Our confidence that evolution occurred centers upon three general arguments. First, we have abundant, direct, observational evidence of evolution in action, from both the field and the laboratory. It ranges from countless experiments on change in nearly everything about fruit flies subjected to artificial selection in the laboratory to the famous British moths that turned black when industrial soot darkened the trees upon which they rest. (The moths gain protection from sharp-sighted bird predators by blending into the background.) Creationists do not deny these observations; how could they? Creationists have tightened their act. They now argue that God only created "basic kinds," and allowed for limited evolutionary meandering within them. Thus toy poodles and Great Danes come from the dog kind and moths can change color, but nature cannot convert a dog to a cat or a monkey to a man.

The second and third arguments for evolution—the case for major changes—do not involve direct observation of evolution in action. They rest upon inference, but are no less secure for that reason. Major evolutionary change requires too much time for direct observation on the scale of recorded human history. All historical sciences rest upon inference, and evolution is no different from geology, cosmology, or human history in this respect. In principle, we cannot observe processes that operated in the past. We must infer them from results that still survive: living and fossil organisms for evolution, documents and artifacts for human history, strata and topography for geology.

The second argument—that the imperfection of nature reveals evolution—strikes many people as ironic, for they feel that evolution should be most elegantly displayed in the nearly perfect adaptation expressed by some organisms—the camber of a gull's wing, or butterflies that cannot be seen in ground litter because they mimic leaves so precisely. But perfection could be imposed by a wise creator or evolved by natural selection. Perfection covers the tracks of past history. And past history—the evidence of descent—is our mark of evolution.

Evolution lies exposed in the *imperfections* that record a history of descent. Why should a rat run, a bat fly, a porpoise swim, and I type this essay with structures built of the same bones unless we all inherited them from a common ancestor? An engineer, starting from scratch, could design better limbs in each case. Why should all the large native mammals of Australia be marsupials, unless they descended from a common ancestor isolated on this island continent? Marsupials are not "better," or ideally suited for Australia; many have been wiped out by placental mammals imported by man from other continents. This principle of imperfection extends to all historical sciences. When we recognize the etymology of September, October, November, and December (seventh, eighth, ninth, and tenth, from the Latin), we know that two additional items (January and February) must have been added to an original calendar of ten months.

The third argument is more direct: transitions are often found in the fossil record. Preserved transitions are not common—and should not be, according to our understanding of evolution (see next section)—but they are not entirely wanting, as creationists often claim. The lower jaw of reptiles contains several bones, that of mammals only one. The non-mammalian jawbones are reduced, step by step, in mammalian ancestors until they become tiny nubbins located at the back of the jaw. The "hammer" and "anvil" bones of the mammalian ear are descendants of these nubbins. How could such a transition be accomplished? the creationists ask. Surely a bone is either entirely in the jaw or in the ear. Yet paleontologists have discovered two transitional lineages of therapsids (the so-called mammal-like reptiles) with a double jaw joint—one composed of the old quadrate and articular bones (soon to become the hammer and anvil), the other of the squamosal and dentary bones (as in modern mammals). For that matter, what better transitional form could we desire than the oldest human, *Australopithecus afarensis*, with its apelike palate, its human upright stance, and a cranial capacity larger than any ape's of the same body size but a full 1,000 cubic centimeters below ours? If God made each of the half dozen human species discovered in ancient rocks, why did he create in an unbroken temporal sequence of progressively more modern features—increasing cranial capacity, reduced face and teeth, larger body size? Did he create to mimic evolution and test our faith thereby?

AN EXAMPLE OF CREATIONIST ARGUMENT

Faced with these facts of evolution and the philosophical bankruptcy of their own position, creationists rely upon distortion and innuendo to buttress their rhetorical claim. If I sound sharp or bitter, indeed I am—for I have become a major target of these practices.

I count myself among the evolutionists who argue for a jerky, or episodic, rather than a smoothly gradual, pace of change. In 1972 my colleague Niles Eldredge and I developed the theory of punctuated equilibrium [*Discover*, October]. We argued that two outstanding facts of the fossil record—geologically "sudden" origin of new species and failure to change thereafter (stasis)—reflect the predictions of evolutionary theory, not the imperfections of the fossil record. In most theories, small isolated populations are the source of new species, and the process of speciation takes thousands or tens of thousands of years. This amount of time, so long when measured against our lives, is a geological microsecond. It represents much less than 1 per cent of the average life span for a fossil invertebrate species—more than 10 million years. Large, widespread, and well established species, on the other hand, are not expected to change very much. We believe that the inertia of large populations explains the stasis of most fossil species over millions of years.

We proposed the theory of punctuated equilibrium largely to provide a different explanation for pervasive trends in the fossil record. Trends, we argued, cannot be attributed to gradual transformation within lineages, but must arise from the differential success of certain kinds of species. A trend, we argued, is more like climbing a flight of stairs (punctuations and stasis) than rolling up an inclined plane.

Since we proposed punctuated equilibria to explain trends, it is infuriating to be quoted again and again by creationists—whether through design or stupidity, I do not know—as admitting that the fossil record includes no transitional forms. Transitional forms are generally lacking at the species level, but are abundant between larger groups. The evolution from reptiles to mammals, as mentioned earlier, is well documented. Yet a pamphlet entitled "Harvard Scientists Agree Evolution Is a Hoax" states: "The facts of punctuated equilibrium which Gould and Eldredge . . . are forcing Darwinists to swallow fit the picture that Bryan insisted on, and which God has revealed to us in the Bible."

Continuing the distortion, several creationists have equated the theory of punctuated equilibrium with a caricature of the beliefs of Richard Goldschmidt, a great early geneticist. Goldschmidt argued, in a famous book published in 1940, that new groups can arise all at once through major mutations. He referred to these suddenly transformed creatures as "hopeful monsters." (I am attracted to some aspects of the non-caricatured version, but Goldschmidt's theory still has nothing to do with punctuated equilibrium.) Creationist Luther Sunderland talks of the "punctuated equilibrium hopeful monster theory" and tells his hopeful readers that "it amounts to tacit admission that anti-evolutionists are correct in asserting there is no fossil evidence supporting the theory that all life is connected to a common ancestor." Duane Gish writes, "According to Goldschmidt, and now apparently according to Gould, a reptile laid an egg from which the first bird, feathers and all, was produced." Any evolutionist who believed such nonsense would rightly be laughed off the intellectual stage; yet the only theory that could ever envision such a scenario for the evolution of birds is creationism—God acts in the egg.

CONCLUSION

I am both angry at and amused by the creationists; but mostly I am deeply sad. Sad for many reasons. Sad because so many people who respond to creationist appeals are troubled for the right reason, but venting their anger at the wrong target. It is true that scientists have often been dogmatic and elitist. It is true that we have often allowed the white-coated, advertising image to represent us—"Scientists say that Brand X cures bunions ten times faster than . . . ." We have not fought it adequately because we derive benefits from appearing as a new priesthood. It is also true that faceless bureaucratic state power intrudes more and more into our lives and removes choices that should belong to individuals and communities. I can understand that requiring that evolution be taught in the schools might be seen as one more insult on all these grounds. But the culprit is not, and cannot be, evolution or any other fact of the natural world. Identify and fight your legitimate enemies by all means, but we are not among them.

I am sad because the practical result of this brouhaha will not be expanded coverage to include creationism (that would also make me sad), but the reduction or excision of evolution from high school curricula. Evolution is one of the half dozen "great ideas" developed by science. It speaks to the profound issues of genealogy that fascinate all of us—the "roots" phenomenon writ large. Where did we come from? Where did life arise? How did it develop? How are organisms related? It forces us to think, ponder, and wonder. Shall we deprive millions of this knowledge and once again teach biology as a set of dull and unconnected facts, without the thread that weaves diverse material into a supple unity?

But most of all I am saddened by a trend I am just beginning to discern among my colleagues. I sense that some now wish to mute the healthy debate about theory that has brought new life to evolutionary biology. It provides grist for creationist mills, they say, even if only by distortion. Perhaps we should lie low and rally round the flag of strict Darwinism, at least for the moment—a kind of old-time religion on our part.

But we should borrow another metaphor and recognize that we too have to tread a straight and narrow path, surrounded by roads to perdition. For if we ever begin to suppress our search to understand nature, to quench our own intellectual excitement in a misguided effort to present a united front where it does not and should not exist, then we are truly lost.

Notes

[1] In George Orwell's novel *1984*, "Newspeak was the official language of Oceania and had been devised to meet the ideological needs of Ingsoc, of English Socialism.... The purpose of Newspeak was not only to provide a medium of expression for the worldview and mental habits proper to the devotees of Ingsoc, but to make all other modes of thought impossible. It was intended that when Newspeak had been adopted once and for all and Oldspeak [Standard English] forgo then, a heretical thought—that is, a thought diverging from the principles of Ingsoc—should be literally unthinkable ... " [from George Orwell "the Principles of Newspeak" in the appendix to *1984.*]

FOCUS: READING REVIEW

1. Explain the two flaws Gould finds in creationist opposition to evolution.
2. What does "falsifiability" mean in science? Explain why the scientific creationist position is not falsifiable.
3. What is Gould's theory of punctuated equilibrium? How does this serve as grounds for contention with scientific creationists?

FOCUS: AUTHOR'S STRATEGIES

1. Is Gould writing for an audience sympathetic with evolutionary or creationist theory? What in the essay indicates this audience?
2. Gould builds his argument from a definition of the words "theory" and "fact." How does he use his definitions to counter creationists' arguments?
3. Gould shifts from using definition as a means of argument to using evidence. How does he construct his argument from evidence?
4. In his conclusions Gould suggests the larger purposes of this essay. What are they?

FOCUS: DISCUSSION AND WRITING

1. In the conclusion Gould says that creationists are angry but at the wrong target. Who or what should they be angry with? Why?
2. Explain what the two sides are in the debate on evolution. Explain objectively and sympathetically the assumptions, arguments, and concerns of each.

Biomedical Advances: A Mixed Blessing?
W. F. Bodmer

W. F. Bodmer, recognized for his important contributions to genetics at Oxford University, gave the address "Biomedical Advances: A Mixed Blessing?" at the distinguished Herbert Spencer Lectures at Oxford in 1973. The Spencer Lectures called upon six prominent lecturers "to examine the notion of progress in science and to reflect on that progress ... both with respect to its consequences and to the obstacles it might encounter." Bodmer's address, from which this selection is excerpted, examines the implications of genetic discovery for social and economic policy. The selection appeared in its entirety in Problems of Scientific Revolution, *edited by Rom Harre.*

My main concern is to discuss the contrast between basic science and its applications, to illustrate the tensions that are created by its applications with some examples from my own field of interest, and to emphasize that the tensions cannot be avoided. Genetics in many people's minds raises rather frightening social problems, fears which are fed by such journalistic phrases as 'genetic engineering' and 'test-tube babies.' Such concerns about biomedical advances are of course nothing new, [but this does not mean that they can be ignored.] Applications of biomedical advances fall into two categories. The first directly affects our health and the physical improvement of our lives. The second is indirect and relates to discoveries which provide insights into the nature of human society. An example of direct applications arises from advances in our understanding of genetic diseases and their detection. One of these is sickle-cell anaemia, which results from an abnormal gene. This could be dealt with by screening individuals to see whether they are carriers, and hope that the knowledge might prevent mating. A more radical approach might be to prevent all carriers from having children. The real problem with the disease is that it occurs in the black population. Any screening or prevention program might carry implications of racial stigmatization. Another inborn error of metabolism, Tay Sach's disease, occurs with a relatively high frequency in Askenazi Jewish populations. It can be detected during pregnancy and the mother can be offered an abortion. This raises two problems: first, people's attitudes toward abortion, and second, the effect that such treatments might have on the eventual frequency of the disease in the population. As an example of indirect applications of science, genetic studies have discovered the uniqueness of each individual. This variability implies that human beings are not equal. This has implications for education. If enough research were to be devoted to genetic differences in response to education, a Utopian goal might suggest that one should identify genotypes more suited to one type of education than another, and then optimize educational procedures to minimize educational costs by matching each type of individual as closely as possible to their best suited occupation. Further, if equality of environment is interpreted literally, then in an equal environment all differences that remain will be genetic. This would lead to a meritocratic society strictly dependent on genetic endowment. My aim in discussing these various examples has been to point out the type of tensions and problems that are raised by the application of new scientific knowledge. Three important points arise. First, the proper application of scientific advances will not happen unless the scientist and non-scientist alike consider the problems and deal with them. Second, the scientist cannot act alone when it comes to applications of science. Third, a good general education in science is needed. Even if biomedical advances are a mixed blessing—they are a blessing we cannot avoid, and it is our job to see to it that the mixture comes out for the best.

My main concern in this lecture is to discuss the contrast between basic science and its applications, to illustrate the tensions that are created by its applications with some examples from my own field of interest, and to emphasize that the tensions must be faced and cannot be avoided. The flow of knowledge will not be stopped or reversed, and even if it were, no problems would thereby be solved.

Genetics is an area that in many people's minds raises rather frightening social problems for our society, fears which are fed by such journalistic phrases as 'genetic engineering' and 'test-tube babies'. This was brought home to me rather vividly when I was returning with my family from a holiday on the Continent the summer before last. As we were confidently driving out along the 'Nothing to Declare' customs lane we were stopped by a rather severe-looking Customs Officer. Having seen from my passport that I was a Professor, he asked me first what University I was at—'Oxford', I said—confidently hoping that that at least would placate him. However, next came the question—'What's your subject?'—'Genetics', I said—silence for a brief moment and then—'Hm, I'd better let you go then hadn't I, otherwise you might turn me into a frog!'

I find this story elicits two very different sorts of reactions. The first is surprise that a Customs Officer should know about genetics and what it was, let alone especially in Oxford, its connection with frogs and, presumably, nuclear transplantation. The existence of such knowledge among 'lay' people must surely be considered as progress, at the very least in the important matter of disseminating science to society. The second reaction, which I must admit was my own immediate reaction, is one of concern that there should be such fear of the geneticist; almost as if he or she were the modern sorcerer, or at best, witch-doctor. This attitude surely represents a basic obstacle to progress in science, certainly of its application and possibly even of its execution if there is a consequent restriction on the freedom to do any research.

Such concerns about biomedical advances (and surely about other advances as well) are of course nothing new. Tissue grafting was recorded by the Egyptians as early as 3500 B.C., though the first proper description of some of the basic techniques was apparently due to Gasparo Tagliacozzi, a professor of anatomy at the University of Bologna in the sixteenth century. The theologians of his time bitterly attacked him, accusing him of impiously interfering with the handiwork of God and attributing his success to the intervention of the 'Evil One'. Towards the end of the eighteenth century the University of Paris banned all such types of operation. A few years ago here in Oxford, Professor Henry Harris, with John Watkins, developed a procedure for efficiently fusing cells from widely differing species, such as man and mouse. From these fused cells one can grow hybrid cells which are now much used in genetical and developmental studies, and in cell biology research in general. One response to Harris and Watkins, paper was a cartoon showing Disney-like characters, including Mickey Mouse, sitting in the London Underground reading the *Daily Mirror,* with a caption 'Who Was Walt Disney, Dad?'. Henry Harris has contrasted this cartoon with one published 163 years earlier in response to Jenner's research on vaccination using cow pox. Jenner is shown vaccinating a group of people, and those already innoculated have grown parts of cows on their arms and faces. The caption reads 'Cow pox. The wonderful effects of the new innoculation'.

The fact that such concerns are not new does not mean that they can be ignored. On the contrary, the increasing rate of advance in knowledge means that accompanying concerns arise more and more frequently and become more and more pressing.

The examples of biomedical advances I shall discuss will not include topical areas like genetic engineering, test tube babies and *in vitro* fertilization, and cloning. The days when, as the satirical columnist of *The San Francisco Chronicle,* Arthur Hoppe, said in response to a somewhat futuristic discussion by Joshua Lederberg, 'genetic engineers will be able to give the unborn child whatever characteristics mum and dad are praying for' are still, fortunately perhaps, a long way off. I should like to concentrate on issues that to my mind raise as many problems, but which are with us today. Better perhaps to deal with today's problems first, before solving those of tomorrow.

Applications of biomedical (and presumably other) advances fall, I believe, into two categories. The first can be called direct and include, for example, the discovery of vaccines, of penicillin, the importance of hygiene, and the development of surgical operations, all of which have direct effects on our health and the physical improvement of our lives. The second type of application is indirect and relates to discoveries which provide insights into the nature of human society that may help in the understanding of its problems.

The first example I should like to discuss, of direct applications, arises from advances in our understanding of genetic diseases and their detection, especially in the foetus *in utero* during comparatively early stages of pregnancy. A large number of diseases are now known that are simply inherited, most of which are extremely rare, occurring with a frequency of less than 1 in 50,000, and a certain proportion of which are well defined biochemically and can be traced to defects in single enzymes. Their biochemical effects can usually be detected in the blood or in cells grown in culture. These diseases are called 'inborn errors of metabolism' and were first so defined and studied by Archibald Garrod who was at one time Regius Professor of Medicine here in Oxford. For most of them there is, so far, no cure. But the first question must be raised as to what can be done about them given the knowledge we now have.

One very well known genetic disease, which is quite common in some populations, is sickle-cell anaemia. This disease, caused by an abnormality of haemoglobin, occurs with a frequency of up to 2–3 per cent in parts of West Africa. Like all so-called 'recessive diseases', affected individuals carry two abnormal genes. However, most of the abnormal genes in the population (which when present in duplicate cause the disease) are found in 'carriers' who have one normal and one abnormal gene, and who are clinically normal and quite healthy. In fact, in those parts of the world where sickle-cell anaemia is common, the carriers have an increased resistance to malaria which most probably accounts for the high frequency of the disease in those areas. Individuals with the severe anaemia, who can only come from matings between carriers, mostly die in their teens, though improved over-all medical care is keeping them alive for longer and longer. There is, however, no specific cure for the disease. What solutions can one suggest for dealing with this extremely important health problem? Since all affected individuals are offspring of matings between two carriers, one possible solution is to try and prevent matings between carriers from taking place. To do this it would be necessary first to screen individuals to see whether they are carriers. Then, perhaps, one might hope that once they know they are, this knowledge will prevent them from mating with other carriers. A more radical approach might be to stop all carriers from having children, which would, 'at a stroke' so to speak, remove the gene from the population. In fact, preventing carriers from mating with each other would not be too severe a restriction on their liberty. More than 75 per cent of the population would still be freely available to choose from. The real problems with these approaches arise in putting them into practice in a population which may not fully comprehend the issues involved. The fact that the disease is one that occurs in the black population naturally creates fear of a racial stigma, especially in the United States where it has been much discussed. Screening has to be done on the blacks and they may not understand why this should be so. Sickle-cell disease in the United States has in fact become a major 'political disease' and the subject of much litigation. In cases where screening has been carried out, carriers may find it hard to get medical insurance and feel stigmatized. Laws have been passed which do not distinguish between carriers of the gene and the diseased individual, only to add to the confusion. It is perhaps a little sad to reflect on the fact that this disease, the first one really to be understood at molecular level, has not, so far, itself benefited greatly from application of this knowledge, though it has contributed enormously to our understanding of many basic biological problems. Tensions created by attempts to apply the new knowledge have, I believe, arisen mainly as a result of misunderstanding and of inadequate education of the general public to appreciate the role of screening programmes.

There is another inborn error of metabolism called Tay Sach's disease, that has been widely studied and which, like PKU, is well defined at the biochemical level.

Infants with this disease weaken within the first six months, suffer from progressive mental and motor deterioration and eventually blindness and paralysis, and generally die within three years. In this disease, carriers of the abnormal gene are detectable. The disease occurs with a relatively high frequency, 1 in 2000, in Askenazi[1] Jewish populations, while in virtually all other populations it has a hundredfold lower frequency. It is, because of its well-understood biochemical nature, of the class of diseases that can be detected *in utero*[2] following the procedure called 'amniocentesis'. A sample of the amniotic fluid which surrounds the foetus can be taken at 14–16 weeks of gestation. This fluid contains cells which can be grown and used for biochemical tests or, if desired, can be examined for their chromosome constitution. When either of these tests reveals an abnormality, then one can offer the mother the possibility of abortion. In the case of Tay Sach's disease, cells from the amniotic fluid can be used to detect whether the foetus suffers from the disease. Thus, one way of guaranteeing normal children, as far as this disease is concerned, to matings between carriers who would otherwise have one quarter of their children affected, is to offer them the possibility of abortion when an affected child is detected. A screening programme among the Askenazi Jewish population of the Baltimore-Washington DC area has been instituted along these lines. Thus, wives are first screened to see whether they are carriers. If they are, then their husbands are also screened. Then, if both husband and wife are carriers, amniocentesis (the process of collecting and testing the amniotic fluid and its cells) is carried out on all their offspring, offering the possibility of abortion for abnormal offspring. In this way, clearly one can in principle avoid having any affected individuals in the population. The procedure is certainly cost-effective in the Askenazi Jewish population because of the high frequency of the disease, though it probably would not be so in other populations. This seems to be a rational and humane programme for dealing with the disease and so far it appears to be working well on a trial basis. Its success clearly depends on having a population which can appreciate the problems involved in such a programme.

There are at least two important questions raised by such programmes of *in utero* detection of genetic disease and subsequent selective abortion. The first of these is, of course, people's attitudes towards abortion. It is often objected to on religious and ethical bases. The second problem is the effect that such treatments might have on the eventual frequency of the disease in the population. In the case of recessive diseases, such as Tay Sachs or PKU, one can actually show that such effects will be very, very slight, since most of the abnormal genes are present in carriers who never produce affected offspring because they are not married to carriers.

Suppose now, however, that it becomes possible to cure a disease such as Tay Sachs. This could be achieved, perhaps, by enzyme therapy, namely by replacing the deficient enzyme much in the way that one gives insulin to a diabetic. Such a cure would undoubtedly be very costly and probably would have to be maintained throughout life. What now should be the decision? Should one cure all affected individuals, or should one continue a programme of selective screening and abortion? This latter is certainly likely to be the cheaper solution. What problems will be raised if the cure turns out not to be complete? It could quite easily result in a comparatively low IQ, that might well be difficult to detect for some time. Is it better not to be born, or to be born maimed or abnormal?

The question is often raised: would it not be possible to remove all abnormal genes from the population by simply preventing carriers of such genes from reproducing? But the point must be made that it can be shown that nearly all of us carry on average, up to four or more such abnormal genes in a single dose, where for the most part they go undetected and have no effect. If we prevent individuals who are carriers of those genes we can now recognize, from mating, we are indeed taking a very arbitrary step dictated simply by which particular diseases we now understand. If we took the more rational approach of stopping all people carrying abnormal genes from reproducing, this would leave few of us, if any, to reproduce. Clearly, any hope of eradicating all such genes from the population is quite unrealistic.

Turning now to an example of indirect applications of science I should like to consider the question of individual genetic differences. Everybody looks different, apart perhaps from identical twins, but how much of these differences are genetic? The outward features, the characteristics by which we usually distinguish people, are not in general simply inherited. But there do exist a number of simply inherited traits, such as the blood groups (like the ABO system) and enzyme differences, for which common variants are found. These simple, genetically determined variations seem to parallel the differences we recognize between people. One of the most striking results of population genetic studies over the last ten years is the uncovering of just how much genetic variability exists in natural populations. Even using presently known genetic systems, the chance is less than one in a million that one should find two identical people. It is now even possible to give a very high probability for positive paternity, rather than simply paternity exclusion. Thus, one can now narrow down very much on the chance of a given child not having come from particular parents.

Transplantation of tissues illustrates, in a striking way, our genetic uniqueness. As most of you probably know, it is not possible, in the absence of appropriate drugs and matching procedures, to graft an organ from one arbitrarily chosen person to another and have it survive for anything but the shortest period of time. The reason that such grafts are rejected by the recipient is that there exist genetic differences between individuals which lead to the recognition of a graft as foreign by his immune system. These differences are rather like blood groups, and so the fact that, in the absence of appropriate medical treatment, all such grafts would be rejected is itself an indication that with respect to just these systems we are all genetically unique. In fact, matching for the more important systems coupled with appropriate drug treatment and careful medical therapy has now made transplantation of the kidney quite a successful medical procedure.

If the variation in the genes we now know and can detect is representative of all genes, then the potential for genetic variability is truly staggering. One can calculate that the probable minimum number of different types of egg or sperm that an individual can produce is 2^{10000}, or $\smile 10^{3000}$, namely 1 followed by 3000 zeros. This can be compared with the total number of sperm that have ever been produced by all human males that have ever lived, which I estimate to be approximately 10^{23} to 10^{24}. Thus, the number of different types of egg or sperm that one individual can produce is some 10^{1000}fold more than the total number of sperm ever produced. Only a very, very small proportion of potential genetic combinations are ever realized. We are all genetically unique, and this genetic uniqueness clearly must apply to behavioural and other attributes as well as to blood type, though specific genetic factors that may be involved in these other traits have not yet been defined.

What are the implications of this variability for our society? Perhaps the most fundamental is with respect to the concept of equality. If equality really means the same, then it is clear that we are not all equal. One must then either say that equality means equality of opportunity, or else accept equal treatment for unequal people. One striking example of the conflict between genetics, with its demonstration of inherited differences between people, and political ideas lies in the former ascendancy of Lysenko[3] in the USSR. Lysenko supported the old and outdated idea of inheritance of acquired characters, largely, perhaps because he felt that it was more in keeping with the political ideas of his country, since it implied that all people could readily be made equal by appropriate environmental manipulation (or perhaps because he saw this belief as a way to gain political power). He dominated biology in Russia and so suppressed its development along modern lines for some twenty or thirty years from the late 1930s, years which covered the major advances in our understanding of molecular biology.

Even though there is much genetic variability in human populations we know there must, nevertheless, be a great deal of scope for environmental effects. The fact that a character is genetic does not by any means imply that it cannot be manipulated by the environment. The cure of PKU by an appropriate diet, and the effect of nutrition on height (which has a very significant genetic component) are simple examples of this. One could even, in principle, conceive of an educational system which compensated for genetic differences in, say, intrinsic ability, by giving less education to the bright and more to the less bright in a way that might truly equalize.

I believe that a common mistake in considering these questions is to imagine that there is a linear scale of quality (IQ in some people's minds) on which high equals good, and low equals bad. The situation is, surely, rather that there simply are differences between people which cannot necessarily be classified as good, bad, high, or low.

There must certainly be implications for education in the existence of genetic differences. Not all will want to learn the same things or learn in the same way, or learn at the same speed. In modern complex societies the need for a variety of individual talents has undoubtedly increased tremendously. Though some educationalists may believe that anybody properly educated can be made proficient in any job, few would surely maintain that the effective cost, however measured, would be the same for each individual. If enough research were to be devoted to genetic differences in response to education, a Utopian goal might suggest that one should identify genotypes more suited to one type of education than another, and then optimize educational procedures to minimize educational costs by matching each type of individual as closely as possible to their best suited occupation. We are still very far from having the sort of knowledge which would allow putting such a programme into practice, perhaps fortunately so. But no educational system will be successful if it ignores the existence of individual variability.

If equality of environment is interpreted literally then, as many have pointed out, in an equal environment all differences that remain will be genetic. It has been suggested that this would lead to a meritocratic society strictly dependent on genetic endowment. Whether this is likely, realistic, or even possible is clearly a moot point, but at the very least we must be aware of the difficulties for the concept of equality in our society given the existence of so much genetic variability.

There are a number of more obvious corrolaries of the existence of genetic variability which follow, for example, from variations in genetic susceptibility to diseases. Mental disease is a particular case in point. Schizophrenia, which occurs with an incidence of one or two per cent in the population, is now generally thought to have a major, if not predominant, genetic component and accounts for a very large fraction of occupied hospital beds. Genetic differences account for the need to match blood for transfusion and transplantation. There are genetically determined allergies and sensitivities to drugs. There are probably genetic factors in alcoholism. Colour blindness is genetically determined and sets some limits to possible occupations. There are almost certainly genetic differences in drug addiction and most probably, also, in tendencies to criminality. All these genetic variations have obvious consequences in our society.

Closely related to the question of individual differences, and often confused with it, is the question of differences between groups of individuals, namely between populations or races. Allegiance to one's own group, be it family, village, country, race, or species seems to me to be so strongly ingrained as to be almost instinctive, and with this allegiance comes its complement racialism. To a biologist a race is just a group of individuals or populations which form some recognizable subdivision of the species. Members of the group share characteristics which, to some extent, distinguish them from members of other groups. Races have traditionally been defined by outwardly obvious features such as skin colour and face shape. Nowadays, however, the only valid approach is to use those individual differences which are simply inherited and which have provided evidence for the genetic uniqueness of the individual. The frequencies of the various genetic types differ from one population to another, and these frequencies can be used to characterize a population. It is important to emphasize that differences between races, as conventionally defined, account for a minority, probably less than 30 per cent, of the total species genetic variability.

Racialism, the belief that some race, usually one's own, is inherently superior and so has a right to dominate, as I have already mentioned, seems to me to follow from a strongly ingrained, almost instinctive, allegiance to one's own group. Many attempts, however, have been made to support racialistic ideas with genetic arguments. The most recent example is the debate on IQ and race differences, notably differences between blacks and whites in the United States, and the question of the extent to which this difference has a genetic component. This is a subject that has been much discussed and I have no time to summarize the arguments here. I should just like to say, however, that many geneticists, including myself, believe that there is no case on present evidence either for assuming, or for not assuming, the existence of a significant genetic component. The data are inadequate and the methodology for answering the question properly is not yet available. Even if there were such an average genetic difference, what relevance would it have to the treatment of the individual, which is the basis for dealing with people in a society free of racial prejudice? The conflict in this example is not created by the scientific knowledge about how we can define population groups using genetic markers. The problem is to use this knowledge for counteracting racialistic tendencies.

There is little doubt that races or populations do seem to have characteristics as a whole which distinguish them in ways that, if these were differences between individuals, one might well think could have a significant genetic component. Yet to a geneticist it is clear that the time available for such differences to arise, especially when taking into account the genetic complexity of the characters that one is usually thinking about, makes it impossible to believe that many, if any, such differences between populations can truly be genetic. Otherwise these characteristics would have to be associated with sufficient biological reproductive advantage to enable the genes determining them to spread quite rapidly through whole populations that are, perhaps, as closely related as the British and the French. Now the cultural spread of a character is quite different from genetic spread. Cultural transmission can be likened to infection, sometimes even to epidemic. The cultural spread of a trait can occur very rapidly because cultural transmission can take place between people of all ages, whether or not they are related, and is not restricted to movement, according to Mendel's laws, from parent to offspring. Most of the population differences that we normally consider must therefore be cultural, and yet we must try and answer the question as to why they often look as though they might be genetic. I think the answer may be relatively simple. Many cultural changes are initiated by a single individual, or at most a small group of individuals, who are dominant within a society. Once initiated, a trait can be rapidly transmitted culturally. The initiator may have had a particular genetic endowment which enabled him to initiate, but human communication allows others to learn without having the genes needed to initiate. We do not all have to be mathematical geniuses like Newton in order to know and use Newtonian mechanics and the calculus.

My aim in discussing these various examples of applications of advances in genetics to society has been to point out the type of tensions and problems that are raised by the applications of new scientific knowledge. There are, perhaps, at least three important points that arise. First, the proper application of scientific advances will not happen unless the scientist and non-scientist alike consider the problems and deal with them. If applications are left to follow their own course without proper consideration, then scientific advances may easily be misapplied. A second point to emphasize is that the scientist cannot act alone when it comes to applications. He is not necessarily the person that knows best what should be done, and so he must communicate with the non-scientist. Lack of communication may lead to invalid arguments as a basis for action. One small example to my mind, comes from the Law Commission's working paper (No. 47) on the injuries to unborn children. In this reference is made to cases in the 1930s of claims that involvement of a mother in an accident during pregnancy might have led to the resulting child having a club foot, a possibility that seems most unlikely scientifically. The third, and to my mind very important point is the need for good general education in science. This should provide people with an understanding of scientific issues, so that applications create less of a problem simply due to misunderstanding, as in the case of genetic screening programmes. This should also allow all members of our society to help make sensible assessments as to what should be done about applications of scientific advances. In each of these three areas, namely the proper consideration of applications of scientific advances, the need to communicate with the non-scientist, and the need to educate, the scientist has a clear responsibility.

I have purposely not dealt with some of the larger philosophical questions that can be raised, such as: what is science and what is the nature of scientific progress? what is the nature of equality? what is for the good of society? Perhaps some of you will thus accuse me of having been prosaic. I am, however, reminded of the story of a wife, who when asked how she and her husband made their decisions said, 'Oh, that's very easy. He makes all the important decisions, such as what to do about the Middle East War, what to do about the world energy crisis and population increases, and whether to impeach President Nixon. I make all the minor decisions, like where we are going to live, what schools the children will go to, where we are going to have our holidays, and what sort of a car we are going to buy.'

The title of my lecture is 'Biomedical advances—a mixed blessing?' Of course one answer to this question might be to have no advances. But as I emphasized at the beginning, I believe that that cannot be—there is no standing still, only moving forward or backward however slowly, and none of us surely would welcome a new Dark Age. Perhaps, occasionally, a brake has to be applied to some research but that can only, in general, be a minor hiccough in the advance of science.

Thus I believe that even if biomedical advances (and of course other scientific advances) are a mixed blessing—they are a blessing we cannot avoid, and it is our job to see to it that the mixture comes out for the best.

Notes

[1] Askenazi: those members of the Jewish population who trace their origins to Eastern Europe.

[2] *in utero*: in the uterus.

[3] Lysenko (1898–1975) was a Soviet agronomist who denied the existence of genes and claimed that the entire organism, not the chromosomes, governs heredity. Based on his theories he stated that wheat could become rye and that crop yields could be greater than other biologists believed. His views won Stalin's favor. The practical application of Lysenko's theories had a devastating effect on Soviet agriculture, and he was later discredited, in part because he falsified data to "prove" his theories.

FOCUS: READING REVIEW

1. What are the categories of applications of biomedical research Bodmer discusses? What are the distinguishing characteristics of each category?
2. Bodmer uses the extended example of genetically caused sickle-cell anemia. What genetic factors govern the disease's transmission? What actions can be taken to prevent the disease? What are the social implications of this action?
3. In the example of Tay Sach's disease, what biomedical advances have enabled detection and control? What social tensions derive from these?
4. What implications does the knowledge of genetic differences have for political and educational thinking?

FOCUS: AUTHOR'S STRATEGIES

1. What is the purpose of Bodmer's essay? What indicates this?
2. Explain how Bodmer's definitions and explanations indicate his audience. What kinds of specialized knowledge does he assume they possess?

FOCUS: DISCUSSION AND WRITING

1. Bodmer believes that the scientists cannot act alone when it comes to applications of science. Explain what role nonscientists could assume to direct scientific application. Consider the problems this would pose for the nonscientist. What would be the advantages and disadvantages of such a solution?
2. Bodmer calls for a good general education in science. Consider your own scientific education (or lack of it), and with Bodmer's essay in mind, evolve a definition of a "good general education in science" and propose a curriculum.

Speculation and Concern
Northrop Frye

Northrop Frye (b. 1921), one of the best recognized and most frequently cited critics of the twentieth century, works primarily in literary studies as the University Professor at the University of Toronto. Because he believes that critical insight derives from the overall structures of literature and these structures embody the essential patterns of human experience, Frye's criticism moves outward from individual literary works to the larger spectrum of human concerns. In "Speculation and Concern," first presented as an address at a conference at the University of Kentucky on what the humanities provide that the sciences do not, Frye examines the fundamental distinction between scientific and artistic views of reality.

What do the humanities provide for human culture that the sciences do not? The best approach to this question is to begin by reversing it. What does science provide for human culture that the arts and the humanities do not provide? The traditional answer, and doubtless the right one, is 'nature'. Science gives us nature, not the understanding or conception of nature. [Science's end is not only to describe and understand what it sees, but to make predictions as well.] [Scientists] see their phenomena in time—or their version of time—as well as space, and their end is rather a vision of nature under law. The genuine basis of a complementary view of the arts and sciences is the distinction between time as externalized by science, where it is really a dimension of space, and time in its other form of the continuous awareness of one's own existence. The role of art, then, is primarily to express the complex of human existence, humanity's awareness of being itself rather than its perception of what is not itself and is outside it. This self-awareness is neither subjective nor objective. It does not quantify existence like science: it qualifies it. The production of art is a stylizing of behaviour like the production of science. As far as the actual man doing the work is concerned, I doubt whether there is any essential psychological difference between the artist and the scientist. But when we consider the finished product only, it is clear that the arts do not stabilize the subject in the same way that science does.

Aristotle spoke of the arts as imitative of nature. But as soon as we examine this conception of imitation, the notion of a continuous relation to the external world begins to dissolve, and we can see that 'nature' exists in the arts only as the content of art, as something that art surrounds and contains. So while science deals with the consolidating of what is there, the arts deal with the expanding of what is here: the circumference of science is the universe, the circumference of the arts is human culture. [Much modern philosophy holds with the view that] reality is primarily what we create, not what we contemplate. [The real world, that is, the human world, has constantly to be created. The reality science studies is only a partial reality. It would be better, however, to] express the contrast between a reality which is there to begin with and the greater reality which, like religious faith or artistic creation, does not exist at all to begin with, but is brought into being through a certain kind of human act.

[Science is a corporate activity, but so is art. When we see literature as a communal enterprise, we see that it is organized by huge containing conceptions called myths.] It is in these myths that the nature of man's concern for his world is most clearly expressed. To sum it up, then: it does not seem to me that the really important difference between the humanities and the sciences is in the difference in their subject-matter. It is rather that science exhibits a method and a mental attitude, of a stabilized subject and an impartial and detached treatment of evidence. The humanities, on the other hand, express in their containing forms, or myths, the nature of the human involvement with the human world. As long as man lives in the world, he will need the perspective and attitude of the scientist; but to the extent that he has created the world he lives in, feels responsible for and has a concern for its destiny, he will need the perspective and attitude of the humanist.

As I understand it, I am being asked to discuss the question: What do the humanities provide for human culture that the sciences do not provide? My own field is literature, and literature seems to belong to two groups: the creative arts, including music and painting, and the verbal disciplines, including history and philosophy. Both may be regarded as humanities, but we have to distinguish them even when we associate them. The question itself is, I suppose, legitimate enough: it is, I take it, simply a matter of trying to indicate the different functions of different things. It is difficult, and perhaps impossible, to contrast the arts and the sciences without a good deal of oversimplifying and making some false or half-true antitheses. There may be some value in over-simplifying the contrast, if one has to do that to make it at all: a more serious difficulty is that nobody is likely to approach such a problem with his mind fully made up, his convictions firmly held, and his tentative and exploratory notions outgrown. In what follows I am thinking aloud, expecting the kind of indulgence that is accorded to such improvisation.

It will not have escaped your notice that I have so far said nothing except 'harrumph'. But there is something to be said for the convention of beginning with an apology, or topos of modesty. This kind of question is often called, as I have just called it, a 'problem', and one expects a problem to be solved. A genuine problem is a specific formulation of experience that can be adequately stated in other terms: to use a common analogy, it is like a knot in a rope that can be untied or retied without affecting the identity of the rope. A question like this is only metaphorically a problem: it is actually a subject of study, and the word solution is not appropriate. All I can do with a subject of study is to individualize it, to make a suggestion or two about how it looks from the standpoint of a literary critic who is living in the mid-twentieth century.

As a subject of study, the question can hardly be called new: a whole line of philosophers from Hegel[1] onward have beaten their brains out over the difference between the knowledge of science and the knowledge of what the Germans call *Geist*, and over the methods and techniques appropriate to the study of history or sociology as distinct from biology or chemistry. It is an appropriate question for a centennial celebration, because it was one of the liveliest issues being debated a hundred years ago. The level of debate has not improved notably in tone since then. No contemporary treatment of the subject known to me matches the lucidity of Walter Bagehot's *Physics and Politics*, published in 1867, or the amiable and urbane discussion of Arnold and Huxley[2] about the proportioning of humanities and sciences in the curriculum of a liberal education. A few years ago we had the Leavis-Snow[3] dispute, where neither contribution was in the least amiable or urbane, and where it is hard to say which of the two documents was the more stupefyingly wrongheaded. Other essays purporting to defend the humanities have all too often a querulous ad self-righteous air, like that of a striptease performer who informs a newspaper reporter that while all the other girls just take off their clothes, she is an authentic artist. And so, after more than a century of giving answers to the question of what is distinctive about the humanities, it is still quite possible that the real answer is 'nothing at all'. Freud concludes his *Future of an Illusion* by saying: 'Science is not an illusion, but it would be an illusion to suppose that we could get anywhere else what it cannot give us.' He was talking about religion, but he may be unconditionally right, beyond the limits of his context, and everything nonscientific, except possibly the creative arts, may be only pre-scientific or pseudo-scientific. And the arts may be an exception only because their function may be a purely ornamental or decorative one. This conference, after all, deals with 'The Humanities and the Quest for Truth', and the arts not only never seem to find truth, but do not even appear to be looking for it very seriously.

The best way to approach our question, I think, is to begin by reversing it, as Freud's phrasing suggests. What does science provide for human culture that the arts and the humanities do not provide? The traditional answer, and doubtless the right one, is 'nature'. What I am saying here is that science gives us nature, not the understanding or conception of nature. This may only be bad grammar, but I mean something more than understanding. The human mind can operate in different ways, but one very obvious way for it to operate is my subject. That is, it can start by saying: Here am I, and I am here. Everything else is there. As soon as the mind does this, nature springs into being, like Athene from Jove's forehead, and reality appears to the mind as objective, as a field. It seems to me that it is peculiarly the function of science to objectify reality, to present the world in its aspect of being there. The world of science is the world of space: as has often been noted, science deals with time as a dimension of space. The subject itself becomes an object in this process, for there is nothing inside the scientist, from the structure of his spine to his infantile complexes, which is not also available for scientific study. Everything is there: nothing is really here except the consciousness with which he studies nature. And this consciousness, or scientific intelligence, is ideally disembodied. The theory of physics, for example, has been complicated, in its more rarefied aspects, by the fact that the scientist possesses a body, and cannot comprehend nature without physical contact. To see the world as an objective field of operation is also to quantify reality, to make it something measured rather than simply seen or heard. Isaiah praises a God 'Who hath measured the waters in the hollow of his hand, and meted out heaven with the span, and comprehended the dust of the earth in a measure, and weighed the mountains in scales, and the hills in a balance'. In science man takes over this traditional function of God, replacing the divine balance by the mathematician's equations.

Because science deals with reality as objective, there is no such thing as subjective science. What this means in practice is that science stabilizes the subject. It assumes a mind in the situation that we think of as sane or normal, ready to accept evidence and follow arguments. Thus science assumes a mind to some extent emancipated from existence, in the state of freedom or detachment that we call clarity. The sense of truth as an ideal, and of the pursuit of truth for its own sake as a virtue, go with the process of objectifying reality on which science is founded. The word truth itself carries with it the sense of a recognition of what is there. So does the sense of facts as given, as irreducible data to be studied in their inherent arrangements instead of being arranged. There may actually be no facts of this kind, but it is important to pretend that there are, that facts lie around immovably where they have been thrown, like rocks carried down by a glacier. As Wallace Stevens says:

> The arrangement contains the desire of
> The artist. But one confides in what has no
> Concealed creator.[4]

What science stands for in human life, then, is the revolt of consciousness against existence, the sense of his own uniqueness in nature that man gets by drawing his mind back from existence and contemplating it as a separated thing. The animal is immersed in existence without consciousness; the human being has consciousness, and consciousness means being capable, up to a point, of seeing existence as external to oneself. Of course, to withdraw from existence means to stop existing, and some philosophers, notably Sartre,[5] even go so far as to associate consciousness with nothingness or non-being. However, it seems clear that conscious human beings can externalize their world and still go on living. Human existence, then, is a complex, of which consciousness is one of many functions, and the concentrated consciousness that produces science is a stylizing or conventionalizing of human behaviour.

I do not wish to suggest that science is founded on a narrowly empirical view of the world: that its end is only to describe and understand what it sees. The physical sciences at least are not simply descriptive, but are based on prediction as well: they see their phenomena in time—or their version of time—as well as space, and their end is rather a vision of nature under law. It is not the experiment but the repeatable experiment that is the key to the understanding of nature in the physical sciences, and the repeatable experiment is what makes prediction possible and gives to science a prophetic quality. Telepathetic communication, poltergeists, mediums, have been approached experimentally and certain typical phenomena recur, but the experiments are not repeatable (except where they are fraudulent),[6] no laws can be established, and so science applied to such things never gets off the ground. Where the phenomena are unconscious or where the units involved are small and numerous, like atoms, molecules or cells, so that there is no practical difference between the highly probable and the certain, the language of science is primarily mathematical. From the natural sciences we move toward the social sciences, where the phenomena are relatively large, few, and complicated, like human beings. Here prediction on a statistical basis is as important as ever, but, except for some specialized aspects, the repeatable experiment is no longer at the centre of the study. In proportion as this is true, the subject tends to be organized verbally rather than mathematically. We then move into what are generally regarded as the humanities. History and philosophy are almost purely verbal, non-experimental, and non-predictive. But accuracy of statement, objectivity of description and dispassionate weighing of evidence, including the accepting of negative evidence, are still required. Hence a scientific element is still present in them that distinguishes history from legend, philosophy from rumination, and, as I think, literary criticism from a good many of the activities that go under that name. From there we move into the creative arts proper, where the requirements even of accurate descriptive statement and the basing of conclusions on fair evidence are no longer made, or at least not in the same way, and where therefore we may feel that we have finally escaped from science. But except for the arts, which pose separate problems, all scholars, whatever their fields, are bound by the same code of honour. All of them have to be as scientific as the nature of their subjects will allow them to be, or abandon all claim to be taken seriously.

The philosophers who moved from Kant[7] and Hegel towards the establishing of modern historical and sociological methods were largely preoccupied with the question of boundary lines. At what point does *Natur* turn into *Geist*? Precisely where do the methods that work in the physical sciences cease to become effective or appropriate? But it is surely possible that there are no boundary lines at all, and that this whole way of looking at knowledge as divided into two complementary bodies is wrong. The crudest form of this view is the one that I call the heart-of-darkness theory. It is a type of argument that used to be fashionable in natural theology (perhaps still is), and has been transferred to the humanities from there. There have been theories among religious apologists that religion, like the ghost of Hamlet's father, or the dancing fairies of Milton's Nativity Ode, belongs to a dark preserve of mystery on which the sun of science has not yet risen. Religion, according to this approach, deals with whatever seems at the moment to be beyond the capacities of science: creation at first, then the origin of life or the human soul, then moral values, and so on—it has to keep moving fairly fast, like the lunatic in Blake's 'Mad Song', to make sure of staying in the dark while science pursues it. Even yet there is a strong popular belief that if we once get hold of something that 'science cannot explain', whether it is extrasensory perception or the principle of indeterminacy or finding underground water with a hazel twig, we have a guarantee of free will and immortality and the existence of God.

The basis of such notions, when applied to the arts, is the assumption that if science deals rationally, factually, impersonally with an external world, the arts can only deal with an inner world of emotion, personality, and value. This really reduces itself to the assumption that if science is objective, the arts must be subjective. But subjective art is as impossible a conception as subjective science. The arts are techniques of communication: they are fostered by schools and groups and depend on convention quite as much as science does. In fact, there seems to be nothing that is really subjective except a rebellion against the stability of the attitude toward the world on which science is based. It is very tiring to keep on being open to involuntary sense impressions, to be detached and clear-headed, to weigh evidence and fit judgements to it, and very easy to relapse into an emotional colouring of experience, such as we get from day-dreaming or bad temper or private memories and associations. But however important and normally human in itself, the individual's emotional colouring of his own experience is not what the arts or the humanities are primarily concerned with. So whenever I read critical theories that begin by saying, in effect, 'Poetry is whatever mere science isn't', I flake out very quickly, because I know that some version of the subjective fallacy[8] is about to follow.

The genuine basis of this complementary view of the arts and sciences is the distinction, already glanced at and most elaborately set out in Bergson,[9] between time as externalized by science, where it is really a dimension of space, and time in its other form of the continuous awareness of one's own existence. This latter does elude science, so here is something that science cannot explain. But nothing else can explain it either, so that is not much help. All explanation contains some traces of scientific method, unless the explanation is really a clouding up of the question, like the doctor's explanation in Molière that opium puts people to sleep because it has a dormative faculty. But while the direct awareness of being cannot be explained, it can, up to a point, be expressed and this expression is the basis of the arts. The role of art, then, is primarily to express the complex of human existence, humanity's awareness of being itself rather than its perception of what is not itself and is outside it. This self-awareness is neither subjective nor objective, for man in himself is both an individual and, no less essentially, a member of the society which is partly inside him; and it is neither rational nor irrational. It does not quantify existence like science: it qualifies it: it tries to express not what is there but what is here, what is involved in consciousness and being themselves. The arts, then, belong to the phase of experience that we have learned to call existential, to an awareness that cannot be external to itself nor have anything external to it.

The production of art is, of course, a stylizing of behaviour like the production of science. As far as the actual man doing the work is concerned, I doubt whether there is any essential psychological difference between the artist and the scientist, any 'creative' factors present in one that are not present in the other. Both have to use the entire mind; both have much the same difficulties in getting that very complicated machine to work. But when we consider the finished product only, it is clear that the arts do not stabilize the subject in the same way that science does.

Emotions, repressed or mythopoeic elements in the subconscious, the manipulating of data, the summoning up of controlled hallucinations (as expressed in the traditional phrase about poetry, *ut pictura poesis*), all have a function in the creation of art. The stabilized subject of science is usually identified with the reason; the unstabilized subject is normally called the imagination. The individual artist is a representative of human imagination, just as the individual scientist is a representative of human reason. But at no point, *qua* artist, is he outside the human world we call culture or civilization, just as the physical scientist, *qua* physical scientist studying 'nature', is never inside it.

I speak, of course, of the arts in the plural because there is a group of them: music, literature, painting, sculpture, architecture, perhaps others. The dance, for instance, is in practice a separate art, though in theory it is difficult to see it as anything but a form of musical expression. It seems inherently unlikely, at the time of writing, that we have yet to develop a new art, despite all the strenuous experiment that there has been, some of it in that direction. Marshall McLuhan[10] says of the new media of communication that 'the medium is the message', and that the content of each medium is the form of another one. This surely means, if I understand it correctly, that each medium is a distinctive art. Thus the 'message' of sculpture is the medium of sculpture, distinct from the message which is the medium of painting. But, as McLuhan also emphasizes, the new media are extensions of the human body, of what we already do with our eyes and ears and throats and hands. Hence they have given us new forms or variations of the arts we now have, and the novelty of these forms constitutes a major imaginative revolution in our time. But though distinctive arts they are not actually new arts: they are new techniques for receiving the impression of words and pictures.

Of these arts, literature is the art of words, and words are also the medium for the humanities and much of the sciences. This suggests that the arts, besides being arts, may also be informing languages for other disciplines. A painting or a poem is a construct: you look first of all at the associative factors in it, the things that make it hold together. But besides having paintings we have pictures of things: that is, there are things outside painting that we understand pictorially. For centuries philosophers expressed themselves in words, taking words for granted, forgetting that there is an art of words, not realizing that the verbal basis of philosophy constitutes a philosophical problem in itself. It seems to have been only in our own time that philosophers and logicians have really tried to become aware of the limitations of form (as distinct from the mere pitfalls or fallacies) inherent in the use of words. Even now their interest seems to be mainly linguistic rather than properly literary, and some philosophers are no ignorant of the source of their own subject that they regularly use 'literary' in a pejorative sense. It is obvious that words lend themselves very readily to being an informing language for a descriptive discipline. Literature was not, up until the Romantic movement at least, regarded as the most impressive thing man does with words, the more objectified structures of theology and philosophy being regarded as higher in status and coming closer to what is called the quest for truth. As compared with music, or even painting, there is always some reference to the outer world implicit in every use of words. Even if in the future we leave painting to the chimpanzees and music to chance, I do not see how literature can ever lose its kernel of externalizable meaning. And yet the capacity of words for informing other disciplines is not unlimited. Compared with mathematics at least, words are incurably associative: multiple meanings lurk in them and the structures of grammar twist them into non-representational forms. It seems more likely that words have a certain radius of descriptive power, and that it is important to determine the approximate limits of that radius.

The other arts seem to differ widely in their powers of being able to inform other studies. Painting and sculpture, like literature, can be employed to represent the external world, and, again like literature, their descriptive or representational aspect has had more prestige in the past than their associative or constructive aspect. We can understand what their informing capacity is if we think not only of painting but of the pictorial arts, including illustrations, sketches, blueprints, diagrams, and models, and not only of sculpture but of the sculptural arts, including three-dimensional models. Some modern painters and sculptors, such as Miró or Giacometti, indicate the inherent relation of their arts with diagram and model very clearly. In some areas, such as geometry, the pictorial and the mathematical overlap, and of course the role of diagram in the sciences, as in the structural formulas of chemistry, is of immense importance. The question of whether light consists of waves or particles is surely, to some extent, a picturing problem. In my *Anatomy of Criticism* I have raised the question of the role of diagram in verbal thought as well. But to what extent and in what ways the pictorial and sculptural arts inform the humanities and sciences I do not know, nor have I read anybody who did know.

Music, on the other hand, has often been said to be the existential art par excellence, the hieratic, self-enclosed expression of 'pure being' with no relation to an externalized order of any kind. Perhaps this is because it is, as Mrs Langer[11] suggests, the art of 'virtual time', the closest expression of the continuous awareness of being which is the core of non-scientific experience. Or perhaps it is only because, up to the rise of electronic music, the music we know has been founded on a set of conventions as arbitrary as chess. On my piano as I write this is a sonata of Clementi called 'Didone Abbandonata': we are supposed to think of the story of Dido while we listen. The finale is a rondo beginning with what for Clementi is a sharp discord, a minor ninth, and the movement is hopefully marked 'con disperazione'. But it soon collapses into the ordinary rondo structure, and by the time we reach the second subject it is clear that poor Dido has been abandoned once more. A greater composer would have been more tactful or created a more compelling musical mood, but that is why the mediocre example illustrates more clearly my point, which is that music is not an informing art: it sets up a powerful centripetal force that resists being drawn into the structure of anything outside itself. We do use metaphors from music a good deal ('harmony', 'overtones', and the like), and the old fables about the music of the spheres suggest that music may have an unsuspected informing power about it. Perhaps the myth of heaven as a place where harp playing is a compulsory cultural accomplishment will come true, and the theology and metaphysics of the future will be understood musically rather than verbally. When I read or try to read Heidegger[12] I get the same feeling that I get when trying to read *Finnegans Wake*, of language dissolving into a mass of associative puns, and language of this kind is surely heading in the direction indicated by the squeals and groans of electronic music.

If words can be used both to construct an art and to inform some of the descriptive disciplines, there seems no reason why we should not think of mathematics, which informs so much of the physical sciences, as an art too. It is a self-contained construct like the arts, and I do not see how it is possible to frame a definition, or even a description, of the arts that would include the five I have listed and exclude mathematics. But mathematics is the art of numerical or quantitative relationships, and so it has a unique capacity for giving order and coherence to the sciences, of providing their descriptions and experiments with the repeatable element of law. In contrast to the other arts, it stabilizes the subject on the 'rational' level, as science does, and is so constantly informing the physical sciences that it is often regarded as simply a part of them. Hence some of the more speculatively minded scientists and philosophers are occasionally surprised to discover that nature has a mathematical form. Of course it has: they put it there. And because it informs science so readily, mathematics practised as an art in its own right is a rare and esoteric achievement, though its tradition can be traced from the semi-occult use of it associated with the name of Pythagoras down to the later work of Einstein.

The rise of modern science involved a new way of looking at the external world which is most lucidly set out in Locke,[13] though it had been there at least since Galileo. According to this the world has secondary qualities which are experienced by sensation, and primary qualities independent of such experience, which can only be weighed and measured. This distinction has a rough but significant analogy to the role of words in rendering the external world as compared with the role of mathematics. Mathematics is the language that can render the world of primary qualities: words never lose their connection with human action and human sensation on which the two primary categories of words, verbs and nouns, are based. To the extent that an electron, for instance, is given a name and made a noun, it becomes a potential object of perception, unlikely as it is that it will ever be an actual one. The radius of verbal information, then, apparently runs between the human body and its environment as perceived and experienced by that body. The non-literary function of words is thus, in the broad Kantian sense, critical: words can be used to explain the human situation, instead of merely expressing it as literature does, but they always remain connected with that situation.

The conception of science, as a systematic understanding of nature under law for which the appropriate language is mathematics, is, of course, a relatively recent one. For thousands of years before the great scientific explosion of the last few centuries, thinkers had been making constructs of the outer world, mainly verbal and pictorial. In these constructs the associative characteristics of the arts from which they were derived are very obvious. Poets find it much easier to live in the Ptolemaic universe than in ours, because it is more associative; modern poets turn from science to occultism because the latter still features associative patterns. Very early the two great containing conceptions of the scientific attitude made their appearance: 'substance', or the objectified world visible and invisible, and 'soul', the ideally disembodied intelligence which contemplates it. These parents then peopled the world with various offspring, ideas, essences, universals, atoms, and the like. The great difficulty with using words, when attempting to deal with primary qualities, is the readiness with which words adapt themselves to what we may call, altering Whitehead's[14] phrase, pseudo-concreteness. Adam named the animals because he could see them, but, as Theseus says in Shakespeare, it is just as easy to name airy nothings, to bestow nouns on and make verbal objects out of things that are not there, or cannot be proved to be there. Again, the prestige of the subject-object relationship meant that attempts to express what is genuinely existential, the human situation itself, could take the form of the *metaphorically* objective. The conception of a spiritual world is a metaphorical verbal object of this kind. With the rise of modern science, words have become more limited in their range. Metaphysics seemed for a time to be taking the form of a verbalized general science, expressing for its age some sense of what scientific activity as a whole is doing. It is more at home, however, with the assumptions on which scientific work is based, because those assumptions are part of the human context of science, and so they can be dealt with critically, which means verbally.

The principle of metaphorical object is of central importance when we try to see what the place of content is in the arts. The activity of consciousness, of externalizing reality, is always part of the whole existential complex. The aspect of painting that reproduces or 'imitates' an outer world exists in painting, as, so to speak, a metaphor of externality. Even music has, in the witty and paradoxical form of 'programme' music, a metaphorical external world of this kind, and literature has it in everything that we call realism. We are constantly using quantitative expressions (e.g. 'I love you very much') as metaphors for things that are not quantities. Aristotle, who approached the arts from a scientific point of view (one of his most illuminating comments on art is in the *Physics*), spoke of the arts as imitative of nature. But as soon as we examine this conception of imitation, the notion of a continuous relation to the external world begins to dissolve, and we can see that 'nature' exists in the art only as the content of art, as something that art surrounds and contains. So while science deals with the consolidating of what is there, the arts deal with the expanding of what is here; the circumference of science is the universe, the circumference of the arts is human culture. In our time the sense of cleavage between the expression of what is here and the study of what is there is very sharp. We tend to feel that whatever is objective or external belongs only to the spatial world of science: every other 'there' is a metaphor derived from that spatial world, and such metaphors no longer carry much conviction. Theology, for example, or at least the Protestant versions of it that I am more familiar with, is now trying to come to terms with the fact that nothing it is talking about is actually 'there'. God is certainly not 'there': he has been deprived of all scientific function and he has no status in the spatial world of science, including the temporal world that can be divided and measured. So whatever the present or future of theology may be, it cannot be the queen of sciences as we now think of science: science deals only with it, and can take no part in an I-Thou dialogue.

For a long time, of course, it was assumed that the study of nature was also the study of a revelation of God, the order and coherence of nature being assumed to be the result of divine design. This view was contemporary with the view that the models of human civilization themselves, the city and the garden, were also of divine origin. But just as man came finally to believe that he had created and was responsible for his own civilization, so he came also to believe that the real basis of science was the correspondence of nature and human reason. Whatever is there in nature, the mind can find something in verbal or mathematical reasoning that will explain, assimilate or inform it. 'The external world is fitted to the mind', as Wordsworth[15] says. So although nature is an externalized reality, it is not, for science, an alien one. In fact, science, as a form of knowledge, could even be thought of as a gigantic human narcissism, the reason falling in love with its own reflection in nature. Whenever there have been anti-scientific trends in human culture, they have usually seized on some aspect of this principle, though their target has been less science itself than the kind of essential philosophy that preceded it. Existentialism, for example, insists that if we think of the external world as a human world, certain elements become primary that are carefully kept out of science: the imminence of death, the feeling of alienation, the pervading sense of accident and of emptiness, and the direct confrontation with something arbitrary and absurd. Once we take away from externality the rational structure that we have put into it, it becomes what Milton calls a universal blank. All science is founded on the equation A equals B, where A is the human reason and B the rationally comprehensible element in nature. The existentialists may be described as the people who have discovered that if A equals B, then A minus B equals nothing.

We notice that existentialists have some difficulty in making their philosophy self-sufficient. Most of the best of them have incorporated it into a religious attitude, and of the atheistic ones, Heidegger went along with the Nazis and Sartre has recently collapsed on the bosom of the Church Marxist. It looks as though the attitude, along with whatever anti-scientific bias it may have, belongs in a larger context which is normally either religious or revolutionary, or both. That larger context is a view, found in very different forms in Blake, Kierkegaard, Nietzsche and D. H. Lawrence,[16] which might be paraphrased somewhat as follows:

Reality is primarily what we create, not what we contemplate. It is more important to know how to construct a human world than to know how to study a non-human one. Science and philosophy are significant as two of the creative things that man does, not as keys to the reality of the world out there. There is a world out there, but science sees it as a world under law, and no vision under law can ever give us the whole truth about anything. Science moves with greatest confidence, and makes its most startling discoveries, in a mechanical and unconscious world. If we remove science from its context and make it not a mental construct but an oracle of reality, the logical conclusion is that man ought to adjust himself to that reality on its terms. Thus moral law imitates natural law, and human life takes on the predictable characteristics of nature as science reveals it. What begins as reason ends in the conditioned reflexes of an insect state, where human beings have become cerebral automata. The real world, that is, the human world, has constantly to be created, and the one model on which we must not create it is that of the world out there. The world out there has no human values, hence we should think of it primarily not as real but as absurd. The existential paradoxes help us to do this, and they thereby reduce the world to the *tohu-wa-bohu*, the waste and void chaos of a world which man has once again to create.

In science applied to the human world, that is, in applied science and technology, we see the mathematical shape of science itself, from the pyramids of Egypt and the highways and aqueducts of Rome to the chessboard cities and cloverleaf intersections of our day. For Blake, and in some degree for Lawrence, these mathematical shapes in human life are symbols of aggression: human life is at its most mathematical and automatic in military operations, and in Blake the pyramid, and more particularly the 'Druid' trilithon, the ancestor of the Roman arch, are symbols of imperialistic hysteria and malevolence. Every advance in technology is likely to cause a immense legal complication in life, as the automobile has done, and the sheeplike panic-stricken stampeding of modern life, of which the totalitarian state is a by-product, is part of a technological way of life. Popular fiction has been exploiting the figure of the mad scientist for over a century, and there really does seem to be such a thing as mad science: psychology used to enslave people, nuclear physics used to exterminate the human race, microbiology suggesting even more lethal methods of trying to improve it. However, even in their most anti-scientific pronouncements such writers as Blake and Lawrence seldom if ever say that science is the direct cause of the sinister will to slavery in modern times. They say rather that man has lost his nerve about taking charge of his own world, through a false theory of knowledge in which he is 'idolatrous to his own shadow', as Blake says, and that this loss of nerve expresses itself as a perversion and parody of science. The world out there is real, but if we *deify* its reality, if we make it an object of imitation, it takes on the outlines of Satan the accuser, belittling us with its vast size in time and space, contemptuous of our efforts to be free of its colossal machinery.

The contrast I am paraphrasing is more conventionally phrased in other writers, and is often put into the form of an antithesis between values and facts. But the word value still has something prefabricated about it, a suggestion of something immutable laid up in a Platonic heaven. It is man's right to create his world that must be safeguarded, and every creation is likely to require a transvaluation of the past. Besides, values are really for the most part still forms of law, and do not get us out of our dilemma. The same is true of the moral categories of Kierkegaard, the 'ethical freedom' of the man who has passed beyond speculation. It would be better to use the existential terms engagement or concern to express the contrast between a reality which is there to begin with and the greater reality which, like religious faith or artistic creation, does not exist at all to begin with, but is brought into being through a certain kind of human act.

Science is increasingly a communal and corporate activity. The humanities are more individualized, and the arts are intensely so: schools and isms in the arts are a sign of youth and immaturity, of an authority not yet established in the single artist. When we think of the scientist as voyaging through strange seas of thought alone, as Wordsworth did Newton, we are probably thinking of him primarily as a mathematician. We are, in contrast to Communist countries, extremely permissive about a writer's loneliness: we allow our writers to retire into what sometimes seem very neurotic fairylands, because they may also be areas of the unstabilized imaginative vision. The result is that communication in and from the arts is a slow and cumbersome business, and that is why we need the dimension of criticism, the vision of artists as a society engaged in a communal enterprise.

As soon as we take this critical perspective on literature, we see that literature is organized by huge containing conceptions which establish the literary societies and the family resemblances among large groups of writers. We call these containing forms myths, and it is in these myths that the nature of man's concern for his world is most clearly expressed. Our own age expresses itself chiefly in the ironic myth, and irony marks the ascendance of a technological society and the tendency of man to imitate the natural law outside him. It is in the ironic mode that the writer deals with the human situation as though it were external to him and as though he were detached from it, and in this mode that he sees human behaviour as mechanized, frustrated, and absurd. If one were to say to almost any serious contemporary writer: 'But I don't like the characters and situations you present to me', he would almost certainly answer: 'That's because I'm trying to tell the truth as I see it.' In our day the writer defends himself in language parallel to the language of science and other objective disciplines. These myths also inform the structures built out of words that exist outside literature, that is, in general, the humanities. Existentialism, with its conceptions of anguish, nausea, and the like, is an ironic philosophy, a fact which accounts for the lack of self-sufficiency I spoke of before. Irony, in literature, is a sophisticated myth, best understood as a frustration or parody of the more primitive comic and romantic myths in which a quest is successfully accomplished. These romantic and comic myths are those that inform Christianity and the revolutionary myth of Marxism. Earlier in this paper I quoted from Freud's *Future of an Illusion*. Religion was a subject Freud had a Freudian block about, mainly because he wanted to be a lawgiving Moses in his own right, contemplating the back parts of his own God. As a literary critic, I am interested in the fact that Freud and Marx are the two most influential thinkers in the world today, that both of them developed an encyclopedic programme that they called scientific, and that nine-tenths of the science of both turns out to be applied mythology.

These mythical expressions of concern, in which man expresses his own attitude to the culture he has built, are subject to a disease of thinking which is best called anxiety, in the Freudian and not the existential sense. We often find that those who are committed to a religious or revolutionary faith have a peculiar difficulty in being intellectually honest in their arguments: their commitment wants to twist and manipulate facts, to maintain tendentious lines of reasoning, to rationalize or simply assert things for which there is no evidence. The record of Christianity is full of persecutions in the name of absurdities, and Marxism is also an anxiety structure, with a sensitive nose for heresies and deviations. The reason for this kind of anxiety is, again, a failure of nerve, a refusal to accept the fact that man continually creates his world anew, a desire to have it fit something outside itself. What is outside, in this sense, cannot be in space: it can only be in time, a pattern established in the past, or to be established in the future, to which all facts and discoveries somehow must be adjusted.

In the sciences it is possible to carry on one's studies with an undeveloped sense of concern. There are scientists who irritably brush off the suggestion that what they are doing may have momentous consequences for good or evil, and that they should be concerned for those consequences. A sense of concern would make such a scientist more presentable as a human being: it would also unite him to the community he lives in, and work against the dehumanizing tendency inherent in all specialization. There is no way of overcoming the barriers of specialization, no way of making a Romance philologist and a solid-state physicist intellectually intelligible to each other. But they are united by being both citizens of their society, and their realization of this makes both Romance philology and solid-state physics liberal arts, studies that liberate mankind. In science this social concern affects the scientist as man, but not so much *qua* scientist. But in the humanities the great poetic myths are also shaping forms: in history, in philosophy, in criticism, a scientific detachment and a humane engagement are fighting each other like Jacob and his angel. That is why the humanities are difficult to characterize, not only in methodology but even as a distinctive group of studies in themselves.

To sum up, then: it does not seem to me that the really important difference between the humanities and the sciences is in the difference in their subject-matter. It is rather that science exhibits a method and a mental attitude, most clearly in the physical sciences, of a stabilized subject and an impartial and detached treatment of evidence which is essential to all serious work in all fields. The humanities, on the other hand, express in their containing forms, or myths, the nature of the human involvement with the human world, which is essential to any serious man's attitude to life. As long as man lives in the world, he will need the perspective and attitude of the scientist; but to the extent that he has created the world he lives in, feels responsible for it and has a concern for its destiny, which is also his own destiny, he will need the perspective and attitude of the humanist.

Notes

[1] Georg Wilhelm Friedrich Hegel (1770–1831), a German philosopher, attempted to understand the universe in terms of faith. He saw knowing the infinite and seeing all things in God as the task of philosophy.

[2] Matthew Arnold (1822–1888), the Victorian poet, engaged Thomas Henry Huxley (1825–1895), the foremost advocate of Darwin, in a debate on the role of science in a liberal education.

[3] F.R. Leavis (1895–1978), a British literary critic and poet, in 1962 debated C.P. Snow (1905–1972) on the topic of science and literature. Snow, a novelist and scientist, diagnoses society's intellectuals as divided into two cultures unable to speak the same language, but he found the scientific culture superior. Leavis advocated the superiority of literature.

[4] "So-and-So Reclining on a Couch," *Collected Poems.* [Frye]

[5] Jean Paul Sartre (1905–1980) was a French philosopher and novelist whose emphasis on human freedom and individual responsibilty identifies him as one of the central existential thinkers.

[6] This refers to what is usually called spiritualism, not to controlled experiments in extrasensory perception and the like, where there is no question of fraud. [Frye]

[7] Immanuel Kant (1724–1804), a German philosopher, argued that we could have knowledge only of experiences in the finite world. In many respects Kant's philosophy advanced scientific philosophy.

[8] subjective fallacy: an erroneous critical approach relying on the view that only the artist's and the critic's subjective emotional experiences inform literature and art.

[9] Henri Bergson (1859–1941), the influential French philosopher, argued that time itself forms philosophy's central ontological concern.

[10] Marshall McLuhan, a Canadian communication theorist, in *The Medium Is the Message* (1965) advanced the theory that the form of a communication medium—print, television, film—influences an audience as much or more than the message contained in the medium.

[11] *Feeling and Form* by Susanne Langer (1953). [Frye]

[12] Martin Heidegger (1889–1976) was a German philosopher who exercised a major influence on existentialism.

[13] John Locke (1632–1704), the English philosopher, initiated the Age of Enlightenment and Reason in England and France, inspired the American Constitution, and influenced western thought for four hundred years after his death. Central to Locke's philosophy is the idea that knowledge derives only from experience and reflection on experience—the senses establish knowledge empirically.

[14] Alfred North Whitehead (1861–1947), an English mathematician and philosopher, examined the implications of science for philosophy. His 1927 essay "Science and the Modern World" attempts to reconcile science and the humanities.

[15] William Wordsworth (1770–1850) was an English Romantic poet and critic.

[16] William Blake (1757–1827) was an English Romantic poet. Soren Kierkegaard (1813–1855), a Danish philosopher and theologian, opposed Hegel's objective philosophy and based his own philosophy on faith and knowledge. His emphasis on the individual quality of religious faith identifies him as a Christian existentialist. Friedrich Nietzsche (1844–1900), a German philosopher, denounced all religion and championed the "morals of

masters," the doctrine of the perfectability of man through forcible self-assertion. The English novelist D.H. Lawrence (1885–1930) created characters motivated by unconscious forces in such novels as *Sons and Lovers* and *The Rainbow*. Despite his reliance on the unconscious, Lawrence mistrusted psychology because it imposed a rational order on what Lawrence saw as mystical.

FOCUS: READING REVIEW

1. How does science define reality? How does this differ from the arts' conception of reality?
2. What are the dual functions of language for the arts? How does science use language?
3. Frye talks of man creating the world he lives in. What does he mean by this? What does he suggest are the distinctions between the world the scientist creates and the world the humanist creates?
4. Frye uses the word myth not to mean "falsehood," but to mean a form of conceptualization that orders human experience. What are the components of Frye's myths?

FOCUS: AUTHOR'S STRATEGIES

1. Frye is addressing an audience of humanists. How does he fit his description of science to their expectations? What objections might a scientist raise to this view?
2. Frye begins his essay with the question he is to discuss. What does he do with the question so he can shape his response? How does he use this?
3. This is an extended comparative analysis with definition. What analytic components frame Frye's essay? What concepts does he define?

FOCUS: DISCUSSION AND WRITING

When identifying the differences between scientists and humanists, Frye states ". . . all scholars, whatever their fields, are bound by the same code of honour. All of them have to be as scientific as the nature of their subjects will allow them to be." How does this compare to Bronowski's discussion of ethics in the sciences?

TOPICS: **Further Research, Synthesis, and Writing in the Natural Sciences**

1. Bronowski says that the scientific community conducts itself with high regard for the values of a democratic society. Because of environmental concerns, research in such areas as nuclear weapons and genetic engineering have given rise to universities and research institutions imposing rules for research on the scientific community. Find out what rules, if any, govern scientific research at your college or university. Write an essay in which you argue for the necessity or lack of necessity for these rules.

2. McCain and Segal and Bronowski acknowledge the distance between science and nonscientists at the same time as they ask for public awareness of science. Select an article from the chapter on work in the natural sciences and use it as a case to support a written argument for or against the importance of lay knowledge in this particular scientific area.

3. Bodmer's essay discusses areas where biomedical research has created social and ethical choices for society. Because people can discover if they carry "defects" like sickle-cell anemia, hemophilia, or Tay Sach's disease, they can choose to avoid or terminate a pregnancy. Write a paper in which you explain to a "lay" audience that may be subject to a genetically transmitted disease what that disease is, how it can be discovered, and what options exist for carriers. You may have to research beyond Bodmer's article for a fuller understanding of the disease.

4. The November 1985 issue of *Psychology Today* featured articles on differences between men and women. Using Weintraub's essay as a model, write an essay summarizing recent findings reported in *Psychology Today*.

5. Consider recent findings on male-female differences and compare them with Weintraub's essay. Write a paper on whether or not men and women think differently, relying on your readings for evidence.

6. Science has led us to prize objectivity and evidence. Consider McCain and Segal's essay in relation to Frye's and write a paper in which you explain the necessity for or limitation of objectivity. Rely on your own experiences—education, entertainment, recreation, relationships—as an arena for your discussion.

7. Ask several family members and friends what they think science is. List seven to ten statements you would have made about science before reading the preceding selections. Make a list of the major ideas you encountered about science (both true and false). Write an extended definition of science focused on reinforcing the positive conceptions, eliminating the misunderstandings, and, if necessary, admitting science's limitations.

8. The essays in this section mentioned several areas in which scientific research affects public policy (evolutionary theory, genetically transmitted diseases, nuclear weapons research, or intelligence testing, for example). Select one of these topics and through further research identify the public policy issue and the principal positions. Write a paper in which you:

    a. identify and give a history of the issue.
    b. summarize each side's position.
    c. assess the strengths and weaknesses of each position's evidence.
    d. present your own argument, based on evidence, stating which position is most valid.

As an example, if you took evolutionary theory, you might examine how it has become a public policy issue in textbook adoptions, school district elections, or curriculum decisions. Be certain to narrow your topic to one policy.

THE
⦿ SOCIAL SCIENCES ⦿

Chapter 4
The
Governing
Assumptions

The social sciences' study of human behavior and interaction ranges from social, political, and economic institutions to the individual person's motivation and behavior. This work largely identifies as its methods the assumptions governing the natural sciences described by McCain and Segal, Huxley, and Bronowski in chapter 1 of this part, "The Governing Assumptions" in the natural sciences. The diversity of human institutions and behavior, however, require an area like psychology to formulate different investigative methods from those of sociology, anthropology, or economics. The essays in this chapter indicate some of the varied approaches in the social sciences.

Articles by Freud and Skinner address the variety in theoretical models governing psychology. "The Mind and Its Workings" presents Freud's theory of the unconscious, which forms the basis of psychoanalytic theory. Skinner, in "The Causes of Behavior," believes that psychological studies should focus not on the mind, as Freud believes, but on observable behavior, which can be studied scientifically. Berger's "Sociology as a Form of Consciousness" identifies sociology as a particular way of viewing human social institutions, one requiring distance, skepticism, and an ability to "see through" society. The branch of anthropology known as ethnography, according to Geertz in "Thick Description: Toward an Interpretive Theory of Culture," calls on the social scientist to objectively record a culture's detailed behavioral data.

The essays included here barely touch the social sciences' breadth. They do, though, indicate recurrent themes: the value of scientific study of human institutions and behavior, the importance of objectivity, and, to some degree, the difficulty in gathering and interpreting data. The essays by Freud and Skinner, especially when read in conjunction with the reviews of Skinner in the chapter on critical responses in the social sciences, reveal how difficult the study of human motivation and behavior can be. The human mind is complex and not yet fully understood; as such, it does not afford a fixed object of study. Not only do the social sciences encounter variable and sometimes elusive subjects, but researchers bring human limitations to their studies, as Geertz suggests. The social sciences, then, despite their commitment to scientific principles and objectivity, must contend with human subjectivity.

The Mind and Its Workings
Sigmund Freud

Sigmund Freud (1865–1939), the father of psychoanalysis, was born in Moravia, but spent most of his life in Vienna. His early career began in medicine, but he gained recognition in psychology from an influential study of hysteria written in collaboration with Josef Breuer. This study found that the conscious mind rejects conflict derived from repressed sex and aggression. This conflict rejection leads to mental disorders. Psychoanalysis seeks to resolve the conflicts by bringing them to the conscious mind through dream analysis and free association. Freud's impact on modern thought has been so great that we frequently use language borrowed from Freud (id, ego, libido, oral fixation) *with considerable imprecision.* The Outline of Psychoanalysis, *from which this selection is taken, outlines briefly, but completely, the fundamental tenets of Freud's theories of psychology. This selection describes the three parts of the human psyche (id, ego, and superego), accounts for instinct's influences on the human psyche, and details sexual development. Finally, in a few short sentences it states the fundamental principle of psychoanalysis: Inhibition in the development of the sexual function manifests itself in disturbance.*

We know two kinds of things about what we call our psyche for we have arrived at our knowledge of the psychical apparatus by studying the individual development of human beings. To the oldest of these psychical agencies we give the name of *id.* It contains everything that is inherited, above all, the instincts. Under the influence of the real external world around us, one portion of the id has undergone a special development and acts as an intermediary between the id and the external world. To this region of our mind we have given the name of *ego.* The ego strives after pleasure and seeks to avoid unpleasure. [The long period of childhood forms a special agency, in which parental influence is prolonged, called the *superego*.] The id and the superego have one thing in common: they both represent the influences of the past, whereas the ego is principally determined by the individual's own experience. The id seeks to satisfy the individual organism's innate needs. The forces which we assume to exist behind the tensions caused by the needs of the id are called *instincts*. We assume the existence of only two basic instincts, *Eros* and *the destructive instinct*.

THE PSYCHICAL APPARATUS

Psycho-analysis makes a basic assumption, the discussion which is reserved to philosophical thought but the justification for which lies in its results. We know two kinds of things about what we call our psyche (or mental life): firstly, its bodily organ and scene of action, the brain (or nervous system) and, on the other hand, our acts of consciousness, whch are immediate data and cannot be further explained by any sort of description. Everything that lies between is unknown to us, and the data to not include any direct relation between these two terminal points of our knowledge. If it existed, it would at the most afford an exact localization of the processes of consciousness and would give us no help towards understanding them.

Our two hypotheses start out from these ends or beginnings of our knowledge. The first is concerned with localization. We assume that mental life is the function of an apparatus to which we ascribe the characteristics of being extended in space and of being made up of several portions—which we imagine, that is, as resembling a telescope or microscope or something of the kind. Notwithstanding some earlier attempts in the same direction, the consistent working-out of a conception such as this is a scientific novelty.

We have arrived at our knowledge of this psychical apparatus by studying the individual development of human beings. To the oldest of these psychical provinces or agencies we give the name of *id*. It contains everything that is inherited, that is present at birth, that is laid down in the constitution—above all, therefore, the instincts, which originate from the somatic organization and which find a first psychical expression here [in the id] in forms unknown to us.

Under the influence of the real external world around us, one portion of the id has undergone a special development. From what was originally a cortical layer, equipped with the organs for receiving stimuli and with arrangements for acting as a protective shield against stimuli, a special organization has arisen which henceforward acts as an intermediary between the id and the external world. To this region of our mind we have given the name of *ego*.

Here are the principal characteristics of the ego. In consequence of the pre-established connection between sense perception and muscular action, the ego has voluntary movement at its command. It has the task of self-preservation. As regards *external* events, it performs that task by becoming aware of stimuli, by storing up experiences about them (in the memory), by avoiding excessively strong stimuli (through flight), by dealing with moderate stimuli (through adaptation) and finally by learning to bring about expedient changes in the external world to its own advantage (through activity). As regards *internal* events, in relation to the id, it performs that task by gaining control over the demands of the instincts, by deciding whether they are to be allowed satisfaction, by postponing that satisfaction to times and circumstances favourable in the external world or by suppressing their excitations entirely. It is guided in its activity by consideration of the tensions produced by stimuli, whether these tensions are present in it or introduced into it. The raising of these tensions is in general felt as *unpleasure* and their lowering as *pleasure*. It is probable, however, that what is felt as pleasure or unpleasure is not the *absolute* height of this tension but something in the rhythm of the changes in them. The ego strives after pleasure and seeks to avoid unpleasure. An increase in unpleasure that is expected and foreseen is met by a *signal of anxiety*; the occasion of such an increase, whether it threatens from without or within, is known as a *danger*. From time to time the ego gives up its connection with the external world and withdraws into the state of sleep, in which it makes far-reaching changes in its organization. It is to be inferred from the state of sleep that this organization consists in a particular distribution of mental energy.

The long period of childhood, during which the growing human being lives in dependence on his parents, leaves behind it as a precipitate the formation in his ego of a special agency in which this parental influence is prolonged. It has received the name of *super-ego*. In so far as this super-ego is differentiated from the ego or is opposed to it, it constitutes a third power which the ego must take into account.

An action by the ego is as it should be if it satisfies simultaneously the demands of the id, of the super-ego and of reality—that is to say, if it is able to reconcile their demands with one another. The details of the relation between the ego and the super-ego become completely intelligible when they are traced back to the child's attitude to its parents. This parental influence of course includes in its operation not only the personalities of the actual parents but also the family, racial and national traditions handed on through them, as well as the demands of the immediate social *milieu* which they represent. In the same way, the super-ego, in the course of an individual's development, receives contributions from later successors and substitutes of his parents, such as teachers and models in public life of admired social ideals. It will be observed that, for all their fundamental difference, the id and the super-ego have one thing in common: they both represent the influences of the past—the id the influence of heredity, the super-ego the influence, essentially, of what is taken over from the other people—whereas the ego is principally determined by the individual's own experience, that is by accidental and contemporary events.

This general schematic picture of a psychical apparatus may be supposed to apply as well to the higher animals which resemble man mentally. A super-ego must be presumed to be present wherever, as is the case with man, there is a long period of dependence in childhood. A distinction between ego and id is an unavoidable assumption. Animal psychology has not yet taken in hand the interesting problem which is here presented.

THE THEORY OF THE INSTINCTS

The power of the id expresses the true purpose of the individual organism's life. This consists in the satisfaction of its innate needs. No such purpose as that of keeping itself alive or of protecting itself from dangers by means of anxiety can be attributed to the id. That is the task of the ego, whose business it also is to discover the most favourable and least perilous method of obtaining satisfaction, taking the external world into account. The super-ego may bring fresh needs to the fore, but its main function remains the limitation of satisfactions.

The forces which we assume to exist behind the tensions caused by the needs of the id are called *instincts*. They represent the somatic demands upon the mind. Though they are the ultimate cause of all activity, they are of a conservative nature; the state, whatever it may be, which an organism has reached gives rise to a tendency to re-establish that state so soon as it has been abandoned. It is thus possible to distinguish an indeterminate number of instincts, and in common practice this is in fact done. For us, however, the important question arises whether it may not be possible to trace all these numerous instincts back to a few basic ones. We have found that instincts can change their aim (by displacement) and also that they can replace one another—the energy of one instinct passing over to another. This latter process is still insufficiently understood. After long hesitancies and vacillations we have decided to assume the existence of only two basic instincts, *Eros*[1] and *the destructive instinct*. (The contrast between the instincts of self-preservation and the preservation of the species, as well as the contrast between ego-love and object-love, fall within Eros.) The aim of the first of these basic instincts is to establish ever greater unities and to preserve them thus—in short, to bind together; the aim of the second is, on the contrary, to undo connections and so to destroy things. In the case of the destructive instinct we may suppose that its final aim is to lead what is living into an inorganic state. For this reason we also call it the *death instinct*. If we assume that living things came later than inanimate ones and arose from them, then the death instinct fits in with the formula we have proposed to the effect that instincts tend towards a return to an earlier state. In the case of Eros (or the love instinct) we cannot apply this formula. To do so would presuppose that living substance was once a unity which had later been torn apart and was now striving towards re-union.

In biological functions the two basic instincts operate against each other or combine with each other. Thus, the act of eating is a destruction of the object with the final aim of incorporating it, and the sexual act is an act of aggression with the purpose of the most intimate union. This concurrent and mutually opposing action of the two basic instincts gives rise to the whole variegation of the phenomena of life. The analogy of our two basic instincts extends from the sphere of living things to the pair of opposing forces—attraction and repulsion—which rule in the inorganic world.

Modifications in the proportions of the fusion between the instincts have the most tangible results. A surplus of sexual aggressiveness will turn a lover into a sex-murderer, while a sharp diminution in the aggressive factor will make him bashful or impotent.

There can be no question of restricting one or the other of the basic instincts to one of the provinces of the mind. They must necessarily be met with everywhere. We may picture an initial state as one in which the total available energy of Eros, which henceforward we shall speak of as 'libido', is present in the still undifferentiated ego-id and serves to neutralize the destructive tendencies which are simultaneously present. (We are without a term analogous to 'libido' for describing the energy of the destructive instinct.) At a later stage it becomes relatively easy for us to follow the vicissitudes[2] of the libido, but this is more difficult with the destructive instinct.

So long as that instinct operates internally, as a death instinct, it remains silent; it only comes to our notice when it is diverted outwards as an instinct of destruction. It seems to be essential for the preservation of the individual that this diversion should occur; the muscular apparatus serves this purpose. When the super-ego is established, considerable amounts of the aggressive instinct are fixated[3] in the interior of the ego and operate there self-destructively. This is one of the dangers to health by which human beings are faced on the path to cultural development. Holding back aggressiveness is in general unhealthy and leads to illness. A person in a fit of rage will often demonstrate how the transition from aggressiveness that has been prevented to self-destructiveness is brought about by diverting the aggressiveness against himself: he tears his hair or beats his face with his fists, though he would evidently have preferred to apply this treatment to someone else. Some portion of self-destructiveness remains within, whatever the circumstances; till at last it succeeds in killing the individual, not, perhaps, until his libido has been used up or fixated in a disadvantageous way. Thus it may in general be suspected that the *individual* dies of his internal conflicts but that the *species* dies of its unsuccessful struggle against the external world if the latter changes in a fashion which cannot be adequately dealt with by the adaptations which the species has acquired.

It is hard to say anything of the behaviour of the libido in the id and in the super-ego. All that we know about it relates to the ego, in which at first the whole available quota of libido is stored up. We call this state absolute, primary *narcissism*. It lasts till the ego begins to cathect[4] the ideas of objects with libido, to transform narcissistic libido into object-libido. Throughout the whole of life the ego remains the great reservoir from which libidinal cathexes are sent out to objects and into which they are also once more withdrawn, just as an amoeba behaves with its pseudopodia.[5] It is only when a person is completely in love that the main quota of libido is transferred on to the object and the object to some extent takes the place of the ego. A characteristic of the libido which is important in life is its *mobility*, the facility with which it passes from one object to another. This must be contrasted with the *fixation* of the libido to particular objects, which often persists throughout life.

There can be no question but that the libido has somatic sources, that it streams to the ego from various organs and parts of the body. This is most clearly seen in the case of that portion of the libido which, from its instinctual aim, is described as sexual excitation. The most prominent of the parts of the body from which this libido arises are known by the name of *'erotogenic zones'*, though in fact the whole body is an erotogenic zone of this kind. The greater part of what we know about Eros—that is to say, about its exponent, the libido—has been gained from a study of the sexual function, which, indeed, on the prevailing view, even it not according to our theory, coincides with Eros. We have been able to form a picture of the way in which the sexual urge, which is destined to exercise a decisive influence on our life, gradually develops out of successive contributions from a number of component instincts, which represent particular erotogenic zones.

Notes

[1] Eros: the love instinct named for the Greek god of love.

[2] vicissitudes: unpredictable changes or variations.

[3] fixated: that which is attached to or stopped at an early stage of psychosexual development.

[4] cathect: to concentrate psychic energy on. The noun form *cathexis* indicates a concentration of psychic energy on one particular person, idea, or aspect of the self.

[5] pseudopodia: the temporary projection of protoplasm in one-cell or some multicell animals, which eats and propels the organism.

FOCUS: **READING REVIEW**

1. What are the three parts of the psyche? What are their principal characteristics? From what do they derive?
2. What is the relationship between id, ego, and superego?
3. Freud ascribes the primary motivation of the id to instinct. What is an instinct? What are the key instincts?
4. What does Freud mean when he says, "When the super-ego is established, considerable amounts of the aggressive instinct are fixated in the interior of the ego and operate there self-destructively."

FOCUS: AUTHOR'S STRATEGIES

1. When Freud asserts "we have arrived at our knowledge of the psychical apparatus by studying the individual development of human beings," what audience does this suggest? What other clues do you find for the audience?
2. Is the language of the piece abstract or concrete, specific or general? What does this indicate about the writer's persona and his relationship with his audience?
3. What is the writer's tone? What does this indicate about his audience and purpose?

FOCUS: DISCUSSION AND WRITING

1. Freud asserts that "holding back aggressiveness is in general unhealthy and leads to illness." Does our society agree or disagree with this notion? Cite instances to illustrate your response.
2. Freud's theory relies on certain assumptions about the mind, the role of sexual development, and the cause of disturbance. What are these assumptions? What other explanations might be offered for the phenomena he considers?
3. This essay is very dense, that is, it refers to many aspects of Freud's theory—the three parts of the psyche; the pursuit of pleasure and avoidance of pain; and the role of childhood experiences in relation to neurosis, the instincts, sex, and aggression. Select one of these subtopics and look it up in an encyclopedia and library card catalogue. Explain the theory more fully using definition and examples.

The Causes of Behavior

B. F. Skinner

B. F. Skinner (b. 1904), a professor of psychology at Harvard University distinguished by his extensive work in behavioral psychology, attended Hamilton College and received his M.A. and Ph.D. in psychology from Harvard. His books Behavior of Organisms *(1938),* Verbal Behavior *(1957),* Beyond Freedom and Dignity *(1971), and* About Behaviorism *(1974), as well as over a hundred articles, have earned him the reputation of the United States's foremost behaviorist. Behaviorism identifies human behavior as a series of responses conditioned by a person's genetic and physical environment. This selection, "The Causes of Behavior," taken from* About Behaviorism, *suggests the differences between psychology that focuses on the human mind (Freud or Jung for example) and psychology as a science of external behavior. In chapter 6, "Critical Responses to the Social Sciences," an essay by Thomas Szasz attacks Skinner and Willard Day defends him.*

Why do people behave as they do? The answer can be reduced to a question about causes. Many of the things we observe just before we behave occur within our body [feelings], and it is easy to take them as the causes of our behavior. The traditional explanation of feelings [mentalisms] is that they are located in a world of nonphysical dimensions called the mind and that they are mental. Physicalism holds that when we introspect or have feelings we are looking at states or activities of our brains. [Structuralists abandon the search for causes and simply describe what people do. Structuralism tells us how people behave but throws very little light on why they behave as they do. But how can a mental event cause or be caused by a physical one? The mentalist problem can be avoided by going directly to the prior physical causes while bypassing intermediate feelings or states of mind—by considering only those facts which can be objectively observed in the behavior of one person in relation to his prior environmental history. This is the approach of methodological behaviorism. Methodological behaviorism rules private events out of bounds because there can be no public agreement about their validity. Radical behaviorism takes a different line. Radical behaviorism restores a balance between mentalism, which keeps attention away from the external antecedent events that might have explained behavior, and methodological behaviorism, which deals exclusively with external events. turning attention away from self-observation and self-knowledge.]

Why do people behave as they do? It was probably first a practical question: How could a person anticipate and hence prepare for what another person would do? Later it would become practical in another sense: How could another person be induced to behave in a given way? Eventually it became a matter of understanding and explaining behavior. It could always be reduced to a question about causes.

We tend to say, often rashly, that if one thing follows another, it was probably caused by it—following the ancient principle of *post hoc, ergo propter hoc* (after this, therefore because of this). Of many examples to be found in the explanation of human behavior, one is especially important here. The person with whom we are most familiar is ourself; many of the things we observe just before we behave occur within our body, and it is easy to take them as the causes of our behavior. If we are asked why we have spoken sharply to a friend, we may reply, "Because I felt angry." It is true that we felt angry before, or as, we spoke, and so we take our anger to be the cause of our remark. Asked why we are not eating our dinner, we may say, "Because I do not feel hungry." We often feel hungry when we eat and hence conclude that we eat because we feel hungry. Asked why we are going swimming, we may reply, "Because I feel like swimming." We seem to be saying, "When I have felt like this before, I have behaved in such and such a way." Feelings occur at just the right time to serve as causes of behavior, and they have been cited as such for centuries. We assume that other people feel as we feel when they behave as we behave.

But where are these feelings and states of mind? Of what stuff are they made? The traditional answer is that they are located in a world of nonphysical dimensions called the mind and that they are mental. But another question then arises: How can a mental event cause or be caused by a physical one? If we want to predict what a person will do, how can we discover the mental causes of his behavior, and how can we produce the feelings and states of mind which will induce him to behave in a given way? Suppose, for example, that we want to get a child to eat a nutritious but not very palatable food. We simply make sure that no other food is available, and eventually he eats. It appears that in depriving him of food (a physical event) we have made him feel hungry (a mental event), and that because he has felt hungry, he has eaten the nutritious food (a physical event). But how did the physical act of deprivation lead to the feeling of hunger, and how did the feeling move the muscles involved in ingestion? There are many other puzzling questions of this sort. What is to be done about them?

The commonest practice is, I think, simply to ignore them. It is possible to believe that behavior expresses feelings, to anticipate what a person will do by guessing or asking him how he feels, and to change the environment in the hope of changing feelings while paying little if any attention to theoretical problems. Those who are not quite comfortable about such a strategy sometimes take refuge in physiology. Mind, it is said, will eventually be found to have a physical basis. As one neurologist recently put it, "Everyone now accepts the fact that the brain provides the physical basis of human thought." Freud believed that his very complicated mental apparatus would eventually be found to be physiological, and early introspective psychologists called their discipline Physiological Psychology. The theory of knowledge called Physicalism holds that when we introspect or have feelings we are looking at states or activities of our brains. But the major difficulties are practical: we cannot anticipate what a person will do by looking directly at his feelings *or* his nervous system, nor can we change his behavior by changing his mind *or* his brain. But in any case we seem to be no worse off for ignoring philosophical problems.

STRUCTURALISM

A more explicit strategy is to abandon the search for causes and simply describe what people do. Anthropologists can report customs and manners, political scientists can take the line of "behavioralism" and record political action, economists can amass statistics about what people buy and sell, rent and hire, save and spend, and make and consume, and psychologists can sample attitudes and opinions. All this may be done through direct observation, possibly with the help of recording systems, and with interviews, questionnaires, tests, and polls. The study of literature, art, and music is often confined to the forms of these products of human behavior, and linguists may confine themselves to phonetics, semantics, and syntax. A kind of prediction is possible on the principle that what people have often done they are likely to do again; they follow customs because it is customary to follow them, they exhibit voting or buying habits, and so on. The discovery of organizing principles in the structure of behavior—such as "universals" in cultures or languages, archetypal patterns in literature, or psychological types—may make it possible to predict instances of behavior that have not previously occurred.

The structure or organization of behavior can also be studied as a function of time or age, as in the development of a child's verbal behavior or his problem-solving strategies or in the sequence of stages through which a person passes on his way from infancy to maturity, or in stages through which a culture evolves. History emphasizes changes occurring in time, and if patterns of development or growth can be discovered, they may also prove helpful in predicting future events.

Control is another matter. Avoiding mentalism (or "psychologism") by refusing to look at causes exacts its price. Structuralism and developmentalism do not tell us why customs are followed, why people vote as they do or display attitudes or traits of character, or why different languages have common features. Time or age cannot be manipulated; we can only wait for a person or a culture to pass through a developmental period.

In practice the systematic neglect of useful information has usually meant that the data supplied by the structuralist are acted upon by others—for example, by decision-makers who in some way manage to take the causes of behavior into account. In theory it has meant the survival of mentalistic concepts. When explanations are demanded, primitive cultural practices are attributed to "the mind of the savage," the acquisition of language to "innate rules of grammar," the development of problem-solving strategies to the "growth of the mind," and so on. In short, structuralism tells us how people behave but throws very little light on why they behave as they do. It has no answer to the question with which we began.

METHODOLOGICAL BEHAVIORISM

The mentalistic problem can be avoided by going directly to the prior physical causes while bypassing intermediate feelings or states of mind. The quickest way to do this is to confine oneself to what an early behaviorist, Max Meyer, called the "psychology of the other one": consider only those facts which can be objectively observed in the behavior of one person in its relation to his prior environmental history. If all linkages are lawful, nothing is lost by neglecting a supposed nonphysical link. Thus, if we know that a child has not eaten for a long time, and if we know that he therefore feels hungry and that because he feels hungry he then eats, then we know that if he has not eaten for a long time, he will eat. And if by making other food inaccessible, we make him feel hungry, and if because he feels hungry he then eats a special food, then it must follow that by making other food inaccessible, we induce him to eat the special food.

Similarly, if certain ways of teaching a person lead him to notice very small differences in his "sensations," and if because he sees these differences he can classify colored objects correctly, then it should follow that we can use these ways of teaching him to classify objects correctly. Or, to take still another example, if circumstances in a white person's history generate feelings of aggression toward blacks, and if those feelings make him behave aggressively, then we may deal simply with the relation between the circumstances in his history and his aggressive behavior.

There is, of course, nothing new in trying to predict or control behavior by observing or manipulating prior public events. Structuralists and developmentalists have not entirely ignored the histories of their subjects, and historians and biographers have explored the influences of climate, culture, persons, and incidents. People have used practical techniques of predicting and controlling behavior with little thought to mental states. Nevertheless, for many centuries there was very little systematic inquiry into the role of the physical environment, although hundreds of highly technical volumes were written about human understanding and the life of the mind. A program of methodological behaviorism became plausible only when progress began to be made in the scientific observation of behavior, because only then was it possible to override the powerful effect of mentalism in diverting inquiry away from the role of the environment.

Mentalistic explanations allay curiosity and bring inquiry to a stop. It is so easy to observe feelings and states of mind at a time and in a place which make them seem like causes that we are not inclined to question further. Once the environment begins to be studied, however, its significance cannot be denied.

Methodological behaviorism might be thought of as a psychological version of logical positivism or operationism, but they are concerned with different issues. Logical positivism or operationism holds that since no two observers can agree on what happens in the world of the mind, then from the point of view of physical science mental events are "unobservables"; there can be no truth by agreement, and we must abandon the examination of mental events and turn instead to how they are studied. We cannot measure sensations and perceptions as such, but we can measure a person's capacity to discriminate among stimuli, and the *concept* of sensation or perception can then be reduced to the *operation* of discrimination.

The logical positivists had their version of "the other one." They argued that a robot which behaved precisely like a person, responding in the same way to stimuli, changing its behavior as a result of the same operations, would be indistinguishable from a real person, even though it would not have feelings, sensations, or ideas. If such a robot could be built, it would prove that none of the supposed manifestations of mental life demanded a mentalistic explanation.

With respect to its own goals, methodological behaviorism was successful. It disposed of many of the problems raised by mentalism and freed itself to work on its own projects without philosophical digressions. By directing attention to genetic and environmental antecedents, it offset an unwarranted concentration on an inner life. It freed us to study the behavior of lower species, where introspection (then regarded as exclusively human) was not feasible, and to explore similarities and differences between man and other species. Some concepts previously associated with private events were formulated in other ways.

But problems remained. Most methodological behaviorists granted the existence of mental events while ruling them out of consideration. Did they really mean to say that they did not matter, that the middle stage in that three-stage sequence of physical-mental-physical contributed nothing—in other words, that feelings and states of mind were merely epiphenomena? It was not the first time that anyone had said so. The view that a purely physical world could be self-sufficient had been suggested centuries before, in the doctrine of psychophysical parallelism, which held that there were two worlds—one of mind and one of matter—and that neither had any effect on the other. Freud's demonstration of the unconscious, in which an awareness of feelings or states of mind seemed unnecessary, pointed in the same direction.

But what about other evidence? Is the traditional *post hoc, ergo propter hoc* argument entirely wrong? Are the feelings we experience just before we behave wholly unrelated to our behavior? What about the power of mind over matter in psychosomatic medicine? What about psychophysics and the mathematical relation between the magnitudes of stimuli and sensations? What about the stream of consciousness? What about the intrapsychic processes of psychiatry, in which feelings produce or suppress other feelings and memories evoke or mask other memories? What about the cognitive processes said to explain perception, thinking, the construction of sentences, and artistic creation? Must all this be ignored because it cannot be studied objectively?

RADICAL BEHAVIORISM

The statement that behaviorists deny the existence of feelings, sensations, ideas, and other features of mental life needs a good deal of clarification. Methodological behaviorism and some versions of logical positivism ruled private events out of bounds because there could be no public agreement about their validity. Introspection could not be accepted as a scientific practice, and the psychology of people like Wilhelm Wundt and Edward B. Titchener was attacked accordingly. Radical behaviorism, however, takes a different line. It does not deny the possibility of self-observation of self-knowledge or its possible usefulness, but it questions the nature of what is felt or observed and hence known. It restores introspection but not what philosophers and introspective psychologists had believed they were "specting," and it raises the question of how much of one's body one can actually observe.

Mentalism kept attention away from the external antecedent events which might have explained behavior, by seeming to supply an alternative explanation. Methodological behaviorism did just the reverse: by dealing exclusively with external antecedent events it turned attention away from self-observation and self-knowledge. Radical behaviorism restores some kind of balance. It does not insist upon truth by agreement and can therefore consider events taking place in the private world within the skin. It does not call these events unobservable, and it does not dismiss them as subjective. It simply questions the nature of the object observed and the reliability of the observations.

The position can be stated as follows: what is felt or introspectively observed is not some nonphysical world of consciousness, mind, or mental life but the observer's own body. This does not mean, as I shall show later, that introspection is a kind of physiological research, nor does it mean (and this is the heart of the argument) that what are felt or introspectively observed are the causes of behavior. An organism behaves as it does because of its current structure, but most of this is out of reach of introspection. At the moment we must content ourselves, as the methodological behaviorist insists, with a person's genetic and environmental histories. What are introspectively observed are certain collateral products of those histories.

The environment made its first great contribution during the evolution of the species, but it exerts a different kind of effect during the lifetime of the individual, and the combination of the two effects is the behavior we observe at any given time. Any available information about either contribution helps in the prediction and control of human behavior and in its interpretation in daily life. To the extent that either can be changed, behavior can be changed.

Our increasing knowledge of the control exerted by the environment makes it possible to examine the effect of the world within the skin and the nature of self-knowledge. It also makes it possible to interpret a wide range of mentalistic expressions. For example, we can look at those features of behavior which have led people to speak of an act of will, of a sense of purpose, of experience as distinct from reality, of innate or acquired ideas, of memories, meanings, and the personal knowledge of the scientist, and of hundreds of other mentalistic things or events. Some can be "translated into behavior," others discarded as unnecessary or meaningless.

In this way we repair the major damage wrought by mentalism. When what a person does is attributed to what is going on inside him, investigation is brought to an end. Why explain the explanation? For twenty-five hundred years people have been preoccupied with feelings and mental life, but only recently has any interest been shown in a more precise analysis of the role of the environment. Ignorance of that role led in the first place to mental fictions, and it has been perpetuated by the explanatory practices to which they gave rise.

A FEW WORDS OF CAUTION

As I noted in the Introduction [to *About Behaviorism,* from which this selection is taken], I am not speaking as *the* behaviorist. I believe I have written a consistent, coherent account, but it reflects my own environmental history. Bertrand Russell once pointed out that the experimental animals studied by American behaviorists behaved like Americans, running about in an almost random fashion, while those of Germans behaved like Germans, sitting and thinking. The remark may have been apt at the time, although it is meaningless today. Nevertheless, he was right in insisting that we are all culture-bound and that we approach the study of behavior with preconceptions. (And so, of course, do philosophers. Russell's account of how people think is very British, very Russellian. Mao Tse-tung's thoughts on the same subject are very Chinese. How could it be otherwise?)

I have not presupposed any technical knowledge on the part of the reader. A few facts and principles will, I hope, become familiar enough to be useful, since the discussion cannot proceed in a vacuum, but the book is not about a science of behavior but about its philosophy, and I have kept the scientific material to a bare minimum. Some terms appear many times, but it does not follow that the text is very repetitious. In later chapters, for example, the expression "contingencies of reinforcement" appears on almost every page, but contingencies are what the chapters are about. If they were about mushrooms, the word "mushroom" would be repeated as often.

Much of the argument goes beyond the established facts. I am concerned with interpretation rather than prediction and control. Every scientific field has a boundary beyond which discussion, though necessary, cannot be as precise as one would wish. One writer has recently said that "mere speculation which cannot be put to the test of experimental verification does not form part of science," but if that were true, a great deal of astronomy, for example, or atomic physics would not be science. Speculation is necessary, in fact, to devise methods which will bring a subject matter under better control.

I consider scores, if not hundreds, of examples of mentalistic usage. They are taken from current writing, but I have not cited the sources. I am not arguing with the authors but with the practices their terms or passages exemplify. I make the same use of examples as is made in a handbook of English usage. (I express my regrets if the authors would have preferred to be given credit, but I have applied the Golden Rule and have done unto others what I should have wished to have done if I had used such expressions.) Many of these expressions I "translate into behavior." I do so while acknowledging that *Traduttori traditori*—Translators are traitors—and that there are perhaps no exact behavioral equivalents, certainly none with the overtones and contexts of the originals. To spend much time on exact redefinitions of consciousness, will, wishes, sublimation, and so on would be as unwise as for physicists to do the same for ether, phlogiston, or *vis viva*.

Finally, a word about my own verbal behavior. The English language is heavy-laden with mentalism. Feelings and states of mind have enjoyed a commanding lead in the explanation of human behavior; and literature, preoccupied as it is with how and what people feel, offers continuing support. As a result, it is impossible to engage in casual discourse without raising the ghosts of mentalistic theories. The role of the environment was discovered very late, and no popular vocabulary has yet emerged.

For purposes of casual discourse I see no reason to avoid such an expression as "I have chosen to discuss . . ." (though I question the possibility of free choice), or "I have in mind . . ." (though I question the existence of a mind), or "I am aware of the fact . . ." (though I put a very special interpretation on awareness). The neophyte behaviorist is sometimes embarrassed when he finds himself using mentalistic terms, but the punishment of which his embarrassment is one effect is justified only when the terms are used in a technical discussion. When it is important to be clear about an issue, nothing but a technical vocabulary will suffice. It will often seem forced or roundabout. Old ways of speaking are abandoned with regret, and new ones are awkward and uncomfortable, but the change must be made.

This is not the first time a science has suffered from such a transition. There were periods when it was difficult for the astronomer not to sound like an astrologer (or to be an astrologer at heart) and when the chemist had by no means freed himself from alchemy. We are in a similar stage in a science of behavior, and the sooner the transition is completed the better. The practical consequences are easily demonstrated: education, politics, psychotherapy, penology, and many other fields of human affairs are suffering from the eclectic use of a lay vocabulary. The theoretical consequences are harder to demonstrate but . . . equally important.

FOCUS: READING REVIEW

1. Skinner describes the study of human behavior as "structuralism." What is structuralism?
2. What is "developmentalism"?
3. What are the limits of structuralism and developmentalism for describing human behavior?
4. What is the "psychology of the other one"? In Skinner's example of teaching a person to classify colored objects or to develop antiblack behavior, how does the "psychology of the other one" operate?
5. From the radical behaviorist's position, what constitutes behavior?

FOCUS: AUTHOR'S STRATEGIES

1. Is Skinner writing for his professional peers or a more general audience? What in his evidence suggests this?
2. This selection seeks to inform its audience about the different schools of psychology. Does the author have a bias? How is this indicated? What does this suggest about his further purposes?
3. How do the questions at the beginning of the essay shape Skinner's comparison?

FOCUS: DISCUSSION AND WRITING

1. Skinner is advancing the case for behavior-oriented psychology over mentalist psychology. Given that Freud would be considered mentalist, explain the difference between mentalism and behaviorism.

2. Skinner uses the example of angry feelings causing an angry response to indicate that we associate a mental experience (feelings) as the cause of a behavior (a physical event). Behaviorism would say that the behavior is a product of prior events "conditioning" a response of harsh words. Consider some behavior of your own—giving gifts, yelling in anger (or sulking silently), studying in a particular fashion, or rewarding yourself with food when you are unhappy. Where did you learn to do this? Did your family respond in the same way? Explain how a previous event or events in your life might explain your behavior.

Sociology as a Form of Consciousness
Peter Berger

Peter Berger was born in 1929 in Vienna, Austria. He attended the University of London, received his M.A. and Ph.D. from the New School for Social Research, and did postdoctoral work at the Lutheran Theological Seminary, the University of Michigan, and Yale Divinity School. Berger taught at the University of North Carolina, Hartford Seminary, the New School for Social Research, CUNY's Brooklyn College, and many European and American universities. In The Noise of Solemn Assemblies *(1961) and* The Precarious Vision *(1961), Berger wrote about his academic field—the sociology of religion. "Sociology as a Form of Consciousness," taken from* Invitation to Sociology: A Humanistic Perspective, *portrays the sociologist as a curious skeptic challenging social assumptions and conventions.*

[Sociology] is constituted by a peculiarly modern form of consciousness. The sociologist thinks of "society" as denoting a large complex of human relationships, as referring to a system of interaction. [Max Weber said] a "social situation" is one in which people orient their actions toward one another. The web of meanings, expectations and conduct resulting from such mutual orientation is the stuff of sociological analysis. To ask sociological questions presupposes that one is interested in looking some distance beyond the commonly accepted or officially defined goals of human actions. Sociological thought is partly [what Nietzsche called] "the art of mistrust." Sociological perspective involves a process of "seeing though" the facades of social structures. The sociologist will be driven time and again, by the very logic of his discipline, to debunk the social systems he is studying. He sees that society works as a system whose conscious and deliberate functions may be at odds with its unconscious and unintended ones.

... The very fact that sociology appeared as a discipline at a certain stage of Western history should compel us to ask further how it is possible for certain individuals to occupy themselves with it and what the preconditions are for this occupation. In other words, sociology is neither a timeless nor a necessary undertaking of the human mind. If this is conceded, the question logically arises as to the timely factors that made it a necessity to specific men. Perhaps, indeed, no intellectual enterprise is timeless or necessary. But religion, for instance, has been well-nigh universal in provoking intensive mental preoccupation throughout human history, while thoughts designed to solve the economic problems of existence have been a necessity in most human cultures. Certainly this does not mean that theology or economics, in our contemporary sense, are universally present phenomena of the mind, but we are at least on safe ground if we say that there always seems to have been human thought directed towards the problems that now constitute the subject matter of these disciplines. Not even this much, however, can be said of sociology. It presents itself rather as a peculiarly modern and Western cogitation. And, as we shall try to argue in this chapter, it is constituted by a peculiarly modern form of consciousness.

The peculiarity of sociological perspective becomes clear with some reflection concerning the meaning of the term "society," a term that refers to the object *par excellence* of the discipline. Like most terms used by sociologists, this one is derived from common usage, where its meaning is imprecise. Sometimes it means a particular band of people (as in "Society for the Prevention of Cruelty to Animals"), sometimes only those people endowed with great prestige or privilege (as in "Boston society ladies"), and on other occasions it is simply used to denote company of any sort (for example, "he greatly suffered in those years for lack of society"). There are other, less frequent meanings as well. The sociologist uses the term in a more precise sense, though, of course, there are differences in usage within the discipline itself. The sociologist thinks of "society" as denoting a large complex of human relationships, or to put it in more technical language, as referring to a system of interaction. The word "large" is difficult to specify quantitatively in this context. The sociologist may speak of a "society" including millions of human beings (say, "American society"), but he may also use the term to refer to a numerically much smaller collectivity (say, "the society of sophomores on this campus"). Two people chatting on a street corner will hardly constitute a "society," but three people stranded on an island certainly will. The applicability of the concept, then, cannot be decided on quantitative grounds alone. It rather applies when a complex of relationships is sufficiently succinct to be analyzed by itself, understood as an autonomous entity, set against others of the same kind.

The adjective "social" must be similarly sharpened for sociological use. In common speech it may denote, once more, a number of different things—the informal quality of a certain gathering ("this is a social meeting—let's not discuss business"), an altruistic attitude on somebody's part ("he had a strong social concern in his job"), or, more generally, anything derived from contact with other people ("a social disease"). The sociologist will use the term more narrowly and more precisely to refer to the quality of interaction, interrelationship, mutuality. Thus two men chatting on a street corner do not constitute a "society," but what transpires between them is certainly "social." "Society" consists of a complex of such "social" events. As to the exact definition of the "social," it is difficult to improve on Max Weber's[1] definition of a "social" situation as one in which people orient their actions towards one another. The web of meanings, expectations and conduct resulting from such mutual orientation is the stuff of sociological analysis.

Yet this refinement of terminology is not enough to show up the distinctiveness of the sociological angle of vision. We may get closer by comparing the latter with the perspective of other disciplines concerned with human actions. The economist, for example, is concerned with the analyses of processes that occur in society and that can be described as social. These processes have to do with the basic problem of economic activity—the allocation of scarce goods and services within a society. The economist will be concerned with these processes in terms of the way in which they carry out, or fail to carry out, this function. The sociologist, in looking at the same processes, will naturally have to take into consideration their economic purpose. But his distinctive interest is not necessarily related to this purpose as such. He will be interested in a variety of human relationships and interactions that may occur here and that may be quite irrelevant to the economic goals in question. Thus economic activity involves relationships of power, prestige, prejudice or even play that can be analyzed with only marginal reference to the properly economic function of the activity.

The sociologist finds his subject matter present in all human activities, but not all aspects of these activities constitute this subject matter. Social interaction is not some specialized sector of what men do with each other. It is rather a certain aspect of all these doings. Another way of putting this is by saying that the sociologist carries on a special sort of abstraction. The social, as an object of inquiry, is not a segregated field of human activity. Rather (to borrow a phrase from Lutheran sacramental theology) it is present "in, with and under" many different fields of such activity. The sociologist does not look at phenomena that nobody else is aware of. But he looks at the same phenomena in a different way.

As a further example we could take the perspective of the lawyer. Here we actually find a point of view much broader in scope than that of the economist. Almost any human activity can, at one time or another, fall within the province of the lawyer. This, indeed, is the fascination of the law. Again, we find here a very special procedure of abstraction. From the immense wealth and variety of human deportment the lawyer selects those aspects that are pertinent (or, as he would say, "material") to his very particular frame of reference. As anyone who has ever been involved in a lawsuit well knows, the criteria of what is relevant or irrelevant legally will often greatly surprise the principals in the case in question. This need not concern us here. We would rather observe that the legal frame of reference consists of a number of carefully defined models of human activity. Thus we have clear models of obligation, responsibility or wrongdoing. Definite conditions have to prevail before any empirical act can be subsumed under one of these headings, and these conditions are laid down by statutes or precedent. When these conditions are not met, the act in question is legally irrelevant. The expertise of the lawyer consists of knowing the rules by which these models are constructed. He knows, within his frame of reference, when a business contract is binding, when the driver of an automobile may be held to be negligent, or when rape has taken place.

The sociologist may look at these same phenomena, but his frame of reference will be quite different. Most importantly, his perspective on these phenomena cannot be derived from statutes or precedent. His interest in the human relationships occurring in a business transaction has no bearing on the legal validity of contracts signed, just as sociologically interesting deviance in sexual behavior may not be capable of being subsumed under some particular legal heading. From the lawyer's point of view, the sociologist's inquiry is extraneous to the legal frame of reference. One might say that, with reference to the conceptual edifice of the law, the sociologist's activity is subterranean in character. The lawyer is concerned with what may be called the official conception of the situation. The sociologist often deals with very unofficial conceptions indeed. For the lawyer the essential thing to understand is how the law looks upon a certain type of criminal. For the sociologist it is equally important to see how the criminal looks at the law.

To ask sociological questions, then, presupposes that one is interested in looking some distance beyond the commonly accepted or officially defined goals of human actions. It presupposes a certain awareness that human events have different levels of meaning, some of which are hidden from the consciousness of everyday life. It may even presuppose a measure of suspicion about the way in which human events are officially interpreted by the authorities, be they political, juridical or religious in character. If one is willing to go as far as that, it would seem evident that not all historical circumstances are equally favorable for the development of sociological perspective.

It would appear plausible, in consequence, that sociological thought would have the best chance to develop in historical circumstances marked by severe jolts to the self-conception, especially the official and authoritative and generally accepted self-conception, of a culture. It is only in such circumstances that perceptive men are likely to be motivated to think beyond the assertions of this self-conception and, as a result, question the authorities. Albert Salomon[2] has argued cogently that the concept of "society," in its modern sociological sense, could emerge only as the normative structures of Christendom and later of the *ancien régime* were collapsing. We can, then, again conceive of "society as the hidden fabric of an edifice, the outside facade of which hides that fabric from the common view. In medieval Christendom, "society" was rendered invisible by the imposing religiopolitical facade that constituted the common world of European man. As Salomon pointed out, the more secular political facade of the absolute state performed the same function after the Reformation had broken up the unity of Christendom. It was with the disintegration of the absolute state that the underlying frame of "society" came into view—that is, a world of motives and forces that could not be understood in terms of the official interpretations of social reality. Sociological perspective can then be understood in terms of such phrases as "seeing through," "looking behind," very much as such phrases would be employed in common speech—"seeing through his game," "looking behind the scenes"—in other words, "being up on all the tricks."

We will not be far off if we see sociological thought as part of what Nietzsche called "the art of mistrust."[3] Now, it would be a gross oversimplification to think that this art has existed only in modern times. "Seeing through" things is probably a pretty general function of intelligence, even in very primitive societies. The American anthropologist Paul Radin has provided us with a vivid description of the skeptic as a human type in primitive culture. We also have evidence from civilizations other than that of the modern West, bearing witness to forms of consciousness that could well be called protosociological. We could point, for instance, to Herodotus or to Ibn-Khaldun.[4] There are even texts from ancient Egypt evincing a profound disenchantment with a political and social order that has acquired the reputation of having been one of the most cohesive in human history. However, with the beginning of the modern era in the West this form of consciousness intensifies, becomes concentrated and systematized, marks the thought of an increasing number of perceptive men. This is not the place to discuss in detail the prehistory of sociological thought, a discussion in which we owe very much to Salomon. Nor would we even give here an intellectual table of ancestors for sociology, showing its connections with Machiavelli, Erasmus, Bacon,[5] seventeenth-century philosophy and eighteenth-century *belles-lettres*—this has been done elsewhere and by others much more qualified than this writer. Suffice it to stress once more that sociological thought marks the fruition of a number of intellectual developments that have a very specific location in modern Western history.

Let us return instead to the proposition that sociological perspective involves a process of "seeing through" the facades of social structures. We could think of this in terms of a common experience of people living in large cities. One of the fascinations of a large city is the immense variety of human activities taking place behind the seemingly anonymous and endlessly undifferentiated rows of houses. A person who lives in such a city will time and again experience surprise or even shock as he discovers the strange pursuits that some men engage in quite unobtrusively in houses that, from the outside, look like all the others on a certain street. Having had this experience once or twice, one will repeatedly find oneself walking down a street, perhaps late in the evening, and wondering what may be going on under the bright lights showing through a line of drawn curtains. An ordinary family engaged in pleasant talk with guests? A scene of desperation amid illness or death? Or a scene of debauched pleasures? Perhaps a strange cult or a dangerous conspiracy? The facades of the houses cannot tell us, proclaiming nothing but an architectural conformity to the tastes of some group or class that may not even inhabit the street any longer. The social mysteries lie behind the facades. The wish to penetrate to these mysteries is an analogon to sociological curiosity. In some cities that are suddenly struck by calamity this wish may be abruptly realized. Those who have experienced wartime bombings know of the sudden encounters with unsuspected (and sometimes unimaginable) fellow tenants in the air-raid shelter of one's apartment building. Or they can recollect the startling morning sight of a house hit by a bomb during the night, neatly sliced in half, the facade torn away and the previously hidden interior mercilessly revealed in the daylight. But in most cities that one may normally live in, the facades must be penetrated by one's own inquisitive intrusions. Similarly, there are historical situations in which the facades of society are violently torn apart and all but the most incurious are forced to see that there was a reality behind the facades all along. Usually this does not happen and the facades continue to confront us with seemingly rocklike permanence. The perception of the reality behind the facades then demands a considerable intellectual effort.

A few examples of the way in which sociology "looks behind" the facades of social structures might serve to make our argument clearer. Take, for instance, the political organization of a community. If one wants to find out how a modern American city is governed, it is very easy to get the official information about this subject. The city will have a charter, operating under the laws of the state. With some advice from informed individuals, one may look up various statutes that define the constitution of the city. Thus one may find out that this particular community has a city-manager form of administration, or that party affiliations do not appear on the ballot in municipal elections, or that the city government partic- ipates in a regional water district. In similar fashion, with the help of some news- paper reading, one may find out the officially recognized political problems of the community. One may read that the city plans to annex a certain suburban area, or that there has been a change in the zoning ordinances to facilitate industrial devel- opment in another area, or even that one of the members of the city council has been accused of using his office for personal gain. All such matters still occur on the, as it were, visible, official or public level of political life. However, it would be an exceedingly naive person who would believe that this kind of information gives him a rounded picture of the political reality of that community. The sociologist will want to know above all the constituency of the "informal power structure" (as it has been called by Floyd Hunter, an American sociologist interested in such studies), which is a configuration of men and their power that cannot be found in any statutes, and probably cannot be read about in the newspapers. The political scientist or the legal expert might find it very interesting to compare the city charter with the constitutions of other similar communities. The sociologist will be far more concerned with discovering the way in which powerful vested interests influence or even control the actions of officials elected under the charter. These vested interests will not be found in city hall, but rather in the executive suites of corporations that may not even be located in that community, in the private man- sions of a handful of powerful men, perhaps in the offices of certain labor unions or even, in some instances, in the headquarters of criminal organizations. When the sociologist concerns himself with power, he will "look behind" the official mechanisms that are supposed to regulate power in the community. This does not necessarily mean that he will regard the official mechanisms as totally ineffective or their legal definition as totally illusionary. But at the very least he will insist that there is another level of reality to be investigated in the particular system of power. In some cases he might conclude that to look for real power in the publicly recognized places is quite delusional.

Take another example. Protestant denominations in this country differ widely in their so-called "polity,"[6] that is, the officially defined way in which the denomination is run. One may speak of an episcopal, a presbyterian or a congregational "polity" (meaning by this not the denominations called by these names, but the forms of ecclesiastical government that various denominations share—for instance, the espiscopal form shared by Episcopalians and Methodists, the congregational by Congregationalists and Baptists). In nearly all cases, the "polity" of a denomination is the result of a long historical development and is based on a theological rationale over which the doctrinal experts continue to quarrel. Yet a sociologist interested in studying the government of American demoninations would do well not to arrest himself too long at these official definitions. He will soon find that the real questions of power and organization have little to do with "polity" in the theological sense. He will discover that the basic form of organization of all denominations of any size is bureaucratic. The logic of administrative behavior is determined by bureaucratic processes, only very rarely by the workings of an episcopal or a congregational point of view. The sociological investigator will then quickly "see through" the mass of confusing terminology denoting officeholders in the ecclesiastical bureaucracy and correctly identify those who hold executive power, no matter whether they be called "bishops," or "stated clerks" or "synod presidents." Understanding denominational organization as belonging to the much larger species of bureaucracy, the sociologist will then be able to grasp the processes that occur in the organization, to observe the internal and external pressures brought to bear on those who are theoretically in charge. In other words, behind the facade of an "episcopal polity" the sociologist will perceive the workings of a bureaucratic apparatus that is not terribly different in the Methodist Church, an agency of the Federal government, General Motors or the United Automobile Workers.

Or take an example from economic life. The personnel manager of an industrial plant will take delight in preparing brightly colored charts that show the table of organization that is supposed to administer the production process. Every man has his place, every person in the organization knows from whom he receives his orders and to whom he must transmit them, every work team has its assigned role in the great drama of production. In reality things rarely work this way—and every good personnel manager knows this. Superimposed on the official blueprint of the organization is a much subtler, much less visible network of human groups, with their loyalties, prejudices, antipathies and (most important) codes of behavior. Industrial sociology is full of data on the operations of this informal network, which always exists in varying degrees of accommodation and conflict with the official system. Very much the same coexistence of formal and informal organization are to be found wherever large numbers of men work together or live together under a system of discipline—military organizations, prisons, hospitals, schools, going back to the mysterious leagues that children form among themselves and that their parents only rarely discern. Once more, the sociologist will seek to penetrate the smoke screen of the official versions of reality (those of the foreman, the officer, the teacher) and try to grasp the signals that come from the "underworld" (those of the worker, the enlisted man, the schoolboy).

Let us take one further example. In Western countries, and especially in America, it is assumed that men and women marry because they are in love. There is a broadly based popular mythology about the character of love as a violent, irresistible emotion that strikes where it will, a mystery that is the goal of most young people and often of the not-so-young as well. As soon as one investigates, however, which people actually marry each other, one finds that the lightning-shaft of Cupid seems to be guided rather strongly within very definite channels of class, income, education, racial and religious background. If one then investigates a little further into the behavior that is engaged in prior to marriage under the rather misleading euphemism of "courtship," one finds channels of interaction that are often rigid to the point of ritual. The suspicion begins to dawn on one that, most of the time, it is not so much the emotion of love that creates a certain kind of relationship, but that carefully predefined and often planned relationships eventually generate the desired emotion. In other words, when certain conditions are met or have been constructed, one allows oneself "to fall in love." The sociologist investigating our patterns of "courtship" and marriage soon discovers a complex web of motives related in many ways to the entire institutional structure within which an individual lives his life—class, career, economic ambition, aspirations of power and prestige. The miracle of love now begins to look somewhat synthetic. Again, this need not mean in any given instance that the sociologist will declare the romantic interpretation to be an illusion. But, once more, he will look beyond the immediately given and publicly approved interpretations. Contemplating a couple that in its turn is contemplating the moon, the sociologist need not feel constrained to deny the emotional impact of the scene thus illuminated. But he will observe the machinery that went into the construction of the scene in its nonlunar aspects—the status index of the automobile from which the contemplation occurs, the canons of taste and tactics that determine the costume of the contemplators, the many ways in which language and demeanor place them socially, thus the social location and intentionality of the entire enterprise.

It may have become clear at this point that the problems that will interest the sociologist are not necessarily what other people may call "problems." The way in which public officials and newspapers (and, alas, some college textbooks in sociology) speak about "social problems" serves to obscure this fact. People commonly speak of a "social problem" when something in society does not work the way it is supposed to according to the official interpretations. They then expect the sociologist to study the "problem" as they have defined it and perhaps even to come up with a "solution" that will take care of the matter to their own satisfaction. It is important, against this sort of expectation, to understand that a sociological problem is something quite different from a "social problem" in this sense.

For example, it is naive to concentrate on crime as a "problem" because law-enforcement agencies so define it, or on divorce because that is a "problem" to the moralists of marriage. Even more clearly, the "problem" of the foreman to get his men to work more efficiently or of the line officer to get his troops to charge the enemy more enthusiastically need not be problematic at all to the sociologist (leaving out of consideration for the moment the probable fact that the sociologist asked to study such "problems" is employed by the corporation or the army). The sociological problem is always the understanding of what goes on here in terms of social interaction. Thus the sociological problem is not so much why some things "go wrong" from the viewpoint of the authorities and the management of the social scene, but how the whole system works in the first place, what are its presuppositions and by what means it is held together. The fundamental sociological problem is not crime but the law, not divorce but marriage, not racial discrimination but racially defined stratification, not revolution but government.

We would contend, then, that there is a debunking motif inherent in sociological consciousness. The sociologist will be driven time and again, by the very logic of his discipline, to debunk the social systems he is studying. This unmasking tendency need not necessarily be due to the sociologist's temperament or inclinations. Indeed, it may happen that the sociologist, who as an individual may be of a conciliatory disposition and quite disinclined to disturb the comfortable assumptions on which he rests his own social existence, is nevertheless compelled by what he is doing to fly in the face of what those around him take for granted. In other words, we would contend that the roots of the debunking motif in sociology are not psychological but methodological. The sociological frame of reference, with its built-in procedure of looking for levels of reality other than those given in the official interpretations of society, carries with it a logical imperative to unmask the pretensions and the propaganda by which men cloak their actions with each other. This unmasking imperative is one of the characteristics of sociology particularly at home in the temper of the modern era.

The debunking tendency in sociological thought can be illustrated by a variety of developments within the field. For example, one of the major themes in Weber's sociology is that of the unintended, unforeseen consequences of human actions in society. Weber's most famous work, *The Protestant Ethic and the Spirit of Capitalism,* in which he demonstrated the relationship between certain consequences of Protestant values and the development of the capitalist ethos, has often been misunderstood by critics precisely because they missed this theme. Such critics have pointed out that the Protestant thinkers quoted by Weber never intended their teachings to be applied so as to produce the specific economic results in question. Specifically, Weber argued that the Calvinist doctrine of predestination led people to behave in what he called an "inner-worldly ascetic" way, that is, in a manner that concerns itself intensively, systematically and selflessly with the affairs of this world, especially with economic affairs. Weber's critics have then pointed out that nothing was further from the mind of Calvin and the other leaders of the Calvinist Reformation. But Weber never maintained that Calvinist thought *intended* to produce these economic action patterns. On the contrary, he knew very well that the intentions were drastically different. The consequences took place regardless of intentions. In other words, Weber's work (and not only the famous part of it just mentioned) gives us a vivid picture of the *irony* of human actions. Weber's sociology thus provides us with a radical antithesis to any views that understand history as the realization of ideas or as the fruit of the deliberate efforts of individuals or collectivities. This does not mean at all that ideas are not important. It does mean that the outcome of ideas is commonly very different from what those who had the ideas in the first place planned or hoped. Such a consciousness of the ironic aspect of history is sobering, a strong antidote to all kinds of revolutionary utopianism.

The debunking tendency of sociology is implicit in all sociological theories that emphasize the autonomous character of social processes. For instance, Émile Durkheim, the founder of the most important school in French sociology, emphasized that society was a reality *sui generis,* that is, a reality that could not be reduced to psychological or other factors on different levels of analysis. The effect of this insistence has been a sovereign disregard for individually intended motives and meanings in Durkheim's study of various phenomena. This is perhaps most sharply revealed in his well-known study of suicide, in the work of that title, where individual intentions of those who commit or try to commit suicide are completely left out of the analysis in favor of statistics concerning various social characteristics of these individuals. In the Durkheimian perspective, to live in society means to exist under the domination of society's logic. Very often men act by this logic without knowing it. To discover this inner dynamic of society, therefore, the sociologist must frequently disregard the answers that the social actors themselves would give to his questions and look for explanations that are hidden from their own awareness. This essentially Durkheimian approach has been carried over into the theoretical approach now called functionalism. In functional analysis society is analyzed in terms of its own workings as a system, workings that are often obscure or opaque to those acting within the system. The contemporary American sociologist Robert Merton has expressed this approach well in his concepts of "manifest" and "latent" functions. The former are the conscious and deliberate functions of social processes, the latter the unconscious and unintended ones. Thus the "manifest" function of antigambling legislation may be to suppress gambling, its "latent" function to create an illegal empire for the gambling syndicates. Or Christian missions in parts of Africa "manifestly" tried to convert Africans to Christianity, "latently" helped to destroy the indigenous tribal cultures and thus provided an important impetus toward rapid social transformation. Or the control of the Communist Party over all sectors of social life in Russia "manifestly" was to assure the continued dominance of the revolutionary ethos, "latently" created a new class of comfortable bureaucrats uncannily bourgeois in its aspirations and increasingly disinclined toward the self-denial of Bolshevik dedication. Or the "manifest" function of many voluntary associations in America is sociability and public service, the "latent" function to attach status indices to those permitted to belong to such associations.

. . . . .

. . . The sociological perspective is a broad, open, emancipated vista on human life. The sociologist, at his best, is a man with a taste for other lands, inwardly open to the measureless richness of human possibilities, eager for new horizons and new worlds of human meaning. It probably requires no additional elaboration to make the point that this type of man can play a particularly useful part in the course of events today.

Notes

[1] Max Weber (1864–1920) was a German sociologist and political economist.

[2] Albert Saloman (1891–1966) was a social researcher and professor.

[3] Friedrich Nietzsche (1844–1900) was a German nihilist philosopher.

[4] Herotodus (485?–425? B.C.) was a classical Greek historian called the Father of History. Ibn-Khaldun (1332–1406) was an Arab historian and sociologist who pioneered the philosophy of history.

[5] Nicolo Machiavelli (1469–1527) was a Florentine statesman and writer on government who advocated deceit and craft. Erasmus (1466?–1536) was the great Dutch Renaissance Christian-humanist philosopher. Francis Bacon (1561–1626), the English philosopher, has often been credited with defining the scientific method of inductive thought.

[6] episcopal, presbyterian, congregational polity: kinds of church governance. *Episcopal* designates governance by bishops and clergy appointed by the bishops. *Presbyterian* designates governance by a council of elders elected by the congregation and by clergy appointed by the presbyters or elders. In *congregational polity,* the congregation directly governs itself and selects its clergy.

FOCUS: READING REVIEW

1. What are the various meanings of the word *society?* What is its special meaning for sociology?
2. What is sociology's special use of the word *social?*
3. How is sociology distinct from economics? from law?
4. What does it mean to ask a "sociological" question?
5. How is sociology "the art of mistrust"?
6. How does sociology "look behind" the social structures? How is this illustrated by the examples of city power, church governance, economic life, and western marriage?
7. How does a sociologist define a "problem"?
8. What is the "debunking motif" in sociological consciousness? How does Berger illustrate this?
9. What characterizes the functional analysis of society?
10. What is the distinction between "manifest" and "latent" functions?

FOCUS: AUTHOR'S STRATEGIES

1. Is Berger writing for other sociologists? Why or why not?
2. For what audience is Berger writing? What clues do you find for this in his language and unexplained assumptions?
3. Berger uses several development strategies. What are they? How do they accomplish his purpose of explanation?

FOCUS: DISCUSSION AND WRITING

1. Berger asserts that the "lightning-shaft of Cupid seems to be guided strongly within very definite channels of class, income, education, racial and religious background." Trying to "see through" the facades, consider couples and marriages you know well—parents, other relatives, friends. What similarities and differences do you find in class, income, education, racial, and religious backgrounds? Using this evidence, oppose or agree with Berger's assertion.
2. Compare and contrast the "manifest" and "latent" functions of some institution with which you are affiliated—a social club, church, political group, school, or community service organization.

Thick Description: Toward an Interpretive Theory of Culture
Clifford Geertz

Clifford Geertz (b. 1926) is professor of social sciences at the Princeton Institute for Advanced Studies. He graduated from Antioch College and received his Ph.D. from Harvard University. A cultural anthropologist, Geertz has done fieldwork in Indonesia and Morocco and published his findings in The Religion of Java *(1960),* The Process of Ecological Change in Indonesia *(1963),* Peddlers and Princes: Social Development and Economic Change in Two Indonesian Towns *(1963), and* The Interpretation of Cultures *(1973), from which this selection is taken. Ethnology, the study of interactions between cultures, forms one branch of anthropology, the study of man. In "Thick Description," Geertz illustrates how the ethnologist must bring objectivity, concern for detail, and background knowledge to his or her fieldwork.*

Doing ethnography is establishing rapport, selecting informants, transcribing texts, taking genealogies, mapping fields, keeping a diary, and so on. What defines it is the notion of "thick description." [Between the "thin description" of the subject's actions and gestures and the "thick description," which explains the actions and gestures, lies the object of ethnography:] a stratified hierarchy of meaningful structures in terms of which [actions and gestures] are produced, perceived, and interpreted. Let me give a not untypical excerpt from my own field journal to demonstrate the sort of piled-up structures of inference and implication through which an ethnographer is continually trying to pick his way. In finished anthropological writings the fact—that what we call our data are really our own constructions of other people's constructions of what they and their compatriots are up to—is obscured because most of what we need to comprehend a particular event, ritual, custom, idea, or whatever is insinuated as background information before the thing itself is directly examined.

From one point of view, doing ethnography[1] is establishing rapport, selecting informants, transcribing texts, taking genealogies, mapping fields, keeping a diary, and so on. But it is not these things, techniques and received procedures, that define the enterprise. What defines it is the kind of intellectual effort it is: an elaborate venture in, to borrow a notion from Gilbert Ryle, "thick description."

Ryle's discussion of "thick description" appears in two recent essays of his (now reprinted in the second volume of his *Collected Papers*) addressed to the general question of what, as he puts it, *"Le Penseur"* is doing: "Thinking and Reflecting" and "The Thinking of Thoughts." Consider, he says, two boys rapidly contracting the eyelids of their right eyes. In one, this is an involuntary twitch; in the other, a conspiratorial signal to a friend. The two movements are, as movements, identical; from an I-am-a-camera, "phenomenalistic"[2] observation of them alone, one could not tell which was twitch and which was wink, or indeed whether both or either was twitch or wink. Yet the difference, however unphotographable, between a twitch and a wink is vast; as anyone unfortunate enough to have had the first taken for the second knows. The winker is communicating, and indeed communicating in a quite precise and special way: (1) deliberately, (2) to someone in particular, (3) to impart a particular message, (4) according to a socially established code, and (5) without cognizance of the rest of the company. As Ryle points out, the winker has not done two things, contracted his eyelids and winked, while the twitcher has done only one, contracted his eyelids. Contracting your eyelids on purpose when there exists a public code in which so doing counts as a conspiratorial signal *is* winking. That's all there is to it: a speck of behavior, a fleck of culture, and—*voilà!*[3]—a gesture.

That, however, is just the beginning. Suppose, he continues, there is a third boy, who, "to give malicious amusement to his cronies," parodies the first boy's wink, as amateurish, clumsy, obvious, and so on. He, of course, does this in the same way the second boy winked and the first twitched: by contracting his right eyelid. Only this boy is neither winking nor twitching, he is parodying someone else's, as he takes it, laughable, attempt at winking. Here, too, a socially established code exists (he will "wink" laboriously, overobviously, perhaps adding a grimace—the usual artifices of the clown); and so also does a message. Only now it is not conspiracy but ridicule that is in the air. If the others think he is actually winking, his whole project misfires as completely, though with somewhat different results, as if they think he is twitching. One can go further: uncertain of his mimicking abilities, the would-be satirist may practice at home before the mirror, in which case he is not twitching, winking, or parodying, but rehearsing; though so far as what a camera, a radical behaviorist, or a believer in protocol sentences would record he is just rapidly contracting his right eyelids like all the others. Complexities are possible, if not practically without end, at least logically so. The original winker might, for example, actually have been fake-winking, say, to mislead outsiders into imagining there was a conspiracy afoot when there in fact was not, in which case our descriptions of what the parodist is parodying and the rehearser rehearsing of course shift accordingly. But the point is that between what Ryle calls the "thin description" of what the rehearser (parodist, winker, twitcher . . .) is doing ("rapidly contracting his right eyelid") and the "thick description" of what he is doing ("practicing a burlesque of a friend faking a wink to deceive an innocent into thinking a conspiracy is in motion") lies the object of ethnography: a stratified hierarchy of meaningful structures in terms of which twitches, winks, fake-winks, parodies, rehearsals of parodies are produced, perceived, and interpreted, and without which they would not (not even the zero-form twitches, which, *as a cultural category,* are as much nonwinks as winks are nontwitches) in fact exist, no matter what anyone did or didn't do with his eyelids.

Like so many of the little stories Oxford philosophers like to make up for themselves, all this winking, fake-winking, burlesque-fake-winking, rehearsed-burlesque-fake-winking, may seem a bit artificial. In way of adding a more empirical note, let me give, deliberately unpreceded by any prior explanatory comment at all, a not untypical excerpt from my own field journal to demonstrate that, however evened off for didactic purposes, Ryle's example presents an image only too exact of the sort of piled-up structures of inference and implication through which an ethnographer is continually trying to pick his way:

The French [the informant said] had only just arrived. They set up twenty or so small forts between here, the town, and the Marmusha area up in the middle of the mountains, placing them on promontories so they could survey the countryside. But for all this they couldn't guarantee safety, especially at night, so although the *mezrag,* trade-pact, system was supposed to be legally abolished it in fact continued as before.

One night, when Cohen (who speaks fluent Berber), was up there, at Marmusha, two other Jews who were traders to a neighboring tribe came by to purchase some goods from him. Some Berbers, from yet another neighboring tribe, tried to break into Cohen's place, but he fired his rifle in the air. (Traditionally, Jews were not allowed to carry weapons; but at this period things were so unsettled many did so anyway.) This attracted the attention of the French and the marauders fled.

The next night, however, they came back, one of them disguised as a woman who knocked on the door with some sort of a story. Cohen was suspicious and didn't want to let "her" in, but the other Jews said, "oh, it's all right, it's only a woman." So they opened the door and the whole lot came pouring in. They killed the two visiting Jews, but Cohen managed to barricade himself in an adjoining room. He heard the robbers planning to burn him alive in the shop after they removed his goods, and so he opened the door and, laying about him wildly with a club, managed to escape through a window.

He went up to the fort, then, to have his wounds dressed, and complained to the local commandant, one Captain Dumari, saying he wanted his 'ar— i.e., four or five times the value of the merchandise stolen from him. The robbers were from a tribe which had not yet submitted to French authority and were in open rebellion against it, and he wanted authorization to go with his *mezrag*-holder, the Marmusha tribal *sheikh,* to collect the indemnity that, under traditional rules, he had coming to him. Captain Dumari couldn't officially give him permission to do this, because of the French prohibition of the *mezrag* relationship, but he gave him verbal authorization, saying, "If you get killed, it's your problem."

So the *sheikh,* the Jew, and a small company of armed Marmushans went off ten or fifteen kilometers up into the rebellious area, where there were of course no French, and, sneaking up, captured the thief-tribe's shepherd and stole its herds. The other tribe soon came riding out on horses after them, armed with rifles and ready to attack. But when they saw who the "sheep thieves" were, they thought better of it and said, "all right, we'll talk." They couldn't really deny what had happened—that some of their men had robbed Cohen and killed the two visitors—and they weren't prepared to start the serious feud with the Marmusha a scuffle with the invading party would bring on. So the two groups talked, and talked, and talked, there on the plain amid the thousands of sheep, and decided finally on five-hundred-sheep damages. The two armed Berber groups then lined up on their horses at opposite ends of the plain, with the sheep herded between them, and Cohen, in his black gown, pillbox hat, and flapping slippers, went out alone among the sheep, picking out, one by one and at his own good speed, the best ones for his payment.

So Cohen got his sheep and drove them back to Marmusha. The French, up in their fort, heard them coming from some distance ("Ba, ba, ba," said Cohen, happily, recalling the image) and said, "What the hell is that?" And Cohen said, "That is my 'ar.'" The French couldn't believe he had actually done what he said he had done, and accused him of being a spy for the rebellious Berbers, put him in prison, and took his sheep. In the town, his family, not having heard from him in so long a time, thought he was dead. But after a while the French released him and he came back home, but without his sheep. He then went to the Colonel in the town, the Frenchman in charge of the whole region, to complain. But the Colonel said, "I can't do anything about the matter. It's not my problem."

Quoted raw, a note in a bottle, this passage conveys, as any similar one similarly presented would do, a fair sense of how much goes into ethnographic description of even the most elemental sort—how extraordinarily "thick" it is. In finished anthropological writings this fact—that what we call our data are really our own constructions of other people's constructions of what they and their compatriots are up to—is obscured because most of what we need to comprehend a particular event, ritual, custom, idea, or whatever is insinuated as background information before the thing itself is directly examined. (Even to reveal that this little drama took place in the highlands of central Morocco in 1912—and was recounted there in 1968—is to determine much of our understanding of it.) There is nothing particularly wrong with this, and it is in any case inevitable. But it does lead to a view of anthropological research as rather more of an observational and rather less of an interpretive activity than it really is. Right down at the factual base, the hard rock, insofar as there is any, of the whole enterprise, we are already explicating: and worse, explicating explications. Winks upon winks upon winks.

Analysis, then, is sorting out the structures of signification[4]—what Ryle called established codes, a somewhat misleading expression, for it makes the enterprise sound too much like that of the cipher clerk when it is much more like that of the literary critic—and determining their social ground[5] and import. Here, in our text, such sorting would begin with distinguishing the three unlike frames of interpretation ingredients in the situation, Jewish, Berber, and French, and would then move on to show how (and why) at that time, in that place, their copresence produced a situation in which systematic misunderstanding reduced traditional form to social farce. What tripped Cohen up, and with him the whole, ancient pattern of social and economic relationships within which he functioned, was a confusion of tongues.

I shall come back to this too-compacted aphorism later, as well as to the details of the text itself. The point for now is only that ethnography is thick description. What the ethnographer is in fact faced with—except when (as, of course, he must do) he is pursuing the more automatized routines of data collection—is a multiplicity of complex conceptual structures, many of them superimposed upon or knotted into one another, which are at once strange, irregular, and inexplicit, and which he must contrive somehow first to grasp and then to render. And this is true at the most down-to-earth, jungle field work levels of his activity: interviewing informants, observing rituals, eliciting kin terms, tracing property lines, censusing households . . . writing his journal. Doing ethnography is like trying to read (in the sense of "construct a reading of") a manuscript—foreign, faded, full of ellipses, incoherencies, suspicious emendations, and tendentious commentaries, but written not in conventionalized graphs of sound but in transient examples of shaped behavior.

Notes

[1] ethnography: recording in writing the distinctive feature of an ethnic group or culture.

[2] phenomenalistic: relating to only those external events or phenomena that can be objectively verified.

[3] *voilà!:* a French exclamatory statement that literally means "look," but carries the connotation of "There you have it! Wow!"

[4] structures of signification: the various levels and kinds of meaning defined by a particular cultural context.

[5] social ground: reference point within the society.

FOCUS: READING REVIEW

1. What is the distinction between "thin" and "thick" description?
2. In the section from the author's journal on the French, the Berbers, and the Jew, what special understanding of ritual and custom would an ethnologist require to clearly describe and interpret the incident?
3. What in the description of the incident in Morocco is interpretation, an analysis of "winks upon winks upon winks"?
4. What does Geertz mean by "transient examples of shaped behavior"? What does the comparison of this with "conventionalized graphs" suggest about the methodology of anthropology as compared to the "hard" sciences?

FOCUS: AUTHOR'S STRATEGIES

1. Although Geertz does not fully define "thick description" initially, how does the example of the boys contracting their eyelids exemplify thick description?
2. Geertz is writing an introduction to ethnography and anthropology. How knowledgeable does he assume his audience to be? How do his definitions (or lack of them) and vocabulary demonstrate this?

FOCUS: DISCUSSION AND WRITING

1. Geertz identifies the task of the ethnologist as "thick description," which grows out of objective observation. Select an event with which you are familiar—dinner in your college dining room; a party, dance, or concert; a laboratory class; a political meeting; a church service or a family get-together—and attend as an observer. Use a tape recorder, film, or a video recorder (if one is available), and also take notes. Write an essay in which you describe the event, relying on your special knowledge whenever necessary to explain the possible meaning of "winks."
2. Geertz illustrates that the anthropologist's ability to record a culture's behavior is dependent upon the observer's knowledge of the culture's rituals and customs. Recount an experience where you have observed or participated in a ritual initially unfamiliar to you—for example, a religious service, a wedding, a holiday celebration, or a friend's family dinner. What aspects were unusual to you? Do you now understand these customs? If so, explain the custom in terms of the culture's traditions. If not, through research, or through asking someone from that culture, discover the explanation.

Chapter 5

The Social Sciences at Work

The essays in this chapter by psychologists, sociologists, and economists represent an exceedingly small part of studies in the social sciences. Maslow, relying on psychological data, appeals for a model of human values. Social psychologists Horner and Goldberg reveal how social institutions and practices affect self-image and prejudice. Psychologist Coles studies a child's responses to racial discrimination and school integration in "When I Draw the Lord." Pearce's essay addresses two themes raised by the other essays—racial and sexual discrimination. In "The Feminization of Ghetto Poverty" Pearce reports economic policy's social consequences for women, particularly black women, employing statistics, an important sociological tool. Galbraith, too, looks at the relationship between social and economic behavior, but from an economist's perspective, in "The Higher Economic Purpose of Women."

Psychological Data and Human Values
Abraham Maslow

Abraham Maslow (1908–1971) taught psychology at Brooklyn College and the University of Wisconsin, and served as chair of the psychology department at Brandeis University. The author of Principles of Abnormal Psychology, Healthy Personality, *and* Toward a Psychology of Being *(from which this selection is taken), Maslow is best known for his work on the hierarchical nature of human needs. According to his theory, satisfied needs drive an individual to seek satisfaction at a higher level. A person first must meet physiological needs, then needs for safety, and then for social affiliation and love before he or she can seek self-esteem and finally, self-actualization. In "Psychological Data and Human Values," Maslow identifies research that leads him to hypothesize the need for self-actualization.*

[From recent evidence] it seems quite clear that all organisms are more self-governing, self-regulating and autonomous [than previously was believed]. [Any capacity inherent in an organism seeks to function; basic needs assure this functioning (self-actualizing). Human needs are hierarchical. The human must fulfill a lower need for food or security, say, before it experiences a higher need for recognition or love. Man's ultimate need for self-actualization represents an ultimate value for mankind. The "peak experiences" derived from meeting each basic need give glimpses of ultimate self-actualization and thereby give validation. From studies of self-actualized human beings, a set of measurable and objectively describable characteristics of the healthy human specimen can be drawn. Furthermore, these characteristics are reinforcing. These findings can be generalized to most of the human species because most people tend toward self-actualization, and, in principle at least, most people are capable of self-actualization.]

Hundreds of experiments have been made that demonstrate a universal inborn ability in all sorts of animals to select a beneficial diet if enough alternatives are presented from among which they are permitted free choice. This wisdom of the body is often retained under less usual conditions, e.g., adrenalectomized[1] animals can keep themselves alive by readjusting their self-chosen diet. Pregnant animals will nicely adjust their diets to the needs of the growing embryo.

We now know this is by no means a perfect widom. These appetites are less efficient, for instance, in reflecting body need for vitamins. Lower animals protect themselves against poisons more efficiently than higher animals and humans. Previously formed habits of preference may quite overshadow present metabolic needs. And most of all, in the human being, and especially in the neurotic human being, all sorts of forces can contaminate this wisdom of the body, although it never seems to be lost altogether.

The general principle is true not only for selection of food but also for all sorts of other body needs as the famous homeostasis experiments have shown.

It seems quite clear that all organisms are more self-governing, self-regulating and autonomous than we thought 25 years ago. The organism deserves a good deal of trust, and we are learning steadily to rely on this internal wisdom of our babies with reference to choice of diet, time of weaning, amount of sleep, time of toilet training, need for activity, and a lot else.

But more recently we have been learning, especially from physically and mentally sick people, that there are good choosers and bad choosers. We have learned, especially from the psychoanalysts, much about the hidden causes of such behavior and have learned to respect these causes.

In this connection we have available a startling experiment, which is pregnant with implications for value theory. Chickens allowed to choose their own diet vary widely in their ability to choose what is good for them. The good choosers become stronger, larger, more dominant than the poor choosers, which means that they get the best of everything. If then the diet chosen by the good choosers if forced upon the poor choosers, it is found that *they* now get stronger, bigger, healthier and more dominant, although never reaching the level of the good choosers. That is, good choosers can choose better than bad choosers what is better for the bad choosers themselves. If similar experimental findings are made in human beings, as I think they will be (supporting clinical data are available aplenty), we are in for a good deal of reconstruction of all sorts of theories. So far as human value theory is concerned, no theory will be adequate that rests simply on the statistical description of the choices of unselected human beings. To average the choices of good and bad choosers, of healthy and sick people is useless. Only the choices and tastes and judgments of healthy human beings will tell us much about what is good for the human species in the long run. The choices of neurotic people can tell us mostly what is good for keeping a neurosis stabilized, just as the choices of a brain injured man are good for preventing a catastrophic breakdown, or as the choices of an adrenalectomized animal may keep *him* from dying but would kill a healthy animal.

I think that this is the main reef on which most hedonistic[2] value theories and ethical theories have foundered. Pathologically motivated pleasures cannot be averaged with healthily motivated pleasures.

Furthermore any ethical code will have to deal with the fact of constitutional differences not only in chickens and rats but also in men, as Sheldon and Morris have shown. Some values are common to all (healthy) mankind, but also some other values will not be common to all mankind, but only to some types of people, or to specific individuals. What I have called the basic needs are probably common to all mankind and are, therefore, shared values. But idiosyncratic needs generate idiosyncratic values.

Constitutional differences in individuals generate preferences among ways of relating to self, and to culture and to the world, i.e., generate values. These researches support and are supported by the universal experience of clinicians with individual differences. This is also true of the ethnological data that make sense of cultural diversity by postulating that each culture selects for exploitation, suppression, approval or disapproval, a small segment of the range of human constiutional possibilities. This is all in line with the biological data and theories and self-actualization theories which show that an organ system presses to express itself, in a word, to function. The muscular person likes to use his muscles, indeed, *has* to use them in order to self-actualize, and to achieve the subjective feeling of harmonious, uninhibited, satisfying functioning which is so important an aspect of psychological health. People with intelligence must use their intelligence, people with eyes must use their eyes, people with the capacity to love have the *impulse* to love and the *need* to love in order to feel healthy. Capacities clamor to be used, and cease their clamor only when they *are* used sufficiently. That is to say, capacities are needs, and therefore are intrinsic values as well. To the extent that capacities differ, so will values also differ.

BASIC NEEDS AND THEIR HIERARCHICAL ARRANGEMENT

It has by now been sufficiently demonstrated that the human being has, as part of his intrinsic construction, not only physiological needs, but also truly psychological ones. They may be considered as deficiencies which must be optimally fulfilled by the environment in order to avoid sickness and subjective illness. They can be called basic, or biological, and likened to the need for salt, or calcium or vitamin D because—

a. The deprived person yearns for their gratification persistently.
b. Their deprivation makes the person sicken and wither.
c. Gratifying them is therapeutic, curing the deficiency-illness.
d. Steady supplies forestall these illnesses.
e. Healthy (gratified) people do not demonstrate these deficiencies.

But these needs or values are related to each other in a hierarchical and developmental way, in an order of strength and of priority. Safety is a more prepotent, or stronger, more pressing, more vital need than love, for instance, and the need for food is usually stronger than either. Furthermore, *all* these basic needs may be considered to be simply steps along the path to general self-actualization, under which all basic needs can be subsumed.

By taking these data into account, we can solve many value problems that philosophers have struggled with ineffectually for centuries. For one thing, it looks as if *there were* a single ultimate value for mankind, a far goal toward which all men strive. This is called variously by different authors self-actualization, self-realization, integration, psychological health, individuation, autonomy, creativity, productivity, but they all agree that this amounts to realizing the potentialities of the person, that is to say, becoming fully human, everything that the person *can* become.

But it is also true that the person himself does not know this. We, the psychologists observing and studying, have constructed this concept in order to integrate and explain lots of diverse data. So far as the person himself is concerned, all *he* knows is that he is desperate for love, and thinks he will be forever happy and content if he gets it. He does not know in advance that he will strive on *after* this gratification has come, and that gratification of one basic need opens consciousness to domination by another, "higher" need. So far as he is concerned, *the* absolute, ultimate value, synonymous with life itself, is whichever need in the hierarchy he is dominated by during a particular period. These basic needs or basic values therefore may be treated *both* as ends and as steps toward a single end goal. It is true that there is a single, ultimate value or end of life and *also* it is just as true that we have a hierarchical and developmental system of values, complexly interrelated.

This also helps to solve the apparent paradox of contrast between Being and Becoming. It is true that human beings strive perpetually toward ultimate humanness, which itself may be anyway a different kind of Becoming and growing. It's as if we were doomed forever to try to arrive at a state to which we could never attain. Fortunately we now know this not to be true, or at least it is not the only truth. There is another truth which integrates with it. We are again and again rewarded for good Becoming by transient states of absolute Being, by peak-experiences. Achieving basic-need gratifications gives us many peak-experiences, each of which are absolute delights, perfect in themselves, and needing no more than themselves to validate life. This is like rejecting the notion that a Heaven lies someplace beyond the end of the path of life. Heaven, so to speak, lies waiting for us through life, ready to step into for a time and to enjoy before we have to come back to our ordinary life of striving. And once we have been in it, we can remember it forever, and feed ourselves on this memory and be sustained in time of stress.

Not only this, but the process of moment-to-moment growth is itself intrinsically rewarding and delightful in an absolute sense. If they are not mountain peak-experiences, at least they are foothill-experiences, little glimpses of absolute, self-validative delight, little moments of Being. Being and Becoming are *not* contradictory or mutually exclusive. Approaching and arriving are both in themselves rewarding.

SELF-ACTUALIZATION: GROWTH

I have published in another place a survey of all the evidence that forces us in the direction of a concept of healthy growth or of self-actualizing tendencies. This is partly deductive evidence in the sense of pointing out that unless we postulate such a concept, much of human behavior makes no sense. This is on the same scientific principle that led to the discovery of a hitherto unseen planet that *had* to be there in order to make sense of a lot of other observed data.

There is also some direct clinical and personological evidence, as well as an increasing amount of test data to support this belief. We can certainly now assert that at least a reasonable, theoretical, and empirical case has been made for the presence within the human being of a tendency toward, or need for growing in a direction that can be summarized in general as self-actualization, or psychological health, and specifically as growth toward each and all of the sub-aspects of self-actualization, i.e., he has within him a pressure toward unity of personality, toward spontaneous expressiveness, toward full individuality and identity, toward seeing the truth rather than being blind, toward being creative, toward being good, and a lot else. That is, the human being is so constructed that he presses toward fuller and fuller being and this means pressing toward what most people would call good values, toward serenity, kindness, courage, honesty, love, unselfishness, and goodness.

It is a delicate matter putting limits on what to claim here and what not. So far as my own studies go, they are based mostly on adults who have, so to speak, "succeeded." I have little information on the non-successes, the ones who dropped out along the way. It is perfectly acceptable to conclude from a study of Olympic medal winners that is in principle possible for a human being to run so fast or jump so high or lift such and such a weight, and that so far as we can tell, any newborn baby might do as well. But this real possibility doesn't tell us anything about statistics and probabilities and likelihood. The situation is about the same for self-actualizing people, as Buhier has justly emphasized.

Furthermore we should be careful to note that the tendency to grow toward full-humanness and health is not the *only* tendency to be found in the human being. In this same person we can also find death-wishes, tendencies to fear, defense and regression, etc.

And yet, few in number though they be, we can learn a great deal about values from the direct study of these highly evolved, most mature, psychologically healthiest individuals, and from the study of the peak moments of average individuals, moments in which they become transiently self-actualized. This is because they are in very real empirical and theoretical ways, most fully human. For instance, they are people who have retained and developed their human capacities, especially those capacities which define the human being and differentiate him from, let us say, the monkey. (This accords with Hartman's axiological approach to the same problem of defining the good human being as the one who has more of the characteristics which define the concept "human being.") From a developmental point of view, they are more fully evolved because not fixated at immature or incomplete levels of growth. This is no more mysterious, or a priori, or question begging than the selection of a type specimen of butterfly by a taxonomist or the most physically healthy young man by the physician. They both look for the "perfect or mature or magnificent specimen" for the exemplar, and so have I. One procedure is as repeatable in principle as the other.

Full humanness can be defined not only in terms of the degree to which the definition of the concept "human" is fulfilled, i.e., the species norm. It also has a descriptive, cataloguing, measurable, psychological definition. We now have from a few research beginnings and from countless clinical experiences some notion of the characteristics both of the fully evolved human being and of the well-growing human being. These characteristics are not only neutrally describable; they are also subjectively rewarding, pleasurable and reinforcing.

Among the objectively describable and measurable characteristics of the healthy human specimen are—

1. Clearer, more efficient perception of reality.
2. More openness to experience.
3. Increased integration, wholeness, and unity of the person.
4. Increased spontaneity, expressiveness; full functioning; aliveness.
5. A real self; a firm identity; autonomy, uniqueness.
6. Increased objectivity, detachment, transcendance of self.
7. Recovery of creativeness.
8. Ability to fuse concreteness and abstractness.
9. Democratic character structure.
10. Ability to love, etc.

These all need research confirmation and exploration but it is clear that such researches are feasible.

In addition, there are subjective confirmations or reinforcements of self-actualization or of good growth toward it. These are the feelings of zest in living, of happiness or euphoria, of serenity, of joy, of calmness, of responsibility, of confidence in one's ability to handle stresses, anxieties, and problems. The subjective signs of self-betrayal, of fixation, of regression, and of living by fear rather than by growth are such feelings as anxiety, despair, boredom, inability to enjoy, intrinsic guilt, intrinsic shame, aimlessness, feelings of emptiness, of lack of identity, etc.

These subjective reactions are also susceptible of research exploration. We have clinical techniques available for studying them.

It is the free choices of such self-actualizing people (in those situations where real choice is possible from among a variety of possibilities) that I claim can be descriptively studied as a naturalistic value system with which the hopes of the observer absolutely have nothing to do, i.e., it is "scientific." I do not say, "He *ought* to choose this or that," but only, "Healthy people, permitted to choose freely, are *observed* to choose this or that." This is like asking, "What *are* the values of the best human beings," rather than, "What *should* be their values?" or, "What *ought* they be?" (Compare this with Aristotle's belief that "it is the things which are valuable and pleasant to a good man that are really valuable and pleasant.")

Furthermore, I think these findings can be generalized to most of the human species because it looks to me (and to others) as if most people (perhaps all) tend toward self-actualization (this is seen most clearly in the experiences in psychotherapy, especially of the uncovering sort), and as if, in principle at least, most people are *capable* of self-actualization.

Notes

¹ adrenalectomized: having had the adrenal glands removed.
² hedonistic: pertaining to the theory that a person always acts in such a way as to seek pleasure and avoid pain.

FOCUS: READING REVIEW

1. What support does Maslow offer for the idea that organisms are self-governing, self-regulating, and autonomous?
2. What are "good choosers" and "bad choosers"? What implications does this have for understanding human behavior?
3. What is self-actualization theory? How does this compare with Skinner's description of the causes of behavior? with Freud's?
4. What does Maslow say psychologists see as mankind's ultimate value? What does any human being see at a given point in his life?
5. What are "peak" moments? What are their implications for values?
6. What implications do free-choice experiments on healthy individuals hold for conceptions of human personality and for understanding the role of man in forming his society?

FOCUS: AUTHOR'S STRATEGIES

1. The writer constructs a complex argument in which he generalizes from specific evidence and then asserts by analogy another general principle that serves as his hypothesis. Explain how this process operates with Maslow's free-choice studies.
2. Maslow writes for a peer audience. How do you know this from kind of evidence, the language, and the assumptions about the audience's knowledge and experience?
3. Having identified Maslow's audience and method, explain how these relate to the writing's purpose.

FOCUS: DISCUSSION AND WRITING

1. Maslow says that the muscular person likes to use his muscles, indeed, has to use them in order to achieve the subjective feeling of harmonious function so important to psychological health. Relate an experience where you have had a "peak experience" because you used an innate ability to its fullest.
2. Maslow asserts that the healthy human being has within him or her a pressure toward spontaneous expressiveness, toward full individuality, toward seeing truth, toward being creative, and toward being good. Do you agree with this assertion? On what evidence does your judgment rest? How would Maslow explain the problem of evil?

Are Women Prejudiced Against Women?
Philip Goldberg

Philip Goldberg (b. 1932), a professor of psychology at Connecticut College, writes on the social and psychological determinants of political behavior. He graduated from Columbia University and received his Ph.D. from the University of Buffalo. This essay, an example of a formal presentation of social science research, examines women's responses to identical professional articles identified with a female author and then with a male.

[Historically studies have shown that both sexes value men more highly than women. This study examines whether women will value a professional writing with a jaundiced eye when they think it is the work of a woman, but praise the same article when its author is a man. To test this hypothesis, 140 college women selected at random were given six professional articles—one each from law, city planning, elementary school teaching, dietetics, linguistics, and art history. The articles were placed in two equal, identical sets of booklets, except that the authors' names were manipulated—the same article bore a male name in one set of booklets, a female name in the other set. The women were asked to answer questions evaluating the competence of the articles. The results indicate that there is clearly a tendency among women to downgrade the work of professionals of their own sex.]

"Woman," advised Aristotle, "may be said to be an inferior man."

Because he was a man, Aristotle was probably biased. But what do women themselves think? Do they, consciously or unconsciously, consider their own sex inferior? And if so, does this belief prejudice them against other women—that is, make them view women, simply because they *are* women, as less competent than men?

According to a study conducted by myself and my associates, the answer to both questions is Yes. Women *do* consider their own sex inferior. And even when the facts give no support to this belief, they will persist in downgrading the competence—in particular, the intellectual and professional competence—of their fellow females.

Over the years, psychologists and psychiatrists have shown that both sexes consistently value men more highly than women. Characteristics considered male are usually praised; those considered female are usually criticized. In 1957 A.C. Sheriffs and J.P. McKee noted that "women are regarded as guilty of snobbery and irrational and unpleasant emotionality." Consistent with this report, E.G. French and G.S. Lesser found in 1964 that "women who value intellectual attainment feel they must reject the woman's role"—intellectual accomplishment apparently being considered, even among intellectual women, a masculine preserve. In addition, ardent feminists like Simone de Beauvoir and Betty Friedan[1] believe that men, in important ways, are superior to women.

Now, is this belief simply prejudice, or are the characteristics and achievements of women really inferior to those of men? In answering this question, we need to draw some careful distinctions.

DIFFERENT OR INFERIOR?

Most important, we need to recognize that there are two distinct dimensions to the issue of sex differences. The first question is whether sex differences exist at all, apart from the obvious physical ones. The answer to this question seems to be a unanimous Yes—men, women, and social scientists agree that, psychologically and emotionally as well are physically, women *are* different from men.

But is being different the same as being inferior? It is quite possible to perceive a difference accurately but to value it inaccurately. Do women automatically view their differences from men as *deficiencies?* The evidence is that they do, and that this value judgment opens the door to anti-female prejudice. For if someone (male or female) concludes that women are inferior, his perceptions of women—their personalities, behavior, abilities, and accomplishments—will tend to be colored by his low expectations of women.

As Gordon W. Allport has pointed out in *The Nature of Prejudice,* whatever the facts about sex differences, anti-feminism—like any other prejudice—*distorts perception and experience.* What defines anti-feminism is not so much believing that women are inferior, as allowing that belief to distort one's perceptions of women. More generally, it is not the partiality itself, but the distortion born of that partiality, that defines prejudice.

Thus, an anti-Semite watching a Jew may see devious or sneaky behavior. But, in a Christian, he would regard such behavior only as quiet, reserved, or perhaps even shy. Prejudice is self-sustaining: It continually distorts the "evidence" on which the prejudiced person claims to base his beliefs. Allport makes it clear that anti-feminism, like anti-Semitism or any other prejudice, consistently twists the "evidence" of experience. We see not what is there, but what we *expect* to see.

The purpose of our study was to investigate whether there is real prejudice by women against women—whether perception itself is distorted unfavorably. Specifically, will women evaluate a professional article with a jaundiced eye when they think it is the work of a woman, but praise the same article when they think its author is a man? Our hypotheses were:

- Even when the work is identical, women value the professional work of men more highly than that of women.
- But when the professional field happens to be one traditionally reserved for women (nursing, dietetics), this tendency will be reversed, or at least greatly diminished.

Some 140 college girls, selected at random, were our subjects. One hundred were used for preliminary work; 40 participated in the experiment proper.

To test the second hypothesis, we gave the 100 girls a list of 50 occupations and asked them to rate "the degree to which you associate the field with men or with women." We found that law and city planning were fields strongly associated with men, elementary-school teaching and dietetics were fields strongly associated with women, and two fields—linguistics and art history—were chosen as neutrals, not strongly associated with either sex.

Now we were ready for the main experiment. From the professional literature of each of these six fields, we took one article. The articles were edited and abridged to about 1500 words, then combined into two equal sets of booklets. The crucial manipulation had to do with the authors' names—the same article bore a male name in one set of booklets, a female name in the other set. An example: If, in set one, the first article bore the name John T. McKay, in set two the same article would appear under the name Joan T. McKay. Each booklet contained three articles by "men" and three articles by "women."

The girls, seated together in a large lecture hall, were told to read the articles in their booklets and given these instructions:

"In this booklet you will find excerpts of six articles, written by six different authors in six different professional fields. At the end of each article you will find several questions . . . . You are not presumed to be sophisticated or knowledgeable in all the fields. We are interested in the ability of college students to make critical evaluations. . . ."

Note that no mention at all was made of the authors' sexes. That information was contained—apparently only by coincidence—in the authors' names. The girls could not know, therefore, what we were really looking for.

At the end of each article were nine questions asking the girls to rate the articles for value, persuasiveness, and profundity—and to rate the authors for writing style, professional competence, professional status, and ability to sway the reader.

On each item, the girls gave a rating of from 1 (highly favorable) to 5 (highly unfavorable).

Generally, the results were in line with our expectations—but not completely. In analyzing these results, we used three different methods: We compared the amount of anti-female bias in the different occupational fields (would men be rated as better city planners, but women as better dieticians?); we compared the amount of bias shown on the nine questions that followed each article (would men be rated more competent, but women as more persuasive?); and we ran an overall comparison, including both fields and rating questions.

Starting with the analysis of bias by occupational field, we immediately ran into a major surprise. (See the table below.) That there is a general bias by women against women, and that it is strongest in traditionally masculine fields, was clearly borne out. But in other fields the situation seemed rather confused. We had expected the anti-female trend to be reversed in traditionally feminine fields. But it appears that, even here, women consider themselves inferior to men. Women seem to think that men are better at *everything*—including elementary-school teaching and dietetics!

Law: A Strong Masculine Preserve

Field of Article	Mean	
	Male	Female
Art History	23.35	23.10
Dietetics	22.05	23.45
Education	20.20	21.75
City Planning	23.10	27.30
Linguistics	26.95	30.70
Law	21.20	25.60

These are the total scores the college girls gave to the six pairs of articles they read. The lowest possible score—9—would be the most favorable; the highest possible score—54—the most critical. While male authors received more favorable ratings in all occupational fields, the differences were statistically significant only in city planning, linguistics, and—especially—law.

Scrutiny of the nine rating questions yielded similar results. On all nine questions, regardless of the author's occupational field, the girls consistently found an article more valuable—and its author more competent—when the article bore a male name. Though the articles themselves were exactly the same, the girls felt that those written by the John T. McKays were definitely more impressive, and reflected more glory on their authors, than did the mediocre offerings of the Joan T. McKays. Perhaps because the world has accepted female authors for a long time, the girls were willing to concede that the female professionals' writing styles were not *far* inferior to those of men. But such a concession to female competence was rare indeed.

Statistical analysis confirms these impressions and makes them more definite. With a total of six articles, and with nine questions after each one, there were 54 points at which comparisons could be drawn between the male authors and the female authors. Out of these 54 comparisons, three were tied, seven favored the female authors—and the number favoring the male authors was 44!

Clearly, there is a tendency among women to downgrade the work of professionals of their own sex. But the hypothesis that this tendency would decrease as the "femaleness" of the professional field increased was not supported. Even in traditionally female fields, anti-feminism holds sway.

Since the articles supposedly written by men were exactly the same as those supposedly written by women, the perception that the men's articles were superior was obviously a distortion. For reasons of their own, the female subjects were sensitive to the sex of the author, and this apparently irrelevant information biased their judgments. Both the distortion and the sensitivity that precedes it are characteristic of prejudice. Women—at least these young college women—are prejudiced against female professionals and, regardless of the actual accomplishments of these professionals, will firmly refuse to recognize them as the equals of their male colleagues.

Is the intellectual double-standard really dead? Not at all—and if the college girls in this study are typical of the educated and presumably progressive segments of the population, it may not even be dying. Whatever lip service these girls pay to modern ideas of equality between men and women, their beliefs are staunchly traditional. Their real coach in the battle of the sexes is not Simone de Beauvoir or Betty Friedan. Their coach is Aristotle.

Notes

[1] Simone de Beauvoir and Betty Friedan are two feminist authors. Beauvoir is best known for *The Second Sex* and Friedan for *The Feminine Mystique.*

FOCUS: READING REVIEW

1. What hypotheses govern Goldberg's experiment? What are his experimental methods?
2. How valid is this sample study in terms of socioeconomic, regional, and numerical samples?
3. What conclusions does he reach? Are his conclusions in the last three paragraphs fully supported by his data? Why or why not?
4. Before reporting the experiment the author asserts that prejudice twists the "evidence" or experience. How does the experiment prove this assertion?

FOCUS: AUTHOR'S STRATEGIES

1. What audience does the introduction indicate? Why?
2. Identify the components of Goldberg's inductive argument.

3. What is the effect of the final statement, "Their real coach in the battle of the sexes is not Simone de Beauvoir or Betty Friedan. Their coach is Aristotle." when you refer back to the first sentence of the essay? Does the writer assure his own experimental objectivity by this?

FOCUS: DISCUSSION AND WRITING

1. Based on your own experience, do you believe that people are prejudiced against women? Would you go to a woman doctor? A woman dentist? Would you confide in a woman rabbi, priest, or minister? Would you consult a woman psychologist? Give reasons for your responses.
2. Does a study such as this reinforce traditional views of women or does it advance equal rights? Explain your reason with specific reference to the essay.

Fail: Bright Women

Matina Horner

Matina Horner (b. 1939) taught psychology and social relations at the University of Michigan and Harvard University before she became president of Radcliffe College in 1972. A graduate of Bryn Mawr, she received her M.A. and Ph.D. in psychology from the University of Michigan. Articles about her research on the relationship between sex-role stereotyping and motivation have appeared in the Journal of Social Issues, Harper's, *and* Psychology Today. *The essay "Fail: Bright Women," which appeared in* Psychology Today *(November 1969), outlines for a popular audience her preliminary research on the relationship between sex and motivation. Although Horner writes here for a popular audience, she conforms to social science report-writing conventions.*

[Consciously or unconsciously girls equate intellectual achievement with loss of femininity. In testing situations a bright woman worries not only about failure, but also about success. If she fails, she is not living up to her own standards of performance; if she succeeds she is not living up to societal expectations about the female role. A sample of 90 girls and 88 boys, all University of Michigan undergraduates, took the standard TAT to measure achievement motivation.] In addition each told a story based on the clue: *After first-term finals, John (Anne) finds himself (herself) at the top of his (her) medical class.* The stories were scored for their "motive to avoid success." [We can see from this small study that achievement motivation in women is much more complex than the same drive in men. Most men do not find many inhibiting forces in their path if they are able and motivated to success.]

Consider Phil, a bright young college sophomore. He has always done well in school, he is in the honors program, he has wanted to be a doctor as long as he can remember. We ask him to tell us a story based on one clue: *"After first-term finals, John finds himself at the top of his medical school class."* Phil writes:

> John is a conscientious young man who worked hard. He is pleased with himself. John has always wanted to go into medicine and is very dedicated . . . John continues working hard and eventually graduates at the top of his class.

Now consider Monica, another honors student. She too has always done well and she too has visions of a flourishing career. We give her the same clue, but with "Anne" as the successful student—*after first-term finals, Anne finds herself at the top of her medical school class.* Instead of identifying with Anne's triumph, Monica tells a bizarre tale:

> Anne starts proclaiming her surprise and joy. Her fellow classmates are so disgusted with her behavior that they jump on her in a body and beat her. She is maimed for life.

Next we ask Monica and Phil to work on a series of achievement tests by themselves. Monica scores higher than Phil. Finally we get them together, competing against each other on the same kind of tests. Phil performs magnificently, but Monica dissolves into a bundle of nerves.

The glaring contrast between the two stories and the dramatic changes in performance in competitive situations illustrate important differences between men and women in reacting to achievement.

In 1953, David McClelland, John Atkinson and colleagues published the first major work on the "achievement motive." Through the use of the Thematic Apperception Test (TAT), they were able to isolate the psychological characteristic of a *need to achieve.* This seemed to be an internalized standard of excellence, motivating the individual to do well in any achievement-oriented situation involving intelligence and leadership ability. Subsequent investigators studied innumerable facets of achievement motivation: how it is instilled in children, how it is expressed, how it relates to social class, even how it is connected to the rise and fall of civilizations. The result of all this research is an impressive and a theoretically consistent body of data about the achievement motive—in men.

Women, however, are conspicuously absent from almost all of the studies. In the few cases where the ladies were included, the results were contradictory or confusing. So women were eventually left out altogether. The predominantly male researchers apparently decided, as Freud had before them, that the only way to understand woman was to turn to the poets. Atkinson's 1958 book, *Motives in*

Fantasy, Action and Society, is an 800-page compilation of all of the theories and facts on achievement motivation in men. Women got a footnote, reflecting the state of the science.

To help remedy this lopsided state of affairs, I undertook to explore the basis for sex differences in achievement motivation. But where to begin?

My first clue came from the one consistent finding on the women: they get higher test-anxiety scores than do the men. Eleanor Maccoby has suggested that the girl who is motivated to achieve is defying conventions of what girls "should" do. As a result, the intellectual woman pays a price in anxiety. Margaret Mead concurs, noting that intense intellectual striving can be viewed as "competitively aggressive behavior." And of course Freud thought that the whole essence of femininity lay in repressing aggressiveness (and hence intellectuality).

Thus consciously or unconsciously the girl equates intellectual achievement with loss of femininity. A bright woman is caught in a double bind. In testing and other achievement-oriented situations she worries not only about failure, but also about success. If she fails, she is not living up to her own standards of performance; if she succeeds, she is not living up to societal expectations about the female role. Men in our society do not experience this kind of ambivalence, because they are not only permitted but actively encouraged to do well.

For women, then, the desire to achieve is often contaminated by what I call the *motive to avoid success*. I define it as the fear that success in competitve achievement situations will lead to negative consequences, such as unpopularity and loss of femininity. This motive, like the achievement motive itself, is a stable disposition within the person, acquired early in life along with other sex-role standards. When fear of success conflicts with a desire to be successful, the result is an inhibition of achievement motivation.

I began my study with several hypotheses about the motive to avoid success:

1. Of course, it would be far more characteristic of women than of men.
2. It would be more characteristic of women who are capable of success and who are career-oriented than of women not so motivated. Women who are not seeking success should not, after all, be threatened by it.
3. I anticipated that the anxiety over success would be greater in competitive situations (when one's intellectual performance is evaluated against someone else's) than in noncompetitive ones (when one works alone). The aggressive, masculine aspects of achievement striving are certainly more pronounced in competitive settings, particularly when the opponent is male. Women's anxiety should therefore be greatest when they compete with men.

I administered the standard TAT achievement motivation measures to a sample of 90 girls and 88 boys, all undergraduates at the University of Michigan. In addition, I asked each to tell a story based on the clue described before: *After first-term finals, John (Anne) finds himself (herself) at the top of his (her) medical school class.* The girls wrote about Anne, the boys about John.

Their stories were scored for "motive to avoid success" if they expressed any negative imagery that reflected concern about doing well. Generally, such imagery fell into three categories:

1. The most frequent Anne story reflected strong fears of social rejection as a result of success. The girls in this group showed anxiety about becoming unpopular, unmarriageable and lonely.

Anne is an acne-faced bookworm. She runs to the bulletin board and finds she's at the top. As usual she smarts off. A chorus of groans is the rest of the class's reply.... She studies 12 hours a day, and lives at home to save money. "Well it certainly paid off. All the Friday and Saturday nights without dates, fun—I'll be the best women doctor alive." And yet a twinge of sadness comes thru—she wonders what she really has ...

Although Anne is happy with her success she fears what will happen to her social life. The male med. students don't seem to think very highly of a female who has beaten them in their field . . . She will be a proud and successful but alas a very *lonely* doctor.

Anne doesn't want to be number one in her class . . . she feels she shouldn't rank so high because of social reasons. She drops down to ninth in the class and then marries the boy who graduates number one.

Anne is pretty darn proud of herself, but everyone hates and envies her.

2. Girls in the second category were less concerned with issues of social approval or disapproval; they were more worried about definitions of womanhood. Their stories expressed guilt and despair over success, and doubts about their femininity or normality.

Unfortunately Anne no longer feels so certain that she really wants to be a doctor. She is worried about herself and wonders if perhaps she isn't normal. . . Anne decides not to continue with her medical work but to take courses that have a deeper personal meaning for her.

Anne feels guilty. . . She will finally have a nervous breakdown and quit medical school and marry a successful young doctor.

Anne is pleased. She had worked extraordinarily hard and her grades showed it. "It is not enough," Anne thinks. "I am not happy." She didn't even want to be a doctor. She is not sure what she wants. Anne says to hell with the whole business and goes into social work—not hardly as glamorous, prestigious or lucrative; but she is happy.

3. The third group of stories did not even try to confront the ambivalence about doing well. Girls in this category simply denied the possibility that any mere woman could be so successful. Some of them completely changed the content of the clue,

or distorted it, or refused to believe it, or absolved Anne of responsibility for her success. These stories were remarkable for their psychological ingenuity:

Anne is a *code name* for a nonexistent person created by a group of med. students. They take turns writing exams for Anne . .

Anne is really happy she's on top, though *Tom is higher than she*—though that's as it should be . . . Anne doesn't mind Tom winning.

Anne is talking to her counselor. Counselor says she will make a fine *nurse.*

It was *luck* that Anne came out on top because she didn't want to go to medical school anyway.

Fifty-nine girls—over 65 percent—told stories that fell into one or another of the above categories. But only eight boys, fewer than 10 percent, showed evidence of the motive to avoid success. (These differences are significant at better than the .0005 level.) In fact, sometimes I think that most of the young men in the sample were incipient Horatio Algers. They expressed unequivocal delight at John's success (clearly John had worked hard for it), and projected a grand and glorious future for him. There was none of the hostility, bitterness and ambivalence that the girls felt for Anne. In short, the differences between male and female stories based on essentially the same clue were enormous.

Two of the stories are particularly revealing examples of this male-female contrast. The girls insisted that Anne give up her career for marriage:

Anne has a boyfriend, Carl, in the same class and they are quite serious . . . She wants him to be scholastically higher than she is. Anne will deliberately lower her academic standing the next term, while she does all she subtly can to help Carl. His grades come up and Anne soon drops out of medical school. They marry and he goes on in school while she raises their family.

But of course the boys would ask John to do no such thing:

John has worked very hard and his long hours of study have paid off . . . He is thinking about his girl, Cheri, whom he will marry at the end of med. school. He realizes he can give her all the things she desires after he becomes established. He will go on in med. school and be successful in the long run.

Success inhibits social life for the girls; it enhances social life for the boys.

Earlier I suggested that the motive to avoid success is especially aroused in competitive situations. In the second part of this study I wanted to see whether the aggressive overtones of competition against men scared the girls away. Would competition raise their anxiety about success and thus lower their performance?

First I put all of the students together in a large competitive group, and gave them a series of achievement tests (verbal and arithmetic). I then assigned them randomly to one of three other experimental conditions. One-third worked on a similar set of tests, each in competition with a member of the same sex. One-third competed against a member of the opposite sex. The last third worked by themselves, a non-competitive condition.

Ability is an important factor in achievement motivation research. If you want to compare two persons on the strength of their *motivation* to succeed, how do you know that any differences in performance are not due to initial differences in *ability* to succeed? One way of avoiding this problem is to use each subject as his own control; that is, the performance of an individual working alone can be compared with his score in competition. Ability thus remains constant; any change in score must be due to motivational factors. This control over ability was, of course, possible only for the last third of my subjects: the 30 girls and 30 boys who had worked alone *and* in the large group competition. I decided to look at their scores first.

Performance changed dramatically over the two situations. A large number of men did far better when they were in competition than when they worked alone. For the women the reverse was true. Fewer than one-third of the women, but more than two-thirds of the men, got significantly higher scores in competition.

When we looked at just the girls in terms of the motive to avoid success, the comparisons were even more striking. As predicted, the students who felt ambivalent or anxious about doing well turned in their best scores when they worked by themselves. Seventy-seven percent of the girls who feared success did better alone than in competition. Women who were low on the motive, however, behaved more like the men: 93 percent of them got higher scores in competition. (Results significant at the .005.)

Female Fear of Success and Performance

	Perform Better Working Alone	Perform Better in Competition
High fear of success	13	4
Low fear of success	1	12

As a final test of motivational differences, I asked the students to indicate on a scale from 1 to 100 "How important was it for you to do well in this situation?" The high-fear-of-success girls said that it was much more important for them to do well when they worked alone than when they worked in either kind of competition. For the low-fear girls, such differences were not statistically significant. Their test scores were higher in competition, as we saw, and they thought that it was important to succeed no matter what the setting. And in all experimental conditions—working alone, or in competition against males or females—high-fear women consistently lagged behind their fearless comrades on the importance of doing well.

The findings suggest that most women will fully explore their intellectual potential only when they do not need to compete—and least of all when they are competing with men. This was most true of women with a strong anxiety about success. Unfortunately, these are often the same women who could be very successful if they were free from that anxiety. The girls in my sample who feared success also tended to have high intellectual ability and histories of academic success. (It is interesting to note that all but two of these girls were majoring in the humanities and in spite of very high grade points aspired to traditional female careers: housewife, mother, nurse, schoolteacher. Girls who did not fear success, however, were aspiring to graduate degrees and careers in such scientific areas as math, physics and chemistry.)

We can see from this small study that achievement motivation in women is much more complex than the same drive in men. Most men do not find many inhibiting forces in their path if they are able and motivated to succeed. As a result, they are not threatened by competition; in fact, surpassing an opponent is a source of pride and enhanced masculinity.

If a woman sets out to do well, however, she bumps into a number of obstacles. She learns that it really isn't ladylike to be too intellectual. She is warned that men will treat ther with distrustful tolerance at best, and outright prejudice at worst, if she pursues a career. She learns the truth of Samuel Johnson's comment, "A man is in general better pleased when he has a good dinner upon his table, than when his wife talks Greek." So she doesn't learn Greek, and the motive to avoid success is born.

In recent years many legal and educational barriers to female achievement have been removed; but it is clear that a psychological barrier remains. The motive to avoid success has an all-too-important influence on the intellectual and professional lives of women in our society. But perhaps there is cause for optimism. Monica may have been Anne maimed for life, but a few of the girls forecast a happier future for our medical student. Said one:

> Anne is quite a lady—not only is she tops academically, but she is liked and admired by her fellow students—quite a trick in a man-dominated field. She is brilliant—but she is also a woman. She will continue to be at or near the top. And . . . always a lady.

FOCUS: READING REVIEW

1. What prompted the author's study on achievement motivation in women?
2. What assumptions underlie Horner's study? What are her experimental hypotheses?

3. What are her experimental procedures? What kinds of problems, if any, do you find in her methods and samples?
4. In what categories does Horner group her findings?
5. What interpretation does Horner offer of her findings? In what ways does the evidence support the interpretation? What other interpretations could have been reached?

FOCUS: AUTHOR'S STRATEGIES

1. The introduction to the essay describes two students' responses to a verbal cue. What have they been asked to do? What differences do you see in their responses? How does the selection of these two responses introduce the rest of the essay?
2. What is the author's purpose? What in the evidence and discussion of the evidence indicates this?
3. What persona reveals itself in the language and tone?

FOCUS: DISCUSSION AND WRITING

1. How do we define achievement and success? Does Horner's study reflect any assumptions about what constitutes success? Explain your own definition of success in relation to Horner's study.
2. Horner looks at a very select sample—college students. How might students in a trade school or people without a college education respond to Horner's definition of achievement and her questions?
3. Are men as confident about success as Horner represents them? In what ways have attitudes changed since this article first appeared in 1969?

When I Draw the Lord, He'll Be a Real Big Man
Robert Coles

Robert Coles (b. 1929) assumed a leading role in the social reforms of the sixties through his work as a social psychologist. A professor of psychiatry at Harvard Medical School, he received his medical training at Columbia University. For his humanitarian work Coles has received the Anisfield-Wolf Award in Race Relations and the Four Freedoms Award from the B'nai B'rith. Besides his major multivolumed work, Children of Crisis, 1967–1978 *from which the selection below is taken, he has written on literature, including* William Carlos Williams: The Knack of Survival in America *(1975),* Walter Percy: An American Search *(1978), and* Flannery O'Connor's South *(1980).* Children of Crisis, 1967–1978, *which received a Pulitzer Prize, has been acclaimed as a landmark of compassionate sociological scholarship. "When I Draw the Lord, He'll Be a Real Big Man," excerpted from the first chapter of the first volume, focuses on southern children during federally enforced school integration's early turbulent days.*

Here the social scientist Coles carefully establishes the background of his research, his methods, and reports his data, but his comfortable narrative interweaving the children's voices with his own engages the reader at a personal as well as an objective level.

Before I ever started my work in the South I had been interested in what the children I treated would tell me with crayons and paints. When I started visiting the four little girls in New Orleans whose entry into the first grades of two white schools occasioned strenuous the objection of mobs and a boycott by most white children, I carried with me paper and crayons. From the very beginning I made a point of asking those girls to draw pictures for me: of their school, their teacher or friends, anything they wanted to draw. Each child's particular life influences what and how he draws. The way these children draw is affected by their racial background. The first Southern child to put my crayons and paints to use was Ruby. She and I started talking when she was six years old, and braving daily mobs to attend an almost empty school building. For a long time Ruby never used brown or black except to indicate soil. She did, however, distinguish between white and Negro people. She drew white people larger and more lifelike. Negroes were smaller, their bodies less intact. Eventually I asked her why she thought twice about how much brown she would give a colored child. She was then eight. She replied directly: "When I draw a white girl, I know she'll be okay, but with the colored it's not so okay. So I try to give the colored as even a chance as I can, even if that's not the way it will end up being." Later, when Ruby was ten, her drawings were less prolific but very accomplished. "Ruby, you know my wife and I were looking at your drawings last night, and we both noticed how differently you draw Negro people now, in contrast to the way you did years ago. Do you think there's any reason for that?" She paused and then spoke out, "Maybe because of all the trouble going to school in the beginning I learned more about my people. Maybe I would have anyway, because when you get older you see yourself and the white kids, and you find out the difference. You try to forget it, and say there is none; and if there is you won't say what it be. Then you say it's my own people, and so I can be proud of them instead of ashamed."

Before I ever started my work in the South I had been interested in what the children I treated would tell me with crayons and paints—and chalk, for I always kept a blackboard in my office, and often a child would suddenly want to use it, then just as quickly apply the eraser to it. Because of my own interests I made a point of asking children whether they would like to sketch whatever came to mind, or indeed draw for me their home, school, parents or friends. Some did so eagerly, some reluctantly; some would have no part of my schemes for a long while, though in the course of treatment those who refused invariably changed their minds, as if they recognized that now they were able to let me know something once unmentionable and as well forbidden to representation.

I kept those files with me when I went South—a stack of drawings made by the middle-class children who make up the major population of a child guidance clinic and a child psychiatrist's private practice. When I started visiting the four little girls in New Orleans whose entry into the first grades of two white schools occasioned the strenuous objection of mobs and a boycott by most white children, I carried with me paper and crayons. From the very beginning I made a point of asking those girls to draw pictures for me: of their school, their teacher or friends, anything they wanted to draw. I also took an interest in the artwork they did in school, always a favorite activity for children in elementary school. There is no doubt about it, they learned that I was interested in their sketches, and without exception they have furnished me an increasing abundance of them over the years.

That same school year (1960–1961) a few white children trickled back to the boycotted schools, in spite of tenacious mobs that in varying strengths constantly besieged the two buildings. I began going to the homes of those children too, and I encouraged those children to draw as well as play games and talk with me. (They were five children from three homes.) During the second year of desegregation, from 1961 to 1962, I continued my studies in New Orleans and expanded them there (while also starting them in Atlanta) just as the city itself, by coming to some terms with its unruly elements, enabled its harassed schools to return gradually to normal. I started interviewing the eight Negro children who were added to the roster of pioneers; they went into three additional elementary schools. (I also expanded the number of white children I was seeing so that I could include their classmates.) All in all in New Orleans I was following up twelve Negro children and twelve white children that second year, as against the four Negro and five white children who in the first year were at one point the entire population of two schools.

In addition to those children I was seeing regularly and continually, I traveled widely in the South, spending a week or two in other villages, towns or cities where younger Negro children were initiating (and white children were experiencing) school desegregation. I lived for a while in Burnsville, North Carolina—a small, rural mountain village—and nearby Asheville, its metropolis. I spent several weeks in Memphis, and later I worked in Birmingham. Finally, in 1964, I divided three months' time between Jackson, Mississippi, and the little farming community of Harmony, near Carthage, Mississippi. In all these instances I tried to gain some impression of how children other than those I knew in New Orleans were managing the social and personal trials of desegregation. At times I felt rude and presumptuous asking children I scarcely knew to draw a picture of their school, a friend, eventually of themselves. Yet these children (and especially their parents) found it easier to draw than to talk; in fact I came to see that they expected me to ask them to *do* something, to test them in some way.

In New Orleans, as the months passed by, a firm relationship between the children and me developed, so that our drawing and painting exercises became more enthusiastic and personal. I encouraged the children to draw whatever they wished. The troubles and joys of their lives gradually took on form and color, and so did their shifting feelings toward me. At times I tried to direct their attention toward one or another concern I had: how they regarded themselves; how they felt they were managing at school; what skin color meant to them, and to others in their neighborhood or the city; why the mobs formed, and to what purpose; how they saw themselves getting along with their white or black classmates; how they viewed their teachers, and how they felt their teachers felt toward them as children, or as representatives of a race or a group of people. (One white child brought me up short at the very beginning of my work by telling me she thought her teacher prejudiced toward her: "She wishes my daddy made more money, so I could dress better. She always talks about the nice kids she used to teach in the Garden District, and how good they behaved. I think she minds me as bad as the nigra girl.")

What have these children had to say in the drawings they have done these past years? Is there any reasonable way to categorize and classify their pictures so that the individual child's feelings are preserved, and yet more general conclusions made possible? I think the answer to the second question is yes, and I will try to show why by describing the interests and concerns these children reveal when they take up crayons or a brush.

Drawings and paintings can be compared in a number of ways: the use of color; the subject matter chosen; the child's command of form; his desire to approximate the real or his ease with whatever fantasies come to mind; his willingness to talk about what he draws and explain it, to expand upon its relevance or significance—for his own life or the lives of others around him. Moreover, anyone who has worked with children and watched them draw over a period of time knows how sensitively the child's activity and performance will respond to his various moods. One day's chaos on paper may give way to another's impressive order and even eloquence. The child's fear and shyness, his doubts and suspicions about adults, especially doctors or visitors to his home, are translated onto the canvas: little may be drawn, mere copying is done, or only "safe" and "neutral" subjects are selected. Often the child may say that he has absolutely nothing on his mind, or that in any event he does not know how to draw. Weeks later that same child may ask for crayons or pick them up quite naturally. What he said in the past is of little concern to him; at last he feels safe, or interested in exchanging ideas and feelings with his doctor, that older starnger who keeps returning to his home.

Any discussion of what a given child (or one of his drawings) has to say about racial matters, school problems or mob scenes must take pains to put the child's social observations, his prejudices and partialities, into the context of his home life. By that I mean to insist upon the young child's strong inclination to reflect his parents' views; but even more, transfer to the neighborhood his personal tensions and struggles, so that other children, not to mention teachers or policemen, take on a meaning to him quite dependent upon how he manages with his parents, brothers and sisters.

I am saying that each child's particular life—his age, his family, his neighborhood, his medical and psychological past history, his intelligence—influences what and how he draws. I am also saying that the way these children draw is affected by their racial background, and what that "fact" means in their particular world (society) at that particular time (period of history). My task in the analysis of these drawings has been not only to understand them, but to learn to appreciate their significance in clinical work with adults. Over the years I have heard grown-up Southerners of both races recall their childhood experiences, their "old" attitudes; but there may be a distinct difference between the memories we have and the actual feelings we once had (or didn't have but now claim to have had) years ago. For that matter, it is often interesting to obtain the reactions of a parent or a teacher to a given drawing. A mother in New Orleans said to me once: "I looked at Mary's picture and all I could see was that she didn't draw it as good that time as she does others." The girl's teacher had this to say about the same picture: "Mary had trouble keeping the drawing accurate. She must have lost interest in it, and the result is a poor picture." Mary herself had the following appraisal to make: "Maybe I tried too hard, but it's a better picture than the easy ones I do." In point of fact, for the first time she had tried (and struggled) to include herself (and her brown skin) in one of the landscapes she usually did so easily.

The first Southern child to put my crayons and paints to use was Ruby. She and I started talking, playing and drawing together when she was six years old, and braving daily mobs to attend an almost empty school building. Upon our first meeting I told Ruby of my interest in drawings, and she showed me some she had done at school and brought home to keep. Over the years she has drawn and painted during most of our talks, so that I now have over two hundred of her productions. Many of the topics were her choice, while other pictures were started in response to my specific suggestion or even request. I would ask her to draw a picture of her school, or of her teacher. I would ask her to paint a picture of anyone she knew, or wanted to portray. I might ask her one day to try putting herself, her brother or her sister on paper, while on another occasion I might ask her to sketch a particular classmate or schoolmate of hers. (For many months there were only two or three of them, the children of the few whites who defied the boycott. We both knew them, and each of us knew that the other spent time with them, Ruby at school and I in visits to their homes.)

For a long time—four months, in fact, Ruby never used brown or black except to indicate soil or the ground; even then she always made sure they were covered by a solid covering of green grass. It was not simply on my account that she abstained from these colors; her school drawings showed a similar pattern. She did, however, distinguish between white and Negro people. She drew white people larger and more lifelike. Negroes were smaller, their bodies less intact. A white girl we both knew to be her own size appeared several times taller. While Ruby's own face lacked an eye in one drawing, an ear in another, the white girl never lacked any features. Moreover, Ruby drew the white girl's hands and legs carefully, always making sure that they had the proper number of fingers and toes. Not so with her own limbs, or those of any other Negro children she chose (or was asked) to picture. A thumb or forefinger might be missing, or a whole set of toes. The arms were shorter, even absent or truncated.

There were other interesting features to her drawings. The ears of Negroes appeared larger than those of white people. A Negro might not have two ears, but the one he or she did have was large indeed. When both were present, their large size persisted. In contrast, quite often a Negro appeared with no mouth—it would be "forgotten"—or she used a thin line to represent the mouth; whereas a white child or adult was likely to have lips, teeth and a full, wide-open mouth. With regard to the nose, Ruby often as not omitted it in both races, though interestingly enough, when it appeared it was in her white classmates a thin orange line.

Hair color and texture presented Ruby with the same kind of challenge that skin color did. So long as she kept away from brown and black crayons or paints she had to be very careful about the hair she drew. White children received blond (yellow) hair, or their hair would be the same orange that outlined their face—always the case with Negro children. Many people of both races had no hair. No Negro child had blond hair.

The first change in all this came when Ruby asked me whether she might draw her grandfather—her mother's father. It was not new for her to ask my permission to draw a particular picture, though this was the first time she had chosen someone living outside of New Orleans. (He has a farm in the Mississippi Delta.) With an enthusiasm and determination that struck me as unusual and worth watching she drew an enormous black man, his frame taking up—quite unusually—almost the entire sheet of paper. Not only did she outline his skin as brown; every inch of him was made brown except for a thick black belt across his midriff. His eyes were large, oval lines of black surrounding the brown irises. His mouth was large, and it showed fine, yellow-colored teeth. The ears were normal in size. The arms were long, stretching to the feet, ending in oversize hands; the left one had its normal complement of fingers, but the right was blessed with six. The legs were thick, and ended in heavily sketched black boots (a noticeable shift from the frayed shoes or bare feet hitherto drawn).

Ruby worked intently right to the end, then instantly told me what her grandfather was doing, and what he had to say. (Often I would ask her what was happening in the place she drew or what the person she painted was thinking.) "That's my momma's daddy and he has a farm that's his and no one else's; and he has just come home to have his supper. He is tired, but he feels real good and soon he is going to have a big supper and then go to bed."

Ruby's father at that time was unemployed. It was not the first time, though never before had he been fired simply because his daughter was going to one school rather than another. He tended to be morose at home. He sat looking at television, or he sat on the front steps of the house carving a piece of wood, throwing it away, hurling the knife at the house's wood, then fetching a new branch to peel, cut and again discard. He also suffered a noticeable loss of appetite—the entire family knew about it and talked about it. The children tried to coax their father to eat. His wife cooked especially tasty chicken or ribs. I was asked for an appetite stimulant—and prescribed a tonic made up of vitamins and some Dexamyl for his moodiness. I gave him a few sleeping pills because he would toss about by the hour and smoke incessantly. (In a house where eight people slept in two adjoining bedrooms with no door between them it seemed essential to do so not only for his sleep but the children's.)

I asked Ruby whether there was any particular reason why she decided to draw her grandfather that day. She told me she had none by shaking her head. She smiled, then picked up the crayons and started drawing again, this time doing a pastoral landscape. Brown and black were used appropriately and freely. When it was finished she took some of her Coke and a cookie, then spoke: "I like it here, but I wish we could live on a farm, too; and Momma says if it gets real bad we can always go there. She says her daddy is the strongest man you can find. She says his arms are as wide as I am, and he can lick anyone and his brother together. She says not to worry, we have a hiding place and I should remember it every day."

She was having no particularly bad time of it, but she was rather tired that day. By then she also knew me long enough to talk about her fears, her periods of exhaustion, her wish for refuge or escape. Only once before Ruby decided to draw her grandfather and a countryside scene had she mentioned her impatience with the mobs, her weariness at their persistence: "They don't seem to be getting tired, the way we thought. Maybe it'll have to be a race, and I hope we win. Some people sometimes think we won't, and maybe I believe them, but not for too long."

It took Ruby several more months to be able to draw or paint a Negro without hesitation or distortion. From the beginning I wondered whether it all was my fault, whether she was in some way intimidated by the strange white doctor who visited her, with his games and crayons, his persistent curiosity about how she was getting along. Though in fact I am sure she was, there is reason to believe that the pictures she drew reflected a larger truth about her feelings than the undeniable one of my somewhat formidable presence. Her mother had saved many of the drawings she did in Sunday school (all-Negro) before either desegregation or strange visitors came into her life, and the same pattern was to be found in them: whites drawn larger and more intact than Negroes; brown and black used with great restraint, just enough to indicate the person's race but no more. It was as if Ruby started drawing all people as white, then turned some of them into Negroes by depriving them of a limb or coloring a small section of their skin (she preferred the shoulder or the stomach) brown.

It seemed to me, then, that on my account Ruby had merely tightened up a preexisting inclination to be confounded and troubled at the representation of racial differences, not to mention the implications those differences had for how people lived. Eventually I asked her why she thought twice about how much brown she would give to a colored child. She was then eight, and we had known one another for two years. She replied directly: "When I draw a white girl, I know she'll be okay, but with the colored it's not so okay. So I try to give the colored as even a chance as I can, even if that's not the way it will end up being."

Two years later Ruby and I could talk even more openly. At ten she was still the outgoing, winning girl she always had been, though of course each time I saw her she was taller, thinner, a bit more composed, a little less the child. She wasn't very much interested in drawing any more. She preferred to talk. She and I looked over many of her drawings and at various intervals she made comments about them, much as if she were a colleague of mine. Almost in that vein I commented that her most recent work was less prolific but very accomplished indeed: "You didn't draw much this past year, but when you did the people were really alive and very accurately shown, and the buildings look as real as can be." She smiled and answered quickly: "I guess when you grow older you can see better, and so you can draw better. My teacher told me last week that my handwriting was getting better, too." A few minutes went by and I decided to persist with my comments on her artwork, this time with a bluntness I can only justify as feeling quite "right" and appropriate at the time: "Ruby, you know my wife and I were looking at your drawings last night, and we both noticed how differently you draw Negro people now, in contrast to the way you did years ago when we first started coming to see you. Do you think there's any reason for that, apart from the fact that you're now a better artist in every way?"

She paused longer than usual, and I began to feel in error for asking the question and nervous about what she might be feeling. I was scurrying about in my mind for a remark that would change the subject without doing so too abruptly when she looked right at me and spoke out: "Maybe because of all the trouble going to school in the beginning I learned more about my people. Maybe I would have anyway; because when you get older you see yourself and the white kids; and you find out the difference. You try to forget it, and say there is none; and if there is you won't say what it be. Then you say it's my own people, and so I can be proud of them instead of ashamed." When she finished she smiled, as if she had delivered a hard speech and was relieved to have it done. I didn't know what to say. On the one hand she was still the same Ruby I had known all those years; yet she now seemed grown-up. Her arms were folded quietly in her lap; her language was so clear, so pointed; and she somehow seemed both content with herself as she was and determined to make something of herself in the future. "Ruby is an exceptionally alert child," one of her teachers wrote on her report card a few days before Ruby and I had this talk. The teacher realized that her pupil had gone through a lot and had gained an order of understanding, or worldliness, that is perhaps rare in elementary school children, at least in more sheltered ones.

FOCUS: READING REVIEW

1. In what terms can a social psychologist analyze children's drawings? What conditions affect a child's drawings?
2. In his description of Ruby, Coles illustrates how drawing reflects changes in the child. What were the changes Ruby underwent? How did her drawings indicate this?
3. What kinds of generalizations does Coles reach about Ruby's experiences? How does he justify these generalizations?

FOCUS: AUTHOR'S STRATEGIES

1. While Coles appeals to a wider audience, he conforms to the conventions of professional writing in the social sciences. What is the background for his research? What are his "experimental" methods?
2. What does Coles's adaptation of the scientific report suggest about his audience?
3. Is Coles's purpose here to report an experiment? Give reasons for your answer. What other purposes does this selection have?

FOCUS: DISCUSSION AND WRITING

Coles is working with a particular group of black children at a particular moment in history. The mere change of language from Coles's "Negro" and "colored" to today's more acceptable "black" suggests that conditions have changed. Would you expect Coles to find similar reactions today in the South or in urban centers? Why or why not?

The Feminization of Ghetto Poverty
Diana M. Pearce

Diana M. Pearce is director of research at the Center for National Policy Review at the Catholic University of America's School of Law in Washington, D.C. She has authored many studies on women and poverty, race and poverty, and segregation in housing and the schools. This article, which appeared in the journal Society, *argues from statistical evidence that poverty in America in the 1980s affects more women and children than men, and that black women, the victims of sexism and racism, are most vulnerable.*

Today, three-quarters of the poor are women and children. The poverty rate for female-headed households has remained steady, but because a significant number of male-headed households have left poverty, and because the number of households headed by women has increased, the proportion of *poor* families maintained by women has risen. Furthermore, families headed by women have experienced a decline in economic status over the past two decades. These trends are appearing even more strongly in the black community. The greater rates of poverty among women can be traced to two distinctly female causes. First of all, women who head their families often bear most or all of the economic burden of raising children. Secondly, because of sex discrimination, occupational segregation in a segmented labor market, and sexual harassment, women who seek to support themselves and their families through paid work are disadvantaged in the labor market. Data indicates that although much of the economic gulf is accounted for by gender, black women experience considerable further disadvantages associated with race. These can be grouped in three areas: trends in racial desegregation in various areas, demographic trends, and welfare programs. Black women also experience qualitative differences in poverty from white women. The low wages afforded women of equal education and experience cannot be explained away as anything except sex discrimination. The poverty of black women, in contrast, is related to more complex factors. For many black men, their own high rates of unemployment and low income make the question of sharing income with their children and their children's mothers moot. Thus black women experience directly and, through black men, indirectly, the effects of racial discrimination. Further, white women stand a much greater chance of leaving poverty through marriage than black women. Black women are more likely to experience what I have called the "workhouse without walls."

The "other America" is a changing neighborhood: men are moving out; women and their children are moving in. This dramatic change is not a reaction to recent fluctuations in the economy, but instead reflects long-term structural shifts both in the labor market and in marriage and childbearing practices. today, three-quarters of the poor are women and children.

The poverty *rate* for female-headed households has remained steady over the past decade, with just under one-third of these families living in poverty. But because a significant number of male-headed households have left poverty, and because the number of households headed by women has increased, the proportion of *poor* families that are maintained by women has risen in the 1970s from 36 percent to more than 50 percent. Moreover, there is evidence that the trend is accelerating. Between 1969 and 1978, there was an annual net increase of 100,000 female-headed families in poverty, but in the two years between 1978 and 1980, the net increase each year was approximately 150,000. Furthermore, according to Reynolds Farley and Suzanne Bianchi, families headed by women have experienced a decline in economic status over the past two decades, with their average income dropping from 77 percent to 62 percent of the average income of white husband-and-wife families, and from 36 percent to 47 percent of black husband-and-wife families.

These trends are appearing even more strongly in the black community. Although the proportion of the poor who are black did not change during the 1970s, the proportion who were in families headed by women increased. Indeed, the decade of the seventies saw a dramatic shift of the burden of poverty among blacks from male-headed to female-headed families. The number of black families in poverty who were maintained by men declined by 35 percent, while the number maintained by women *increased* by 62 percent. In the course of one decade, black female-headed families increased from about one-half to three-fourths of all poor black families.

Some elements of the experience of being poor are common to all women; that is, they are a function of gender. Others, however, are the effect of race, though even these are experienced differently by men and women, as we shall see.

Though poor women share many characteristics in common with poor men (such as low education, lack of market-relevant job skills, or location in job-poor areas), the greater rates of poverty among women can be traced to two distinctly female causes. First of all, women who head their families often bear most or all of the economic burden of raising the children. Secondly, because of sex discrimination, occupational segregation in a segmented labor market, and sexual harassment, women who seek to support themselves and their families through paid work are disadvantaged in the labor market.

If a woman is married, even if she is employed outside the home, she shares substantially in the resources obtained by her husband. That transfer drops off dramatically when the parents no longer live together. In 1975, for example, only 25 percent of the women eligible actually received child support, and for more than half of those, the annual income from child-support payments was less than $1,500. If the parents were never married, the picture is even worse; only 5 percent of these fathers provide child support. Ironically, a woman is better off if her husband is dead, for widows are the best protected against income loss following the loss of a spouse and are therefore least likely to be poor. However, receipt of such transfers is unlikely to provide much of a bulwark against poverty; the average amount as of 1978 was about $1,800, and the duration is generally only a few years.

Accordingly, many women seek income through paid employment. For all too many, this goes against their lifelong expectations and preparations. Although it is true that most women today expect to work or have worked, sex-role socialization in general and vocational preparation in particular do not prepare women to be the *primary* breadwinner. Instead, the traditional emphasis has been on jobs, rather than careers, and on making job choices that emphasize flexibility and adaptability, rather than income potential. Thus, women faced with the necessity of being the sole source of support for themselves and their children are handicapped.

These handicaps are reinforced by a highly discriminatory labor market. Despite increased attention given this problem—including litigation and legislation—continuing high levels of *occupational segregation* of women stand in marked contrast to the decline of racial segregation in employment and education. Women who work full time continue to earn only 59 cents on the dollar earned by men who work full time. And while we do not know with precision the magnitude of the problem, it is increasingly evident that large numbers of women experience sexual harassment and thereby incur heavy economic, as well as personal, costs in lost recommendations, denied promotions, abrupt dismissals, and demotions.

BEING BLACK, FEMALE, AND POOR

The inequality experienced by women in the labor market has been conceptualized by some as confinement to the secondary sector of a dual labor market. According to the dual-economy theory, jobs and industries are readily divided into primary and the secondary sectors, and this division is reinforced by barriers that make it difficult for workers to move from one sector to another. In the primary sector, jobs are characterized by good pay and fringe benefits, job security, a high degree of unionization, good working conditions, and due process in job rights. In contrast, the secondary sector includes work in marginal industries; these jobs are low-paying, often seasonal or sporadic, less likely to be unionized, and offer little protection against the vagaries of either the individual employer or the ups and downs of the marketplace.

The duality of the labor market is complemented and reinforced by a parallel duality in the welfare system. There is a primary welfare sector in which benefits are conferred as a right, often (but not always) because they have been "earned." One is not stigmatized by receipt of these benefits, nor must one demonstrate poverty or suffer degrading, detailed investigations of one's lifestyle. The benefits are more generous, often with minimum or national levels set by the federal government. Not only are benefit levels relatively generous, but one does not have to exhaust one's resources to qualify; nor are benefits reduced in proportion to other income. Examples of primary-welfare-sector benefits include unemployment compensation and social security.

In contrast, the secondary welfare sector is characterized by benefits that are much lower, on the average, and highly variable across states and even across localities within a state. Since such benefits are a privilege, not received by right, they may be revoked arbitrarily and for different reasons in different places. They may be, and usually are, reduced in proportion to other income. Receipt of welfare, in the eyes of the public and many recipients, is stigmatizing and demoralizing.

For those in the secondary sector of either the labor market or the welfare system, escape is difficult. This is especially so for women and minorities. For a variety of reasons, the welfare system and related training and jobs programs (such as WIN and CETA) do not overcome the labor-market barriers faced by women. For example, training is often for traditionally female occupations, such as clerical work or food service, occupations that do not pay wages adequate to support a woman and even one child. The stubborn obsession with getting women off welfare and into jobs as quickly as possible, with no attention to their special needs (e.g., for child care or fringe benefits that include adequate health insurance), has long-term results that are counterproductive. Those who accept or are forced to take economically marginal jobs in the secondary sector quickly find that they do not have access to the primary welfare sector when they lose or are laid off from these jobs. They are then forced to depend on impoverished secondary-welfare-sector programs. Thus, the interlocking secondary welfare system and secondary labor market reinforce a vicious circle of welfare dependency and marginal work.

Women and minorities are concentrated in the secondary welfare sector. As shown in Table 1, whereas men are slightly overrepresented and women underrepresented in the primary welfare sector, there is a severe sex discrepancy in the secondary sector. Less than half of white men receive secondary-sector benefits according to their proportion in the population, while three times the number of white women—and six times the number of black women—receive income from the secondary welfare sector according to their proportions in the population.

Many, of course, receive income from earnings as well as from transfer programs, but since the receipt of primary-sector benefits is strongly associated with previously held primary-sector *jobs*, the figures in Table 1 indicate implicitly the effect of differential participation not only in the primary and secondary welfare sectors, but also in the primary and secondary labor markets. (Theoretically, one could receive income from primary as well as from secondary welfare programs, but Census Bureau data show that few actually do.)

If one compares poverty rates across gender and race categories, several conclusions suggest themselves. First, the poverty rate for those receiving benefits (and perhaps, also, earnings) in the secondary sector (67.7%) is more than eleven times the rate for those in the primary sector (5.5%). Second, within each sector, the poverty rates are greater for blacks than for whites, and greater for women than for men; but the gender differentials are greater than the racial ones. In this connection, the differences in poverty rates between black and white men within each sector are quite small, whereas there is a substantial added disadvantage to being both black and female. The "double" disadvantage experienced by black women is actually, in quantitative terms, a geometrically increasing "quadruple" disadvantage.

TABLE 1   Primary versus Secondary Welfare Sectors, 1978

	All Household Heads		Primary Sector[a]		Secondary Sector[b]	
	Percentage	Poverty Rate	Percentage	Poverty Rate	Percentage	Poverty Rate
Men[c]						
white	79.2	4.7	81.5	4.0	30.2	35.7
black	6.2	11.8	7.3	7.2	10.1	36.9
SUBTOTAL	85.4	5.3	88.8	4.3	40.3	36.1
Women[d]						
white	10.4	23.5	8.9	10.4	28.7	66.8
black	4.2	50.6	2.3	32.3	30.9	75.8
SUBTOTAL	14.6	31.4	11.2	15.1	59.6	71.2
Total	100.0		100.0	5.5	100.0	67.7

[a] Includes unemployment and workmen's compensation, veterans' benefits
[b] Includes all types of cash public assistance (aid to families with dependent children, general assistance, etc.)
[c] Both male-only and husband-and-wife households
[d] Female householder, no husband
Source: U.S. Census Bureau, *Characteristics of the Population below the Poverty Level: 1978*, Series P-60, No. 124

SPECIAL EFFECTS

It is clear from the data that although much of the economic gulf is accounted for by gender, black women experience considerable further disadvantages associated with race. These disadvantages can be grouped into three areas for purposes of discussion: trends in racial desegregation in various areas, demographic trends, and welfare programs.

Considerable occupational desegregation has been experienced by both men and women. This has meant an exodus from extremely low-paying jobs (often irregular and part-time), particularly in household service, that have been race/sex "occupational ghettoes." But because *sex* segregation levels, which have always been higher than those of race, have remained quite high, and because the wages of women have remained at less than 60 percent of men's wages, black men have benefited more from the racial desegregation of occupations than black women. Thus, statistics purporting to show that black women are closing the gap on white women faster than black men are on white men are misleading. The use of white women as a benchmark is inappropriate, for it eliminates the effects of gender. If one compares the progress of black men and black women to that of white men, then at present rates black men will catch up to white men in 35 years, but it will take black women 135 years to achieve occupational parity with white men.

In other areas, there have been parallel developments. For example, as Robert Crain and Rita Mehard have pointed out, school desegregation has opened up opportunities for black students of both sexes and, therefore, has resulted in increased achievement levels. Continued sex segregation of vocational programs, however, has the consequence of channeling women students into lower-paying occupations. For obvious economic reasons, housing desegregation, has been experienced disproportionately by two-parent, two-income black families. In sum, racial desegregation has had a much greater impact on families with a male householder.

More than 40 percent of black families, and more than 50 percent of those with children, are headed by a single parent (almost all of whom are women). This is partly related to high divorce rates, but several other factors have contributed to the growth of single-parent homes. One of these is the high ratio of out-of-wedlock births—now at about 55 percent for blacks. Many of these children are born to teenagers. Black women tend to marry or remarry at lower rates than white women, and they tend to remain single longer if they do marry. This is, in part, because of a shortage of black men of marriageable age. For example, the ratio (in the resident population) of black women to men, ages 20 to 49 is 1.16 (the white ratio is 1.01); in other words, there are sixteen "extra" black women for every hundred black men.

This imbalance in the sex ratio is the result of several factors, including higher levels of suicide and homicide among black men and an incredible incarceration rate for young black men—phenomena that are directly related to very high levels of poverty, underemployment, and unemployment. While it is true that *being a single parent* causes poverty, it is also clear that the widespread poverty among young black men, and their less-than-cheerful prospects for future economic stability, is an important *cause* of the formation of single-parent households among blacks. The converse also holds, so that marriage is as much the result of economic security, well-being, and upward mobility as it is the cause of economic well-being among families. In this connection, Farley and Bianchi find that the black community is not becoming polarized along traditional class lines (such as occupation or education), but that there is a polarization along *marital-status* lines. Two-parent families are increasing their economic status while families headed by women become poorer, opening up a different kind of schism in black America.

All of the factors noted above play a part in the racial differences seen in patterns of welfare use. Keeping in mind that these differences are relative, and that there is high degree of overlap among the factors, I will briefly examine some of the differences between white and black women who are welfare recipients.

White women tend more often to be divorced (as opposed to being single or separated). They also tend to come to welfare with more resources (including education, work experience, and even ownership of a house and/or a more favorable residential location vis-à-vis job opportunities. On the other hand, white women are also less likely to be employed and are more likely to go on welfare as a result of the loss of a husband's earnings. Because of this combination of more immediate need and yet greater "long-run" resources, white women not only tend to be on welfare for shorter periods of time, they are also more fully dependent during the time that they are on welfare. In contrast, more black women come to welfare as a result of unemployment and underemployment. Whereas white women often leave welfare because they have obtained a job or remarried (or both), black women are less likely to find a job—at least one providing sufficient income to support themselves and their family—and are less likely to marry or remarry.

In sum, white women tend more often to use welfare for shorter periods of time, even though welfare accounts for most (if not all) of their income while they are on welfare. Black women who head households, in contrast, are more likely to use welfare for longer periods of time, but in conjunction with earnings and other sources of income (e.g., child support), and are less likely to be totally dependent upon welfare, particularly over a period of years. Again, it should be remembered that these racial differences are relative. It should be emphasized, too, that the differences between women householders who use welfare and those that do not are not all that great. Data reported by Martin Rein and Lee Rainwater show that among those who were heavily dependent on welfare over a seven-year period, almost 30 percent of annual income came from earnings, while among low-income families who did not use welfare during that period, about 70 percent of annual income came from earnings. Phillip AuClaire estimates that about 58 percent of the annual income of long-term welfare recipients who were also employed came from earnings.

THE WORKHOUSE WITHOUT WALLS

Black women experience quantitatively more poverty than either black men or white women, no matter what the circumstances or income source. But there is also an important qualitative difference not made explicit by the above discussion. The various causes of white women's poverty can be traced back to a single, fundamental source—sexism, perpetuated mainly by white men. Only in a sexist society can the breakup of a marriage actually improve the economic well-being of the father, cause the mother and children to suffer a large drop in economic status, and permit most fathers to provide little or no support to their children. The low wages afforded women of equal education and experience cannot be explained away as anything except sex discrimination. The poverty of black women, in contrast, is related to more complex factors. Black men are rarely in the position of employers and, therefore, are hardly able to determine the wage scales of women vis-à-vis men. And for many black men, their own high rates of unemployment and low income make the question of sharing income with their children and their children's mothers moot. Thus, in addition to the sources of poverty experienced by all women—the economic burden of children, labor-market discrimination and duality, a welfare system that provides penurious benefits and no training/support system—black women experience directly and, through black men, indirectly, the effects of racial discrimination.

A further qualitative difference experienced by black women is that their poverty has a more permanent, or at least, indefinite quality. They, of course, bear the burden of poverty in the black community, a community that as a whole has long had much more poverty than the white community. Thus, because of the greater economic resources in the white community, white women stand a much greater chance of leaving poverty through marriage than black women. Black women are more likely to experience what I have called the "workhouse without walls," in which they support themselves through a combination of earnings, welfare, child support, and other transfers, whether concurrently or serially.

It is evident that, within the black community, there is a growing gulf between two-parent, two-earner families and families headed by women. It is also clear that the high unemployment rates among black youth which contribute to the formation of single-parent families, together with the sexism in the labor/welfare system which locks women householders into poverty, are resulting in increasing proportions of black children being born into and/or growing up in families that must struggle every day with poverty.

FOCUS: READING REVIEW

1. What reasons does Pearce give for the increase in poverty among women and children? What evidence does she give to indicate this increase?
2. What characteristics do poor women share with poor men? What are the peculiarly female aspects of poverty?
3. How are women handicapped by their employment expectations?
4. What is the dual-economy theory? How does this affect women?
5. What trends make the black woman particularly vulnerable to poverty? How does this compare with white women?

FOCUS: AUTHOR'S STRATEGIES

1. What is Pearce's thesis? What tone does the statement of this thesis establish for the essay? What purpose and audience do these suggest?
2. Pearce begins by giving statistics on poverty trends. The remaining essay analyzes a series of interrelated causes and effects. What are the elements of this analysis? How does Pearce relate the causes and effects?
3. This article relies on a single set of statistics. Do the statistics support the writer's conclusions? What other ways might these be interpreted?

FOCUS: DISCUSSION AND WRITING

Pearce's essay relies on "dry" statistics. What do these statistics mean in human terms?

The Higher Economic Purposes of Women
John Kenneth Galbraith

John Kenneth Galbraith (b. 1908), a distinguished professor of economics at Harvard University, has served as a presidential advisor on economics and United States ambassador to India. He received his education at the University of Toronto, the University of California, Berkeley, and Cambridge University in England. His writings include The Great Crash *(1955),* The Affluent Society *(1958), and the collection of essays* Annals of an Abiding Liberal *(1979). As a writer Galbraith wears many hats—economist, political activist, social critic, even literary critic. Here observing a social phenomenon—specifically society's recruitment of well-educated upper-middle-class women as household managers—Galbraith lends economic analysis and interpretation. Inspired by his experience as a Radcliffe College trustee in the 1950s, "The Higher Economic Purpose of Women," which appeared in* Ms. Magazine *(1974), still lends insight into a segment of our society.*

[In the 1950s the trustees of Radcliffe College felt their responsibility was to help women prepare themselves for their life's work: the care of home, husband, and children. While the rhetorical commitment of women to home and husband as career has been weakened since, the economic ideas by which they are kept persuaded to serve economic interests are still almost completely intact.] The decisive economic contribution of women in the developed industrial society is rather simple—to make possible a continuing and more or less unlimited increase in the sale and use of consumer goods. The test of success in modern economic society is the annual rate of increase in Gross National Product. The large corporation seeks relentlessly to get larger. That expansion requires an expanding or growing economy (manpower, capital, and materials) for increased production as well as increased consumption. Just as the production of goods and services requires management, so does consumption. The higher the standard of living, that is to say the greater the consumption, the more demanding is this management. In earlier times administration was the function of a menial servant class. [In modern industrial societies this administration is the function that wives perform.] It seems likely that the responsible, high-bracket, suburban woman's managerial effectiveness, derived from her superior education, her accumulating experience as well as her expanding array of facilitating gadgetry and services, keeps her more or less abreast of her increasingly large and complex task. Thus the danger of a ceiling on consumption does not seem imminent. That these women are instruments of the economic system is concealed by modern neoclassical economic theory. Further, society uses its persuasive powers to convince women that consumption is happiness and that, however onerous its associated toil, it all adds up to greater happiness for themselves and their families. If women were to see and understand how they are used—that they are the facilitating agents of consumption—they might reject its administration as a career, return to a less demanding urban life, and see that they can serve purposes which are their own.

In the nineteen-fifties, for reasons that were never revealed to me, for my relations with academic administrators have often been somewhat painful, I was made a trustee of Radcliffe College. It was not a highly demanding position. Then, as now, the college had no faculty of its own, no curriculum of its own and, apart from the dormitories, a gymnasium and a library, no academic plant of its own. We were a committee for raising money for scholarships and a new graduate center. The meetings or nonmeetings of the trustees did, however, encourage a certain amount of reflection on the higher education of women, there being no appreciable distraction. This reflection was encouraged by the mood of the time at Harvard. As conversation and numerous formal and informal surveys reliably revealed, all but a small minority of the women students felt that they were a failure unless they were firmly set for marriage by the time they got their degree. I soon learned that my fellow trustees of both sexes thought this highly meritorious. Often at our meetings there was impressively solemn mention of our responsibility, which was to help women prepare themselves for their life's work. Their life's work, it was held, was care of home, husband and children. In inspired moments one or another of my colleagues would ask, "Is there anything so important?"

Once, and rather mildly, for it was more to relieve tedium than to express conviction, I asked if the education we provided wasn't rather expensive and possibly also ill-adapted for these tasks, even assuming that they were combined with ultimate service to the New Rochelle Library and the League of Women Voters. The response was so chilly that I subsided. I've never minded being in a minority, but I dislike being thought eccentric.

It was, indeed, mentioned that a woman should be prepared for what was called a *second* career. After her children were raised and educated, she should be able to essay a re-entry into intellectual life—become a teacher, writer, researcher or some such. All agreed that this was a worthy, even imaginative design which did not conflict with *basic* responsibilities. I remember contemplating but censoring the suggestion that this fitted in well with the common desire of husbands at about this stage in life to take on new, younger and sexually more inspiring wives.

In those years I was working on the book that eventually became *The Affluent Society*. The task was a constant reminder that much information solemnly advanced as social wisdom is, in fact, in the service of economic convenience—the convenience of some influential economic interest. I concluded that this was so of the education of women and resolved that I would one day explore the matter more fully. This I have been doing in these last few years, and I've decided that while the rhetorical commitment of women to home and husband as a career has been weakened in the interim, the economic ideas by which they are kept persuaded to serve economic interests are still almost completely intact. Indeed, these ideas are so generally assumed that they are very little discussed.

Women are kept in the service of economic interests by ideas that they do not examine and that even women who are professionally involved as economists continue to propagate, often with some professional pride. The husband, home and family that were celebrated in those ghastly Radcliffe meetings are no longer part of the litany. But the effect of our economic education is still the same.

Understanding of this begins with a look at the decisive but little-perceived role of women in modern economic development and at the economic instruction by which this perception is further dulled.

The decisive economic contribution of women in the developed industrial society is rather simple—or at least it so becomes once the disguising myth is dissolved. It is, overwhelmingly, to make possible a continuing and more or less unlimited increase in the sale and use of consumer goods.

The test of success in modern economic society, as all know, is the annual rate of increase in Gross National Product. At least until recent times this test was unquestioned; a successful society was one with a large annual increase in output, and the most successful society was the one with the largest increase. Even when the social validity of this measure is challenged, as on occasion it now is, those who do so are only thought to be raising an interesting question. They are not imagined to be practical.

Increasing production, in turn, strongly reflects the needs of the dominant economic interest, which in modern economic society, as few will doubt, is the large corporation. The large corporation seeks relentlessly to get larger. The power, prestige, pay, promotions and perquisites of those who command or who participate in the leadership of the great corporation are all strongly served by its expansion. That expansion, if it is to be general, requires an expanding or growing economy. As the corporation became a polar influence in modern economic life, economic growth became the accepted test of social performance. This was not an accident. It was the predictable acceptance of the dominant economic value system.

Economic growth requires manpower, capital and materials for increased production. It also, no less obviously, requires increased consumption, and if population is relatively stable, as in our case, this must be increased per-capita consumption. But there is a further and equally unimpeachable truth which, in economics at least, has been celebrated scarcely at all: just as the production of goods and services requires management or administration, so does their consumption. The one is no less essential than the other. Management is required for providing automobiles, houses, clothing, food, alcohol and recreation. And management is no less required for their possession and use.

The higher the standard of living, that is to say the greater the consumption, the more demanding is this management. The larger the house, the more numerous the automobiles, the more elaborate the attire, the more competitive and costly the social rites involving food and intoxicants, the more complex the resulting administration.

In earlier times this administration was the function of a menial servant class. To its great credit, industrialization everywhere liquidates this class. People never remain in appreciable numbers in personal service if they have alternative employment. Industry supplies this employment, so the servant class, the erstwhile managers of consumption, disappears. If consumption is to continue and expand, it is an absolute imperative that a substitute administrative force be found. This, in modern industrial societies, is the function that wives perform. The higher the family income and the greater the complexity of the consumption, the more nearly indispensible this role. Within broad limits the richer the family, the more indispensably menial must be the role of the wife.

It is, to repeat, a vital function of economic success as it is now measured. Were women not available for managing consumption, an upper limit would be set thereon by the administrative task involved. At some point it would become too time-consuming, too burdensome. We accept, without thought, that a bachelor of either sex will lead a comparatively simple existence. (We refer to it as the bachelor life.) That is because the administrative burden of a higher level of consumption, since it must be assumed by the individual who consumes, is a limiting factor. When a husband's income passes a certain level, it is expected that his wife will be needed "to look after the house" or simply "to manage things." So, if she has been employed, she quits her job. The consumption of the couple has reached the point where it requires full-time attention.

Although without women appropriately conditioned to the task there would be an effective ceiling on consumption and thus on production and economic expansion, this would not apply uniformly. The ceiling would be especially serious for high-value products for the most affluent consumers. The latter, reflecting their larger share of total income—the upper 20 percent of income recipients received just under 42 percent of all income in 1977—account for a disproportionate share of total purchases of goods. So women are particularly important for lifting the ceiling on this kind of consumption. And, by a curious quirk, their doing so opens the way for a whole new range of consumer products—washing machines, dryers, dishwashers, vacuum cleaners, automatic furnaces, sophisticated detergents, cleaning compounds, tranquilizers, pain-relievers—designed to ease the previously created task of managing a high level of consumption.

Popular sociology and much associated fiction depict the extent and complexity of the administrative tasks of the modern diversely responsible, high-bracket, suburban woman. But it seems likely that her managerial effectiveness, derived from her superior education, her accumulating experience as well as her expanding array of facilitating gadgetry and services, keeps her more or less abreast of her increasingly large and complex task. Thus the danger of a ceiling on consumption, and therefore on economic expansion, caused by the exhaustion of her administrative capacities does not seem imminent. One sees here, more than incidentally, the economic rationale, even if it was unsuspected for a long time by those involved, of the need for a superior education for the upper-bracket housewife. Radcliffe prepared wives for the higher-income family. The instinct that this required superior intelligence and training was economically sound.

The family of higher income, in turn, sets the consumption patterns to which others aspire. That such families be supplied with intelligent, well-educated women of exceptional managerial competence is thus of further importance. It allows not only for the continued high-level consumption of these families, but it is important for its demonstration effect for families of lesser income.

That many women are coming to sense that they are instruments of the economic system is not in doubt. But their feeling finds no support in economic writing and teaching. On the contrary, it is concealed, and on the whole with great success, by modern neoclassical economics—the everyday economics of the textbook and classroom. This concealment is neither conspiratorial nor deliberate. It reflects the natural and very strong instinct of economics for what is convenient to influential economic interest—for what I have called the convenient social virtue. It is sufficiently successful that it allows many hundreds of thousands of women to study economics each year without their developing any serious suspicion as to how they will be used.

The general design for concealment has four major elements:

First, there is the orthodox identification of an increasing consumption of goods and services with increasing happiness. The greater the consumption, the greater the happiness. This proposition is not defended; it is again assumed that only the philosophically minded will cavil. They are allowed their dissent, but, it is held, no one should take it seriously.

Second, the tasks associated with the consumption of goods are, for all practical purposes, ignored. Consumption being a source of happiness, one cannot get involved with the problems in managing happiness. The consumer must exercise choice; happiness is maximized when the enjoyment from an increment of expenditure for one object of consumption equals that from the same expenditure for any other object or service. As all who have ever been exposed, however inadequately, to economic instruction must remember, satisfactions are maximized when they are equalized at the margin.

Such calculation does require some knowledge of the quality and technical performance of goods as well as thought in general. From it comes the subdivision of economics called consumer economics; this is a moderately reputable field that, not surprisingly, is thought especially appropriate for women. But this decision-making is not a burdensome matter. And once the decision between objects of expenditure is made, the interest of economics is at an end. No attention whatever is given to the effort involved in the care and management of the resulting goods.[1]

The third requisite for the concealment of women's economic role is the avoidance of any accounting for the value of household work. This greatly helps it to avoid notice. To include in the Gross National Product the labor of housewives in managing consumption, where it would be a very large item which would increase as consumption increases, would be to invite thought on the nature of the service so measured. And some women would wonder if the service was one they wished to render. To keep these matters out of the realm of statistics is also to help keep them innocuously within the sacred domain of the family and the soul. It helps sustain the pretense that, since they are associated with consumption, the toil involved is one of its joys.

The fourth and final element in the concealment is more complex and concerns the concept of the household. The intellectual obscurantism that is here involved is accepted by all economists, mostly without thought. It would, however, be defended by very few.

The avowed focus of economics is the individual. It is the individual who distributes her or his expenditures so as to maximize satisfactions. From this distribution comes the instruction to the market and ultimately to the producing firm that makes the individual the paramount power in economic society. (There are grave difficulties with this design, including the way in which it reduces General Motors to the role of a mere puppet of market forces, but these anomalies are not part of the present story.)

Were this preoccupation with the individual pursued to the limit, namely to the individual, there would be grave danger that the role of women would attract attention. There would have to be inquiry as to whether, within the family, it is the husband's enjoyments that are equalized and thus maximized at the margin. Or, in his gallant way, does he defer to the preference system of his wife? Or does marriage unite only men and women whose preference schedules are identical? Or does marriage make them identical?

Investigation would turn up a yet more troublesome thing. It would be seen that, in the usual case, the place and style of living accord with the preferences and needs of the member of the family who makes the money—in short, the husband. Thus, at least partly, his titles: "head of the household," "head of the family." And he would be seen to have a substantial role in decisions on the individual objects of expenditure. But the management of the resulting house, automobile, yard, shopping and social life would be by the wife. It would be seen that this arrangement gives the major decisions concerning consumption extensively to one person and the toil associated with that consumption to another. There would be further question as to whether consumption decisions reflect with any precision or fairness the preferences of the person who has the resulting toil. Would the style of life and consumption be the same if the administration involved were equally shared?

None of these questions gets asked, for at precisely the point they obtrude, the accepted economics abruptly sheds its preoccupation with the individual. The separate identities of men and women are merged into the concept of the household. The inner conflicts and compromises of the household are not explored; by nearly universal consent, they are not the province of economics. The household, by a distinctly heroic simplification, is assumed to be the same as an individual. It thinks, acts and arranges its expenditures as would an individual; it is so treated for all purposes of economic analysis.

That, within the household, the administration of consumption requires major and often tedious effort, that decisions on consumption are heavily influenced by the member of the household least committed to such tasks, that these arrangements are extremely important if consumption is to expand, are all things that are thus kept out of academic view. Those who study and those who teach are insulated from such adverse thoughts. The concept of the household is an outrageous assault on personality. People are not people; they are parts of a composite or collective that is deemed somehow to reflect the different or conflicting preferences of those who make it up. This is both analytically and ethically indefensible. But for concealing the economic function of women even from women it works.

One notices, at this point, an interesting convergence of economics with politics. It has long been recognized that women are kept on political leash primarily by urging their higher commitment to the family. Their economic role is also concealed and protected by submerging them in the family or household. There is much, no doubt, to be said for the institution of the family. And it is not surprising that conservatives say so much.

In modern society power rests extensively on persuasion. Such reverse incentives as flogging, though there are law-and-order circles that seek their revival, are in limbo. So, with increasing affluence, is the threat of starvation. And even affirmative pecuniary reward is impaired. For some, at least, enough is enough—the hope for more ceases to drive. In consequence, those who have need for a particular behavior in others resort to persuasion—to instilling the belief that the action they need is reputable, moral, virtuous, socially beneficent or otherwise good. It follows that what women are persuaded to believe about their social role and, more important, what they are taught to overlook are of prime importance in winning the requisite behavior. They must believe that consumption is happiness and that, however onerous its associated toil, it all adds up to greater happiness for themselves and their families.

If women were to see and understand how they are used, the consequence might be a considerable change in the pattern of their lives, especially in those income brackets where the volume of consumption is large. Thus, suburban life sustains an especially large consumption of goods, and, in consequence, is especially demanding in the administration required. The claims of roofs, furniture, plumbing, crabgrass, vehicles, recreational equipment and juvenile management are all very great. This explains why unmarried people, regardless of income, favor urban living over the suburbs. If women understood that they are the facilitating instrument of this consumption and were led to reject its administration as a career, there would, one judges, be a general return to a less demanding urban life.

More certainly there would be a marked change in the character of social life. Since they are being used to administer consumption, women are naturally encouraged to do it well. In consequence, much social activity is, in primary substance, a competitive display of managerial excellence. The cocktail party or dinner party is, essentially, a fair, more refined and complex than those at which embroidery or livestock are entered in competition but for the same ultimate purpose of displaying and improving the craftsmanship or breed. The cleanliness of the house, the excellence of the garden, the taste, quality and condition of the furnishings and the taste, quality and imagination of the food and intoxicants and the deftness of their service are put on display before the critical eye of those invited to appraise them. Comparisons are made with other exhibitors. Ribbons are not awarded, but the competent administrator is duly proclaimed a good housekeeper, a gracious hostess, a clever manager or, more simply, a really good wife. These competitive social rites and the accompanying titles encourage and confirm women in their role as administrators and thus facilitators of the high levels of consumption on which the high-production economy rests. It would add measurably to economic understanding were they so recognized. But perhaps for some it would detract from their appeal.

However, the more immediate reward to women from an understanding of their economic role is in liberalizing the opportunity for choice. What is now seen as a moral compulsion—the diligent and informed administration of the family consumption—emerges as a service to economic interests. When so seen, the moral compulsion disappears. Once women see that they serve purposes which are *not* their own, they will see that they can serve purposes which *are* their own.

Notes

¹ There is a branch of learning—home economics or home science—that does concern itself with such matters. This field is a nearly exclusive preserve of women. It has never been accorded any serious recognition by economists or scholars generally; like physical education or poultry science, it is part of an academic underworld. And home economists or home scientists, in their natural professional enthusiasm for their subject matter and their natural resentment of their poor academic status, have sought to elevate their subject, homemaking, into a thing of unique dignity, profound spiritual reward, infinite social value as well as great nutritional significance. Rarely have they asked whether it cons women into a role that is exceedingly important for economic interest and also highly convenient for the men and institutions they are trained to serve. Some of the best home economists were once students of mine. I thought them superbly competent in their commitment to furthering a housewifely role for women. [Galbraith]

FOCUS: READING REVIEW

1. This essay asserts that "women are kept in the service of economic interests by ideas that they do not examine." What is the primary economic contribution of women in developed industrial society?
2. Galbraith states that modern neoclassical economics is an economics of "concealment." What does it conceal and how does it achieve this concealment?
3. What does the author mean by the statement that in modern society power rests on persuasion? What are women being persuaded to do? How are they persuaded?

FOCUS: AUTHOR'S STRATEGIES

1. For what audience is Galbraith writing? How do his explanations of economic theory indicate this?
2. What purposes does Galbraith seek? What in the essay reveals these purposes?
3. Galbraith's expertise as an economist provides evidence on which he bases his argument. What are the economic "facts"? Are any of these facts subject to another interpretation? If so, which ones, and how might they be interpreted differently?

FOCUS: DISCUSSION AND WRITING

1. How do women contribute to increased production? Do you agree or disagree? In what other ways are women called to serve the economy? Has increasing the number of women in the labor force changed the nature of their contribution?
2. Galbraith begins with an experience he had in the fifties, but he writes from a seventies perspective. To what degree do women still find themselves being educated for a "second career"?
3. What socioeconomic group is Galbraith considering here? Are his considerations significantly different for this group today? From your observations of people you know, defend your position.
4. What changes would occur if women understood they are primarily facilitating consumption? If women made these changes how would American life-styles change? How would this affect the economy?

Chapter 6
Critical Responses
in the
Social Sciences

Because they touch important parts of peoples lives, issues in the social sciences often provoke response and controversy. In this chapter you will find articles responding directly to social science studies or articles that critically address those issues the social sciences study. Two essays, Szasz's "A Critique of Skinner's Behaviorism" and Day's "A Defense of Skinner's Behaviorism," respond to Skinner's essay in chapter 5 on the social sciences' governing assumptions. Szasz asserts that Skinner's psychology deprives people of meaning and significance in their lives. He argues from definitions of Skinner's language and from his own assumption that man derives dignity from existence as more than a mere organism. Day attacks Szasz's logic and reaffirms the theoretical assumptions of behavioral psychology. Also considering specific studies, "Television at the Crossroads" (Gerbner et al.) reviews studies of television's effect on children's academic performance. This article objects to the studies on experimental grounds.

A considerable proportion of writing on society comes from writers criticizing the social institutions themselves and not the study of these institutions done by social scientists. One such essay, Martin Luther King's "Letter from Birmingham Jail," objects to the upholding of racial segregation by social and political institutions.

A Critique of Skinner's Behaviorism

Thomas Szasz

Thomas Szasz (b. 1920), a psychoanalyst and professor of psychiatry at the State University of New York's Upstate Medical Center, advocates a humanistic approach in psychology. Born in Budapest, Hungary, he received his A.B. and M.D. at the University of Cincinnati and his psychiatric training at the Chicago Institute of Psychoanalysis. His writings include Ethics of Psychoanalysis *(1965),* Ideology and Insanity *(1970), and* The Age of Madness *(1973). This essay, written as a review of B.F. Skinner's* About Behaviorism, *objects to behavioral theory's dehumanization of man. Szasz concerns himself not with the theory alone, but with the kind of language Skinner must create to replace the traditional language of human experience. The confrontation between humanistic and behaviorist psychology becomes particularly apparent when you read this together with Willard Day's response which follows.*

About Behaviorism is not a book at all, but a dictionary that furnishes us with the equivalents, in Skinnerese, of ordinary English words. Skinner is out to destroy language and substitute his own. [Skinner's ideas are not new, his understanding of physiology is inaccurate and his use of language imprecise.] As Skinner warms to his subject, he reveals more and more about his willingness to do away with persons qua agents. There are no individuals, no agents—there are only organisms. Skinner is, or aspires to be, one of the great destroyers of meaning and hence, of man. Skinner has constructed a world of acts without actors, of conditioning without conditioners, of slaves without masters, of politics without politicians, of the good life without ethics, of man without language.

One of the things that distinguishes persons from animals is that, for reasons familiar enough, persons cannot simply live: they must have, or must feel that they have, some reason for doing so. In other words, men, women, and children must have some sense and significance in and for their lives. If they do not, they perish. Hence, I believe that those who rob people of the meaning and significance they have given their lives kill them and should be considered murderers, at least metaphysically. B.F. Skinner is such a person and, like all of the others, he fascinates—especially his intended victims.

But, it may be objected, Skinner has no political or military power at his command. How, then, could he inflict such a grave injury on mankind? The answer is as simple as is Skinner's mentality. Man qua organism is an animal; to destroy it, one must kill it. Man qua person is the animal that uses language; to destroy him, one must destroy his language. This, it seems to me, is what Skinner is out to accomplish. Perhaps more than any of his earlier books, *About Behaviorism* makes this crystal clear. It is not really a book at all, but a dictionary: it furnishes us with the equivalents, in Skinnerese, of ordinary English words.

Simply put, what Skinner is out to do is to destroy ordinary language and to substitute his own language for it. It is a sort of one-man Esperanto effort. Skinner puts it this way: "I consider scores, if not hundreds, of examples of mentalistic usage. They are taken from current writings, but I have not cited the sources . . . Many of these expressions I 'translate into behavior.'" That is, indeed, what the whole book is about: translation—from English into "behavior." Skinner's pride at citing what others have said, without giving their names, is of interest in this connection. "I am not arguing with the authors," he explains, as if references served the sole purpose of identifying enemies. It seems to me that his not naming names is consistent with his general thesis that there are, and should be, no individuals. Books without authors are simply a part of Skinner's grand design of acts without actors—his master plan for world conquest.

What about Skinner's own acts, his speaking and writing? Is he not an agent and an author? Not really, says Skinner. In the first place, you and I may speak and write, but not Skinner; Skinner exhibits "verbal behavior." I am not kidding. "Finally, a word about my own verbal behavior," he writes in a chapter titled "The Causes of Behavior." Skinner thus disclaims writing in a language, which is asserting a falsehood, or having a style, which is asserting a truth. Instead, he claims to be exhibiting physiological behavior, which is reductionism[1] of the stupidest sort. But this is what he espouses: "For purposes of casual discourse, I see no reason to avoid such an expression as 'I have chosen to discuss . . . (though I question the possibility of free choice) . . . .' When it is important to be clear about an issue, nothing but a technical vocabulary will suffice. It will often seem forced or roundabout. Old ways of speaking are abandoned with regret, and new ones are awkward and uncomfortable, but the change must be made." To what? To Skinnerese. Why? To aggrandize Skinner.

Here is another sample of how Skinner sees the world and proposes to explain it: "A small part of the universe is contained within the skin of each of us. There is no reason why it should have any special physical status because it lies within this boundary and eventually we will have a complete account of it from anatomy and physiology." So what else is new? Physicalism, biologism, reductionism, scientism—all have had much more eloquent spokesmen than Skinner. Why all the fuss about him, then? Perhaps because he is a Harvard professor who is ignorant both of his own sources (for example, Auguste Comte) and of the many important critics of scientism (from John Stuart Mill to F.A. Hayek), thus making it not only possible but positively respectable for millions to believe that the drivel between the covers of his book is both new and good.

Skinner loves anatomy and physiology, although, so far as I can make out, he knows nothing about either. Perhaps this allows him to think that these "disciplines" can somehow explain everything. How else are we to account for such statements as these: "The human species, like all other species, is the product of natural selection. Each of its members is an extremely complex organism, a living system, the subject of anatomy and physiology." What is this, an excerpt from a biology lecture to bright second-graders? No. It is Skinner's introduction to his explanation of "innate behavior." There is more, much more, of this. Two more sentences should suffice: "But what is felt or introspectively observed is not an important part of the physiology which fills the temporal gap in an historical analysis . . . " and "The experimental analysis of behavior is a rigorous, extensive, and rapidly advancing branch of biology . . . . "

Next, we come to Skinner's key concepts: "operant behavior" and "reinforcement." "A positive reinforcer," he explains, "strengthens any behavior that produces it: a glass of water is positively reinforcing when we are thirsty: and if we then draw and drink a glass of water, we are more likely to do so again on similar occasions. A negative reinforcer strengthens any behavior that reduces or terminates it: when we take off a shoe that is pinching, the reduction of pressure is negatively reinforcing, and we are more likely to do so again when a shoe pinches." Well, I simply do not understand this, but that may be because I have not grasped the fine points of Skinner's language—excuse me, "verbal behavior." Water relieves thirst. Taking off a tight shoe relieves pain. Why call one a "positive reinforcer" and the other a "negative reinforcer"? I have no satisfactory answer to this question. Skinner thinks he does, and I herewith quote it: "The fact that operant conditioning, like all physiological processes, is a product of natural selection throws light on the question of what kinds of consequences are reinforcing and why. The expressions 'I like Brahms,' 'I love Brahms,' 'I enjoy Brahms,' and 'Brahms pleases me,' may easily be taken to refer to feelings but they can be taken as statements that the music of Brahms is reinforcing."

Well, I like Brahms, but I do not like Skinner. But do not be misled: this is neither an expression of my ill feelings toward Skinner nor an act of criticism of his work. Ill feelings, as Skinner himself has just explained, do not exist; so I merely experience Skinner as "negatively reinforcing." And in view of Skinner's definition of a "forceful act," mine is surely not a critical one. "Depriving a person of something he needs or wants is not a forceful act," he asserts without any qualifications. Depriving a person of property or of liberty or even of air are thus *not* forceful acts. Skinner does not tell us what *is* a forceful act.

Although force may not be Skinner's forte, he feels very confident about being able to explain why people gamble, climb mountains, or invent things: "All gambling systems are based on variable-ratio schedules of reinforcement, although their effects are usually attributed to feelings. . . . The same variable-ratio schedule affects those who explore, prospect, invent, conduct scientific research, and compose works of art, music, or literature . . . . " The irony of it all is that Skinner keeps contrasting himself to Freud, whom, in these respects, he resembles and imitates. Freud attributed creativity to the repression and sublimation of all sorts of nasty "drives," from anality to homosexuality. Skinner attributes them to "schedules of reinforcement." Anything will do, so long as it reduces the artist to the level of robot or rat.

As Skinner warms to his subject, he reveals more and more about his willingness to do away—in his science and perhaps elsewhere—with persons qua agents. "In a behavioral analysis," he writes, "a person is an organism, a member of the human species, which has acquired a repertoire of behavior." In a word, an animal. He then continues: "The person who asserts his freedom by saying, '*I* determine what I shall do next,' is speaking of freedom in or from a current situation: the *I* who thus seems to have an option is the product of a history from which it is not free and which in fact determines what it will now do." That takes care of my personal responsibility for writing this review. I did not write it at all: a "locus" did. I do not believe that, but Skinner evidently does: "A person is not an originating agent; he is a locus, a point at which many genetic and environmental conditions come together in a joint effect."

Skinner has an absolutely unbounded love for the idea that there are no individuals, no agents—that there are only organisms, animals: "The scientific analysis of behavior must, I believe, assume that a person's behavior is controlled by his genetic and environmental histories rather than by the person himself as an initiating, creative agent." This view leads inexorably to his love affair with the image of every human being as a controlled object, with no room, or word, for either controlling others (for example, tyranny), or for controlling oneself (for example, self-discipline). The "feeling" of freedom creates some problems for this scheme, but Skinner talks his way out of it, at least to his own satisfaction. He explains that "the important fact is not that we feel free when we have been positively reinforced, *but that we do not tend to escape or counterattack.* [Italics Skinner's.] Feeling free is an important hallmark of a kind of control distinguished by the fact that it does not breed countercontrol."

It is in the chapter titled "The Question of Control" that Skinner explains how, in the world he is designing, everyone will be controlled, everyone will feel free, and *mirabile visu,*[2] no one will control! As this is the capstone in the triumphal arch leading to his Utopia, I will quote Skinner rather than try to paraphrase what he says—for he is, after all, quite unparaphrasable:

> The design of human behavior implies, of course, control and possibly the question most often asked of the behaviorist is this: Who is to control? The question represents the age-old mistake of looking to the individual rather than to the world in which he lives. It will not be a benevolent dictator, a compassionate therapist, a devoted teacher, or a public-spirited industrialist who will design a way of life in the interests of everyone. We must look instead at the conditions under which people govern, give help, teach, and arrange incentive systems in particular ways. In other words, we must look to the culture as a social environment. Will a culture evolve in which no individual will be able to accumulate vast power and use it for his own aggrandizement in ways which are harmful to others? Will a culture evolve in which individuals are not so much concerned with their own actualization and fulfillment that they do not give serious attention to the future of the culture? These questions, and many others like them, are the questions to be asked rather than who will control and to what end. No one steps outside the causal stream. No one really intervenes.

No one "intervenes." Everyone is an "effect." Amen.

But enough is enough. I wrote at the beginning of this review that human beings cannot live without meaning; that they either create or destroy meaning; and that, in my opinion, Skinner is, or aspires to be, one of the great destroyers of meaning, and, hence, of man. This is the note on which I now want to elaborate and on which I want to end.

Although languages, George Steiner observed in *Language and Silence,* "have great reserves of life," these reserves are not inexhaustible: ". . . there comes a breaking point. Use a language to conceive, organize, and justify Belsen; use it to make out specifications for gas ovens; use it to dehumanize man during twelve years of calculated bestiality. Something will happen to it. . . . Something of the lies and sadism will settle in the marrow of the language."

Others—in particular, Orwell[3]—have suggested that what has happened to the German language under the influence of Nazism has happened to other modern languages under the influence of bureaucratization, collectivization, and technicalization. Skinnerese is accordingly just one of the depersonalized scientific idioms of our age—a member of the family of languages for loathing and liquidating man. What distinguishes Skinnerese from its sister languages—such as legalese, medicalese, or psychoanalese—is the naive but infectious enthusiasm of its author for world destruction through the conscious and deliberate destruction of language.

Skinner devotes a whole chapter of *About Behaviorism* to language. Aptly titled "Verbal Behavior," it is devoted to the destruction of the idea of language. "Relatively late in its history," Skinner begins, "the human species underwent a remarkable change: its vocal musculature came under operant control." Skinner then explains why he wants to get rid of the word "language": "The very difference between 'language' and 'verbal behavior' is an example of a word requiring 'mentalistic explanations.' Language has the character of a thing, something a person acquires and possesses. . . . A much more productive view is that verbal behavior is behavior. It has a special character only because it is reinforced by its effects on people. . . ." Translation: Do not say "language" if you want to be positively reinforced by Dr. Skinner.

Perhaps realizing that much of what he says is an attempt to replace a generally accepted metaphor with a metaphor of his own choosing, Skinner reinterprets metaphor as well: "In verbal behavior one kind of response evoked by a merely similar stimulus is called metaphor." He evidently prefers this to Aristotle's definition, according to which we use metaphor when we give something a name that rightly belongs to something else.

Finally, Skinner redefines "truth" itself. This definition is so revealing of his effort and so repellent in its effect (at least on me), that I shall end my series of quotations with it:

> The truth of a statement is limited by the sources of the behavior of the speaker, the control exerted by the current setting, the effects of similar settings in the past, the effects upon the listener leading to precision or to exaggeration or falsification, and so on.

Honest to God, this is what Skinner says is truth. He does not say what is false-hood. Or what is fakery. He does not have to: he displays them.

These, then are the reasons that I consider Skinner to be just another megalo-maniacal destroyer, or would-be destroyer, of mankind—one of many from Plato to Timothy Leary.[4] But Skinner has the distinction, in this company, of being more simple-minded than most, and hence being able to advocate a political system no one has thought of before: namely, one in which all are ruled and no one rules! Plato envisioned a Utopia in which people are perfectly ruled by perfect philosopher-kings: here everyone was destroyed qua person, save for the rulers. Lenin, Stalin, and Hitler had their own versions of Utopia: like Plato's, their Uto-pias were characterized by the destruction, actual or metaphorical, of large classes of mankind; but some individuals were still considered to be agents. Skinner has gone all of these one better. He has constructed a world of acts without actors, of conditioning without conditioners, of slaves without masters, of politics without politicians, of the good life without ethics, of man without language. It is an achievement worthy of a Harvard professor.

Notes

[1] reductionism: a procedure or theory that reduces complex data or phenomena to simple terms. In the sciences reductionism generally tries to use a single set of laws to describe all scientific processes.

[2] *mirabile visu:* wonderful to see.

[3] George Orwell (1903–1950), a twentieth-century British novelist and essayist, wrote *Animal Farm* and *1984.* In *1984* Newspeak, the language of Oceania, obliterated former knowledge and allowed only politically acceptable ideas.

[4] Timothy Leary, in the sixties, advocated a society built on psychedelic experiences.

FOCUS: READING REVIEW

1. On what grounds does Szasz object to Skinner?
2. Szasz makes some direct attacks on Skinner. What are they?
3. To what aspect of Skinner's language does Szasz object? How does he phrase his own objections? What effect does this have on the reader's opinion of Skinner?
4. How does Szasz justify his position that Skinner is another "megalomaniacal destroyer, or would-be destroyer, of mankind"?

FOCUS: AUTHOR'S STRATEGIES

1. This is a critical analysis. What are the analytic components? What criteria exist for the author's judgments?
2. Szasz opens with a syllogism. What are the syllogism's premises and conclusion? How does Szasz build his essay on this?
3. What tone does Szasz's language create? What persona does the tone create? What audi-ence do the tone and persona suggest?

FOCUS: **DISCUSSION AND WRITING**

1. Review Skinner's essay, "The Causes of Behavior," in Chapter 4 on social science's governing assumptions (pp. 000–000). Does Szasz focus his discussion on Skinner's central issues? Explain where you feel Szasz is justified in his criticisms and where he distorts Skinner. Why?
2. Szasz objects to Skinner's use of language. Analyze Szasz's use of language, particularly its connotative meaning. Explain the effect of Szasz's language.

A Defense of Skinner's Behaviorism: Comments on Professor Szasz's Review
Willard F. Day

Willard F. Day (b. 1926), a professor of psychology at the University of Nevada, Reno, edits the journal Behaviorism. *He received his A.B., M.A., and Ph.D. degrees from the University of Virginia and specializes in behavior analysis and behaviorist theory. This response, which defends Skinner for defining psychological knowledge in measurable terms, objects to Szasz's review for its nonscientific attack. By comparing Day with Szasz, you will see the very different kinds of assumptions that underlie humanistic and behaviorist psychology.*

I can find little in Szasz's remarks on *About Behaviorism* that should put behaviorism on the defensive. Behaviorism succeeds better than many other perspectives in bringing to the fore an awareness of the many difficulties of a conceptual nature that characterize most contemporary claims to psychological knowledge. As a review of *About Behaviorism* Professor's Szasz's remarks leave something to be desired. Skinner's primary purpose in the book is to reply to the common objections to behaviorism, [which he does by numbering twenty objections and responding to them]. I happen to feel that some of the discussions offered by Skinner in his final "Summing Up" appear to fare less well than others as effective rebuttal.

There is, however, new material of importance in *About Behaviorism*. The most striking thing about Professor Szasz's remarks is their ad hominem nature: he shifts the discussion from the merits of what has been said to issues associated with the saying of it. Szasz does not *discuss* what Skinner says, but why he says it. Szasz's commentary functions largely to guide the readers to a perception of Skinner's evil motives.

I remember when, as a graduate student, I first tried to read B. F. Skinner's book *Science and Human Behavior*, shortly after it came out in 1953. When I reached page 177, I suddenly hurled the book across the room. Even though I had been reading alone, I swore out loud that I would never open the book again. This incident remains the only instance in my life when I have thrown any book across a room or taken any oath that I would never open a particular book. Needless to say, since then I have had innumerable occasions to refer to *Science and Human Behavior*. The latest was only a month ago, when, in preparing a lengthy paper for the Nebraska Symposium on Motivation, I felt that material from that book would best illustrate details of how the "translations" Skinner frequently makes of mentalistic explanations are related to the interpretative practices of behaviorists when they analyze what animals actually do in laboratory situations.

I have been asked to write something of a "defense" of behaviorism, in view of the outspoken nature of Professor Szasz's remarks on Skinner's latest book, *About Behaviorism*. Actually, I can find little in what Szasz has had to say that should put behaviorism on the defensive. Behaviorism, as an intellectual outlook in psychology, seems to stand pretty well on its own feet, and one of the reasons it is important today is that it succeeds better than many other perspectives in bringing to the fore an awareness of the many difficulties of a conceptual nature that characterize most contemporary claims to psychological knowledge. At least in Skinner's work, in its opposition to traditional "methodological" behaviorism, we have a coherent account of science as the behavior of scientists that challenges the precepts of logical positivism[1], which have become tacitly incorporated into the epistemological underpinnings of much of experimental psychology itself. Again, at least in Skinner's work, his attack on the conceptual ramifications of stimulus-response reflex psychology goes far enough to constitute a powerful challenge to the conceptual underpinnings of much current theorizing in connection with cognitive processes, the storage and retrieval of "information," and attempts to view human functioning on the analogue of computers and feedback servo-mechanisms. Behaviorism today must carry the torch for "determinism"[2] in psychology. Yet the current concern with determinism is not simply a philosophical issue. Under the banner of determinism, behaviorism today must stand for the legitimacy of any robust psychological knowledge itself, at least to the extent that we engage seriously the question whether psychological factors *ever* truly determine any aspect of human functioning in a causal fashion. In the face of the growing interest in humanistic approaches to psychotherapy, with the attendant conceptual confusion associated with struggles to clarify what is meant by psychological freedom, behaviorism must stand today as the champion of a psychology that would keep itself responsive to new knowledge in such related scientific disciplines as biology, ethology, and neurophysiology. In the face of growing confidence in the intelligibility of psychoanalytically derived insights, behaviorism today forces attention to the issue of precisely to what extent it is accurate to look for the explanation of people's behavior in their *intentions*, either conscious or unconscious.

It would seem to me that, as a review of *About Behaviorism*, Professor Szasz's remarks leave something to be desired. In what follows I will first say something about the book, so that the reader can have some idea of what goes on in it. I will conclude with a relatively brief discussion of what Professor Szasz has had to say, more or less by way of giving the reader a sample of behaviorist reasoning.

I do not have the space here to provide the closely detailed review of *About Behaviorism* that the importance of the book merits. A lengthy review by Roger Schnaitter will be forthcoming in the March issue of the *Journal of the Experimental Analysis of Behavior*, and I recommend it to the reader interested in how *About Behaviorism* is connected to the issues most currently under discussion among behaviorists. However, in its structure, *About Behaviorism* lends itself particularly easily to impartial review. Skinner's primary purpose in the book is to reply to the most common objections to behaviorism. In the introduction, Skinner lists by number twenty "of the things commonly said about behaviorism or the science of behavior." In the final chapter, a "Summing Up," Skinner returns to the numbered objections, as based on the preceding discussion constituting the body of the book. The dimensions of an adequate discussion of the book follow naturally: the objections could again be taken up in order, and the adequacy of Skinner's treatment of them could be straightforwardly assessed. With respect to the twenty objections themselves, Skinner says, "They are all, I believe, wrong. . . . These contentions represent, I believe, an extraordinary misunderstanding of the achievements and significance of a scientific enterprise."

Since the body of the book develops material that bears upon the objections, the reader can get some notion of the range of issues discussed by looking at a selection from among the numbered objections:

1. It ignores consciousness, feelings, and states of mind. . . .
3. It formulates behavior simply as a set of responses to stimuli, thus representing a person as an automaton, robot, puppet, or machine.
4. It does not attempt to account for cognitive processes.
5. It has no place for intention or purpose. . . .
7. It assigns no role to a self or sense of self. . . .
9. It limits itself to the prediction and control of behavior and misses the essential nature or being a man. . . .
16. It dehumanizes man; it is reductionistic and destroys man *qua* man. . . .
19. It regards abstract ideas such as morality or justice as fictions.
20. It is indifferent to the warmth and richness of human life, and it is incompatible with the creation and enjoyment of art, music, and literature and with love for one's fellow man.

So far as I can see, Skinner's list of the bona fide objections most commonly raised to his views is reasonably complete. Professor Szasz's objection would appear to be of another order: the whole thing is doubletalk, maliciously intended. Yet I find Skinner trying more conspicuously here than anywhere else in his writing to *listen* to the core of the objections responsibly raised by his critics.

As a person relatively familiar with the corpus of Skinner's work, I would argue that the intellectual outlook inherent in contemporary behaviorism meets, on the whole, fairly nicely most of the objections commonly raised against it, quite independently of the new contribution in *About Behaviorism*. I happen to feel personally that some of the discussions offered by Skinner in his final "Summing Up" appear to fare less well than others as effective rebuttal. An example is Skinner's lengthy discussion of Objection 16—namely, that behaviorism dehumanizes man. Granted that it is generally difficult to verbalize coherently precisely what the humanistic psychologist is after in his advocacy of "human potential," Skinner's rebuttal misses the mark when the issue is treated by him in terms of the human capacity to choose, have purposes, and behave creatively. More-relevant rebuttal would discuss current interest in such matters as self-assertion, the importance of coming to know what one's feelings really are, and the range of dimensions often taken to be involved in personal growth. The following paragraph, extracted from a lengthy discussion, is representative of Skinner's treatment of the topic:

> What is usually meant in saying that behaviorism dehumanizes man is that it neglects important capacities which are not to be found in machines or animals, such as the capacity to choose, have purposes, and behave creatively. But the behavior from which we infer choice, intention, and originality is within reach of a behavioral analysis, and it is not clear that it is wholly out of reach of other species. Man is perhaps unique in being a moral animal, but not in the sense that he possesses morality; he has constructed a social environment in which he behaves with respect to himself and others in moral ways.

Of course. However, he would have done better, for example, to point out how widely behavior-modification techniques are employed to strengthen self-assertive behavior; or to call attention to how it has been largely the behaviorists who have argued that we should not expect people to know how to verbalize their feelings to begin with, unless differential reinforcement has been made fairly directly contingent upon them; or to call for a reasonably objective description of precisely what the behavior patterns are that we take to be the signs of significant personal growth; and so on.

I have said that there is new material of importance in *About Behaviorism.* Let me briefly identify the nature of some of it. In this book, Skinner comes closer than in any other of his works to presenting his views as coherent philosophy. Throughout the book there is a keen sense of Skinner's taking a firm stance on certain issues somewhat more ambiguously formulated in the past. A sharp distinction is drawn between the experimental analysis of behavior (an aspect of empirical science) and *behaviorism,* which is a philosophical perspective and is presumably subject to techniques of critical assessment properly a part of the discipline of professional philosophy. Skinner links behaviorism tightly with the fortunes of the philosophical position known as central-state materialism and referenced as *physicalism* in the index. Thus Skinner's perspective, which he refers to as *radical* behaviorism, differs markedly from *methodological* behaviorism, a popular psychological outlook linked to logical positivism and operationism, which are rejected.

Not unexpectedly, much of the discussion in the book bears upon the persistent indictment of mentalism. What Skinner means by mentalism is particularly clearly presented here: mentalism is the belief that inner states and feelings can *cause* behavior. Philosophers will want to focus quickly on the stance repeatedly taken by Skinner with respect to explanation. Mental concepts do not explain because they are given meaning to begin with in response to behavior, and behavior is susceptible to causal explanation. Only *causal* explanations are genuinely explanatory. Without question the most interesting thing philosophically about the book is the highly original formulation of the notion of cause itself that it contains. The causes of behavior are taken to be properties only of contingencies, of which there are two kinds: contingencies of survival and contingencies of reinforcement. Intentionality in behavior reflects the functioning of causal contingencies. The philosophical problem of agency is explicitly engaged, and it is argued that the self is not a concept that can be called upon to explain the initiation of action. The commitment to determinism is explicit, yet the conception of determinism that Skinner holds is not as recherché[3] as professional philosophical conceptualizations of the problem are sometimes likely to be. Skinner's conception of determinism is refreshingly uncomplex, and it maps nicely onto what psychologists are always getting at when they feel they have knowledge of *any* psychological determinants of behavior.

Skinner's radical behaviorism differs from its popular misrepresentation principally in connection with the role of private events. Private events are a legitimate subject of scientific investigation, a conclusion that follows from their physical nature. Private events can exercise antecedent *control* over behavior (as in self-descriptive verbal behavior), yet they do not explain behavior in a causal way. The concepts of cause and of control are different. Consequently, the penultimate[4] chapter in the book, on "What Is Inside the Skin?" is particularly important. The discussion throughout the body of the book drives toward this apical[5] chapter. In it the reader is invited to choose between radical behaviorism and traditional mentalistic psychology. Rational grounds bearing on such a choice are discussed in terms of such criteria as "Simplicity," "Use in Control," "Use in Prediction," "Use in Interpretation," "How Far Back?" (in a person's history must psychological explanation continue), "Relation to Other Sciences," and "Is Choice Necessary?" The choice is set up at the outset of the chapter in the following way. (The first paragraph quoted below contains a particularly concise statement of the philosophical perspective developed in the book.)

A behavioristic analysis rests on the following assumptions: A person is first of all an organism, a member of a species and a subspecies, possessing a genetic endowment of anatomical and physiological characteristics, which are the product of the contingencies of survival to which the species has been exposed in the process of evolution. The organism becomes a person as it acquires a repertoire of behavior under the contingencies of reinforcement to which it is exposed during its life-time. The behavior it exhibits at any moment is under the control of a current setting. It is able to acquire such a repertoire under such control because of processes of conditioning which are also part of its genetic endowment.

In the traditional mentalistic view, on the other hand, a person is a member of the human species who behaves as he does *because of* [italics added] many internal characteristics or possessions, among them sensations, habits, intelligence, opinions, dreams, personalities, moods, decisions, fantasies, skills, percepts, thoughts, virtues, intentions, abilities, instincts, daydreams, incentives, acts of will, joy, compassion, perceptual defenses, beliefs, complexes, expectancies, urges, choice, drives, ideas, responsibilities, elation, memories, needs, wisdom, wants, a death instinct, a sense of duty, sublimation, impulses, capacities, purposes, wishes, an id, repressed fears, a sense of shame, extraversion, images, knowledge, interests, information, a superego, propositions, experiences, attitudes, conflicts, meanings, reaction formations, a will to live, consciousness, anxiety, depression, fear, reason, libido, psychic energy, reminiscences, inhibitions, and mental illnesses.

How are we to decide between these two views?

There is an initial matter. It is a gross failure to perceive what is perhaps the central point of the book for Szasz to report that according to Skinner, feelings, such as the ill feelings Szasz confesses that he has toward Skinner, do not exist. *Of course* behaviorists recognize that people have feelings. Their claim is simply that, to continue to speak of this instance, the specifics of what Szasz has had to say in his review are not *caused* by his ill feelings.

However, the most striking thing about Professor Szasz's remarks is their ad hominem[6] nature. The professional community rightly disparages debate of this kind, and perhaps I can briefly illustrate what the behaviorist is up to in his opposition to "the traditional mentalistic view" by commenting on the ad hominem structure of Szasz's review.

Ad hominem argumentation is generally deplored because, in shifting the discussion from the merits of what has been said to issues associated with the saying of it, the socially adaptive consequences of the rational assessment of ideas are preempted. Szasz does not *discuss* what Skinner says, but why he says it. Material quoted from the book is left hanging for the reader's reaction: Szasz's commentary functions largely to guide the reader to a perception of Skinner's evil motives. Skinner is said to be motivated toward his own personal aggrandizement. In this he is out to destroy the meaningfulness of people's lives. Since man differs from animals largely in his capacities for language, Skinner wants first to destroy language. The widespread interest in Skinner's thought follows from the motivational structure of those among us who are "fascinated" by what Harvard professors have to say.

It is the fact that Szasz tries to make sense out of Skinner's book primarily by attempting to assess his motives that interests me here, not the particular motives that he claims to be at work. Yet it is to some extent relevant to the important differences between behaviorism and other professional approaches that in writing his book Skinner is seen to be a "megalomaniacal destroyer" by a psychiatrist. The behaviorist calls attention to the fact that in making this motivational assessment

Szasz is exercising a form of judgement for which under more private circumstances other members of his profession would be paid. Yet my point is broader than one of simply calling attention to how it is that Szasz may easily be challenged in his assessment of Skinner's motives. The important thing about behaviorism is its insistence that it is wrong to begin with to think that we can best make sense out of what people do by speculating about their motives and intentions. Szasz's review is preeminently an example of the kind of mentalism that behaviorism is trying to correct.

Entirely apart from issues of ad hominem argument. Szasz is well within the scope of issues of concern to psychology in wanting to give an account of what Skinner is doing in writing his book, a concern that falsely seems to imply an intentional answer when it is expressed as a concern with *why* Skinner wrote the book. For the behaviorist, it is largely a professionally maladaptive move to believe that the *why* questions we so often ask of behavior are best answered by a specification of intentions. For the behaviorist, to ask "Why did Skinner write his book?" is to ask for information that would best be provided by a functional analysis of his behavior in doing so. The extraordinary professional achievement in Skinner's book *Verbal Behavior* lies precisely in the direction it points toward an analysis of what we are doing when we think and speak, one which accounts for the functioning of language in terms of the consequences it generates, rather than in terms of motives and intentions, either conscious or unconscious, which the speaker must be thought to have in mind.

Just how this is done, how it is that we can make sense of behavior by taking into account the environmental setting in which it occurs and the reinforcing consequences that it produces, is the business of behaviorism. The dramatically increasing interest in Skinner's work is similarly to be explained. People continue to read Skinner because it has been reinforcing to them to do so. People do not read Skinner because they are gullible victims of a diabolical mastermind, much less because they are somehow attracted by verbal confusion. People do so precisely because they have found that the realities of the human situation become much more meaningful, make much more sense, when viewed from within a perspective that is largely the result of Skinner's innovative thought. Granted, Skinner is difficult. Granted, also, there are conceptual problems within the current formulation of behaviorism that remain to be worked out. But the matter is by no means simply one of the intentional lynching of language, nor is any solution to be found in the lynching, in the language of a book review, of a behaviorist.

Notes

[1] logical positivism: a movement in philosophy which tests all statements by reference to experience or the structure of language and is concerned with the unification of the sciences through a common logical language.

[2] determinism: the doctrine that everything, especially one's choice of action, is determined by a sequence of causes independent of one's will.

³ recherché: too refined or too studied.

⁴ penultimate: next to last.

⁵ apical: at the highest point of interest.

⁶ *ad hominem:* appealing to one's prejudices rather than to reason, often by attacking the opponent rather than addressing the issues.

FOCUS: READING REVIEW

1. Day dismisses Szasz's review as "malicious doubletalk." Is Szasz malicious? If so, why? How does he employ "doubletalk"?
2. How descriptive is Day's summary of the *ad hominem* nature of Szasz's review?
3. Day states, "People continue to read Skinner because it has been reinforcing for them to do so." Explain this statement and tell why Day takes this position.

FOCUS: AUTHOR'S STRATEGIES

1. Compare Day's definition of "mentalism" with Skinner's use of the word. Does Day's definition of mentalism clarify Skinner's use? How does this compare with Szasz's understanding of the concept? Explain how Day uses this as part of his evidence.
2. According to Day, Skinner asserts that the need for behaviorism exists when one considers the options. To illustrate the strength of Skinner's position, he then quotes an extensive comparison between the behaviorist and the mentalist views. What is the effect of using this quotation? Does it achieve its intended purpose?
3. For what audience is Day writing? What in his language and discussion of Skinner suggest this?

FOCUS: DISCUSSION AND WRITING

1. Day lists a range of objections generally raised against behaviorism. Based on your reading of Skinner in chapter 4, are these objections valid? How does Szasz contend with these objections in his review?
2. The dialogue between Szasz and Day indicates two views on psychology's purpose. Explain how each sees this purpose. Explain how you would propose to reconcile these two extremes.

Television at the Crossroads: Fact, Fantasies, and Schools

George Gerbner, Larry Gross, Michael Morgan, and Nancy Signorielli

George Gerbner, professor of communications, dean of the Annenberg School of Communications at the University of Pennsylvania and editor of the Journal of Communication, *has written extensively on mass communication and recently edited* Mass Media in Changing Cultures. *Larry Gross, professor of communications at the Annenberg School of Communications and co-editor of* Studies in Visual Communication, *does research in the area of cultural determinants of symbolic behavior. Michael Morgan, assistant professor of communications at the University of Massachusetts, specializes in role socialization and academic achievement. Nancy Signorielli, a research administrator for the Annenberg School of Communications, studies television images and their effects upon people's conceptions. This article, which appeared in the journal* Society, *critiques a National Association of Broadcasters' Television Information Office (TIO) report on the relationship between high levels of television watching and low academic performance. Gerbner et al. propose alternate ways of interpreting the TIO study's data and argue that causation is far more complex than the study indicates.*

[Whether television harms, helps, or has no effect on academic achievement is a question of long-standing scholarly and popular debate.] Some claim that television has created a brighter, more aware generation, with greater knowledge of the people and cultures of the world. Some argue television can stimulate reading, increase vocabulary, expand general knowledge, and help develop critical faculties. [For those who view the medium's effect as negative], it is tempting to connect the apparent decline in school performance with the rise of television. The problem with this conclusion is that many other things have happened in the last thirty years to account for the decline. An article by Briller and Miller, which states the view of the Television Information Office (TIO) of the National Association of Broadcasters points this out. The central flaw in the TIO presentation is the way in which it frames the issues. It asks whether television is the cause of decline in academic performance, rather than the question that should be asked: "Does television viewing exert an independent influence on academic achievement, and if so, for whom, under what conditions, and in which direction?" [The TIO report's contention that television viewing is not "the" cause of scholastic decline is correct; but contrary to the TIO's interpretations, the bulk of research (reviewed in this essay) supports the argument that those who spend more time watching television will get lower test scores and that some groups of students are more vulnerable, particularly poor readers.]

Whether television harms, helps, or has no effect on academic achievement is a question of long-standing scholarly and popular debate. As with the issue of television's impact on aggressive behavior, it provokes strong opinions on all sides. These are often based more on wishful thinking than on objective, scientific analysis. As with television and violence, the issues and the research are often more complex than they appear at first glance. In some ways, these concerns are nothing new. We do not have to look far back to find the most popular mass media of earlier days accused of causing similarly dire consequences—whether the medium was movies, comic books, or even fiction (the reading of which is generally endorsed today).

Television is different from other media in some important ways. The television set is on in the average American home more than six and a half hours a day. Children are born into a new symbolic environment and grow up absorbing thousands of stories told by television each year. There is no longer any need to go outside of the home—to church, to school—or to learn to read in order to encounter the broader culture. The ritualistic nature of the activity and the quantity of time children and adolescents spend watching television makes it a historically unprecedented phenomenon. We assume that there might be equally unprecedented consequences.

Some claim that television has created a brighter, more aware generation, with greater knowledge of the people and the cultures of the world. Some argue television can stimulate reading, increase vocabulary, expand general knowledge, and help develop critical faculties.

Many who view the medium's effects as negative tend to be far more vocal, outspoken, and adamant about their position. To support their case, they are also more likely to cite research studies or reports of those studies in the press, which, unfortunately, often exaggerate or sensationalize the data. Some of these critics point to troubling social developments, such as the steady decline in Scholastic Aptitude Test (SAT) scores and the existence of millions of functionally illiterate adults. Critics note that the longer we live with television, the worse these situations become. Similarly, veteran teachers complain about new crops of bleary-eyed pupils with short attention spans, whose frames of reference seem entirely determined by television. There is no potential source of these ills as easy to target for the blame as television.

It is tempting to connect the apparent decline in school performance with the rise of television and let that be the end of the discussion. The problem with such "self-evident," "commonsense" conclusions is that many other things have happened in the last thirty years that might account for the decline. A recent attempt to point this out is the preceding article by Briller and Miller, which states the views of the Television Information Office (TIO) of the National Association of Broadcasters. It attempts to refute the often heard claim that television adversely affects academic achievement. It criticizes one well-known study that purports to show that heavy viewers get lower test scores; discusses other studies that show no such relationship; considers other factors that negatively affect school achievement; and presents research that implies television has made "significant contributions to children's education."

The central flaw in the TIO presentation is the way in which it frames the issues. It asks, in essence, whether television is *the* cause of declines in academic performances: "If there is a decline in . . . [children's] ability to read and in their academic achievement, is it the fault of television?" The answer is, "Of course not." The question that should be asked—one that leads to a sharply different answer—is: "Does television viewing exert an independent influence on academic achievement, and if so, for whom, under what conditions, and in which direction?"

WHAT THE RESEARCH SAYS

Research on television's effect on school achievement dates back to the earliest days of television. The past few years have seen a rapid increase in the number of studies on the topic and in-depth reviews of those studies. Within the past two years alone, the question has been the focus of special sessions at conferences of the American Educational Research Association, the Conference on Culture and Communication, and the International Communication Association. The amount of attention paid to the subject shows no signs of diminishing.

In addition to the work done by academic researchers, the Departments of Education in various states (including Rhode Island, Connecticut, Pennsylvania, Texas, and California) have attempted to determine whether amount of television viewing relates systematically to students' achievement scores. These state assessment programs have provided results from many thousands of students. Taken all together, they point to a firm conclusion: Those students who say they spend relatively more time watching television are more likely to get lower scores on achievement tests. There can be no doubt or disagreement about the consistency of this finding across numerous studies all over the country. Even the TIO acknowledges the basic finding that heavy viewing tends to be associated with lower test scores.

The controversy is not over whether or not students who watch more television get lower test scores. It concerns the kinds of interpretations and inferences that have been (or may be) drawn from that finding. Specifically, these revolve around two central issues that are tightly intertwined: (1) the size of the relationship, and (2) the impact of controls for important background factors.

The TIO charges that the relationships found in one highly publicized study (conducted by the California State Department of Education) were termed "very strong," but are more properly characterized as weak. We do not disagree, but we also do not share the conclusion that weak relationships are irrelevant, and that television is somehow "off the hook" just because the observable relationships between television and achievement are weak.

The size of an effect is less important than the direction and consistency of its contribution. Small effects may have far-reaching consequences, in spheres ranging from consumer product sales to election results to geothermal temperature changes. There is a wide gap between small effects and no effects. Small overall effects may also hide larger ones for statistical reasons. For example, most American children may be so heavily exposed to television that our instruments are only able to detect the tip of the iceberg. More importantly, small effects observed over an entire population may be masking much larger effects in certain subgroups; these may show systematic evidence of greater susceptibility.

The TIO attempts to bolster its case for minimal television effects by citing two articles, one by Susan B. Neuman and the other by Lilya Wagner. Both of these discuss, in very general terms, about a dozen studies conducted between the early 1950s and the mid-1970s.

Neuman is quoted as concluding that, across all studies, regardless of the specific research designs or measures being used, "the relationship between the amount of television viewed and reading achievement in the schools was *not* significant." This is not quite accurate; several of the studies cited by Neuman show significant correlations between television viewing and numerous areas of achievement. The Neuman article (and the TIO report) ignore other studies which find substantial associations. The criterion of statistical significance can be misleading, since many of these studies were based on small numbers of children; the same coefficients, if found in larger samples, would have generated the opposite conclusion. The Neuman paper is of remarkably little value in attempting to understand research findings, since none at all are presented beyond the unqualified statements that we quoted. Neuman mysteriously contrasts "survey" and "correlation" as opposing research designs and misrepresents the use of controls for intelligence quotient in these studies, claiming that all but two used such controls. Virtually none of these studies even considered controlling for IQ.

TIO quotes Wagner's "verdict" that "A student's academic standing in an educational system based largely on reading does not appear to be greatly influenced by TV," but ignores the next sentence: "Creativity does seem to be hampered because of television's one-way transaction." Wagner's also notes:

> Students of lower intelligence watch more TV while those of higher ability turn to reading with increasing frequency as they mature. However, if they continue their extensive TV viewing, their ability to achieve declines.

Some studies Neuman and Wagner cite are seriously flawed. One, for example, asked students for their own subjective judgments of how television has affected their reading habits. Such data could hardly represent convincing evidence one way or the other.

Others have reviewed the same (and more) research evidence in considerably greater detail and come up with different conclusions. Robert Hornik discusses most of these same studies in a 1978 article in the *American Educational Research Journal.* He points out critical methodological and analytical limitations that severely challenge their validity. He notes that the strongest of these studies reveals negative trends and that one "cannot help but wonder whether inadequate design or measurement, whether failure to introduce the right control variable, might not have resulted in underestimates of these negative trends." In a 1979 article in the *Review of Educational Research,* Hornik evaluates evidence from more studies:

There are a few studies which find inconsistent relationships between television use and schooling outcomes. . . . However, the great majority of studies find a negative association between number of hours of television watching and level of school achievement or reading ability. . . . In particular, when students beyond the fourth grade level are tested, hours of television watching is always negatively associated with achievement and reading skills.

Even more recently, in the *American Educational Research Journal* in 1982, Patricia Williams and her colleagues published the results of a "research synthesis" on television and achievement. This study systematically consolidated the data from all available studies on the topic as of 1979, about twice as many as either Neuman or Wagner considered. (Some of the studies relied upon by Neuman and Wagner were discarded by Williams et al. because they provided inadequate statistical information.) In this synthesis, the authors find a preponderance of negative associations and conclude that there is a small but overwhelmingly consistent negative association between viewing and achievement.

Their research synthesis does not include a half dozen or so recent studies, all showing consistent negative relationships, such as the California Education Department project. References to even more studies showing comparable negative relationships can be found in a review of the research by Michael Morgan and Larry Gross in the National Institute of Mental Health's report on *Television and Behavior: Ten Years of Scientific Progress and Implications for the Eighties.* That review also presents data from a national sample of adults, showing that those who watch more television have significantly lower scores on a verbal intelligence test. None of these reviews, nor the implications of the studies they evaluate, are acknowledged in the TIO report.

We have been considering only the overall association between amount of television viewing and scholastic achievement, but neither television nor its consequences operate in a vacuum. Television viewing is part and parcel of various constellations of factors, many of which also affect achievement. Many of the early studies of television and achievement failed to control for these factors.

Controls for such factors as IQ and social class must be implemented for two reasons. First, even if there is a demonstrable and stable association between television viewing and achievement, it may be spurious; that is, some other variable, such as IQ, may be the true cause of both amount of viewing and achievement, and thereby be responsible for any apparent relationship between them. When the true cause is statistically removed, the association may disappear entirely. Second, whether or not various background factors account for the observed relationship, there may be systematically different associations between television and achievement within different subgroups in the sample. There can be a strong negative association within one subgroup and a positive association within another. These different patterns would then cancel each other out in the overall comparison and lead to the misleading conclusion of a small negative association.

The TIO report muddles and confuses these concepts. In discussing the California Education Department study, TIO states that

> The report claims that "the relationship was very strong, and none of several other factors—such as socioeconomic status and English language fluency—that were analyzed substantially affected it."
>
> Analysis of the data shows socioeconomic factors to have been one of the major—if not *the* major—influences on test scores results.

This rebuttal is a non sequitur. We live in a universe of multiple causality. To say that automobiles are the major cause of air pollution is not to say that factories have no effect. Similarly, whatever the impact of variables such as social class and IQ on achievement, they have no necessary, intrinsic bearing on whether or not television also has an influence. Controls for those background factors would have to be shown to eliminate the relationships between television and achievement—that there are no such relationships within any of the different IQ or social class groups. This is not the case.

Other variables have profound but subtle effects on the relationship between television and achievement, in ways not dealt with by TIO. Intelligence quotient is probably the strongest known predictor of achievement scores. In an article in the *Journal of Broadcasting* in 1980, Michael Morgan and Larry Gross point out that there appears to be no dispute over the relatively strong relationship between television viewing and IQ: heavier television viewers have lower IQs than light viewers, and those with higher IQs watch less television. Apparent relationships between viewing and test scores may be merely an artifact of IQ: high-IQ students watch less and score better, low-IQ students watch more and score worse. In some areas of achievement (especially mathematics skills) this seems to be the case; television has no independent relationship to achievement above and beyond the effects of IQ. In some other areas, notably reading comprehension and language usage, significant associations between television and achievement persist even after IQ is taken into account.

Most importantly, the associations are not the same at all IQ levels. These overall assessments mask systematic variations within different subgroups.... [The] data show an enhanced negative relationship between television and achievement among high-IQ students, and a small positive association among low-IQ students, especially among girls. The resulting pattern is one of convergence among heavy viewers of otherwise divergent groups, with heavy viewing being associated with the "center" of achievement. In each IQ group, heavy viewers have the score that is closest to the midpoint percentile.

This is exactly what the California Education Department study found, using controls for social class and English fluency, for most areas of achievement and at most ages. The relationships between amount of viewing and achievement were slightly positive among students from lower socioeconomic levels and for students with limited English fluency; in their counterpart subgroups, stronger negative associations emerged. The TIO report interprets these patterns as evidence for no effects.

More researchers in the field are uncovering the same results. Jerome and Dorothy Singer, in a paper presented at the 1983 Conference on Culture and Communication in Philadelphia, found this type of convergence when their sample was partitioned according to social class divisions. Richard Kohr, in a 1979 presentation to the National Council for Measurement in Education, found stronger negative associations between television viewing and achievement among students whose parents have more education (based on data from 90,000 Pennsylvania students). The research synthesis by Patricia Williams and her colleagues also concluded that the negative associations between television viewing and achievement are strongest for high-IQ students.

These findings are paralleled in research conducted by our Cultural Indicators Project at The Annenberg School of Communications, University of Pennsylvania, on television's contributions to viewers' conceptions of social reality. In this work, the process of convergence among heavy viewers has been called "mainstreaming," on the premise that television's portrayals of life and society represent the mainstream of our culture. In general, stronger evidence that television cultivates conceptions of reality has been found within groups who, as light viewers, are least likely to be part of that mainstream. The result is a homogenization of heavy viewers from otherwise different groups; television viewing seems to override or diminish the effects of other factors. The phenomenon of mainstreaming has been found to explain group differences in cultivation patterns in terms of images of violence, sex-role stereotypes, health-related beliefs and practices, science, and other issues. In articles in the *Journal of Communication* and the *Public Opinion Quarterly,* we extend the theory of mainstreaming to television's contributions to political orientations and attitudes.

Variables that mediate relationships between television viewing and achievement in ways that reveal mainstreaming are not limited to social class and IQ. A whole range of personal, social, family, and other factors have been found to make a difference in systematic and theoretically meaningful ways. These are some of the major results we have found:

- Students with higher educational and occupational aspirations get higher achievement scores, but they show stronger negative associations between amount of viewing and those scores.
- Students who devote most of their attention to television while they are watching reveal stronger negative relationships between viewing and achievement; students who engage in many activities while viewing show smaller associations.
- More studious, home-oriented students, who spend more time on homework, chores, religion, art, and music, show stronger negative associations between television and achievement.
- Students whose parents are less involved in their viewing show stronger negative associations. Parental involvement in the viewing experience—whether restrictive and protective or characterized by an active, critical viewing orientation—reduces

or eliminates the associations. The more students argue with their parents about how much television and what shows they watch, the greater the negative associations.

- The more socially isolated the student, the stronger the effect. Students who are more integrated into cohesive peer groups reveal weaker relationships between television and achievement.

When we talk about television's implications for academic achievement we are not talking about any simple, clear-cut associations. The TIO report's contention that television viewing is not "the" cause of scholastic decline is correct; but contrary to TIO's interpretations, the bulk of research evidence supports the argument that those who spend more time watching television will get lower test scores and that some groups of students are more vulnerable. In study after study, reading skills in particular are negatively associated with heavy viewing.

FOCUS: READING REVIEW

1. What are the positions on the relation between television viewing and academic achievement?
2. The TIO supports its position with studies by Neuman and Wagner. What does each of these studies assert? What are this article's objections to these studies?
3. What kinds of evidence do Gerbner and his associates offer in support of their position?
4. What experimental controls do the authors suggest to improve the validity of studies on the relation between television viewing and achievement? Why should these be implemented?
5. What other factors besides IQ and social class influence the relation between television viewing and academic achievement?
6. What conclusions does the article reach? Are these supported by the evidence the authors have provided?

FOCUS: AUTHOR'S STRATEGIES

1. This essay reviews the methods of several studies about the effects of television on children's school performance. What is the purpose of this essay?
2. The authors summarize several studies on television's effects. How do they link their discussion of these studies?
3. On what grounds do the authors object to the studies? What criteria are implicit in these objections?

FOCUS: DISCUSSION AND WRITING

1. The authors discuss several factors that alter the effects of abundant television viewing. Explain how these factors might alter television's negative effects. Rely on your own observations and experiences to support your explanation.
2. Take a position for or against a program in schools and homes restricting television viewing. Rely on evidence from this essay to support your position.

Erotica and Pornography: A Clear and Present Difference

Gloria Steinem

Gloria Steinem (b. 1934), a prominent feminist leader, founded and edits Ms. Magazine. *Since her graduation from Smith College, she has contributed articles to* Esquire, Vogue, Life, Cosmopolitan, *and* Ms. *"Erotica and Pornography," which first appeared in* Ms., *defines pornography and from this definition argues that pornography's brutalization of women robs women and sexual relationships of integrity.*

For humans alone, sexuality can be and often is primarily a way of bonding. We developed this through our ability to affect our own evolution. But as an emotional result of this spiraling path away from other animals, we seem to alternate between periods of exploring our unique abilities and periods of fear that sometimes sends us back to the comfort of the animal world. We have explored our sexuality as separable from conception, yet we also have times of suspicion that sex is not complete—or even legal or intended-by-god—if it cannot end in conception. No wonder the concepts of "erotica" and "pornography" can be so crucially different, and yet so confused. Both assume that sexuality can be separated from conception. Both may be equally "shocking." This gross condemnation of all sexuality that isn't harnessed to childbirth and marriage has been increased by the current backlash against women's progress. Defending against such reaction in turn leads to another temptation: to merely declare that all nonprocreative sex is good. In fact, however, this human activity can be both constructive and destructive. The origins of "erotica" and "pornography" indicate this. "Erotica" is rooted in *eros* or passionate love, and "pornography" begins with a root meaning "prostitution" or "female captives." The difference is clear in the words. It becomes even more so by example. Perhaps one could simply say that erotica is about sexuality, but pornography is about power and sex-as-weapon. At the moment, fear of change is increasing both the indiscriminate repression of all nonprocreative sex in the religious and "conservative" male world, and the pornographic vengeance against women's sexuality in the secular world of "liberal" or "radical" men. Until we untangle the lethal confusion of sex with violence, there will be more pornography and less erotica.

Human beings are the only animals that experience the same sex drive at times when we can—and cannot—conceive.

Just as we developed uniquely human capacities for language, planning, memory, and invention along our evolutionary path, we also developed sexuality as a form of expression; a way of communicating that is separable from our need for sex as a way of perpetuating ourselves. For humans alone, sexuality can be and often is primarily a way of bonding, of giving and receiving pleasure, bridging differentness, discovering sameness, and communicating emotion.

We developed this and other human gifts through our ability to change our environment, adapt physically, and in the long run, to affect our own evolution. But as an emotional result of this spiraling path away from other animals, we seem to alternate between periods of exploring our unique abilities to forge new boundaries, and feelings of loneliness in the unknown that we ourselves have created; a fear that sometimes sends us back to the comfort of the animal world by encouraging us to exaggerate our sameness.

The separation of "play" from "work," for instance, is a problem only in the human world. So is the difference between art and nature, or an intellectual accomplishment and a physical one. As a result, we celebrate play, art, and invention as leaps into the unknown; but any imbalance can send us back to nostalgia for our primate past and the conviction that the basics of work, nature, and physical labor are somehow more worthwhile or even moral.

In the same way, we have explored our sexuality as separable from conception: a pleasurable, empathetic bridge to strangers of the same species. We have even invented contraception—a skill that has probably existed in some form since our ancestors figured out the process of birth—in order to extend this uniquely human difference. Yet we also have times of atavistic[1] suspicion that sex is not complete—or even legal or intended-by-god—if it cannot end in conception.

No wonder the concepts of "erotica" and "pornography" can be so crucially different, and yet so confused. Both assume that sexuality can be separated from conception, and therefore can be used to carry a personal message. That's a major reason why, even in our current culture, both may be called equally "shocking" or legally "obscene," a word whose Latin derivative means "dirty, containing filth." This gross condemnation of all sexuality that isn't harnessed to childbirth and marriage has been increased by the current backlash against women's progress. Out of fear that the whole patriarchal structure might be upset if women really had the autonomous power to decide our reproductive futures (that is, if we controlled the most basic means of production), right-wing groups are not only denouncing prochoice abortion literature as "pornographic," but are trying to stop the sending of all contraceptive information through the mails by invoking obscenity laws. In fact, Phyllis Schlafly[2] recently denounced the entire Women's Movement as "obscene."

Not surprisingly, this religious, visceral backlash has a secular, intellectual counterpart that relies heavily on applying the "natural" behavior of the animal world to humans. That is questionable in itself, but these Lionel Tiger[3]-ish studies make their political purpose even more clear in the particular animals they select and the habits they choose to emphasize. The message is that females should accept their "destiny" of being sexually dependent and devote themselves to bearing and rearing their young.

Defending against such reaction in turn leads to another temptation: to merely reverse the terms, and declare that all nonprocreative sex is good. In fact, however, this human activity can be as constructive or destructive, moral or immoral, as any other. Sex as communication can send messages as different as life and death; even the origins of "erotica" and "pornography" reflect that fact. After all, "erotica" is rooted in *eros* or passonate love, and thus in the idea of positive choice, free will, the yearning for a particular person. (Interestingly, the definition of erotica leaves open the question of gender.) "Pornography" begins with a root meaning "prostitution" or "female captives," thus letting us know that the subject is not mutual love, or love at all, but domination and violence against women. (Though, of course, homosexual pornography may imitate this violence by putting a man in the "feminine" role of victim.) It ends with a root meaning "writing about" or "description of" which puts still more distance between subject and object, and replaces a spontaneous yearning for closeness with objectification and a voyeur.

The difference is clear in the words. It becomes even more so by example.

Look at any photo or film of people making love; really making love. The images may be diverse, but there is usually a sensuality and touch and warmth, an acceptance of bodies and nerve endings. There is always a spontaneous sense of people who are there because they *want* to be, out of shared pleasure.

Now look at any depiction of sex in which there is clear force, or an unequal power that spells coercion. It may be very blatant, with weapons of torture or bondage, wounds and bruises, some clear humiliation, or an adult's sexual power being used over a child. It may be much more subtle: a physical attitude of conqueror and victim, the use of race or class difference to imply the same thing, perhaps a very unequal nudity, with one person exposed and vulnerable while the other is clothed. In either case, there is no sense of equal choice or equal power.

The first is erotic: a mutually pleasurable, sexual expression between people who have enough power to be there by positive choice. It may or may not strike a sense-memory in the viewer, or be creative enough to make the unknown seem real; but it doesn't require us to identify with a conqueror or a victim. It is truly sensuous, and may give us a contagion of pleasure.

The second is pornographic: its message is violence, dominance, and conquest. It is sex being used to reinforce some inequality, or to create one, or to tell us the lie that pain and humiliation (ours or someone else's) are really the same as pleasure. If we are to feel anything, we must identify with conqueror or victim. That means we can only experience pleasure through the adoption of some degree of sadism or masochism. It also means that we may feel diminished by the role of conqueror, or enraged, humiliated, and vengeful by sharing identity with the victim.

Perhaps one could simply say that erotica is about sexuality, but pornography is about power and sex-as-weapon—in the same way we have come to understand that rape is about violence, and not really about sexuality at all.

Yes, it's true that there are women who have been forced by violent families and dominating men to confuse love with pain; so much so that they have become masochists. (A fact that in no way excuses those who administer such pain.) But the truth is that, for most women—and for men with enough humanity to imagine themselves into the predicament of women—true pornography could serve as aversion therapy for sex.

Of course, there will always be personal differences about what is and is not erotic, and there may be cultural differences for a long time to come. Many women feel that sex makes them vulnerable and therefore may continue to need more sense of personal connection and safety before allowing any erotic feelings. We now find competence and expertise erotic in men, but that may pass as we develop those qualities in ourselves. Men, on the other hand, may continue to feel less vulnerable, and therefore more open to such potential danger as sex with strangers. As some men replace the need for submission from childlike women with the pleasure of cooperation from equals, they may find a partner's competence to be erotic, too.

Such group changes plus individual differences will continue to be reflected in sexual love between people of the same gender, as well as between women and men. The point is not to dictate sameness, but to discover ourselves and each other through sexuality that is an exploring, pleasurable, empathetic part of our lives; a human sexuality that is unchained both from unwanted pregnancies and from violence.

But that is a hope, not a reality. At the moment, fear of change is increasing both the indiscriminate repression of all nonprocreative sex in the religious and "conservative" male world, and the pornographic vengeance against women's sexuality in the secular world of "liberal" or "racial" men. It's almost futuristic to debate what is and is not truly erotic, when many women are again being forced into compulsory motherhood, and the number of pornographic murders, tortures, and woman-hating images are on the increase in both popular culture and real life.

It's a familiar division: wife or whore, "good" woman who is constantly vulnerable to pregnancy or "bad" woman who is unprotected from violence. *Both* roles would be upset if we were to control our own sexuality. And that's exactly what we must do.

In spite of all our atavistic suspicions and training for the "natural" role of motherhood, we took up the complicated battle for reproductive freedom. Our bodies had borne the health burden of endless births and poor abortions, and we had a greater motive for separating sexuality and conception.

Now we have to take up the equally complex burden of explaining that all nonprocreative sex is *not* alike. We have a motive: our right to a uniquely human sexuality, and sometimes even to survival. As it is, our bodies have too rarely been enough our own to develop erotica in our own lives, much less in art and literature. And our bodies have too often been the objects of pornography and the woman-hating, violent practice that it preaches. Consider also our spirits that break a little each time we see ourselves in chains or full labial display for the conquering male viewer, bruised or on our knees, screaming a real or pretended pain to delight the sadist, pretending to enjoy what we don't enjoy, to be blind to the images of our sisters that really haunt us—humiliated often enough ourselves by the truly obscene idea that sex and the domination of women must be combined.

Sexuality *is* human, free, separate—and so are we.

But until we untangle the lethal confusion of sex with violence, there will be more pornography and less erotica. There will be little murders in our beds—and very little love.

Notes

[1] atavistic: inherited from ancestors more remote than the parents.

[2] Phyllis Schlafly strongly advocates traditional roles of wife, homemaker, and mother for women.

[3] Lionel Tiger, an anthropologist, assigns human cultural patterns, including stereotyped sex roles, to evolutionary instincts.

FOCUS: READING REVIEW

1. What assumption underlies both erotica and pornography?
2. What is the patriarchal structure? Why does Steinem suggest that condemnation of all sexuality not tied to childbirth and marriage is threatening to the patriarchal structure?
3. Steinem moves from the discussion of pornography to a discussion of the erotic differences between men and women. What are these differences? What reasons does she offer for them?

FOCUS: AUTHOR'S STRATEGIES

1. The author uses the definition of pornography and erotica as a foundation for arguing for women's sexual integrity. Explain how she builds her definition. How does she move from defining to arguing?
2. What assumptions does the author hold about her readers' political and social prejudices? What in the language and examples illustrates this?
3. What end does this essay seek? Will the audience she writes for be able to seek this end?

FOCUS: DISCUSSION AND WRITING

What dangers does Steinem find in pornography? Are these the only dangers pornography poses to a society? Explain how important the issue of pornography is.

Letter from Birmingham Jail

Martin Luther King, Jr.

*Martin Luther King, Jr. (1929–1968), led the American civil rights move-
ment in the sixties. After receiving his Ph.D. in 1955 from Boston University's School of Theology, he returned to his native South first to serve as a
minister and then to become president of the Southern Christian Leadership
Conference, a group seeking civil rights. King advocated that blacks, in the
nonviolent tradition of Gandhi, should resist laws that denied blacks places
next to whites in classrooms, in buses, in restaurants, in rest rooms, and at
drinking fountains. "Letter from Birmingham Jail," was written in response
to a statement by eight white clergymen condemning the nonviolent demonstrations in Birmingham, Alabama. King, in jail at the time he wrote the
letter, had been arrested for participating in the demonstrations. According
to King, he began the letter on margins of the newspaper which carried the
clergymen's statement, continued it on scraps of paper supplied by a "Negro
trusty," and concluded on a pad his attorneys were "eventually permitted" to
leave him. The letter outlines the steps of a nonviolent campaign and justifies their use in Birmingham. Its power derives both from its carefully constructed argument and from its persuasive appeals.*

Since I feel that you are men of genuine good will and your criticisms are sincerely
set forth, I would like to answer your statement. You have been influenced by the
argument of "outsiders coming in." As president of the Southern Christian Leadership Conference, I, along with members of my staff, am here because I was invited
here and because injustice is here. You deplore the demonstrations that are presently
taking place in Birmingham. These are unfortunate, but it is even more unfortunate
that the white power structure left no other alternative. In a nonviolent campaign
there are four basic steps: (1) collection of the facts to determine whether injustices
are alive; (2) negotiation; (3) self-purification; and (4) direct action. We have gone
through all of these steps in Birmingham. One of the basic points in your statement is
that our acts are untimely. History is the long and tragic story of the fact that privileged groups seldom give up their privileges voluntarily. I have never yet engaged in
a direct action movement that was "well timed," according to the timetable of those
who have not suffered unduly from the disease of segregation. You express a great
deal of anxiety over our willingness to break laws. There are *just* laws and there are
unjust laws. I would be the first to advocate obeying just laws. Conversely, one has a
moral responsibility to disobey unjust laws. I must confess that I have been disappointed with the white moderate who is more devoted to "order" than to justice. I
had also hoped that the white moderate would reject the myth of time. You spoke of
our activity in Birmingham as extreme. But as I continued to think about the matter
I gradually gained a bit of satisfaction from being considered an extremist. Was not
Jesus an extremist in love? Amos an extremist for justice? Maybe the South, the

nation, and the world are in dire need of creative extremists. I have also been disappointed with the white Church and its leadership. I see the Church as the body of Christ. But, oh! How we have blemished and scarred that body through social neglect and fear of being nonconformist. But even if the Church does not come to the aid of justice, I have no despair about the future. I have no fear about the outcome of our struggle in Birmingham. We will reach the goal of freedom in Birmingham and all over the nation, because the goal of America is freedom.

MARTIN LUTHER KING, JR.
Birmingham City Jail
April 16, 1963

Bishop C. C. J. CARPENTER
Bishop JOSEPH A. DURICK
Rabbi MILTON L. GRAFMAN
Bishop PAUL HARDIN
Bishop NOLAN B. HARMON
The Rev. GEORGE M. MURRAY
The Rev. EDWARD V. RAMAGE
The Rev. EARL STALLINGS

My dear Fellow Clergymen,

While confined here in the Birmingham City Jail, I came across your recent statement calling our present activities "unwise and untimely." Seldom, if ever, do I pause to answer criticism of my work and ideas. If I sought to answer all of the criticisms that cross my desk, my secretaries would be engaged in little else in the course of the day and I would have no time for constructive work. But since I feel that you are men of genuine good will and your criticisms are sincerely set forth, I would like to answer your statement in what I hope will be patient and reasonable terms.

I think I should give the reason for my being in Birmingham, since you have been influenced by the argument of "outsiders coming in." I have the honor of serving as president of the Southern Christian Leadership Conference, an organization operating in every Southern state with headquarters in Atlanta, Georgia. We have some eighty-five affiliate organizations all across the South—one being the Alabama Christian Movement for Human Rights. Whenever necessary and possible we share staff, educational and financial resources with our affiliates. Several months ago our local affiliate here in Birmingham invited us to be on call to engage in a nonviolent direct action program if such were deemed necessary. We readily consented and when the hour came we lived up to our promises. So I am here, along with several members of my staff, because we were invited here. I am here because I have basic organizational ties here. Beyond this, I am in Birmingham because injustice is here. Just as the eighth century prophets left their little villages and carried their "thus saith the Lord" far beyond the boundaries of their home town, and just as the Apostle Paul left his little village of Tarsus and carried the gospel of Jesus Christ to practically every hamlet and city of the Graeco-Roman world, I too am compelled to carry the gospel of freedom beyond my particular home town. Like Paul, I must constantly respond to the Macedonian call for aid.

Moreover, I am cognizant of the interrelatedness of all communities and states. I cannot sit idly by in Atlanta and not be concerned about what happens in Birmingham. Injustice anywhere is a threat to justice everywhere. We are caught in an inescapable network of mutuality tied in a single garment of destiny. Whatever affects one directly affects all indirectly. Never again can we afford to live with the narrow, provincial "outside agitator" idea. Anyone who lives inside the United States can never be considered an outsider anywhere in this country.

You deplore the demonstrations that are presently taking place in Birmingham. But I am sorry that your statement did not express a similar concern for the conditions that brought the demonstrations into being. I am sure that each of you would want to go beyond the superficial social analyst who looks merely at effects, and does not grapple with underlying causes. I would not hesitate to say that it is unfortunate that so-called demonstrations are taking place in Birmingham at this time, but I would say in more emphatic terms that it is even more unfortunate that the white power structure of this city left the Negro community with no other alternative.

In any nonviolent campaign there are four basic steps: (1) collection of the facts to determine whether injustices are alive; (2) negotiation; (3) self-purification; and (4) direct action. We have gone through all of these steps in Birmingham. There can be no gainsaying of the fact that racial injustice engulfs this community. Birmingham is probably the most thoroughly segregated city in the United States. Its ugly record of police brutality is known in every section of this country. Its unjust treatment of Negroes in the courts is a notorious reality. There have been more unsolved bombings of Negro homes and churches in Birmingham than any city in this nation. These are the hard, brutal, and unbelievable facts. On the basis of these conditions Negro leaders sought to negotiate with the city fathers. But the political leaders consistently refused to engage in good faith negotiation.

Then came the opportunity last September to talk with some of the leaders of the economic community. In these negotiating sessions certain promises were made by the merchants—such as the promise to remove the humiliating racial signs from the stores. On the basis of these promises Rev. Shuttlesworth and the leaders of the Alabama Christian Movement for Human Rights agreed to call a moratorium on any type of demonstrations. As the weeks and months unfolded we realized that we were the victims of a broken promise. The signs remained. As in so many experiences of the past we were confronted with blasted hopes, and the dark shadow of a deep disappointment settled upon us. So we had no alternative except that of preparing for direct action, whereby we would present our very bodies as a means of laying our case before the conscience of the local and national community. We were not unmindful of the difficulties involved. So we decided to go through a process of self-purification. We started having workshops on non-violence and repeatedly asked ourselves the questions, "Are you able to accept blows without retaliating?" "Are you able to endure the ordeals of jail?"

We decided to set our direct action program around the Easter season, realizing that with the exception of Christmas, this was the largest shopping period of the year. Knowing that a strong economic withdrawal program would be the by-product of direct action, we felt that this was the best time to bring pressure on the merchants for the needed changes. Then it occurred to us that the March election was ahead, and so we speedily decided to postpone action until after elec-tion day. When we discovered that Mr. Connor was in the run-off, we decided again to postpone action so that the demonstrations could not be used to cloud the issues. At this time we agreed to begin our nonviolent witness the day after the run-off.

This reveals that we did not move irresponsibly into direct action. We too wanted to see Mr. Connor defeated; so we went through postponement after post-ponement to aid in this community need. After this we felt that direct action could be delayed no longer.

You may well ask, "Why direct action? Why sit-ins, marches, etc.? Isn't negoti-ation a better path?" You are exactly right in your call for negotiation. Indeed, this is the purpose of direct action. Nonviolent direct action seeks to create such a crisis and establish such creative tension that a community that has constantly refused to negotiate is forced to confront the issue. It seeks so to dramatize the issue that it can no longer be ignored. I just referred to the creation of tension as a part of the work of the nonviolent resister. This may sound rather shocking. But I must confess that I am not afraid of the word tension. I have earnestly worked and preached against violent tension, but there is a type of constructive nonviolent tension that is necessary for growth. Just as Socrates felt that it was necessary to create a tension in the mind so that individuals could rise from the bondage of myths and half-truths to the unfettered realm of creative analysis and objective appraisal, we must see the need of having nonviolent gadflies to create the kind of tension in society that will help men rise from the dark depths of prejudice and racism to the majestic heights of understanding and brotherhood. So the purpose of the direct action is to create a situation so crisis-packed that it will inevitably open the door to negotiation. We, therefore, concur with you in your call for nego-tiation. Too long has our beloved Southland been bogged down in the tragic at-tempt to live in monologue rather than dialogue.

One of the basic points in your statement is that our acts are untimely. Some have asked, "Why didn't you give the new administration time to act?" The only answer that I can give to this inquiry is that the new administration must be prodded about as much as the outgoing one before it acts. We will be sadly mis-taken if we feel that the election of Mr. Boutwell will bring the millennium to Birmingham. While Mr. Boutwell is much more articulate and gentle than Mr.

Connor, they are both segregationists dedicated to the task of maintaining the status quo. The hope I see in Mr. Boutwell is that he will be reasonable enough to see the futility of massive resistance to desegregation. But he will not see this without pressure from the devotees of civil rights. My friends, I must say to you that we have not made a single gain in civil rights without determined legal and nonviolent pressure. History is the long and tragic story of the fact that privileged groups seldom give up their privileges voluntarily. Individuals may see the moral light and voluntarily give up their unjust posture; but as Reinhold Niebuhr has reminded us, groups are more immoral than individuals.

We know through painful experience that freedom is never voluntarily given by the oppressor; it must be demanded by the oppressed. Frankly I have never yet engaged in a direct action movement that was "well timed," according to the time-table of those who have not suffered unduly from the disease of segregation. For years now I have heard the word "Wait!" It rings in the ear of every Negro with a piercing familiarity. This "wait" has almost always meant "never." It has been a tranquilizing thalidomide, relieving the emotional stress for a moment, only to give birth to an ill-formed infant of frustration. We must come to see with the distinguished jurist of yesterday that "justice too long delayed is justice denied." We have waited for more than three hundred and forty years for our constitutional and God-given rights. The nations of Asia and Africa are moving with jet-like speed toward the goal of political independence, and we still creep at horse and buggy pace toward the gaining of a cup of coffee at a lunch counter.

I guess it is easy for those who have never felt the stinging darts of segregation to say wait. But when you have seen vicious mobs lynch your mothers and fathers at will and drown your sisters and brothers at whim; when you have seen hate filled policemen curse, kick, brutalize, and even kill your black brothers and sisters with impunity; when you see the vast majority of your twenty million Negro brothers smothering in an air-tight cage of poverty in the midst of an affluent society; when you suddenly find your tongue twisted and your speech stammering as you seek to explain to your six-year-old daughter why she can't go to the public amusement park that has just been advertised on television, and see tears welling up in her little eyes when she is told that Funtown is closed to colored children, and see the depressing clouds of inferiority begin to form in her little mental sky, and see her begin to distort her little personality by unconsciously developing a bitterness toward white people; when you have to concoct an answer for a five-year-old son asking in agonizing pathos: "Daddy, why do white people treat colored people so mean?"; when you take a cross country drive and find it necessary to sleep night after night in the uncomfortable corners of your automobile because no motel will accept you; when you are humiliated day in and day out by nagging signs reading "white" men and "colored"; when your first name becomes "nigger" and your middle name becomes "boy" (however old you are) and your last name becomes "John," and when your wife and mother are never given the respected title "Mrs."; when you are harried by day and haunted by night by the fact that you are a Negro, living constantly at tiptoe stance never quite knowing what to expect next, and plagued with inner fears and outer resentments; when you are forever fighting a degenerating sense of "nobodiness";—then you will understand why we find it difficult to wait. There comes a time when the cup of endurance runs over, and men are no longer willing to be plunged into an abyss of injustice where they experience the bleakness of corroding despair. I hope, sirs, you can understand our legitimate and unavoidable impatience.

You express a great deal of anxiety over our willingness to break laws. This is certainly a legitimate concern. Since we so diligently urge people to obey the Supreme Court's decision of 1954 outlawing segregation in the public schools, it is rather strange and paradoxical to find us consciously breaking laws. One may well ask, "How can you advocate breaking some laws and obeying others?" The answer is found in the fact that there are two types of laws. There are *just* laws and there are *unjust* laws. I would be the first to advocate obeying just laws. One has not only a legal but moral responsibility to obey just laws. Conversely, one has a moral responsibility to disobey unjust laws. I would agree with Saint Augustine that "An unjust law is no law at all."

Now what is the difference between the two? How does one determine when a law is just or unjust? A just law is a man-made code that squares with the moral law or the law of God. An unjust law is a code that is out of harmony with the moral law. To put it in the terms of Saint Thomas Aquinas, an unjust law is a human law that is not rooted in eternal and natural law. Any law that uplifts human personality is just. Any law that degrades human personality is unjust. All segregation statutes are unjust because segregation distorts the soul and damages the personality. It gives the segregator a false sense of superiority and the segregated a false sense of inferiority. To use the words of Martin Buber, the great Jewish philosopher, segregation substitutes an "I-it" relationship for the "I-thou" relationship, and ends up relegating persons to the status of things. So segregation is not only politically, economically, and sociologically unsound, but it is morally wrong and sinful. Paul Tillich has said that sin is separation. Isn't segregation an existential expression of man's tragic separation, an expression of his awful estrangement, his terrible sinfulness? So I can urge men to obey the 1954 decision of the Supreme Court because it is morally right, and I can urge them to disobey segregation ordinances because they are morally wrong.

Let us turn to a more concrete example of just and unjust laws. An unjust law is a code that a majority inflicts on a minority that is not binding on itself. This is *difference* made legal. On the other hand a just law is a code that a majority compels a minority to follow that it is willing to follow itself. This is *sameness* made legal.

Let me give another explanation. An unjust law is a code inflicted upon a minority which that minority had no part in enacting or creating because they did not have the unhampered right to vote. Who can say the legislature of Alabama which set up the segregation laws was democratically elected? Throughout the state of Alabama all types of conniving methods are used to prevent Negroes from becoming registered voters and there are some counties without a single Negro registered to vote despite the fact that the Negro constitutes a majority of the population. Can any law set up in such a state be considered democratically structured?

These are just a few examples of unjust and just laws. There are some instances when a law is just on its face but unjust in its application. For instance, I was arrested Friday on a charge of parading without a permit. Now there is nothing wrong with an ordinance which requires a permit for a parade, but when the ordinance is used to preserve segregation and to deny citizens the First Amendment privilege of peaceful assembly and peaceful protest, then it becomes unjust.

I hope you can see the distinction I am trying to point out. In no sense do I advocate evading or defying the law as the rabid segregationist would do. This would lead to anarchy. One who breaks an unjust law must do it *openly, lovingly* (not hatefully as the white mothers did in New Orleans when they were seen on television screaming "nigger, nigger, nigger") and with a willingness to accept the penalty. I submit that an individual who breaks a law that conscience tells him is unjust, and willingly accepts the penalty by staying in jail to arouse the conscience of the community over its injustice, is in reality expressing the very highest respect for law.

Of course there is nothing new about this kind of civil disobedience. It was seen sublimely in the refusal of Shadrach, Meshach, and Abednego to obey the laws of Nebuchadnezzar because a higher moral law was involved. It was practiced superbly by the early Christians who were willing to face hungry lions and the excruciating pain of chopping blocks, before submitting to certain unjust laws of the Roman Empire. To a degree academic freedom is a reality today because Socrates practiced civil disobedience.

We can never forget that everything Hitler did in Germany was "legal" and everything the Hungarian freedom fighters did in Hungary was "illegal." It was "illegal" to aid and comfort a Jew in Hitler's Germany. But I am sure that, if I had lived in Germany during that time, I would have aided and comforted my Jewish brothers even though it was illegal. If I lived in a communist country today where certain principles dear to the Christian faith are suppressed, I believe I would openly advocate disobeying these antireligious laws.

I must make two honest confessions to you, my Christian and Jewish brothers. First I must confess that over the last few years I have been gravely disappointed with the white moderate. I have almost reached the regrettable conclusion that the Negroes' great stumbling block in the stride toward freedom is not the White Citizens' "Counciler" or the Ku Klux Klanner, but the white moderate who is more devoted to "order" than to justice; who prefers a negative peace which is the absence of tension to a positive peace which is the presence of justice; who constantly says "I agree with you in the goal you seek, but I can't agree with your methods of direct action"; who paternalistically feels that he can set the time-table for another man's freedom; who lives by the myth of time and who constantly advises the Negro to wait until a "more convenient season." Shallow understanding from people of good will is more frustrating than absolute misunderstanding from people of ill will. Lukewarm acceptance is much more bewildering than outright rejection.

I had hoped that the white moderate would understand that law and order exist for the purpose of establishing justice, and that when they fail to do this they become the dangerously structured dams that block the flow of social progress. I had hoped that the white moderate would understand that the present tension in the South is merely a necessary phase of the transition from an obnoxious negative peace, where the Negro passively accepted his unjust plight, to a substance-filled positive peace, where all men will respect the dignity and worth of human personality. Actually, we who engage in nonviolent direct action are not the creators of tension. We merely bring to the surface the hidden tension that is already alive. We bring it out in the open where it can be seen and dealt with. Like a boil that can never be cured as long as it is covered up but must be opened with all its pus-flowing ugliness to the natural medicines of air and light, injustice must likewise be exposed, with all of the tension its exposing creates, to the light of human conscience and the air of national opinion before it can be cured.

In your statement you asserted that our actions, even though peaceful, must be condemned because they precipitate violence. But can this assertion be logically made? Isn't this like condemning the robbed man because his possession of money precipitated the evil act of robbery? Isn't this like condemning Socrates because his unswerving commitment to truth and his philosophical delvings precipitated the misguided popular mind to make him drink the hemlock? Isn't this like condemning Jesus because His unique God consciousness and never-ceasing devotion to His will precipitated the evil act of crucifixion? We must come to see, as federal courts have consistently affirmed, that it is immoral to urge an individual to withdraw his efforts to gain his basic constitutional rights because the quest precipitates violence. Society must protect the robbed and punish the robber.

I had also hoped that the white moderate would reject the myth of time. I received a letter this morning from a white brother in Texas which said: "All Christians know that the colored people will receive equal rights eventually, but is it possible that you are in too great of a religious hurry? It has taken Christianity almost 2000 years to accomplish what it has. The teachings of Christ take time to come to earth." All that is said here grows out of a tragic misconception of time. It is the strangely irrational notion that there is something in the very flow of time that will inevitably cure all ills. Actually time is neutral. It can be used either destructively or constructively. I am coming to feel that the people of ill will have used time much more effectively than the people of good will. We will have to repent in this generation not merely for the vitriolic words and actions of the bad people, but for the appalling silence of the good people. We must come to see that human progress never rolls in on wheels of inevitability. It comes through the tireless efforts and persistent work of men willing to be coworkers with God, and without this hard work time itself becomes an ally of the forces of social stagnation.

We must use time creatively, and forever realize that the time is always ripe to do right. Now is the time to make real the promise of democracy, and transform our pending national elegy into a creative psalm of brotherhood. Now is the time to lift our national policy from the quicksand of racial injustice to the solid rock of human dignity.

You spoke of our activity in Birmingham as extreme. At first I was rather disappointed that fellow clergymen would see my nonviolent efforts as those of the extremist. I started thinking about the fact that I stand in the middle of two opposing forces in the Negro community. One is a force of complacency made up of Negroes who, as a result of long years of oppression, have been so completely drained of self-respect and a sense of "somebodiness" that they have adjusted to segregation, and of a few Negroes in the middle class who, because of a degree of academic and economic security, and because at points they profit by segregation, have unconsciously become insensitive to the problems of the masses. The other force is one of bitterness and hatred and comes perilously close to advocating violence. It is expressed in the various black nationalist groups that are springing up over the nation, the largest and best known being Elijah Muhammad's Muslim movement. This movement is nourished by the contemporary frustration over the continued existence of racial discrimination. It is made up of people who have lost faith in America, who have absolutely repudiated Christianity, and who have concluded that the white man is an incurable "devil." I have tried to stand between these two forces saying that we need not follow the "do-nothingism" of the complacent or the hatred and despair of the black nationalist. There is the more excellent way of love and nonviolent protest. I'm grateful to God that, through the Negro church, the dimension of nonviolence entered our struggle. If this philosophy had not emerged I am convinced that by now many streets of the South would be flowing with floods of blood. And I am further convinced that if our white brothers dismiss us as "rabble rousers" and "outside agitators"—those of us who are working through the channels of nonviolent direct action—and refuse to support our nonviolent efforts, millions of Negroes, out of frustration and despair, will seek solace and security in black nationalist ideologies, a development that will lead inevitably to a frightening racial nightmare.

Oppressed people cannot remain oppressed forever. The urge for freedom will eventually come. This is what has happened to the American Negro. Something within has reminded him of his birthright of freedom; something without has reminded him that he can gain it. Consciously and unconsciously, he has been swept in by what the Germans call the *Zeitgeist*, and with his black brothers in Africa, and his brown and yellow brothers of Asia, South America, and the Caribbean, he is moving with a sense of cosmic urgency toward the promised land of racial justice. Recognizing this vital urge that has engulfed the Negro community, one should readily understand public demonstrations. The Negro has many pent-up resentments and latent frustrations. He has to get them out. So let him march sometime; let him have his prayer pilgrimages to the city hall; understand why he must have sit-ins and freedom rides. If his repressed emotions do not come out in these nonviolent ways, they will come out in ominous expressions of violence. This is not a threat; it is a fact of history. So I have not said to my people, "Get rid of your discontent." But I have tried to say that this normal and healthy discontent can be channeled through the creative outlet of nonviolent direct action. Now this approach is being dismissed as extremist. I must admit that I was initially disappointed in being so categorized.

But as I continued to think about the matter I gradually gained a bit of satisfaction from being considered an extremist. Was not Jesus an extremist in love? "Love your enemies, bless them that curse you, pray for them that despitefully use you." Was not Amos an extremist for justice—"Let justice roll down like waters and righteousness like a mighty stream." Was not Paul an extremist for the gospel of Jesus Christ—"I bear in my body the marks of the Lord Jesus." Was not Martin Luther King an extremist—"Here I stand; I can do none other so help me God." Was not John Bunyan an extremist—"I will stay in jail to the end of my days before I make a butchery of my conscience." Was not Abraham Lincoln an extremist—"This nation cannot survive half slave and half free." Was not Thomas Jefferson an extremist—"We hold these truths to be self evident that all men are created equal." So the question is not whether we will be extremist but what kind of extremist will we be. Will we be extremists for hate or will we be extremists for love? Will we be extremists for the preservation of injustice—or will we be extremists for the cause of justice? In that dramatic scene on Calvary's hill three men were crucified. We must never forget that all three were crucified for the same crime—the crime of extremism. Two were extremists for immorality, and thus fell below their environment. The other, Jesus Christ, was an extremist for love, truth, and goodness, and thereby rose above His environment. So, after all, maybe the South, the nation, and the world are in dire need of creative extremists.

I had hoped that the white moderate would see this. Maybe I was too optimistic. Maybe I expected too much. I guess I should have realized that few members of a race that has oppressed another race can understand or appreciate the deep groans and passionate yearnings of those that have been oppressed, and still fewer have the vision to see that injustice must be rooted out by strong, persistent, and determined action. I am thankful, however, that some of our white brothers have grasped the meaning of this social revolution and committed themselves to it. They are still all too small in quantity, but they are big in quality. Some like Ralph McGill, Lillian Smith, Harry Golden, and James Dabbs have written about our struggle in eloquent, prophetic, and understanding terms. Others have marched with us down nameless streets of the South. They have languished in filthy, roach-infested jails, suffering the abuse and brutality of angry policemen who see them as "dirty nigger lovers." They, unlike so many of their moderate brothers and sisters, have recognized the urgency of the moment and sensed the need for powerful "action" antidotes to combat the disease of segregation.

Let me rush on to mention my other disappointments. I have been so greatly disappointed with the white Church and its leadership. Of course there are some notable exceptions. I am not unmindful of the fact that each of you has taken some significant stands on this issue. I commend you, Rev. Stallings, for your Christian stand on this past Sunday, in welcoming Negroes to your worship service on a nonsegregated basis. I commend the Catholic leaders of this state for integrating Springhill College several years ago.

But despite these notable exceptions I must honestly reiterate that I have been disappointed with the Church. I do not say that as one of those negative critics who can always find something wrong with the Church. I say it as a minister of the gospel, who loves the Church; who was nurtured in its bosom; who has been sustained by its spiritual blessings and who will remain true to it as long as the cord of life shall lengthen.

I had the strange feeling when I was suddenly catapulted into the leadership of the bus protest in Montgomery several years ago that we would have the support of the white Church. I felt that the white ministers, priests, and rabbis of the South would be some of our strongest allies. Instead, some have been outright opponents, refusing to understand the freedom movement and misrepresenting its leaders; all too many others have been more cautious than courageous and have remained silent behind the anesthetizing security of stained glass windows.

In spite of my shattered dreams of the past, I came to Birmingham with the hope that the white religious leadership of the community would see the justice of our cause and, with deep moral concern, serve as the channel through which our just grievances could get to the power structure. I had hoped that each of you would understand. But again I have been disappointed.

I have heard numerous religious leaders of the South call upon their worshippers to comply with a desegregation decision because it is the law, but I have longed to hear white ministers say follow this decree because integration is morally right and the Negro is your brother. In the midst of blatant injustices inflicted upon the Negro, I have watched white churches stand on the sideline and merely mouth poius irrelevancies and sanctimonious trivialities. In the midst of a mighty struggle to rid our nation of racial and economic injustice, I have heard so many ministers say, "Those are social issues with which the Gospel has no real concern," and I have watched so many churches commit themselves to a completely otherworldly religion which made a strange distinction between body and soul, the sacred and the secular.

So here we are moving toward the exit of the twentieth century with a religious community largely adjusted to the status quo, standing as a tail light behind other community agencies rather than a headlight leading men to higher levels of justice.

I have travelled the length and breadth of Alabama, Mississippi, and all the other Southern states. On sweltering summer days and crisp autumn mornings I have looked at her beautiful churches with their spires pointing heavenward. I have beheld the impressive outlay of her massive religious education buildings.

Over and over again I have found myself asking: "Who worships here? Who is their God? Where were their voices when the lips of Governor Barnett dripped with words of interposition and nullification? Where were they when Governor Wallace gave the clarion call for defiance and hatred? Where were their voices of support when tired, bruised, and weary Negro men and women decided to rise from the dark dungeons of complacency to the bright hills of creative protest?"

Yes, these questions are still in my mind. In deep disappointment, I have wept over the laxity of the Church. But be assured that my tears have been tears of love. There can be no deep disappointment where there is not deep love. Yes, I love the Church; I love her sacred walls. How could I do otherwise? I am in the rather unique position of being the son, the grandson, and the great grandson of preachers. Yes, I see the Church as the body of Christ. But, oh! How we have blemished and scarred that body through social neglect and fear of being nonconformist.

There was a time when the Church was very powerful. It was during that period when the early Christians rejoiced when they were deemed worthy to suffer for what they believed. In those days the Church was not merely a thermometer that recorded the ideas and principles of popular opinion; it was a thermostat that transformed the mores of society. Wherever the early Christians entered a town the power structure got disturbed and immediately sought to convict them for being "disturbers of the peace" and "outside agitators." But they went on with the conviction that they were a "colony of heaven" and had to obey God rather than man. They were small in number but big in commitment. They were too God-intoxicated to be "astronomically intimidated." They brought an end to such ancient evils as infanticide and gladiatorial contest.

Things are different now. The contemporary Church is so often a weak, ineffectual voice with an uncertain sound. It is so often the arch-supporter of the status quo. Far from being disturbed by the presence of the Church, the power structure of the average community is consoled by the Church's silent and often vocal sanction of things as they are.

But the judgment of God is upon the Church as never before. If the Church of today does not recapture the sacrificial spirit of the early Church, it will lose its authentic ring, forfeit the loyalty of millions, and be dismissed as an irrelevant social club with no meaning for the twentieth century. I am meeting young people every day whose disappointment with the Church has risen to outright disgust.

Maybe again I have been too optimistic. Is organized religion too inextricably bound to the status quo to save our nation and the world? Maybe I must turn my faith to the inner spiritual Church, the church within the Church, as the true *ecclesia* and the hope of the world. But again I am thankful to God that some noble souls from the ranks of organized religion have broken loose from the paralyzing chains of conformity and joined us as active partners in the struggle for freedom. They have left their secure congregations and walked the streets of Albany, Georgia, with us. They have gone through the highways of the South on torturous rides for freedom. Yes, they have gone to jail with us. Some have been kicked out of their churches and lost the support of their bishops and fellow ministers. But they have gone with the faith that right defeated is stronger than evil triumphant. These men have been the leaven in the lump of the race. Their witness has been the spiritual salt that has preserved the true meaning of the Gospel in these troubled times. They have carved a tunnel of hope through the dark mountain of disappointment.

I hope the Church as a whole will meet the challenge of this decisive hour. But even if the Church does not come to the aid of justice, I have no despair about the future. I have no fear about the outcome of our struggle in Birmingham, even if our motives are presently misunderstood. We will reach the goal of freedom in Birmingham and all over the nation, because the goal of America is freedom. Abused and scorned though we may be, our destiny is tied up with the destiny of America. Before the pilgrims landed at Plymouth, we were here. Before the pen of Jefferson etched across the pages of history the majestic words of the Declaration of Independence, we were here. For more than two centuries our foreparents labored in this country without wages; they made cotton "king"; and they built the homes of their masters in the midst of brutal injustice and shameful humiliation—and yet out of a bottomless vitality they continued to thrive and develop. If the inexpressible cruelties of slavery could not stop us, the opposition we now face will surely fail. We will win our freedom because the sacred heritage of our nation and the eternal will of God are embodied in our echoing demands.

I must close now. But before closing I am impelled to mention one other point in your statement that troubled me profoundly. You warmly commended the Birmingham police force for keeping "order" and "preventing violence." I don't believe you would have so warmly commended the police force if you had seen its angry violent dogs literally biting six unarmed, nonviolent Negroes. I don't believe you would so quickly commend the policemen if you would observe their ugly and inhuman treatment of Negroes here in the city jail; if you would watch them push and curse old Negro women and young Negro girls; if you would see them slap and kick old Negro men and young Negro boys; if you will observe them, as they did on two occasions, refuse to give us food because we wanted to sing our grace together. I'm sorry that I can't join you in your praise for the police department.

It is true that they have been rather disciplined in their public handling of the demonstrators. In this sense they have been rather publicly "nonviolent." But for what purpose? To preserve the evil system of segregation. Over the last few years I have consistently preached that nonviolence demands that the means we use must be as pure as the ends we seek. So I have tried to make it clear that it is wrong to use immoral means to attain mortal ends. But now I must affirm that it is just as wrong, or even more so, to use moral means to preserve immoral ends. Maybe Mr. Connor and his policemen have been rather publicly nonviolent, as Chief Prichett was in Albany, Georgia, but they have used the moral means of nonviolence to maintain the immoral end of flagrant racial injustice. T.S. Eliot has said that there is no greater treason than to do the right deed for the wrong reason.

I wish you had commended the Negro sit-inners and demonstrators of Birmingham for their sublime courage, their willingness to suffer, and their amazing discipline in the midst of the most inhuman provocation. One day the South will recognize its real heroes. They will be the James Merediths, courageously and with a majestic sense of purpose, facing jeering and hostile mobs and the agonizing loneliness that characterizes the life of the pioneer. They will be old, oppressed, battered Negro women, symbolized in a seventy-two year old woman of Montgomery, Alabama, who rose up with a sense of dignity and with her people decided not to ride the segregated buses, and responded to one who inquired about her tiredness with ungrammatical profundity: "My feets is tired, but my soul is rested." They will be young high school and college students, young ministers of the gospel and a host of the elders, courageously and nonviolently sitting in at lunch counters and willingly going to jail for conscience sake. One day the South will know that when these disinherited children of God sat down at lunch counters they were in reality standing up for the best in the American dream and the most sacred values in our Judeo-Christian heritage, and thus carrying our whole nation back to great wells of democracy which were dug deep by the founding fathers in the formulation of the Constitution and the Declaration of Independence.

Never before have I written a letter this long (or should I say a book?). I'm afraid that it is much too long to take your precious time. I can assure you that it would have been much shorter if I had been writing from a comfortable desk, but what else is there to do when you are alone for days in the dull monotony of a narrow jail cell other than write long letters, think strange thoughts, and pray long prayers?

If I have said anything in this letter that is an overstatement of the truth and is indicative of an unreasonable impatience, I beg you to forgive me. If I have said anything in this letter that is an understatement of the truth and is indicative of my having a patience that makes me patient with anything less than brotherhood, I beg God to forgive me.

I hope this letter finds you strong in the faith. I also hope that circumstances will soon make it possible for me to meet each of you, not as an integrationist or a civil rights leader, but as a fellow clergyman and a Christian brother. Let us all hope that the dark clouds of racial prejudice will soon pass away and the deep fog of misunderstanding will be lifted from our fear-drenched communities and in some not too distant tomorrow the radiant stars of love and brotherhood will shine over our great nation with all of their scintillating beauty.

Yours for the cause of
Peace and Brotherhood

MARTIN LUTHER KING, JR.

FOCUS: READING REVIEW

1. What are the criticisms to which King responds? (Some are explicit and some implied.)
2. King defines the distinction between "just" and "unjust" laws. What are the distinguishing features of each? What kind of evidence does he offer in support of civil disobedience to unjust laws?
3. What are King's criticisms of the church and organized religion in the South? What evidence does he offer in support of his criticisms?

FOCUS: AUTHOR'S STRATEGIES

1. One of the ways King responds to criticism is to counter with his own critical assertions. What are some of these criticisms? What kind of evidence does he offer for his assertions?
2. What are the stages in a nonviolent action campaign? How does King use this process analysis as an organizational principle of his argument?
3. Part of the power of King's rhetoric rests in his word choice. Sometimes he uses language to advance a rational argument, sometimes to affect his audience's emotions. Which use of language predominates? Cite examples and explain how they affect the audience.

FOCUS: DISCUSSION AND WRITING

1. The issue of just and unjust laws provides a ground for civil disobedience. Identify a law in our society that is unjust, and, using King's definition, explain why it is unjust. What course of action would you advocate to change this law? Why?
2. Write a letter to protest an injustice apparent to you.

TOPICS: Further Research, Synthesis, and Writing in the Social Sciences

1. Freud, Skinner, and Maslow represent central areas of psychological studies. Based on the essays included here, write a paper for a lay audience defining psychology and explaining the central differences between psychoanalysis, humanistic psychology, and behavioral psychology.

2. Design an experiment similar to Philip Goldberg's or Matina Horner's. Write an essay in which you state your hypothesis, review the literature (use Horner or Goldberg as a source), describe your experiment, report your findings, and explain your conclusions. You might wish to research more recent studies than Horner's and Goldberg's.

3. Gerbner et al. examine the findings of important studies on the relation between television viewing and children's school performance. Locate the articles they critique as well as at least two more studies on television and school performance. Using the dialogue between Gerbner et al. and their predecessors and your other sources as evidence, write an essay directed to parents or educators on responsible television viewing for children.

4. Pearce's essay relies on statistical evidence. Using sources like the recent census, *Facts on File,* and newspaper files, gather statistical evidence on a topic of social concern—divorce, changing birthrate in various segments of the population, women in various levels of the work force, reverse discrimination against men, immigration, or tax payment rates, for example. Write a paper presenting and interpreting the evidence to support a thesis statement about the social issue.

5. The essays by Coles and King suggest that racial discrimination occurred in the South at a particular point in history. How real is racial discrimination today? Write an essay on whether or not racial prejudice and discrimination exist today. Rely on research as well as personal experiences for evidence.

6. The essays in the social science section raise several issues for further reading and research: the causes of human behavior, the effects of prejudice, the nature of the American economy, and the effects of media. Select one of these categories, narrow your topic within manageable limits, and locate at least three different views on your topic. Write an essay in which you summarize, compare and contrast, and critique these views.

↘ HISTORY ↙

Chapter 7

The Governing Assumptions

History records human experience—political, social, scientific, cultural, and artistic. Some historians concern themselves with the past's legacy and others with recording and interpreting the present. Central to understanding historical studies is an appreciation of the relationship between historians and facts. Some historians view facts as scientific evidence and regard themselves as social scientists; others see their task so bound up with literature, art, and philosophy that they view themselves as humanists. This chapter presents the discussion among historians on the relations between fact and interpretation that defines the historian's role.

In "History as a Literary Art" Morison admits that while the historian needs to be objective and accurate, he must give form to the amorphous mass of facts. Carr's essay "The Historian and the Facts" suggests two extreme views of history. In one, the historian, as discoverer of facts, pieces together a puzzle which is complete when all the facts are present; in the other, the historian, as selector of facts, paints a picture. By defining historical fact and describing the process by which a fact becomes a historical fact, Carr illustrates that neither extreme accurately depicts the historian's task. In "The Premises of Inquiry" Muller finds our interest in history to be "more poetic than practical or scientific" because the past is the source of our identity. Despite this, the historian must be concerned with the literal truth and rely on the relative objectivity of the scientific community for evidence.

History as a Literary Art

Samuel Eliot Morison

Samuel Eliot Morison (1887–1976) wrote twenty-nine United States histo-
ries, and earned the tribute, "Too few statesmen have spoken like Winston
Churchill and John F. Kennedy; too few historians have written like
Samuel Eliot Morison." Morison received his Ph.D. from Harvard Univer-
sity, where he later taught for forty years. During his academic career, he
served as visiting professor at the University of California, Berkeley, and
Oxford University. World War II took him away from his academic duties
to become the U.S. Navy's war historian, and he later rose to the rank of
Rear Admiral in the Naval Reserve. Morison's writings include The Mari-
time History of Massachusetts, *the textbook* Growth of the American Republic, *which he coauthored with Henry Steele Commager,* The European
Discovery of America, *and* The Life of Christopher Columbus. *"History as*
a Literary Art," which appears in the essay collection By Land and Sea,
calls for well-written history and offers some concrete suggestions on how
to write well.

A whole generation of historians has passed without producing any really great works
on American history—books with fire in the eye to make a young man want to fight
for his country in war or live to make it a better country in peace. The American
public has become so sated by dull history textbooks in school and college that it
won't read history. [To remedy this, young people writing in history should attain
style. This can be accomplished by a writer getting what he has to say clearly in his
mind and dashing it off. Then he can revise for the three prime qualities of historical
composition—clarity, vigor, and objectivity. Beyond this the writer of history can
improve his writing by broadening his literary experience.]

Exploring American history has been a very absorbing and exciting business now
for three quarters of a century. Thousands of graduate students have produced
thousands of monographs on every aspect of the history of the Americas. But the
American reading public for the most part is blissfully ignorant of this vast output.
When John Citizen feels the urge to read history, he goes to the novels of Kenneth
Roberts or Margaret Mitchell, not to the histories of Professor this or Doctor that.
Why?

Because American historians, in their eagerness to present facts and their laudable concern to tell the truth, have neglected the literary aspects of their craft.
They have forgotten that there is an art of writing history.

Even the earliest colonial historians, like William Bradford and Robert
Beverley, knew that; they put conscious art into their narratives. And the historians of our classical period, Prescott and Motley, Irving and Bancroft, Parkman

and Fiske, were great literary craftsmen. Their many-volumed works sold in sufficient quantities to give them handsome returns; even today they are widely read.
But the first generation of seminar-trained historians, educated in Germany or by
teachers trained there, imagined that history would tell itself, provided one was
honest, thorough, and painstaking. Some of them went so far as to regard history
as pure science and to assert that writers thereof had no more business trying to be
"literary" than did writers of statistical reports or performers of scientific experiments. Professors warned their pupils (quite unnecessarily) against "fine writing,"
and endeavored to protect their innocence from the seductive charm of Washington Irving or the masculine glamour of Macaulay. And in this flight of history
from literature the public was left behind. American history became a bore to the
reader and a drug on the market; even historians with something to say and the
talent for saying it (Henry Adams, for instance) could not sell their books. The
most popular American histories of the period 1890–1905 were those of John
Fiske, a philosopher who had no historical training, but wrote with life and movement.

Theodore Roosevelt in his presidential address before the American Historical
Association in 1912 made a ringing plea to the young historian to do better: "He
must ever remember that while the worst offense of which he can be guilty is to
write vividly and inaccurately, yet that unless he writes vividly he cannot write
truthfully; for no amount of dull, painstaking detail will sum up the whole truth
unless the genius is there to paint the truth."

And although American historians cannot hope, as Theodore Roosevelt did, to
"watch the nearing chariots of the champions," or to look forward to the day when
"for us the war-horns of King Olaf shall wail across the flood, and the harps sound
high at festivals in forgotten halls," we may indeed "show how the land which the
pioneers won slowly and with incredible hardship was filled in two generations by
the overflow from the countries of western and central Europe." We may describe
the race, class, and religious conflicts that immigration has engendered, and trace
the rise of the labor movement with a literary art that compels people to read
about it. You do not need chariots and horsemen, harps and war-horns, to make
history interesting.

Theodore Roosevelt's trumpet call fell largely on deaf ears, at least in the academic historical profession. A whole generation has passed without producing any
really great works on American history. Plenty of good books, valuable books, and
new interpretations and explorations of the past; but none with fire in the eye,
none to make a young man want to fight for his country in war or live to make it a
better country in peace. There has been a sort of chain reaction of dullness.
Professors who have risen to positions of eminence by writing dull, solid, valuable
monographs that nobody reads outside the profession, teach graduate students to
write dull, solid, valuable monographs like theirs; the road to academic security is
that of writing dull, solid, valuable monographs. And so the young men who have a
gift for good writing either leave the historical field for something more exciting,
or write more dull, solid, valuable monographs. The few professional historians

who have had a popular following or appeal during the last thirty years are either men like Allan Nevins who were trained in some juicier profession like journalism, or men and women like the Beards who had the sense to break loose young from academic trammels.

In the meantime, the American public has become so sated by dull history textbooks in school and college that it won't read history unless it is disguised as something else under a title such as *The Flowering of Florida, The Epic of the East,* or *The Growth of the American Republic.* Or, more often, they get what history they want from historical novels.

Now, I submit, this is a very bad situation. The tremendous plowing up of the past by well-trained scholars is all to the good, so far as it goes. Scholars know more about America's past than ever; they are opening new furrows and finding new artifacts, from aboriginal arrowheads to early twentieth-century corset stays. But they are heaping up the pay dirt for others. Journalists, novelists, and free-lance writers are the ones who extract the gold; and they deserve every ounce they get because they are the ones who know how to write histories that people care to read. What I want to see is a few more Ph.D.'s in history winning book-of-the-month adoptions and reaping the harvest of dividends. They can do it, too, if they will only use the same industry in presenting history as they do in compiling it.

Mind you, I intend no disparagement of historians who choose to devote their entire energies to teaching. Great teachers do far more good to the cause of history than mediocre writers. Such men, for instance, as the late H. Morse Stephens, who stopped writing (which he never liked) as soon as he obtained a chair in this country, and the late Edwin F. Gay, who never began writing, inspired thousands of young men and initiated scores of valuable books. Thank God for these gifted teachers, I say; universities should seek out, encourage, and promote them far more than they do. My remarks are addressed to young people who have the urge to write history, and wish to write it effectively.

There are no special rules for writing history; any good manual of rhetoric or teacher of composition will supply the rules for writing English. But what terrible stuff passes for English in Ph.D. dissertations, monographs, and articles in historical reviews! Long, involved sentences that one has to read two or three times in order to grasp their meaning; poverty in vocabulary, ineptness of expression, weakness in paragraph structure, frequent misuse of words, and, of late, the introduction of pseudoscientific and psychological jargon. There is no fundamental cure for this except better teaching of English in our schools and colleges, and by every teacher, whatever his other subject may be. If historical writing is infinitely better in France than in America, and far better in the British Isles and Canada than in the United States, it is because every French and British teacher of history drills his pupils in their mother tongue, requiring a constant stream of essays and reports, and criticizing written work, not only as history, but as literature. The American university teacher who gives honor grades to students who have not yet learned to write English, for industrious compilations of facts or feats of memory, is wanting in professional pride or competence.

Of course, what we should all like to attain in writing history is style. "The sense for style," says Whitehead in his *Aims of Education*, "is an aesthetic sense, based on admiration for the direct attainment of a foreseen end, simply and without waste. Style in art, style in literature, style in science, style in logic, style in practical execution, have fundamentally the same aesthetic qualities, namely, attainment and restraint. Style, in its finest sense, is the last acquirement of the educated mind; it is also the most useful. It pervades the whole being . . . Style is the ultimate morality of mind."

Unfortunately, there is no royal road to style. It cannot be attained by mere industry; it never be achieved through imitation, although it may be promoted by example. Reading the greatest literary artists among historians will help; but do not forget that what was acceptable style in 1850 might seem turgid today. We can still read Macaulay with admiration and pleasure; we can still learn paragraph structure and other things from Macaulay; but anyone who tried to imitate Macaulay today would be a pompous ass.

Just as Voltaire's ideal curé advises his flock not to worry about going to heaven, but to do right and probably by God's grace they will get there, so the young writer of history had better concentrate on day-by-day improvement in craftsmanship. Then, perhaps, he may find someday that his prose appeals to a large popular audience; that, in other words, he has achieved style through simple, honest, straightforward writing.

A few hints as to the craft may be useful to budding historians. First and foremost, *get writing!* Young scholars generally wish to secure the last fact before writing anything, like General McClellan refusing to advance (as people said) until the last mule was shod. It is a terrible strain, isn't it, to sit down at a desk, with your notes all neatly docketed, and begin to write? You pretend to your wife that you mustn't be interrupted; but, actually, you welcome a ring of the telephone, a knock at the door, or a bellow from the baby as an excuse to break off. Finally, after smoking sundry cigarettes and pacing about the house two or three times, you commit a lame paragraph or two to paper. By the time you get to the third, one bit of information you want is lacking. What a relief! Now you must go back to the library or the archives to do some more digging. That's where you are happy! And what you turn up there leads to more questions and prolongs the delicious process of research. Half the pleas I have heard from graduate students for more time or another grant-in-aid are mere excuses to postpone the painful drudgery of writing.

There is the "indispensablest beauty in knowing how to get done," said Carlyle. In every research there comes a point, which you should recognize like a call of conscience, when you must get down to writing. And when you once are writing, go on writing as long as you can; there will be plenty of time later to shove in the footnotes or return to the library for extra information. Above all, *start* writing. Nothing is more pathetic than the "gonna" historian, who from graduate school on is always "gonna" write a magnum opus but never completes his research on the subject, and dies without anything to show for a lifetime's work.

Dictation is usually fatal to good historical writing. Write out your first draft in longhand or, if you compose easily on the typewriter, type it out yourself, revise with pencil or pen, and have it retyped clean. Don't stop to consult your notes for every clause or sentence; it is better to get what you have to say clearly in your mind and dash it off; then, after you have it down, return to your notes and compose your next few pages or paragraphs. After a little experience you may well find that you think best with your fingers on the typewriter keys or your fountain pen poised over the paper. For me, the mere writing of a few words seems to point up vague thoughts and make jumbled facts array themselves in neat order. Whichever method you choose, composing before you write or as you write, do not return to your raw material or verify facts and quotations or insert footnotes until you have written a substantial amount, an amount that will increase with practice. It is significant that two of our greatest American historians, Prescott and Parkman, were nearly blind during a good part of their active careers. They had to have the sources read to them and turn the matter over and over in their minds before they could give anything out; and when they gave, *they gave!*

Now, the purpose of this quick, warm synthesis between research, thinking, and writing is to attain the three prime qualities of historical composition—clarity, vigor, and objectivity. You must think about your facts, analyze your material, and decide exactly what you mean before you can write it so that the average reader will understand. Do not fall into the fallacy of supporting that "facts speak for themselves." Most of the facts that you excavate, like other relics of past human activity, are dumb things; it is for you to make them speak by proper selection, arrangement, and emphasis. Dump your entire collection of facts on paper, and the result will be unreadable if not incomprehensible.

So, too, with vigor. If your whole paragraph or chapter is but a hypothesis, say so at the beginning, but do not bore and confuse the reader with numerous "but"s, "except"s, "perhaps"s, and "possibly"s. Use direct rather than indirect statements, the active rather than the passive voice, and make every sentence and paragraph an organic whole. Above all, if you are writing historical narrative make it move. Do not take time out in the middle of a political or military campaign to introduce special developments or literary trends, as McMaster did to the confusion of his readers. Place those admittedly important matters in a chapter or chapters by themselves so that you do not lose your reader's attention by constant interruption.

That brings us to the third essential quality—objectivity. Keep the reader constantly in mind. You are not writing history for yourself or for the professors who are supposed to know more about it than you do. Assume that you are writing for intelligent people who know nothing about your particular subject but whom you wish to interest and attract. I once asked the late Senator Beveridge why his *Life of John Marshall,* despite its great length and scholarly apparatus, was so popular. He replied: "The trouble with you professors of history is that you write for each other. I write for people almost completely ignorant of American history, as I was when I began my research."

A few more details. Even if the work you are writing does not call for footnotes, keep them in your copy until the last draft, for they will enable you to check up on your facts, statements, and quotations. And since accuracy is the prime virtue of the historian, this checking must be done, either by the author or by someone else. You will be surprised by the mistakes that creep in between a first rough draft and a final typed copy. And the better you write, the more your critics will enjoy finding misquotations and inaccuracies.

The matter of handling quotations seems to be a difficult one for young historians. There is nothing that adds so much to the charm and effectiveness of a history as good quotations from the sources, especially if the period is somewhat remote. But there is nothing so disgusting to the reader as long, tedious, broken quotations in small print, especially those in which, to make sense, the author has to interpolate words in brackets. Young writers are prone to use quotations in places where their own words would be better, and to incorporate in the text source excerpts that belong in footnotes or appendices. Avoid ending chapters with quotations, and never close your book with one.

Above all, do not be afraid to revise and rewrite. Reading aloud is a good test—historians' wives have to stand a lot of that! A candid friend who is not an historian, and so represents the audience you are trying to reach, is perhaps the best "dog" to try it on. Even if he has little critical sense, it is encouraging to have him stay awake. My good friend Lucien Price years ago listened with a pained expression to a bit of my early work. "Now, just what do you mean by that?" he asked after a long, involved, pedantic, and quote-larded paragraph. I told him in words of one syllable, or perhaps two. "Fine!" said he. "I understand that. Now write down what you said; throw the other away!"

Undoubtedly the writer of history can enrich his mind and broaden his literary experience as well as better his craftsmanship by his choice of leisure reading. If he is so fortunate as to have had a classical education, no time will be better spent in making him an effective historian than in reading Latin and Greek authors. Both these ancient languages are such superb instruments of thought that a knowledge of them cures slipshod English and helps one to attain a clear, muscular style. All our greatest historical stylists—notably Prescott, Parkman, Fiske, and Frederick J. Turner—had a classical education and read the ancient historians in the original before they approached American history.

If you have little Latin and less Greek and feel unable to spare the time and effort to add them to your stock of tools, read the ancient classics in the best literary translations, such as North's Plutarch, Rawlinson's Herodotus, Gilbert Murray's Euripides, and, above all, Jowett's or Livingstone's Thucydides. Through them you will gain the content and spirit of the ancient classics, which will break down your provincialism, refresh your spirit, and give you a better philosophical insight into the ways of mankind than most of such works as the new science of psychology has brought forth. Moreover, you will be acquiring the same background as many of the great Americans of past generations, thus aiding your understanding of them.

The reading of English classics will tend in the same direction, and will also be a painless and unconscious means of improving your literary style. Almost every English or American writer of distinction is indebted to Shakespeare and the English Bible. The Authorized Version is not only the great source book of spiritual experience of English-speaking peoples; it is a treasury of plain, pungent words and muscular phrases, beautiful in themselves and with long associations, which we are apt to replace by smooth words lacking in punch, or by hackneyed or involved phrases. Here are a few examples chosen in five minutes from my desk Bible: I Samuel 1:28: "I have lent him to the Lord." What an apt phrase for anyone bringing up his son for the Church! Why say "loaned" instead of "lent"? Isaiah 22:5: "For it is a day of trouble, and of treading down, and of perplexity." In brief, just what we are going through today. But most modern historians would not feel that they were giving the reader his money's worth unless they wrote: "It is an era of agitation, of a progressive decline in the standard of living, and of uncertainty as to the correct policy." Romans 11:25: "Wise in your own conceits." This epigram has often been used, but a modern writer would be tempted to express the thought in some such cumbrous manner as "Expert within the limits of your own fallacious theories."

Of course much of the Biblical phraseology is obsolete, and there are other literary quarries for historians. You can find many appropriate words, phrases, similes, and epigrams in American authors such as Mark Twain, Emerson, and Thoreau. I have heard an English economist push home a point to a learned audience with a quotation from *Alice in Wonderland;* American historians might make more use of *Huckleberry Finn.*

The historian can learn much from the novelist. Most writers of fiction are superior to all but the best historians in characterization and description. If you have difficulty in making people and events seem real, see if you cannot learn the technique from American novelists such as Sherwood Anderson, Joseph Hergesheimer, and Margaret Mitchell. For me, the greatest master of all is Henry James. He used a relatively simple and limited vocabulary; but what miracles he wrought with it! What precise and perfect use he makes of words to convey the essence of a human situation to the reader! If you are not yet acquainted with Henry James, try the selection of his shorter novels and stories edited by Clifton Fadiman, and then read some of the longer novels, like *Roderick Hudson* and *The American.* And, incidentally, you will learn more about the top layers of American and European society in the second half of the nineteenth century than you can ever glean from the works of social historians.

What is the place of imagination in history? An historian or biographer is under restrictions unknown to a novelist. He has no right to override facts by his own imagination. If he is writing on a remote or obscure subject about which few facts are available, his imagination may legitimately weave them into a pattern. But to be honest he must make clear what is fact and what is hypothesis. The quality of imagination, if properly restrained by the conditions of historical discipline, is of great assistance in enabling one to discover problems to be solved, to grasp the significance of facts, to form hypotheses, to discern causes in their first beginnings, and, above all, to relate the past creatively to the present. There are many opportunities in historical narrative for bold, imaginative expressions. "A complete statement in the imaginative form of an important truth arrests attention," wrote Emerson, "and is repeated and remembered." Imagination used in this way invests an otherwise pedestrian narrative with vivid and exciting qualities.

Finally, the historian should have frequent recourse to the book of life. The richer his personal experience, the wider his human contacts, the more likely he is to effect a living contact with his audience. In writing, similes drawn from the current experience of this mechanical age, rather than those rifled from the literary baggage of past eras, are the ones that will go home to his reader. Service on a jury or a local committee may be a revelation as to the political thoughts and habits of mankind. A month's labor in a modern factory would help any young academician to clarify his ideas of labor and capital. A camping trip in the woods will tell him things about Western pioneering that he can never learn in books. The great historians, with few exceptions, are those who have not merely studied, but lived; and whose studies have ranged over a much wider field than the period or subject of which they write.

The veterans of World War II who, for the most part, have completed their studies in college or graduate school should not regard the years of their war service as wasted. Rather should they realize that the war gave them a rich experience of life, which is the best equipment for an historian. They have "been around"; they have seen mankind at his best and his worst; they have shared the joy and passion of a mighty effort; and they can read man's doings in the past with far greater understanding than if they had spent these years in sheltered academic groves.

To these young men especially, and to all young men I say (as the poet Chapman said to the young Elizabethan): "Be free, all worthy spirits, and stretch yourselves!" Bring all your knowledge of life to bear on everything that you write. Never let yourself bog down in pedantry and detail. Bring history, the most humane and noble form of letters, back to the proud position she once held; knowing that your words, if they are read and remembered, will enter into the stream of life, and perhaps move men to thought and action centuries hence, as do those of Thucydides after more than two thousand years.

FOCUS: READING REVIEW

1. In his lament over losing the American public as history readers, Morison suggests the value of reading history. What is it?
2. What are the weaknesses Morison finds in most historical writing?
3. What constitutes style?
4. What process for writing does Morison advocate?
5. What are the prime qualities of historical writing?

6. What will a history writer gain from reading the classics, the Bible, Shakespeare, and American authors?

FOCUS: AUTHOR'S STRATEGIES

1. Morison clearly defines his purpose and audience. What is his purpose? Who is his audience? How does he shape his writing to accomplish this purpose?
2. What different development strategies does the author use? How do they contribute to the "liveliness" of his writing?

FOCUS: DISCUSSION AND WRITING

1. When Morison states "Most of the facts that you excavate, like other relics of past human activity, are dumb things; it is for you to make them speak by proper selection, arrangement, and emphasis," what does he suggest about historical writing's objectivity and accuracy?
2. Select an example of historical writing and explain how it complies or fails to comply with Morison's criteria of "clarity, vigor, and objectivity."
3. Select a piece of dull historic writing and rewrite it using Morison's suggestions to meet the criteria of "clarity, vigor, and objectivity."

The Historian and the Facts
Edward Hallett Carr

Edward Hallett Carr (1892–1982), a distinguished British historian and fellow of Trinity College, Cambridge, earned acclaim for his fourteen-volume The History of Soviet Russia. *At Cambridge in 1961, Carr presented "The Historian and the Facts" as one in a series of lectures entitled "What Is History," later published as a book. This selection contrasts the nineteenth-century historian's view that history is constantly being reshaped and rewritten. Standing between these two extremes, Carr distinguishes the historical from the ordinary fact and demonstrates how historians select and emphasize historical facts to shape history.*

What is history? [Nineteenth-century historians on the whole agreed] that the task of the historian was "simply to show how it really was"—[to get the facts]. Many later historians "take refuge in skepticism, or at least in the doctrine that, since all historical judgments involve persons and points of view, one is as good as another and there is no 'objective' historical truth." [To Carr, a historian's accuracy is a necessary condition of his work, but not his essential function. Establishing the basic facts rests not on any quality in the facts themselves, but on a decision of the historian. Tracing the fate of historical documents from the German Weimar Republic, ultimately destroyed by Hitler, illustrates this.]

What is history? Lest anyone think the question meaningless or superfluous, I will take as my text two passages relating respectively to the first and second incarnations of *The Cambridge Modern History*. Here is Acton in his report of October 1896 to the Syndics of the Cambridge University Press on the work which he had undertaken to edit:

> It is a unique opportunity of recording, in the way most useful to the greatest number, the fullness of the knowledge which the nineteenth century is about to bequeath. . . . By the judicious division of labour we should be able to do it, and to bring home to every man the last document, and the ripest conclusions of international research.
>
> Ultimate history we cannot have in this generation; but we can dispose of conventional history, and show the point we have reached on the road from one to the other, now that all information is within reach, and every problem has become capable of solution.[1]

And almost exactly sixty years later Professor Sir George Clark, in his general introduction to the second *Cambridge Modern History*, commented on this belief of Acton and his collaborators that it would one day be possible to produce "ultimate history," and went on:

> Historians of a later generation do not look forward to any such prospect. They expect their work to be superseded again and again. They consider that knowledge of the past has come down through one or more human minds, has been "processed" by them, and therefore cannot consist of elemental and impersonal atoms which nothing can alter. . . . The exploration seems to be endless, and some impatient scholars take refuge in scepticism, or at least in the doctrine that, since all historical judgments involve persons and points of view, one is as good as another and there is no "objective" historical truth.[2]

Where the pundits contradict each other so flagrantly the field is open to enquiry. I hope that I am sufficiently up-to-date to recognize that anything written in the 1890's must be nonsense. But I am not yet advanced enough to be committed to the view that anything written in the 1950's necessarily makes sense. Indeed, it may already have occurred to you that this enquiry is liable to stray into something even broader than the nature of history. The clash between Acton and Sir George Clark is a reflection of the change in our total outlook on society over the interval between these two pronouncements. Acton speaks out of the positive belief, the clear-eyed self-confidence of the later Victorian age; Sir George Clark echoes the bewilderment and distracted scepticism of the beat generation. When we attempt to answer the question, What is history?, our answer, consciously or unconsciously, reflects our own position in time, and forms part of our answer to the broader question, what view we take of the society in which we live. I have no fear that my subject may, on closer inspection, seem trivial. I am afraid only that I may seem presumptuous to have broached a question so vast and so important.

The nineteenth century was a great age for facts. "What I want," said Mr. Gradgrind in *Hard Times*, "is Facts. . . . Facts alone are wanted in life." Nineteenth-century historians on the whole agreed with him. When Ranke in the 1830's, in legitimate protest against moralizing history, remarked that the task of the historian was "simply to show how it really was (*wie es eigentlich gewesen*)" this now very profound aphorism had an astonishing success. Three generations of German, British, and even French historians marched into battle intoning the magic words, *"Wie es eigentlich gewesen"* like an incantation—designed, like most incantations, to save them from the tiresome obligation to think for themselves. The Positivists,[3] anxious to stake out their claim for history as a science, contributed the weight of their influence to this cult of facts. First ascertain the facts, said the positivists, then draw your conclusions from them. In great Britain, this view of history fitted in perfectly with the empiricist[4] tradition which was the dominant strain in British philosophy from Locke to Bertrand Russell. The empirical theory of knowledge presupposes a complete separation between subject and object. Facts, like sense-impressions, impinge on the observer from outside, and are independent of his consciousness. The process of reception is passive: having received the data, he then acts on them. *The Shorter Oxford English Dictionary*, a useful but tendentious work of the empirical school, clearly marks the separation of the two processes by defining a fact as "a datum of experience as distinct from conclusions." This is what may be called the common-sense view of history. History consists of a corpus of ascertained facts. The facts are available to the historian in documents, inscriptions, and so on, like fish on the fishmonger's slab. The historian collects them, takes them home, and cooks and serves them in whatever style appeals to him. Acton, whose culinary tastes were austere, wanted them served plain. In his letter of instructions to contributors to the first *Cambridge Modern History* he announced the requirement "that our Waterloo must be one that satisfies French and English, German and Dutch alike; that nobody can tell, without examining the list of authors where the Bishop of Oxford laid down the pen, and whether Fairbairn or Gasquet, Liebermann or Harrison took it up."[5] Even Sir George Clark, critical as he was of Acton's attitude, himself contrasted the "hard core of facts" in history with the "surrounding pulp of disputable interpretation"[6]—forgetting perhaps that the pulpy part of the fruit is more rewarding than the hard core. First get your facts straight, then plunge at your peril into the shifting sands of interpretation—that is the ultimate wisdom of the empirical, common-sense school of history. It recalls the favourite dictum of the great liberal journalist C.P. Scott: "Facts are sacred, opinion is free."

Now this clearly will not do. I shall not embark on a philosophical discussion of the nature of our knowledge of the past. Let us assume for present purposes that the fact that Caesar crossed the Rubicon and the fact that there is a table in the middle of the room are facts of the same or of a comparable order, that both these facts enter our consciousness in the same or in a comparable manner, and that both have the same objective character in relation to the person who knows them. But, even on this bold and not very plausible assumption, our argument at once runs into the difficulty that not all facts about the past are historical facts, or are treated as such by the historian. What is the criterion which distinguishes the facts of history from other facts about the past?

What is a historical fact? This is a crucial question into which we must look a little more closely. According to the common-sense view, there are certain basic facts which are the same for all historians and which form, so to speak, the backbone of history—the fact, for example, that the Battle of Hastings was fought in 1066. But this view calls for two observations. In the first place, it is not with facts like these that the historian is primarily concerned. It is no doubt important to know that the great battle was fought in 1066 and not in 1065 or 1067, and that it was fought at Hastings and not at Eastbourne or Brighton. The historian must not get these things wrong. But when points of this kind are raised, I am reminded of Housman's remark that "accuracy is a duty, not a virtue."[7] To praise a historian for his accuracy is like praising an architect for using well-seasoned timber or properly mixed concrete in his building. It is a necessary condition of his work, but not his essential function. It is precisely for matters of this kind that the historian is entitled to rely on what have been called the "auxiliary sciences" of history—archaeology, eipgraphy, numismatics, chronology, and so forth. The historian is not required to have the special skills which enable the expert to determine the origin and period of a fragment of pottery or marble, to decipher an obscure inscription, or to make the elaborate astronomical calculations necessary to establish a precise date. These so-called basic facts which are the same for all historians commonly belong to the category of the raw materials of the historian rather than of history itself. The second observation is that the necessity to establish these basic facts rests not on any quality in the facts themselves, but on an *a priori* decision of the historian. In spite of C.P. Scott's motto, every journalist knows today that the most effective way to influence opinion is by the selection and arrangement of the appropriate facts. It used to be said that facts speak for themselves. This is, of course, untrue. The facts speak only when the historian calls on them: it is he who decides to which facts to give the floor, and in what order of context. It was, I think, one of Pirandello's characters who said that a fact is like a sack—it won't stand up till you've put something in it. The only reason why we are interested to know that the battle was fought at Hastings in 1066 is that historians regard it as a major historical event. It is the historian who has decided for his own reasons that Caesar's crossing of that petty stream, the Rubicon, is a fact of history, whereas the crossing of the Rubicon by millions of other people before or since interests nobody at all. The fact that you arrived in this building half an hour ago on foot, or on a bicycle, or in a car, is just as much a fact about the past as the fact that Caesar crossed the Rubicon. But it will probably be ignored by historians. Professor Talcott Parsons once called science "a selective system of cognitive orientations to reality."[8] It might perhaps have been put more simply. But history is, among other things, that. The historian is necessarily selective. The belief in a hard core of historical facts existing objectively and independently of the interpretation of the historian is a preposterous fallacy, but one which is very hard to eradicate.

Let us take a look at the process by which a mere fact about the past is transformed into a fact of history. At Stalybridge Wakes in 1850, a vendor of gingerbread, as the result of some petty dispute, was deliberately kicked to death by an angry mob. Is this a fact of history? A year ago I should unhesitatingly have said "no." It was recorded by an eyewitness in some little-known memoirs;[9] but I had never seen it judged worthy of mention by any historian. A year ago Dr. Kitson Clark cited it in his Ford lectures in Oxford.[10] Does this make it into a historical fact? Not, I think, yet. Its present status, I suggest, is that it has been proposed for membership of the select club of historical facts. It now awaits a seconder and sponsors. It may be that in the course of the next few years we shall see this fact appearing first in footnotes, then in the text, of articles and books about nineteenth-century England, and that in twenty or thirty years' time it may be a well established historical fact. Alternatively, nobody may take it up, in which case it will relapse into the limbo of unhistorical facts about the past from which Dr. Kitson Clark has gallantly attempted to rescue it. What will decide which of these two things will happen? It will depend, I think, on whether the thesis or interpretation in support of which Dr. Kitson Clark cited this incident is accepted by other historians as valid and significant. Its status as a historical fact will turn on a question of interpretation. This element of interpretation enters into every fact of history.

May I be allowed a personal reminiscence? When I studied ancient history in this university many years ago, I had as a special subject "Greece in the period of the Persian Wars." I collected fifteen or twenty volumes on my shelves and took it for granted that there, recorded in these volumes, I had all the facts relating to my subject. Let us assume—it was very nearly true—that those volumes contained all the facts about it that were then known, or could be known. It never occurred to me to enquire by what accident or process of attrition that minute selection of facts, out of all the myriad facts that must have once been known to somebody, had survived to become *the* facts of history. I suspect that even today one of the fascinations of ancient and mediaeval history is that it gives us the illusion of having all the facts at our disposal within a manageable compass: the nagging distinction between the facts of history and other facts about the past vanishes because the few known facts are all facts of history. As Bury, who had worked in both periods, said, "the records of ancient and mediaeval history are starred with lacunae."[11] History has been called an enormous jig-saw with a lot of missing parts. But the main trouble does not consist of the lacunae. Our picture of Greece in the fifth century B.C. is defective not primarily because so many of the bits have been accidentally lost, but because it is, by and large, the picture formed by a tiny group of people in the city of Athens. We know a lot about what fifth-century Greece looked like to an Athenian citizen; but hardly anything about what it looked like to a Spartan, a Corinthian, or a Theban—not to mention a Persian, or a slave or other non-citizen resident in Athens. Our picture has been pre-selected and predetermined for us, not so much by accident as by people who were consciously or unconsciously imbued with a particular view and thought the facts which supported that view worth preserving. In the same way, when I read in a modern history of the Middle Ages that the people of the Middle Ages were deeply concerned with religion, I wonder how we know this, and whether it is true. What we know as the facts of mediaeval history have almost all been selected for us by generations of chroniclers who were professionally occupied in the theory and practice of religion, and who therefore thought it supremely important, and recorded everything relating to it, and not much else. The picture of the Russian peasant as devoutly religious was destroyed by the revolution of 1917. The picture of mediaeval man as devoutly religious, whether true or not, is indestructible, because nearly all the known facts about him were pre-selected for us by people who believed it, and wanted others to believe it, and a mass of other facts, in which we might possibly have found evidence to the contrary, has been lost beyond recall. The dead hand of vanished generations of historians, scribes, and chroniclers has determined beyond the possibility of appeal the pattern of the past. "The history we read," writes Professor Barraclough, himself trained as a mediaevalist, "though based on facts, is, strictly speaking, not factual at all, but a series of accepted judgments."[12]

But let us turn to the different, but equally grave, plight of the modern historian. The ancient or mediaeval historian may be grateful for the vast winnowing process which, over the years, has put at his disposal a manageable corpus of historical facts. As Lytton Strachey said in his mischievous way, "ignorance is the first requisite of the historian, ignorance which simplifies and clarifies, which selects and omits."[13] When I am tempted, as I sometimes am, to envy the extreme competence of colleagues engaged in writing ancient or mediaeval history, I find consolation in the reflexion that they are so competent mainly because they are so ignorant of their subject. The modern historian enjoys none of the advantages of this built-in ignorance. He must cultivate this necessary ignorance for himself—the more so the nearer he comes to his own times. He has the dual task of discovering the few significant facts and turning them into facts of history, and of discarding the many insignificant facts as unhistorical. But this is the very converse of the nineteenth-century heresy that history consists of the compilation of a maximum number of irrefutable and objective facts. Anyone who succumbs to this heresy will either have to give up history as a bad job, and take to stamp-collecting or some other form of antiquarianism, or end in a madhouse. It is this heresy, which during the past hundred years has had such devastating effects on the modern historian, producing in Germany, in Great Britain, and in the United

States a vast and growing mass of dry-as-dust factual histories, of minutely specialized monographs, of would-be historians knowing more and more about less and less, sunk without trace in an ocean of facts. It was, I suspect, this heresy—rather than the alleged conflict between liberal and Catholic loyalties—which frustrated Acton as a historian. In an early essay he said of his teacher Döllinger: "He would not write with imperfect materials and to him the materials were always imperfect."[14] Acton was surely here pronouncing an anticipatory verdict on himself, on that strange phenomenon of a historian whom many would regard as the most distinguished occupant the Regius Chair of Modern History in this university has ever had—but who wrote no history. And Acton wrote his own epitaph in the introductory note to the first volume of the *Cambridge Modern History*, published just after his death, when he lamented that the requirements pressing on the historian "threaten to turn him from a man of letters into the compiler of an encyclopedia."[15] Something had gone wrong. What had gone wrong was the belief in this untiring and unending accumulation of hard facts as the foundation of history, the belief that facts speak for themselves and that we cannot have too many facts, a belief at that time so unquestioning that few historians then thought it necessary—and some still think it unnecessary today—to ask themselves the question: What is history?

The nineteenth-century fetishism of facts was completed and justified by a fetishism of documents. The documents were the Ark of the Covenant in the temple of facts. The reverent historian approached them with bowed head and spoke of them in awed tones. If you find it in the documents, it is so. But what, when we get down to it, do these documents—the decrees, the treaties, the rent-folls, the blue books, the official correspondence, the private letters and diaries—tell us? No document can tell us more than what the author of the document thought—what he thought had happened, what he thought ought to happen or would happen, or perhaps only what he wanted others to think he thought, or even only what he himself thought he thought. None of this means anything until the historian has got to work on it and deciphered it. The facts, whether found in documents or not, have still to be processed by the historian before he can make any use of them: the use he makes of them is, if I may put it that way, the processing process.

Let me illustrate what I am trying to say by an example which I happen to know well. When Gustav Stresemann, the Foreign Minister of the Weimar Republic,[16] died in 1929, he left behind him an enormous mass—300 boxes full—of papers, official, semi-official, and private, nearly all relating to the six years of his tenure of office as Foreign Minister. His friends and relatives naturally thought that a monument should be raised to the memory of so great a man. His faithful secretary Bernhardt got to work; and within three years there appeared three massive volumes, of some 600 pages each, of selected documents from the 300 boxes, with the impressive title *Stresemanns Vermächtnis*.[17] In the ordinary way the documents themselves would have mouldered away in some cellar or attic and disappeared forever; or perhaps in a hundred years or so some curious scholar would have come upon them and set out to compare them with Bernhardt's text. What happened was far more dramatic. In 1945 the documents fell into the hands of the British and the American governments, who photographed the lot and put the photostats at the disposal of scholars in the Public Records Office in London and in the National Archives in Washington, so that, if we have sufficient patience and curiosity, we can discover exactly what Bernhardt did. What he did was neither very unusual nor very shocking. When Stresemann died, his Western policy seemed to have been crowned with a series of brilliant successes—Locarno, the admission of Germany to the League of Nations, the Dawes and Young plans and the American loans, the withdrawal of allied occupation armies from the Rhineland. This seemed the important and rewarding part of Stresemann's foreign policy; and it was not unnatural that it should have been over-represented in Bernhardt's selection of documents. Stresemann's Eastern policy, on the other hand, his relations with the Soviet Union, seemed to have led nowhere in particular; and, since masses of documents about negotiations which yielded only trivial results were not very interesting and added nothing to Stresemann's reputation, the process of selection could be more rigorous. Stresemann in fact devoted a far more constant and anxious attention to relations with the Soviet Union, and they played a far larger part in his foreign policy as a whole, than the reader of the Bernhardt selection would surmise. But the Bernhardt volumes compare favorably, I suspect, with many published collections of documents on which the ordinary historian implicitly relies.

This is not the end of my story. Shortly after the publication of Bernhardt's volumes, Hitler came into power. Stresemann's name was consigned to oblivion in Germany, and the volumes disappeared from circulation: many, perhaps most, of the copies must have been destroyed. Today *Stresemanns Vermächtnis* is a rather rare book. But in the West Streseman's reputation stood high. In 1935 an English publisher brought out an abbreviated translation of Bernhardt's work—a selection from Bernhardt's selection; perhaps one third of the original was omitted. Sutton, a well-known translator from the German, did his job competently and well. The English version, he explained in the preface, was "slightly condensed, but only by the omission of a certain amount of what, it was felt, was more ephemeral matter ... of little interest to English readers or students."[18] This again is natural enough. But the result is that Streseman's Eastern policy, already under-represented in Bernhardt, recedes still further from view, and the Soviet Union appears in Sutton's volumes merely as an occasional and rather unwelcome intruder in Stresemann's predominantly Western foreign policy. Yet it is safe to say that, for all except a few specialists, Sutton and not Bernhardt—and still less the documents themselves—represents for the Western world the authentic voice of Stresemann. Had the documents perished in 1945 in the bombing, and had the remaining Bernhardt volumes disappeared, the authenticity and authority of Sutton would never have been questioned. Many printed collections of documents gratefully accepted by historians in default of the originals rest on no securer basis than this.

But I want to carry the story one step further. Let us forget about Bernhardt and Sutton, and be thankful that we can, if we choose, consult the authentic papers of a leading participant in some important events of recent European history. What do the papers tell us? Among other things they contain records of some hundreds of Stresemann's conversations with the Soviet ambassador in Berlin and of a score or so with Chicherin. These records have one feature in common. They depict Stresemann as having the lion's share of the conversations and reveal his arguments as invariably well put and cogent, while those of his partner are for the most part scanty, confused, and unconvincing. This is a familiar characteristic of all records of diplomatic conversations. The documents do not tell us what happened, but only what Stresemann thought had happened, or what he wanted others to think, or perhaps what he wanted himself to think, had happened. It was not Sutton or Bernhardt, but Stresemann himself, who started the process of selection. And, if we had, say, Chicherin's records of these same conversations, we should still learn from them only what Chicherin thought, and what really happened would have to be reconstructed in the mind of the historian. Of course, facts and documents are essential to the historian. But do not make a fetish of them. They do not by themselves constitute history; they provide in themselves no ready-made answer to this tiresome question: What is history?

At this point I should like to say a few words on the question of why nineteenth-century historians were generally indifferent to the philosophy of history. The term was invented by Voltaire, and has since been used in different senses; but I shall take it to mean, if I use it at all, our answer to the question: What is history? The nineteenth century was, for the intellectuals of Western Europe, a comfortable period exuding confidence and optimism. The facts were on the whole satisfactory; and the inclination to ask and answer awkward questions about them was correspondingly weak. Ranke piously believed that divine providence would take care of the meaning of history if he took care of the facts; and Burckhardt with a more modern touch of cynicism observed that "we are not initiated into the purposes of the eternal wisdom." Professor Butterfield as late as 1931 noted with apparent satisfaction that "historians have reflected little upon the nature of things and even the nature of their own subject."[19] But my predecessor in these lectures, Dr. A.L. Rowse, more justly critical, wrote of Sir Winston Churchill's *The World Crisis*—his book about the First World War—that, while it matched Trotsky's *History of the Russian Revolution* in personality, vividness, and vitality, it was inferior in one respect: it had "no philosophy of history behind it."[20] British historians refused to be drawn, not because they believed that history had no meaning, but because they believed that its meaning was implicit and self-evident. The liberal nineteenth-century view of history had a close affinity with the economic doctrine of *laissez-faire*—also the product of a serene and self-confident outlook on the world. Let everyone get on with his particular job, and the hidden hand would take care of the universal harmony. The facts of history were themselves a demonstration of the supreme fact of a beneficent and apparently infinite progress towards higher things. This was the age of innocence, and historians walked in the Garden of Eden, without a scrap of philosophy to cover them, naked and unashamed before the god of history. Since then, we have known Sin and experienced a Fall; and those historians who today pretend to dispense with a philosophy of history are merely trying, vainly and self-consciously, like members of a nudist colony, to recreate the Garden of Eden in their garden suburb. Today the awkward question can no longer be evaded.

Notes

[1] *The Cambridge Modern History: Its Origins, Authorship and Production* (Cambridge University Press, 1907), pp. 10–12. [Carr]

[2] *The New Cambridge Modern History,* I (Cambridge University Press, 1957), pp. xxiv–xxv. [Carr]

[3] Positivists base knowledge solely on data derived from sense experience and deny speculation about the search for ultimate origins. Positivists generally held a high regard for scientific evidence and the interrelationship of scientific knowledge.

[4] Empiricists hold that practical experience is the only source of knowledge.

[5] Action, *Lectures on Modern History* (London: Macmillan & Co., 1906), p. 318 [Carr]

[6] Quoted in *The Listener* (June 19, 1952), p. 992. [Carr]

[7] M. Mamlius, *Astronomicon: Liber Primus,* 2nd ed. (Cambridge University Press, 1937), p. 87. [Carr]

[8] Talcott Parsons and Edward A. Shils, *Toward a General Theory of Action,* 3rd ed. (Cambridge, Mass.: Harvard University Press, 1954), p. 167. [Carr]

[9] Lord George Sanger, *Seventy Years a Showman* (London: J. M. Dent and Sons, 1926), pp. 188–189. [Carr]

[10] These will shortly be published under the title *The Making of Victorian England.* [Carr]

[11] John Bagnell Bury, *Selected Essays* (Cambridge University Press, 1930), p. 52.

[12] Geoffrey Barraclough, *History in a Changing World* (London: Basil Blackwell and Mott, 1955), p. 14. [Carr]

[13] Lytton Strachey, Preface to *Eminent Victorians.* [Carr]

[14] Quoted in George P. Gooch, *History and Historians in the Nineteenth Century* (London: Longmans, Green and Company, 1952), p. 385. Later Acton said of Döllinger that "it was given his to form him philosophy of history on the largest induction ever available to man" (*History of Freedom and other Essays* [London: Macmillan & Co., 1907], p. 435). [Carr]

[15] *The Cambridge Modern History,* I (1902), p. 4. [Carr]

[16] Wiemar Republic: German Republic (1919–1933) created by a constitutional assembly at Weimar in 1919 and dissolved after Hitler became chancellor.

[17] *Stresemanns Vermächtnis: Stresemann's Legacy.*

[18] Gustav Stresemann, *His Diaries, Letters, and Papers* (London: Macmillan & Co., 1935), I, Editor's Note. [Carr]

[19] Herbert Butterfield, *The Whig Interpretation of History* (London: George Bell & Sons, 1931), p. 67. [Carr]

[20] Alfred L. Rowse, *The End of an Epoch* (London: Macmillan & Co., 1947), pp. 282–83. [Carr]

FOCUS: READING REVIEW

1. What is Acton's view of history? How does it compare with Clark's? What does each historian's view indicate about his society's outlook?
2. What did the nineteenth century want in history? How did this relate to the period's philosophy?
3. What distinguishes historical facts from other facts from the past? What is a basic fact? What is the process by which a mere fact becomes a historical fact?
4. Why does Carr state that facts do not speak for themselves? Who speaks?
5. Explain how our view of the Middle Ages has been shaped by historians rather than by facts.
6. What role do documents play in history? What information do they provide?
7. When Stresemann's secretary, Bernhardt, edited Stresemann's papers, what guided his selection process? How were these documents further transformed? What does this illustrate about the "truth" of history?

FOCUS: AUTHOR'S STRATEGIES

1. Carr takes on the large task of answering the question, "What Is History?" To do this he establishes a definite persona. Where does he clearly communicate this persona?
2. What does Carr's persona tell you about his audience? What does the information he presents indicate about the audience?
3. How do the two alternative views of history Carr presents initially enable him to define his own view?

FOCUS: DISCUSSION AND WRITING

1. You have studied history throughout school. How did your textbooks present American heroes? How did they present the Soviet Union? The English side of the Revolutionary War? What philosophy of history did these textbooks have?
2. Select one of the essays from the next chapter and identify the historical facts; then explain how the writer shapes those facts by his or her view of history.

The Premises of Inquiry

Herbert J. Muller

Herbert J. Muller (1905–1967) received his education at Cornell University and taught at Purdue University and Indiana University. His book Freedom in the Ancient World *(1961–1962) received a Phi Beta Kappa award for most distinguished book in philosophy, religion, and history. Muller writes about the philosophy of history in* Science and Criticism *(1943),* The Loom of History *(1958),* The Individual in a Revolutionary World *(1965),* Freedom in the Modern World *(1967), and* The Uses of the Past *(1952), the source for this selection. Here Muller questions whether the study of history can be "scientific," and answers that as a complex of factors, including human will, history cannot lay claim to universal truth.*

Only by a historical analysis can we determine how we got into the latest mess, and how we might get out of it. [Although the historian composes his narrative, selecting, shaping, and coloring, history must always aim at literal truth.] The most objective history conceivable, [however], is still a selection and an interpretation, necessarily governed by some special interests and based on some particular belief. [Further, history does not always possess scientific certainty] because we cannot isolate, measure, or graph the multiple forces that determine it. Nor can we ignore the human agency in history, or escape the implication that within limits it is a free agency. Respect for conscious human purposes calls for conscious ethical judgment about whatever significance we find in history. These judgments must see in perspective not only our own nation but our civilization. To accomplish this we must think in universal terms—discern the basic uniformities and continuities that make an intelligible history; we must accept cultural relativism. [The admission of relativity and uncertainty does not destroy knowledge but enables higher objectivity, a full understanding of past and present.]

1. Although the practical value of a knowledge of history is commonly exaggerated, since men do not appear to learn readily from the mistakes of their ancestors, and historians themselves are not always conspicuous for their wisdom, I suppose that few would deny the practical necessity of this knowledge. When Henry Ford, in the good old boom days, said that 'history is bunk,' he merely illustrated the ignorance of the hard-headed industrial leaders who were leading the country straight to a crash. History has also been described as a series of messes, but only by a historical analysis can we determine how we got into the latest mess, and how we might get out of it. The very idea that we are in a mess involves assumptions about the 'natural' course of affairs, as do all policies for dealing with it. Practical men who distrust 'mere theory' are especially fond of pointing out that 'history shows' something or other—usually showing that they are fearful of all change and incapable of learning from the failures of their conservative forebears. In any event, we are forever drawing upon the past. It not only constitutes all the 'experience' by which we have learned: it is the source of our major interests, our claims, our rights, and our duties. It is the source of our very identity. In an eternal present, which is a specious present, the past is all we know. And as the present is forever slipping back, it reminds us that we too shall in time belong wholly to the past.

For such reasons our interest in history is more poetic than practical or scientific. It begins as a childlike interest in the obvious pageantry and exciting event; it grows as a mature interest in the variety and complexity of the drama, the splendid achievements and the terrible failures; it ends as a deep sense of the mystery of man's life—of all the dead, great and obscure, who once walked the earth, and of the wonderful and awful possibilities of being a human being. 'History is neither written nor made without love or hate,' Mommsen wrote. The historian is inevitably an artist of a kind as he composes his narrative, selecting, shaping, coloring. The greater historians, from Herodotus to Toynbee, have generally been distinguished for their imaginative reach and grasp, not necessarily the soundness of their conclusions. Gibbon remains one of the greatest, despite his apparent prejudice and his untrustworthiness in detail, because of his artistic mastery of an epic theme.

Nevertheless history must always aim at literal truth. As Trevelyan said, its very poetry consists in its truth. 'It is the fact about the past that is poetic'—the fact that this was the actual drama of actual men, and that these men are no more. A lover of history loves it straight, without chasers of fancy; he is especially irritated by merely picturesque history, or by such bastard offspring as the fictionized biography. This concern for literal truth helps to explain why historians, the lovers of the past, have been more disposed to condemn their predecessors than poets have been. Over two thousand years ago Polybius noted how each successive historian 'makes such a parade of minute accuracy, and inveighs so bitterly when refuting others, that people come to imagine that all other historians have been mere dreamers.' So the scientific historians of the last century inveighed against the dreamers before them, and have in turn been ridiculed in this century.

In this view, one might wonder just where the truth comes out, and why one should put any trust in the latest version of it. It is always easy to be cynical about history, as 'a pack of tricks we play on the dead.' Yet it is impossible to deny the impressive advance that has been made in the last hundred years. Historians have built up an immense body of factual knowledge, knowledge that is no less genuine because it is subject to different theoretical interpretations. They have systematically widened, deepened, and clarified the sources of knowledge by philological, paleographical, archaelogical, and ethnological research. They have come to realize the importance of commonplace, everyday events, in particular the economic activities that have been neglected in favor of the political and military. They have learned a great deal about the influence of both the physical and the cultural environment, what lies below factual history and above it. They have become aware of evolution, of origins and growths, of the history of history itself. Their very ignorance is suffused with knowledge, which at least keeps them from being ignorant of their ignorance.

The progress in historical knowledge, accordingly, has not been a steady advance toward absolute truth, a steady reduction in the number of universal laws to be discovered. It has been a progressive clarification, a fuller consciousness of what has happened, and how and why. When historians offer some fifty different reasons for the fall of the Roman Empire, we may at first be simply confused; yet we have a better understanding of the fall than if we assumed there was only one reason, or no reason except Fate. In spite of all their disagreement, moreover, historians are now generally agreed in discounting the most obvious explanation, that Rome succumbed to barbarian invasions; they have a deeper insight than the great Gibbon had, and perceive the dry rot that had set in during the Golden Age he celebrated. For they now have the advantage of a vast, international, cooperative enterprise, conducted in a scientific spirit. Although every historian remains fallible and subject to bias, his work remains subject to correction and criticism by his fellows, in professional journals and congresses. The relative objectivity of contemporary social science, as Karl Popper points out, is due not to the impartiality of all the social scientists, but to the publicity and community of the scientific method.

2. A particular gain is summed up in my second proposition—the very awareness that historians can never attain the impersonal exactitude to which they must always aspire. There can be no 'pure history'—history-in-itself, recorded from nobody's point of view, for nobody's sake. The most objective history conceivable is still a selection and an interpretation, necessarily governed by some special interests and based on some particular beliefs. It can be more nearly objective if these interests and beliefs are explicit, out in the open, where they can be freely examined and criticized. Historians can more nearly approach the detachment of the physicist when they realize that the historical 'reality' is symbolic, not physical, and that they are giving as well as finding meanings. The important meanings of history are not simply there, lined up, waiting to be discovered.

Up to a point, all this implies something like Croce's principle, that true history is always contemporary history—history 'for the occasion,' of what is alive for us. The past has no meaningful existence except as it exists for us, as it is given meaning by us. In piety and justice we try to see it as it was, or as it seemed to the men who lived it, but even this poetic interest is not disinterested; in our contemplation of the drama we see what is most pertinent for our own hopes and fears. Hence the past keeps changing with the present. Every age has to rewrite its history, re-create the past; in every age a different Christ dies on the Cross, and is resurrected to a different end. Today the Peloponnesian War and the decline of the Roman Empire have a special significance for us that they could not have had for the Middle Ages or the Renaissance; by the same token, they will have a different significance for a Hindu or Chinese than for a Western historian. Our task is to create a 'usable past,' for our own living purposes.

Yet this admission of relativity does not permit us to create whatever we have a mind to, make over the past to suit ourselves. Old Testament and early Christian historians could freely tamper with the facts because they knew the divine plan of history; the only important use of facts was to illustrate the all-important religious truth. We cannot simply stick to the facts but we cannot disregard them either, and must derive our meanings from them in the knowledge that they are both stubborn and ambiguous. Our distinctive interests and beliefs make it possible for history to be relatively disinterested and impartial. Through Marx, Freud, Sumner, Pareto, Boas, Spengler, and many others, we have become more aware of the inveterate habit of rationalization and the sources of bias—the class interests, the *mores,* the conditioned reflexes of culture, the unconscious assumptions, the 'climate of opinion.' Although we can never entirely escape or control our climate, never attain a God's-eye view, we can more freely discount and supplement—at least when we read the other fellow's history. The very crisis of our civilization is in this aspect an aid to understanding. In a stabler society we might expect to have a simpler, stabler past, whose primary meaning was the wisdom of the ancestors. We are not naturally wiser than our ancestors; but the revolutionary conditions of our thought and life have forced a realization of relativity and complexity, the uncertainties of all history, and the ambiguities of the good old days that somehow led to these very bad days.

3. Meanwhile the most apparent reason why we cannot generalize about history with scientific certainty and precision is that we cannot isolate, measure, or graph the multiple forces that determine it. Race, the natural environment, the pressure of surrounding cultures, technological inventions and discoveries, genius or great leadership, institutions economic, political, and religious—the complex, continuous interaction of these and other factors defies equation or controlled experiment. Considered separately, even a seemingly incidental factor may look decisive. Thus Simkhovitch argued plausibly that hay has been a major influence. The introduction of grass seed and clovers, by which soil can be restored in a few years, was 'the greatest of revolutions, the revolution against the supreme law, the law of the land, the law of diminishing returns and of soil exhaustion'; the Roman failure to make hay was a basic reason for the decline of their empire. Hans Zinsser argued as plausibly for the importance of rats, lice, and fleas, the carriers of diseases that have decided more decisive battles and campaigns than has brilliant generalship; the Roman Empire was also fatally weakened by terrible plagues. But we cannot measure the relative importance of such factors, much less explain history by them. With hay, and without plagues, history in this century looks more complex than ever.

A further complication is that the 'natural' causes we can point to often have unpredictable, disproportionate, seemingly unnatural results. Cortez and a handful of adventurers confronted the mighty Aztec empire, a civilization in some respects superior to their own; but they toppled the empire and destroyed the civilization because they had gunpowder. This historic event is quite understandable—and it is supremely irrational, philosophically absurd. History is full of still more trifling, fortuitous events that had momentous consequences. In 1920, for example, the pacific King Alexander of Greece died of blood-poisoning, due to the bite of a pet monkey; a general election led to the recall of King Constantine, who thereupon started a disastrous war on the Turks. Winston Churchill observed, 'A quarter of a million persons died of that monkey's bite.'

Needless to add, causes go much deeper than the immediate event that sets off a historic train of events. The deeper we go, however, the more ramifications we find; and I stress the incalculables and imponderables because analysts are always prone to reduce the interaction of many forces to the action of a single force, such as race, environment, or economic activity, and then to 'explain' history by it. Tocqueville remarked that an exaggerated system of general causes is a consolation to second-rate historians as well as statesmen: 'it can always furnish a few mighty reasons to extricate them from the most difficult part of their work, and it indulges the indolence or incapacity of their minds, while it confers upon them the honors of deep thinking.' If the desire for great laws of history is quite natural, rooted in the ancient notion that 'nature loves simplicity,' the laws so far proclaimed prove only that man loves simplicity, and that he has not really found it. They are always arbitrary, man-made laws that men can break, as they cannot break the law of gravitation. Just as conservative businessmen appeal to inviolable laws of supply and demand, which they are the first to violate whenever they get a monopoly, so Communists appeal to iron laws of history and inevitable outcomes to justify their efforts to make history come out to suit themselves, and to excuse their merciless liquidation of Marxist-lawsbreakers.

4. This is to repeat my fourth assumption: that we cannot ignore the human agency in history, cannot escape the implication that within limits it is a free agency.[1] Historians have been stressing the deep, impersonal, unconscious processes that govern social change, as in the growth of a vast industrial civilization that nobody had planned and few understood. They have accordingly tended to minimize the power of ideas and ideals, or even to deny this power. The complexities that make it difficult to find the great law of history also strengthen the impression that man has no real freedom to make his history. Yet the problems we face are clearly of man's own making. However unplanned, the industrial revolution was a vast human effort, a conscious exploitation of new power got by scientific ideas and ideals. 'Invention is the mother of necessity.'

The fundamental fact is that man is the only culture-building animal. Culture means a man-made environment, which is primarily a mythical or 'spiritual' environment. In this enterprise he is aided by the seeming biological handicap of prolonged infancy and immaturity, during which he learns what his ancestors have made. The kind of culture he builds is conditioned by the natural environment but not determined by it; his creativity or freedom of action is indicated by the variety of Indian cultures developed on the American plains, or the long series of different societies in the same environment of Asia Minor. And the most powerful influence on him is the unseen environment of his own creation. We may deny, for example, the validity of belief in the supernatural, but we cannot deny its tremendous power. It has often proved stronger than the elemental impulses of self-interest and self-preservation, inducing men to give up their worldly goods, to deny the claims of their senses, to mortify their flesh, to welcome martyrdom—to defy the oldest laws of nature and society, in order to devote themselves to biologically preposterous behavior. Civilization, or culture grown more varied and complex, represents a more conscious, determined, resourceful effort to master the natural environment and set up a world of man's own. Amid its complexities one may see only that the individual is a product of his society, which in turn is a product of impersonal forces. Nevertheless the whole enterprise of civilization is a rare human creation, a triumph of mind and will; and the impersonal forces work only through the ideas and beliefs of men.

Similarly with the influence of great men. In the revulsion against the 'hero' theory of history, proposed by such thinkers as Fichte, Hegel, and Carlyle, historians have tended to picture the great men as mere agents of impersonal forces, and thereby to reduce the issue to a false antithesis—whether they make history or are made by it. The actual problem is to determine both their effect on their environment and its effect on them. Many seem dispensable despite their greatness; if Columbus had not discovered America or Watt invented the steam engine, it seems fairly certain that somebody else would have before long. Other men of greater genius, who achieved what nobody else could have, had little apparent influence on the course of history; despite my conviction that Shakespeare was the greatest writer who ever lived, I cannot believe that his work made any appreciable difference to the subsequent history of Western civilization, or even of literature. Still others—in particular many famous generals and monarchs—owe their fame more to their accidental position than to qualities of greatness; like the little Dutch boy who saved the dykes, Sidney Hook has remarked, they needed only a finger and the chance of happening by at the right moment. All the heroes of history required the great moment or the right moment, the forces to work with. Had Alexander the Great been born in Macedon three centuries earlier or three centuries later than he was, he could never have embarked on his conquest.

Yet the great man may indeed be epoch-making, by the decisions he makes, the direction he gives to the forces at his disposal. Although it is clear—in retrospect—that the time was ripe for such adventurers as Alexander, Mohammed, Jenghiz Kahn, and Lenin,[2] their *success* was not clearly inevitable. Their will—even their whim—made a profound difference in history. Moreover, the mere ideal of greatness is a force. All peoples have clung to it, and responded to it; all have their national heroes. If the immediate achievements of the hero may be discounted, the hero as symbol, or even the mythical hero, continues to make history.

Although the admission of such imponderables is likely to be displeasing to scientists and philosophers who want strict law and order, it does not destroy all possibility of lawfulness and predictability. The 'spiritual' forces are still recognizable universal forces. At any rate, here are the given terms of our problem. The scientific determinist himself must reckon with the power of beliefs, sacred traditions, new ideas, great leaders, simply because they are among the most recognizable, determinable causes in history. Otherwise he is forced back on a kind of mystical, inhuman fatalism that would be fatal to the historical sense. If everything that has happened is the only thing that could possibly have happened, we might as well close the book. The reason we don't is that even the determinists and fatalists are always implying that there were real alternatives, and that men made the wrong choice. Whatever we believe in theory, we continue in practice to think and act as if we were not puppets.

5. It is this inescapable sense of human responsibility that fills the past with poignant 'might-have-beens,' and the future with portentous 'ifs.' And so the idea

that history is made, and suffered, by men is not pure idealization. As we recognize the real power of knowledge, reason, and conscious aspiration, we are forced to recongize the greater power of inertia, ignorance, stupidity, and irrationality. The very respect for conscious human purposes calls for stress on the human obstacles to their fulfillment. It calls, finally, for conscious ethical judgment. My fifth proposition is that such judgments are implicity in whatever significance we find in history, and had better be explicit.

Conflict and change are the essence of the drama. As we study the great historic conflicts we naturally take sides; as we study the great changes we as naturally judge that they were for better or worse. When we talk of the progress or decadence of a society we are implying some standards of value. When we lament any of the tragedies of history, such as the decline and fall of Rome, we are committing ourselves to the values of civilization; we are refusing to rejoice with the Huns, who no doubt were proud and happy enough during the worst days of Rome. The most impartial, objective historians are constantly passing judgment on leaders and policies. Their factual narratives are full of such adjectives as wise, cruel, just, unscrupulous, benevolent, brutal, corrupt, vicious—adjectives that seem factually accurate only because of the general agreement on the ethical standards implicit in these judgments. And none are prone to judge more freely, or more harshly, than those—like the Puritans and Marxists—who ostensibly believe in predestination[3] or determinism.[4]

Here again the very advances in our knowledge and understanding have tended to obscure the ethical issues, the judgments finally required by the faith in reason that has produced this knowledge. In our awareness of evolution and cultural relativity we can understand any stupidity or atrocity by simply dating it. We can excuse Aristotle and St. Paul for taking slavery for granted; we can appreciate the exalted fervor that led the noblest Crusaders to rejoice in the massacre of heathens; we can see that it was piety and ignorance, not mere sadism, that burned old women at the stake as witches. We can do a fine justice, indeed, to the past. Still, we do condemn—we just condemn—the cruelties of slavery, fanaticism, and witch-burning. In being charitable to the doer of the deed, we cannot afford to condone the deed itself. And least of all can we afford to explain away our own shortcomings as historic necessities. Although the irresponsibility of America after the First World War was quite understandable and predictable, it was not strictly inevitable. It was a moral and intellectual failure, for which Americans were responsible. They have learned something from it, and must continue to learn; for in all history no nation has faced such staggering responsibilities as face America today.

6. It is therefore a commonplace that we must establish some kind of world order, and cannot hope to do so without breadth of understanding and sympathy. Our scientific, esthetic, moral, and urgently practical interest alike call out my sixth proposition, of the need for an anthropological view of our history, an effort to see in perspective not only our nation but our civilization. Although this may

seem to be a harmless exercise, in practice it will meet violent opposition. It involves what practical men call globaloney or un-Americanism, and what pious men call indifference to principles or betrayal of the true faiths. It involves still another contradiction of our age: that we now have a far wider view of history than our ancestors, a view in which we can appreciate the astonishing variety of human aspiration and achievement, and that we have also developed stronger prejudices than any other civilization, raised new barriers to understanding and community.

The ugliest example is racial prejudice. Even though few reputable historians continue to find the key to civilization in the innate superiority of the white, the Nordic, or the Anglo-Saxon race, this vulgar theory still colors the thought and feeling of a great many men who do not openly commit themselves to it. In the Anglo-Saxon world, indeed, feeling about color is so strong and deep that men assume it is instinctive, and even the tolerant are likely to be repelled by the thought of racial intermarriage; whereas such feeling has actually been rare in history. All peoples have been pleased to regard themselves as superior, but few have identified their superiority with the color of their skin. And since the great majority of the world's population are what Americans call colored, and consider naturally inferior, it becomes necessary to repeat that this attitude is strictly a prejudice, inconsistent with the principles of democracy and Christianity, and with no scientific basis whatever. Biologically, races are not pure or sharply defined, racial differences are only a small fraction of man's common inheritance, and the clearest differences—as between white skin and yellow, long heads and broad, straight hair and kinky—have no clear importance for survival. Historically, mixed races have usually produced the golden ages, all races have proven capable of civilization, and no race has led the way throughout history. The 100 percent American today is a parvenu who owes 99 percent of his civilization to a mongrel antiquity.

More common in history is the prejudice of nationalism, based on the universal 'in-group' feeling. It is not simply an ugly sentiment, or a refuge for scoundrels. It has inspired high ideals of duty, devotion to the common welfare, sacrifice for a greater good. It has fertilized Western culture with a rich variety of national traditions. Yet the historic claim to national sovereignty, with the sentiment of devotion to one's country right or wrong and the natural conclusion that it is practically always right, is now an apparent anachronism. And if such ancient sentiments will scarcely be eradicated by a study of world history, at least they should not be fortified by historians. Until recently, most histories were national histories, written from a nationalistic point of view; today most school texts are still of this provincial kind. They give a false idea of the self-sufficiency and the manifest destiny of the nation. They slight the common foundations, the unity and continuity of Western civilization, and the great indebtedness to other civilizations. They foster the common misconceptions of the past that are much more dangerous than simple ignorance of the past.

Less conspicuous but still pervasive is religious prejudice, the exclusiveness that has distinguished Western civilization from all others except Islam. Despite the

growth of tolerance, most Christans still assume that theirs is the only true religion, and that their Christian duty is to convert the rest of the world. The rest of
the world, which happens to include the great majority of mankind, still resents
this assumption; and in the light of religious history it does look like an arrogant
assumption. One may reasonably argue that Christ is the most nearly perfect
symbol of the one God that all the higher religions have sought to comprehend.
One cannot reasonably take for granted the certain truth of an exclusive divine
revelation: a revelation that was granted to an obscure group at a particular moment in history, that was recorded by fallible men in narratives marked by manifest inconsistencies, that cannot be proved by independent reason, and that Christians themselves have never been able to agree upon, much less to embody in a
Christian society. Yet Western writers, including historians, cling to the parochial
attitude symbolized in our calendar. The appearance of Christ is regarded as the
turning point of all history, and the confused records of his appearance as conclusive proof of a higher truth known only to Westerners.

This religious self-righteousnes is both cause and symptom of a general cultural
chauvinism. All peoples, to repeat, have tended to assume the superiority of their
culture. (Thus the Eskimos of Greenland believed that the white men came there
to learn good manners and morals from them.) With its technological triumphs,
however, Western culture has been able to achieve an unprecedented domination
of all other cultures, and to express an almost unprecedented contempt for them.
The early stages of this domination involved such savagery as the extermination of
Indians and enslavement of Negroes, who were thereupon called savages. The
later stages involved an economic exploitation that was less atrocious, more offensive because of the increasingly sanctimonious talk about the white man's burden,
and the constant insistence on his moral and religious superiority. And though
contemporaries are both more curious and more sympathetic, even borrowing
freely from the 'backward' peoples, there is still too little regard for their rights or
respect for their customs, and too little appreciation of the significance and the
value of cultural diversity. One result is that almost all Western nations are
plagued by the problem of cultural minorities, intensified by racial, religious, and
even linguistic prejudice.

The point here is not merely the moral need of a better understanding of other
peoples. It is the intellectual need of a better understanding of ourselves, and of
our possibile destiny. Toynbee suggests an apt analogy in his account of the great
emperor Babur, who founded a mighty empire in India about 1500. As a Turk,
Babur was the agent of manifest destiny, ruling at the heart of civilization; for
centuries Turkish people had been riding out to conquer, spreading from
Mongolia to Algeria and the Ukraine, and they now dominated most of the civilized world except China. As a cultivated man, Babur knew that some Frankish
barbarians had threatened civilization by invading the holy lands of Islam centuries before, though of course they had finally been thrown out; and no doubt he
knew that these rude infidels still existed on a corner of the peninsula of Asia

known as Europe, though he never bothered to mention them in his brilliant auto-biography. He also failed to note that some Frankish ships had reached India a few years before he did. For he could never have dreamed that descendants of these infidels were going to dominate the whole world, including incidentally his own empire. Three hundred years later, Toynbee notes, the great Egyptian historian Al-Gabarti still looked at the world from Babur's point of view. In recording the events of an extraordinary year, Al-Gabarti remarked somberly that 'the most portentous was the cessation of the Pilgrimage' from Egypt to Mecca, an unprece-dented event that showed again how Allah alone ruled history; for this was the year when Napoleon descended on Egypt.

No more can we predict the fantastic course that history will have taken some centuries hence, or be sure what are the most portentous events taking place today. But we can at least imagine the possibilities. We might be somewhat wiser, and less self-righteous, if we did not take for granted that the future belongs to America, or even to the West. We might learn, as Toynbee remarks, from our great historic achievement. 'By making history we have transcended our own his-tory'—laying the foundations of a world order, making possible the union of man-kind. Easterners have been forced to learn from this achievement of the West; many have profited from the study of both their history and ours, gaining a per-spective on civilizations in clash and in crisis. Westerners remain more provincial than Babur, without his excuse for short-sightedness.

7. Indeed, we might well go further than Toynbee, and question his own seem-ingly provincial assumption that it is the Christian God who rules history. If we try to think in really universal terms, we cannot talk easily of universal truths. The eternal verities we hear so much about usually look like selected beliefs of our own society, and in a long view they turn out to be mutable. History itself is the dead-liest enemy of the Eternal and Absolute. The whole history of thought is a refuta-tion of the finality to which thinkers have endlessly aspired. I conclude, accord-ingly, that in first and last matters we cannot conclude with absolute certainty.

But I should at once add that the admission of *ultimate* uncertainty does not mean *complete* uncertainty. The absolutist tradition of Christendom leads men to assume that if we don't have absolute standards we can't have any standards, and that if we are not standing on the Rock of Ages we are standing on nothing. Actu-ally, we can and do know plenty of objective truths without knowing the whole or final Truth. Beneath the manifold diversity of human history, more specifically, we can discern the basic uniformities and continuities that make it an intelligible history, not a chaos. They are implicit in the common structure of man, and the common requirements of social existence in the natural world. Thus all societies have to deal with the problems of birth, growth, education, sex, toil, and death. All display an esthetic sense, an interest in creating beauty; all have and enforce a code of morality, which generally comes down to something like the Golden Rule; all recognize the existence of unseen forces greater than man, which remain high and unseen whether they are called demons, God, or energy; all have standards of excellence, values that defy mortality. The very diversity in their ways of life points to such fundamental truths as the remarkable adaptability of man, and the universal power of custom or habit in fixing any one way of life.

In general, the uniformities and continuities of human experience are what make significant thought possible; the manifold possibilities of experience are what make critical thought necessary. Hence a refusal on principle to say the last word about human history is not a refusal to say any word, or to pass any firm judgment. Rather, it defines the conditions of judgment. Say that our most cherished beliefs are matters of opinion and it is then our business to get sound opinions, based on honest thought and the best available knowledge; only a fool will say that any opinion is as good as any other opinion—and even a fool is apt to seek expert opinion when he gets sick. Say that our final preferences are matters of taste and it is then our business to cultivate good taste; cultivated men may dispute the relative merits of Donne and Shelley, but they can and do agree that both are better poets than Eddie Guest. Because of the flagrant disagreement among the wise men, we are apt to forget the very general agreement on who were the great men—and to overlook the implication of this agreement, the tacit admission that there are diverse forms of goodness and greatness. As for history, we are confronted by societies embodying radically different ways of life, but it remains our business to judge the historical consequences of those ways. We can hope to make more intelligent judgments if we are aware of the many ways, and do not take for granted that our own is necessary or necessarily superior to all others.

Here, it seems to me, is the basic problem of thoughtful men today. We do not know the final truth about God and the world; the most certain knowledge we do have about the history of man belies all pretense to absolute certainty. We must nevertheless have principles, standards, faiths; many men have been demoralized by a shallow relativism that denies us the right to judge anyone or anything, while we perforce keep judging. The problem, then, is to maintain principle and morale in the face of ultimate uncertainty, on grounds that permit both the faith and the tolerance required by the pursuit of truth and goodness; just as the problem for statesmen is to compromise and reconcile without a cynical indifference to principle, in order to accomodate fundamentally different ways of life in a world order. The immediate objection to all partisans of absolute truth is that they evade the given terms of this problem.

8. I am therefore led to my final assumption, that the admission of a principle of relativity and uncertainty should not be simply depressing. It does not destroy all possibility of knowledge and judgment. Rather, it is the outcome of comprehensive knowledge, and the means to further knowledge of man's history. It enables a higher objectivity, a fuller understanding of present and past. It enables wiser choices among the possibilities open to us—among goods that are no less real because they are relative, and that are more relevant than arbitrary absolutes. Above all, this principle encourages a positive faith in positive values: of liberality, breadth of spirit, hospitality to new ideas, willingness to adventure, humility in admitting one's own fallibility and the limitations of the human mind—of the tolerance that is indispensable for the pursuit of truth, for social harmony, and for

simple humanity. If these are not the highest values, none are more essential to the hopes of world order and peace.

They also entail obvious dangers, of confusion, halfheartedness, demoralization, despair. One cannot be confident that mankind is yet ready or able to surrender the ancient illusion of certainty in its idealisms. Nevertheless this illusion intensifies the confusion and dismay of our times. It obscures the actual uncertainty in which men have always lived and which they take for granted in daily life. It obscures the goods that actually sustain men—such goods as creative work, appreciation of beauty, friendship and love, or simple comradeliness—and that do not require metaphysical or supernatural sanctions. It obscures the living faith of Western democracy. Thus seven Princeton professors asserted in a manifesto, 'The Spiritual Basis of Democracy,' that democracy cannot endure without a belief in an 'objective moral and spiritual order' established by a 'cosmic spiritual power'; whereas this belief is not logically required by a faith in democracy, which is rather an agreement on the right to disagree peaceably about religious or any other belief. And those who do believe in such a divine order are as likely to support an authoritarian regime—and historically they usually have.

All in all, we doubtless suffer from too much doubt. But we are likely to suffer much more because too many men are too sure of themselves.

Notes

[1] I feel free to waive the metaphysical problem of free will. Although it may be hard to see just how man can go his own way in a presumably lawful universe (not to mention the theological assumption of an omnipotent God who wills all), his freedom is less mysterious if it is not conceived as a purely spiritual state, an ability to be utterly unaffected by the world about him. Most plainly, it is the ability to do things in and to the world. And this is not only compatible with lawful necessities but increased by a knowledge of such necessities. Knowing the law of gravitation, I cannot be carefree and jump off a cliff; but I am free to save my neck—or if I choose, to kill myself in this manner. Science, which has fathered the doctrine of determinism, is the most striking example of man's determination and ability to bend nature to his own purposes. [Muller]

[2] Alexander the Great (356-323 B.C.), King of Macedonia, spread Greek culture through military conquests from Asia Minor to Egypt to India; Mohammed (1432-1481), the Ottoman sultan, known as "the conqueror," transformed Constantinople into Istanbul, consolidating the Ottoman Empire; Jenghiz Khan (1162?-1227) conquered land from the Black Sea to the Pacific; and Lenin (1870-1924) led Russia's Communist revolution of 1917 and served as premier of the U.S.S.R. between 1917 and 1924.

[3] predestination: the theological doctrine that at the Creation, God conceived a plan for all events, including which people would be saved.

[4] determinism: the doctrine that a sequence of causes independent of individual will determine all events, especially the individual's choice of action.

FOCUS: **READING REVIEW**

1. What does the past provide?
2. What have been historians' achievements in the twentieth century? What relationship do these achievements have with truth?
3. How does Muller see history as a manifestation of the scientific method? How can history approach the exactness of a physicist?
4. What is the relativity that Muller finds in history? Can history truly be scientific and relative at the same time?
5. What are the varied forces that shape history?
6. What role does human agency have in history?
7. How does finding significance in history involve an ethical sense?
8. What is an anthropological view of history? What prejudices would Muller have us lay aside?
9. How can relativity and uncertainty be a means to further knowledge?

FOCUS: **AUTHOR'S STRATEGIES**

1. Given the author's casual and frequent reference to historic events, to what audience is this essay directed?
2. What assumptions about the value of human endeavor and the value of knowledge underlie Muller's essay? What do these suggest about his purpose?
3. Muller makes extensive use of illustration. Select one example and explain what the illustration accomplishes.

FOCUS: **DISCUSSION AND WRITING**

1. Muller says that despite our awareness of cultural relativity which allows us to understand any stupidity or atrocity, we still hold a moral position. What historic events do we condemn? How do we explain these events? By our condemnation, what values do we affirm? Do these values encourage a nationalistic view or a more universal view of history?
2. Muller subscribes to the conviction that human beings, as well as complex forces, shape history. Based on your knowledge of history and/or current events, explain how one individual affected the course of history. How might history have been affected had the person not lived? (Some examples might include famous American presidents like Washington, Lincoln, Franklin D. Roosevelt, or John Kennedy; leaders of other countries; great scientists; or such infamous leaders as Hitler or Stalin.)

Chapter 8
History
at Work

The work of responsible historians balancing fact and interpretation appears in this chapter. In "The Greek Mind" and "The Achievement of Rome" respectively, Kitto and Muller argue that Greek and Roman values made possible their great civilizations. Recounting the bubonic plague's movement across Europe in the thirteenth century and assessing its toll on family, church, and government, Tuchman's "This Is the End of the World" shows how a natural event can radically change the face of history. Kitto, Muller, and Tuchman analyze causal relationships; for them, history is the product of human masses. But for some historians, great people shape nations' and causes' destinies. For Catton in "End and Beginning," Booth's assassination of Lincoln and Stanton's response to it prevented a real truce between North and South after the American Civil War. Here the actions of two men, Booth and Stanton, led to an enmity which colored Reconstruction and over a hundred years of American race relations. While Catton looks at the effect of great men on history, Brodie looks at the personal life of one of history's great men, Thomas Jefferson. "My Head and My Heart" studies Jefferson's relationship with Maria Cosway during his tenure as minister to France from the young American republic. From her analysis of Jefferson's letter "My Head and My Heart" and other documents, Brodie argues that the relationship was intimate. Jefferson's letter follows Brodie's essay. Here you will be able to see a historian constructing a historical narrative from data.

The Greek Mind

H.D.F. Kitto

H.D.F. Kitto (1897–1982) taught Greek at the University of Glasgow before joining the faculty at the University of Bristol, where he was a professor of Greek for more than fifteen years. During his academic career, he served as a visiting professor at Cornell University, Brandeis University, and the University of California. An authority in his field, Professor Kitto wrote numerous books on Greek literature and history. The London Times *noted* The Greeks *(1951), the source for this selection, to be a "remarkable introduction to Classical Greece." "The Greek Mind" demonstrates that Greek language and literature informed the ancient Greek's understanding of his world.*

A sense of the wholeness of things is perhaps the most typical feature of the Greek mind. [The Greek language illustrates this wholeness in its use of the words *kalos* (beautiful), *hamartia* (fault), and particularly *aretê* (excellence). The heroic ideal of *arete* was so deep and wide that it was the ideal of the age.]

A sense of the wholeness of things is perhaps the most typical feature of the Greek mind. We have already met some notable expressions of this—the way in which Homer, for all his love of the particular detail and the individual character, yet fixes it firmly into a universal frame; the way in which so many Greeks are several things at once, as Solon is political and economic reformer, man of business, and poet; the way in which the polis itself is not a machine for governing, but something which touches almost the whole of life. The modern mind divides, specializes, thinks in categories: the Greek instinct was the opposite, to take the widest view, to see things as an organic whole. The speeches of Cleon and Diodotus showed precisely the same thing: the particular issue must be generalized.

Let us now try to illustrate this 'wholeness' a little further, beginning with that very Greek thing, the Greek language.

He who is beginning Greek is in constant difficulties with certain words which, he thinks, ought to be simple, and in fact are, but at first seem unexpectedly difficult. There is the word 'kalos' and its opposite 'aischros'. He is told that the former means 'beautiful'. He knows the Latin equivalent, 'pulcher', and is quite happy. He reads of a 'kalê polis', a 'beautiful city'; Homer calls Sparta 'kalligynaikos', 'city of beautiful women'; all is well. But then he reads that Virtue is 'beautiful', that it is a 'beautiful' thing to die for one's country, that the man of great soul 'strives to attain the beautiful'; also that a good weapon or a commodious harbour is 'beautiful'. He concludes that the Greek took an essentially aesthetic view of things; and the conclusion is confirmed when he finds that the word 'aischros', the Latin 'turpis', the English 'base' or 'disgraceful', also means 'ugly', so that a man can be 'base' not only in character but also in appearance. How charming of the Greeks to turn Virtue into Beauty and Vice into Ugliness!

But the Greek is doing nothing of the sort. It is we who are doing that, by dividing concepts into different, though perhaps parallel categories, the moral, the intellectual, the aesthetic, the practical. The Greek did not: even the philosophers were reluctant to do it. When Plato makes Socrates begin an argument by saying, 'You will agree that there is something called the Kalon', we may be sure that he is going to bamboozle the other man by sliding gently from kalon, 'beautiful', to kalon, 'honourable'. The word really means something like 'worthy of warm admiration', and may be used indifferently in any of these categories—rather like our word 'fine'. We have words like this in English: the word 'bad' can be used of conduct, poetry or fish, in each case meaning something quite different, but in Greek this refusal to specialize the meaning is habitual.

The word 'hamartia' means 'error', 'fault', 'crime' or even 'sin'; literally, it means 'missing the mark', 'a bad shot'. We exclaim, 'How intellectualist these Greeks were! Sin is just "missing the mark"; better luck next time!' Again we seem to find confirmation when we find that some of the Greek virtues seem to be as much intellectual as moral—a fact that makes them untranslatable, since our own vocabulary must distinguish. There is 'Sôphrosynê', literally 'whole-minded-ness' or 'unimpaired-mindedness'. According to the context it will mean 'wisdom', 'prudence', 'temperateness', 'chastity', 'sobriety', 'modesty', or 'self-control', that is, something entirely intellectual, something entirely moral, or something intermediate. Our difficulty with the word, as with *hamartia*, is that we think more in departments. *Hamartia*, 'a bad shot', does not mean 'Better luck next time'; it means rather that a mental error is as blameworthy, and may be as deadly, as a moral one.

And then, to complete our education, we find that in regions where we should use intellectual terms, in political theory for example, Greek uses words heavily charged with a moral content. 'An aggressive policy' is likely to be *adikia*, 'injustice', even if it is not *hybris*, 'wanton wickedness'; while 'aggrandizement' or 'profiteering' is *pleonexia*, 'trying to get more than your share', which is both an intellectual and a moral error, a defiance of the laws of the universe.

Let us turn back to Homer for a moment. The poet of the *Iliad* had what some misguided people today think the most necessary qualification for the artist: he was class-conscious. He writes only of kings and princes; the ordinary soldier plays no part in the poem. Moreover, these kings and princes are portrayed sharply with all the limitations of their class and time; they are proud, fierce, vengeful, glorying in war though at the same time hating it. How could it happen then that such heroes could become exemplars and a living inspiration to the later bourgeoisie? Because, being Greeks, they could not see themselves in any context but the widest possible, namely as men. Their ideal was not a specifically knightly ideal, like Chivalry or Love: they called it *aretê*—another typically Greek word. When we meet it in Plato we translate it 'Virtue' and consequently miss all the flavour of it. 'Virtue', at least in modern English, is almost entirely a moral word; *aretê* on the other hand is used indifferently in all the categories and means simply 'excellence'. It may be limited of course by its context; the *aretê* of a race-horse is speed, of a cart-horse strength. If it is used, in a general context, of a man it will connote excellence in the ways in which a man can be excellent—morally, intellectually, physically, practically. Thus the hero of the *Odyssey* is a great fighter, a wily schemer, a ready speaker, a man of stout heart and broad wisdom who knows that he must endure without too much complaining what the gods send; and he can both build and sail a boat, drive a furrow as straight as anyone, beat a young braggart at throwing the discus, challenge the Phaeacian youth at boxing, wrestling or running; flay, skin, cut up and cook an ox, and be moved to tears by a song. He is in fact an excellent all-rounder; he has surpassing *aretê*. So too has the hero of the older poem, Achilles—the most formidable of fighters, the swiftest of runners, and the noblest of soul; and Homer tells us, in one notable verse, how Achilles was educated. His father entrusted the lad to old Phoenix, and told Phoenix to train him to be 'A maker of speeches and a doer of deeds'. The Greek hero tried to combine in himself the virtues which our own heroic age divided between the knight and the churchman.

That is one reason why the epic survived to be the education of a much more civilized age. The heroic ideal of *aretê*, though firmly rooted in its own age and circumstances, was so deep and wide that it could become the ideal of an age that was totally different.

In the passage which I translated from the *Iliad* there is one detail that strikes me as being extremely Greek. 'His heart within his shaggy breast was torn, whether he should . . . slay Atreus' son, or put away his wrath'. Tennyson, translating Virgil, writes, of a similar moment:

> This way and that dividing his swift mind.

The mind, to be sure, is not the heart, but we should be astonished if Tennyson, or Virgil, in mentioning either heart or mind, had at the same time mentioned a physical detail of the body in which this heart or mind resided. Homer finds it perfectly natural to notice that the chest is a hairy one. He sees the whole man at once.

It is not a point to emphasize, but it does introduce another aspect of this wholeness of mind, one in which the Greeks contrasted sharply with the 'barbarians' and with most modern peoples. The sharp distinction which the Christian and the Oriental world has normally drawn between the body and the soul, the physical and the spiritual, was foreign to the Greek—at least until the time of Socrates and Plato. To him there was simply the whole man. That the body is the tomb of the soul is indeed an idea which we meet in certain Greek mystery-religions, and Plato, with his doctrine of immortality, necessarily distinguished sharply between body and soul; but for all that, it is not a typical Greek idea. The Greek made physical training an important part of education, not because he said to himself, 'Look here, we mustn't forget the body', but because it could never occur to him to train anything but the whole man. It was as natural for the polis to have gymnasia as to have a theatre or warships, and they were constantly used by men of all ages, not only for physical but also for mental exercise.

But it is the Games, local and international, which most clearly illustrate this side of the Greek mind. Among us it is sometimes made a reproach that a man 'makes a religion of games'. The Greek did not do this, but he did something perhaps more surprising: he made games part of his religion. To be quite explicit, the Olympian Games, the greatest of the four international festivals, were held in honour of Zeus of Olympia, the Pythian Games in honour of Apollo, the Panathenaic Games in honour of Athena. Moreover, they were held in the sacred precinct. The feeling that prompted this was a perfectly natural one. The contest was a means of stimulating and displaying human *aretê*, and this was a worthy offering to the god. In the same way, games were held in honour of a dead hero, as to Patroclus in the *Iliad*. But since *aretê* is of the mind as well as of the body, there was not the slightest incongruity or affectation in combining musical contests with athletic; a contest in flute-playing was an original fixture in the Pythian Games—for was not Apollo himself 'Lord of the Lyre'?

It was *arete* that the games were designed to test—the *aretê* of the whole man, not a merely specialized skill. The usual events were a sprint, of about 200 yards, the long race (1½ miles), the race in armour, throwing the discus, and the javelin, the long jump, wrestling, boxing (of a very dangerous kind), and chariot-racing. The great event was the pentathlon: a race, a jump, throwing the discus, and the javelin, and wrestling. If you won this, you were a man. Needless to say, the Marathon race was never heard of until modern times: the Greeks would have regarded it as a monstrosity. As for the skill shown by modern champions in games like golf or billiards, the Greeks would certainly have admired it intensely, and thought it an admirable thing—in a slave, supposing that one had no better use for a slave than to train him in this way. Impossible, he would say, to acquire skill like this and at the same time to live the proper life of a man and a citizen. It is this feeling that underlies Aristotle's remark that a gentleman should be able to play the flute—but not too well.

The victor in one of the great games was a Man. He was indeed almost something more, a Hero, and was treated as such by his fellow-citizens. Public honours were paid him—which might include the grant of dinner in the town-hall at the public expense for the rest of his life (something to off-set the Crown of Wild Olive), and, especially among the Dorians, the custom grew of commissioning a poet-composer to write a solemn choral hymn in his honour, for performance at a banquet or at some religious festival. So it came about that of the two most majestic and serious poets of the early fifth century, Aeschylus and Pindar, the latter is known to us entirely (but for some fragments of other poems) as a writer of victory-odes. A strange idea to us, that a serious poet should write odes to athletes. What is more surprising is to find, in such an ode, a passage like this:

He who wins, of a sudden, some noble prize
In the rich years of youth
Is raised high with hope; his manhood takes wings;
He has in his heart what is better than wealth.
But brief is the season of man's delight.
Soon it falls to the ground; some dire decision uproots it.
–Thing of a day! such is man; a shadow of a dream.
Yet when god-given splendour visits him
A bright radiance plays over him, and how sweet is life!
–Aegina, dear mother, guide this city in the path of liberty
Through Zeus, and with the favour of Aeacus the Hero,
And Peleus, and stout Telamon, and Achilles.

This is grand poetry, even when uprooted from its original Greek. For a worthy parallel one has to turn to *Ecclesiastes*. It is the conclusion of an ode written to celebrate the victory in the boys' wrestling match at Delphi of a young gentleman from Aegina.

Not all of Pindar's odes are as sombre as this, by any means. When he wrote this one he was quite an old man, and the Aeginetans—a kindred Dorian people for whom he had very friendly feelings—were menaced by Athens; hence the solemn invocation of Aeginetan heroes at the close. But the seriousness of it is not in the least unusual. Pindar thinks not of the mere athletic event—which he never condescends to describe—but of the *aretê* shown by the victor; and from this it is natural enough, for a Greek poet, to pass to any form of *aretê*, whether in the individual or in the polis. The victory is seen in the widest context.

To Pindar, physical, moral and intellectual excellence—and, be it added, plain Wealth—were all parts of the one whole; one reason, perhaps, why Pindar can make a man feel, while the spell is on him, that he is the only real poet who has ever written. This high conception of the Games, transmuted though it may be, by Pindar, into something higher than the ordinary man's conception, was real enough; but it was nevertheless 'a thing of a day'. 'A bright radiance was on it, and a god-given splendour', but this complete fusion of the physical, the intellectual, the moral, the spiritual and the sensuous disintegrated. Some twenty years after Pindar's death Euripides wrote a scathing passage on Olympic victors, men of brawn and no mind, who receive the adulation of a city to which they contribute nothing; and Pindar himself wrote an ode, his only perfunctory one, for a certain Xenophon of Corinth who seems to have been a semi-professional pot-hunter and nothing more.

This instinct for seeing things as a whole is the source of the essential sanity of Greek life. The Greeks had their passions; their political records are no freer than other peoples' from paroxysms of savagery; the hungry exile would ruin his city if only he could return and rule, whether he was oligarch or democrat. But their standard, in all their activities, was a sane balance. It is difficult to think of a Greek who can be called a fanatic; the religious excesses of the East or of the

Middle Ages find no place in the life of Classical Greece—nor for that matter the less interesting excesses of our own age, such as commercialism. The Greek knew mystical ecstacy, and sought it, in cults of Dionysus, but this was one part of a definite scheme of things. There is great significance in the religious legend that for three months in the year Apollo left Delphi and Dionysus took his place. Euripides draws a portrait of a fanatic—Hippolytus, the pure and virginal worshipper of the virgin goddess Artemis, who will pay no honour to the love-goddess Aphrodite. He is the kind of whom the Middle Ages might have made a saint; Euripides makes of him a tragic misfit; Man must worship both these goddesses, antagonistic though they may seem. Hippolytus is destroyed by the Aphrodite whom he slights, and his Artemis can do nothing to protect him.

FOCUS: READING REVIEW

1. What is the most typical feature of the Greek mind? How does this compare with modern thought?
2. In what ways does the modern misread the concepts of *kalos* (beauty) and *aischros* (ugly)?
3. How did the Olympic games reflect Greek life's wholeness?
4. What role did passions play in the Greek mind?

FOCUS: AUTHOR'S STRATEGIES

1. Kitto has developed his picture of the Greek mind from a series of facts and interpretations. What historical facts are at the center of his study? What part of this selection shows the historian interpreting and shaping the facts?
2. What persona do you find in this selection? What in Kitto's tone and information builds this persona?
3. Explain how Kitto uses a comparative analysis of language to define the Greek mind.

FOCUS: DISCUSSION AND WRITING

1. Explain the concept of *aretê*. How does this differ from our concept of success or excellence?
2. The Greek mind saw the "wholeness of things." Do we think today in terms of wholeness or parts? Point to specific experiences—education, careers, media, religion—to illustrate your answer.
3. The Greek concept of human wholeness dictated the program of the *gymnasia*. Considering your own college curriculum, explain to what degree we seek to educate for human wholeness.

The Achievement of Rome
Herbert J. Muller

In this selection Muller chronicles the historic events that created Rome's greatness and then analyzes the causes, distinctive features, and legacy of the Roman achievement. "The Achievement of Rome," taken from The Uses of the Past, *reflects several of the premises in Muller's essay "The Premises of Inquiry" in chapter 7. We see the "complex of factors"—including the force of human character and ideals—shaping history, and we encounter the historian making value judgments. (Biographical information on Muller precedes "The Premises of Inquiry.")*

The Roman Empire remains one of the greatest historic achievements of man. We owe a tribute to the achievements of the Romans, who were in truth creators and even saviors of a sort. What they saved first of all was the legacy of Greece; they gave it their own practical bent, however. The practical sense of the Romans also led to some original contributions, notably their monumental architecture and their engineering achievements. [Another secular but still majestic achievement was the Roman law, which is still incorporated in Western law.] The main principles of Roman justice are indispensable for any system of international law, or any hope of a world order. No better key to the success of the Romans exists than the vague, unscientific, old-fashioned concept of 'character,' a character marked by courage, temperance, grave dignity, and a high sense of duty.

Never before, wrote Polybius, had Fortune 'accomplished such a work, achieved such a triumph,' as the establishment of the Roman Empire. 'What man is so indifferent or so idle that he would not wish to know how and under what form of government almost all the inhabited world came under the single rule of the Romans in less than fifty-three years?' Polybius was a Greek, however. The Romans were less curious, and had less understanding of what they had wrought in these fifty years (220–168 B.C.). They had not consciously set out to rule the world. They had emerged as the greatest power in the Mediterranean by defeating Carthage, in a terrific life-and-death struggle; then one conquest led to another almost in spite of them, and the rolling stone gathered an empire. Some of their senators even tried to circumvent the designs of Fortune, opposing further expansion as a threat to their rule at home. For Rome itself, in fact, the immediate result of the epoch-making triumph was corruption, class war, increasing chaos. Nevertheless the Roman Empire continued to expand, during a century of bloody civil war, until it finally destroyed the Roman Republic.

When the great Augustus restored peace and order, he deliberately called a halt to the career of conquest. Beginning as an unscrupulous, ruthless politician, he ended as the wise, just statesman who established the famous Principate, a monarchy under an elaborate cloak of republican forms—perhaps the most pious hoax in political history. In his old age, deeply troubled by the moral corruption that accompanied the peace and prosperity he had restored to Rome, Augustus thought he had failed. A century later Tacitus was still disposed to agree with him. The greatest of Roman historians had little idea of the momentous history the Empire was making; aware chiefly of its attendant evils, he pined for the grand old days of the Republic. (The Romans in turn apparently had little idea of Tacitus' own greatness, since his friend Pliny is the only known writer to refer to him until three hundred years later, when Marcellinus—a Greek—set about a continuation of the histories.) Yet the creation of Augustus stood up for some centuries. It has been hailed as 'the supreme achievement in the history of statesmanship.' It led the Romans to inscribe the motto *Æternitas* on their coins, and to cling to this illusion while their empire was crumbling, undergoing a still bloodier anarchy than had resulted from its rise. After Rome was sacked by Alaric in the year 410, the poet Rutilius christened it the 'Eternal City'; when Rome finally 'fell,' in the year 476 according to our history texts, contemporaries did not notice its fall— as Ferdinand Lot remarks, it fell without a sound. A few decades later the chronicler Cassidorus saw nothing exceptional in the events of this famous year. And in fact it did not mark the fall of an empire. The Western provinces were taken over by the Germans, who for all practical purposes had long controlled them; but the Eastern Roman Empire went on.

Such, in rough outline, is the story of the Roman Empire, which has haunted Western historians ever since, and whose fall has been considered 'the most important problem of universal history.' Easterners may add ironic postscripts. The rise and fall of Rome did not shake the whole world; it had little effect on the older, wealthier, more populous East. Neither was its endurance so remarkable. Although Westerners are pleased to observe that some great nations have not lasted as long as it took Rome to fall, it can hardly match the East for longevity. Compared to Egypt, which endured for some thousands of years (and remained a major source of the wealth of Rome), it was a flash in the pan. So now our universal historians are tending to reduce it to just another empire. To Spengler it was a mere 'civilization,' the inevitably sordid, futile dying phase of Hellenic culture; he echoes the verdict that the grandeur of Rome was 'a violent and vulgar fraud.' To Toynbee it was a mere 'universal state,' which is the next to the last stage of a disintegrating society; he holds that in this stage the only role for creative personalities is that of savior, and the great Romans were not saviors. They even persecuted the followers of the true Saviour.

Nevertheless the Roman Empire remains one of the greatest historic achievements of man. If the abysmal Dark Ages that followed it are an ironic comment on its presumptions as an Eternal City, they also deepen the tragedy of its fall, which appears as the worst setback in the history of civilization. For East and West alike Rome is far more significant than Egypt, as the grandest symbol of the ideals of universal peace, law, and order that men are again seeking to realize. Created by force and fraud, like all other empires—created almost absent-mindedly, and full of anomalies to the end—it became different from all other empires by aspiring to be a genuine commonwealth. Its greater rulers were concerned with the welfare of their subject peoples, not merely with the power, wealth, and glory of the Romans; after Augustus these peoples were not merely resigned to Roman rule but were grateful for it. It is unique in the extravagant tributes it elicited from its subjects. One example is the oration of Aristeides, a Greek contemporary of Marcus Aurelius:

> Before the establishment of your empire the World was in confusion, upside down, adrift and out of control; but as soon as you Romans intervened the turmoils and factions ceased, and life and politics were illumined by the dawn of an era of universal order... You Romans are the only rulers known to History who have reigned over freemen... The lustre of your rule is unsullied by any breath of ungenerous hostility; and the reason is that you yourselves set the example of generosity by sharing all your power and privileges with your subjects ... with the result that in your day a combination has been achieved which previously appeared quite impossible—the combination of consummate power with consummate benevolence... Rome is a citadel which has all the peoples of the Earth for its villagers. And Rome has never failed those who have looked to her.

Rome soon did fail them—wretchedly. Within a generation after Aristeides the empire was convulsed by military anarchy; and the benevolent Marcus Aurelius, the inspiration of this tribute, himself touched off the anarchy by fondly naming his worthless son Commodus as his successor. As with the Greeks, the failure was not a tragic accident—it was a moral and intellectual failure. But it deserves our study because it was a great tragic drama in its own right, not merely an epilogue to the tragedy of Greece. We too owe a tribute to the achievements of the Romans, who were in truth creators and even saviors of a sort.

What they saved first of all was the legacy of Greece. Far less brilliant, original, and versatile than the Greeks, the Romans were content to borrow most of their culture from them. They gave it their own practical bent, however, translating it into terms more suitable for universal use. They were able to transmit it to the barbaric West and thereby to lay the foundations of modern Europe.[1] Thus they systematized education, bequeathing the seven liberal arts to the Middle Ages. They adapted Greek philosophy to daily needs, applying it to government and recasting it into a philosophy of life available to men without high gifts. They developed the type of cultivated gentleman or man of the world—the type of Cicero, Horace, and Pliny the Younger, who were less spontaneous and exciting than the Greeks but more moderate, urbane, and sensible. Even their pompous rhetoricians did a valuable service by consolidating the power and prestige of the word, siring the profession of letters; in time these bores had such progeny as Petrarch, Montaigne, and Voltaire.

The practical sense of the Romans also led to some original contributions, notably their monumental architecture. While the Greeks stuck to their simple post and lintel, the Romans exploited the possibilities of the arch, the dome, and the vault to erect baths, palaces, amphitheatres, and government buildings, which provide a model for public buildings to this day. (Grand Central Station is among their countless offspring.) Still more characteristic were their engineering achievements, such as the famous roads, bridges, and aqueducts. As Frontinus contemplated the fourteen aqueducts, totaling some thirteen thousand miles, that brought Rome as much water as any modern city has, he made a typically Roman remark: 'Who will venture to compare with these mighty conduits the idle Pyramids, or the famous but useless works of the Greeks?' This is the Philistine talking: celebrating size and utility, revealing the deep-seated contempt of the Romans for mere artists, betraying the reason why their art was mostly anonymous, given to shoddy reproductions, and often coarse, gross, even brutal. Yet only a snob, with a vulgar fear of being vulgar, can dismiss the Romans as mere Philistines. In their great building enterprises they often displayed a bold imagination, a vigorous sense of form-and-function, that produced a genuine grandeur. Their architecture was more humanistic than the Greek in that it contributed much more to civic life; nor were they betraying culture when they added the sewer, the bath, and the house with central heating. They built many splendid cities that were pleasant both to live in and to look at. Their mode of life was at once more comfortable and hygienic than the common life of Europe today, and more gracious than the American.[2]

At least the mighty aqueducts are clearly more admirable than the 'idle Pyramids,' which served no purpose whatever except to gratify the monstrous conceit of the Pharaohs. By contrast with such aspirations to immortality, another secular achievement of the Romans appears still more majestic. This was the Roman law. A code that was at first designed to provide for the commercial needs of foreigners in their cities, in time it generated provisions binding on both foreigners and citizens, and finally, under the influence of Greek philosophical ideas, became the *Jus Gentium*—a universal law such as the Greeks never developed. Much Roman law is still incorporated in Western law, where it may be an anachronism, but its everlasting importance lies in its basic principles. The foundation of Justice, Cicero had declared, was a Law 'implanted in Nature,' discoverable by 'right reason,' and therefore available to all men by virtue of their natural endowments of reason. This 'true law' was universal and inalterable, 'valid for all nations and all times,' above mere custom and opinion; it could not be abolished by any legislation. It implied, as the later jurist Ulpian explicitly declared, that 'all men are equal.' Roman law accordingly protected the individual against the state.[3]

Apart from the shortcomings of Roman legal practice, one may question even the ideal theory of an eternal law independent of man and society, authored by 'Nature.' At least men of reason have not yet been able to reach agreement on the dictates of this absolute, immutable law. Yet they may agree—as the English-speaking peoples in particular have agreed—that the basic law of the land should be above the wishes of any one man or group, and should guarantee rights not subject to majority opinion. Universal principles of equity may be grounded on uniformities in the nature of man and social life, instead of on a deified Nature. They may be just as valid for our time if we grant that they were not valid for the ape-man, and may not be valid for the man of A.D. 1,000,000. The main principles of Roman justice, at any rate, are indispensable for any system of international law, or any hope of a world order. Their law remains their greatest intellectual and moral achievement, their chief contribution to a free society. And it was the foundation of the enduring glory of their empire—an empire that was first won by military conquest but really won by law and peace.

'Rome made a city what was once a world,' Rutilius could sing after it had been sacked. The consciousness of this world mission dawned under Augustus, who inspired Virgil's *Aeneid*—one of the noblest monuments to new ideals in the history of new eras. So grievous were the travails of Aeneas—'so great was the labor of founding the Roman race'—because he was founding a world: the rise of Rome meant 'a new hope for the human race, a hope of peace, of order, of civilization.' In the political terms of Marcus Aurelius, it meant 'a state in which there is the same law for all, a policy of equal rights and freedom of speech, and the idea of a kingly government that most of all respects the freedom of the governed.' Here was the fulfillment of the classical ideal toward which later Greek thinkers had been groping: an Earthly City in which the State is supreme, subordinating the claims of the individual, but subjecting its great power to the claims of natural reason and equity, and devoting itself to the service of man. The *polis* was now *cosmopolis*. 'The whole of this Universe is to be regarded as one single commonwealth of gods and men,' wrote Cicero. 'For me as Antoninus,' added Marcus Aurelius, 'my city and fatherland is Rome, but as man, the world.' His highest obligation, he took for granted, was to the world; and because he took it for granted, and really meant it, he threw in no cant about the white man's burden.

Needless to add, Rome fell short of this ideal; yet it came near enough to haunt the mind of Europe ever since. For it did more than conceive an abstract idealism—such idealism may also be found in Ikhnaton, Ashoka, Akbar,[4] and other great emperors in other societies. Rome alone succeeded in embodying the ideal in a heterogeneous empire, maintaining it through different dynasties. It provided such material means to unity as its superb system of roads, which made travel easier, faster, and safer than it was in Europe and the Near East until the last century. It planted cities everywhere, introducing the vigorous civic life of the Hellenistic East to western Europe. Above all, it brought the *Pax Romana*—the longest period of continuous peace in the annals of imperial history. After Augustus deliberately refrained from further aggression there were occasional campaigns on the borders, but chiefly for defensive purposes. Within the empire there were no serious rebellions except for the uprisings of the intractable Hebrews. For almost two hundred years the Mediterranean world enjoyed a relative peace that it has never known since, least of all in the last hundred years.

According to Toynbee, this period was the 'Indian summer' of the Hellenic society. We can now see that it was the prelude to disaster, and so must presently consider the reasons for the disaster. Yet transitory as it was, the Roman achievement was vastly impressive, Toynbee oversimplifies both the success and the failure of the empire when he treats it as merely a phase of the 'Hellenic society.' If the Greeks provided the cultural foundations of the Mediterranean world, they failed to organize and unify it, make it a real society. The immediate question is why the Romans succeeded where the brilliant Greeks failed.

As usual, the answer is not simply inspiring. The men who made the empire were not crusaders; and none had the Hebrew faith in a heavenly kingdom on earth, or the modern faith in progress. Nor was religion the inspiration of the Romans. Their ancient religion was wholly practical, a matter of pious prudence rather than deep faith or lofty aspiration. Their countless gods for the occasions of daily life were vague or abstract, 'earth-spirits' who required a scrupulous observance of traditional ceremonies but promised no rewards in a life to come; their priests, in the words of Dean Inge, were 'professors of spiritual jurisprudence,' carefully carrying out the letter of the prescribed contract long after the origin or meaning of the contract had been lost sight of. (G.F. Moore notes that when the antiquarian Varro set out to collect and classify the ancient rituals he found 'gods whose names were perpetuated in the calendar, but whose cult had long since been extinct; priesthoods and sodalities whose functions had been forgotten; rites whose motive and meaning no man knew.') After Augustus, the emperors were added to the old gods, but this new cult induced no more exaltation; although Orientals worshiped the emperors during their lifetime, the practical Romans waited until they had died, and then set them up as deities only if they had earned the honor by good works. When the Romans turned to the mystery religions their more spiritual faith did not carry them to greater heights; the gain in spirituality was a loss in vitality. The faith that made Rome great was essentially secular. The real religion of Rome, as of Periclean Athens, was patriotism.

At the same time, the famed political genius of the Romans calls for serious qualification. Certainly no practical genius was displayed in their institutions. Their Republic was a fantastic system of checks and balances, seemingly designed to prevent any hope of efficiency and continuity. Among its elaborate impracticalities were two consuls, who could veto each other and were changed annually, and ten tribunes, each of whom could veto the consuls and all the rest of the tribunes. While the supreme authority theoretically rested in the popular assembly, the government was in fact run by the aristocratic Senate, which constitutionally had no control over either legislation or executive action, and displayed its astuteness most conspicuously in thwarting or nullifying the will of the voters. When this system broke down, with the rise of the powerful generals and volunteer armies who won the empire that the Senate did not want and could not run, Augustus set up the Principate, which retained all the forms of the Republic and emptied them of political substance. Priding himself upon his constitutionalism, Augustus nevertheless gave supreme power to the Emperor; while supposed to rule in the interests of the State, the Emperor alone decided what those interests were. The popular assembly soon disappeared while the Senate came to act chiefly as an imperial rubber stamp or publicity bureau. And although everything depended on the character and ability of the emperor, there was no one customary or constitutional procedure for choosing him—he might be designated by the ruling emperor, the Senate, or the army.

The apparent political genius of the Romans, in short, was their ability to keep a preposterous system working. They were much like the English in their reverence for forms, their reliance on tradition rather than logic, their habit of muddling through. At best, their practical sense made them more adaptable than the subtler, more ingenious Greeks; sustained by their ancient forms, they could take liberties untroubled by theoretical inconsistencies, or unaware of them. The genius of Augustus in particular lay in his unconscious blend of conservatism and realism. Always maintaining a pious regard for the Senate and the old families, he built his Principate on the enterprising middle class, whose interest in commerce was scorned by the old families. He made it the administrative class, creating the civil service that the aristocratic Republic had failed to set up. The basis of his Principate was not a constitution but a bureaucracy. The guarantor of law and order in his Empire was the institution of red tape, which has also been called the mother of freedom.

Ultimately, I can find no better key to the success of the Romans than the vague, unscientific, old-fashioned concept of 'character.' This does not really explain history, since the origin and persistence of character have in turn to be explained; neither does character guarantee historic success. Nevertheless it is a social reality, and none is more important for our human purposes. Although Livy was unaware of major factors that are now commonplaces of historical knowledge, he was not merely naïve when he made the central theme of his history the faith of the Romans in themselves and their ancient virtues, *gravitas, pietas,* and *simplicitas.*[5] As early as Polybius men were deploring the moral corruption of Rome—the notorious corruption that persisted over six centuries, providing an endless text for Christian preachers and prophets of doom. Yet the famous iron character of the Romans also persisted. They clung to the ideal of discipline they had introduced—an ideal that outside of Sparta was seldom realized by the supposedly measured Greeks. They continued to produce their great types of the soldier, the magistrate, the senator, the proconsul—models of courage, temperance, grave dignity, and high sense of duty. The middle class elevated by Augustus and his successors carried on the tradition of public spirit. The emperors themselves, for all the vicious weaklings and despots among them, maintained a remarkably high average of responsible, patriotic rule. History cannot match the century of Nerva, Trajan, Hadrian, Antoninus Pius, and Marcus Aurelius—a succession of emperors who differed in temperament and policy but alike ruled as devoted servants, not masters of the commonwealth.

As old-fashioned is the most apparent source of this strength of character—the Roman family. Famous for their public spirit, the Romans were nevertheless devoted to domestic life and created the home as we know it (or knew it until this century). Woman had an honored position, as wife and mother; the sense of duty to the parents and the spirits of the ancestors was almost as strong as in China; the household gods—the *Lares* and *Penates*—were the most vital of the deities, long surviving the official religion. Such loyalty to family and home helps to explain why the Romans were more consistently and profoundly patriotic than the early Greeks, whose religion was also patriotism. In their all-engrossing public life, the Greeks were apt to talk too much, get lost in generalities and abstractions, or make a habit of dispute; at least they might have been less volatile and erratic if they had known the privacy, sobriety, and security of the ancestral home. The distinctive virtues of the Romans were also strengthened by their less civilized religion. Unimaginative, unreasoned, and unexalted, it instilled piety and order by endless ritual, solemnizing all phases of public and private life, uniting the family and the nation.

This severe Roman character had severe limitations, which will concern us later. At his best, the good Roman was more admirable than attractive. Straitlaced, distrustful of individuality and genius, suspicious of art and speculative thought, indifferent even to science, incapable of understanding Plato, Archimedes, and Christ alike—'he could only rule the world,' Will Durant concludes. Still, we should first admire his gravity; and if we are sympathetic we may see him unbend. Even the scandal-mongering Suetonius presents some attractive pictures of the Caesars. Thus we see the Emperor Vespasian, the old soldier and commoner, with his habitual 'expression of one who was straining at stool,' complaining of the wearisome pomp on the day of his triumph, ridiculing the efforts to dress up his lowly ancestors, and on his deathbed remarking, 'Alas, I think I am becoming a god.'

Indeed, the Romans could not have ruled the world so long and so well had they not had a measure of flexibility. In their grave pride, their sureness of themselves, they were capable of a liberality that for practical purposes was more beneficial than the intellectual liberality of Athens. Like the Greeks, they were free from religious bigotry.[6] 'If the gods are insulted,' said the matter-of-fact Emperor Tiberius, 'let them see to it themselves.' The Romans likewise had relatively little racial and cultural prejudice. While looking down on the Greeks as effete, they also paid them many tributes, including the supreme tribute of going to school under them. They regarded their more gifted slaves as potential citizens, permitting them to earn their freedom, and as freedmen to rise to high positions. (Tenney Frank observes that slaves in the Roman Empire had better opportunities than the mass of workers in Europe until recent times.) Hence they enlisted good will by respecting the customs as well as protecting the legal rights of their provincials. They were content with a commonwealth that was indeed a wealth of diverse cultures. In effect, the basic aim of their empire was not uniformity but unity.

This wisdom was discarded after the empire became Christian; the emperors now sought to impose religious uniformity. When medieval Europe tried to recover the Roman universal ideal it made the same mistake; later it was torn by strife because both Catholics and Protestants insisted on the necessity of uniform belief. Today, as men again seek to revive the *Pax Romana* in a world order, they are again wrangling in the conviction that the one world must be all democratic, or all capitalistic, or all communistic. Even high-minded idealists are apt to conceive the ideal as political or religious uniformity; they merely tolerate cultural differences, as an unfortunate necessity. I should say that the Roman ideal of unity amid diversity is not only the most we can hope for—it is the best we could ask for.

Notes

[1] German historians are fond of talking of the lusty, original genius of the Teutonic peoples and their potentially splendid culture. The fact remains, however, that these peoples did not build a civilization all by themselves. Directly or indirectly, they were educated by the Romans. [Muller]

[2] The famous American bathroom, incidentally, incorporates only one process of the elaborate Roman bath—a unique institution that is now known as the Turkish bath, because it was borrowed by the Turks from Byzantium. This civilized institution was completely destroyed by the barbarians of the West, with the aid of Christian ascetics; and when civilization rose anew in the Middle Ages it clung to the squalor of the Orient. As H.J. Randall observes, the ages of faith have been ages of dirt. [Muller]

[3] On such counts the Roman law was an advance beyond the Code of Hammurabi, the most famous legal achievement of the ancient East. Although this Code included many humane provisions, and in a Prologue announced Hammurabi's divine mission "to prevent the strong from oppressing the weak," it contained nothing about the rights of the people against the state. [Muller]

[4] Ikhnaton (?-1358? B.C.) was king and religious reformer in Egypt. Akbar (1542-1605) served as the Mogul emperor of Hindustan.

[5] *gravitas, pietas, simplicitas:* literally, weight, piety, and simplicity. "Weight" carries the connotation of solemnity and earnestness.

[6] The notorious persecution of the Christians was not really an exception, for its motives were political rather than religious. In their fear of idolatry, the Christians refused to make the nominal obeisances required by the imperial cult—a patriotic duty comparable to saluting the flag; all who paid such perfunctory respects to the emperor were free to worship their own gods. (At that, the Jews were exempted from these ceremonial requirements, as a peculiar people; the Christians got into trouble only when they separated themselves from the Jews and became still more peculiar.) Until Diocletian, moreover, the persecution sprang largely from popular hostility to a sect known as "enemies of the human race" because they rejoiced in the prospect of the imminent destruction of Rome, in a universal holocaust. Given all the other popular superstitions about the infernal Christians—such as their reputation for cannibalism, owing to the custom of eating the flesh and blood of the Son of Man—it is surprising that they escaped with so little persecution. The number of victims was greatly exaggerated by later monks, with whom the manufacture of martyrs

became a thriving industry. Thus the bones of many ordinary Romans in the catacombs of Rome became the bones of saints. [Muller]

FOCUS: READING REVIEW

1. According to Muller, how did the Romans come to rule the world?
2. Why was the Roman empire one of "the greatest historic achievements of man"?
3. What aspects of the Greek culture did the Romans borrow?
4. What were the original contributions of the "practical" Romans?
5. What was the key to Rome's success? To what evidence does Muller point to support this?
6. What lesson does the Roman achievement have for modern man?
7. What values in Rome emerge as values admired by the author?

FOCUS: AUTHOR'S STRATEGIES

1. Muller combines historical narrative and process analysis, with an analysis of Rome's achievements. What are the time demarcations in the process analysis? What are the analytic components of Rome's achievement?
2. The author presents several historians' views of Rome. What does this contribute to your understanding of the author's purpose?
3. Muller creates for the modern reader a picture of Rome colored by interpretation. What facts does he provide? How does his selection and emphasis shape the meaning he offers?

FOCUS: DISCUSSION AND WRITING

1. How does the Roman ideal Muller identifies compare with America's ideals?
2. Using Muller's analytic components, compare and contrast Rome's achievement with America's achievement. Cite specific historical events to illustrate your comparative analysis.
3. Muller says that the real religion of Rome was patriotism. Can you make a similar assertion about the United States? What features in American society illustrate your view?

This Is the End of the World

Barbara Tuchman

Barbara Tuchman (b. 1912) began her writing career as a staff writer and foreign correspondent for Nation *magazine following her graduation from Radcliffe College. Although she had published three earlier books, her 1962 study of World War I,* The Guns of August, *won her critical acclaim, a Pulitzer Prize, and recognition for historical accuracy. She followed this with* The Proud Tower *(1966) and* Stilwell and the American Experience in China *(1971), which also received a Pulitzer Prize. A* Distant Mirror

*(1978) chooses an individual person's life, Enguerrand de Coucy, as a ve-
hicle for a narrative about the fourteenth century. Her study examines both
political and economic history's large patterns and society's minute details—marriage, religion, work, taxes. The chapter "This Is the End of the
World" chronicles the spread of the bubonic plague—the black death.
Tuchman's vivid language re-creates the horror that must have accompanied the disease's decimation of a huge population.*

[The bubonic plague, the black death, entered Europe in 1347 through Sicily on
Genoese trading ships from the Crimea. It spread throughout Europe, accomplishing
its kill within four to six months in a given area.] Although the mortality rate was
erratic, ranging from one fifth in some places to nine tenths or almost total elimination in others, the overall estimate of modern demographers is that "a third of Europe died." [In human terms this meant that people died without last rites, deserted
villages sank back into wilderness, monasteries disappeared, work on cathedrals
stopped, the rich fled to country villas, and the urban poor died in burrows. Both rich
and poor died, with particularly high mortality rates among priests and physicians.]
Ignorance of the illness's cause augmented the horror. [Although learned doctors
looked to astral influence], the people at large saw but one explanation—the wrath of
God. If the plague were punishment, there had to be terrible sin to have occasioned
it. The result was an underground lake of guilt in the soul.

In October 1347, two months after the fall of Calais, Genoese trading ships put
into the harbor of Messina in Sicily with dead and dying men at the oars. The
ships had come from the Black Sea port of Caffa (now Feodosiya) in the Crimea,
where the Genoese maintained a trading post. The diseased sailors showed strange
black swellings about the size of an egg or an apple in the armpits and groin. The
swellings oozed blood and pus and were followed by spreading boils and black
blotches on the skin from internal bleeding. The sick suffered severe pain and died
quickly within five days of the first symptoms. As the disease spread, other symptoms of continuous fever and spitting of blood appeared instead of the swellings or
buboes. These victims coughed and sweated heavily and died even more quickly,
within three days or less, sometimes in 24 hours. In both types everything that
issued from the body—breath, sweat, blood from the buboes and lungs, bloody
urine, and blood-blackened excrement—smelled foul. Depression and despair accompanied the physical symptoms, and before the end "death is seen seated on the
face."

The disease was bubonic plague, present in two forms: one that infected the
bloodstream, causing the buboes and internal bleeding, and was spread by contact;
and a second, more virulent pneumonic type that infected the lungs and was
spread by respiratory infection. The presence of both at once cause the high mortality and speed of contagion. So lethal was the disease that cases were known of
persons going to bed well and dying before they woke, of doctors catching the
illness at a bedside and dying before the patient. So rapidly did it spread from one

to another that to a French physician, Simon de Covino, it seemed as if one sick person "could infect the whole world." The malignity of the pestilence appeared more terrible because its victims knew no prevention and no remedy.

The physical suffering of the disease and its aspect of evil mystery were expressed in a strange Welsh lament which saw "death coming into our midst like black smoke, a plague which cuts off the young, a rootless phantom which has no mercy for fair countenance. Woe is me of the shilling in the armpit! It is seething, terrible . . . a head that gives pain and causes a loud cry . . . a painful angry knob . . . Great is its seething like a burning cinder . . . a grievous thing of ashy color." Its eruption is ugly like the "seeds of black peas, broken fragments of brittle sea-coal . . . the early ornaments of black death, cinders of the peelings of the cockle weed, a mixed multitude, a black plague like halfpence, like berries. . . ."

Rumors of a terrible plague supposedly arising in China and spreading through Tartary (Central Asia) to India and Persia, Mesopotamia, Syria, Egypt, and all of Asia Minor had reached Europe in 1346. They told of a death toll so devastating that all of India was said to be depopulated, whole territories covered by dead bodies, other areas with no one left alive. As added up by Pope Clement VI at Avignon, the total of reported dead reached 23,840,000. In the absence of a concept of contagion, no serious alarm was felt in Europe until the trading ships brought their black burden of pestilence into Messina while other infected ships from the Levant carried it to Genoa and Venice.

By January 1348 it penetrated France via Marseille, and North Africa via Tunis. Shipborne along coasts and navigable rivers, it spread westward from Marseille through the ports of Languedoc to Spain and northward up the Rhône to Avignon, where it arrived in March. It reached Narbonne, Montpellier, Carcassonne, and Toulouse between February and May, and at the same time in Italy spread to Rome and Florence and their hinterlands. Between June and August it reached Bordeaux, Lyon, and Paris, spread to Burgundy and Normandy, and crossed the Channel from Normandy into southern England. From Italy during the same summer it crossed the Alps into Switzerland and reached eastward to Hungary.

In a given area the plague accomplished its kill within four to six months and then faded, except in the larger cities, where, rooting into the close-quartered population, it abated during the winter, only to reappear in spring and rage for another six months.

In 1349 it resumed in Paris, spread to Picardy, Flanders, and the Low Countries, and from England to Scotland and Ireland as well as to Norway, where a ghost ship with a cargo of wool and a dead crew drifted offshore until it ran aground near Bergen. From there the plague passed into Sweden, Denmark, Prussia, Iceland, and as far as Greenland. Leaving a strange pocket of immunity in Bohemia, and Russia unattacked until 1351, it had passed from most of Europe by mid-1350. Although the mortality rate was erratic, ranging from one fifth in some places to nine tenths or almost total elimination in others, the overall estimate of modern demographers[1] has settled—for the area extending from India to Iceland—around the same figure expressed in Froissart's[2] casual words: "a third of the world died." His estimate, the common one at the time, was not an inspired guess but a borrowing of St. John's figure for mortality from plague in Revelation, the favorite guide to human affairs of the Middle Ages.

A third of Europe would have meant about 20 million deaths. No one knows in truth how many died. Contemporary reports were an awed impression, not an accurate count. In crowded Avignon, it was said, 400 died daily; 7,000 houses emptied by death were shut up; a single graveyard received 11,000 corpses in six weeks; half the city's inhabitants reportedly died, including 9 cardinals or one third of the total, and 70 lesser prelates. Watching the endlessly passing death carts, chroniclers let normal exaggeration take wings and put the Avignon death toll at 62,000 and even at 120,000, although the city's total population was probably less than 50,000.

When graveyards filled up, bodies at Avignon were thrown into the Rhône until mass burial pits were dug for dumping the corpses. In London in such pits corpses piled up in layers until they overflowed. Everywhere reports speak of the sick dying too fast for the living to bury. Corpses were dragged out of homes and left in front of doorways. Morning light revealed new piles of bodies. In Florence the dead were gathered up by the Compagnia della Misericordia—founded in 1244 to care for the sick—whose members wore red robes and hoods masking the face except for the eyes. When their efforts failed, the dead lay putrid in the streets for days at a time. When no coffins were to be had, the bodies were laid on boards, two or three at once, to be carried to graveyards or common pits. Families dumped their own relatives into the pits, or buried them so hastily and thinly "that dogs dragged them forth and devoured their bodies."

Amid accumulating death and fear of contagion, people died without last rites and were buried without prayers, a prospect that terrified the last hours of the stricken. A bishop in England gave permission to laymen to make confession to each other as was done by the Apostles, "or if no man is present then even to a woman," and if no priest could be found to administer extreme unction, "then faith must suffice." Clement VI found it necessary to grant remissions of sin to all who died of the plague because so many were unattended by priests. "And no bells tolled," wrote a chronicler of Siena, "and nobody wept no matter what his loss because almost everyone expected death. . . . And people said and believed, 'This is the end of the world.' "

In Paris, where the plague lasted through 1349, the reported death rate was 800 a day, in Pisa 500, in Vienna 500 to 600. The total dead in Paris numbered 50,000 or half the population. Florence, weakened by the famine of 1347, lost three to four fifths of its citizens, Venice two thirds, Hamburg and Bremen, though smaller in size, about the same proportion. Cities, as centers of transportation, were more likely to be affected than villages, although once a village was infected, its death rate was equally high. At Givry, a prosperous village in Burgundy of

1,200 to 1,500 people, the parish register records 615 deaths in the space of fourteen weeks, compared to an average of thirty deaths a year in the previous decade. In three villages of Cambridgeshire, manorial records show a death rate of 47 percent, 57 percent, and in one case 70 percent. When the last survivors, too few to carry on, moved away, a deserted village sank back into the wilderness and disappeared from the map altogether, leaving only a grass-covered ghostly outline to show where mortals once had lived.

In enclosed places such as monasteries and prisons, the infection of one person usually meant that of all, as happened in the Franciscan convents of Carcassonne and Marseille, where every inmate without exception died. Of the 140 Dominicans at Montpellier only seven survived. Petrarch's brother Gherardo, member of a Carthusian monastery, buried the prior and 34 fellow monks one by one, sometimes three a day, until he was left alone with his dog and fled to look for a place that would take him in. Watching every comrade die, men in such places could not but wonder whether the strange peril that filled the air had not been sent to exterminate the human race. In Kilkenny, Ireland, Brother John Clyn of the Friars Minor, another monk left alone among dead men, kept a record of what had happened lest "things which should be remembered perish with time and vanish from the memory of those who come after us." Sensing "the whole world, as it were, placed within the grasp of the Evil One," and waiting for death to visit him too, he wrote, "I leave parchment to continue this work, if perchance any man survive and any of the race of Adam escape this pestilence and carry on the work which I have begun." Brother John, as noted by another hand, died of the pestilence, but he foiled oblivion.

The largest cities of Europe, with populations of about 100,000, were Paris and Florence, Venice and Genoa. At the next level, with more than 50,000, were Ghent and Bruges in Flanders, Milan, Bologna, Rome, Naples, and Palermo, and Cologne. London hovered below 50,000, the only city in England except York with more than 10,000. At the level of 20,000 to 50,000 were Bordeaux, Toulouse, Montpellier, Marseille, and Lyon in France, Barcelona, Seville, and Toledo in Spain, Siena, Pisa, and other secondary cities in Italy, and the Hanseatic trading cities of the Empire. The plague raged through them all, killing anywhere from one third to two thirds of their inhabitants. Italy, with a total population of 10 to 11 million, probably suffered the heaviest toll. Following the Florentine bankruptcies, the crop failures and workers' riots of 1346-47, the revolt of Cola di Rienzi that plunged Rome into anarchy, the plague came as the peak of successive calamities. As if the world were indeed in the grasp of the Evil One, its first appearance on the European mainland in January 1348 coincided with a fearsome earthquake that carved a path of wreckage from Naples up to Venice. Houses collapsed, church towers toppled, villages were crushed, and the destruction reached as far as Germany and Greece. Emotional response, dulled by horrors, underwent a kind of atrophy epitomized by the chronicler who wrote, "And in these days was burying without sorrowe and wedding without friendschippe."

In Siena, where more than half the inhabitants died of the plague, work was abandoned on the great cathedral, planned to be the largest in the world, and never resumed, owing to loss of workers and master masons and "the melancholy and grief" of the survivors. The cathedral's truncated transept still stands in permanent witness to the sweep of death's scythe. Agnolo di Tura, a chronicler of Siena, recorded the fear of contagion that froze every other instinct. "Father abandoned child, wife husband, one brother another," he wrote, "for this plague seemed to strike through the breath and sight. And so they died. And no one could be found to bury the dead for money or friendship. ... And I, Angolo di Tura, called the Fat, buried my five children with my own hands, and so did many others likewise."

There were many to echo his account of inhumanity and few to balance it, for the plague was not the kind of calamity that inspired mutual help. Its loathsomeness and deadliness did not herd people together in mutual distress, but only prompted their desire to escape each other. "Magistrates and notaries refused to come and make the wills of the dying," reported a Franciscan friar of Piazza in Sicily; what was worse, "even the priests did not come to hear their confessions." A clerk of the Archbishop of Canterbury reported the same of English priests who "turned away from the care of their benefices from fear of death." Cases of parents deserting children and children their parents were reported across Europe from Scotland to Russia. The calamity chilled the hearts of men, wrote Boccaccio in his famous account of the plague in Florence that serves as introduction to the *Decameron*. "One man shunned another ... kinsfolk held aloof, brother was forsaken by brother, oftentimes husband by wife; nay, what is more, and scarcely to be believed, fathers and mothers were found to abandon their own children to their fate, untended, unvisited as if they had been strangers." Exaggeration and literary pessimism were common in the 14th century, but the Pope's physician, Guy de Chauliac, was a sober, careful observer who reported the same phenomenon: "A father did not visit his son, nor the son his father. Charity was dead."

Yet not entirely. In Paris, according to the chronicler Jean de Venette, the nuns of the Hôtel Dieu or municipal hospital, "having no fear of death, tended the sick with all sweetness and humility." New nuns repeatedly took the places of those who died, until the majority "many times renewed by death now rest in peace with Christ as we may piously believe."

When the plague entered northern France in July 1348, it settled first in Normandy and, checked by winter, gave Picardy a deceptive interim until the next summer. Either in mourning or warning, black flags were flown from church towers of the worst-stricken villages of Normandy. "And in that time," wrote a monk of the abbey of Fourcarment, "the mortality was so great among the people of Normandy that those of Picardy mocked them." The same unneighborly reaction was reported of the Scots, separated by a winter's immunity from the English. Delighted to hear of the disease that was scourging the "southrons," they gathered forces for an invasion, "laughing at their enemies." Before they could move, the savage mortality fell upon them too, scattering some in death and the rest in panic to spread the infection as they fled.

In Picardy in the summer of 1349 the pestilence penetrated the castle of Coucy to kill Enguerrand's mother, Catherine, and her new husband. Whether her nine-year-old son escaped by chance or was perhaps living elsewhere with one of his guardians is unrecorded. In nearby Amiens, tannery workers, responding quickly to losses in the labor force, combined to bargain for higher wages. In another place villagers were seen dancing to drums and trumpets, and on being asked the reason, answered that, seeing their neighbors die day by day while their village remained immune, they believed they could keep the plague from entering "by the jollity that is in us. That is why we dance." Further north in Tournai on the border of Flanders, Gilles li Muisis, Abbot of St. Martin's, kept one of the epidemic's most vivid accounts. The passing bells rang all day and all night, he recorded, because sextons were anxious to obtain their fees while they could. Filled with the sound of mourning, the city became oppressed by fear, so that the authorities forbade the tolling of bells and the wearing of black and restricted funeral services to two mourners. The silencing of funeral bells and of criers' announcements of deaths was ordained by most cities. Siena imposed a fine on the wearing of mourning clothes by all except widows.

Flight was the chief recourse of those who could afford it or arrange it. The rich fled to their country places like Boccaccio's young patricians of Florence, who settled in a pastoral palace "removed on every side from the roads" with "wells of cool water and vaults of rare wines." The urban poor died in their burrows, "and only the stench of their bodies informed neighbors of their death." That the poor were more heavily afflicted than the rich was clearly remarked at the time, in the north as in the south. A Scottish chronicler, John of Fordun, stated flatly that the pest "attacked especially the meaner sort and common people—seldom the magnates." Simon de Covino of Montpellier made the same observation. He ascribed it to the misery and want and hard lives that made the poor more susceptible, which was half the truth. Close contact and the lack of sanitation was the unrecognized other half. It was noticed too that the young died in greater proportion than the old; Simon de Covino compared the disappearance of youth to the withering of flowers in the fields.

In the countryside peasants dropped dead on the roads, in the fields, in their houses. Survivors in growing helplessness fell into apathy, leaving ripe wheat uncut and livestock untended. Oxen and asses, sheep and goats, pigs and chickens ran wild and they too, according to local reports, succumbed to the pest. English sheep, bearers of the precious wool, died throughout the country. The chronicler Henry Knighton, canon of Leicester Abbey, reported 5,000 dead in one field alone, "their bodies so corrupted by the plague that neither beast nor bird would touch them," and spreading an appalling stench. In the Austrian Alps wolves came down to prey upon sheep and then, "as if alarmed by some invisible warning, turned and fled back into the wilderness." In more remote Dalmatia bolder wolves descended upon a plague-stricken city and attacked human survivors. For want of herdsmen, cattle strayed from place to place and died in hedgerows and ditches. Dogs and cats fell like the rest.

The dearth of labor held a fearful prospect because the 14th century lived close to the annual harvest both for food and for next year's seed. "So few servants and laborers were left," wrote Knighton, "that no one knew where to turn for help." The sense of a vanishing future created a kind of dementia of despair. A Bavarian chronicler of Neuberg on the Danube recorded that "Men and women . . . wandered around as if mad" and let their cattle stray "because no one had any inclination to concern themselves about the future." Fields went uncultivated, spring seed unsown. Second growth with nature's awful energy crept back over cleared land, dikes crumbled, salt water reinvaded and soured the lowlands. With so few hands remaining to restore the work of centuries, people felt, in Walsingham's words, that "the world could never again regain its former prosperity."

Though the death rate was higher among the anonymous poor, the known and the great died too. King Alfonso XI of Castile was the only reigning monarch killed by the pest, but his neighbor King Pedro of Aragon lost his wife, Queen Leonora, his daughter Marie, and a niece in the space of six months. John Cantacuzene, Emperor of Byzantium, lost his son. In France the lame Queen Jeanne and her daughter-in-law Bonne de Luxemburg, wife of the Dauphin, both died in 1349 in the same phase that took the life of Enguerrand's mother. Jeanne, Queen of Navarre, daughter of Louis X, was another victim. Edward III's second daughter, Joanna, who was on her way to marry Pedro, the heir of Castile, died in Bordeaux. Women appear to have been more vulnerable than men, perhaps because, being more housebound, they were more exposed to fleas. Boccaccio's mistress Fiammetta, illegitimate daughter of the King of Naples, died, as did Laura, the beloved—whether real or fictional—of Petrarch. Reaching out to us in the future, Petrarch cried, "Oh happy posterity who will not experience such abysmal woe and will look upon our testimony as a fable."

In Florence Giovanni Villani, the great historian of his time, died at 68 in the midst of an unfinished sentence: " . . . *e dure questo pistolenza fino a . . .* (in the midst of this pestilence there came to an end . . .)." Siena's master painters, the brothers Ambrogio and Pietro Lorenzetti, whose names never appear after 1348, presumably perished in the plague, as did Andrea Pisano, architect and sculptor of Florence. William of Ockham and the English mystic Richard Rolle of Hampole both disappear from mention after 1349. Francisco Datini, merchant of Prato, lost both his parents and two siblings. Curious sweeps of mortality afflicted certain bodies of merchants in London. All eight wardens of the Company of Cutters, all six wardens of the Hatters, and four wardens of the Goldsmiths died before July 1350. Sir John Pulteney, master draper and four times Mayor of London, was a victim, likewise Sir John Montgomery, Governor of Calais.

Among the clergy and doctors the mortality rate was naturally high because of the nature of their professions. Out of 24 physicians in Venice, 20 were said to have lost their lives in the plague, although, according to another account, some were believed to have fled or to have shut themselves up in their houses. At Montpellier, site of the leading medical school, the physician Simon de Covino reported that, despite the great number of doctors, "hardly one of them escaped." In Avignon, Guy de Chauliac confessed that he performed his medical visits only because he dared not stay away for fear of infamy, but "I was in continual fear." He claimed to have contracted the disease but to have cured himself by his own treatment; if so, he was one of the few who recovered.

Clerical mortality varied with rank. Although the one-third toll of cardinals reflects the same proportion as the whole, this was probably due to their concentration in Avignon. In England, in strange and almost sinister procession, the Archbishop of Canterbury, John Stratford, died in August 1348, his appointed successor died in May 1349, and the next appointee three months later, all three within a year. Despite such weird vagaries, prelates in general managed to sustain a higher survival rate than the lesser clergy. Among bishops the deaths have been estimated at about one in twenty. The loss of priests, even if many avoided their fearful duty of attending the dying, was about the same as among the population as a whole.

Government officials, whose loss contributed to the general chaos, found, on the whole, no special shelter. In Siena four of the nine members of the governing oligarchy died, in France one third of the royal notaries, in Bristol 15 out of the 52 members of the Town Council or almost one third. Tax-collecting obviously suffered, with the result that Philip VI was unable to collect more than a fraction of the subsidy granted him by the Estates in the winter of 1347–48.

Lawlessness and debauchery accompanied the plague as they had during the great plague of Athens of 430 B.C., when according to Thucydides, men grew bold in the indulgence of pleasure: "For seeing how the rich died in a moment and those who had nothing immediately inherited their property, they reflected that life and riches were alike transitory and they resolved to enjoy themselves while they could." Human behavior is timeless. When St. John had his vision of plague in Revelation, he knew from some experience or race memory that those who survived "repented not of the work of their hands. . . . Neither repented they of their murders, nor of their sorceries, nor of their fornication, nor of their thefts."

Ignorance of the cause augmented the sense of horror. Of the real carriers, rats and fleas, the 14th century had no suspicion, perhaps because they were so familiar. Fleas, though a common household nuisance, are not once mentioned in contemporary plague writings, and rats only incidentally, although folklore commonly associated them with pestilence. The legend of the Pied Piper arose from an outbreak of 1284. The actual plague bacillus, *Pasturella pestis,* remained undiscovered for another 500 years. Living alternately in the stomach of the flea and the bloodstream of the rat who was the flea's host, the bacillus in its bubonic form was transferred to humans and animals by the bite of either rat or flea. It traveled by virtue of *Rattus rattus,* the small medieval black rat that lived on ships, as well as by the heavier brown or sewer rat. What precipitated the turn of the bacillus from innocuous to virulent form is unknown, but the occurrence is now believed to have taken place not in China but somewhere in central Asia and to have spread along the caravan routes. Chinese origin was a mistaken notion of the 14th century based on real but belated reports of huge death tolls in China from drought, famine, and pestilence which have since been traced to the 1330s, too soon to be responsible for the plague that appeared in India in 1346.

The phantom enemy had no name. Called the Black Death only in later recurrences, it was known during the first epidemic simply as the Pestilence or Great Mortality. Reports from the East, swollen by fearful imaginings, told of strange tempests and "sheets of fire" mingled with huge hailstones that "slew almost all," or a "vast rain of fire" that burned up men, beasts, stones, trees, villages, and cities. In another version, "foul blasts of wind" from the fires carried the infection to Europe "and now as some suspect it cometh round the seacoast." Accurate observation in this case could not make the mental jump to ships and rats because no idea of animal- or insect-borne contagion existed.

The earthquake was blamed for releasing sulfurous and foul fumes from the earth's interior, or as evidence of a titanic struggle of planets and oceans causing waters to rise and vaporize until fish died in masses and corrupted the air. All these explanations had in common a factor of poisoned air, of miasmas and thick, stinking mists traced to every kind of natural or imagined agency from stagnant lakes to malign conjunction of the planets, from the hand of the Evil One to the wrath of God. Medical thinking, trapped in the theory of astral influences, stressed air as the communicator of the disease, ignoring sanitation or visible carriers. The existence of two carriers confused the trail, the more so because the flea could live and travel independently of the rat for as long as a month and, if infected by the particularly virulent septicemic form of the bacillus, could infect humans without reinfecting itself from the rat. The simultaneous presence of the pneumonic form of the disease, which was indeed communicated through the air, blurred the problem further.

The mystery of the contagion was "the most terrible of all the terrors," as an anonymous Flemish cleric in Avignon wrote to a correspondent in Bruges. Plagues had been known before, from the plague of Athens (believed to have been typhus) to the prolonged epidemic of the 6th century A.D., to the recurrence of sporadic outbreaks of the 12th and 13th centuries, but they had left no accumulated store of understanding. That the infection came from contact with the sick or with their houses, clothes, or corpses was quickly observed but not comprehended. Gentile da Foligno, renowned physician of Perugia and doctor of medicine at the universities of Bologna and Padua, came close to respiratory infection when he surmised that poisonous material was "communicated by means of air breathed out and in." Having no idea of microscopic carriers, he had to assume that the air was corrupted by planetary influences. Planets, however, could not explain the ongoing contagion. The agonized search for an answer gave rise to such theories as transference by sight. People felt ill, wrote Guy de Chauliac, not only by remaining with the sick but "even by looking at them." Three hundred years later Joshua Barnes, the 17th century biographer of Edward III, could write that the power of infection had entered into beams of light and "darted death from the eyes."

Doctors struggling with the evidence could not break away from the terms of astrology, to which they believed all human physiology was subject. Medicine was the one aspect of medieval life, perhaps because of its links with the Arabs, not shaped by Christian doctrine. Clerics detested astrology, but could not dislodge its influence. Guy de Chauliac, physician to three popes in succession, practiced in obedience to the zodiac. While his *Cirurgia* was the major treatise on surgery of its time, while he understood the use of anesthesia made from the juice of opium, mandrake, or hemlock, he nevertheless prescribed bleeding and purgatives by the planets and divided chronic from acute diseases on the basis of one being under the rule of the sun and the other of the moon.

In October 1348 Philip VI asked the medical faculty of the University of Paris for a report on the affliction that seemed to threaten human survival. With careful thesis, antithesis, and proofs, the doctors ascribed it to a triple conjunction of Saturn, Jupiter, and Mars in the 40th degree of Aquarius said to have occurred on March 20, 1345. They acknowledged, however, effects "whose cause is hidden from even the most highly trained intellects." The verdict of the masters of Paris became the official version. Borrowed, copied by scribes, carried abroad, translated from Latin into various vernaculars, it was everywhere accepted, even by the Arab physicians of Cordova and Granada, as the scientific if not the popular answer. Because of the terrible interest of the subject, the translations of the plague tracts stimulated use of national languages. In that one respect, life came from death.

To the people at large there could be but one explanation—the wrath of God. Planets might satisfy the learned doctors, but God was closer to the average man. A scourge so sweeping and unsparing without any visible cause could only be seen as Divine punishment upon mankind for its sins. It might even be God's terminal disappointment in his creature. Matteo Villani compared the plague to the Flood in ultimate purpose and believed he was recording "the extermination of mankind." Efforts to appease Divine wrath took many forms, as when the city of Rouen ordered that everything that could anger God, such as gambling, cursing, and drinking, must be stopped. More general were the penitent processions authorized at first by the Pope, some lasting as long as three days, some attended by as many as 2,000, which everywhere accompanied the plague and helped to spread it.

Barefoot in sackcloth, sprinkled with ashes, weeping, praying, tearing their hair, carrying candles and relics, sometimes with ropes around their necks or beating themselves with whips, the penitents wound through the streets, imploring the mercy of the Virgin and saints at their shrines. In a vivid illustration for the *Très Riches Heures* of the Duc de Berry, the Pope is shown in a pentinent procession attended by four cardinals in scarlet from hat to hem. He raises both arms in supplication to the angel on top of the Castel Sant'Angelo, while white-robed priests bearing banners and relics in golden cases turn to look as one of their number, stricken by the plague, falls to the ground, his face contorted with anxiety. In the rear, a gray-clad monk falls beside another victim already on the ground as the townspeople gaze in horror. (Nominally the illustration represents a 6th century plague in the time of Pope Gregory the Great, but as medieval artists made no distinction between past and present, the scene is shown as the artist would have seen it in the 14th century.) When it became evident that these processions were sources of infection, Clement VI had to prohibit them.

In Messina, where the plague first appeared, the people begged the Archbishop of neighboring Catania to lend them the relics of St. Agatha. When the Catanians refused to let the relics go, the Archbishop dipped them in holy water and took the water himself to Messina, where he carried it in a procession with prayers and litanies through the streets. The demonic, which shared the medieval cosmos with God, appeared as "demons in the shape of dogs" to terrify the people. "A black dog with a drawn sword in his paws appeared among them, gnashing his teeth and rushing upon them and breaking all the silver vessels and lamps and candlesticks on the altars and casting them hither and thither. . . . So the people of Messina, terrified by this prodigious vision, were all strangely overcome by fear."

The apparent absence of earthly cause gave the plague a supernatural and sinister quality. Scandinavians believed that a Pest Maiden emerged from the mouth of the dead in the form of a blue flame and flew through the air to infect the next house. In Lithuania the Maiden was said to wave a red scarf through the door or window to let in the pest. One brave man, according to legend, deliberately waited at his open window with drawn sword and, at the fluttering of the scarf, chopped off the hand. He died of his deed, but his village was spared and the scarf long preserved as a relic in the local church.

Beyond demons and superstition the final hand was God's. The Pope acknowledged it in a Bull of September 1348, speaking of the "pestilence with which God is afflicting the Christian people." To the Emperor John Cantacuzene it was manifest that a malady of such horrors, stenches, and agonies, and especially one bringing the dismal despair that settled upon its victims before they died, was not a plague "natural" to mankind but "a chastisement from Heaven." To Piers Plowman "these pestilences were for pure sin."

The general acceptance of this view created an expanded sense of guilt, for if the plague were punishment there had to be terrible sin to have occasioned it. What sins were on the 14th century conscience? Primarily greed, the sin of avarice, followed by usury, worldliness, adultery, blasphemy, falsehood, luxury, irreligion. Giovanni Villani, attempting to account for the cascade of calamity that had fallen upon Florence, concluded that it was retribution for the sins of avarice and usury that oppressed the poor. Pity and anger about the condition of the poor, especially victimization of the peasantry in war, was often expressed by writers of the time and was certainly on the conscience of the century. Beneath it all was the daily condition of medieval life, in which hardly any act or thought, sexual, mercantile, or military, did not contravene the dictates of the Church. Mere failure to fast or attend mass was sin. The result was an underground lake of guilt in the soul that the plague now tapped.

That the mortality was accepted as God's punishment may explain in part the vacuum of comment that followed the Black Death. An investigator has noticed that in the archives of Périgord references to the war are innumerable, to the plague few. Froissart mentions the great death but once, Chaucer gives it barely a glance. Divine anger so great that it contemplated the extermination of man did not bear close examination.

Notes

[1] Demographers study the statistical evidence regarding the distribution, density, and vital statistics of populations.

[2] Jean Froissart (1337?–1410) was a French chronicler and poet.

FOCUS: READING REVIEW

1. How did the bubonic plague enter Europe? How long did it take to spread from its port of entry to England?
2. What kind of evidence does Tuchman give of the plague's devastation? What does she suggest about the problems of historicity in comparing death reports with population figures? What kinds of records are available to suggest actual effects?
3. What was the plague's effect on the sense of community? What examples illustrate this?
4. Among what group of people was the plague most devastating and why?
5. Why did lawlessness and debauchery accompany the plague?
6. What were some of the reports of natural catastrophe that accompanied the plague? Why did these arise?
7. What popular explanations were offered for the plague's cause? What do these demonstrate about the medieval world?
8. Why is the bubonic plague rarely referred to in the literature of the years following it?

FOCUS: AUTHOR'S STRATEGIES

1. Tuchman presents an event familiar to history in a way that re-creates the experiences for the modern reader. What in her language and in her kinds of examples brings immediacy to the black death?
2. The author organizes this essay spatially and temporally. Explain how this operates.
3. What other development strategy, besides space and time, is present in this essay?

FOCUS: **DISCUSSION AND WRITING**

1. The greatest terror of the black death was the "mystery of the contagion." Do we still experience terror in the face of disease? To what degree does the scientific understanding of disease shape popular response to cancer, heart disease, herpes, or AIDS? To what degree do we respond superstitiously?
2. Have you ever experienced a disaster in your community? Fire? Flood? Crime? Earthquake? How did the event affect the sense of community? Compare this to the response in the Middle Ages to the black death.

My Head and My Heart
Fawn M. Brodie

Fawn Brodie (1915–1981) was best known for Thomas Jefferson: An Intimate History *(1974), from which this selection is taken. Brodie graduated from the University of Utah, received her M.A. from the University of Chicago, and taught history at U.C.L.A. Her other writings include* No Man Knows My History *(1945), a biography of Joseph Smith, the founder of the Mormon church;* Thaddeus Stevens: Scourge of the South *(1959); and* The Devil Drives: A Life of Sir Richard Burton *(1967). "My Head and My Heart" examines Thomas Jefferson's relationship with Maria Cosway during Jefferson's tenure as U.S. minister to France. Brodie's study reconstructs the relationship from letters, particularly the letter "My Head and My Heart," which follows the selection.*

Thomas Jefferson and Maria Cosway spent their first afternoon at a most unlikely spot for the beginning of a romance, the big, new, noisy Paris grain market. The company [also] included two artists from London, and Richard Cosway [Maria's husband]. Jefferson knew in advance of "the merits and talents" of the Cosways, that the husband, [Richard], was the most skillful miniature painter in England and that his wife, [Maria], presided over one of London's most fashionable salons. If ever a man fell in love in a single afternoon, it was Jefferson. In the first few days after their meeting Jefferson spent his days in a dizzying round of visits to Paris landmarks. When Richard Cosway began serious work on his miniatures, Jefferson and Maria began to see each other alone. Jefferson sought out some of the most idyllic spots in all the environs of Paris. His happiness spilled out in letters to his friends, and in these weeks he turned also to reading and writing about the poetry of love. The question of whether or not Jefferson and Maria Cosway became lover and mistress during these weeks has been answered in the negative with extraordinary finality by a good many writers. [This is curious as] the nuances and overtones in Jefferson's letters are richly suggestive, and the writers most certain of Jefferson's continuing chastity minimize or ignore the relevant fact that Maria Cosway returned to Paris for a second autumn without her husband and stayed almost four months. Furthermore,

Jefferson kept copies of his letters to Maria and all of Maria's to him: this was the one love affair he was clearly willing to share with history. [In October of 1786 the Cosways returned to England, after which Jefferson wrote the great love letter known as "My Head and My Heart."] Many scholars look at the letter as a debate between the head and the heart, and insist that the head (Jefferson) puts the heart (Maria) in its place. To say this is to ignore all the subsequent letters Jefferson wrote to Maria, and to forget their months together in the autumn of 1787. Taken as a whole the letter is a remarkable declaration of passion.

What a mass of happiness had we travelled over!

JEFFERSON TO MARIA COSWAY, October 12, 1786[1]

Thomas Jefferson and Maria Cosway spent their first afternoon together at the most unlikely spot for the beginning of a romance. This was the Halle aux Bleds, the big, new, noisy Paris grain market, crowded with peasants and merchants, and smelling of hay, flax, and barley. It was, nevertheless, one of the attractions of the day, famous for its giant dome—130 feet across—constructed of wooden ribs in such a fashion that the interior was flooded with light. Outside rose an old Renaissance column with circular steps inside, where visitors who climbed to the top were told that it had been built for Catherine de Medici, wife of Henry II, who climbed it often with her astrologer to learn the will of the stars.

Jefferson had mixed feelings about going on the excursion at all. "The Halle aux bleds might have rotted down before I should have gone to see it," he later wrote.[2] But John Trumbull, the young American artist Jefferson had recently met in London who was presently staying with him as he worked out the design of his planned canvas of the signing of the Declaration of Independence, persuaded him to go, promising him amusing company. It consisted of two artists from London, Richard Cosway and his wife. Thinking that he might at least see architecture worth copying for a market in Richmond, Jefferson acquiesced. What he saw there, he wrote later to Maria, was "the most superb thing on earth." But he was not writing "of a parcel of sticks and chips put together in pens," but the lady "to whom he had been presented."[3]

Maria Louisa Catherine Cecilia (Hadfield) Cosway was a fragile, languorously feminine woman of twenty-seven, with luminous blue eyes, exquisite skin, and a halo of golden curls. Though of English parentage, she spoke with a marked Italian accent, having been born and educated in Florence, and must have seemed to Jefferson exotic in a way that most Englishwomen were not. Her husband was a small man, shorter even than his wife, invariably dressed with foppish elegance. He was forty-four, close to Jefferson's age, and had been married for only three years. He was bouncy and cheerful; in his wife's words, *"toujours riant, toujours gai,"*[4] but also fulsome and sycophantic.[5] English critics would describe him as "an absurd little coxcomb," "a preposterous little Dresden china manikin." James Northcote dismissed him as "one of those butterfly characters that nobody minded, so that his opinion went for nothing."[6]

Though he was mocked for his pretentiousness in dress, especially a mulberry silk coat ornamented with strawberries, and was described as having a face like a monkey, Cosway in painting self-portraits not surprisingly showed a handsome man, with no trace in his face either of dandyism, or of the cruelty with which he treated his wife. Everyone in the bohemian London court circle in which they moved knew that Maria was wretchedly unhappy. James Northcote, who said she married out of necessity when her mother's money was exhausted, wrote that "she always despised him." And Jefferson, with the special sensitivity of a man in need of love, must have seen this the first afternoon.

Trumbull had told Jefferson in advance of "the merits and talents" of the Cosways, so he must have known that the husband was the most skillful miniature painter in England and that his wife presided over one of London's most fashionable salons.[7] Cosway's Schomberg House was full of European paintings and exotic furniture—Japanese screens, escritoires[8] of ebony inlaid with mother-of-pearl, exquisitely enameled and jeweled boxes, mosaic tables set with jasper, bloodstone, and lapis lazuli, tortoise-shell musical clocks, and Persian carpets—many of which were discreetly sold to the wealthy Londoners who frequented the celebrated Sunday-night musicals, when Maria entertained by playing and singing Italian songs. Whether Trumbull knew that Cosway also secretly painted pornographic pictures on snuffboxes which sold at exorbitant prices is not clear, though it was common enough knowledge in the lively gambling and libertine circle of the Prince of Wales.[9]

After the death of her father in Florence, Maria had wanted to join a nunnery, but her mother, who was Protestant, would have none of it. Upon coming to England, she had been sheltered by the artist Angelica Kauffmann, then the toast of London. Sir Joshua Reynolds[10] admired Maria's drawings, and like everyone else was charmed by the gentle simplicity of her manner. She was taught by the artist Henry Fuseli, and was said to have been engaged for a time to a composer, a Dr. Parsons. But it was Cosway in the end who in the very crassest sense finally purchased her, settling upon her £2,800, and promising to care for her mother until her death.[11] "As I meant to be a nun," Maria wrote later, "I found the convent I had chosen would have taken me without a fortune; and also found a *husband* who did the same."[12]

After the marriage Cosway improved Maria's English and painting technique, and then set her up as the leading ornament in his grandiose mansion. She told her friends she was afraid of him at first but came to love him, a genteel fiction few believed.[13] Bitter unpublished letters from Maria to her husband written years after their estrangement and still buried in her papers in the convent school in Italy which she founded suggest that there had been an initial period of some happiness, followed by her despairing realization that he was having affairs with men as well as women. One of them reads as follows:

Remember my good Mr. Cos: how many years we were happy. My wishes were to second and follow yours. . . . until you began to divied Your thoughts, first with occupations in Bedford Square, & a Miss P. Afterwards with Hammersmith and then L. . . . Lastly with the Udneys and this ended our happiness.[14]

But in the first years after their marriage she had been flattered by the continuing publicity; Allan Cunningham wrote that for a time "nothing was talked of but the great youth and talent of Mrs. Cosway; one half of the carriages who stopped at her husband's door contained sitters ambitious of the honours of her pencil."[15] James Boswell, one of her admirers, accused her of treating men like dogs. Cosway saw to it that his wife's pictures were exhibited in the Academy, along with those of Mary Moser, who would one day be his mistress, and of Angelica Kauffmann. No reputable art critic took any of this female talent seriously. "It was not that women were not often very clever (cleverer than many men)," William Hazlitt wrote, "but there was a point of excellence which they never reached." Even Angelica Kauffmann, he said, had "an effeminate and feeble look in all her works. . . . There was not a man's hand in it . . . something with strength and muscle."[16]

Horace Walpole composed for the *Morning Chronicle* a poem of mixed derision and praise, "Verses on Seeing Mrs. Cosway's Pallett":

Behold this strange chaotic mass,
Where colours in confusion lie,
Where rival tints commix'd appear,
Here tints for water, *there* for sky.
Kept in imagination's glow,
See now the lovely artist stand!
Grand visions beaming on her mind,
The magic pencil in her hand.[17]

John Wolcott, writing under the pseudonym Peter Pindar, would write maliciously of both the Cosways:

What vanity was in your skulls
To make you act so like two fools,
To expose your daubs tho' made with wondrous pains out
Could Raphael's angry ghost arise,
He'd catch a pistol up and blow your brains out.[18]

Actually Cosway had a formidable talent, deserving something of George C. Williamson's appraisal that he was "the most brilliant miniature painter" of eighteenth-century England. George III detested him—"Among *my* painters there are no fops,"[19] he said—but the Prince of Wales admired his talent and commissioned him to paint miniatures of two of his mistresses, Perdita Robinson and Mrs. Fitzherbert. (The latter miniature he was said to be clutching when he died.) Perdita, whose lovely face was immortalized by Gainsborough[20] and Sir Joshua

Reynolds as well as by Cosway, had become a friend to Maria Cosway and they planned to publish a book together, with Maria as illustrator. Abandoned by the Prince of Wales for the more seductive Mrs. Fitzherbert, Perdita had captured the affection of Colonel Banastre Tarleton, whose dragoons[21] had very nearly captured Jefferson at Monticello. She was in Paris with Tarleton in the same September that Maria Cosway met Jefferson, helping with the memoirs of his American campaign, and it is one of the entertaining minor coincidences of history that Jefferson and Tarleton in 1786 were both in Paris and in love with two women who eventually published a book together.[22]

Whether Jefferson ever heard that a secret passage ran from Schomberg House to the quarters of the Prince of Wales and that the Prince had seduced, or tried to seduce, Maria Cosway must remain a mystery.[23] That Trumbull or Maria herself had brought word of the Prince's libertine habits is clear enough from a letter Jefferson wrote to Abigail Adams a week after he met the Cosways. He had heard a rumor of an attempted assassination of George III and wrote to her in some alarm, "No man upon earth has my prayers for his continuance of life more sincerely than him. . . . The Prince of Wales on the throne, Lansdowne and Fox in the ministry, and we are undone!"[24] Jefferson never recognized that the Prince was one of the wittiest and cleverest of all the princes of Europe. Later he described his entourage to John Jay[25] as that of "the lowest, the most illiterate and profligate persons in the kingdom, without choice of rank or merit, and with whom the subjects of the conversation are only horses, drinking-matches, bawdy houses, and in terms the most vulgar." The young nobility, who begin by associating with him, he said, "soon leave him, disgusted with the insupportable profligacy of his society."[26]

What Jefferson was told in advance about Maria Cosway is irrelevant, for if ever a man fell in love in a single afternoon it was he. Though he had a dinner invitation from the Duchess d'Anville, he canceled it with a note, pleading the pressure of newly arrived correspondence, and the visitors to the Halle aux Bleds all drove off happily in a carriage to the Parc de St. Cloud, where they dined, strolled through the gallery, past the cascading fountains in the garden, and then came back to Paris to see the fireworks display, *Spectacle Pyrrhique des Sieurs Ruggieri,* on the rue St. Lazare. Having learned that Maria played both harp and harpsichord, and still loath to say goodbye, Jefferson persuaded them to go on to the home of Johann Baptiste Krumpholtz, whose wife, Julie, a distinguished harpist, entertained them to a late hour. "If the day had been as long as a Lapland summer day," Jefferson wrote to Maria later, he would "still have contrived means . . . to have filled it. . . . When I came home at night and looked back to the morning, it seemed to have been a month agone."[27]

Maria Cosway, like Martha Wayles,[28] was small, exquisite, and feminine as well as being a musician. Importantly too, she seemed to be in need of rescue, trapped like a delicate butterfly in a monstrous web of lascivious intrigue spun by the Prince of Wales. That she was genuinely in need of rescue we know by what happened to her later in life, but when she and Jefferson first met the necessity of rescue was already an old theme in Maria Cosway's life. Maria's mother had had five children born to her before Maria, of whom four had inexplicably died in the night. Charles Hadfield, her father, certain that there had been foul play, though the nurses had been different with each child, hired a governess to watch the nurse when Maria was born.

"One day," Maria wrote, "a Maid servant went into the nursery, took me in her Arms, & said pretty little Creature, I have sent four to heaven, I hope to send you also." The governess, "struck at this extraordinary speech, ran to my father, proper enquiries were made," and the girl went to an asylum for the insane.[29] Maria wrote of her father not only as her rescuer, but also as a man who "had a great taste & knowledge of the Arts & sciences," and who had "in every way contrived to furnish my mind. . . . Everybody knows what my father was and the education he gave me. My gratitude has never ceased."[30] The resemblance in this respect to Jefferson and his own daughter is striking. James Northcote, who had met Maria in Rome in 1788 when she was eighteen, said "she had been the object of adoration of an indulgent father, who, unfortunately for her had never checked the growth of her imperfections." Northcote had found her "not unhandsome" and talented, but also "active, ambitious, proud, and restless."[31] Jefferson saw only "music, modesty, beauty, and that softness of disposition which is the ornament of her sex."[32]

In the first few days after their meeting Jefferson wrote no letters, spending his days in a dizzying round of visits to the Louvre, the Palais Royale, the Bibliothèque du Roi, the "new church of Ste. Geneviève" (converted during the Revolution into the Panthéon), and to Versailles.[33] Accompanying Trumbull and Jefferson in the Cosway entourage was an aging scholar, Pierre François Hugues, known as d'Hancarville, who followed Maria about in humble adoration, and whose legacy of scores of affectionate letters Maria preserved, along with the first note Jefferson sent her, an envelope later inscribed by him to her husband, and a portrait painted of Jefferson by John Trumbull.[34] The Cosways introduced Jefferson to the Polish hero Thaddeus Kosciusko, and to Jacques Louis David,[35] whose enormous canvases Maria greatly admired. They visited the salons of sculptors Jean Antoine Houdon and Augustin Pagou. So the shy diplomat, who had been describing himself as a "savage from Virginia," and who had been consorting with scholars and diplomats, found himself thrust into the insouciant, bohemian life of the artists.

When Richard Cosway began serious work on his miniatures for the Duchesse d'Orléans, and Trumbull went off on a tour of Germany, Jefferson and Maria began to see each other alone. Jefferson's duties as minister were not onerous; they left him free the better part of every afternoon. He saw his daughter chiefly on Sundays, and his evenings were almost always his own. Later he reminded Maria of their expeditions together:

How beautiful was every object! the Port de Neuilly, the hills along the Seine, the rainbows of the machine of Marly, the terras of St. Germains, the chateaux, the gardens, the statues of Marly, the pavillion of Lucienne. Recollect too Madrid, Bagatelle, the King's garden, the Dessert.[36]

Maria Kimball, in *Jefferson: The Scene of Europe,* reconstructed with loving detective work descriptions of what all these gardens, grottoes, intimate restaurants, and inns were like in 1786, and one can see in reading her pages that Jefferson sought out some of the most idyllic spots in all the environs of Paris. What he wrote of as "the Dessert" was really the Désert de Retz, an elaborate *anglo-chinois* garden four miles from St. Germain, containing a grotto, a replica of a ruined Gothic church, a Chinese *orangerie,* a *temple de repose,* and a *temple au dieu Pan.* It also included an enormous column, sixty-five feet in diameter and four stories high, built to look like a ruin, which especially excited Jefferson. "How grand the ideas excited by the remains of such a column!" he wrote to Maria. "The spiral staircase too was beautiful. The wheels of time moved on with a rapidity of which those of our carriage gave but a faint idea, and yet in the evening, when one took a retrospect of the day, what a mass of happiness had we travelled over!"[37]

He could not contain this new happiness, which spilled over in letters to his friends. To Abigail Adams he wrote on August 9, 1786, when he had been seeing Maria Cosway for less than a week:

Here we have singing, dauncing, laugh, and merriment. No assassinations, no treasons, rebellions nor other dark deeds. When our king goes out, they fall down and kiss the earth where he has trodden; and then they go to kissing one another. And this is the truest wisdom. They have as much happiness in one year as an Englishman in ten.[38]

To the Adamses' new son-in-law, William Stephens Smith, he wrote a long letter on August 10, tedious with business details, but containing a cheerful, totally irrelevant aside, "for beauty is ever leading us astray."[39] And in a letter to George Wythe on August 13 in which he launched into his usual strictures about the malevolence of the kings, nobles, and priests, he nevertheless described the French people as having "the most benevolent, the most gay, and amiable character of which the human form is susceptible."[40]

In these weeks he turned also to reading and writing about the poetry of love. The poems a man chooses to copy or memorize usually speak to him in some special fashion, and under the guise of a scholarly inquiry into patterns of meter and rhyme, later titled "Thoughts on English Prosody," Jefferson caressed a great many beautiful lines. As he himself wrote of these selections, mostly from Milton, Gray, Collins, Shenstone, and Pope, "I chose, too, the most pregnant passages, those wherein every word teems with latent meaning."[41] Some were reflections on his dead wife:

Ye who e'er lost an angel, pity me!

O how self-fettered was my groveling soul!
To every sod which wraps the dead . . .

But most were appropriate to the new love:

He sung and hell consented
To hear the poet's prayer
Stern Proserpine relented
And gave him back the fair

. . .

And I loved her the more when I heard
Such tenderness fall from her tongue.

. . .

With her how I stray'd amid fountains and bowers!
Or loiter'd behind, and collected the flowers!
Then breathless with ardor my fair one pursued,
And to think with what kindness my garland she view'd!
But be still, my fond heart! this emotion give o'er;
Fain would'st thou forget thou must love her no more.[42]

Near the end of his compilation, as Maria Cosway's return to London became certain, he included the melancholy lines:

I mourn
I sigh
I Burn
I die
Let us part—
Let us part
Will you break
My poor heart?[43]

Maria Cosway was as sensitive to Jefferson's loneliness as he was to her unhappiness, and almost from the beginning she felt the power of the clutching hand of his dead wife. After her return to London she wrote to him: "Are you to be painted in future ages sitting solitary and sad, on the beautiful Monticello, tormented by the shadow of a woman who will present you a deform'd rod, twisted and broken, instead of the emblematical instrument belonging to the Muses, held by Genius, inspired by wit, from which all that is pleasing, beautifull and happy can be describ'd to entertain?"[44] After reading Jefferson's *Notes on the State of Virginia,* which he had given to her as a present, she wrote passionately: "Oh how I wish My self in those delightful places! Those enchanted Grotto's! Those Magnificent Mountains rivers, &c. &c.! Why am I not a Man that I could sett out immediatly and satisfy My Curiosity, indulge My sight with wonders!"[45]

The question whether or not Jefferson and Maria Cosway became lover and mistress during these weeks has been answered in the negative with extraordinary finality by a good many writers. Nathan Schachner wrote, "There is absolutely no evidence nor reason to believe the relation was anything but platonic." Thomas Fleming insisted, "There was no hope, no future to this infatuation. The lady was married, and too religious to commit adultery." Merrill Peterson, as we have already noted, described it as a pleasant game, with no "ardent desire," and Winthrop Jordan dismissed it as a "superficially frantic flirtation," a mere bagatelle, where the love was "play," and the "affair" was nonexistent. Saul Padover said "the affair was brief and apparently not successful," and Dixon Wecter wrote with contempt, "At forty-three" Jefferson was "older than Franklin at seventy-five."

Only Dumas Malone, of all the male biographers and historians, has been willing to concede that Jefferson "fell deeply in love during that golden September" and to suggest that if ever as a widower he engaged in "illicit lovemaking . . . this was the time."[46] Helen Bullock, who edited the Maria Cosway–Jefferson letters in 1945 with great discretion, let the correspondence speak for itself, but one of her chapters is called "Peep into Elysium." And Maria Kimball described the romance as "one of the most momentous experiences of Jefferson's life."[47]

The insistence of many of these writers that Jefferson remained continent is a curiosity suggesting that something is at work here that has little to do with scholarship.[48] The nuances and overtones in his letters are richly suggestive, and the writers most certain of Jefferson's continuing chastity minimize or ignore the relevant fact that Maria Cosway returned to Paris for a second autumn without her husband and stayed almost four months. Moreover, Jefferson kept copies of his own letters to Maria, and all of Maria Cosway's to him. His failure to destroy them tells us that he knew that his daughters would one day probably read them, if not a larger audience. This was one love affair he was clearly willing to share with history.

On September 18, 1786, about six weeks after their original meeting, Jefferson and Maria were walking along the Seine westward from the Place Louis XV. In attempting to jump over a fence—whether to retrieve a blowing scarf in the wind or simply in sheer exuberant good spirits one can only guess—he fell very hard and dislocated his right wrist. This at least was the diagnosis of the French surgeons who ineptly treated it, though it would seem from his subsequent agony and failure to recover that he certainly broke a bone, as his daughter Martha believed. "How the right hand became disabled," Jefferson wrote cryptically to William Stephens Smith, "would be a long story for the left to tell. It was one of those follies from which good cannot come but ill may."[49]

Jefferson's daughter described the accident in later years as if her father had been walking with a man:

He frequently walked as far as seven miles in the country. Returning from one of those rambles, he was joined by some friend, and being earnestly engaged in conversation he fell and fractured his wrist. He said nothing at the moment, but holding his suffering limb with the other hand, he continued the conversation till he arrived near to his own house, when, informing his companion of the accident, he left him to send for the surgeon. The fracture was a compound one, and probably much swollen before the arrival of the surgeon; it was not *set*, and remained ever after weak and stiff.[50]

Whether Jefferson really deceived Martha, or whether she never really exorcised her jealousy for Mrs. Cosway and deliberately misled Jefferson's biographer is uncertain.

Maria, frantic to see Jefferson after the accident, had a problem getting away from her husband. On the second day she sent him a note: "I meant to have had the pleasure of seeing you *Twice,* and I have appeared a Monster for not having sent to know how you was, the *whole* day." She had planned a morning visit, she said, but her husband had "kill'd My project, I had proposed to him, by burying himself among Pictures and forgetting the hours." She had come late at night, she said, too late to do anything but prove "a disturbance to your Neighbours." Whether she was alone or with her husband is not clear—here the letter is mutilated. But she promised to return the following morning.[51]

Marie Kimball, who dismisses Maria Cosway as "a spoiled, egocentric young woman, with a very limited emotional capacity," and even Dumas Malone, who describes her more charitably as "a lovely, talented capricious creature—half woman and half child," mistakenly believe that the fractured wrist brought an end to the "summer idyl." Malone wrote positively that Jefferson did not join the Cosways until October 4, more than two weeks after the accident, when he went to say goodbye to them both.[52] Both biographers seem to have forgotten that the absence of letters is evidence not of their failure to see each other but the contrary. That Jefferson did see her, perhaps often, is evident from a note Maria wrote to him on October 5, which makes clear that he had been begging her to go out in the carriage with him on an excursion of some sort, and that she had feared it would do his wrist some damage. "You repeatedly said it wou'd do you no harm," she remembered.[53] When she did agree to this excursion on October 4 she had to give Jefferson the dreaded but long expected news that her husband was insisting—despite her protestation that "nothing seems redy"—that they leave for London the next day.[54]

The effect on Jefferson was catastrophic. He described it later in a letter to Maria as if he were talking to himself: "Remember the last night. You knew your friends were to leave Paris to-day. This was enough to throw you into agonies. All night you tossed us from one side of the bed to the other. No sleep, no rest. The poor crippled wrist too, never left one moment in the same position, now up, now down, now here, now there; was it to be wondered at if all it's pains returned?"[55] The next morning he sent for the surgeon, who, he said, could not "devine the cause of this extraordinary change."[56] Unable to go for the farewell visit, as he had planned, Jefferson sent off a little note, laboriously written with his left hand, of necessity somewhat formal, since he knew Cosway would be with Maria when she received it.

> I have passed the night in so much pain that I have not closed my eyes. It is with infinite regret therefore that I must relinquish your charming company for that of the Surgeon whom I have sent for to examine into the cause of this change. I am in hopes it is only the having rattled a little too freely over the pavement yesterday. If you do go, god bless you wherever you go. Present me in the most friendly terms to Mr. Cosway, and let me hear of your safe arrival in England. Addio Addio.
> Let me know if you do not go today.[57]

The Cosways did delay their departure one more day, and Jefferson not only left his home to pay a final visit but even traveled with them the first several miles to the Pavillon de St. Denis. D'Hancarville, also saying goodbye, went along as an unhappy fourth in the carriage. What Cosway thought about these two men who insisted on such a prolonged farewell to his pretty wife is not hard to imagine. He was used to a world of amorous intrigue, and had liaisons of his own. Still, he had a keen sense of property if not propriety, and eventually decided firmly if unsuccessfully against permitting his wife to come back to Paris.

After bidding farewell at St. Denis, Jefferson turned on his heel and walked away, as he put it, "more dead than alive." He and d'Hancarville climbed into a crowded carriage to return to Paris, "like recruits for the Bastille,[58] not having soul enough to give orders to the coachman," and proceeded to console each other with "a mutual confession of distress."[59] Once back at his own hearth Jefferson began to write the great love letter known as "My Head and My Heart," what Julian Boyd properly calls "one of the notable love letters in the English language."[60] In a contrived though not unusual eighteenth-century conceit, he wrote in the form of a dialogue, with first his Head speaking, and then his Heart. Though laboriously written with his left hand, the letter covered twelve pages and exceeded four thousand words. The original has never been found, but Jefferson kept a press copy, as he did of almost all of the subsequent letters he sent to Maria, thus making it possible for him to read and reread their total correspondence in a special reliving of their hours together.

"My Head and My Heart" is so important a window to Jefferson's inner life, and has been the subject of such divergent and contradictory interpretations, that it is here reproduced in full in an Appendix so that every reader may have a look at it himself. Jefferson wrote it in great wretchedness of spirit, and also in considerable physical pain. The wrist did not heal properly, his fingers continued to be swollen for over a year, and some of the muscles permanently atrophied so that he carried about with him for the rest of his life a reminder of his infatuation in what was a real disablement. The immediate suffering compounded his sense of loss, but also revived his old conviction that love invariably brings pain and loss. So the letter can be read on several levels.

Many scholars look at the letter as a debate, and insist that the head emerges triumphant over the heart. Julian Boyd sees it as proof that "reason was not only enthroned as a chief disciplinarian of his life, but also . . . a sovereign to whom the Heart yielded a ready and full allegiance." Merrill Peterson writes that "in the end the head (Jefferson) coolly put the heart (Maria) in its place. Reason and sentiment might divide life between them, yet, for him, one was the master, the other the servant."[61] To say this is to ignore all the subsequent letters Jefferson wrote to Maria, and to forget their months together in the autumn of 1787. "My Head and My Heart" was the first of many tender letters; it is the longest and the most complicated. The dialogue is less a debate than a searching examination of himself, a portrait in words laid in the lap of a woman who was herself far more gifted with the brush and with the harpischord than with the pen. As a self-portrait there is nothing in the Jefferson literature to compare with it. What he pictures is a deeply tormented man—"the divided empire," he calls it—a man who would be controlled by science and reason debating with a man controlled by sentiment and passion.

It is also, taken as a whole, a remarkable declaration of passion. Falling in love again had brought not only an ecstasy of affection but also a kind of ecstasy of self-knowledge he felt compelled to share. His Head cried out—I have been punished so often by love—"Advance with caution"—"The art of life is the art of avoiding pain"—"Our own share of miseries is sufficient"—"You rack our whole system when you are parted from those you love." Such phrases, attributed to the Head, in their totality became a cry for love, for reassurance, for the promise of renewal. And his Heart spoke with even greater anguish:

> I am indeed the most wretched of all earthly beings. Overwhelmed with grief, every fibre of my frame distended beyond it's natural powers to bear, I would willingly meet whatever catastrophe should leave me no more to feel or to fear. . . .
>
> I feel more fit for death than life. But when I look back on the pleasures of which it is the consequence, I am conscious they were worth the price I am paying. . . . Hope is sweeter than despair, and they were too good to mean to deceive me. In the summer said the gentleman; but in the spring, said the lady: and I should love her forever, were it only for that!

One sees, too, thinly disguised in this letter, Jefferson's fantasy that the Cosways will visit America, that the husband will die and Maria will be left, to be cherished and comforted at "our own dear Monticello" where with majesty "we ride above the storms." I hope in god no circumstance may ever make either seek asylum from grief," he protests, but who was better equipped to comfort a widow than himself:

> Deeply practised in the school of affliction, the human heart knows no joy which I have not lost, no sorrow of which I have not drank! Fortune can present no grief of unknown form to me! Who then can so softly bind up the wound of another as he who has felt the same wound himself? But Heaven forbid they should ever know a sorrow!

Let the Cosways come to America, he said, they would find not a nation of anarchy, as the mendacious British press contended, but a people "occupied as we are in opening rivers, digging navigable canals, making roads, building public schools, establishing academies, erecting busts and statues to our great men, protecting religious freedom, abolishing sanguinary punishments, reforming and improving our laws in general"—a nation behaving in fact exactly like Thomas Jefferson.

In a burst of scorn he caricatured his own manner of living since his wife's death:

> Let the gloomy Monk, sequestered from the world, seek unsocial pleasures in the bottom of his cell! Let the sublimated philosopher grasp visionary happiness while pursuing phantoms dressed in the garb of truth! Their supreme wisdom is supreme folly: and they mistake for happiness the mere absence of pain. Had they ever felt the solid pleasure of one generous spasm of the heart, they would exchange for it all the frigid speculations of their lives.

He finished the letter with conventional good wishes for Richard Cosway, adding moodily, "My health is good, except my wrist which mends slowly, and my mind which mends not at all, but broods constantly over your departure."[62]

Jefferson spent several days writing this letter. He had no sooner sealed the envelope than a letter arrived from John Trumbull, who when returning from Germany had unexpectedly come upon the Cosways in Antwerp. When they told him of Jefferson's accident to his wrist, Trumbull at once wrote his sympathy, and took the opportunity to describe his German tour in detail. Maria Cosway, weary and disconsolate after riding almost all night in the rain, had scribbled a small note in Italian as a postscript.

> I am adding a couple of lines to ask you how you are. I hope the trip to St. Dennys did not cause you to remember us painfully, [and that] I shall soon receive news of your complete recovery, which will give infinite pleasure to your always obliged and affectionate Friend, Maria Cosway.—Mr. Cosway adds his compliments to mine. We arrived here Sunday, three hours past midnight.[63]

When Jefferson received Trumbull's letter and glanced at the signature, he thought for one happy moment the whole letter was from Maria. Discovering quickly that hers was only a four-line postscript, he wrote with a disappointment that came very close to rage:

> Just as I had sealed the enclosed I received a letter of good length, dated Antwerp, with your name at the bottom. I prepared myself for a feast. I read two or three sentences: looked again at the signature to see if I had not mistaken it. It was visibly yours. Read a sentence or two more. Diable! Spelt your name distinctly. There was not a letter of it omitted. Began to read again. In fine after reading a little and examining the signature, alternately, half a dozen times, I found that your name was to four lines

only instead of four pages. I thank you for the four lines however because they prove you think of me. Little indeed, but better little than none. To shew how much I think of you I send you the enclosed letter. . . . I will even allow you twelve days to get through it. . . . I send you the song I promised. Bring me in return its subject, *Jours heureux!*

The song was from Sacchini's *Dardanus:*

Jours heureux, espoir enchanteur!
Prix charmant d'un amour si tendre!
Je vais la voir, je vais l'entendre,
Je vais retrouver le bonheur![64]

Adding this letter to his twelve-page "dialogue," Jefferson sent them off to London in a packet in care of John Trumbull, with specific instructions to "deliver it personally." He and Maria had worked out a plan which they hoped would circumvent interception either by her husband or by the spies in the post office, who Jefferson believed regularly read all his mail. Maria was to deliver her letters to Trumbull, who would either find a trusted friend to carry them, or send them to Paris by way of Jefferson's banker, "Mr. Grand," on the rue Neuve des Capucins.[65] Trumbull, who had lived through a scandal in America, with a child born out of wedlock, could be counted on to be compassionate. Jefferson trusted him totally. "Lay all my affections at her feet," he wrote in one letter, and in another, "Kneel to Mrs. Cosway for me, and lay my soul in her lap."[66] On the occasions when Trumbull was not available he used the regular mail service, disguising his seal and omitting his signature. Trumbull was a willing accomplice, and discretion itself. Even fifty years later, when about to publish his autobiography and diary of the period, he reported that the pages of his diary which covered the dates of the Jefferson-Cosway meetings in Paris were torn out and lost.[67]

Back in London Maria fell into melancholy. The delay between Jefferson's letters, she wrote, meant "the punishment of Tantalus." To the twelve-page letter she replied in English and Italian:

My heart is . . . ready to burst. . . . Your letter could employ me for some time, an hour to Consider every word, to every sentence I could write a volume . . .
Amid the fog and smoke, sadness seems (to reign) in every heart. . . . I must return as soon as possible to my occupations in order not to feel the rigor of the Melancholy which is inspired by this unpleasant climate. . . . Everything is tranquil, quiet and gloomy, there are no Bells ringing. . . . (your letters) will never be long enough.[68]

Cosway's biographer, who knew nothing of the Jefferson affair, would write later of Maria's "depression, dullness of spirits, and nervous agitation," which were "alleviated only by her trips to Paris."[69]

On November 17, 1786, having heard nothing from Jefferson for several weeks, Maria sent him a book of songs and duets she had herself composed, and wrote, impatiently:

But what does this silence mean. . . . I have awaited the post with so much anxiety and lo each time it arrives without bringing any letters from Paris, I am really worried. . . . After the pain of separation is past, one lives in continual anxiety. . . . The weather here is very bad, melancholy, sad. . . . Night Thoughts, before the fire, and when the imagination is well warmed up, one could go cool off in a river.[70]

On November 19, Jefferson was writing for the first time with his right hand.

I write with pain and must be short. This is good news for you; for were the hand able to follow the effusions of the heart, that would cease to write only when this shall cease to beat. . . . When sins are dear to us we are but too prone to slide into them again. The act of repentance itself is often sweetened with the thought that it clears our account for a repetition of the same sin.[71]

Ten days later he wrote, "I am determined when you come next not to admit the idea that we are ever to part again. But are you to come again? I dread the answer to this question, and that my poor heart has been duped by the fondness of its wishes. . . . Say many kind things, and say them without reserve. They will be food for my soul."[72]

Evidence of Jefferson's despair escaped in letters to others than Maria. To Eliza House Trist he wrote on December 15, 1786, "I am burning the candle of life without present pleasure, or future object. A dozen or twenty years ago this scene would have amused me. But I am past the age for changing habits. I take all the fault on myself, as it is impossible to be among a people who wish more to make one happy."[73]

Fully expecting that Maria would return to Paris in the spring, he made no effort to find an excuse to go to England. Though he had been enchanted by the English gardens on his visit in the spring of 1786, he detested the court and the people and had vowed never to return. Impatient and teasing, though it was still midwinter, he wrote on December 24, "It is time therefore you should be making your arrangements, packing your baggage."

I was so unlucky when very young, as to read the history of Fortunatus. He had a cap of such virtues that when he put it on his head, and wished himself anywhere, he was there. I have been all my life sighing for this cap. Yet if I had it, I question if I should use it but once. I should wish myself with you, and not wish myself away again. . . . I am always thinking of you. . . . I will believe you intend to go to America, to draw the Natural bridge . . . that I shall meet you there, and visit with you all those grand scenes. . . . I had rather be deceived, than live without hope.[74]

But Cosway resorted to delay and postponement, and when Maria wrote that their trip would not take place until summer Jefferson decided to take a spring trip to Italy. He promised himself a tour of the Roman antiquities in southern France, and wanted to see something of Maria's birthplace in Italy. He did not get as far south as Florence, but did tour northern Italy as well as southern France, and got a very respectful opinion of the Alps, which made him less chauvinistic though no less affectionate toward his Virginia mountains. Even on this trip his letters to others reflected the state of his heart. To Madame de Tessé he wrote from Nîmes, "Here I am, Madam, gazing whole hours at the Maison quarrée, like a lover at his mistress."[75] Upon his return he wrote to Maria Cosway beseeching:

> But I am born to lose everything I love. Why were you not with me? So many enchanting scenes which only wanted your pencil to consecrate them to fame. . . . Come then, my dear Madam, and we will breakfast every day à l'Angloise, hie away to the Desert, dine under the bowers of Marly, and forget that we are ever to part again.[76]

Maria meanwhile was in despair lest her husband cancel his summer plans.

> I do not know that we shall come to Paris this year. I fear not. My husband begins to doubt it. . . . Why lead me to hope? It seems a dream to have been there and I now wish it to be real.[77]

At some time during the summer, when Cosway decided absolutely against a return to Paris, she found the courage to come by herself. There surely was a letter to Jefferson telling him of this decision, but if so he destroyed it. In fact, in none of the letters Jefferson wrote to Maria, and in none of those he kept of hers, is there evidence that she came to Paris alone in the second autumn. Thus Jefferson demonstrated that he could be as discreet as Trumbull. But come alone she did, as we learn from other sources, and she stayed over three months.

"My Head and My Heart"

Jefferson to Maria Cosway, Paris, October 12, 1786 (*Papers*, Boyd, X, 443–53)

[MY DEAR] MADAM

Having performed the last sad office of handing you into your carriage at the Pavillon de St. Denis, and seen the wheels get actually into motion, I turned on my heel and walked, more dead than alive, to the opposite door, where my own was awaiting me. Mr. Danquerville was missing. He was sought for, found, and dragged down stairs. [We] were crammed into the carriage, like recruits for the Bastille, and not having [sou]l enough to give orders to the coachman, he presumed Paris our destination, [and] drove off. After a considerable interval, silence was broke with a "je suis vraiment affligé du depart de ces bons gens." This was the signal for a mutual confession [of dist]ress. We began immediately to talk of

Mr. and Mrs. Cosway, of their goodness, their [talents], their amability, and tho we spoke of nothing else, we seemed hardly to have entered into matter when the coachman announced the rue St. Denis, and that we were opposite Mr. Danquerville's. He insisted on descending there and traversing a short passage to his lodgings. I was carried home. Seated by my fire side, solitary and sad, the following dialogue took place between my Head and my Heart.

Head. Well, friend, you seem to be in a pretty trim.

Heart. I am indeed the most wretched of all earthly beings. Overwhelmed with grief, every fibre of my frame distended beyond it's natural powers to bear, I would willingly meet whatever catastrophe should leave me no more to feel or to fear.

Head. These are the eternal consequences of your warmth and precipitation. This is one of the scrapes into which you are ever leading us. You confess your follies indeed: but still you hug and cherish them, and no reformation can be hoped, where there is no repentance.

Heart. Oh my friend! This is no moment to upbraid my foibles. I am rent into fragments by the force of my grief! If you have any balm, pour it into my wounds: if none, do not harrow them by new torments. Spare me in this awful moment! At any other I will attend with patience to your admonitions.

Head. On the contrary I never found that the moment of triumph with you was the moment of attention to my admonitions. While suffering under your follies you may perhaps be made sensible of them, but, the paroxysm over, you fancy it can never return. Harsh therefore as the medecine may be, it is my office to administer it. You will be pleased to remember that when our friend Trumbull used to be telling us of the merits and talents of these good people, I never ceased whispering to you that we had no occasion for new acquaintance; that the greater their merit and talents, the more dangerous their friendship to our tranquillity, because the regret at parting would be greater.

Heart. Accordingly, Sir, this acquaintance was not the consequence of my doings. It was one of your projects which threw us in the way of it. It was you, remember, and not I, who desired the meeting, at Legrand & Molinos. I never trouble myself with domes nor arches. The Halle aux bleds might have rotted down before I should have gone to see it. But you, forsooth, who are eternally getting us to sleep with your diagrams and crotchets, must go and examine this wonderful piece of architecture. And when you had seen it, oh! it was the most superb thing on earth! What you had seen there was worth all you had yet seen in Paris! I thought so too. But I meant it of the lady and gentleman to whom we had been presented, and not of a parcel of sticks and chips put together in pens. You then, Sir, and not I, have been the cause of the present distress.

Head. It would have been happy for you if my diagrams and crotchets had gotten you to sleep on that day, as you are pleased to say they eternally do. My visit to Legrand & Molinos had publick utility for it's object. A market is to be built in Richmond. What a commodious plan is that of Legrand & Molinos: especially if we put on it the noble dome of the Halle aux bleds. If such a bridge as they shewed us can be thrown across the Schuylkill at Philadelphia, the floating bridges taken up, and the navigation of that river opened, what a copious resource will be added, of wood and provisions, to warm and feed the poor of that city. While I was occupied with these objects, you were dilating with your new acquaintances, and contriving how to prevent a separation from them. Every soul of you had an engagement for the day. Yet all these were to be sacrificed, that you might dine together. Lying messengers were to be dispatched into every quarter of the city with apologies for your breach of engagement. You particularly had the effrontery [to] send word to the Dutchess Danville that, in the moment we were setting out to d[ine] with her, dispatches came to hand which required immediate attention. You [wanted] me to invent a more ingenious excuse; but I knew you were getting into a scrape, and I would have nothing to do with it. Well, after dinner to St. Cloud, from St. Cloud to Ruggieri's, from Ruggieri to Krumfoltz, and if the day had been as long as a Lapland summer day, you would still have contrived means, among you, to have filled it.

Heart. Oh! my dear friend, how you have revived me by recalling to my mind the transactions of that day! How well I remember them all, and that when I came home at night and looked back to the morning, it seemed to have been a month agone. Go on then, like a kind comforter, and paint to me the day we went to St. Germains. How beautiful was every object! the Port de Neuilly, the hills along the Seine, the rainbows of the machine of Marly, the terras of St. Germains, the chateaux, the gardens, the [statues] of Marly, the pavillon of Lucienne. Recollect too Madrid, Bagatelle, the King's garden, the Dessert. How grand the idea excited by the remains of such a column! The spiral staircase too was beautiful. Every moment was filled with something agreeable. The wheels of time moved on with a rapidity of which those of our carriage gave but a faint idea, and yet in the evening, when one took a retrospect of the day, what a mass of happiness had we travelled over! Retrace all those scenes to me, my good companion, and I will forgive the unkindness with which you were chiding me. The day we went to St. Germains was a little too warm, I think, was not it?

Head. Thou art the most incorrigible of all the beings that ever sinned! I reminded you of the follies of the first day, intending to deduce from thence some useful lessons for you, but instead of listening to these, you kindle at the recollection, you retrace the whole series with a fondness which shews you want nothing but the opportunity to act it over again. I often told you during it's course that you were imprudently engaging your affections under circumstances that must cost you a great deal of pain: that the persons indeed were of the greatest merit, possessing good sense, good humour, honest hearts, honest manners, and eminence in a lovely art: that the lady had moreover qualities and accomplishments, belonging to her sex, which might form a chapter apart for her: such as music, modesty, beauty, and that softness of disposition which is the ornament of her sex and charm of ours. But that all these considerations would increase the pang of separation: that their stay here was to be short: that you rack our whole system when you are parted from those you love, complaining that such a separation is worse than death, inasmuch as this ends our sufferings, whereas that only begins them: and that the separation would in this instance be the more severe as you would probably never see them again.

Heart. But they told me they would come back again the next year.

Head. But in the mean time see what you suffer: and their return too depends on so many circumstances that if you had a grain of prudence you would not count upon it. Upon the whole it is improbable and therefore you should abandon the idea of ever seeing them again.

Heart. May heaven abandon me if I do!

Head. Very well. Suppose then they come back. They are to stay here two months, and when these are expired, what is to follow? Perhaps you flatter yourself they may come to America?

Heart. God only knows what is to happen. I see nothing impossible in that supposition, and I see things wonderfully contrived sometimes to make us happy. Where could they find such objects as in America for the exercise of their enchanting art? especially the lady, who paints landscape so inimitably. She wants only subjects worthy of immortality to render her pencil immortal. The Falling spring, the Cascade of Niagara, the Passage of the Potowmac thro the Blue mountains, the Natural bridge. It is worth a voiage across the Atlantic to see these objects; much more to paint, and make them, and thereby ourselves, known to all ages. And our own dear Monticello, where has nature spread so rich a mantle under the eye? mountains, forests, rocks, rivers. With what majesty do we there ride above the storms! How sublime to look down into the workhouse of nature, to see her clouds, hail, snow, rain, thunder, all fabricated at our feet! And the glorious Sun, when rising as if out of a distant water, just gilding the tops of the mountains, and giving life to all nature!—I hope in god no circumstance may ever make either seek an asylum from grief! With what sincere sympathy I would open every cell of my composition to receive the effusion of their woes! I would pour my tears into their wounds: and if a drop of balm could be found at the top of the Cordilleras, or at the remotest sources of the Missouri, I would go thither myself to seek and to bring it. Deeply practised in the school of affliction, the human heart knows no joy which I have not lost, no sorrow of which I have not drank! Fortune can present no grief of unknown form to me! Who then can so softly bind up the wound of another as he who has felt the same wound himself? But Heaven forbid they should ever know a sorrow!—Let us turn over another leaf, for this has distracted me.

Head. Well. Let us put this possibility to trial then on another point. When you consider the character which is given of our country by the lying newspapers of London, and their credulous copyers in other countries; when you reflect that all Europe is made to believe we are a lawless banditti, in a state of absolute anarchy, cutting one another's throats, and plundering without distinction, how can you expect that any reasonable creature would venture among us?

Heart. But you and I know that all this is false: that there is not a country on earth where there is greater tranquillity, where the laws are milder, or better obeyed: where every one is more attentive to his own business, or meddles less with that of others: where strangers are better received, more hospitably treated, and with a more sacred respect.

Head. True, you and I know this, but your friends do not know it.

Heart. But they are sensible people who think for themselves. They will ask of impartial foreigners who have been among us, whether they saw or heard on the spot any instances of anarchy. They will judge too that a people occupied as we are in opening rivers, digging navigable canals, making roads, building public schools, establishing academies, erecting busts and statues to our great men, protecting religious freedom, abolishing sanguinary punishments, reforming and improving our laws in general, they will judge I say for themselves whether these are not the occupations of a people at their ease, whether this is not better evidence of our true state than a London newspaper, hired to lie, and from which no truth can ever be extracted but by reversing everything it says.

Head. I did not begin this lecture my friend with a view to learn from you what America is doing. Let us return then to our point. I wished to make you sensible how imprudent it is to place your affections, without reserve, on objects you must so soon lose, and whose loss when it comes must cost you such severe pangs. Remember the last night. You knew your friends were to leave Paris to-day. This was enough to throw you into agonies. All night you tossed us from one side of the bed to the other. No sleep, no rest. The poor crippled wrist too, never left one moment in the same position, now up, now down, now here, now there; was it to be wondered at if all it's pains returned? The Surgeon then was to be called, and to be rated as an ignoramus because he could not devine the cause of this extraordinary change.—In fine, my friend, you must mend your manners. This is not a world to live at random in as you do. To avoid these eternal distresses, to which you are for ever exposing us, you must learn to look forward before you take a step which may interest our peace. Everything in this world is matter of calculation. Advance then with caution, the balance in your hand. Put into one scale the pleasures which any object may offer; but put fairly into the other the pains which are to follow, and see which preponderates. The making an acquaintance is not a matter of indifference. When a new one is proposed to you, view it all round. Consider what advantages it presents, and to what inconveniences it may expose you. Do not bite at the bait of pleasure till you know there is no hook beneath it. The art of life is the art of avoiding pain: and he is the best pilot who steers clearest of the rocks and shoals with which it is beset. Pleasure is always before us; but misfortune is at our side: while running after that, this arrests us. The most effectual means of being secure against pain is to retire within ourselves, and to suffice for our own happiness. Those, which depend on ourselves, are the only pleasures a wise man will count on: for nothing is ours which another may deprive us of. Hence the inestimable value of intellectual pleasures. Ever in our power, always leading us to something new, never cloying, we ride, serene and sublime, above the concerns of this mortal world, contemplating truth and nature, matter and motion, the laws which bind up their existence, and that eternal being who made and bound them up by these laws. Let this be our employ. Leave the bustle and tumult of society to those who have not talents to occupy themselves without them. Friendship is but another name for an alliance with the follies and the misfortunes of others. Our own share of miseries is sufficient: why enter then as volunteers in those of another? Is there so little gall poured into our own cup that we must needs help to drink that of our neighbor? A friend dies or leaves us: we feel as if a limb was cut off. He is sick: we must watch over him, and participate of his pains. His fortune is shipwrecked: ours must be laid under contribution. He loses a child, a parent or a partner: we must mourn the loss as if it was our own.

Heart. And what more sublime delight than to mingle tears with one whom the hand of heaven hath smitten! To watch over the bed of sickness, and to beguile it's tedious and it's painful moments! To share our bread with one to whom misfortune has left none! This world abounds indeed with misery: to lighten it's burthen we must divide it with one another. But let us now try the virtues of your mathematical balance, and as you have put into one scale the burthens of friendship, let me put it's comforts into the other. When languishing then under disease, how grateful is the solace of our friends! How are we penetrated with their assiduities and attentions! How much are we supported by their encouragements and kind offices! When Heaven has taken from us some object of our love, how sweet is it to have a bosom whereon to recline our heads, and into which we may pour the torrent of our tears! Grief, with such a comfort, is almost a luxury! In a life where we are perpetually exposed to want and accident, yours is a wonderful proposition, to insulate ourselves, to retire from all aid, and to wrap ourselves in the mantle of self-sufficiency! For assuredly nobody will care for him who cares for nobody. But friendship is precious not only in the shade but in the sunshine of life: and thanks to a benevolent arrangement of things, the greater part of life is sunshine. I will recur for proof to the days we have lately passed. On these indeed the sun shone brightly! How gay did the face of nature appear! Hills, vallies, chateaux, gardens, rivers, every object wore it's liveliest hue! Whence did they borrow it? From the presence of our charming companion. They were pleasing, because she seemed pleased. Alone, the scene would have been dull and insipid: the participation of it with her gave it relish. Let the gloomy Monk, sequestered from the world, seek unsocial pleasures in the bottom of his cell! Let the sublimated philosopher grasp visionary happiness while pursuing phantoms dressed in the garb of truth! Their supreme wisdom is supreme folly: and they mistake for happiness the mere absence of pain. Had they ever felt the solid pleasure of one generous spasm of the heart, they would exchange for it all the frigid speculations of their lives, which you have been vaunting in such elevated terms. Believe me then, my friend, that that is a miserable arithmetic which would estimate friendship at nothing, or at less than nothing. Respect for you has induced me to enter into this discussion, and to hear principles uttered which I detest and abjure. Respect for myself now obliges me to recall you into the proper limits of your office. When nature assigned us the same habitation, she gave us over it a divided empire. To you she allotted the field of science, to me that of morals. When the circle is to be squared, or the orbit of a comet to be traced: when the arch of greatest strength, or the solid of least resistance is to be investigated, take you the problem: it is yours: nature has given me no cognisance of it. In like manner in denying to you the feelings of sympathy, of benevolence, of gratitude, of justice, of love, of friendship, she has excluded you from their controul. To these she has adapted the mechanism of the heart. Morals were too essential to the happiness of man to be risked on the incertain combinations of the head. She laid their foundation therefore in sentiment, not in science. That she gave to all, as necessary to all: this to a few only, as sufficing with a few. I know indeed that you pretend authority to the sovereign controul of our conduct in all it's parts: and a respect for your grave saws and maxims, a desire to do what is right, has sometimes induced me to conform to your counsels. A few facts however which I can readily recall to your memory, will suffice to prove to you that nature has not organised you for our moral direction. When the poor wearied souldier, whom we overtook at Chickahominy with his pack on his back, begged us to let him get up behind our chariot, you began to calculate that the road was full of souldiers, and that if all should be taken up our horses would fail in their journey. We drove on therefore. But soon becoming sensible you had made me do wrong, that tho we cannot relieve all the distressed we should relieve as many as we can, I turned about to take up the souldier; but he had entered a bye path, and was no more to be found: and from that moment to this I could never find him out to ask his forgiveness. Again, when the poor woman came to ask a charity in Philadelphia, you whispered that she looked like a drunkard, and that half a dollar was enough to give her for the alehouse. Those who want the dispositions to give, easily find reasons why they ought not to give. When I sought her out afterwards, and did what I should have done at first, you know that she employed the money immediately towards placing her child at school. If our country, when pressed with wrongs at the point of the bayonet, had been governed by it's heads instead of it's hearts, where should we have been now? hanging on a gallows as high as Haman's. You began to calculate and to compare wealth and numbers: we threw up a few pulsations of our warmest blood: we supplied enthusiasm against wealth and numbers: we put our existence to the hazard, when the hazard seemed against us, and we saved our country: justifying at the same time the ways of Providence, whose precept is to do always what is right, and leave the issue to him. In short, my friend, as far as my recollection serves me, I do not know that I ever did a good thing on your suggestion, or a dirty one without it. I do for ever then disclaim your interference in my province. Fill paper as you please with triangles and squares: try how many ways you can hang and combine them together. I shall never envy nor controul your sublime delights. But leave me to decide when and where friendships are to be contracted. You say I contract them at random, so you said the woman at Philadelphia was a drunkard. I receive no one into my esteem till I know they are worthy of it. Wealth, title, office, are no recommendations to my friendship. On the contrary great good qualities are requisite to make amends for their having wealth, title and office. You confess that in the present case I could not have made a worthier choice. You only object that I was so soon to lose them. We are not immortal ourselves, my friend; how can we expect our enjoiments to be so? We have no rose without it's thorn; no pleasure without alloy. It is the law of our existence; and we must acquiesce. It is the condition annexed to all our pleasures, not by us who receive, but by him who gives them. True, this condition is pressing cruelly on me at this moment. I feel more fit for death than life. But when I look back on the pleasures of which it is the consequence, I am conscious they were worth the price I am paying. Notwithstanding your endeavors too to damp my hopes, I comfort myself with expectations of their promised return. Hope is sweeter than despair, and they were too good to mean to deceive me. In the summer, said the gentleman; but in the spring, said the lady: and I should love her forever, were it only for that! Know then, my friend, that I have taken these good people into my bosom: that I have lodged them in the warmest cell I could find: that I love them, and will continue to love them thro life: that if misfortune should dispose them on one side of the globe, and me on the other, my affections shall pervade it's whole mass to reach them. Knowing then my determination, attempt not to disturb it. If you can at any time furnish matter for their amusement, it will be the office of a good neighbor to do it. I will in like manner seize any occasion which may offer to do the like good turn for you with Condorcet, Rittenhouse, Madison, La Cretelle, or any other of those worthy sons of science whom you so justly prize.

I thought this is a favorable proposition whereon to rest the issue of the dialogue. So I put an end to it by calling for my nightcap. Methinks I hear you wish to heaven I had called a little sooner, and so spared you the ennui of such a tedious sermon. I did not interrupt them sooner because I was in a mood for hearing sermons. You too were the subject; and on such a thesis I never think the theme long; not even if I am to write it, and that slowly and awkwardly, as now, with the left hand. But that you may not be discoraged from a correspondence which begins so formidably, I will promise you on my honour that my future letters shall be of a reasonable length. I will even agree to express but half my esteem for you, for fear of cloying you with too full a dose. But, on your part, no curtailing. If your letters are as long as the bible, they will appear short to me. Only let them be brim full of affection. I shall read them with the dispositions with which Arlequin in les deux billets spelt the words "je t'aime" and wished that the whole alphabet had entered into their composition.

We have had incessant rains since your departure. These make me fear for your health, as well as that you have had an uncomfortable journey. The same cause has prevented me from being able to give you any account of your friends here. This voiage to Fountainbleau will probably send the Count de Moutier and the Marquise de Brehan to America. Danquerville promised to visit me, but has not done it as yet. De latude comes sometimes to take family soupe with me, and entertains me with anecdotes of his five and thirty years imprisonment. How fertile is the mind of man which can make the Bastille and Dungeon of Vincennes yeild interesting anecdotes. You know this was for making four verses on Mme. de Pompadour. But I think you told me you did not know the verses. They were these. "Sans esprit, sans sentiment, Sans etre belle, ni neuve, En France on peut avoir le premier amant: Pompadour en est l'epreuve." I have read the memoir of his three escapes. As to myself my health is good, except my wrist which mends slowly, and my mind which mends not at all, but broods constantly on your departure. The lateness of the season obliges me to decline my journey into the South of France. Present me in the most friendly terms to Mr. Cosway, and receive me into your own recollection with a partiality and a warmth, proportioned, not to my own poor merit, but to the sentiments of sincere affection and esteem with which I have the honour to be, my dear Madam, your most obedient humble servant,

TH: JEFFERSON

Notes

[1] Jefferson to Maria Cosway, October 12, 1786, *Papers,* Boyd, X, 446; see Appendix II.

[2] See Appendix II. The dome of the Halle aux Bleds was constructed by Legrand and Molinos. The building was torn down in the 1880s to make way for the present Bourse du Commerce. The Medici column is still standing. Boyd (*Papers,* X, 435) reproduces a picture by Merechal of the Halle aux Bleds just as Jefferson saw it in 1786.

[3] Quoted by William Hazlitt, in George C. Williamson, *Richard Cosway, R.A.* (London, 1905), 55.

[4] *toujours riant, toujours gai:* always laughing, always gay. [ed.]

[5] sycophantic: seeking favor through flattery.[ed.]

[6] William Hazlitt, in *Conversations with James Northcote,* Edmund Gosse, ed. (London, 1894), 99. (James Northcote [1746–1831]: English painter who studied under Sir Joshua Reynolds. [(ed.)].

[7] salon: a regular gathering of distinguished persons in a private residence. [ed.]

[8] *escritoires:* writing desks. [ed.]

[9] Allan Cunningham, *The Lives of the Most Eminent British Painters, Sculptors and Architects,* 6 vols. (London, 1829-33), VI, 6.

[10] Sir Joshua Reynolds (1723–1792): a major English portrait painter. [ed.]

[11] Ellen C. Clayton, *English Female Artists,* 2 vols. (London, 1876), I, 316; Williamson, *Richard Cosway,* 20.

[12] Maria Cosway to M. Changers, July 11, 1816, Ms., Collegio di Maria SS. Bambina, Lodi, Italy.

[13] Williamson, *Richard Cosway,* 20.

[14] Maria Cosway to Richard Cosway, March 22, 1815, Ms., Maria Cosway Letterbook, Lodi, Italy. Maria Cosway also wrote to a Mrs. Chambers, May 29, 1816, " . . . the moment he gave himself to Hammersmith, began to lead him from me and from his home. . . . Hammersmith was drop'd for another acquaintance which kept him farther from me. peevish, cross, we were not happ." Ms., Letterbook, Lodi, Italy.

[15] Cunningham, *Lives of the Most Eminent British Painters,* VI, 10.

[16] Hazlitt, *Conversations with James Northcote,* 62.

[17]January 1784, reproduced in Horace Walpole, *Anecdotes of Painting in England, 1760-1795, with Some Account of the Principal Artists . . .* , F.W. Hilles and P.B. Daghlian, eds., 5 vols. (New Haven, 1937), V, 127-28.

[18]Quoted in Williamson, *Richard Cosway,* 43. Wolcott called Cosway "The Tiny Cosmetic," and caricaturist Mat Darley made an etching of him with the title "The Macaroni Miniature Painter." The title stuck to him for life. Williamson, *Richard Cosway,* 31.

[19] Williamson, *Richard Cosway,* 52.

[20] Thomas Gainsborough (1727-1788): English portrait painter. [ed.]

[21] dragoon: a soldier armed with a short musket. [ed.]

[22] See Marguerite Steen, *The Lost One: A Biography of Mary (Perdita) Robinson* (London, 1937), 190-91. Jefferson mentioned the volume, *Progress of Female Virtue and Female Dissipation,* which contained a set of aquatint engravings by Maria Cosway, in a letter to his daughter Martha Jefferson Randolph, October 7, 1804. *Family Letters,* 262. He had seen a magazine account.

[23] This gossip was reported in Williamson, *Richard Cosway,* 28, 49.

[24] Jefferson to Abigail Adams, August 9, 1786, *Papers,* Boyd, X, 202.

[25] John Jay (1745-1779) served as president of the Continental Congress, a diplomat, and first Supreme Court Chief Justice. [ed.]

[26] Jefferson to John Jay, January 11, 1789, Papers, Boyd, XIV, 430.

[27] Jefferson to Maria Cosway, October 12, 1789. See Appendix II.

[28] Martha Wayles, Jefferson's wife, died in 1782, prior to his ministry in France. [ed.]

[29] Maria Cosway to Allan Cunningham, Lodi, May 24, 1830, Williamson, *Richard Cosway,* 17.

[30] Maria Cosway to Allan Cunningham, Williamson, *Richard Cosway,* and Maria Cosway to M. Chambers, July 11, 1816, Maria Cosway Papers, Lodi, Italy.

[31] Williamson, *Richard Cosway,* 18.

[32] Jefferson to Maria Cosway, October 12, 1786. See Appendix II.

[33] The Louvre, former residence to the French kings in Paris, became an art gallery. The Palais Royale (Royal Palace) was built as Cardinal Richelieu's residence in the seventeenth century. The Bibliothèque du Roi was the king's library and the Panthéon a Paris church begun in 1764. Versailles, the palace and gardens built by Louis XIV outside Paris, housed the French monarchy in the seventeenth and eighteenth centuries. [ed.]

[34] Jefferson's visits can be reconstructed by a careful checking of his account book, his October 12, 1786, letter to Maria Cosway, and *Autobiography of Colonel John Trumbull, Patriot-Artist, 1756-1843,* Theodore Sizer, ed. (New Haven, 1953). The Cosway friendships in Paris were detailed in Williamson, *Richard Cosway.* D'Hancarville, whom Jefferson referred to as Mr. Danquerville, was a classical archaeologist and antiquarian who in 1785 had published a book on Greek art, notable for its sophistication in relating art to ancient religious phallic worship. *Recherches sur l'orgine, l'esprit et les progres des arts de la Grece; sur leurs connections avec les arts et la religion des plus anciens peuple connus . . .* (London, 1785). His letters to Maria Cosway may be seen in the Museo Circo, Lodi, Italy. Only one of Jefferson's original letters to Maria Cosway was preserved. See *Papers,* Boyd, X, 432n. The others published by Julian Boyd and Helen Bullock are taken from Jefferson's own press copies, preserved by his heirs. The envelope addressed to Richard Cosway, Stratford Place, London, in Jefferson's hand, along with Trumbull's portrait of Jefferson, are in the Collegio di Maria SS. Bambina, Lodi, Italy. See *Papers,* Boyd, X, xxxix, 466.

[35] Jacques Louis David was the chief French painter of the French Revolution, the Consulate and the First Empire. [ed.]

[36] Jefferson's account book includes the following: September 7, "pd seeing Machine of Marly 6 f the chateau 6f Pd Petit towards dinner at Marly 12f pd at Lowechienne f"; September 8, "pd at Concert Spiritual 6f"; September 9, "pd. seeing Gardes marbles 12 f"; September 14, "pd seeing machine 3f"; September, 16, "pd seeing Desert 12 f."

[37] Jefferson to Maria Cosway, October 12, 1786. See Appendix II.

[38] Jefferson to Abigail Adams, August 9, 1786, *Papers,* Boyd, X, 203.

[39] Jefferson to William Stephens Smith, August 9, 1786, *Papers,* Boyd, X, 223.

[40] Jefferson to George Wythe, August 13, 1786, *Papers,* Boyd, X, 244.

[41] *Writings,* L. and B., XVIII, 438. In 1785 Jefferson had purchased a twenty-two-volume set of Bell's English poets (account book, October 13, 1785). His "Thoughts on English Prosody," mistakenly dated by editors Lipscomb and Berger as having been written in 1789, was actually written between August and September 18, 1786, as Julian Boyd has pointed out. Some of the revisions were written with Jefferson's left hand, after the dislocation or breaking of his wrist September 18, 1786. See *Papers,* Boyd, X, 498n. See also Jefferson to Chasteliux, October 1786, *Papers,* Boyd, X, 498.

[42] *Writings,* L. and B., XVIII, 426, 430, 434.

[43] *Writings,* L. and B., XVIII, 443.

[44] Maria Cosway to Jefferson, February 15, 1787, *Papers,* Boyd, XI, 148–49. The letter was delivered to Jefferson personally by d'Hancarville, *Papers,* Boyd, XI, 150n.

[45] Maria Cosway to Jefferson, February 15, 1787, *Papers,* Boyd, XI, 149.

[46] Schachner, *Jefferson,* 317; Thomas Fleming, *The Man from Monticello: An Intimate Life of Thomas Jefferson* (New York, 1969), 136; Peterson, *Jefferson and the New Nation,* 348; Jordan, *White over Black,* 462; Saul Padover, *Jefferson* (New York, 1942), 140; Dixon Wecter, *The Hero in America* (New York, 1945), 154; Malone, *Jefferson and the Rights of Man,* 72.

[47] Kimball, *Jefferson: The Scene of Europe,* 159.

[48] See Fawn M. Brodie, "Jefferson Biographers and the Psychology of Canonization," *Journal of Interdisciplinary History* II (1971), 155–71.

[49] Jefferson to William Stephens Smith, October 22, 1786, *Papers,* Boyd, X, 478. Lyman Butterfield discovered a letter among the papers of William Temple Franklin which established the date and place of the accident. Le Veillard wrote to Franklin September 20, 1786, "Day before yesterday Mr. Jefferson dislocated his right wrist when attempting to jump over a fence in the 'Petit Cours.'" See Lyman Butterfield and Howard C. Rice, "Jefferson's Earliest Note to Maria Cosway with Some New Facts and Conjectures on His Broken Wrist," *William and Mary Quarterly,* 3rd series, V (1948), 26–33, 620–21. *Papers,* Boyd, X, 432n.

[50] Quoted in Randall, *Jefferson,* I, 456.

[51] Maria Cosway to Jefferson, September 20, 1786, *Papers,* Boyd, X, 393.

[52] Kimball, *Jefferson: The Scene of Europe,* 168–69; Malone, *Jefferson and the Rights of Man,* 72, 74.

[53] Maria Cosway to Jefferson, October 5, 1786, *Papers,* Boyd, X, 433.

[54] *Ibid.*

[55] Jefferson to Maria Cosway, October 12, 1786. See Appendix II.

[56] *Ibid.*

[57] Jefferson to Maria Cosway, October 5, 1786, *Papers,* Boyd, X, 431–32.

58 Bastille: Paris prison that was stormed and destroyed during the French Revolution in 1789. [ed.]

59 Jefferson to Maria Cosway, October 12, 1-86. See Appendix II.

60 *Papers,* Boyd, X, 453n. Balzac also left copies of his love letters.

61 *Papers,* Boyd, X, 453n; Peterson, *Jefferson and the New Nation,* 349.

62 Jefferson to Maria Cosway, October 12, 1786. See Appendix II.

63 Maria Cosway to Jefferson, October 9, 1786, *Papers,* Boyd, X, 441. This note is in Italian, appended to a letter by John Trumbull. Boyd gives the original and a translation. Several scholars have mistakenly believed that this four-line note was Maria Cosway's reply to the twelve-page letter from Jefferson, "My Head and My Heart."

64 Jefferson to Maria Cosway, October 13, 1786, *Papers,* Boyd, X, 458-59.

65 Jefferson to John Trumbull, October 13, 1786, *Papers,* Boyd, X, 460.

66 Jefferson to John Trumbull, February 23, 1787, August 26, 1788, *Papers,* Boyd, XI, 181, XIII, 546.

67 "I very much regret the loss of these twenty days," Trumbull wrote, ". . . I distinctly recollect, however . . . that Mr. Jefferson joined our party almost daily; and here commenced his acquaintance with Mrs. Cosway, of whom very respectful mention is made in his published correspondence." Trumbull, *Autobiography,* 120.

68 Maria Cosway to Jefferson, October 30, 1786, *Papers,* Boyd, X, 494-96. Julian Boyd filled in what he believed might have been the original words, in the holes gnawed by mice or rats, and he translated the Italian.

69 Williamson, *Richard Cosway,* 44-49.

70 Maria Cosway to Jefferson, November 17, 1786, translated from the Italian, *Papers,* Boyd, X, 538-39.

71 Jefferson to Maria Cosway, November 19, 1786, *Papers,* Boyd, X, 542.

72 Jefferson to Maria Cosway, November 29, 1786, *Papers,* Boyd, X, 555.

73 Jefferson to Eliza House Trist, December 15, 1786, *Papers,* Boyd, X, 600.

74 Jefferson to Maria Cosway, December 24, 1786, *Papers,* Boyd, X, 627.

75 Jefferson to Madame de Tessé, March 20, 1787, *Papers,* Boyd, XI, 226.

76 Jefferson to Maria Cosway, July 1, 1787, *Papers,* Boyd, XI, 520.

77 Maria Cosway to Jefferson, July 9, 1787, *Papers,* Boyd, XI, 569.

FOCUS: READING REVIEW

1. What was the nature of the Maria Cosway's relationship with her husband? What kinds of evidence does Brodie offer to support this? Why does she include this information?
2. Brodie presents the historians' judgments that Jefferson did not have an affair with Maria Cosway. What could be at work "that has little to do with scholarship"? How is Jefferson's accident used to disprove the affair by some historians? How does Brodie use it?
3. What interpretations do scholars offer to the "My Head and My Heart" letter? What evidence does Brodie offer for her interpretation?

FOCUS: AUTHOR'S STRATEGIES

1. The author's conscientious use of evidence suggests both a clear purpose and a particular audience. What is this purpose? Who is the audience? How does the evidence indicate these?

2. Brodie constructs a case of circumstantial evidence to suggest Jefferson's growing affections for Maria when she describes their explorations in Paris. How does she accomplish this? What is her evidence? What interpretation does she offer?

FOCUS: DISCUSSION AND WRITING

1. In terms of historical fact and creating a case, why does Brodie include the following statement? "Whether Jefferson ever heard that a secret passage ran from Schomberg House to the quarters of the Prince of Wales and that the Prince had seduced, or tried to seduce, Maria Cosway must remain a mystery."
2. Using Brodie's case for Jefferson's affair with Maria Cosway as an illustration, make a case for or against the possibility of historical objectivity.

The End and Beginning

Bruce Catton

Bruce Catton (1899–1978), the popular Civil War historian and longtime editor of American Heritage, *began his writing career as a journalist. In the 1940s he turned to writing about the Civil War, and* Stillness at Appomattox *won a 1953 Pulitzer Prize. Catton combined accurate historical research with lively, vivid writing in* The Centennial History of the Civil War *(1961–1965),* Gettysburg: The Final Fury *(1974),* Grant Takes Command *(1969), and* The Civil War *(1971), from which "The End and Beginning" is excerpted. Here Booth's assassination of Lincoln and Stafford's vindictiveness toward the South alter the shape of Reconstruction. For historian Catton, individual men create destiny.*

If no one could say exactly why the Civil War had come about in the first place, no one could quite say what it meant now that it was finished. Of all men, Abraham Lincoln came the closest to understanding what had happened. He believed that both sides shared in the blame for the war, just as they had shared in the cost of it. Out of such a belief had to come a determination that both sections must also share in the victory. The peace that would come out of the war must, in Lincoln's view, be broad enough and humane enough to mean some sort of gain for everyone in the land. To his great lieutenants, Grant and Sherman, Lincoln gave a glimpse of his policy, so when Johnston surrendered, Sherman was guided by what he thought Lincoln wanted. Two things, however, were wrong: Sherman appears to have gone beyond anything Lincoln was prepared to offer—and when he and Johnston met to discuss surrender terms Lincoln was dead, and the atmosphere in which Northern politicians could be magnanimous and farsighted had been fatally poisoned. Lincoln died early on the morning of April 15, and his death left the Republican radicals—the men who hated the South and hoped to see stern punishment inflicted on it—in full control of the Federal government. Lincoln's death brought an anger so black that Lincoln's own vision was blotted out. The Union was reconstructed at the price of bitterness and injustice, with much work left for later generations to do.

The war had lasted for four years and it had consumed hundreds of thousands of lives and billions of dollars in treasure. It had destroyed one of the two American ways of life forever, and it had changed the other almost beyond recognition; and it ended as it had begun, in a mystery of darkness and passion. If no one could say exactly why it had come about in the first place, no one could quite say what it meant now that it was finished. (A century of reflection has not wholly answered either riddle.) Things done by men born generations after Appomattox would continue to shed light on the significance of this greatest of all convulsions of the American spirit.

Of all men, Abraham Lincoln came the closest to understanding what had happened; yet even he, in his final backward glance, had to confess that something that went beyond words had been at work in the land. When he tried to sum it up, delivering his second inaugural address on March 4, 1865, he could do no more than remind his countrymen that they had somehow done more than they intended to do, as if without knowing it they had served a purpose that lay far beyond their comprehension.

"Neither party," he said, "expected for the war the magnitude or the duration which it has already attained. Neither anticipated that the cause of the conflict might cease with, or even before, the conflict itself should cease." (As he spoke, the Federal Congress had passed the thirteenth amendment[1] and seventeen states had already ratified it; and in Richmond, the Congress of the Confederacy was preparing to vote regiments of slaves into the Confederate service. Slavery was dead no matter how the war came out.) "Both read the same Bible and pray to the same God, and each invokes His aid against the other. ... The prayers of both could not be answered; that of neither has been answered fully. The Almighty has His own purposes."

It was a thing to brood over, this war with its terrible cost and its veiled meanings, and the wisest man could perhaps do little more than ask searching questions about it. As he went on with his speech Lincoln was doing nothing less than remind the people of America that they could not hope to understand what they had done and what had been done to them without examining the central riddle of human existence. As the war storm slowly ebbed he left one of the great questions for all men to ponder: "If we shall suppose that American slavery is one of those offenses which, in the providence of God, must needs come, but which, having continued through His appointed time, He now wills to remove, and that He gives to both North and South, this terrible war, as the woe due to those by whom the offense came, shall we discern therein any departure from those divine attributes which the believers in a living God always ascribe to Him?"

This question was propounded by a man who believed that both sides shared in the blame for the war, just as they had shared in the cost of it. Out of such a belief had to come a determination that both sections must also share in the victory. The peace that would come out of the war must, in Lincoln's view, be broad enough and humane enough to mean some sort of gain for everyone in the land—for the Northerner who had fought to reunite the country and to end slavery, for the Southerner who had fought against that goal, for the Negro who had humbly endured the struggle. In such a peace there could be no question of any punitive measures, any more than there could be any question of seeking to restore what the war had destroyed. If there was a triumph to celebrate, it was not the triumph of one set of men over another set, but of all men together over a common affliction.

To his great lieutenants, Grant and Sherman, Lincoln gave a glimpse of his policy in a meeting on board Lincoln's steamer *River Queen* at City Point, just before the beginning of the last campaign of the war. It was a policy rather than a detailed program, summarized in Lincoln's homely injunction: "Let 'em up easy." He wanted to see the Confederate armies disbanded and the men back at work on their farms and in the shops, and he wanted civil governments re-established in the secessionist states at the earliest possible moment. Sherman got the impression that Lincoln was perfectly willing to deal with the existing state governments in the South in order to maintain order, until Congress could provide for a more permanent arrangement. When Sherman returned to North Carolina to finish the job against Johnston, he took with him the conviction that Lincoln wanted a peace of reconciliation with no particular concern about formalities.

So when Johnston surrendered, Sherman was guided by what he thought Lincoln wanted. Two things, however, were wrong: Sherman appears to have gone beyond anything Lincoln was prepared to offer—and when he and Johnston met to discuss surrender terms Lincoln was dead, and the atmosphere in which Northern politicians could be magnanimous and farsighted had been fatally poisoned.

Johnston was brought to bay a few days after Lee surrendered. The Union army, more than 80,000 strong, was in camp around Raleigh, North Carolina. Johnston had fewer than half that many men, and not all of them were fully armed and organized. He and Sherman met near a place called Durham's Station, aware that Lee had given up and that the only task remaining was to get the Confederacy out of existence as smoothly as possible, and on April 18 they agreed on a document. Considering the fact that Sherman was looked upon as the South's most pitiless enemy, the hard man of war who struck without compassion and laid waste whole states without remorse, it was an amazing agreement.

To begin with, it covered not simply Johnston's army, but all of the remaining armed forces of the Confederacy. (Johnston had no authority over these, but he had with him the Confederate Secretary of War, General John C. Breckinridge, and Breckinridge's word would be binding.) It went far beyond the terms Grant had given Lee. Confederate regiments were to march to their respective state capitals, deposit their weapons there, and then disband, each man signing a pledge not to take up arms again. Each state government would be recognized as lawful once its officers had taken oath to support the Constitution of the United States. No one was to be punished for the part he had taken in bringing on or supporting secession, all political rights were to be guaranteed, and the rights of person and property as defined in the Federal Constitution were to be fully respected—which might, conceivably, give slavery a new lease on life. All in all, this treaty—for it was a treaty of peace, rather than a simple surrender document—gave all that any Southerner in this spring of 1865 could hope to ask; and by this time there was not a chance in the world that the government in Washington would ratify it.

Lincoln himself would almost certainly have modified it. From the moment when Confederate surrender became an imminent probability, he had insisted that generals in the field were not to concern themselves with political questions; they should give liberal terms to the surrendering armies, but all issues involving the readmission of the states to the Union, the restoration of civil and political rights, and the abolition of slavery, they were to leave in the President's hands. (Sherman apparently had missed this particular point.) To bring the seceded states back into full relationship with the rest of the Union would take the most delicate kind of political finesse, and Lincoln proposed to handle all of this himself. Congress would not be in session until late in the fall, and it was just possible that Lincoln could have his moderate reconstruction program well enough established by that time so that the bitter-enders in House and Senate could not upset it, but he never would have let any general set the pattern for him.

But an actor named John Wilkes Booth had chosen this moment to upset everything. On Good Friday evening, April 14—driven by an insane compulsion of hatred and perverted loyalty to a cause which he had never felt obliged to fight for as a soldier—Booth strode into the President's box at Ford's Theatre in Washington, fired a bullet into Lincoln's brain, vaulted from the box to the stage, and rode off desperately through the night, fancying that if he could just reach Confederate territory he would be hailed as a hero and a savior. His twisted, inadequate mind was never able to see that his trigger finger had done the South more harm than all the lawless bummers in Sherman's army.

In all American history there is no stranger story than the story of the plot that took Lincoln's life. Booth had been conspiring for months, doing it flamboyantly, dramatically, in a way that fairly invited detection. He had first nourished a crack-brained plan to kidnap Lincoln alive and take him down to Richmond, shifting to a scheme for wholesale murder after Lee surrendered and Richmond was captured. He planned to kill Lincoln, Grant, Vice-President Johnson, and Secretary of State Seward, and he conspired with a weird set of dim-witted incompetents who could hardly have carried out a plan to rob a corner newsstand. The odds that the whole scheme would fall of its own weight were fantastically long. And yet, somehow—the luck of the American people just then being out—the thing worked. Lincoln was assassinated; Seward barely escaped death when one of Booth's minions forced a way into his sickroom and slashed him with a knife. The plot to kill Grant and Johnson missed fire, but the central, disastrous feature of the plan worked. Lincoln died.

Lincoln died early on the morning of April 15, and his death left the Republican radicals—the men who hated the South and hoped to see stern punishment inflicted on it—in full control of the Federal government. Vice-President Andrew Johnson had demanded that treason be made odious: now he was President, with full power to make the peace as stern as anyone could wish, and although he would finally come to see that Lincoln's policy was the better one, and would wreck his career trying to put it into effect, he was surrounded by men of great force and determination who would put Lincoln's ideas into the grave along with Lincoln's lifeless body.

For the immediate present the Federal government would be effectively operated by Secretary of War Stanton, who made himself something very like a dictator during the first week or two of Johnson's regime.

Stanton was a man of immense drive; ruthless, often arrogant, of an incurably suspicious nature. The task of unraveling Booth's mad plot was in his hands, and as the details of the scheme came to light Stanton was convinced that Booth was no lone-wolf operator, but was in fact an agent for the Confederate government itself. In part this deduction came simply because Stanton was always ready to believe the worst, especially where his enemies were concerned; and in part it rested on the fact that the Confederate government had been operating that fifth-column business in the North, with agents trying to burn Northern cities, wreck railroads, seize military prison camps, and raid Yankee banks. The War Department had collected a great deal of information about this operation, some of it false, some of it true. It knew, among other things, that these operations had been directed by Confederate agents established in Canada, and it also knew that Booth himself had recently been in Canada. Under the circumstances it is hardly surprising that a man like Stanton should suspect that Booth might be a part of the Southern conspiracy which had been keeping Federal counter-espionage operatives so busy.

Stanton did more than suspect: he informed the nation, without any qualifications, that Lincoln had been murdered by Jefferson Davis' agents, and that the whole tragedy was a direct part of the dying Confederate war effort. That he was never able to prove a word of this—it soon became clear that no one in Richmond had had anything at all to do with the murder, and that Booth had been as much an irresponsible fanatic as John Brown had been when he descended on Harpers Ferry—made no difference whatever. The damage was done; in the terrible revulsion of feeling that swept across the North few people would bother to speak out for the sort of peace Lincoln himself had wanted.

Stanton and the other bitter-enders saw to it that no one in the North was allowed to get over his grief quickly. Lincoln's body lay in state beneath the Capitol dome, and there was a state funeral in the White House. Then, in a special train, the body was taken back to Springfield, Illinois, for burial—taken there in the most roundabout way imaginable, put on display in New York and Chicago and in many other cities, made the occasion for the most elaborately contrived funeral procession in American history. Millions of Americans saw it. Those who could not file past the open casket, in places where it was on display, at least could gather by the railroad tracks and watch the train as it moved slowly past. Millions of people took part in this parade of sorrow. It lasted for two weeks, and although the grief which was expressed was undoubtedly sincere, the whole affair amounted to turning a knife in a wound—turning it again and again, so that the shock of sorrow and outraged indignation which had gone all across the North might continue to be felt.

In trying to capitalize on the nation's tragedy the radicals had something real and deep to work with. The millions who stood in silence to watch the funeral car, with its black bunting, drift past on its way to Illinois were the people who had supported Lincoln through thick and thin. They had provided the armies that he had called into being. They had sustained him at the polls when the issue was in doubt. He had spoken to their hearts, in a way no one else had ever done, when he explained the ultimate meaning of the war in his address at Gettysburg and groped for the unattainable truth in his second inaugural. He had expressed the best that was in them, speaking not so much to them as for them, and he had gone with them through four years of trial by doubt and fire. As the war ended they had come to understand his greatness: and now, when he was struck down at the very moment of his triumph, they felt an anger so black that Lincoln's own vision was blotted out.

The first step was to undo what Sherman had tried to do. His treaty with Johnston went first to Grant, who could see that Sherman had done much more than any general was authorized to do. Grant sent the papers on to Stanton and suggested that the whole cabinet might want to consider them. The cabinet did want to consider them, and it disapproved them in short order; Grant was ordered to go to Sherman at once, to cancel the armistice which was a part of the Sherman-Johnston agreement, and to resume hostilities. Grant obeyed and Johnston was notified that the deal was off. There was no more fighting, as he promptly surrendered on terms identical with those Grant had given Lee.

None of this disturbed Sherman greatly. He could see that he had tried to exercise powers which belonged to the civil government, and when he was overruled he was ready to accept the fact quietly. What infuriated him was the way Stanton used the whole episode to inflame public opinion.

For Stanton made a public announcement concerning the Sherman-Johnston agreement in a way which strongly suggested that Sherman was disloyal or crazy. This agreement, Stanton declared, practically recognized the Confederacy, re-established the secessionist state governments, put arms and ammunition in the hands of Rebels, permitted the re-establishment of slavery, possibly made the Northern taxpayer responsible for debts run up by the Confederate government, and left the defeated Rebels in position to renew the rebellion whenever they saw fit.

An announcement of this kind, coming at the moment when the electorate was still in a state of shock because of Lincoln's assassination, and coming also at a time when the complicity of the Confederate government in Booth's murder plot was being proclaimed as an established fact, was a stunner. It raised Sherman to a high pitch of rage, and made him one of Stanton's most devout and enduring enemies; but this did no particular damage, since Sherman was a good hater and Stanton already had many enemies, and the public outcry that was raised against the general eventually subsided. In a few years no one in the North or the South would remember that Sherman had nearly wrecked his career in his attempt to befriend the South, and he would be enshrined as an unstained hero in the North and as an unmitigated villain in Southern memories. The real harm that was done was the mortal injury that was inflicted on the Lincolnian policy which Sherman, however clumsily, had tried to put into effect.

For the basis of Lincoln's whole approach to reconstruction was the belief that the broken halves of the Union could be fitted together without bitterness and in a spirit of mutual understanding and good will. The war was over, and there was no undoing of anything that had happened. No one had really intended that things should go as they had gone; the responsibility for it all was strangely divided, just as the almost unendurable suffering and heartache had been divided . . . the Almighty did indeed have His own purposes, and now it was up to the people of both sections to try to adjust themselves to those purposes and to work together in the adjustment. But by the time Lincoln's body had finished its long journey and lay in the tomb at Springfield, an atmosphere had been created in the North which put such an effort out of reach. President Johnson would try to make the effort, but he had not a fraction of Lincoln's political skill, and the job was too much for him. He was never able to use what might have been his greatest asset—the wholehearted support which the two most famous Northern generals, Grant and Sherman, would have given to an attempt to put Lincoln's policy into effect.

No one in the North, after Lincoln's death, had anything approaching the prestige which these two soldiers had, and Johnson could have used them if he had known how. But Sherman's experience following the rejection of his "treaty" left him embittered, deeply disgusted with anything smacking of politics; thereafter he would be nothing but the soldier, letting the people at Washington commit any folly they chose to commit, and President Johnson never understood how to soften him. And Grant before long became estranged, not because he opposed what Johnson wanted to do, but simply because Johnson could not handle him. In the end he would be counted among Johnson's enemies because the radicals were able to take advantage of Johnson's clumsiness and Grant's own political innocence.

So things happened in the familiar and imperfect way that every American knows about. The Union was reconstructed, at last, at the price of bitterness and injustice, with much work for later generations to do. A measure of the amount of work bequeathed to these later generations is the fact that nearly a century after Appomattox the attempt to work out a solution for the race problem—that great untouchable which, many layers down, lay at the abyssal depth of the entire conflict—would still be looked upon as a sectional matter and would still be productive of sectional discord. In the anger and suspicion of the reconstruction era the chance that the thing might be approached rationally, so that it could perhaps be solved rather than simply shoved aside and ignored, flickered out like a candle's flame in a gale of wind.

Nothing could be done rationally at that time because wars do not leave men in a rational mood. Bone-weary of fighting in 1865, the American people greatly desired magnanimity and understanding and a reasonable handling of vexing problems; but those virtues had gone out of fashion, and they could not immediately be re-established. What happened after the war ended grew out of the hot barren years when anger and suspicion went baying down the trail of violence: the years in which bitter appeals to unleashed emotion had made the fury of a few the common affliction of all ... years of desperate battles, of guerrilla snipings and hangings, with a swinging torch for town and home place and the back of a hard hand to silence dissent. These had created the atmosphere in which men tried to put the Union back together, to turn enmity into friendship, and to open the door of freedom for a race that had lain in bondage. The wonder is not that the job was done so imperfectly, but that it was done at all.

For it was done, finally; if not finished, at least set on the road to completion. It may be many years before the job is really completed; generations before the real meaning and the ultimate consequences of the Civil War are fully comprehended. We understand today a little more than could be understood in 1865, but the whole truth remains dim.

Here was the greatest and most moving chapter in American history, a blending of meanness and greatness, an ending and a beginning. It came out of what men were, but it did not go as men had planned it. The Almighty had His own purposes.

Notes

[1] The Thirteenth Amendment prohibited slavery.

FOCUS: READING REVIEW

1. What did Lincoln see as the Civil War's final triumph? What kind of a peace did he envision? How did the treaty designed by Johnston and Sherman reflect his concerns? Why did the treaty fail?
2. Why did Booth's "trigger finger" do "the South more harm than all the lawless bummers in Sherman's army"?
3. How did Stanton marshal Northern sentiment against the South following Lincoln's death?
4. What was the legacy of Lincoln's death and Stanton's power? How is it easier to understand the Civil War now than it was in 1865? What still remains to be understood?

FOCUS: AUTHOR'S STRATEGIES

1. Catton writes for an audience familiar with Lincoln's assassination. How does his language rekindle his audience's interest at yet another retelling?
2. Besides informing his audience about these important historic events, what purpose does Catton seek to achieve? How do the introduction and conclusion indicate this?
3. The essay's larger structure is chronological, but embedded in this recounting of historical process is a causal analysis. On what events does Catton focus? What are the effects of those events?

FOCUS: DISCUSSION AND WRITING

1. What philosophy of history does the following passage suggest? "And yet, somehow—the luck of the American people just then being out—the thing worked. Lincoln was assassinated. . . ."
2. What is your understanding of the "meaning and consequence" of the Civil War? How does this compare with Lincoln's own view in his Second Inaugural Address?
3. Does Catton take a biased position toward or against either the North or the South? Point to passages in the essay to support your position.

Chapter *9*
Critical Responses
to
Historical Studies

For better or worse, each generation's historians return to historical problems with new evidence and new perspectives. The essays in chapters 7 and 8 introduced the idea that historical studies engage in a process of accumulation and revision, hoping to move toward a more accurate image of the past. The selections in this chapter reflect and respond to historical reevaluation. In "Past Masters," Frances FitzGerald finds recent changes in American history textbooks disconcerting. These recent texts, she finds, demythologize heroes and question traditional values. Her study considers an extreme case of historical subjectivity; historical revision fares better in Potter's essay, "Abundance and the Turner Hypothesis." Here Potter examines Frederick Jackson Turner's theory that the seemingly boundless frontier shaped American character. Potter objects to Turner's generalizations and imprecise language. He then refines Turner's view, presents historical evidence, and concludes that economic abundance, and not merely limitless land, has shaped the American character.

Past Masters

Frances FitzGerald

Frances FitzGerald (b. 1940), an American freelance journalist, won a Pulitzer Prize in general nonfiction for her work reporting the Vietnam War, later collected in Fire in the Lake: The Vietnamese and Americans in Viet Nam *(1973). Her interests have since turned to American history and to how a given era's prejudices change history books.* America Revised *(1979), the source for "Past Masters," published her study. This selection analyzes the changes in American history textbooks in the late 1960s and early 1970s and argues that these changes revised history.*

Those of us who grew up in the fifties believed in the permanence of our American-history textbooks. But now the textbook histories have changed. Columbus, a minor character now, is far from being the only personage to have suffered from time and revision. Modern scholarship and modern perspectives have found their way into children's books. The history texts now hint at a certain level of unpleasantness in American history. The histories of the fifties were implacable; America was perfect. In the new texts the past is no highway to the present; it is a collection of issues and events that do not fit together and that lead in no single direction. The present is now a tangle of problems. Even more surprising, whereas in the fifties all texts represented the same political view, current texts follow no pattern of orthodoxy. The political diversity in the books is matched by a diversity of pedagogical approach. In these books, history is clearly not a list of agreed-upon facts but a welter of events which must be ordered by the historian.

Those of us who grew up in the fifties believed in the permanence of our American-history textbooks. To us as children, those texts were the truth of things: they were American history. It was not just that we read them before we understood that not everything that is printed is the truth, or the whole truth. It was that they, much more than other books, had the demeanor and trappings of authority. They were weighty volumes. They spoke in measured cadences: imperturbable, humorless, and as distant as Chinese emperors. Our teachers treated them with respect, and we paid them abject homage by memorizing a chapter a week. But now the textbook histories have changed, some of them to such an extent that an adult would find them unrecognizable.

One current junior-high-school American history begins with a story about a Negro cowboy called George McJunkin. It appears that when McJunkin was riding down a lonely trail in New Mexico one cold spring morning in 1925 he discovered a mound containing bones and stone implements, which scientists later proved belonged to an Indian civilization ten thousand years old. The book goes on to say that scientists now believe there were people in the Americas at least twenty thousand years ago. It discusses the Aztec, Mayan, and Incan civilizations and the meaning of the word "culture" before introducing the European explorers.[1]

Another history text—this one for the fifth grade—begins with the story of how Henry B. Gonzalez, who is a member of Congress from Texas, learned about his own nationality. When he was ten years old, his teacher told him he was an American because he was born in the United States. His grandmother, however, said, "The cat was born in the oven. Does that make him bread?" After reporting that Mr. Gonzalez eventually went to college and law school, the book explains that now "some people say that people of the United States are more like a salad bowl than a melting pot."[2]

Poor Columbus! He is a minor character now, a walk-on in the middle of American history. Even those books that have not replaced his picture with a Mayan temple or an Iroquois mask do not credit him with discovering America—even for the Europeans. The Vikings, they say, preceded him to the New World, and after that the Europeans, having lost or forgotten their maps, simply neglected to cross the ocean again for five hundred years. Columbus is far from being the only personage to have suffered from time and revision. Captain John Smith, Daniel Boone, and Wild Bill Hickok—the great self-promoters of American history—have all but disappeared, taking with them a good deal of the romance of the American frontier. General Custer has given way to Chief Crazy Horse; General Eisenhower no longer liberates Europe single-handed; and, indeed, most generals, even to Washington and Lee, have faded away, as old soldiers do, giving place to social reformers such as William Lloyd Garrison and Jacob Riis. A number of black Americans have risen to prominence: not only George Washington Carver but Frederick Douglass and Martin Luther King, Jr. W.E.B. Du Bois now invariably accompanies Booker T. Washington. In addition, there is a mystery man called Crispus Attucks, a fugitive slave about whom nothing seems to be known for certain except that he was a victim of the Boston Massacre and thus became one of the first casualties of the American Revolution. Thaddeus Stevens has been reconstructed—his character changed, as it were, from black to white, from cruel and vindictive to persistent and sincere. As for Teddy Roosevelt, he now champions the issue of conservation instead of charging up San Juan Hill. No single President really stands out as a hero, but all Presidents—except certain unmentionables in the second half of the nineteenth century—seem to have done as well as could be expected, given difficult circumstances.

Of course, when one thinks about it, it is hardly surprising that modern scholarship and modern perspectives have found their way into children's books. Yet the changes remain shocking. Those who in the sixties complained of the bland optimism, the chauvinism, and the materialism of their old civics texts did so in the belief that, for all their protests, the texts would never change. The thought must have had something reassuring about it, for that generation never noticed when its complaints began to take effect and the songs about radioactive rainfall and houses made of ticky-tacky began to appear in the textbooks. But this is what happened.

The history text texts now hint at a certain level of unpleasantness in American history. Several books, for instance, tell the story of Ishi, the last "wild" Indian in the continental United States, who, captured in 1911 after the massacre of his tribe, spent the final four and a half years of his life in the University of California's museum of anthropology, in San Francisco. At least three books show the same stunning picture of the breaker boys, the child coal miners of Pennsylvania—ancient children with deformed bodies and blackened faces who stare stupidly out from the entrance to a mine. One book quotes a soldier on the use of torture in the American campaign to pacify the Philippines at the beginning of the century. A number of books say that during the American Revolution the patriots tarred and feathered those who did not support them, and drove many of the loyalists from the country. Almost all the present-day history books note that the United States interned Japanese-Americans in detention camps during the Second World War.

Ideologically speaking, the histories of the fifties were implacable, seamless. Inside their covers, America was perfect: the greatest nation in the world, and the embodiment of democracy, freedom, and technological progress. For them, the country never changed in any important way: its values and its political institutions remained constant from the time of the American Revolution. To my generation—the children of the fifties—these texts appeared permanent just because they were so self-contained. Their orthodoxy, it seemed, left no handholds for attack, no lodging for decay. Who, after all, would dispute the wonders of technology or the superiority of the English colonists over the Spanish? Who would find fault with the pastorale of the West or the Old South? Who would question the anti-Communist crusade? There was, it seemed, no point in comparing these visions with reality, since they were the public truth and were thus quite irrelevant to what existed and to what any one privately believed. They were—or so it seemed—the permanent expression of mass culture in America.

But now the texts have changed, and with them the country that American children are growing up into. The society that was once uniform is now a patchwork of rich and poor, old and young, men and women, blacks, whites, Hispanics, and Indians. The system that ran so smoothly by means of the Constitution under the guidance of benevolent conductor Presidents is now a rattletrap affair. The past is no highway to the present; it is a collection of issues and events that do not fit together and that lead in no single direction. The word "progress" has been replaced by the word "change": children, the modern texts insist, should learn history so that they can adapt to the rapid changes taking place around them. History is proceeding in spite of us. The present, which was once portrayed in the concluding chapters as a peaceful haven of scientific advances and Presidential inaugurations, is now a tangle of problems: race problems, urban problems, foreign-policy problems, problems of pollution, poverty, energy depletion, youthful rebellion, assassination, and drugs. Some books illustrate these problems dramatically. One, for instance, contains a picture of a doll half buried in a mass of untreated sewage; the caption reads, "Are we in danger of being overwhelmed by the products of our society and wastage created by their production? Would you agree with this photographer's interpretation?"[3] Two books show the same picture of an old black woman sitting in a straight chair in a dingy room, her hands folded in graceful resignation;[4] the surrounding text discusses the problems faced by the urban poor and by the aged who depend on Social Security. Other books present current problems less starkly. One of the texts concludes sagely:

> Problems are part of life. Nations face them, just as people face them, and try to solve them. And today's Americans have one great advantage over past generations. Never before have Americans been so well equipped to solve their problems. They have today the means to conquer poverty, disease, and ignorance. The technetronic age has put that power into their hands.[5]

Such passages have a familiar ring. Amid all the problems, the deus ex machina of science still dodders around in the gloaming of pious hope.

Even more surprising than the emergence of problems is the discovery that the great unity of the texts has broken. Whereas in the fifties all texts represented the same political view, current texts follow no pattern of orthodoxy. Some books, for instance, portray civil-rights legislation as a series of actions taken by a wise, paternal government; others convey some suggestion of the social upheaval involved and make mention of such people as Stokely Carmichael and Malcolm X. In some books, the Cold War has ended; in others, it continues, with Communism threatening the free nations of the earth.

The political diversity in the books is matched by a diversity of pedagogocal approach. In addition to the traditional narrative histories, with their endless streams of facts, there are so-called "discovery," or "inquiry," texts, which deal with a limited number of specific issues in American history. These texts do not pretend to cover the past; they focus on particular topics, such as "stratification in Colonial society" or "slavery and the American Revolution," and illustrate them with documents from primary and secondary sources. The chapters in these books amount to something like case studies, in that they include testimony from people with different perspectives or conflicting views on a single subject. In addition, the chapters provide background information, explanatory notes, and a series of questions for the student. The questions are the heart of the matter, for when they are carefully selected they force students to think much as historians think: to define the point of view of the speaker, analyze the ideas presented, question the relationship between events, and so on. One text, for example, quotes Washington, Jefferson, and John Adams on the question of foreign alliances and then asks, "What did John Adams assume that the international situation would be after the American Revolution? What did Washington's attitude toward the French alliance seem to be? How do you account for his attitude?" Finally, it asks, "Should a nation adopt a policy toward alliances and cling to it consistently, or should it vary its policies toward other countries as circumstances change?"[6] In these books, history is clearly not a list of agreed-upon facts or a sermon on politics but a babble of voices and a welter of events which must be ordered by the historian.

In matters of pedagogy, as in matters of politics, there are not two sharply differentiated categories of books; rather, there is a spectrum. Politically, the books run from moderate left to moderate right; pedagogically, they run from the traditional history sermons, through a middle ground of narrative texts with inquiry-style questions and of inquiry texts with long stretches of narrative, to the most rigorous of case-study books. What is common to the current texts—and makes all of them different from those of the fifties—is their engagement with the social sciences. In eighth-grade histories, the "concepts" of social science make fleeting appearances. But these "concepts" are the very foundation stones of various elementary-school social-studies series. The 1970 Harcourt Brace Jovanovich series, for example, boasts in its preface of "a horizontal base or ordering of conceptual schemes" to make its "vertical arm of behavioral themes."[7] What this means is not entirely clear, but the books do proceed from easy questions to hard ones, such as—in the sixth-grade book—"How was interaction between merchants and citizens different in the Athenian and Spartan social systems?" Virtually all the American-history texts for older children include discussions of "role," "status," and "culture." Some of them stage debates between eminent social scientists in roped-off sections of the text; some include essays on economics or sociology; some contain pictures and short biographies of social scientists of both sexes and of diverse races. Many books seem to accord social scientists a higher status than American Presidents.

Quite as striking as these political and pedagogical alterations is the change in the physical appearance of the texts. The schoolbooks of the fifties showed some effort in the matter of design: they had maps, charts, cartoons, photographs, and an occasional four-color picture to break up the columns of print. But beside the current texts they look as naïve as Soviet fashion magazines. The print in the fifties books is heavy and far too black, the colors muddy. The photographs are conventional news shots—portraits of Presidents in three-quarters profile, posed "action" shots of soldiers. The other illustrations tend to be Socialist-realist-style drawings (there are a lot of hefty farmers with hoes in the Colonial-period chapters) or incredibly vulgar made-for-children paintings of patriotic events. One painting shows Columbus standing in full court dress on a beach in the New World from a perspective that could have belonged only to the Arawaks. By contrast, the current texts are paragons of sophisticated modern design. They look not like *People* or *Family Circle* but, rather, like *Architectural Digest* or *Vogue*. One of them has an Abstract Expressionist design on its cover, another a Rauschenberg-style collage, a third a reproduction of an American primitive painting. Inside, almost all of them have a full-page reproduction of a painting of the New York school—a Jasper Johns flag, say, or "The Boston Massacre," by Larry Rivers. But these reproductions are separated only with difficulty from the overall design, for the time charts in the books look like Noland stripe paintings, and the distribution charts are as punctilious as Albers' squares in their color gradings. The amount of space given to illustrations is far greater than it was in the fifties; in fact, in certain "slow-learner" books the pictures far outweigh the text in importance. However, the illustrations have a much greater historical value. Instead of made-up paintings or anachronistic sketches, there are cartoons, photographs, and paintings drawn from the periods being treated. The chapters on the Colonial period will show, for instance, a ship's carved prow, a Revere bowl, a Copley painting—a whole gallery of Early Americana. The nineteenth century is illustrated with nineteenth-century cartoons and photographs—and the photographs are all of high artistic quality. As for the twentieth-century chapters, they are adorned with the contents of a modern-art museum.

The use of all this art and high-quality design contains some irony. The nineteenth-century photographs of child laborers or urban slum apartments are so beautiful that they transcend their subjects. To look at them, or at the Victor Gatto painting of the Triangle shirtwaist-factory fire, is to see not misery or ugliness but an art object. In the modern chapters, the contrast between style and content is just as great: the color photographs of junkyards or polluted rivers look as enticing as *Gourmet's* photographs of food. The book that is perhaps the most stark in its description of modern problems illustrates the horrors of nuclear testing with a pretty Ben Shahn picture of the Bikini explosion, and the potential for global ecological disaster with a color photograph of the planet swirling its mantle of white clouds.[8] Whereas in the nineteen-fifties the texts were childish in the sense that they were naïve and clumsy, they are now childish in the sense that they are polymorphous-perverse. American history is not dull any longer; it is a sensuous experience.

The surprise that adults feel in seeing the changes in history texts must come from the lingering hope that there is, somewhere out there, an objective truth. The hope is, of course, foolish. All of us children of the twentieth century know, or should know, that there are no absolutes in human affairs, and thus there can be no such thing as perfect objectivity. We know that each historian in some degree creates the world anew and that all history is in some degree contemporary history. But beyond this knowledge there is still a hope for some reliable authority, for some fixed stars in the universe. We may know journalists cannot be wholly unbiased and that "balance" is an imaginary point between two extremes, and yet we hope that Walter Cronkite will tell us the truth of things. In the same way, we hope that our history will not change—that we learned the truth of things as children. The texts, with their impersonal voices, encourage this hope, and therefore it is particularly disturbing to see how they change, and how fast.

Slippery history! Not every generation but every few years the content of American-history books for children changes appreciably. Schoolbooks are not, like trade books, written and left to their fate. To stay in step with the cycles of "adoption" in school districts across the country, the publishers revise most of their old texts or substitute new ones every three or four years. In the process of revision, they not only bring history up to date but make changes—often substantial changes—in the body of the work. History books for children are thus more contemporary than any other form of history. How should it be otherwise? Should students read histories written ten, fifteen, thirty years ago? In theory, the system is reasonable—except that each generation of children reads only one generation of schoolbooks. That transient history is those children's history forever—their particular version of America.

Notes

[1] Wood, Gabriel, and Biller, *American* (1975), p. 3.
[2] King and Anderson, *The United States* (sixth level), Houghton Mifflin Social Studies Program (1976), pp. 15–16.
[3] Sellers et al., *As It Happened* (1975), p. 812.
[4] Graff, *The Free and the Brave*, 2nd ed. (1972), p. 696; and Graff and Krout, *The Adventure*, 2nd ed. (1973), p. 784.
[5] Wood, Gabriel, and Biller, *America* (1975), p. 812.
[6] Fenton, gen. ed., *A New History of the United States*, grade eleven (1969), p. 170.
[7] Brandwein et al., *The Social Sciences* (1975), introduction to all books.
[8] Ver Steeg and Hofstadter, *A People* (1975), pp. 772–73.

FOCUS: READING REVIEW

1. What about history textbooks of the fifties gave them the demeanor of authority?
2. How has Columbus suffered from time and revision? What does the different focus on the origins of the United States suggest about the views of those who have revised U.S. history?
3. How have history texts altered the concept of progress? What are some examples of this? Why has this change occurred?
4. What changes in approaches for teaching history have occurred? What does this suggest about the methods of historical studies?
5. What is the relation of social science to history in the new texts?
6. What is the nature of the physical appearance of the new texts? On what grounds does FitzGerald object to the appearance?
7. Which history textbooks, those of the fifties or the later ones, does FitzGerald prefer and why?

FOCUS: AUTHOR'S STRATEGIES

1. The author develops this essay through a comparative analysis. What are the components of the two groups of textbooks she examines? How does she order this in her writing?
2. FitzGerald's bias weights this essay. What is her preference? How does she use comparison and contrast to present her opinion? What in her language indicates bias?
3. For what audience is FitzGerald writing? How does her evidence suggest this audience? How do her assumptions about the values that history should teach indicate her audience?

FOCUS: DISCUSSION AND WRITING

1. After reading FitzGerald's comparison of old and new history texts, which texts do you feel give a more accurate presentation of history and why?
2. Compare and contrast FitzGerald's view of history with Muller's views in "The Premises of Inquiry" (pp. 327–338).
3. FitzGerald implies that school textbooks should teach children a particular view of the United States. What is this view? Agree or disagree with this viewpoint, offering reasons based on your own experiences with learning history.

Abundance and the Turner Hypothesis
David M. Potter

David M. Potter (1910–1971), one of the United States' most distinguished historians, studied at Emory University and Yale, where he earned a Ph.D. and then taught there for nineteen years. He left Yale to become Coe Professor of American History at Stanford. Potter received special appointments to the Harmsworth Lectureship at Oxford University, the Walgreen Lectureship at the University of Chicago, and the Commonwealth Fund Lectureship at London University. His best known works are Lincoln and the Succession Crises *(1942 and 1979),* People of Plenty: Economic Abundance and the American Character *(1954), and* Nationalism and Sectionalism in America, 1775–1877 *(1961). This essay, taken from the* People of Plenty, *examines Frederick Jackson Turner's famous hypothesis that the frontier experience formed the American character's independence, economic equality, and democracy. Potter sets out Turner's inaccuracies and then proposes his own refinement of Turner's hypothesis. This essay provides a fine example of critical analysis and refutation.*

No historian can overlook the fact that American history has long provided a classic formula for defining and explaining the American character: this is Frederick Jackson Turner's frontier hypothesis. Turner declared that, on the frontier, the "perennial rebirth" of society present in the westward expansion and the continuous touch with primitive society "furnish the forces dominating American character." To Turner "the most significant thing about the American frontier is that it lies at the hither edge of free land." The real key to Turner's thought is in Turner's predilection for the social ideal of agrarian democracy. When abundance operated within an agragrian context—in the form of free land for farmers—Turner seized upon it, while refusing to recognize the operation of abundance outside this selected context. Yet, clearly it is not merely the greater endowment of land which has differentiated America's growth from Europe's. It is the greater supply, also, of timber, of iron, of copper, or petroleum, of coal, of hydroelectric power. Because of this land and because of Turner's concealed agrarianism, it becomes important to consider more closely the frontier situation as Turner conceived it. The frontier was the place where free land lay at the edge of settlement; the place where institutions no longer towered over the individual man; the place where European complexity gave way to American simplicity; and the place where democratic growth and change was repeatedly re-enacted as a process and reaffirmed as a principle. The "frontier of settlement . . . carried with it individualism, democracy, and nationalism."

With this outline of the frontier hypothesis in mind, we can determine to what extent the frontier was the context of abundance and to what extent it explains what abundance alone cannot explain. By confining his explanation of Americanism to the conditions of the pioneer stage of our development, Turner implied that nothing distinctively American would be left after the pioneer stage passed. Further, by limiting his recognition of abundance to free land, he limited his recognition of successive American democratic readjustments. By failing to recognize that the frontier was only one form of American abundance, Turner cut himself off from the insight that other forms of abundance had superseded the frontier even before the supply of free land had been exhausted. In reality, it was abundance in any form, including the frontier form, rather than the frontier in any unique sense, which wrought some of the major results in the American experience. American abundance has remained of primary significance both in the frontier phase and in the vast industrial phase which has dominated American life.

No historian can overlook the fact that American history has long provided a classic formula for defining and explaining the American character: this is Frederick Jackson Turner's frontier hypothesis. In any appraisal of what history has to contribute, therefore, it is inevitable that we should return ultimately to the Turner theory. And in any evaluation of the factor of abundance, it is vital to establish what relation, if any, existed between the frontier influence specifically and the general influence of economic abundance. Thus I find myself coming around as all American historians do sooner or later, to that much-debated formulation which the young professor from Wisconsin proposed to the sages of the American Historical Association when they met at Chicago in 1893.

Turner's paper on "The Significance of the Frontier in American History" was not only a turning point in the development of American historical writing; it was also, in the most explicit sense, an explanation of American character, and might, with perfect validity, have been entitled "The Influence of the Frontier on American Character." Passages throughout the essay may be cited to justify this assertion. For instance, Turner declared that, on the frontier, the "perennial rebirth" of society, the "fluidity of American life, this expansion westward with its new opportunities, its continuous touch with the simplicity of primitive society furnish the forces dominating American character." And, again, "to the frontier, the American intellect owes its striking characteristics."[1]

In any analysis of American character, therefore, Turner and his ideas must be considered with the utmost care. Fortunately, this does not mean that we need undertake any general critique of the entire body of Turner's thought. That is a broad field which has been traversed repeatedly by opposing critics—with Avery

O. Craven, Joseph Schafer, and Frederic L. Paxson guarding the essential points of the Turner position and with a number of writers, including Charles A. Beard, Louis Hacker, Fred A. Shannon, James C. Malin, Carlton J.H. Hayes, Murray Kane, Benjamin F. Wright, Jr., and Carter Goodrich in collaboration with Sol Davidson, conducting the assault on specific sectors, while George Wilson Pierson, in a series of articles, has provided a very searching analysis and review of the entire question.[2]

But, in so far as the frontier hypothesis is related to the factor of abundance, it behooves us to take account of it here. Turner himself said, "the Western wilds, from the Alleghenies to the Pacific, constituted the richest free gift that was ever spread out before civilized man. . . . Never again can such an opportunity come to the sons of men."[3] And, specifically linking this opportunity with the frontier, he added, "The most significant thing about the American frontier is that it lies at the hither edge of free land."

Of course, it should be recognized at once that Turner conceived of other factors besides abundance as being present in the frontier condition. To name only two, there was a temporary lowering of civilized standards, and there was a weakening of the power of traditional institutions such as church and school, with a corresponding enhancement of the stature of the individual.

Therefore we are dealing with abundance as one in a complex of factor, and it becomes important to determine, as far as we can, how much of the influence of what Turner called the "frontier" lay in its being on the outskirts of civilization and how much lay in its function as the locus of maximum access to unused resources. The question is a critical one because, if the factor of abundance was really primary, if the most significant thing about the frontier was, as Turner himself asserted, its contiguity to free land, then we ought to recognize the primacy of abundance and speak of the influence of abundance, in whatever form it occurs, and not restrictively in only one of its manifestations—the frontier manifestation. Do we really mean the influence of the frontier, or do we mean the influence of a factor that was especially conspicuous in the frontier situation but that also operated apart from it upon many other parts of American experience?[4] In so far as the latter is what we mean, we might justifiably regard Turner's famous paper as being, in essence, a study of the significance of economic abundance in American history.

In grappling with this problem, we cannot expect, unfortunately, to secure as much precise guidance as we might wish from an analysis of Turner's own writings. His conception of the frontier was nothing if not a protean one. Sometimes he seems to think of the frontier as a geographical region, as when he says that "the Western wilds from the Alleghenies to the Pacific" were the special area where nature conferred a unique bounty or that a new order of Americanism emerged when "the mountains rose between the pioneer and the seaboard." Sometimes he conceives of a condition, the existence at the edge of settlement of an unused area of free land. In this sense the frontier becomes, as Dixon Ryan Fox said, simply "the edge of the unused." Sometimes, again, he conceives of it as a process: "The peculiarity of American institutions is the fact that they have been compelled to adapt themselves to the changes of an expanding people—to the changes involved in crossing a continent, in winning a wilderness, and in developing at each area of this progress out of the primitive economic and political conditions of the frontier into the complexity of city life." Avery O. Craven has summarized this idea of process very effectively in a paraphrase of the concept as he construes it: "The basic idea . . . was what American history, through most of its course, presents a series of recurring social evolutions in diverse geographical areas as a people advance to colonize a continent. The chief characteristic is expansion; the chief peculiarity of institutions, constant readjustment. . . . Into . . . raw and differing areas men and institutions and ideas poured from older basins, there to return to a more or less primitive state and then to climb slowly back toward complexity. . . . The process was similar in each case, with some common results but always with 'essential differences' due to time and place."[5]

Certainly, then, if Turner did not use the term "frontier" to mean various things at various times, at least he used it in a way that placed heavy stress first on one aspect, then on another, with very little notice to the reader that the cluster of ideas back of the term was being substantially changed. No doubt he was right in the view that a whole complex of factors was associated with the westward advance of settlement and that all these factors ought to be taken into account. But his technique, very frustrating to many critics of the last two decades, was instead of treating the separate constituents as separate constituents, to fuse all and discuss them interchangeably under the rubric "frontier." George Wilson Pierson, who has made a careful analysis of this shifting concept, remarks ruefully that, to Turner, "the West was rough (a geographic factor) and it was empty (a sociological force). Perhaps, then, Turner's greatest achievement was his successful marriage of these two dissimilar forces in the single phrase, *free land*."[6]

The real key, however, to Turner's thought—both in its strength and in its limitations—will never be grasped if we suppose that this elusiveness of definition was simply the result of a vagueness of mind or an indifference to analysis. It is rather, as Henry Nash Smith has recently argued, the result of Turner's personal predilection for one special social ideal—the ideal of agrarian democracy. As Smith expresses this, "from the time of Franklin down to the end of the frontier period almost a century and a half later, the West had been a constant reminder of the importance of agriculture in American society. It had nourished an agrarian philosophy and an agrarian myth that purported to set forth the character and destinies of the nation. The philosophy and the myth affirmed an admirable set of values, but they ceased very early to be useful in interpreting American society as a whole, because they offered no intellectual apparatus for taking account of the industrial revolution. A system which revolved about a half-mystical conception of nature and held up as an ideal a rudimentary type of agriculture was powerless to confront issues arising from the advance of technology. Agrarian theory encouraged men to ignore the industrial revolution altogether, or to regard it as an unfortunate and anomalous violation of the natural order of things. In the . . .

sphere of historical scholarship, for example, the agrarian emphasis of the frontier hypothesis has tended to divert attention from the problems created by industrialization for a half-century during which the United States has become the most powerful industrial nation in the world." Turner's "problem"—the one that he set for himself—was "to find a basis for democracy in some aspect of civilization as he observed it about him in the United States. His determined effort in this direction showed that his mind and his standards of social ethics were subtler and broader than the conceptual system within which the frontier hypothesis had been developed, but he was the prisoner of the assumptions he had taken over from the agrarian tradition."[7]

Applying this dictum specifically to the factor of abundance, one can readily verify Smith's general observations. What happened was that, when abundance operated within an agrarian context—in the form of free land for farmers—Turner seized upon it, but with a tendency to identify the factor with the context, to attribute to the context the results that followed from the operation of the factor, while refusing to recognize the operation of the factor when it occurred outside the selected context.[8]

In this connection it would be misleading to say that Turner refused to admit the existence of nonagrarian frontiers. On the contrary, he mentioned them explicitly and specified also that various frontiers offered various conditions and inducements. In his own words, "the unequal rate of advance compels us to distinguish the frontier into the trader's frontier, the rancher's frontier, or the miner's frontier, and the farmer's frontier."

But, although these dissimilarities forced him grudgingly—"compelled" him, in his own revealing phrase—to give formal recognition to a variety of frontiers, they conspicuously failed to compel him to broaden his concept of the frontier sufficiently to accommodate them. When he came to such matters as the exploitation of salt, coal, oil, and other mineral resources, he would neither separate them out, thus conceding the limitations of his agrarian hypothesis, nor include them actively in his calculations, thus modifying and qualifying the agrarian tenor of his theme.

The arbitrary restrictiveness of this agrarian preoccupation is shown very clearly, it seems to me, in a statement by Carl Becker, who was one of Turner's most brilliant and most faithful followers. Becker said, "The United States has always had, until very recently, more land than it could use and fewer people than it needed." Certainly this premise would be difficult to refute. Then he continues: "This is not only the fundamental economic difference between the United States and European countries, but it is a condition which has more influence than any other in determining the course of American history."[9] Today the United States has, perhaps, as large an industrial capacity as the rest of the world, and it was well on the way to such leadership when Becker wrote; yet the factor which he offers as the key to the fundamental economic difference between America and the Old World turns its back upon this major development of our economic life. Clearly, it is not merely the greater endowment of land which has differentiated America's growth from Europe's. It is the greater supply, also, of timber, of iron, of copper, of petroleum, of coal, of hydroelectric power. By some mystic process these may be subsumed under the term "land," but if we should speak of land in this sense, as meaning everything except sea and air, we ought at least to recognize that it is in this form too broad for the agrarians to claim a franchise on it. Indeed, it then becomes more nearly equivalent to physical abundance, or at least potential physical abundance, than to soil.

Because of these anomalies and because of the presence of concealed agrarian dogma in what purports to be an environmental analysis, it becomes important to consider a little more closely what the elements were in the frontier situation as Turner conceived it. I have already suggested that he was by no means schematic in his approach to this question, but I think we may agree in identifying his major points of stress. As I have already observed, he constantly recurred to the factor of plenty in the form of free land. Sometimes he touched this theme as a lyric chord, as when he said, "American democracy was born of no theorist's dream; it was not carried in the *Susan Constant* to Virginia, nor in the *Mayflower* to Plymouth. It came out of the American forest, and it gained new strength each time it touched a new frontier. Not the Constitution, but free land and an abundance of natural resources open to a fit people, made the democratic type of society in America for three centuries."[10] Sometimes he dealt with the same thought in more analytical economic terms, as when he explained the precise motives that stimulated the westward push: "The farmers [of settled areas] who lived on soil whose returns were diminished by unrotated crops were offered the virgin soil of the frontier at nominal prices. Their growing families demanded more lands, and these were dear. The competition of the unexhausted, cheap, and easily tilled prairie lands compelled the farmer either to go west and continue the exhaustion of the soil on a new frontier, or to adopt intensive culture. Thus the census of 1890 shows, in the Northwest, many counties in which there is an absolute or a relative decrease of population. These states have been sending farmers to advance the frontier on the plains and have themselves begun to turn to intensive farming and to manufacture." But, whether in didactic or in poetic terms, Turner reiterated constantly the factor of abundance, which he recognized most frequently, but not invariably, in the form of land.

Another feature of the frontier which Turner consistently emphasized as important was the fact that it temporarily emancipated the individual from institutional controls. Often though he returned to this point, it seems to me that he never did develop it with real clarity; but there is one formulation of the idea in his statement that "we have the complex European life sharply precipitated by the wilderness into the simplicity of primitive conditions." This, I take it, means two things: It means that the system of division of labor, prevalent in complex societies, breaks down, and the individual is obliged to diversify his activities—to produce his own food, to minister to his own soul, to educate his own children, to doctor his own ailments, to provide his own police protection, and to be a true self-sufficing man. It means also that, since he, as an individual, has gone ahead of organized society, leaving it to follow him, he is not overshadowed by the weight of institutions, and his stature as an individual is correspondingly greater.

Another factor that Turner regarded as intrinsic was the way in which the frontier dictated a temporary lowering of the standards of civilization. The pioneers, of course, accepted this regression only because they expected it to pay off in a raising of standards later; but for the first phase, at least, there was an inescapable reduction: "The wilderness masters the colonist ... It strips off the garments of civilization and arrays him in the hunting shirt and the moccasin. It puts him in the log cabin of the Cherokee and Iroquois and runs an Indian palisade around him. Before long he has gone to planting Indian corn and plowing with a sharp stick; he shouts the war cry and takes the scalp in orthodox Indian fashion."

It is difficult to be certain whether or not Turner viewed this change with a romantic primitivism that caused him to take pleasure in it; but in any case he certainly regarded it as the most transitory of conditions. Frederic L. Paxson, paraphrasing Turner, expresses the concept well when he says that "as the pioneer trudged ahead of his little procession, along the rugged trails that pierced the mountain gaps, he was only incidentally living in the present. The future filled his mind; a future beginning with the rough shack that must shelter him for his first season; but a future of field after field of fertile land, of houses and livestock, of growing family and the education and religion that it needed."[11]

Along with these factors there was also, as I have suggested previously, the element of successive readjustments, of "perennial rebirth," of constant changes moving in a kind of rhythmic cycle, "the changes involved in crossing a continent, in winning a wilderness, and in developing at each area of this progress out of the primitive economic and political conditions of the frontier into the complexity of city life." Always, of course, this cycle was a democratic one.

Most of the things which the frontier meant to Turner are embraced, I believe, by one or another of these factors. It was the place where free land lay at the edge of settlement; the place where institutions no longer towered over the individual man; the place where European complexity gave way to American simplicity; and the place where democratic growth and change was repeatedly re-enacted as a process and reaffirmed as a principle.

But how did these elements in the pioneer experience impinge upon the American character? What was their influence in shaping the traits of the American people? Here Turner's analysis is somewhat more explicit, and it is, in fact, easier to know what he meant by the "influence of the frontier" than what he meant by the "frontier" itself. First of all, he was confident that the frontier promoted nationalism: the pioneer looked to the national government to adopt the measures he needed—to provide him with internal improvements, to administer the public domain, and still more to accord to the area in which he had settled territorial status and, later, statehood; moreover, the pioneer, on the frontier, mingled with other settlers from other states and even from other countries. Here was the true melting pot, and "on the tide of the Father of Waters, North and South met and mingled into a nation." "It was," he said, "this nationalizing tendency of the West that transformed the democracy of Jefferson into the national republicanism of Monroe and the democracy of Andrew Jackson. The West of the War of 1812, the West of Clay and Benton and Harrison and Andrew Jackson, shut off by the Middle States and the mountains from the coast sections, had a solidarity of its own with national tendencies." Second, he was equally confident that the frontier had fostered democracy: "The most important effect of the frontier has been in the promotion of democracy here and in Europe." In this connection Turner often cited the liberal suffrage provisions with which the frontier states came into the Union and the reactive effects of these provisions upon the political arrangements in the older states. Third, he also credited the frontier with stimulating the spirit of individualism: "Complex society," he felt, "is precipitated by the wilderness into a kind of primitive organization based on the family. The tendency is anti-social. It produces antipathy to control." And with each family occupying land of its own, very largely on a self-sufficing basis, there was, in fact, every reason why the individual should feel a minimum need to be cared for by society, and there-fore a minimum tolerance for control by society. This was true only on the farmer's frontier, of course, and Turner himself recognized that other frontiers might not be individualistic at all. He himself stated this limitation, saying, "But when the arid lands and the mineral resources of the Far West were reached, no conquest was possible by the old individual pioneer methods. Here expensive irri-gation works must be constructed, coöperative activity was demanded in utiliza-tion of the water supply, capital beyond the reach of the small farmer was re-quired. In a word, the physiographic province itself decreed that the destiny of this new frontier should be social rather than individual."[12] But, as was character-istic with him, though he might give lip service to the existence of a variety of frontiers, it always turned out that the farmer's frontier was the one he was really talking about, and the others lay somewhere beyond the periphery of his thought. And the farmer's frontier was unquestionably individualistic. Thus he did not hesitate to rank individualism with his other factors and to declare that the "fron-tier of settlement ... carried with it individualism, democracy, and nationalism."

These three were, in a sense, his triad—factors to which he often recurred. But however important they may be and however deeply they may be imbedded in the character, they can hardly be described as "traits of character" or "qualities of mind" in the ordinary sense; and we must therefore go one step further, to ask: How did Turner conceive that the frontier made the pioneer unlike other people? The complete answer, of course, runs through the whole body of his work, but there is a very good summary answer near the end of his famous essay. "To the frontier," he said, "the American intellect owes its striking characteristics. That coarseness and strength combined with acuteness and inquisitiveness; that prac-tical, inventive turn of mind, quick to find expedients; that masterful grasp of material things, lacking in the artistic but powerful to effect great ends; that rest-less, nervous energy; that dominant individualism, working for good and for evil, and withal that buoyancy and exuberance which comes with freedom—these are traits of the frontier, or traits called out elsewhere because of the existence of the frontier."

Such, then, were the main elements of the frontier hypothesis, as Turner developed it: West of the Alleghenies lay a vast expanse of fertile and unsettled land which became available almost free to those who would cultivate it. Across this area, a frontier or edge of settlement pushed steadily west, and along this frontier individuals who had advanced ahead of society's usual institutional controls accepted a lowering of standards at the time for the sake of progress in the future. Constantly repeating over again a democratic experience, they reinforced the national democratic tradition. All these conditions, of course, influenced the mental traits of those who were directly or indirectly involved in the process, and especially their nationalism, their democracy, and their individualism were stimulated. Certain other qualities—a coarseness, combined with a strength, a practicality and materialism of mind, a restless energy, and a measure of buoyancy or exuberance—were all traceable to this frontier influence.

With this outline of the frontier hypothesis in mind, we can now revert to the question: To what extent was the frontier merely the context in which abundance occurred? To what extent does it explain developments which the concept of abundance alone could not explain?

At times Turner himself seemed almost to equate the frontier with abundance, as, for instance, when he said, "These free lands promoted individualism, economic equality, freedom to rise, democracy."[13] It is probably valid to criticize him for this. But if there was a fallacy in his failure to distinguish between these coinciding factors and his consequent practice of treating qualities which were intrinsically derived from abundance as if they were distinctive to the frontier, it would be the same fallacy in reverse to treat qualities which were intrinsically frontier qualities as if they were attributable to abundance. Bearing this caveat in mind, we can hardly deny that there were a number of influences which were peculiar to the frontier or to abundance in its distinctive frontier form and which did not operate outside the frontier phase. For instance, the pioneer's necessity of submitting to hardships and low living standards as the price of higher standards must certainly have stimulated his optimism and his belief in progress. Similarly, one can hardly doubt that the mingling of peoples on the frontier and their urgent need for federal legislative measures must have stimulated the growth of nationalism just as Turner said. And again, at an even deeper level, it is hard to doubt that the frontier projection of the individual ahead of society and the self-sufficing way of life on the edge of settlement must have greatly stimulated American individualism.

But even to say that Turner was right in all these matters is not to say that he took a comprehensive view of the American experience. By confining his explanation of Americanism to the conditions of the pioneer stage of our development, he placed himself in the position of implying that nothing distinctively American would be left, except as a residue, after the pioneer stage had been passed. By limiting his recognition of abundance to its appearance in the form of free land, he limited his recognition of successive American democratic readjustments to the successive settlement of new areas of free land, and thus he cut himself off from a recognition of the adjustments to technological advance, to urban growth, and to the higher standard of living, all of which have contributed quite as much as the frontier to the fluidity and facility for change in American life. Further, by failing to recognize that the frontier was only one form in which America offered abundance, he cut himself off from an insight into the fact that other forms of abundance had superseded the frontier even before the supply of free land had been exhausted, with the result that it was not really the end of free land but rather the substitution of new forms of economic activity which terminated the frontier phase of our history.

Perhaps it may be in order to say a few words more about each of these points. In the first place, then, by making the frontier the one great hopeful factor in our experience, Turner gave us every cause to feel alarm and pessimism about the conditions that would follow the disappearance of the frontier. As he himself expressed it, "since the days when the fleet of Columbus sailed into the waters of the New World, America has been another name for opportunity. . . . He would be a rash prophet who should assert that the expansive character of American life has now entirely ceased. Movement has been its dominant fact, and, unless this training has no effect upon a people, the American energy will continually demand a wider field for its exercise. But never again will such gifts of free land offer themselves. . . . Now, four centuries from the discovery of America, at the end of a hundred years of life under the Constitution, the frontier has gone, and with its going has closed the first period of American history."

The tone of foreboding in this statement is easily transformed into a defeatist lament or into a conviction that, without the frontier, freedom and opportunity are endangered. To take but one of a good many possible illustrations, Governor Philip La Follette, in his message to the Wisconsin legislature in 1931, observed that "in the days of our pioneer fathers, the free land of the frontier gave this guarantee of freedom and opportunity," but that no such natural safeguard remained in operation after the passing of the frontier.[14]

Some years ago Dixon Ryan Fox pointed out this defeatist corollary of the frontier hypothesis and suggested that broader definition of a frontier which I have already mentioned—namely, "the edge of the unused." This would imply, of course, that science has its frontiers, industry its frontiers, technology its frontiers, and that so long as Americans can advance their standards of living and maintain the fluidity of their lives and their capacity for change along these frontiers, the disappearance of the agrarian frontier is not at all critical. In terms of abundance, Turner was correct in saying, "Never again will such gifts of free land offer themselves," but his implication that nature would never again offer such bounty is open to challenge, for the frontiers of industry, of invention, and of engineering have continued to bring into play new resources quite as rich as the unbroken sod of the western frontier.

A second point which I believe Turner's agrarian orientation caused him to overlook was the broad variety of factors which have worked to cause unceasing change and development in America and thereby have conditioned the American to a habit of constant adjustment, constant adaptation to new circumstances, and constant readiness to accept or experiment with what is new. It was "to the frontier" that he attributed "that practical inventive turn of mind, quick to find expedients," to it that he credited the fact that Americans were "compelled to adapt themselves to the changes of an expanding people." But clearly it is not "the simplicity of primitive society" which requires new expedients and inventive ability; on the contrary, primitive society was highly repetitive in its patterns and demanded stamina more than talent for innovation; it was an increasingly complex society of rapid technological change, far away from the frontier, which demanded range and flexibility of adjustment. No amount of concentration upon the frontier will give us an awareness of the way in which the American home has been readjusted to the use first of gas and later of electricity; of the way in which American business has been readjusted to the typewriter and the comptometer; of the way in which American communication has been adjusted to the telegraph, the telephone, the radio, and even the motion picture; and of the way in which the American community has been readjusted to the railroad, the streetcar, and the automobile. One has only to compare an old, pre-automobile city, like Boston, with a new, post-automobile city, like Houston, Texas, with its supermarkets, its drive-in restaurants, and its other facilities for automotive living, to appreciate that this is true. Are not these constant changes more important in maintaining the fluidity of American life, in perpetuating the habit of expecting something different, than any number of successive removals to new areas of free land?

A third and final aspect in which the agrarian perspective proved too limiting is in the fact that Turner did not recognize that the attraction of the frontier was simply as the most accessible form of abundance, and therefore he could not conceive that other forms of abundance might replace it as the lodestone to which the needle of American aspirations would point. To him the frontier remained the polar force until it was exhausted; America must turn to second-best resources after this unparalleled opportunity of the frontier had passed. Yet, in fact, what happened was that, as early as the mid-century, if not earlier, American industrial growth, relying upon the use of other forms of abundance than soil fertility, began to compete with the frontier in the opportunities which it offered, and the migration of Americans began to point to the cities rather than to the West.[15] Later, this same industrial growth provided a general standard of living so high that people were no longer willing to abandon it for the sake of what the frontier promised. This can be stated almost in the terms of a formula: The frontier, with its necessity for some reduction of living standards, could attract people from settled areas so long as the existing standards in those areas did not exceed a certain maximum (people would accept a certain unfavorable differential in their current standards for the sake of potential gain). But when existing city standards exceeded this maximum, when the differential became too great, people would no longer accept it even for all the future rewards that the frontier might promise. To leave a primitive agrarian community and settle in primitive agrarian isolation was one thing, but to leave refrigeration, electric lighting, running water, hospitals, motion pictures, and access to highways was another, and, as these amenities and others like them were introduced, the frontier distinctly lost the universality of its lure. As George W. Pierson says, "When cars, movies, and radios become essentials of the accepted standard of living, subsistence farming is repugnant even to the starving. Measured, therefore, against this concept of a changing fashion or standard of living, it may be suggested that the lure of the land began in Tudor England before there was any available, and ceased in the United States before the available supply gave out."[16] In short, the frontier ceased to operate as a major force in American history not when it disappeared—not when the superintendent of the census abandoned the attempt to map a frontier boundary—but when the primary means of access to abundance passed from the frontier to other focuses in American life.

It is now sixty years since Turner wrote his famous essay. For two-thirds of this period his ideas commanded vast influence and indiscriminate acceptance, and then they encountered a barrage of criticism as severe as it was belated. Some aspects of his thought have received such devastating analysis that no historian today would be likely to make the error of adopting them. For instance, historians today would be wary of the agrarian assumptions in Turner's formulation. But the geographical determinism or environmentalism of Turner still possesses great vitality. The strength of its appeal was demonstrated again in 1952 more strikingly, perhaps, than ever before in this country, with the publication by Walter P. Webb of another and a broader restatement of the frontier hypothesis—not for the United States alone, this time, but for the entire planet.

Webb's *Great Frontier* cuts free of both the restrictive Americanism and the restrictive agrarianism of Turner to propose the thesis that the world frontier, opened up by the age of discovery, was "inherently a vast body of wealth without proprietors," that it precipitated a "sudden, continuing, and ever-increasing flood of wealth" upon the centers of Western civilization, thus inaugurating a period of boom which lasted about four hundred years and during which all the institutions—economic, political, and social—evolved to meet the needs of a world in boom.

In his explicit recognition that the very essence of the frontier was its supply of unappropriated wealth, Webb has clarified a vital factor which remained obscure in Turner, for Turner seemed to sense the point without clearly stating it, and Turner always neglected forms of wealth other than soil fertility. Webb, with his attention to the precious metals and even more with his focus upon the importance of "that form of wealth classed as Things or commodities," everlastingly breaks the link between agrarian thought and the frontier doctrine. Through his clear perception of the part played by abundance, he has demonstrated in thorough and convincing fashion the validity of the precise point which I have attempted to put forward in this analysis.

If it were only a question of whether the frontier has significance intrinsically as a locus of wealth, therefore, my comment would be only to echo Professor Webb;

but there is another question: whether the *only* significant source of modern wealth is the frontier. Webb seems to contend that it is, for he asserts that "it was the constant distribution on a nominal or free basis of the royal or public domain that kept the boom going and that gave a peculiar dynamic quality to Western civilization for four centuries,"[17] and his discussion is pervaded with dark forebodings for the future of a world which no longer commands such a stock of untapped resources.

The theme of American abundance, which is, of course, New World abundance and therefore, in large measure, frontier abundance, is, in many respects, fully in accord with Professor Webb's theme and at first glance might appear identical with it. But, at the point where Webb attributes to the frontier an exclusive function, my argument diverges from his. American abundance has been in part freely supplied by the bounty of nature, but it has also been in part socially created by an advancing technology, and neither of these factors can explain modern society without the other. Abundance, as a horse-breeder might say, is by technology out of environment. Professor Webb has treated the subject as if environment bred abundance by spontaneous generation.

To approach the matter more explicitly, let us consider the basis of our present standard of living, which reflects the supply of goods of all kinds. This standard results not merely from our stock of resources, for primitive peoples with bare subsistence standards have possessed the same resources for as long as fifty thousand years. It results also from our ability to convert these resources into socially useful form—that is, from our productive capacity. Our productive capacity, in turn, depends not only on the raw materials, which are ready to hand, but even more upon our ability to increase, through mechanization, the volume of goods which can be turned out by each worker. If I may allude again to a previously used illustration, an infinite supply of free land would never, by itself, have raised our standard of living very far, for it would never have freed us from the condition in which more than 70 percent of our labor force was required to produce food for our population. But, when technology enabled 11 percent of our labor force to produce food for our population, it freed 60 percent to engage in other activities—that is, to create other goods which would become part of the standard of living.

No doubt it is true that in many societies the level of living will be controlled by the scarcity of resources (e.g., by lack of soil fertility), and certainly there is good reason to feel concern lest such controls should come into play in the future as world population multiplies and world resources are expended. But in most of the societies with which history has had to deal, it was the limited productivity of the worker rather than the absolute lack of resources in the environment which fixed the maximum level for the standard of living. In these societies where technology has been the limiting factor, it would clearly be fallacious to seek the explanation for an increase of wealth solely in the increasing supply of resources, since the society already possessed resources which it was not using.

In practice, however, the forces of technology and environment constantly interact and cannot be isolated. Because they do interact, it might be argued, with some force, that the richness of supply of resources has stimulated the technology—that the spectacle of vast riches waiting to be grasped has inspired men to devise new means for grasping them—and that, in this sense, the great frontier precipitated the new technology. But, without denying either the attractiveness of, or the elements of truth in, such an interpretation, which would buttress the Webb thesis, I think we should recognize that historically the technological revolution seemed to precede the age of discovery. From the time of the Crusades, four centuries before Columbus and Da Gama, western Europe was in transition. The use of gunpowder, the art of printing, improvements in navigation, the revival of commerce, the development of various sciences, and the whole pervasive change known as the Renaissance—all these had paved the way not only for the great geographical discoveries but also for the industrial transformation of Europe. Viewing the matter in this way, it might be argued that what really happened was that an advancing technology opened up a whole new range of potentialities, including the physical resources of the New World, rather than that the epic geographical discoveries called into being a new technology.

Probably it is as fruitless to seek the dynamics of economic change solely in technology as it is to seek them solely in environment. Certainly nothing would be gained by minimizing the environmental factor, and it is not my purpose to assert either that technology can operate without materials or that Webb's Malthusian concern for the future is unjustified. But precisely because the factor of abundance is of capital significance, it is important that it should not become identified with doctrines of geographical determinism. And precisely because Webb's formulation is one of the first fully developed treatments of this factor, it is unfortunate that he should accept geographical determinism as a necessary part of his position. When he rejects what he calls "the Fallacy of New Frontiers," he is not only attacking a glib and overworked slogan, but he is also attacking the belief that science may find new potentialities in physical materials that are currently regarded as valueless—something which science has repeatedly done in the past. When he asserts that "science can do much, but . . . it is not likely soon to find a new world or make the one we have much better than it is," he offers two propositions of very unequal tenor: the prospect of science's finding a new world is indeed remote, but the entire history of science for several centuries would justify our expectation that, if not perverted to the uses of war, it may make our world a great deal better.

If abundance is to be properly understood, it must not be visualized in terms of a storehouse of fixed and universally recognizable assets, reposing on shelves until humanity, by a process of removal, strips all the shelves bare. Rather, abundance resides in a series of physical potentialities, which have never been inventoried at the same value for any two cultures in the past and are not likely to seem of identical worth to different cultures in the future. As recently as twenty years ago, for example, society would not have counted uranium among its important assets.

When abundance exercises a function in the history of man, it is not as an absolute factor in nature to which man, as a relative factor, responds. Rather, it is as a physical and cultural factor, involving the interplay between man, himself a geological force, and nature, which holds different meanings for every different human culture and is therefore relative.

In short, abundance is partly a physical and partly a cultural manifestation. For America, from the eighteenth to the twentieth century, the frontier was the focus of abundance, physically because the land there was virgin and culturally because the Anglo-Americans of that time were particularly apt at exploiting the new country.[18] At this lowest threshold of access to abundance, the pioneers found an individualism and a nationalism which they might not have found at other thresholds. But, though physically the frontier remained the site of virgin land, cultural changes gave to the people an aptitude for exploiting new industrial potentialities and thus drew the focus of abundance away from the frontier. But this change of focus itself perpetuated and reinforced the habits of fluidity, of mobility, of change, of the expectation of progress, which have been regarded as distinctive frontier traits. The way in which this happened suggests that it was, in reality, abundance in any form, including the frontier form, rather than the frontier in any unique sense, which wrought some of the major results in the American experience. The frontier remained of primary significance precisely as long as it remained the lowest threshold of access to America's abundance; it ceased to be primary when other thresholds were made lower, and not when the edge of unsettled land ceased to exist. American abundance, by contrast, has remained of primary significance both in the frontier phase and in the vast industrial phase which has dominated American life for the past three-quarters of a century. American development and the American character are too complex to be explained by any single factor, but, among the many factors which do have to be taken into account, it is questionable whether any has exerted a more formative or more pervasive influence than the large measure of economic abundance which has been so constantly in evidence.

Notes

[1] All quotations from Turner, except where otherwise noted, are taken from "The Significance of the Frontier in American History," using the revised form which appeared in his *The Frontier in American History* (New York: Henry Holt & Co., 1920).

[2] For a bibliography of this literature, with reference not only to the controversial writers, but also to studies of Turner's precursors, his influence, his thought, and his method, by Herman C. Nixon, Everett E. Edwards, Fulmer Mood, and Merle Curti, respectively, see Ray Allen Billington, *Westward Expansion* (New York: Macmillian Co., 1949), pp. 760–61.

[3] "Contributions of the West to American Democracy," in *The Frontier in American History*, p. 261.

[4] "To Turner, however, 'the most significant thing about the American frontier' is not that historically it represents a vast domain of natural resources ready to be transformed

into capital through the medium of reproductive process, but that it lies geographically at the 'hither edge of free land' " (Murray Kane, "Some Considerations on the Frontier Concept of Frederick Jackson Turner," *Mississippi Valley Historical Review*, XXVII [1940], 389).

"One of the major deficiencies of the Turner approach was the failure to see that free raw materials stood in almost exactly the same relation to the opportunity for industrial urbanism as the hither edge of free land did to agriculture" (James C. Malin, "Mobility and History," *Agricultural History*, XVII [1943], 178.)

[5] "Frederick Jackson Turner," in William T. Hutchinson (ed.), *Marcus W. Jernegan Essays in American Historiography* (Chicago: University of Chicago Press, 1937), p. 254.

[6] George Wilson Pierson, "The Frontier and American Institutions," *New England Quarterly*, XV (1942), 252.

[7] Henry Nash Smith, *Virgin Land* (Cambridge, Mass.: Harvard University Press, 1950), pp. 258–59.

[8] "Absorption in the Turner philosophy, centering around agriculture, seems to have diverted attention from the significant and all-important fact that there was still opportunity, created by the fluidity of society based on the industrial urbanism" (Malin, *loc. cit.*).

[9] *The United States: An Experiment in Democracy* (New York: Harper & Bros., 1920), p. 143.

[10] "The West and American Ideals," in *The Frontier in American History*, p. 293.

[11] *When the West Is Gone* (New York: Henry Holt & Co., 1930), p. 39.

[12] "Contributions of the West to American Democracy," in *The Frontier in American History*, p. 258.

[13] *Ibid.,* p. 259.

[14] James C. Malin observes that the doctrine of closed space caused "the hysterical conservation movement of the early twentieth century. It remained for the apologists of the New Deal, however, and especially such men as Rexford G. Tugwell and Henry A. Wallace [author of *New Frontiers*], to invoke in extreme form the prestige of the Turner tradition to justify governmental regulation of American life as a substitute for the vanished frontier. . . . In effect it was a repudiation of the America of Turner, accompanied by the application of an unwanted corollary from his own teaching" (*op. cit.,* p. 177).

[15] Walter P. Webb, *The Great Frontier* (Boston: Houghton Mifflin Co., 1952), p. 374, quotes Carl, in John Steinbeck's "The Red Pony" (1945), "No, no place to go, Jody. Every place is taken. But that's not the worst—no, not the worst. Westering has died out of the people. Westering isn't a hunger any more. It's all done."

[16] *Op. cit.,* p. 239.

[17] *Op. cit.,* p. 413.

[18] Pierson asks, "What about the Spaniards, who had the run of the whole hemisphere? Did the Mississippi Valley make them democratic, prosperous and numerous? In a word, do not the level of culture and the 'fitness' of a society for the wilderness, matter more than the wilderness? . . . If today a new continent were to rise out of the Pacific Ocean, are we so sure that it would encourage small freeholds, not corporation or governmental monopolies?" (*op. cit.,* p. 253).

FOCUS: READING REVIEW

1. What does Turner's frontier hypothesis say about abundance and the American frontier? What other factors are present in the frontier condition?

2. What was Turner's conception of the frontier? What problem does this pose for Turner's critics?
3. What was Turner's agrarian preoccupation? How does this fail to account for a full explanation of American life?
4. How did the frontier influence social and political institutions like the national government, the family, and democracy?
5. What problems does Potter find in Turner making the frontier the "one great hopeful factor in our experience"?
6. What is the "defeatist corollary to the frontier hypothesis"?
7. Why does the "primitivism" of the frontier fail to explain American inventiveness?
8. What other kinds of abundance does Potter find Turner failing to account for?
9. What is Potter's definition of abundance? How has abundance affected America?

FOCUS: AUTHOR'S STRATEGIES

1. A substantial portion of this essay recounts the views of historians toward Turner's work. Why are they included? What do they suggest about Potter's audience?
2. Potter employs the pattern of a critical analysis. What are the components of his analysis of Turner? What are his criteria for objecting to Turner's theory? What does he add to Turner to create a theory that will meet his criteria?

FOCUS: DISCUSSION AND WRITING

1. Do you experience the promise of American abundance Potter finds in the American experience? If yes, what signs of abundance support this promise? If no, where in America have we lost the promise of abundance?
2. Turner cites the American frontier as the cause of "individualism, democracy, and nationalism." Are these still principal characteristics of Americans? Give concrete examples to support your answer.

TOPICS: Further Research, Synthesis, and Writing in History

1. Other than Muller, find the work of a historian on Rome's achievement. Write an essay comparing and contrasting this interpretation with Muller's.
2. Locate the Jefferson biographers Brodie refers to in "My Head and My Heart." Read their treatments of Jefferson's relationship with Maria Cosway. Relying on these studies and your own reading of Jefferson's letter, write a critique of Brodie's essay. Be sure to consider the degree to which historians "interpret" and account for their disagreements.
3. Locate a history of the Civil War and Reconstruction written from a perspective other than the "great men" view of history. Compare and contrast this essay with Catton's in terms of "fact" and "interpretation."
4. Using Morison's criteria for lively history, compare and contrast two or more essays in these chapters, and comment on them critically.

❮ ARTS AND LITERATURE ❯

Chapter 10

The Governing Assumptions

In "Criticism, Visible and Invisible," Northrop Frye identifies examining a work's distinctive experience as literary criticism's central task. To accomplish this, "the central activity of criticism is essentially one of establishing a context for the works being studied." We can borrow from Frye to define art criticism's task generally as one of establishing contexts for works being studied. The art critic, then, is really the student of art objects and their contexts. The essays in this chapter set the goals for critical studies and suggest the pitfalls. Frye's initial essay identifies bringing the reader closer to a work so that he or she can "possess" it as the critical task. Criticism should establish a relationship of identification and not merely one of knowledge between audience and art. Knowledge, however, plays a central role in identification because it provides access. Frye's essay can be compared to Eliot's "Tradition and the Individual Talent." For Eliot a work of art derives its meaning and value from its tradition—the art which has gone before. For both Frye and Eliot, tradition influences the creative experience and knowledge of tradition leads the critic to art.

From reading Frye and Eliot, we may believe we can experience a work of art if we have enough objective information about art and its tradition. The selections by Gombrich and Booth call this objectivity into question. In "The Conditions of

Illusion," Gombrich demonstrates the degree to which a percipient must enter into artistic conventions to understand an artistic experience. Viewing art requires subjective experience. According to Booth in "Beliefs and the Reader," readers are motivated by their own interests. By understanding that readers cannot be neutral toward values, impartial toward characters, or unimpassioned toward events, we can better understand literature. By heightening our awareness of subjectivity, both Gombrich and Booth offer a way to consider how art communicates. We will probably not be able to study art with scientific precision, but we should be able to approach the knowledge which is criticism's aim.

Criticism, Visible and Invisible
Northrop Frye

Northrop Frye, who has been identified as a mythic critic, is himself often impatient with the confusion deriving from critical schools and critical identities. He has appealed again and again for employing critical reason and approaching criticism systematically. In his essay "Speculation and Concern" (pp. 167–180), Frye indicates that, like science, literary studies should proceed objectively. The difference between science and literary studies lies in the objects of consideration. While science looks outside of humankind to nature, literature returns humankind to itself. This essay, "Criticism, Visible and Invisible," indicates how criticism can bring readers closer to possessing that artistic experience which is at the human center. Criticism, according to Frye, educates a reader about all the contexts which distinguish a literary work. This essay first appeared in the journal College English. *More information about Frye and his other writings appears in the introduction to "Speculation and Concern," in chapter 3.*

There is a distinction, certainly as old as Plato and possibly as old as the human mind, between two levels of understanding. Plato calls them the level of *nous* and the level of *dianoia,* knowledge of things and knowledge about things. Literature presents the same distinction. There is the *dianoia* of literature, or criticism, which constitutes the whole of what can be directly taught and learned about literature. Beyond this is the experience of literature itself. What criticism can do, to point beyond itself, is to try to undermine the student's sense of the ultimate objectivity of the literary work. The student is confronted by an alien structure of imagination, set over against him, strange in its conventions and often in its values. It is not to remain so: it must become possessed by and identified with the student. Criticism cannot make this act of possession for the student; what it can do is weaken those tendencies within criticism that keep the literary work objective and separated. All methods of criticism and teaching are bad if they encourage persisting separation of student and literary work: all methods are good if they try to overcome it. The tendency to persistent separation is the result of shifting the critical attention from the object of literary experience to something else, usually something in the critic's mind. The end of criticism and teaching is not an aesthetic but an ethical and participating end. To treat literature seriously as a social and moral force is to pass into the genuine experience of it.

I wish all teachers of English could feel that they were concerned with the whole of a student's verbal, or in fact imaginative, experience, not merely with the small part of it that is conventionally called literacy. The incessant verbal bombardment addresses the same part of the mind that literature addresses. If the critic is deeply concerned with evaluation, and with separating the good from the bad in literature, then he should address the entire area of verbal experience. The distinction of good and bad should consider the affinities in structure and imagery between the 'best' and the 'worst' of what every young person reads or listens to. The difference between good and bad is not something inherent in literary works themselves, but the difference between two ways of using literary experience. Propaganda and advertising encourage a passive response by merging what is said with a stimulating way of saying it. Literature actively engages the reader. Literary education is not doing the whole of its proper work unless it marshals the verbal imagination against the assaults of advertising and propaganda that try to bludgeon it into passivity. By its central activity, creating a historical, biographical, and literary context, criticism enables the distinction between passive and active approaches to verbal experience, and the inner possession of literature as an imaginative force.

There is a distinction, certainly as old as Plato and possibly as old as the human mind, between two levels of understanding. I say levels, because one is nearly always regarded as superior to the other, whether in kind or in degree. Plato calls them, in his discussion of the divided line in the *Republic,* the level of *nous* and the level of *dianoia,* knowledge of things and knowledge about things. Knowledge about things preserves the split between subject and object which is the first fact in ordinary consciousness. 'I' learn 'that': what I learn is an objective body of facts set over against me and essentially unrelated to me. Knowledge of things, on the other hand, implies some kind of identification or essential unity of subject and object. What is learned and the mind of the learner become interdependent, indivisible parts of one thing.

Three principles are involved in this conception. First, learning about things is the necessary and indispensable prelude to the knowledge of things: confrontation is the only possible beginning of identity. Second, knowledge about things is the limit of teaching. Knowledge of things cannot be taught: for one thing, the possibility that there is some principle of identity that can link the knower and the known in some essential relation is indemonstrable. It can only be accepted, unconsciously as an axiom or deliberately as an act of faith. He who knows on the upper level knows that he knows, as a fact of his experience, but he cannot impart this knowledge directly. Third, *nous* is (or is usually considered to be) the same knowledge as *dianoia:* it is the relation between knower and known that is different. The difference is that something conceptual has become existential: this is the basis of the traditional contrast between knowledge and wisdom.

This distinction is of great importance in religion: Maritain's *Degrees of Knowledge* is one of many attempts to distinguish a lower comprehension from a higher apprehension in religious experience. When St. Thomas Aquinas remarked on his death-bed that all his work seemed to him so much straw, he did not mean that his books were worthless, but that he himself was passing from the *dianoia* to the *nous* of what he had been writing about. I mention the religious parallel only to emphasize a principle which runs through all education: that what Plato calls *nous* is attainable only through something analogous to faith, which implies habit or consistent will, the necessary persistence in pursuing the goals of the faith.

I am dealing here, however, only with the application of the principle of two levels of knowledge to the ordinary learning process. Here the clearest illustration is that of a manual skill. In beginning to learn a skill like driving a car, a conscious mind comes into contact with an alien and emotionally disturbing object. When the skill is learned, the object ceases to be objective and becomes an extension of the personality, and the learning process has moved from the conscious mind to something that we call unconscious, subconscious, instinctive, or whatever best expresses to us the idea of unmediated unity. We think of this subconscious, usually, as more withdrawn, less turned outward to the world, than the consciousness: yet it is far less solipsistic. It is the nervous novice who is the solipsist[1]: it is the trained driver, with a hidden skill that he cannot directly impart to others, who is in the community of the turnpike highway, such as it is.

Literature presents the same distinction. There is the *dianoia* of literature, or criticism, which constitutes the whole of what can be directly taught and learned about literature. I have explained elsewhere that it is impossible to teach or learn literature: what one teaches and learns is criticism. We do not regard this area of direct teaching and learning as an end but as a means to another end. A person who is absorbed wholly by knowledge about something is what we ordinarily mean by a pedant. Beyond this is the experience of literature itself, and the goal of this is something that we call vaguely the cultivated man, the person for whom literature is a possession, a possession that cannot be directly transmitted, and yet not private, for it belongs in a community. Nothing that we can teach a student is an acceptable substitute for the faith that a higher kind of contact with literature is possible, much less for the persistence in that faith which we call the love of reading. Even here there is the possibility of pedantry: literature is an essential part of the cultivated life, but not the whole of it, nor is the form of the cultivated life itself a literary form.

The great strength of humanism,[2] as a conception of teaching literature, was that it accepted certain classics or models in literature, but directed its attention beyond the study of them to the possession of them, and insisted on their relevance to civilized or cultivated life. We spoke of pedantry, and there was undoubtedly much pedantry in humanism, especially at the level of elementary teaching, but not enough to destroy its effectiveness. Browning's[3] grammarian was not a pedant, because he settled *hoti*'s business and based *oun* in the light of a blindingly clear vision of a community of knowledge. The act of faith in literary experience which humanism defended was closely associated with a more specific faith in the greatness of certain Greek and Latin classics. The classics were great, certainly, and produced an astonishingly fertile progeny in the vernaculars. But the conception of literature involved tended to be an aristocratic one, and had the limitations of aristocracy built into it. It saw literature as a hierarchy of comparative greatness, the summit of which provided the standards for the critics.

In the philologists of the nineteenth century, dealing with the vernaculars[4] themselves, one sometimes detects a late humanistic pedantry which takes the form of critical arrogance. All too often the philologists, one feels, form an initiated clique, with literary standards and models derived (at several removes) from the 'great' poets, which are then applied to the 'lesser' ones. Old-fashioned books on English literature which touch on 'lesser' poets, such as Skelton and Wyatt[5] in the early sixteenth century, maintain an attitude toward them of slightly injured condescension. Criticism of this sort had to be superseded by a democratizing of literary experience, not merely to do justice to underrated poets, but to revise the whole attitude to literature in which a poet could be judged by standards derived from another poet, however much 'greater'. Every writer must be examined on his own terms, to see what kind of literary experience he can supply that no one else can supply in quite the same way. The objection 'But Skelton isn't as great a poet as Milton' may not be without truth, but it is without critical point. Literary experience is far more flexible and varied than it was a century ago, but hierarchical standards still linger, and the *subjection* of the critic to the uniqueness of the work being criticized is still not a wholly accepted axiom. Also, the relevance to criticism of what used to be regarded as sub-literary material, primitive myths and the like, is still resisted in many quarters.

All teaching of literature, which is literary *dianoia* or criticism, must point beyond itself, and cannot get to where it is pointing. The revolution in the teaching of English associated with the phrase 'new criticism'[6] began by challenging the tendency (less a tendency of teachers, perhaps, than of examination-haunted students) to accept knowledge about literature as a substitute for literary experience. The new critics set the object of literary experience directly in front of the student and insisted that he grapple with it and not try to find its meaning or his understanding of it in the introduction and footnotes. So far, so good. No serious teaching of literature can ever put the object of literary experience in any other position. But new criticism was criticism too: it developed its own techniques of talking about the work, and providing another critical counterpart of the work to read instead. No method of criticism, as such, can avoid doing this. What criticism can do, to point beyond itself, is to try to undermine the student's sense of the ultimate objectivity of the literary work. That, I fear, is not a very intelligible sentence, but the idea it expresses is unfamiliar. The student is confronted by an alien structure of imagination, set over against him, strange in its conventions and often in its values. It is not to remain so: it must become possessed by and identified with the student. Criticism cannot make this act of possession for the student; what it can do is weaken those tendencies within criticism that keep the literary work objective and separated. Criticism, in order to point beyond itself, needs to be actively iconoclastic about itself.

The metaphor of 'taste' expresses a real truth in criticism, but no metaphor is without pitfalls. The sense of taste is a contact sense: the major arts are based on the senses of distance, and it is easy to think of critical taste as a sublimation, the critic being an astral gourmet and literature itself being, as Plato said of rhetoric, a kind of disembodied cookery. This gastronomic metaphor is frequently employed by writers, for instance at the opening of *Tom Jones*,[7] though when recognized as a metaphor it is usually only a joke. It suggests that the literary work is presented for enjoyment and evaluation, like a wine. The conception of taste is a popular one because it confers great social prestige on the critic. The man of taste is by definition a gentleman, and a critic who has a particular hankering to be a gentleman is bound to attach a good deal of importance to his taste. A generation ago the early essays of Eliot owed much of their influence and popularity to their cavalierism,[8] their suggestion that the social affinities of good poetry were closer to the landed gentry than to the Hebrew prophets. Taste leads to a specific judgement: the metaphor of the critic as 'judge' is parallel to the metaphor of taste, and the assumption underlying such criticism is usually that the test of one's critical ability is a value-judgement on the literary work.

If this is true, the critic's contribution to literature, however gentlemanly, seems a curiously futile one, the futility being most obvious with negative judgements. Ezra Pound, T.S. Eliot, Middleton Murry, F.P. Leavis,[9] are only a few of the eminent critics who have abused Milton. Milton's greatness as a poet is unaffected by this: as far as the central fact of his importance in literature is concerned, these eminent critics might as well have said nothing at all. A journal interested in satire recently quoted a critic as saying that satire must have a moral norm and that Fielding's *Jonathan Wild* was a failure because no character in it represented a moral norm. The question was referred to me, and I said, somewhat irritably, that of course a moral norm was essential to satire, but it was the reader and not the satirist who was responsible for supplying it. My real objection, however, was to the critical procedure involved in the 'X is a failure because' formula. No critical principle can possibly follow the 'because' which is of any importance at all compared to the fact of *Jonathan Wild*'s position in the history of satire and in eighteenth-century English culture. The fact is a fact about literature, and, as I have tried to show elsewhere, nothing can follow 'because' except some kind of pseudo-critical moral anxiety. Thus: 'King Lear is a failure because it is indecorous to represent a king on the stage as insane.' We recognize this statement to be nonsense, because we are no longer burdened with the particular social anxiety it refers to, but all such anxieties are equally without content. Matthew Arnold[10] decided that 'Empedocles on Etna' was a failure because its situation was one 'in which the suffering finds no vent in action; in which a continuous state of mental distress is prolonged, unrelieved by incident, hope, or resistance; in which there is everything to be endured, nothing to be done'. These phrases would exactly describe, for instance, Eliot's 'Prufrock', one of the most penetrating poems of our time, or a good deal of Arnold's contemporary, Baudelaire. We cannot question Arnold's sincerity in excluding his poem from his 1853 volume, but all he demonstrated by excluding it was his own anxious fear of irony.

The attitude that we may call critical dandyism, where the operative conceptions are vogue words of approval or the reverse, like 'interesting' or 'dreary', is an extreme but logical form of evaluating criticism, where the critic's real subject is his own social position. Such criticism belongs to the wrong side of Kierkegaard's[11] 'either-or' dialectic: it is an attitude for which the work of art remains permanently a detached object of contemplation, to be admired because the critic enjoys it or blamed because he does not. Kierkegaard himself was so impressed by the prevalence of this attitude in art that he called it the aesthetic attitude, and tended to identify the arts with it. We do not escape from the limitations of the attitude by transposing its judgements from an aesthetic into a moral key. F.R. Leavis has always commanded a good deal of often reluctant respect because of the moral intensity he brings to his criticism, and because of his refusal to make unreal separations between moral and aesthetic values. Reading through the recent reprint of *Scrutiny*, one feels at first that this deep concern for literature, whether the individual judgements are right or wrong, is the real key to literary experience, and the real introduction that criticism can make to it. But as one goes on one has the feeling that this concern, which is there and is a very real virtue, gets deflected at some crucial point, and is prevented from fully emerging out of the shadow-battles of anxieties. Perhaps what the point is is indicated by such comments of Leavis himself as 'the poem is a determinate thing: it is *there*', and, 'unappreciated, the poem isn't *there*'. An insistence on the 'thereness' or separation of critic and literary work forces one, for all one's concern, to go on playing the same 'aesthetic' game. The paradox is that the 'aesthetic' attitude is not a genuinely critical one at all, but social: concern makes the social reference more impersonal, but does not remove it.

Evaluating criticism is mainly effective as criticism only when its valuations are favourable. Thus Ezra Pound, in the middle of his *Guide to Kulchur*, expresses some disinterested admiration for the lyrical elegies of Thomas Hardy, and the effect, in that book, is as though a garrulous drunk had suddenly sobered up, focused his eyes, and begun to talk sense. But, of course, if my argument suggests that everything which has acquired some reputation in literature should be placed 'beyond criticism', or that histories of literature should be as bland and official as possible, I should merely be intensifying the attitude I am attacking, turning the verbal icon into a verbal idol. My point is a very different one, and it begins with the fact that the work of literature is 'beyond criticism' now: criticism can do nothing but lead into it.

There are two contexts in which a work of literature is potential, an internal context and an external one. Internally, the writer has a potential theme and tries to actualize it in what he writes. Externally, the literary work, actualized in itself, becomes a potential experience for student, critic, or reader. A 'bad' poem or novel is one in which, so the critic feels, a potential literary experience has not been actualized. Such a judgement implies a consensus: the critic speaks for all critics, even if he happens to be wrong. But an actualized work of literature may still fail to become an actualized experience for its reader. The judgement here implies withdrawal from a consensus: however many critics may like this, I don't. The first type of judgement belongs primarily to the critical reaction to contemporary literature, reviewing and the like, where a variety of new authors are struggling to establish their authority. The second type belongs primarily to the tactics of critical pressure groups that attempt to redistribute the traditional valuations of the writers of the past in order to display certain new writers, usually including themselves, to better advantage. There is no genuinely critical reason for 'revaluation'. Both activities correspond in the sexual life to what Freud calls the 'polymorphous perverse', the preliminaries of contact with the object. Judicial criticism, or reviewing, is necessarily imcomplete: it can never free itself from historical variables, such as the direct appeal of certain in-group conventions to the sophisticated critic. The kind of criticism that is expressed by the term 'insight', the noticing of things in the literary work of particular relevance to one's own experience, is perhaps the nearest that criticism can get to demonstrating the value of what it is dealing with. Insight criticism of this kind, however, is a form of divination, an extension of the principle of *sortes Virgilianae*: it is essentially random both in invention and in communication.

In short, all methods of criticism and teaching are bad if they encourage the persisting separation of student and literary work: all methods are good if they try to overcome it. The tendency to persistent separation is the result of shifting the critical attention from the object of literary experience to something else, usually something in the critic's mind, and this deprives criticism of content. I know that I have said this before, but the same issues keep turning up every year. This year the issue was raised by Professor Rowse's book on Shakespeare. The questions usually asked about Shakespeare's sonnets, such as who was W.H., have nothing to do with Shakespeare's sonnets or with literary criticism, and have only been attached to criticism because, owing to Shakespeare's portentous reputation, critics have acquired an impertinent itch to know more about his private life than they need to know. It seemed to Professor Rowse that such questions were properly the concern of a historian, and he was quite right. True, he had no new facts about the sonnets and added nothing to our knowledge of this alleged subject, but his principle was sound. But Professor Rowse went further. It occurred to him that perhaps literary criticism was not a genuine intellectual discipline at all, and that there could be no issues connected with it that could not be better dealt with by someone who did belong to a genuine discipline, such as history. One of his sentences, for instance, begins: 'A real writer understands better than a mere critic'. Literary criticism ought to be profoundly grateful to Professor Rowse for writing so bad a book: it practically proves that writing a good book on Shakespeare is a task for a mere critic. Still, the fact that a responsible scholar in a related field could assume, in 1964, that literary criticism was a parasitic pseudo-subject with no facts to build with and no concepts to think with, deserves to be noted.

I do not believe, ultimately, in a plurality of critical methods, though I can see a division of labour in critical operations. I do not believe that there are different 'schools' of criticism today, attached to different and irreconcilable metaphysical assumptions: the notion seems to me to reflect nothing but the confusion in critical theory. In particular, the notion that I belong to a school or have invented a school of mythical or archetypal criticism reflects nothing but confusion about me. I make this personal comment with some hesitation, in view of the great generosity with which my books have been received, but everyone who is understood by anybody is misunderstood by somebody. It is true that I call the elements of literary structure myths, because they are myths; it is true that I call the elements of imagery archetypes, because I want a word which suggests something that changes its context but not its essence. James Beattie, in *The Minstrel*, says of the poet's activity:

From Nature's beauties, variously compared
And variously combined, he learns to frame
Those forms of bright perfection

and adds a footnote to the last phrase: 'General ideas of excellence, the immediate archetypes of sublime imitation, both in painting and in poetry'. It was natural for an eighteenth-century poet to think of poetic images as reflecting 'general ideas of excellence'; it is natural for the twentieth-century critic to think of them as reflecting the same imagery in other poems. But I think of the term as indigenous to criticism, not as transferred from Neoplatonic philosophy or Jungian psychology. However, I would not fight for a word, and I hold to no 'method' of criticism beyond assuming that the structure and imagery of literature are central considerations of criticism. Nor, I think, does my practice of criticism illustrate the use of a patented critical method of my own different in kind from the approaches of other critics.

The end of criticism and teaching, in any case, is not an aesthetic but an ethical and participating end: for it, ultimately, works of literature are not things to be comtemplated but powers to be absorbed. This completes the paradox of which the first half has already been given. The 'aesthetic' attitude, persisted in, loses its connection with literature as an art and becomes socially or morally anxious: to treat literature seriously as a social and moral force is to pass into the genuine experience of it. The advantage of using established classics in teaching, the literary works that have proved their effectiveness, is that one can skip preliminary stages and clear everything out of the way except understanding, which is the only road to possession. At the same time it is easy for understanding to become an end in itself too. The established classics are, for the most part, historically removed from us, and to approach them as new works involves a certain historical astigmatism: but to consider them as historical documents only is again to separate student and literary work. In teaching manual skills, such as car-driving, an examination can test the skill on the higher level; but an examination in English literature cannot pass beyond the level of theoretical knowledge. We may guess the quality of a student's literary experience from the quality of his writing, but there is no assured way of telling from the outside the difference between a student who knows literature and a student who merely knows about it.

Thus the teaching of literature, an activity of criticism which attempts to cast its bread on the waters without knowing when or how or by whom it will be picked up, is involved in paradox and ambiguity. The object of literary experience must be placed directly in front of the student, and he should be urged to respond to it and accept no substitutes as the end of his understanding. Yet it does not matter a tinker's curse what a student thinks and feels about literature until he can think and feel, which is not until he passes the stage of stock response. And although the cruder forms of stock response can be identified and the student released from them, there are subtler forms that are too circular to be easily refuted. There is, for instance, critical narcissism, or assuming that a writer's 'real' meaning is the critic's own attitude (or the opposite of it, if the reaction is negative). There is no 'real' meaning in literature, nothing to be 'got out of it' or abstracted from the total experience; yet all criticism seems to be concerned with approaching such a meaning. There is no way out of these ambiguities: criticism is a phoenix preoccupied with constructing its own funeral pyre, without any guarantee that a bigger and better phoenix will manifest itself as a result.

A large part of criticism is concerned with commentary, and a major work of literature has a vast amount of commentary attached to it. With writers of the size of Shakespeare and Milton, such a body of work is a proper and necessary part of our cultural heritage; and so it may be with, say, Melville or Henry James or Joyce or T.S. Eliot. The existence of a large amount of commentary on a writer is a testimony to the sense of the importance of that writer among critics. As the first critic in *The Pooh Perplex* says, on the opening page of the book: 'Our ideal in English studies is to amass as much commentary as possible upon the literary work, so as to let the world know how deeply we respect it.' An important critical principle is concealed in this remark. It is an illusion that only great literature can be commented on, and that the existence of such commentary proves or demonstrates its greatness. It is a writer's merits that make the criticism on him rewarding, as a rule, but it is not his merits that make it possible. The techniques of criticism can be turned loose on anything whatever. If this were not so, a clever parody like *The Pooh Perplex* could hardly make its point. Hence a mere display of critical dexterity or ingenuity, even as an act of devotion, is not enough: criticism, to be useful both to literature and to the public, needs to contain some sense of the progressive or the systematic, some feeling that irrevocable forward steps in understanding are being taken. We notice that all the contributors to *The Pooh*

Perplex claim to be supplying the one essential thing needed to provide this sense of progress, though of course none of them does. Thus the piling up of commentary around the major writers of literature may in itself simply be another way of barricading those writers from us.

Yeats tells us that what fascinates us is the most difficult among things not impossible. Literary criticism is not in so simple a position. Teaching literature is impossible; that is why it is difficult. Yet it must be tried, tried constantly and indefatigably, and placed at the centre of the whole educational process, for at every level the understanding of words is as urgent and crucial a necessity as it is on its lowest level of learning to read and write. Whatever is educational is also therapeutic. The therapeutic power of the arts has been intermittently recognized, especially in music since David played his harp before Saul, but the fact that literature is essential to the mental health of society seldom enters our speculations about it. But if I am to take seriously my own principle that works of literature are not so much things to be studied as powers to be possessed, I need to face the implications of that principle.

I wish all teachers of English, at every level, could feel that they were concerned with the whole of a student's verbal, or in fact imaginative, experience, not merely with the small part of it that is conventionally called literary. The incessant verbal bombardment that students get from conversation, advertising, the mass media, or even such verbal games as Scrabble or cross-word puzzles, is addressed to the same part of the mind that literature addresses, and it does far more to mould their literary imagination that poetry or fiction. It often happens that new developments in literature meet with resistance merely because they bring to life conventions that the critics had decided were sub-literary. Wordsworth's *Lyrical Ballads* met with resistance of this kind, and in our day teachers and critics who think literature should be a matter of direct feeling and are prejudiced against the verbal puzzle find that their students, unlike themselves, are living in the age of *Finnegans Wake*.[12] There is a real truth, for all of what has been said above, in the belief that the critic is deeply concerned with evaluation, and with separating the good from the bad in literature. But I would modify this belief in three ways. First, as just said, the area of literature should not be restricted to the conventionally literary, but expanded to the entire area of verbal experience. Hence the evaluating activity should not be concerned solely with civil wars in the conventionally literary field. Second, the distinction of good and bad is not a simple opposing of the conventionally literary to the conventionally sub-literary, a matter of demonstrating the superiority of Henry James to Mickey Spillane. On the contrary, it seems to me that an important and neglected aspect of literary teaching is to illustrate the affinities in structure and imagery between the 'best' and the 'worst' of what every young person reads or listens to.

Third, if I am right in saying that literature is a power to be possessed, and not a body of objects to be studied, then the difference between good and bad is not something inherent in literary works themselves, but the difference between two ways of using literary experience. The belief that good and bad can be determined as inherent qualities is the belief that inspires censorship, and the attempt to establish grades and hierarchies in literature itself, to distinguish what is canonical from what is apocryphal, is really an 'aesthetic' form of censorship. Milton remarked in *Areopagitica*[13] that a wise man would make a better use of an idle pamphlet than a fool would of Holy Scripture, and this, I take it, is an application of the gospel principle that man is defiled not by what goes into him but by what comes out of him. The question of censorship takes us back to the metaphor of taste by a different road, for censorship is apparently based on an analogy between mental and physical nourishment, what is censorable being inherently poisonous. But there is something all wrong with this analogy: it has often been pointed out that the censor himself never admits to being adversely affected by what he reads. We need to approach the problem that censorship fails to solve in another way.

In primitive societies art is closely bound up with magic: the creative impulse is attached to a less disinterested hope that its products may affect the external world in one's favour. Drawing pictures of animals is part of a design to catch them; songs about bad weather are partly charms to ensure good weather. The magical attachments of primitive art, though they may have stimulated the creative impulse, also come to hamper it, and as society develops they wear off or become isolated in special ritual compartments. Many works of art, including Shakespeare's *Tempest,* remind us that the imaginative powers are released by the renunciation of magic. In the next stage of civilization the magical or natural attachment is replaced by a social one. Literature expresses the preoccupations of the society that produced it, and it is pressed into service to illustrate other social values, religious or political. This means that it has an attachment to other verbal structures in religion or history or morals which is allegorical. Here, too, is something that both hampers and stimulates the creative impulse. Much of Dante's *Commedia* and Milton's *Paradise Lost* is concerned with political and religious issues that we regard now as merely partisan or superstitious. The poems would never have been written without the desire to raise these issues, and as long as we are studying the poems the issues are relevant to our study. But when we pass from the study to the possession of the poems, a dialectical separation of a permanent imaginative structure from a mass of historical anxieties takes place. This is the critical principle that Shelley was attempting to formulate in his *Defence of Poetry,* and in fact the Romantic movement marks the beginning of a third stage in the attachments of the arts, and one that we are still in.

This third stage (to some extent 'decadent', as the first one is primitive, though we should be careful not to get trapped by the word) is both social and magical, and is founded on the desire to make art act kinetically on other people, startling, shocking, or otherwise stimulating them into a response of heightened awareness. It belongs to an age in which kinetic verbal stimulus, in advertising, propaganda, and mass media, plays a large and increasing role in our verbal experience. Sometimes the arts try to make use of similar techniques, as the Italian Futurist movement did, but more frequently the attempt is to create a kind of counter-stimulus. In the various shocking, absurd, angry, and similar conventions in contemporary art one may recognize a strong kinetic motivation. Even in the succession of fashions there is something of this, for the succession of vogues and movements in the arts is part of the economy of waste. Most cultivated people realize that they should overlook or ignore these attachments in responding to the imaginative product itself, and meet all such assaults on their sense of decorum with a tolerant aplomb that sometimes infuriates the artist still more. Here again, the attachment begins as a stimulus and may eventually become a hindrance, unless the artist is astute enough to detach himself at the point where the hindrance begins.

It is the critic's task, in every age, to fight for the autonomy of the arts, and never under any circumstances allow himself to be seduced into judging the arts, positively or negatively, by their attachments. The fact that, for instance, Burroughs's *Naked Lunch* is written in the convention of the psychological shocker does not make it either a good or a bad book, and the fashion for pop-art painting is neither good because painters ought to rediscover content nor bad because they ought not. But an essential part of the critic's strategy, to the extent that the critic is a teacher, is in leading his students to realize that in responding to art without attachments they are at the same time building up a resistance to kinetic stimulus themselves. Literary education is not doing the whole of its proper work unless it marshals the verbal imagination against the assaults of advertising and propaganda that try to bludgeon it into passivity. This is a battle that should be fought long before university, because university comes too late in a student's life to alter his mental habits more than superficially. I think of a public school teacher I know who got his grade-eight students to analyse the rhetorical devices in a series of magazine advertisements. The effect was so shattering that he thought at first he must be working with too young an age group: children who were contemptuous of Santa Claus and the stork were still not ready to discover that advertising was no more factual than the stories they told their parents. Eventually, however, he realized that he was right, and that he had uncovered a deeper level of literary response than literature as such can ordinarily reach at that age.

The direct response to a verbal kinetic stimulus persists into adult life, and is, of course, what makes the propaganda of totalitarian states effective for their own people. Such response is not an inability to distinguish rhetorical from factual statement, but a will to unite them. Even though a Communist, for example, understands the difference between what is said and the political necessity of saying it, he has been conditioned to associate rhetoric and fact when they are produced in a certain area of authority, not to separate them. In the democracies we are not trained in this way, but we are continually being persuaded to fall into the habit, by pressure groups trying to establish the same kind of authority, and by certain types of entertainment in which the kinetic stimulus is erotic. I recently saw a documentary movie of the rock-and-roll singer Paul Anka. The reporter pried one of the squealing little sexballs out of the audience and asked her what she found so ecstatic about listening to Anka. She said, still in a daze: 'He's so *sincere.*' The will to unite rhetorical and direct address is very clear here.

The central activity of criticism, which is the understanding of literature, is essentially one of establishing a context for the works of literature being studied. This means relating them to other things: to their context in the writer's life, in the writer's time, in the history of literature, and above all in the total structure of literature itself, or what I call the order of words. Relation to context accounts for nearly the whole of the factual basis of criticism, the aspect of it that can progress through being verified or refuted by later criticism. This central activity itself has a further context, a lower and an upper limit, with which I have been mainly concerned in this paper. On the lower limit is criticism militant, a therapeutic activity of evaluation, or separating the good from the bad, in which good and bad are not two kinds of literature, but, respectively, the active and the passive approaches to verbal experience. This kind of criticism is essentially the defence of those aspects of civilization loosely described as freedom of speech and freedom of thought. On the higher limit is criticism triumphant, the inner possession of literature as an imaginative force to which all study of literature leads, and which is criticism at once glorified and invisible.

We remember the discussion in Joyce's *Portrait* in which the characteristics of beauty are said to be *integritas, consonantia,* and *claritas;* unity, harmony, and radiance. Poet and critic alike struggle to unify and to relate; the critic, in particular, struggles to demonstrate the unity of the work of literature he is studying and to relate it to its context in literature. There remains the peculiar *claritas* or intensity, which cannot be demonstrated in either literature or criticism, though all literature and criticism point toward it. No darkness can comprehend any light; no ignorance or indifference can ever see any *claritas* in literature itself or in the criticism that attempts to convey it, just as no saint in ordinary life wears a visible gold plate around his head. All poet or critic can do is to hope that somehow, somewhere, and for someone, the struggle to unify and to relate, because it is an honest struggle and not because of any success in what it does, may be touched with a radiance not its own.

Notes

[1] A solipsist believes that the self can be aware of nothing but its own experiences.

[2] Humanism usually indicates a doctrine centered in human endeavor. Humanities as a discipline grew from the study of classical literature emphasized by Renaissance humanist scholars.

[3] Robert Browning's (1812–1899) grammarian, who appeared in the 1855 poem "A Grammarian's Funeral," was not a pedant, because in settling "*hoti's* business," he concerned himself with statements introduced by "because" (hotis) or facts denoted by such statements. Browning's grammarian thus concerned himself with reason and fact rather than intellectualism for its own sake.

[4] Vernaculars are languages spoken by common people. For example, during the Middle Ages, although Latin was Europe's official language for learning and law, the common people spoke their native languages like French, German, Italian, or English.

[5] John Skelton (1460–1529) was one of the earliest Tudor poets in England. Sir Thomas Wyatt (1503–1542), an English poet, wrote lyrics which reflected native English rather than the Italian influences embraced by most early English Renaissance poets.

[6] New Criticism refers to twentieth-century literary criticism's reaction against earlier biographical, historical, and moral criticism, which drew attention away from the literary text. Although diverse, New Critics generally share a conviction that criticism requires precision, method, theory, and close textual reading.

[7] Chapter 1 of Henry Fielding's *Tom Jones* bears the title "The Introduction to the Work or Bill of Fare to the Feast." The chapter itself analogizes literary taste to the varieties of taste found among diners at an inn and likens the writer's craft to the cook's ability to dress up his meats. Fielding will, he says, "represent human nature . . . to the keen appetite of our reader."

[8] Cavalierism carries a nonchalant and seemingly nonserious attitude toward life.

[9] Ezra Pound (1885–1972) and T.S. Eliot (1886–1965), both poets and critics, took a classical perspective which emphasized that art relies on the experiences and culture of the past and embodies "disinterested" emotion. (Eliot's essay "Tradition and the Individual Talent" is the next selection in this chapter.) Their critical stance responded directly to J. Middleton Murry's (1889–1957) Romantic emphasis on imagination and feeling. F.R. Leavis (1895–1978), one of the midtwentieth century's most influential literary critics, advocated I.A. Richard's practical criticism (that is, criticism based on close analysis of the literary text) as a unique opportunity for developing general "critical awareness."

[10] Matthew Arnold (1822–1888), the Victorian poet and literary critic, developed English literary criticism into a discipline of its own right.

[11] The Danish philosopher and theologian Soren Kierkegaard's (1813–1855) reputation as the founder of modern existentialism places him as a central twentieth-century philosopher.

[12] *Finnegan's Wake* (1939), James Joyce's last novel, presents the vast story of a symbolic Irishman's cosmic dream. Joyce creates a dream language reverberating in puns derived from every conceivable source in history. The language combines several languages, fits together varied words, and recombines syllables.

[13] *Areopagitica* (1644), John Milton's great prose work, argued for the "freedom on unlicensed printing."

FOCUS: READING REVIEW

1. Explain Frye's distinction between "knowledge of things" and "knowledge about things." What kind of relationship does the knower form with the knowledge in each circumstance?
2. What relationship does Frye find between taste, judgment, and criticism?
3. What is the aesthetic attitude? Why does Frye object to it as a critical position?
4. What is the relationship between potential and actualized literature? How can this relationship serve as a means of distinguishing between good and bad literature?

FOCUS: AUTHOR'S STRATEGIES

1. Who is Frye's audience? What specific passages indicate this?
2. Frye's purpose is explaining the function of criticism. Explain how he uses definition and comparative analysis to accomplish this.

FOCUS: **DISCUSSION AND WRITING**

1. Frye says, "It is impossible to teach or learn literature. What one teaches and learns is criticism." How does this define criticism? What distinction does he suggest between criticism and literature?
2. Frye advocates experiencing literature as a "social and moral force." How can literature be social? How can it be moral?
3. Frye comments that "incessant verbal bombardment does more to shape the literary imagination than poetry or fiction." What examples of "verbal bombardment" have shaped your imagination? To what degree has literature shaped your imagination?
4. In the example of a documentary movie on Paul Anka how does the audience member's response, "He's so sincere," unite rhetorical and direct address? Cite instances from advertising or television that unite rhetorical and direct address.

Tradition and the Individual Talent
T.S. Eliot

T.S. Eliot (1888–1965) revolutionized British and American poetry in the 1920s with the publication of The Wasteland *in 1922. Though a rich pattern of image and illustration, the poem juxtaposes past civilization and its origins with the contemporary world to show horror at modern man's fragmented, alienated experience. Born in Boston, Eliot grew up in St. Louis, Missouri. He attended Harvard University, the Sorbonne in Paris, and Oxford University. While in Europe, he became an involuntary expatriate in London because of the outbreak of World War I in 1914. During this time Eliot formed ties with Ezra Pound and other experimental writers and thinkers, and he chose to remain in England following the war. His conversion to the Anglican church and his connection to England led him to become a British subject in 1927. His later poetry,* Ash Wednesday *(1930) and* Four Quartets *(1943), and his plays* Murder in the Cathedral *(1935) and* The Cocktail Party *(1949) reflect his movement from despair to faith. Eliot's critical theory, perhaps best illustrated by "Tradition and the Individual Talent," asks that poetry incorporate the legacy of its literary predecessors and objectify emotion in concrete imagery. Eliot's critical writings and poetry influenced modern distrust of emotion and sentiment in literature.*

In English writing we seldom speak of tradition, though we occasionally apply its name in deploring its absence. Certainly the word is not likely to appear in our appreciations of living or dead writers. One of the facts that might come to light in articulating what passes in our minds when we read a book and feel an emotion about it is our tendency to insist, when we praise a poet, upon those aspects of his work in which he least resembles anyone else. Whereas if we approach a poet without this prejudice we shall often find that not only the best, but the most individual parts of his work may be those in which the dead poets, his ancestors, assert their immortality most vigorously. Tradition involves the historical sense which compels a man to write not merely with his own generation in his bones, but with a feeling that the whole of the literature of Europe from Homer and within it the whole of the literature of his own country has a simultaneous existence. No artist has his complete meaning alone: he must be set for contrast and comparison among the dead. He must be judged by the standards of the past. What is to be insisted upon is that the poet must develop or procure the consciousness of the past and that he should continue to develop this consciousness throughout his career. What happens is a continual surrender of himself as he is at the moment to something which is more valuable. There remains to define this process of depersonalization and its relation to the sense of tradition. The more perfect the artist, the more completely separate in him will be the man who suffers and the mind which creates. The poet's mind is in fact a receptacle for seizing and storing up numberless feelings, phrases, images, which remain there until all the particles which can unite to form a new compound are present together. The poet has not a 'personality' to express, but a particular medium in which impressions and experiences combine in peculiar and unexpected ways. The business of the poet is not to find new emotions, but to use the ordinary ones and, in working them up into poetry, to express feelings which are not in actual emotions at all. Poetry is not a turning loose of emotion, but an escape from emotion; it is not the expression of personality, but an escape from personality. To divert interest from the poet to the poetry is a laudable aim: for it would conduce to a juster estimation of actual poetry, good and bad.

I

In English writing we seldom speak of tradition, though we occasionally apply its name in deploring its absence. We cannot refer to 'the tradition' or to 'a tradition'; at most, we employ the adjective in saying that the poetry of So-and-so is 'traditional' or even 'too traditional'. Seldom, perhaps does the word appear except in a phrase of censure. If otherwise, it is vaguely approbative,[1] with the implication, as to the work approved, of some pleasing archaeological reconstruction. You can hardly make the word agreeable to English ears without this comfortable reference to the reassuring science of archaeology.

Certainly the word is not likely to appear in our appreciations of living or dead writers. Every nation, every race, has not only its own creative, but its own critical turn of mind; and is even more oblivious of the shortcomings and limitations of its critical habits than of those of its creative genius. We know, or think we know, from the enormous mass of critical writing that has appeared in the French language the critical method or habit of the French; we only conclude (we are such unconscious people) that the French are 'more critical' than we, and sometimes even plume ourselves a little with the fact, as if the French were the less spontaneous. Perhaps they are; but we might remind ourselves that criticism is as inevitable as breathing, and that we should be none the worse for articulating what passes in our minds when we read a book and feel an emotion about it, for criticizing our own minds in their work of criticism. One of the facts that might come to light in this process is our tendency to insist, when we praise a poet, upon those aspects of his work in which he least resembles anyone else. In these aspects or parts of his work we pretend to find what is individual, what is the peculiar essence of the man. We dwell with satisfaction upon the poet's difference from his predecessors, especially his immediate predecessors; we endeavour to find something that can be isolated in order to be enjoyed. Whereas if we approach a poet without this prejudice we shall often find that not only the best, but the most individual parts of his work may be those in which the dead poets, his ancestors, assert their immortality most vigorously. And I do not mean the impressionable period of adolescence, but the period of full maturity.

Yet if the only form of tradition, of handing down, consisted in following the ways of the immediate generation before us in a blind or timid adherence to its successes, 'tradition' should positively be discouraged. We have seen many such simple currents soon lost in the sand; and novelty is better than repetition. Tradition is a matter of much wider significance. It cannot be inherited, and if you want it you must obtain it by great labour. It involves, in the first place, the historical sense, which we may call nearly indispensable to anyone who would continue to be a poet beyond his twenty-fifth year; and the historical sense involves a perception, not only of the pastness of the past, but of its presence; the historical sense compels a man to write not merely with his own generation in his bones, but with a feeling that the whole of the literature of Europe from Homer and within it the whole of the literature of his own country has a simultaneous existence and composes a simultaneous order. This historical sense, which is a sense of the timeless as well as of the temporal and of the timeless and of the temporal together, is what makes a writer traditional. And it is at the same time what makes a writer most acutely conscious of his place in time, of his own contemporaneity.

No poet, no artist of any art, has his complete meaning alone. His significance, his appreciation is the appreciation of his relation to the dead poets and artists. You cannot value him alone; you must set him, for contrast and comparison, among the dead. I mean this as a principle of aesthetic, not merely historical, criticism. The necessity that he shall conform, that he shall cohere, is not one-sided; what happens when a new work of art is created is something that happens simultaneously to all the works of art which preceded it. The existing monuments form an ideal order among themselves, which is modified by the introduction of the new (the really new) work of art among them. The existing order is complete before the new work arrives; for order to persist after the supervention of novelty, the *whole* existing order must be, if ever so slightly, altered; and so the relations, proportions, values of each work of art toward the whole are readjusted; and this is conformity between the old and the new. Whoever has approved this idea of order, of the form of European, of English literature will not find it preposterous that the past should be altered by the present as much as the present is directed by the past. And the poet who is aware of this will be aware of great difficulties and responsibilities.

In a peculiar sense he will be aware also that he must inevitably be judged by the standards of the past. I say judged, not amputated, by them; not judged to be as good as, or worse or better than, the dead; and certainly not judged by the canons of dead critics. It is a judgment, a comparison, in which two things are measured by each other. To conform merely would be for the new work not really to conform at all; it would not be new, and would therefore not be a work of art. And we do not quite say that the new is more valuable because it fits in; but its fitting in is a test of its value—a test, it is true, which can only be slowly and cautiously applied, for we are none of us infallible judges of conformity. We say: it appears to conform, and is perhaps individual, or it appears individual, and may conform; but we are hardly likely to find that it is one and not the other.

To proceed to a more intelligible exposition of the relation of the poet to the past: he can neither take the past as a lump, an indiscriminate bolus, nor can he form himself wholly on one or two private admirations, nor can he form himself wholly upon one preferred period. The first course is inadmissible, the second is an important experience of youth, and the third is a pleasant and highly desirable supplement. The poet must be very conscious of the main current, which does not at all flow invariably through the most distinguished reputations. He must be quite aware of the obvious fact that art never improves, but that the material of art is never quite the same. He must be aware that the mind of Europe—the mind of his own country—a mind which he learns in time to be much more important than his own private mind—is a mind which changes, and that this change is a development which abandons nothing *en route,* which does not superannuate either Shakespeare, or Homer, or 'the rock drawing of the Magdalenian draughtsmen. That this development, refinement perhaps, complication certainly, is not, from the point of view of the artist, any improvement. Perhaps not even an improvement from the point of view of the psychologist or not to the extent which we imagine; perhaps only in the end based upon a complication in economics and machinery. But the difference between the present and the past is that the conscious present is an awareness of the past in a way and to an extent which the past's awareness of itself cannot show.

Someone said: 'The dead writers are remote from us because we *know* so much more than they did'. Precisely, and they are that which we know.

I am alive to a usual objection to what is clearly part of my programme for the *métier* of poetry. The objection is that the doctrine requires a ridiculous amount of erudition (pedantry), a claim which can be rejected by appeal to the lives of poets in any pantheon. It will even be affirmed that much learning deadens or perverts poetic sensibility. While, however, we persist in believing that a poet ought to know as much as will not encroach upon his necessary receptivity and necessary laziness, it is not desirable to confine knowledge to whatever can be put into a useful shape for examinations, drawing-rooms, or the still more pretentious modes of publicity. Some can absorb knowledge, the more tardy must sweat for it. Shakespeare acquired more essential history from Plutarch than most men could from the whole British Museum. What is to be insisted upon is that the poet must develop or procure the consciousness of the past and that he should continue to develop this consciousness throughout his career.

What happens is a continual surrender of himself as he is at the moment to something which is more valuable. The progress of an artist is a continual self-sacrifice, a continual extinction of personality.

There remains to define this process of depersonalization and its relation to the sense of tradition. It is in this depersonalization that art may be said to approach the condition of science. I therefore invite you to consider, as a suggestive analogy, the action which takes place when a bit of finely filiated platinum is introduced into a chamber containing oxygen and sulphur dioxide.

II

Honest criticism and sensitive appreciation is directed not upon the poet but upon the poetry. If we attend to the confused cries of the newspaper critics and the susurrus[2] of popular repetition that follows, we shall hear the names of poets in great numbers; if we seek not Blue-book knowledge but the enjoyment of poetry, and ask for a poem, we shall seldom find it. I have tried to point out the importance of the relation of the poem to other poems by other authors, and suggested the conception of poetry as a living whole of all the poetry that has ever been written. The other aspect of this Impersonal theory of poetry is the relation of the poem to its author. And I hinted, by an analogy, that the mind of the mature poet differs from that of the immature one not precisely in any valuation of 'personality', not being necessarily more interesting, or having 'more to say', but rather by being a more finely perfected medium in which special, or very varied, feelings are at liberty to enter into new combinations.

The analogy was that of the catalyst. When the two gases previously mentioned are mixed in the presence of a filament of platinum, they form sulphurous acid. This combination takes place only if the platinum is present; nevertheless the newly formed acid contains no trace of platinum, and the platinum itself is apparently unaffected: has remained inert, neutral, and unchanged. The mind of the poet is the shred of platinum. It may partly or exclusively operate upon the experience of the man himself; but, the more perfect the artist, the more completely separate in him will be the man who suffers and the mind which creates; the more perfectly will the mind digest and transmute the passions which are its material.

The experience, you will notice, the elements which enter the presence of the transforming catalyst, are of two kinds: emotions and feelings. The effect of a work of art upon the person who enjoys it is an experience different in kind from any experience not of art. It may be formed out of one emotion, or may be a combination of several; and various feelings, inhering for the writer in particular words or phrases or images, may be added to compose the final result. Or great poetry may be made without the direct use of any emotion whatever: composed out of feelings solely. Canto XV[3] of the *Inferno* (Brunetto Latini) is a working up of the emotion evident in the situation; but the effect, though single as that of any work of art, is obtained by considerable complexity of detail. The last quatrain gives an image, a feeling attaching to an image, which 'came', which did not develop simply out of what precedes, but which was probably in suspension in the poet's mind until the proper combination arrived for it to add itself to. The poet's mind is in fact a receptacle for seizing and storing up numberless feelings, phrases, images, which remain there until all the particles which can unite to form a new compound are present together.

If you compare several representative passages of the greatest poetry you see how great is the variety of types of combination, and also how completely any semi-ethical criterion of 'sublimity' misses the mark. For it is not the 'greatness', the intensity, of the emotions, the components, but the intensity of the artistic process, the pressure, so to speak, under which the fusion takes place, that counts. The episode of Paolo and Francesca employs a definite emotion, but the intensity of the poetry is something quite different from whatever intensity in the supposed experience it may give the impression of. It is no more intense, furthermore, than Canto XXVI, the voyage of Ulysses, which has not the direct dependence upon an emotion. Great variety is possible in the process of transmutation of emotion: the murder of Agamemnon, or the agony of Othello, gives an artistic effect apparently closer to a possible original than the scenes from Dante. In the *Agamemnon,* the artistic emotion approximates to the emotion of an actual spectator; in *Othello* to the emotion of the protagonist himself. But the difference between art and the event is always absolute; the combination which is the murder of Agamemnon is probably as complex as that which is the voyage of Ulysses. In either case there has been a fusion of elements. The ode of Keats contains a number of feelings which have nothing particular to do with the nightingale, but which the nightingale, partly perhaps because of its attractive name, and partly because of its reputation, served to bring together.

The point of view which I am struggling to attack is perhaps related to the metaphysical theory of the substantial unity of the soul: for my meaning is, that the poet has, not a 'personality' to express, but a particular medium, which is only a medium and not a personality, in which impressions and experiences combine in peculiar and unexpected ways. Impressions and experiences which are important for the man may take no place in the poetry, and those which become important in the poetry may play quite a negligible part in the man, the personality.

I will quote a passage which is unfamiliar enough to be regarded with fresh attention in the light—in darkness—of these observations:

And now methinks I could e'en chide myself
For doating on her beauty, though her death
Shall be revenged after no common action.
Does the silkworm expend her yellow labours
For thee? For thee does she undo herself?
Are lordships sold to maintain ladyships
For the poor benefit of a bewildering minute?
Why does yon fellow falsify highways,
And put his life between the judge's lips,
 To refine such a thing—keeps horse and men
To beat their valours for her? . . .

In this passage (as is evident if it is taken in its context) there is a combination of positive and negative emotions: an intensely strong attraction toward beauty and an equally intense fascination by the ugliness which is contrasted with it and which destroys it. This balance of contrasted emotion is in the dramatic situation to which the speech is pertinent, but that situation alone is inadequate to it. This is, so to speak, the structural emotion, provided by the drama. But the whole effect, the dominant tone, is due to the fact that a number of floating feelings, have an affinity to this emotion by no means superficially evident, have combined with it to give us a new art emotion.

It is not in his personal emotions, the emotions provoked by particular events in his life, that the poet is in any way remarkable or interesting. His particular emotions may be simple, or crude, or flat. The emotion in his poetry will be a very complex thing, but not with the complexity of the emotions of people who have very complex or unusual emotions in life. One error, in fact, of eccentricity in poetry is to seek for new human emotions to express; and in this search for novelty in the wrong place it discovers the perverse. The business of the poet is not to find new emotions, but to use the ordinary ones and, in working them up into poetry, to express feelings which are not in actual emotions at all. And emotions which he has never experienced will serve his turn as well as those familiar to him. Consequently, we must believe that 'emotion recollected in tranquillity'[4] is an inexact formula. For it is neither emotion, nor recollection, nor, without distortion of meaning, tranquillity. It is a concentration, and a new thing resulting from the concentration, of a very great number of experiences which to the practical and active person would not seem to be experiences at all; it is a concentration which does not happen consciously or of deliberation. These experiences are not 'recollected', and they finally unite in an atmosphere which is 'tranquil' only in that it is a passive attending upon the event. Of course this is not quite the whole story. There is a great deal, in the writing of poetry, which must be conscious and deliberate. In fact, the bad poet is usually unconscious where he ought to be conscious, and conscious where he ought to be unconscious. Both errors tend to make him 'personal'. Poetry is not a turning loose of emotion, but an escape from emotion; it is not the expression of personality, but an escape from personality. But, of course, only those who have personality and emotions know what it means to want to escape from these things.

III

δ δὲ νοῦς ἴσως θειότερόν τι καὶ ἀπαθές ἐστιν.

This essay proposes to halt at the frontier of metaphysics or mysticism, and confine itself to such practical conclusions as can be applied by the responsible person interested in poetry. To divert interest from the poet to the poetry is a laudable aim: for it would conduce to a juster estimation of actual poetry, good and bad. There are many people who appreciate the expression of sincere emotion in verse, and there is a smaller number of people who can appreciate technical excellence. But very few know when there is an expression of *significant* emotion, emotion which has its life in the poem and not in the history of the poet. The emotion of art is impersonal. And the poet cannot reach this impersonality without surrendering himself wholly to the work to be done. And he is not likely to know what is to be done unless he lives in what is not merely the present, but the present moment of the past, unless he is conscious, not of what is dead, but of what is already living.

Notes

   [1] approbative: showing approval.
   [2] susurrus: a whispering, murmuring sound.
   [3] *Inferno*: The first book of Dante's *Divine Comedy.*
   [4] "emotion recollected in tranquillity": In his *Preface to the Lyrical Ballads,* William Wordsworth, the great English Romantic poet, observed that all good poetry is "powerful emotion recollected in tranquillity." This defines for Romantic poetry the relation of emotion to art, a concept Eliot denies.

FOCUS: READING REVIEW

1. What is tradition in relation to art?
2. What is historical sense and what does it provide?
3. What difficulties and responsibilities lie with the poet who works within tradition?
4. What role does individuality have in Eliot's view?
5. What is the distinction between a young and a mature poet?
6. Explain how the poet is like platinum in Eliot's analogy.
7. What role does Eliot give to "feelings" in poetry? What does he value more highly than feeling?

FOCUS: AUTHOR'S STRATEGIES

1. Who is Eliot's audience—poet or critic? What in the essay indicates this?
2. Eliot's argument relies on defining key concepts. What are they? How do his definitions differ from conventional usage? How does he shape his essay from these definitions?

3. What end does Eliot seek for poetry and for criticism? What does this indicate about the essay's purpose?

FOCUS: DISCUSSION AND WRITING

1. Explain Eliot's statement "Poetry is not a turning loose of emotion; but an escape from emotion: it is not the expression of personality, but an escape from personality."
2. Based on this essay, what criteria would you expect Eliot to employ in judging poetry?

Beliefs and the Reader
Wayne Booth

Wayne Booth (b.1921) is George M. Pullman Professor of English at the University of Chicago, where he was educated. In this selection, taken from The Rhetoric of Fiction *(1961), Booth considers the literary interests of the reader and demonstrates that reading is a subjective experience which the author depends on to achieve fiction's effects. Literature creates between an author and his audience a relationship which communicates value and involvement.* The Rhetoric of Fiction, *an important critical study, makes readers more aware of narrative technique. Other of Booth's works include* The Rhetoric of Irony *(1974),* Now Don't Try to Reason with Me *(1970), and* The Knowledge Most Worth Having *(1967), which he edited.*

The values which interest us, and which are thus available for technical manipulation in fiction, may be roughly divided into three kinds. (1) Intellectual or cognitive: We have, or can be made to have, strong intellectual curiosity about "the facts," the true interpretation, the true reasons, the true origins, the true motives, or the truth about life itself. (2) Qualitative: We have or can be made to have a strong desire to see any pattern or form completed or to experience a further development of qualities. We seek an end of a causal chain, the fulfillment of our expectation from literary conventions, or the completion of a pattern. We also seek the fulfillment of the promise of style, meaning, character portrayal, or tone which a work makes in its first few pages. We might call this kind "aesthetic." (3) Practical: We have or can be made to have a strong desire for the success or failure of those we love or hate, admire or detest; or we can be made to cope for or fear a change in the quality of a character. Much of what looks like purely aesthetic or intellectual quality in a character may in fact have a moral dimension that is highly effective. We might call this kind "human." Since men do have strong intellectual, qualitative, and practical interests, there is no reason why great novels cannot be written relying primarily on any one kind. But it is clear that no great work is based solely on one interest.

TYPES OF LITERARY INTEREST (AND DISTANCE)

The values which interest us, and which are thus available for technical manipulation in fiction, may be roughly divided into three kinds: (1) Intellectual or cognitive: We have, or can be made to have, strong intellectual curiosity about "the facts," the true interpretation, the true reasons, the true origins, the true motives, or the truth about life itself. (2) Qualitative: We have or can be made to have, a strong desire to see any pattern or form completed, or to experience a further development of qualities of any kind. We might call this kind "aesthetic," if to do so did not suggest that a literary form using this interest was necessarily of more artistic value than one based on other interests. (3) Practical: We have or can be made to have, a strong desire for the success or failure of those we love or hate, admire or detest; or we can be made to hope for or fear a change in the quality of a character. We might call this kind "human," if to do so did not imply that 1 and 2 were somehow less than human. This hope or fear may be for an intellectual change in a character or for a change in his fortune; one finds this practical aspect even in the most uncompromising novel of ideas that might seem to fall entirely under 1. Our desire may, second, be for a change of quality in a character; one finds this practical aspect even in the purely "aesthetic" novel of sensibility that might seem to fall entirely under 2. Finally, our desire may be for a moral change in a character, or for a change in his fortune—that is, we can be made to hope for or to fear particular moral choices and their results.

Intellectual interests.—We always want to find out the facts of the case, whether the simple material circumstances, as in most mystery stories, or psychological or philosophical truths which explain the external circumstances. Even in so-called plotless works we are pulled forward by a desire to discover the truth about the world of the book. In works relying heavily on this interest, we know that the book is completed when we once see the complete picture. In Hermann Hesse's *Siddhartha,* for example, our major interest is in Siddhartha's quest for the truth about how a man should live. If we do not think that the question of how a man should live is important, or that this author's insights on the question are likely to prove valuable, we can never care very much for this novel, even though we may enjoy some of the lesser pleasures offered by it. In many serious modern novels we look for an answer to the question, "What do these lives *mean*?" In others we look for completed patterns of theme, image, or symbol.

Very few imaginative works, however, rely entirely on a desire for intellectual completion. The pure literary forms that belong properly to this kind of suspense are the philosophical treatise which arouses our curiosity about an important question and the purely ratiocinative[1] detective novel.

Completion of qualities.—Most imaginative works, even those of a kind that might seem to be cognitive or didactic in the sense of being built only on speculative or intellectual interests, rely in part on interests very different from intellectual curiosity; they make us desire a quality. Though some of the qualities which some works provide are often discussed under cognitive terms like "truth" and "knowledge," clearly the satisfaction we receive from the following qualities is to some degree distinct from the pleasure of learning.

a. *Cause-effect.*—When we see causal chain started, we demand—and demand in a way that is only indirectly related to mere curiosity—to see the result. Emma[2] meddles, Tess[3] is seduced, Huck[4] runs away—and we demand certain consequences. This kind of sequence, so strongly stressed by Aristotle in his discussion of plot, is, as we have seen, often played down or even deplored by modern critics and novelists. Yet our desire for causal completion is one of the strongest of interests available to the author. Not only do we believe that certain causes do in life product certain effects; in literature we believe that they should. Consequently, we ordinary readers will go to great lengths, once we have been caught up by an author who knows how to make use of this interest, to find out whether our demands will be met.

The suspension from cause to effect is of course closely related, on the one hand, to curiosity—that is, to a cognitive interest; we know that whatever fulfillment of our expectations we are given will be given with a difference, and we are inevitably curious about what the difference will be. All good works surprise us, and they surprise us largely by bringing to our attention convincing cause-and-effect patterns which were earlier played down. We can predict that disaster will result from Achilles' anger; we could never predict the generosity to Priam as a crucial part of the "disaster," even though when it comes it can be seen to follow properly as a result from other causes in Achilles' nature and situation.[5]

On the other hand, this interest is easily confused with practical interests, which are described below. It is qualitative, nonetheless, because it operates quite independently of our interests in the welfare of human beings. In fact it can conflict with those interests. The hero commits a crime—and we are torn between our appetite for the proper effect, discovery and punishment, and our practical desire for his happiness.

b. *Conventional expectations.*—For experienced readers a sonnet[6] begun calls for a sonnet concluded; an elegy[7] begun in blank verse calls for an elegy completed in blank verse. Even so amorphous a genre as the novel, with hardly any established conventions, makes use of this kind of interest: when I begin what I think is a novel, I expect to read a novel throughout unless the author can, like Sterne,[8] transform my idea of what a novel can be.

We seem to be able to accept almost anything as a literary convention, no matter how inherently improbable. Even the most outlandish of mannerisms, like Euphuism[9] or Finneganswakism,[10] can perform the essential task of maintaining our sense of the artistic integrity of *this* work as distinct from all others and as distinct from life. Again, authors may surprise us by violating conventions, but only so long as conventional expectations are available in a given public to be played upon. When everyone prides himself on violating conventions, there is nothing left to violate; the fewer the conventions the fewer the surprises.

c. *Abstract forms.*—There seems to lie behind each convention some more general pattern of desires and gratifications that it serves. Balance, symmetry, climax, repetition, contrast, comparison—some pattern derived from our experience is probably imitated by every successful convention. The conventions which continue to give pleasure when they are no longer fashionable are based on patterns of reaction that lie very deep. Fashions in verse form come and go, for example, but meter and rhyme and the other musical devices of poetry do not lose their importance.

With the surrender of verse, and with no conventional agreement whatever about what is good narrative prose style, writers of longer narratives have been forced to engage in a constant search for new ways of giving body to abstract forms.

d. *"Promised" qualities.*—In addition to these qualities, common to many works, each work promises in its early pages a further provision of distinctive qualities exhibited in those pages. Whether the quality is a pecular stylistic or symbolic brilliance, an original kind of wit, a unique sublimity, irony, ambiguity, illusion of reality, profundity, or convincing character portrayal, there is an implied promise of more to come.

Our interest in these qualities may be static; we do not hope for or find a change in the quality but simply move forward looking for more of the same. Some good works rely heavily on this kind of interest (Montaigne's *Essays,* Burton's *Anatomy of Melancholy,* collections of table talk and facetiae, modern novels of stylistic experimentation like Gertrude Stein's *Melanctha*). Many of the realistic and naturalistic novels which were once popular and which now seem tedious relied somewhat too heavily on the sustained appeal of what was often call truth. Reading for the first time a novel dealing in the new vivid way with any new subject matter—whether the social reality about prostitution, slums, or the wheat market or the psychological reality about Irish Jews or American psychopaths—many readers were so fascinated by the new sense of reality, quite aside from the appeal of the facts as information, that little else was needed to carry them through to the end. But once this quality had become common, its appeal faded. Now that most commercial writers know how to portray violent physical reality, for example, with a vividness that would at one time have established an international reputation, only those novels which provide something more than physical reality survive.

The same danger threatens interest in any technique, even when the inherently more interesting procedure is adopted of providing some progressive change in the quality. Following James's[11] masterful explorations of what "composition" could do for the novel, it was easy to believe that the reader's interest in technique was an adequate substitute for other interests, rather than at best a useful adjunct and at worst a harmful distraction. And some novels were written which encouraged this interest. When James and his eleven colleagues wrote *The Whole Family: A Novel by Twelve Authors* (1908), each author writing one chapter, each chapter using a different central intelligence to throw a different light on the events, no reader could help being mainly interested in the point of view rather than in what the point of view revealed: "I wonder what James will make of *his* chapter?" But even with this much "suspense" introduced, interest in technique alone is likely to prove trivial.

Practical interests.—If we look closely at our reactions to most great novels, we discover that we feel a strong concern for the characters as people; we care about their good and bad fortune. In most works of any significance, we are made to admire or detest, to love or hate, or simply to approve or disapprove of at least one central character, and our interest in reading from page to page, like our judgment upon the book after reconsideration, is inseparable from this emotional involvement. We care, and care deeply, about Raskolnikov and Emma, about Father Goriot and Dorothea Brooke.[12] Whatever happens to them, we wish them well. It is of course true that our desires concerning the fate of such imagined people differ markedly from our desires in real life. We will accept destruction of the man we love, in a literary work, if destruction is required to satisfy our other interests; we will take pleasure in combinations of hope and fear which in real life would be intolerable. But hope and fear are there, and the destruction or salvation is felt in a manner closely analogous to the feelings by such events in real life.

Any characteristic, mental, physical, or moral, which in real life will make me love or hate other men will work the same effect in fiction. But there is a large difference. Since we are not in a position to profit from or be harmed by a fictional character, our judgment is disinterested, even in a sense irresponsible. We can easily find our interests magnetized by characters who would be unbearable as acquaintances. But the fact remains that what I am calling practical interests, and particularly moral qualities as inferred from characteristic choices or as stated directly by the author, have always been an important basis for literary form. Our interest in the fate of Oedipus and Lear, of David Copperfield and Richard Feverel, of Stephen Dedalus and Quentin Compson,[13] springs in part from our conviction that they are people who matter, people whose fate concerns us not simply because of its meaning or quality, but because we care about them as human beings.

Such concerns are not simply a necessary but impure base, as Ortega[14] would have it, to "make contemplation possible" but "with no aesthetic value or only a reflected or secondary one." In many first-rate works they are the very core of our experience. We may refuse assent when an author tries to manipulate us too obviously or cheaply with a casual bestowal of goodness or intellectual brilliance or beauty or charm. We all have use for epithets like "melodramatic" to apply against abuses of this kind. But this does not mean that human interest in itself is cheap. It is true that our involvement in the fate of Raskolnikov is not different in kind from the involvement sought by the most sentimental of novels. But in the great work we surrender our emotions for reasons that leave us with no regrets, no inclination to retract, after the immediate spell is past. They are, in fact, reasons which we should be ashamed *not* to respond to.

The best of these has always been the spectacle of a good man facing moral choices that are important. Our current neglect of moral terms like "good man" and "bad man" is really unfortunate if it leads us to overlook the role that moral judgment plays in most of our worthwhile reading. There is a story of the psychoanalyst who listened patiently and without judgment to the criminal self-revelations of his patient—until suddenly, as the patient was leaving, the analyst was filled with surprised revulsion. Try as we will to avoid terms like "moral" and "good"—and despite the mounting chorus against relativism, many still do try—we cannot avoid judging the characters we know as morally admirable or contemptible, any more than we can avoid judgments on their intellectual ability. We may tell ourselves that we do not condemn stupidity and viciousness, but we believe that men ought not to be stupid and vicious nonetheless. We may explain the villain's behavior by relating him to his environment, but even to explain away is to admit that something requires excuse.

Actually, there has been less of a retreat from moral judgment than appears on the surface, because of the shift, in modern fiction, to new terms for goodness and wickedness. Modern literature is in fact full of conventionally "virtuous" villains, fatally flawed by their blind adherence to outmoded norms, or by their intolerance of true but unconventional goodness (the missionaries in Maugham's "Rain," the "quiet American" in Greene's novel).[15] Perhaps the prototype is Huck Finn's Miss Watson, who is determined to "live so as to go to the good place." It is easy for the author to make us agree with Huck, who "couldn't see no advantage in going where she was going, so I made up my mind I wouldn't try for it." But few have ever made the mistake of thinking that Huck has repudiated virtue in repudiating Miss Watson's idea of virtue.

Much of what looks like purely aesthetic or intellectual quality in a character may in fact have a moral dimension that is highly effective, though never openly acknowledged between author and reader. When compared with Dickens, for example, James Joyce may seem explicitly amoral. Joyce's overt interests are entirely in matters of truth and beauty. Conventional moral judgments never occur in his books except in mockery. And yet the full force of *A Portrait of the Artist* depends on the essentially moral quality of Stephen's discovery of his artistic vocation and of his integrity in following where it leads. His repudiations of conventional morality—his refusal to enter the priesthood, his rejection of communion, his decision to become an exile—are in fact read as signs of aesthetic integrity—that is, of superior morality. Joyce would probably never call him a "good" boy, though later an older and mellower Joyce was willing to describe Bloom as "a good man," a "complete man."[16] For us Stephen is, in part, a good boy. His pursuit of his own vision is uncompromising; he is headed for Joyce's heaven. We may pretend that we read Joyce objectively and disinterestedly, without the sentimental involvements required of us in Victorian fiction. But most of us would never get beyond page one if the novel were only a portrait of an aesthetic sensibility receiving its Joycean epiphanies.

Whatever Joyce's intentions, for example, with such episodes as the cruel pandybatting of the innocent Stephen, Joyce clearly profits from our irresistible sympathy for the innocent victim. Once such sympathy is established, each succeeding episode is felt deeply, not simply contemplated. The Victorian hero often enough won our sympathies because his heart was in the right place. Many modern heroes win our allegiance because their aesthetic sensibilities will not be denied, or because they live life to the hilt, or simply because they are victims of their surroundings. This is indeed a shift of emphasis, but we should not let popular talk about the "affective fallacy" deceive us: the very structure of fiction and, hence, of our aesthetic apprehension of it is often built of such practical, and in themselves seemingly "non-aesthetic," materials.

COMBINATIONS AND CONFLICTS OF INTERESTS

Since men do have strong intellectual, qualitative, and practical interests, there is no reason why great novels cannot be written relying primarily on any one kind. But it is clear that no great work is based on only one interest. Whenever a work tends toward an exclusive reliance on intellectual interests, on the contemplation of qualities, or on practical desires we all look for adjectives to whip the offender with; a mere "novel of ideas," a mere "desiccated form," a mere "tear-jerker" will offend all but the small handful of critics and authors who are momentarily absorbed in pushing one interest to the limit. But it is a rare critic who can distinguish the novels that are really marred by narrowness from those "narrow" novels which, like Jane Austen's, develop a wide range of interests within a narrow social setting.

In any case, for good or ill, we all seem convinced that a novel or play which does justice to our interest in truth, in beauty, and in goodness is superior to even the most successful "novel of ideas," "well-made play," or "sentimental novel"—to name only a selection from the partialities that conventional labels describe. Our emotional concern in Shakespeare is firmly based on intellectual, qualitative, and moral interests. It is a serious mistake to talk as if this richness were simply a matter of stuffing in something for the pit and something else for the gallery. To separate the plot, the manifold qualitative pleasures (including the patterns of imagery and the rich bawdry), or the profound intellectual import and to erect one of the fragments as superior to the others is precisely what a direct experience of the plays teaches us not to do. We experience a miraculous unity of what might have remained dissociated but for Shakespeare's ability to involve our minds, hearts, and sensibilities simultaneously.

Notes

[1] ratiocinative: given solely to a reasoned train of thought.

[2] Emma is the central, often self-centered character in Jane Austen's novel *Emma* (1816).

³ Tess, caught in a web of fate, is Thomas Hardy's heroine in *Tess of the D'Urbervilles* (1891).

⁴ Huck Finn, Mark Twain's hero in *The Adventures of Huckleberry Finn* (1884), struggles between civilization's demands and freedom on the river.

⁵ Achilles and Priam contest against each other in Homer's epic *The Iliad*.

⁶ A sonnet contains fourteen lines of iambic pentameter verse in a set rhyme scheme.

⁷ An elegy is a serious poem written in alternating pentameter and hexameter lines, usually about death or lost love.

⁸ Laurence Sterne wrote the then unconventional English novel *Tristram Shandy* between 1760 and 1767. Sterne moved the narrative focus from characters' actions to their mind and motivations.

⁹ John Lyly employed highly affected and ornate language in *Euphues* (1579).

¹⁰ James Joyce created the punning language blend of "Finneganswakism" in his novel *Finnegan's Wake* (1939).

¹¹ Henry James sought to create in his fiction an intense illusion of "experiencing life as seen by a fine mind subject to realistic human limitations." (Booth, *The Rhetoric of Fiction*, p. 42.)

¹² These characters appear in the following novels: Raskolnikov in Fëdor Dostoevski's *Crime and Punishment* (Russian, 1866); Emma in Jane Austen's *Emma* (English, 1816); Father Goriot in Honoré de Balzac's *Père Goriot* (French, 1835); and Dorothea Brooke in George Eliot's *Middlemarch* (English, 1871–1872).

¹³ These characters appear in the following works: Oedipus in *Oedipus Rex* by Sophocles; Lear in Shakespeare's *King Lear;* David Copperfield in Charles Dickens's *David Copperfield* (English, 1849); Richard Feverel in George Meredith's *The Ordeal of Richard Feverel* (English, 1871–1872); Stephen Dedalus in *A Portrait of the Artist* by James Joyce (Irish, 1916); Quentin Compson in William Faulkner's *Absalom, Absalom!* (American, 1936) and his *The Sound and the Fury* (1929).

¹⁴ In "The Dehumanization of Art and Other Writings on Art and Culture," the Spanish critic Juan Ortega y Gassett found the "preoccupation with the human content" of a work incompatible with aesthetic enjoyment.

¹⁵ The English novelist Somerset Maugham wrote the short story "Rain" in 1919. The quiet American appears in Graham Greene's novel *The Quiet American* (English, 1955).

¹⁶ Quoted from Frank Budgen in R. Ellman, *James Joyce* (New York, 1959), p. 449. [Booth]

FOCUS: READING REVIEW

1. What are the categories of values which interest a reader of fiction?
2. Explain the reader's interest in intellectual completion. What are the ways in which authors can engage this?
3. What are a reader's practical interests in fiction?

FOCUS: AUTHOR'S STRATEGIES

1. What is the author's purpose? What passages indicate this?
2. What audience does Booth's constant reference to novels and their characters suggest?

3. In what ways does this essay sharpen the audience's understanding of fiction? How does Booth organize the essay to accomplish this?

FOCUS: DISCUSSION AND WRITING

1. Consider a fictional work you particularly admire and explain how the author engages your interests.
2. Booth says that a great literary work engages the reader's intellectual, qualitative, and moral interests simultaneously. Using this as a criteria for greatness, argue for or against the greatness of a novel or short story you have recently read.

The Conditions of Illusion
E. H. Gombrich

E. H. Gombrich (b. 1890), a British art historian and aesthetician born and educated in Vienna, served as a trustee of the British Museum, the director of the Warburg Institute at the University of London, and professor of art at University College, London. Gombrich has significantly influenced recent understanding of how art has developed and how we perceive the visual arts. His influential book Art and Illusion, *from which this selection is taken, presents his A. W. Mellon Lectures in the Fine Arts given at the National Gallery of Art in Washington, D.C. in 1956. In this study he shows that the artist's ability to reproduce what he sees is limited by the techniques and conventions he knows. Through continuous trial and error, employing technological developments, and learning new formulae and skills, artists have refined and reformed their representation of reality. In "The Conditions of Illusion" Gombrich demonstrates that art is a "give and take" experience between artist and viewer in which both rely on conventions. He thus finds some subjectivity in the creative and viewing experiences. By recognizing this visual subjectivity and understanding the conventions of illusion and representation, the viewer's understanding of art will move from emotional over-interpretation of the image to appreciation of an artwork in its historic, social, and artistic context.*

All representation relies to some extent on what we have called "guided projection." Psychologists class the problem of picture reading with what they call "the perception of symbolic material." The basic facts were described by William James when he said, "When we listen to a person speaking or read a page of print, much of what we think we see or hear is supplied from our memory." I had an opportunity to study this aspect of perception in a practical context during the war when I was employed for six years at a listening post, where we kept constant watch on radio transmissions from friend and foe. My experience enabled me to appreciate that a message selects from an "ensemble of possible states." The possibility exists in the language and the contexts in which it is used. At the slightest auditory hint, the receptor jumps ahead and anticipates the whole message. To the student of the visual image, these experiences are of relevance because they show how the context of actions creates conditions of illusion.

The mind, having received of sense a small beginning of remembrance, runneth on infinitely, remembring all what is to be remembred. Our senses therefore, which stand as it were at the entry of the mind, having received the beginning of anything, and having proffered it to the mind; the mind likewise receiveth this beginning, and goeth over all what followeth: the lower part of a long and slender pike being but slightly shaken, the motion runneth thorough the whole length of the pike, even to the speares-head ... so does our mind need but a small beginning to the remembrance of the whole matter.

AFTER MAXIMUS TYRIUS AS IN FRANCISCUS JUNIUS,
The Painting of the Ancients

I

The examples in the last chapter have confirmed the ideas which Philostratus attributes to his hero Apollonius of Tyana, the idea that "those who look at works of painting and drawing must have the imitative faculty" and that "no one could understand the painted horse or bull unless he knew what such creatures are like." All representation relies to some extent on what we have called "guided projection." When we say that the blots and brushstrokes of the impressionist landscapes "suddenly come to life," we mean we have been led to project a landscape into these dabs of pigment.

Psychologists class the problem of picture reading with what they call "the perception of symbolic material." It is a problem which has engaged the attention of all who investigate effective communication, the reading of texts or displays or the hearing of signals. The basic facts were described by William James with his usual lucidity in his *Talks to Teachers* before the turn of the century:

"When we listen to a person speaking or read a page of print, much of what we think we see or hear is supplied from our memory. We overlook misprints, imagining the right letters, though we see the wrong ones; and how little we actually hear, when we listen to speech, we realize when we go to a foreign theatre; for there what troubles us is not so much that we cannot understand what the actors say as that we cannot hear their words. The fact is that we hear quite as little under similar conditions at home, only our mind, being fuller of English verbal associations, supplies the requisite material for comprehension upon a much slighter auditory hint."

It so happens I had an opportunity to study this aspect of perception in a severely practical context during the war. I was employed for six years by the

British Broadcasting Corporation in their "Monitoring Service," or listening post, where we kept constant watch on radio transmissions from friend and foe. It was in this context that the importance of guided projection in our understanding of symbolic material was brought home to me. Some of the transmissions which interested us most were often barely audible, and it became quite an art, or even a sport, to interpret the few whiffs of speech sound that were all we really had on the wax cylinders on which these broadcasts had been recorded. It was then we learned to what an extent our knowledge and expectations influence our hearing. You had to know what might be said in order to hear what was said. More exactly, you selected from your knowledge of possibilities certain word combinations and tried projecting them into the noises heard. The problem then was a twofold one—to think of possibilities and to retain one's critical faculty. Anyone whose imagination ran away with him, who could hear any words—as Leonardo could in the sound of bells—could not play that game. You had to keep your projection flexible, to remain willing to try out fresh alternatives, and to admit the possibility of defeat. For this was the most striking experience of all: once your expectation was firmly set and your conviction settled, you ceased to be aware of your own activity, the noises appeared to fall into place and to be transformed into the expected words. So strong was this effect of suggestion that we made it a practice never to tell a colleague our own interpretation if we wanted him to test it. Expectation created illusion.

` While I was struggling with these practical tasks, I did not know that these problems of transmission and reception of communication—terms such as "message" and "noise"—were destined to become a most important, not to say fashionable, field of study under the name of "Information Theory." The technical and mathematical aspects of this science will always remain a closed book to me, but my experience enabled me to appreciate at least one of its basic concepts, the function of the message to select from an "ensemble of possible states." The knowledge of possibilities in the monitor is the knowledge of the language and the contexts in which it is used. If there is only one possibility, his receptor apparatus is likely to jump ahead and anticipate the result at what William James called the slightest "auditory hint." But it also follows from this theory that where there is only one such possibility the hint is in itself redundant and there is, in fact, no special message. The word we must expect in a given context will not add to our "information." We receive no message in the strict sense of the word when a friend enters a room and says "good morning." The word has no function to select from an ensemble of possible states, though situations are conceivable in which it would have.

The most interesting consequence of this way of looking at communication is the general conclusion that the greater the probability of a symbol's occurrence in any given situation, the smaller will be its information content. Where we can anticipate we need not listen. It is in this context that projection will do for perception.

The difficulty in distinguishing between the two in seeing as well as in hearing was well brought out in a fiendish experiment. The subjects were seated in the dark in front of a screen and were told their sensitivity to light was to be tested. At the request of the experimenter, the assistant projected a very faint light onto the screen and slowly increased its intensity, each person being asked to record exactly when he perceived it. But once in a while when the experimenter made the request no light was, in fact, shown. It was found that the subjects still saw it appearing. Their firm expectation of the sequence of events had actually led to a hallucination.

I suspect there is no class of people better able to bring about such phantom perceptions than conjurers. They set up a train of expectations, a semblance of familiar situations, which makes our imagination run ahead and complete it obligingly without knowing where we have been tricked. There are simple parlor tricks which show the problem in its most elementary form. Anyone who can handle a needle convincingly can make us see a thread which is not there. The conjuring trick is turned into art when a magician such as Charlie Chaplin performs a dance with a pair of forks and a couple of rolls that turn into nimble legs in front of our eyes.

II

To the student of the visual image, these experiences are of relevance because they show how the context of action creates conditions of illusion. When the hobbyhorse leans in the corner, it is just a stick; as soon as it is ridden, it becomes the focus of the child's imagination and turns into a horse. The images of art, we remember, also once stood in context of action. It must have been an uncanny sight to see the painting of a bison belabored with spears in the darkness of the cave—if our ideas about these origins are right. What we do know is that the fetishes and cult images of early cultures stood in such contexts of action; they were bathed, anointed, clothed, and carried in procession. What wonder that illusion settled on them and that the faithful saw them smiling, frowning, or nodding behind the clouds of incense.

FOCUS: **READING REVIEW**

1. What does the quotation from William James suggest about the ways in which different people perceive art?
2. How does expectation affect perception? Explain how Gombrich's examples illustrate this.
3. How does incompleteness in visual representation affect the viewer?

FOCUS: **AUTHOR'S STRATEGIES**

1. The author explains a difficult concept in communication theory by relating a personal experience. Identify his discussion of theory, and explain how he relates the personal experience to this discussion.
2. How do the assumptions and definitions indicate the audience for which Gombrich is writing?

FOCUS: **DISCUSSION AND WRITING**

1. What does Gombrich's study suggest about the percipient's role as he or she views pictorial art?
2. Look carefully at a painting that represents an object. Explain how the painter's object differs from a real object. What in your own experience enabled you to recognize the real object in the painted object?

Chapter 11
Studies in
Art and
Literature

When we encounter a work of art, each of us brings to the experience our own preferences and prejudices. For some of us words on a page evoke a rich imaginative experience. Others of us respond to music's rhythms, melodies, and harmonies. Still others thrill at rich visual composition. We respond, to some degree, subjectively. Criticism should enhance rather than deny this experience if one accepts Frye's discussion in "Criticism, Visible and Invisible." The critic directs the art respondent to nuances which heighten the understanding of imaginative responses. This chapter's selections seek to draw the reader closer to poetry, music, architecture, and the dramatic and visual arts. The writers employ various critical approaches and focus the reader's attention on different aspects of the artistic experience. The essays by Bradley and Jarrell immerse the reader in the literature; they examine Shakespeare's *Macbeth* and Robert Frost's "Home Burial" respectively by retelling the literary events, explaining words and passages, and offering interpretation. Both critics leave the reader with a sense that he or she has encountered a discussion about real, living people. Writing in Eliot's vein, Copland ("The Pleasures of Music") and Gombrich ("Harmony Attained") emphasize the importance the political and social milieu assumes for understanding art. This critical approach contrasts directly with Pater's "Leonardo da Vinci." Pater draws attention to the painter's life and personality and responds subjectively to the art. The remaining essays in the chapter on architecture and film examine the relationship between art and society. In their architectural studies, "Escape to Islip" and "The Getty," Wolfe and Didion respectively consider people's responses to buildings and building styles as a measure of the society as well as the architecture. In "Underground Man," Kael looks at film as artistic creation in her consideration of writing, directing, and performance, but through her consideration of violence, she also looks at modern society's image depicted in film.

Robert Frost's "Home Burial"
Randall Jarrell

Randall Jarrell (1914–1965), in his thirty-year career as a poet, critic, and literature teacher, frequently insisted that truth lay in ordinary people's experiences. This conviction informs his essay on Robert Frost's "Home Burial." Here Jarrell's understanding of grief's effect on a marriage and his insights about emotion combine with a close reading of the poem's language, rhythms, and images to illuminate the main experience of Frost's poem. Jarrell began his college career as a psychology major, but his encounter with the well-known writer and critic John Crowe Ransom at Vanderbilt University drew him to major in literature. During his academic career Jarrell taught at the University of Texas, Austin; Sarah Lawrence College; and the University of North Carolina. His writings include three books of criticism, including the posthumous The Third Book of Criticism *(1970), which contains this selection;* Pictures from an Institution, *a 1954 novel satirizing academic life; three children's books—*The Gingerbread Rabbit *(1963),* The Bat Poet *(1964),* The Animal Family *(1965); and several volumes of poetry.*

"Home Burial," a poem about a neurotic woman in an extreme situation, is a fairly long but extraordinarily concentrated poem. The poem begins with a vertical ballet of indecision toward and away from a fearful but mesmerically attractive object, something hard to decide to leave and easy to decide to return to. When the man asks: "What is it you see / From up there always—for I want to know," the word "always" tells us that all this has gone on many times before, and that he has seen it—without speaking of it—a number of times before. In response to the woman's rhetorical question, "What is it—what?" the man goes on explaining, to himself, and to mankind, and to her too, in slow rumination about it and about it. In the line, "The little graveyard where my people are!" we feel not only the triumph of the slow person at last comprehending, but also the tender, easy accustomedness of habit—for him the graves are not the healed scars of old agonies, but are something as comfortable as the photographs in the family album.

Next, to show her how well he understands, the man shows her how ill he understands. He says about his family's graves: "We haven't to mind *those*." When he says this, it is as if he had touched, with a crude desecrating hand, the sacred, forbidden secret upon which her existence depends. When he asks if a man can't speak of his dead child, the woman responds that he can't. Following this, the man begins a long and slow appeal which ends with her moving the door latch. His next appeal to her to let him into her grief is an attempt to get her to replace her exclusive relationship with her child with the restored relationship of a man and wife grieving together over their dead child. The man condemns her for exceeding the reasonable social norm of guilt.

The man has talked at length during the first two-thirds of the poem; she has responded in three- or four-word phrases or motions without words. For the rest of the poem she talks at length, as everything that has been shut up inside her pours out. His open attack has elicited her anger. The woman had watched from a window as the man dug his own child's grave and for his actions she condemns him. The husband's digging seemed to the wife a kind of brutally unfeeling, secular profanation of her holy grief. Unconsciously the wife has far more compelling reasons to be appalled at this job. The man's actions have a sexual force and a sexual power in contrast to the woman's passive suffering. When the woman sees her husband digging, she can blame him for the child's death. She is able to substitute for passive suffering and guilt an active loathing and condemnation. Further, in the disaster of her child's death, her husband's crime, her one consolation is that she is inconsolable; she has grieved for months as her husband was not able to grieve even for hours. If he could hear and respond to what she actually has said, there would be some hope for them. But he doesn't; instead he dumps her into the pigeonhole of the crying woman and then tries to manage her as one manages a child. Then at the moment when the depths have been opened, someone happens to come down the road, and this someone who can affect public opinion becomes more important than anything she has said. Her final words are full of a longing, despairing, regretful realization of a kind of final impossibility: "How can I make you—" His last line, "I will," refers to the brute force he will use to bring her back if she leaves.

"Home Burial" and "The Witch of Coös" seem to me the best of all Frost's dramatic poems—though "A Servant to Servants" is nearly as good. All three are poems about women in extreme situations; neurotic or (in "A Servant to Servants") psychotic women. The circumstances of the first half of his life made Frost feel for such women a sympathy or empathy that amounted almost to identification. He said that, "creature of literature that I am," he had learned to "make a virtue of my suffering / From nearly everything that goes on round me," and that "Kit Marlowe taught me how to say my prayers: / 'Why, this is Hell, nor am I out of it.' " It is with such women that he says this—this and more than this: the Pauper Witch of Grafton's

Up where the trees grow short, the mosses tall,
I made him gather me wet snow berries
On slippery rocks beside a waterfall.
I made him do it for me in the dark.
And he liked everything I made him do . . .

shows us, as few passages can, that for a while the world was heaven too.

"Home Burial" is a fairly long but extraordinarily concentrated poem; after you have known it long enough you feel almost as the Evangelist did, that if all the things that could be said about it were written down, "I suppose that even the world itself could not contain the books that should be written." I have written down a few of these things; but, first of all, here is "Home Burial" itself:

He saw her from the bottom of the stairs
Before she saw him. She was starting down,
Looking back over her shoulder at some fear.
She took a doubtful step and, then undid it
To raise herself and look again. He spoke
Advancing toward her: "What is it you see
From up there always—for I want to know."
She turned and sank upon her skirts at that,
And her face changed from terrified to dull.
He said to gain time: "What is it you see,"
Mounting until she cowered under him.
"I will find out now—you must tell me, dear."
She, in her place, refused him any help
With the least stiffening of her neck and silence.
She let him look, sure that he wouldn't see,
Blind creature; and awhile he didn't see.
But at last he murmured, "Oh," and again, "Oh."
"What is it—what?" she said.

                    "Just that I see."

"You don't," she challenged. "Tell me what it is."
"The wonder is I didn't see at once.
I never noticed it from here before.
I must be wonted to it—that's the reason.
The little graveyard where my people are!
So small the window frames the whole of it.
Not so much larger than a bedroom, is it?
There are three stones of slate and one of marble,
Broad-shouldered little slabs there in the sunlight
On the sidehill. We haven't to mind *those*.
But I understand: it is not the stones,
But the child's mound—"

                    "Don't, don't, don't, don't," she cried.

She withdrew shrinking from beneath his arm
That rested on the banister, and slid downstairs;
And turned on him with such a daunting look,
He said twice over before he knew himself:
"Can't a man speak of his own child he's lost?"

"Not you! Oh, where's my hat? Oh, I don't need it!
I must get out of here. I must get air.
I don't know rightly whether any man can."

"Amy! Don't go to someone else this time.
Listen to me. I won't come down the stairs."
He sat and fixed his chin between his fists.
"There's something I should like to ask you, dear."

"You don't know how to ask it."

                              "Help me, then."

Her fingers moved the latch for all reply.

"My words are nearly always an offence.
I don't know how to speak of anything
So as to please you. But I might be taught,
I should suppose. I can't say I see how.
A man must partly give up being a man
With women-folk. We could have some arrangement
By which I'd bind myself to keep hands off
Anything special you're a-mind to name.
Though I don't like such things 'twixt those that love.
Two that don't love can't live together without them.
But two that do can't live together with them."
She moved the latch a little. "Don't—don't go.
Don't carry it to someone else this time.
Tell me about it if it's something human.
Let me into your grief. I'm not so much
Unlike other folks as your standing there
Apart would make me out. Give me my chance.
I do think, though, you overdo it a little.
What was it brought you up to think it the thing
To take your mother-loss of a first child
So inconsolably—in the face of love.
You'd think his memory might be satisfied—"

"There you go sneering now!"

                             "I'm not, I'm not!

You make me angry. I'll come down to you.
God, what a woman! And it's come to this,
A man can't speak of his own child that's dead."

"You can't because you don't know how to speak.
If you had any feelings, you that dug
With your own hand—how could you?—his little grave;
I saw you from that very window there,
Making the gravel leap and leap in air,
Leap up, like that, like that, and land so lightly
And roll back down the mound beside the hole.
I thought, Who is that man? I didn't know you.
And I crept down the stairs and up the stairs

To look again, and still your spade kept lifting.
Then you came in. I heard your rumbling voice
Out in the kitchen, and I don't know why,
But I went near to see with my own eyes.
You could sit there with the stains on your shoes
Of the fresh earth from your own baby's grave
And talk about your everyday concerns.
You had stood the spade up against the wall
Outside there in the entry, for I saw it."

"I shall laugh the worst laugh I ever laughed.
I'm cursed. God, if I don't believe I'm cursed."

"I can repeat the very words you were saying.
'Three foggy mornings and one rainy day
Will rot the best birch fence a man can build.'
Think of it, talk like that at such a time!
What had how long it takes a birch to rot
To do with what was in the darkened parlor.
You *couldn't* care! The nearest friends can go
With anyone to death, comes so far short
They might as well not try to go at all.
No, from the time when one is sick to death,
One is alone, and he dies more alone.
Friends make pretense of following to the grave,
But before one is in it, their minds are turned
And making the best of their way back to life
And living people, and things they understand.
But the world's evil. I won't have grief so
If I can change it. Oh, I won't, I won't!"

"There, you have said it all and you feel better.
You won't go now. You're crying. Close the door.
The heart's gone out of it: why keep it up.
Amy! There's someone coming down the road!"
"*You*—oh, you think the talk is all. I must go—
Somewhere out of this house. How can I make you—"

"If—you—do!" She was opening the door wider.
"Where do you mean to go? First tell me that.
I'll follow and bring you back by force. I *will!*—"

The poem's first sentence, "He saw her from the bottom of the stairs / Before she saw him," implies what the poem very soon states: that, knowing herself seen, she would have acted differently—she has two sorts of behavior, behavior for him to observe and spontaneous immediate behavior. "She was starting down, / Looking back over her shoulder at some fear" says that it is *some fear,* and not a specific feared object, that she is looking back at; and, normally, we do not look back over our shoulder at what we leave, unless we feel for it something more than fear. "She took a doubtful step" emphasizes the queer attraction or fascination that the fear has for her; her departing step is not sure it should depart. "She took a doubtful step and then *undid* it": the surprising use of *undid* gives her withdrawal of the tentative step a surprising reality. The poem goes on: "To raise herself and look again." It is a little vertical ballet of indecision toward and away from a fearful but mesmerically attractive object, something hard to decide to leave and easy to decide to return to. "He spoke / Advancing toward her": having the old line end with "spoke," the new line begin with "advancing," makes the very structure of the lines express the way in which he looms up, gets bigger. (Five lines later Frost repeats the effect even more forcibly with: "He said to gain time: 'What is it you see,' / Mounting until she cowered under him.") Now when the man asks: "What is it you see / From up there always—for I want to know," the word "always" tells us that all this has gone on many times before, and that he has seen it—without speaking of it—a number of times before. The phrase "for I want to know" is a characteristic example of the heavy, willed demands that the man makes, and an even more characteristic example of the tautological, rhetorical announcements of his actions that he so often makes, as if he felt that the announcement somehow justified or excused the action.

The poem goes on: "She turned and sank upon her skirts at that. ... " The stairs permit her to subside into a modest, compact, feminine bundle; there is a kind of smooth deftness about the phrase, as if it were some feminine saying: "When in straits, sink upon your skirts." The next line, "And her face changed from terrified to dull," is an economically elegant way of showing how the terror of surprise (perhaps with another fear underneath it) changes into the dull lack of response that is her regular mask for him. The poem continues: "He said to gain time"—to gain time in which to think of the next thing to say, to gain time in which to get close to her and gain the advantage of his physical nearness, his physical bulk. His next "What is it you see" is the first of his many repetitions; if one knew only this man one would say, "Man is the animal that repeats." In the poem's next phrase, "Mounting until she cowered under him," the identity of the vowels in "mounting" and "cowered" physically connects the two, makes his mounting the plain immediate cause of her cowering. "I will find out now" is another of his rhetorical announcements of what he is going to do: "this time you're going to tell me, I'm going to make you." But this heavy-willed compulsion changes into sheer appeal, into reasonable beseeching, in his next phrase: "You must tell me, dear." The "dear" is affectionate intimacy, the "must" is the "must" of rational necessity; yet the underlying form of the sentence is that of compulsion. The poem goes on: "She, in her place, refused him any help. ..." The separated phrase "in her place" describes and embodies, with economical brilliance, both her physical and spiritual lack of outgoingness, forthcomingness; she brims over none of her contours, remains sitting upon her skirts upon her stairstep, in feminine exclusion. "Refused him any help / With the least stiffening of her neck and silence": she doesn't say Yes, doesn't say No, doesn't say; her refusal of any answer is worse than almost any answer. "The least stiffening of her neck," in its concise reserve, its slight precision, is more nearly conclusive than any larger gesture of rejection. He, in extremities, usually repeats some proverbial or rhetorical generalization; at such moments she usually responds either with a particular, specific sentence or else with something more particular than any sentence: with some motion or gesture.

The next line, "She let him look, sure that he wouldn't see," reminds one of some mother bird so certain that her nest is hidden that she doesn't even flutter off, but sits there on it, risking what is no risk, in complacent superiority. "Sure that he wouldn't see, / Blind creature": the last phrase is quoted from her mind, is her contemptuous summing up. "And awhile he didn't see"; but at last when he sees, he doesn't tell her what it is, doesn't silently understand, but with heavy slow comprehension murmurs, "Oh," and then repeats, "Oh." It is another announcement of what he is doing, a kind of dramatic rendition of his understanding. (Sometimes when we are waiting for someone, and have made some sound or motion we are afraid will seem ridiculous to the observer we didn't know was there, we rather ostentatiously look at our watch, move our face and lips into a "What on earth could have happened to make him so late?" as a way of justifying our earlier action. The principle behind our action is the principle behind many of this man's actions.) With the undignified alacrity of someone hurrying to reestablish a superiority that has been questioned, the woman cries out like a child: "What is it—what?" Her sentence is, so to speak, a rhetorical question rather than a real one, since it takes it for granted that a correct answer can't be made. His reply, "Just that I see," shows that his unaccustomed insight has given him an unaccustomed composure; she has had the advantage, for so long, of being the only one who knows, that he for a moment prolongs the advantage of being the only one who knows that he knows. The immediate following " 'You don't,' she challenged. 'Tell me what it is' " is the instant, childishly assertive exclamation of someone whose human position depends entirely upon her knowing what some inferior being can never know; she cannot let another second go by without hearing the incorrect answer that will confirm her in her rightness and superiority.

The man goes on explaining, to himself, and to mankind, and to her too, in slow rumination about it and about it. In his "The wonder is I didn't see at once. / I never noticed it from here before. / I must be wonted to it—that's the reason," one notices how "wonder" and "once" prepare for "wonted," that provincial-, archaic-sounding word that sums up—as "used" never could—his reliance on a habit or accustomedness which at last sees nothing but itself, and hardly sees that; and when it does something through itself, beyond itself, slowly marvels. In the next line, "The little graveyard where my people are!" we feel not only the triumph of the slow person at last comprehending, but also the tender, easy accustomedness of habit, of long use, of a kind of cozy social continuance—for him the graves are not the healed scars of old agonies, but are something as comfortable and accustomed as the photographs in the family album. "So small the window frames the whole of it," like the later "Broad-shouldered little slabs there in the sunlight / On the sidehill," not only has this easy comfortable acceptance, but also has the regular feel of a certain sort of Frost nature description: this is almost the only place in the poem where for a moment we feel that it is Frost talking first and the man talking second. But the man's "Not so much larger than a bedroom, is it?"—an observation that appeals to her for agreement—carries this comfortable acceptance to a point at which it becomes intolerable: the only link between the bedroom and the graveyard is the child conceived in their bedroom and buried in that graveyard. The sentence comfortably establishes a connection which she cannot bear to admit the existence of—she tries to keep the two things permanently separated in her mind. (What he says amounts to his saying about their bedroom: "Not so much smaller than the graveyard, is it?") "There are three stones of slate and one of marble, / Broad-shouldered little slabs there in the sunlight / On the sidehill" has a heavy tenderness and accustomedness about it, almost as if he were running his hand over the grain of the stone. The "little" graveyard and "little" slabs are examples of our regular way of making something acceptable or dear by means of a diminutive.

Next, to show her how well he understands, the man shows her how ill he understands. He says about his family's graves: "We haven't to mind *those*"; that is, we don't have to worry about, grieve over, my people: it is not your obligation to grieve for them at all, nor mine to give them more than their proper share of grief, the amount I long ago measured out and used up. But with the feeling, akin to a sad, modest, relieved, surprised pride, with which he regularly responds to his own understanding, he tells her that he does understand: what matters is not the old stones but the new mound, the displaced earth piled up above the grave which he had dug and in which their child is buried.

When he says this, it is as if he had touched, with a crude desecrating hand, the sacred, forbidden secret upon which her existence depends. With shuddering hysterical revulsion she cries: "Don't, don't, don't, don't." (If the reader will compare the effect of Frost's four *don't*'s with the effect of three or five, he will see once more how exactly accurate, perfectly effective, almost everything in the poem is.) The poem continues: "She withdrew shrinking from beneath his arm / That rested on the banister, and slid downstairs"; the word "slid" says, with vivid indecorousness, that anything goes in extremities, that you can't be bothered, then, by mere appearance or propriety; "slid" has the ludicrous force of actual fact, is the way things are instead of the way we agree they are. In the line "And turned on him with such a daunting look," the phrase "turned on him" makes her resemble a cornered animal turning on its pursuer; and "with such a daunting look" is the way he phrases it to himself, is quoted from his mind as "blind creature" was quoted from hers. The beautifully provincial, old-fashioned, folk-sounding "daunting" reminds one of the similar, slightly earlier "wonted," and seems to make immediate, as no other word could, the look that cows him. The next line, "He said twice over before he knew himself," tells us that repetition, saying something twice over, is something he regresses to under stress; unless he can consciously prevent himself from repeating, he repeats. What he says twice over (this is the third time already that he has repeated something) is a rhetorical question, a querulous, plaintive appeal to public opinion: "Can't a man speak of his own child he's lost?" He does not say specifically, particularly, with confidence in himself: "I've the right to speak of our dead child"; instead he cites the acknowledged fact that any member of the class *man* has the acknowledged right to mention, just to mention, that member of the class of his belongings, *his own child*—and he has been unjustly deprived of this right. "His own child he's lost" is a way of saying: "You act as if he were just yours, but he's just as much just mine; that's an established fact." "Can't a man speak of his own child he's lost" has a magnificently dissonant, abject, aggrieved querulousness about it, in all its sounds and all its rhythms; "Can't a man" prepares us for the even more triumphantly ugly dissonance (or should I say consonance?) of the last two words in her "I don't know rightly whether any man can."

Any rhetorical question demands, expects, the hearer's automatic agreement; there is nothing it expects less than a particular, specific denial. The man's "Can't a man speak ..." means "Isn't any man allowed to speak ...," but her fatally specific answer, "Not you!" makes it mean, "A man cannot—is not able to—speak, if the man is you." Her "Oh, where's my hat?" is a speech accompanied by action, means: "I'm leaving. Where's the hat which social convention demands that a respectable woman put on, to go out into the world?" The immediately following "Oh, I don't need it!" means: in extremities, in cases when we come down to what really matters, what does social convention or respectability really matter? Her "I must get out of here. I must get air" says that you breathe understanding and suffocate without it, and that in this house, for her, there is none. Then, most extraordinarily, she gives a second specific answer to his rhetorical question, that had expected none: "I don't know rightly whether any man can." The line says: "Perhaps it is not the individual *you* that's to blame, but man in general; perhaps a woman is wrong to expect that any man can speak—really *speak*—of his dead child."

His "Amy! Don't go to someone else this time" of course tells us that another time she *has* gone to someone else; and it tells us the particular name of this most particular woman, something that she and the poem never tell us about the man. The man's "Listen to me. I won't come down the stairs" tells us that earlier he *has* come down the stairs, hasn't kept his distance. It (along with "shrinking," "cowered," and many later things in the poem) tells us that he has given her reason to be physically afraid of him; his "I won't come down the stairs" is a kind of euphemism for "I won't hurt you, won't even get near you."

The poem's next sentence, "He sat and fixed his chin between his fists"—period, end of line—with its four short *i*'s, its "fixed" and "fists," fixes him in baffled separateness; the sentence fits into the line as he fits into the isolated perplexity of his existence. Once more he makes a rhetorical announcement of what he is about to do, before he does it: "There's something I should like to ask you, dear." The sentence tiptoes in, gentle, almost abjectly mollifying, and ends with a reminding "dear"; it is an indirect rhetorical appeal that expects for an answer at least a grudging: "Well, go ahead and ask it, then." His sentence presupposes the hearer's agreement with what it implies: "Anyone is at least allowed to *ask,* even if afterwards you refuse him what he asks." The woman once more gives a direct, crushing *particular* answer: "You don't know how to ask it." "Anyone may be allowed to ask, but *you* are not because you are not able to ask"; we don't even need to refuse an animal the right to ask and be refused, since if we gave him the right he couldn't exercise it. The man's "Help me, then," has an absolute, almost abject helplessness, a controlled childlike simplicity, that we pity and sympathize with; yet we can't help remembering the other side of the coin, the heavy, brutal, equally simple and helpless anger of his later *I'll come down to you.*

The next line, "Her fingers moved the latch for all reply" (Like the earlier "She . . . refused him any help / With the least stiffening of her neck and silence"; like / "And turned on him with such a daunting look"; like the last "She moved the latch a little"; like the last "She was opening the door wider"), reminds us that the woman has a motion language more immediate, direct, and particular than words—a language she resorts to in extremities, just as he, in extremities, resorts to a language of repeated proverbial generalizations. "Home Burial" starts on the stairs but continues in the doorway, on the threshold between the old life inside and the new life outside.

The man now begins his long appeal with the slow, heavy, hopeless admission that "My words are nearly always an offence." This can mean, "Something is nearly always wrong with me and my words," but also can mean—does mean, underneath—that she is to be blamed for nearly always finding offensive things that certainly are not meant to offend. "I don't know how to speak of anything /

So as to please you" admits, sadly blames himself for, his baffled ignorance, but it also suggests that she is unreasonably, fantastically hard to please—if the phrase came a little later in his long speech he might pronounce it "so as to please *you*." (Whatever the speaker intends, there are no long peacemaking speeches in a quarrel; after a few sentences the speaker always has begun to blame the other again.) The man's aggrieved, blaming "But I might be taught, I should suppose" is followed by the helpless, very endearing admission: "I can't say I see how"; for the moment he removes the blame from her, and his honesty of concession makes us unwilling to blame him. He tries to summarize his dearly bought understanding in a generalization, almost a proverb: "A man must partly give up being a man / With women-folk." The sentence begins in the dignified regretful sunlight of the main floor, in "A man must partly give up being a man," and ends huddled in the basement below, in "With women-folk." He doesn't use the parallel, coordinate "with a woman," but the entirely different "with women-folk"; the sentence tries to be fair and objective, but it is as completely weighted a sentence as "A man must partly give up being a man with the kiddies," or "A man must partly give up being a man with Bandar-log." The sentence presupposes that the right norm is a man being a man with men, and that some of this rightness and normality always must be sacrificed with that special case, that inferior anomalous category, "women-folk."

He goes on: "We could have some arrangement [it has a hopeful, indefinite, slightly helter-skelter sound] / By which I'd bind myself to keep hands off"—the phrase "bind myself" and "keep hands off" have the primitive, awkward materiality of someone taking an oath in a bad saga; we expect the sentence to end in some awkwardly impressive climax, but get the almost ludicrous anticlimax of "Anything special you're a-mind to name." And, too, the phrase makes whatever she names quite willful on her part, quite unpredictable by reasonable man. His sensitivity usually shows itself to be a willing, hopeful form of insensitivity, and he himself realizes this here, saying, "Though I don't like such things 'twixt those that love." Frost then makes him express his own feeling in a partially truthful but elephantine aphorism that lumbers through a queerly stressed line a foot too long ("Two that don't love can't live together without them") into a conclusion ("But two that do can't live together with them") that has some of the slow, heavy relish just in being proverbial that the man so often shows. (How hard it is to get through the monosyllables of the two lines!) His words don't convince her, and she replies to them without words: "She moved the latch a little." He repeats in grieved appeal: "Don't—don't go. / Don't carry it to someone else this time." (He is repeating an earlier sentence, with "Don't go" changed to "Don't carry it.") The next line, "Tell me about it if it's something human," is particularly interesting when it comes from him. When is something inside a human being not human, so that it can't be told? Isn't it when it is outside man's understanding, outside all man's categories and pigeonholes—when there is no proverb to say for it? It is, then, a waste or abyss impossible to understand or manage or share with another. His next appeal to her, "Let me into your grief," combines an underlying sexual metaphor with a child's "Let me in! let me in!" This man who is so much a member of the human community feels a helpless bewilderment at being shut out of the little group of two of which he was once an anomalous half; the woman has put in the place of this group a group of herself-and-the-dead-child, and he begs or threatens—reasons with her as best he can—in his attempt to get her to restore the first group, so that there will be a man-and-wife grieving over their dead child.

He goes on: "I'm not so much / Unlike other folks as your standing there / Apart would make me out." The "standing there / Apart" is an imitative, expressive form that makes her apart, shows her apart. Really her apartness makes him out *like* other folks, all those others who make pretense of following to the grave, but who before one's back is turned have made their way back to life; but he necessarily misunderstands her, since for him being like others is necessarily good, being unlike them necessarily bad. His "Give me my chance"—he doesn't say *a* chance—reminds one of those masculine things fairness and sportsmanship, and makes one think of the child's demand for justice, equal shares, which follows his original demand for exclusive possession, the lion's share. "Give me my chance" means: "You, like everybody else, must admit that anybody deserves a chance—so give me mine"; he deserves his chance not by any particular qualities, personal merit, but just by virtue of being a human being. His "I do think, though, you overdo it a little" says that he is forced against his will to criticize her for so much exceeding (the phrase "a little" is understatement, politeness, and caution) the norm of grief, for mourning more than is usual or reasonable; the phrase "overdo it a little" manages to reduce her grief to the level of a petty social blunder. His next words, "What was it brought you up to think it the thing / To take your mother-loss of a first child / So inconsolably—in the face of love," manage to crowd four or five kinds of condemnation into a single sentence. "What was it brought you up" says that it is not your essential being but your accidental upbringing that has made you do this—it reduces the woman to a helpless social effect. "To think it the thing" is particularly insulting because it makes her grief a mere matter of fashion; it is as though he were saying, "What was it brought you up to think it the thing to wear your skirt that far above your knees?" The phrase "to take your mother-loss of a first child" pigeonholes her loss, makes it a regular, predictable category that demands a regular, predictable amount of grief, and no more. The phrase "So inconsolably—in the face of love" condemns her for being so unreasonable as not to be consoled by, for paying no attention to, that unarguably good, absolutely general thing, love; the generalized *love* makes demands upon her that are inescapable, compared to those which would be made by a more specific phrase like "in the face of my love for you." The man's "You'd think his memory might be satisfied" again condemns her for exceeding the reasonable social norm of grief; condemns her, jealously, for mourning as if the dead child's demands for grief were insatiable.

Her interruption, "There you go sneering now!" implies that he has often before done what she calls "sneering" at her and her excessive sensitivity; and, conscious of how hard he has been trying to make peace, and unconscious of how much his words have gone over into attack, he contradicts her like a child, in righteous anger: "I'm not, I'm not!" His "You make me angry" is another of his rhetorical, tautological announcements about himself, one that is intended somehow to justify the breaking of his promise not to come down to her; he immediately makes the simple childish threat, "I'll come down to you"—he is repeating his promise, "I won't come down to you," with the "not" removed. "God, what a woman!" righteously and despairingly calls on God and public opinion (that voice of the people which is the voice of God) to witness and marvel at what he is being forced to put up with: the fantastic, the almost unbelievable wrongness and unreasonableness of this woman. "And it's come to this," that regular piece of rhetorical recrimination in quarrels, introduces his *third* use of the sentence "Can't a man speak of his own child he's lost"; but this time the rhetorical question is changed into the factual condemnation of "A man can't speak of his own child that's dead." This time he doesn't end the sentence with the more sentimental, decorous, sympathy-demanding "that's lost," but ends with the categorical "that's dead."

Earlier the woman has given two entirely different, entirely specific and unexpected answers to this rhetorical question of his; this time she has a third specific answer, which she makes with monosyllabic precision and finality: "You can't because you don't know how to speak." He has said that it is an awful thing not to be permitted to speak of his own dead child; she replies that it is not a question of permission but of ability, that he is too ignorant and insensitive to be *able* to speak of his child. Her sentence is one line long, and it is only the second sentence of hers that has been that long. He has talked at length during the first two-thirds of the poem, she in three- or four-word phrases or in motions without words; for the rest of the poem she talks at length, as everything that has been shut up inside her begins to pour out. She opens herself up, now—is far closer to him, striking at him with her words, than she has been sitting apart, in her place. His open attack has finally elicited from her, by contagion, her open anger, so that now he is something real and unbearable to attack, instead of being something less than human to be disregarded.

The first sentence has indicted him; now she brings in the specific evidence for the indictment. She says: "If you had any feelings, you that dug / With your own hand"—but after the three stabbing, indicting stresses of

$$\acute{\text{y}}\text{our } \acute{\text{o}}\text{wn h}\acute{\text{a}}\text{nd}$$

she breaks off the sentence, as if she found the end unbearable to go on to; interjects, her throat tightening, the incredulous rhetorical question, "how could you?"—and finishes with the fact that she tries to make more nearly endurable, more euphemistic, with the tender word "little": "his little grave." The syntax of the sentence doesn't continue, but the fact of things continues; she says, "I saw you from that very window there."

$$/ \quad / \quad \quad / \quad \quad \quad /$$
That very window there

has the same stabbing stresses, the same emphasis on a specific, damning actuality, that

$$/ \quad / \quad \quad /$$
your own hand

had—and that, soon,

$$/ \quad / \quad /$$
my own eyes

and

$$/ \quad / \quad \quad /$$
your own baby's grave

and other such phrases will have. She goes on: "Making the gravel leap and leap in air, / Lead up, like that, like that, and land so lightly / And roll back down the mound beside the hole." As the sentence imitates with such terrible life and accuracy the motion of the gravel, her throat tightens and aches in her hysterical repetition of "like that, like that": the sounds of "leap and leap in air, / Leap up, like that, like that, and land so lightly" are "le! le! le! li! li! la! li!" and re-create the sustained hysteria she felt as she first watched; inanimate things, the very stones, leap and leap in air, or when their motion subsides land "so lightly," while the animate being, her dead child, does not move, will never move. (The foxes have holes, and the birds of the air have nests; but the Son of man hath not where to lay his head.) Her words "leap and leap in air, / Leap up, like that, like that" keep the stones alive! alive! alive!—in the words "and land" they all start to die away, but the following words "so lightly" make them alive again, for a last moment of unbearable contradiction, before they "*roll* back *down* the *mound* beside the *hole*." The repeated *o*'s (the line says "oh! ow! ow! oh!") make almost crudely actual the abyss of death into which the pieces of gravel and her child fall, not to rise again. The word "hole" (insisted on even more by the rhyme with "roll") gives to the grave the obscene actuality that watching the digging forced it to have for her.

She says: "I thought, Who is that man? I didn't know you." She sees the strange new meaning in his face (what, underneath the face has meant all along) so powerfully that the face itself seems a stranger's. If her own husband can do something so impossibly alien to all her expectations, he has never really been anything but alien; all her repressed antagonistic knowledge about his insensitivity comes to the surface and masks what before had masked it. In the next sentence, "And I crept down the stairs and up the stairs / To look again," the word "crept" makes her a little mouselike thing crushed under the weight of her new knowledge. But the truly extraordinary word is the "and" that joins "down the stairs" to "up the stairs." What is so extraordinary is that she sees nothing extraordinary about it: the "and" joining the two coordinates hides from her, shows that she has repressed, the thoroughly illogical, contradictory nature of her action; it is like saying: "And I ran out of the fire and back into the fire," and seeing nothing strange about the sentence.

Her next words, "and still your spade kept lifting," give the man's tool a dead, mechanical life of its own; it keeps on and on, crudely, remorselessly, neither guided nor halted by spirit. She continues: "Then you came in. I heard your rumbling voice / Out in the kitchen"; the word "rumbling" gives this great blind creature an insensate weight and strength that are, somehow, hollow. Then she says that she did something as extraordinary as going back up the stairs, but she masks it, this time, with the phrase "and I don't know why." She doesn't know why, it's unaccountable, "But I went near to see with my own eyes." Her "I don't know why" shows her regular refusal to admit things like these; she manages by a confession of ignorance not to have to make the connections, consciously, that she has already made unconsciously.

She now says a sentence that is an extraordinarily conclusive condemnation of him: "You could sit there with the stains on your shoes / Of the fresh earth from your own baby's grave / And talk about your everyday concerns." The five hissing or spitting *s*'s in the strongly accented "sit," "stains," "shoes"; the whole turning upside down of the first line, with four trochaic feet followed by one poor iamb; the concentration of intense, damning stresses in

$$\text{/ \quad / \quad / \quad / \quad / \quad /}$$
fresh earth of your own baby's grave

—all these things give an awful finality to the judge's summing up, so that in the last line, "And talk about your everyday concerns," the criminal's matter-of-fact obliviousness has the perversity of absolute insensitivity: Judas sits under the cross matching pennies with the soldiers. The poem has brought to life an unthought-of literal meaning of its title: this is home burial with a vengeance, burial *in* the home; the fresh dirt of the grave stains her husband's shoes and her kitchen floor, and the dirty spade with which he dug the grave stands there in the entry. As a final unnecessary piece of evidence, a last straw that comes long after the camel's back is broken, she states: "You had stood the spade up against the wall / Outside there in the entry, for I saw it." All her pieces of evidence have written underneath them, like Goya's drawing, that triumphant, traumatic, unarguable I SAW IT.

The man's next sentence is kind of summing-up-in-little of his regular behavior, the ways in which (we have come to see) he *has* to respond. He has begged her to let him into her grief, to tell him about it if it's something human; now she lets him into not her grief but her revolted, hating condemnation of him; she does tell him about it and it isn't human, but a nightmare into which he is about to fall. He says, "I shall laugh the worst laugh I ever laughed. / I'm cursed. God, if I don't believe I'm cursed." The sounds have the gasping hollowness of somebody hit in the stomach and trying over and over to get his breath—of someone nauseated and beginning to vomit: the first stressed vowel sounds are "agh! uh! agh! uh! agh! uh!" He doesn't reply to her, argue with her, address her at all, but makes a kind of dramatic speech that will exhibit him in a role public opinion will surely sympathize with, just as he sympathizes with himself. As always, he repeats, "laugh," "laugh," and "laughed," "I'm cursed" and "I'm cursed" (the rhyme with "worst" gives almost the effect of another repetition); as always, he announces beforehand what he is going to do, rhetorically appealing to mankind for justification and sympathy. His "I shall laugh the worst laugh I ever laughed" has the queer effect of seeming almost to be quoting some folk proverb. His "I'm cursed" manages to find a category of understanding in which to pigeonhole this nightmare, makes him a reasonable human being helpless against the inhuman powers of evil—the cursed one is not to blame. His "God, if I don't believe I'm cursed" is akin to his earlier "God, what a woman!"—both have something of the male's outraged, incredulous, despairing response to the unreasonableness and immorality of the female. He responds hardly at all to the exact situation; instead he demands sympathy for, sympathizes with himself for, the impossibly unlucky pigeonhole into which Fate has dropped him.

His wife then repeats the sentence that, for her, sums up everything: "I can repeat the very words you were saying. / 'Three foggy mornings and one rainy day / Will rot the best birch fence a man can build.' " We feel with a rueful smile that he has lived by proverbs and—now, for her—dies by them. He has handled his fresh grief by making it a part of man's regular routine, man's regular work; and by quoting man's regular wisdom, that explains, explains away, pigeonholes, anything. Nature tramples down man's work, the new fence rots, but man still is victorious, in the secure summing up of the proverb.

/   /   /
The best birch fence

is, so far as its stresses are concerned, a firm, comfortable parody of all those stabbing stress systems of hers. In his statement, as usual, it is not *I* but *a man.* There is a resigned but complacent, almost relishing wit about this summing up of the transitoriness of human effort: to understand your defeat so firmly, so proverbially, is in a sense to triumph. He has seen his ordinary human ambition about that ordinary human thing, a child, frustrated by death; so there is a certain resignation and pathos about his saying what he says. The word "rot" makes the connection between the fence and the child, and it is the word "rot" that is unendurable to the woman, since it implies with obscene directness: how many foggy mornings and rainy days will it take to rot the best flesh-and-blood child a man can have? Just as, long ago at the beginning of the poem, the man brought the bedroom and the grave together, he brings the rotting child and the rotting fence together now. She says in incredulous, breathless outrage: "Think of it, talk like that at such a time!" (The repeated sounds, *th, t, t, th, t, t,* are thoroughly expressive.) But once more she has repressed the connection between the two things: she objects to the sentence not as what she knows it is, as rawly and tactlessly relevant, but something absolutely irrelevant, saying: "What had how long it takes a birch to rot / To do with"—and then she puts in a euphemistic circumlocution, lowers her eyes and lowers the shades so as not to see—"what was in the darkened parlor."

But it is time to go back and think of just what it was the woman saw, just how she saw it, to make her keep on repeating that first occasion of its sight. She saw it on a holy and awful day. The child's death and burial were a great and almost unendurable occasion, something that needed to be accompanied with prayer and abstention, with real grief and the ritual expression of grief. It was a holy or holiday that could only be desecrated by "everyday concerns"; the husband's digging seemed to the wife a kind of brutally unfeeling, secular profanation of that holy day, her holy grief. Her description makes it plain that her husband dug strongly and well. And why should he not do so? Grief and grave digging, for him, are in separate compartments; the right amount of grief will never flow over into the next compartment. To him it is the workaday, matter-of-fact thing that necessarily comes first; grieving for the corpse is no excuse for not having plenty of food at the wake. If someone had said to him: "You dig mighty well for a man that's just lost his child," wouldn't he have replied: "Grief's no reason for doing a bad job"? (And yet, the muscles tell the truth; a sad enough man shovels badly.) When, the grave dug and the spade stood up in the entry, he went into the kitchen, he may very well have felt: "A good job," just as Yakov, in *Rothschild's Fiddle,* taps the coffin he has made for wife and thinks: "A good job."

But unconsciously, his wife has far more compelling reasons to be appalled at this job her husband is doing. Let me make this plain. If we are told how a woman dreams of climbing the stairs, and of looking out through a window at a man digging a hole with a spade—digging powerfully, so that the gravel leaps and leaps into the air, only to roll back down into the hole; and still the man's spade keeps lifting and plunging down, lifting and plunging down, as she watches in fascinated horror, creeps down the stairs, creeps back up against her will, to keep on watching; and then, she doesn't know why, she has to go to see with her own eyes the fresh earth staining the man's shoes, has to see with her own eyes the man's tool stood up against the wall, in the entrance to the house—if we are told such a dream, is there any doubt what *sort* of dream it will seem to us? Such things have a sexual force, a sexual meaning, as much in our waking hours as in our dreams—as we know from how many turns of speech, religious rites, myths, tales, works of art. When the plowman digs his plow into the earth, Mother Earth, to make her bear, this does not have a sexual appropriateness only in the dreams of neurotic patients—it is something that we all understand, whether or not we admit that we understand. So the woman understood her husband's digging. If the spade, the tool that he stands up in the entry, stands for man's workaday world, his matter-of-fact objectivity and disregard of emotion, it also stands for his masculinity, his sexual power; on this holy day he brings back into the house of grief the soiling stains of fresh earth, of this digging that, to her, is more than digging.

That day of the funeral the grieving woman felt only misery and anguish, passive suffering; there was nobody to blame for it all except herself. And how often women do blame themselves for the abnormality or death of a baby! An old doctor says they keep blaming themselves; they should have done this, that, something; they forget all about their husbands; often they blame some doctor who, by not coming immediately, by doing or not doing something, was responsible for it all: the woman's feeling of guilt about other things is displaced onto the child's death. Now when this woman sees her husband digging the grave (doing what seems to her, consciously, an intolerably insensitive thing; unconsciously, an indecent thing) she *does* have someone to blame, someone upon whom to shift her own guilt: she is able to substitute for passive suffering and guilt an active loathing and condemnation—as she blames the man's greater guilt and wrongness her own lesser guilt can seem in comparison innocence and rightness. (The whole matrix of attitudes available to her, about woman as Madonna-and-child and man as brute beast, about sexuality as a defiling thing forced upon woman, helps her to make this shift.) The poem has made it easy for us to suspect a partial antagonism or uncongeniality, sexually, between the weak oversensitive woman and the strong insensitive man, with his sexual force so easily transformed into menace. (The poem always treats it in that form.) The woman's negative attitudes have been overwhelmingly strengthened, now; it is plain that since the child's death there has been no sort of sexual or emotional union between them.

To her, underneath, the child's death must have seemed a punishment. Of whom for what? Of them for what they have done—sexual things are always tinged with guilt; but now her complete grief, her separateness and sexual and emotional abstention, help to cancel out her own guilt—the man's matter-of-fact physical obliviousness, his desire to have everything what it was before, reinforce his own guilt and help to make it seem absolute. Yet, underneath, the woman's emotional and physiological needs remain unchanged, and are satisfied by this compulsory symptomatic action of hers—this creeping up the stairs, looking, looking, creeping down and then back up again, looking, looking; she stares with repudiating horror, with accepting fascination, at this obscenely symbolic sight. It is not the child's mound she stares at, but the scene of the crime, the site of this terrible symbolic act that links sexuality and death, the marriage bed and the grave. (Afterwards she had gone down into the kitchen to see the man flushed and healthy, breathing a little harder after physical exertion; her words "I heard your *rumbling* voice / Out in the kitchen" reminds us of that first telling description of him on the stairs, "*Mounting* until she *cowered* under him." Her first response to the sight, "I thought: Who *is* that man? I didn't know you," makes him not her husband but a stranger, a guilty one, whom she is right to remain estranged from, must remain estranged from.) Her repeated symptomatic act has the consciousness of obsessional-compulsive symptoms, not the unconsciousness of hysterical blindness or paralysis: she is conscious of what she is doing, knows how it all began; and yet she cannot keep from doing it, does not really know why she does it, and is conscious only of a part of the meaning it has for her. She has isolated it, and refuses to see its connections, consciously, because the connections are so powerful unconsciously: so that she says, "And I crept down the stairs *and* up the stairs"; says "*And I don't know why,* / But I went near to see with my own eyes"; says, "What had how long it takes a birch to rot / To do with what was in the darkened parlor?"

This repeated symptomatic action of hers satisfies several needs. It keeps reassuring her that she is right to keep herself fixed in separation and rejection. By continually revisiting this scene, by looking again and again at—so to speak—this indecent photograph of her husband's crime, she is making certain that she will never come to terms with the criminal who, in the photograph, is committing the crime. Yet, underneath, there is a part of her that takes guilty pleasure in the crime, that is in identifying complicity with the criminal. A symptom or symptomatic action is an expression not only of the defense against the forbidden wish, but also of the forbidden wish.

If the reader doubts that this symptomatic action of hers has a sexual root, he can demonstrate it to himself by imagining the situation different in one way. Suppose the wife had looked out of the window and seen her husband animatedly and matter-of-factly bargaining to buy a cemetery lot from one of the next day's funeral guests. She would have been angered and revolted. But would she have crept back to look again? have gone into the kitchen so as to see the bargainer with her own eyes? have stared in fascination at the wallet from which he had taken the money? Could she as easily have made a symptom of it?

After she has finished telling the story of what she had seen, of what he had done, she cries: "You *couldn't* care!" The words say: "If you could behave as you behaved, it proves that you didn't care and, therefore, that you couldn't care; if you, my own husband, the child's own father, were unable to care, it proves that it must be impossible for anyone to care." So she goes on, not about him but about everyone: "The nearest friends can go / With anyone to death, comes so far short / They might as well not try to go at all." The sentence has some of the rueful, excessive wit of Luther's "In every good act the just man sins"; man can do so little he might as well do nothing. Her next sentence, "No, from the time when one is sick to death, / One is alone, and he dies more alone," tolls like a lonely bell for the human being who grieves for death and, infected by what she grieves for, dies alone in the pesthouse, deserted by the humanity that takes good care not to be infected. When you truly feel what death is, you must die: all her phrases about the child's death and burial make them her own death and burial.

She goes on: "Friends make pretense of following to the grave, / But before one is in it, their minds are turned"—her "make pretense" blames their, his, well-meant hypocrisy; her "before one is in it" speaks of the indecent haste with which he hurried to dig the grave into which the baby was put, depriving her of it—of the indecent haste with which he forgot death and wanted to resume life. The phrases "their minds are turned" and "making the best of their way back" are (as so often with Frost) queerly effective adaptations of ordinary idioms, of "their backs are turned" and "making the best of things"; these are the plain roots, in the woman's mind, of her less direct and more elaborate phrases. But when we have heard her whole sentence: "Friends make pretense of following to the grave, / But before one is in it, their minds are turned / And making the best of their way back to life / And living people, and things they understand," we reply: "As they must." She states as an evil what we think at worst a necessary evil; she is condemning people for not committing suicide, for not going down into the grave with the corpse and dying there. She condemns the way of the world, but it is the way of any world that continues to be a world: the world that does otherwise perishes. Her "But the world's evil. I won't have grief so / If I can change it. Oh, I won't, I won't!" admits what grief is to everybody else; is generally; and says that she will change the universal into her own contradictory particular if she can: the sentence has its own defeat inside it. What this grieving woman says about grief is analogous to a dying woman's saying about death: "I won't have death so if I can change it. Oh, I won't, I won't!" Even the man responds to the despairing helplessness in her "Oh, I won't, I won't!" She is still trying to be faithful and unchanging in her grief, but already she has begun to be faithless, has begun to change. Saying "I never have colds any more," an hour or two before one has a cold, is one's first unconscious recognition that one has caught cold; similarly, she says that other people forget and change but that she never will, just when she has begun to change—just when, by telling her husband the cause of her complete separation, she has begun to destroy the completeness of the separation. Her "Oh, I won't, I won't!" sounds helplessly dissolving, running down; already contains within it the admission of what it denies. Her "I won't have grief so" reminds us that grief *is* so, is by its very nature a transition to something that isn't grief. She knows it too, so that she says that everybody else is that way, the world is that way, but they're wrong, they're evil; *someone* must be different; *someone* honorably and quixotically, at no matter what cost, must contradict the nature of grief, the nature of the world.

All this is inconceivable to the man: if everybody is that way, it must be right to be that way; it would be insanity to think of any other possibility. She has put grief, the dead child, apart on an altar, to be kept separate and essential as long as possible—forever, if possible. He has immediately filed away the child, grief, in the pigeonhole of man's wont, man's proverbial understanding: the weight is off his own separate shoulders, and the shoulders of all mankind bear the burden. In this disaster of her child's death, her husband's crime, her one consolation is that she is inconsolable, has (good sensitive woman) grieved for months as her husband (bad insensitive man) was not able to grieve even for hours. Ceasing to grieve would destroy this consolation, would destroy the only way of life she has managed to find.

And yet she has begun to destroy them. When she says at the end of the poem: "How can I make you—" understand, see, she shows in her baffled, longing despair that she *has* tried to make him understand; has tried to help him as he asked her to help him. Her "You *couldn't* care," all her lines about what friends and the world necessarily are, excuse him in a way, by making him a necessarily insensitive part of a necessarily insensitive world that she alone is sensitive in: she is the one person desperately and forlornly trying to be different from everyone else, as she tries to keep death and grief alive in the middle of a world intent on its own forgetful life. At these last moments she does not, as he thinks, "set him apart" as "so much / Unlike other folks"; if he could hear and respond to what she actually has said, there would be some hope for them. But he doesn't; instead of understanding her special situation, he dumps her into the pigeonhole of the crying woman—any crying woman—and then tries to *manage* her as one manages a child. She does try to let him into her grief, but he won't go; instead he tells her that now she's had her cry, that now he feels better, that the heart's gone out of it, that there's really no grief left for him to be let into.

The helpless tears into which her hard self-righteous separateness has dissolved show, underneath, a willingness to accept understanding; she has denounced him, made a clean breast of things, and now is accessible to the understanding or empathy that he is unable to give her. Women are oversensitive, exaggerate everything, tell all, weep, and then are all right: this is the pigeonhole into which he drops her. So rapid an understanding can almost be called a form of stupidity, of not even trying really to understand. The bewitched, uncanny, almost nauseated helplessness of what he has said a few lines before: "I shall laugh the worst laugh I ever laughed. / I'm cursed. God, if I don't believe I'm cursed," has already changed into a feeling of mastery, of the strong man understanding and managing the weak hysterical woman. He is the powerful one now. His "There, you have said it all and you feel better. / You won't go now" has all the grownup's condescension toward the child, the grownup's ability to make the child do something simply by stating that the child is about to do it. The man's "You're crying. Close the door. / The heart's gone out of it: why keep it up" shows this quite as strikingly; he feels that he can manipulate her back into the house and into his life, back out of the grief that—he thinks or hopes—no longer has any heart in it, so that she must pettily and exhaustingly "keep it up."

But at this moment when the depths have been opened for him; at this moment when the proper management might get her back into the house, the proper understanding get her back into his life; at this moment that it is fair to call the most important moment of his life, someone happens to come down the road. Someone who will see her crying and hatless in the doorway; someone who will go back to the village and tell everything; someone who will shame them in the eyes of the world. Public opinion, what people will say, is more important to him than anything she will do; he forgets everything else, and expostulates: "Amy! There's someone coming down the road!" His exclamation is full of the tense, hurried fear of social impropriety, of public disgrace; nothing could show more forcibly what he *is* able to understand, what he *does* think of primary importance. Her earlier "Oh, where's my hat? Oh, I don't need it!" prepares for, is the exact opposite of, his "Amy! There's someone coming down the road!"

She says with incredulous, absolute intensity and particularity, *"You—"*

That italicized *you* is the worst, the most nearly final thing that she can say about him, since it merely points to what he is. She doesn't go on; goes back and replies to his earlier sentences: "oh, you think the talk is all." Her words have a despairing limpness and sadness: there is no possibility of his being made to think anything different, to see the truth under the talk. She says: "I must go—" and her words merely recognize a reality—"Somewhere out of this house." Her final words are full of a longing, despairing, regretful realization of a kind of final impossibility: "How can I make you—" The word that isn't said, that she stops short of saying, is as much there as anything in the poem. All her insistent anxious pride in her own separateness and sensitiveness and superiority is gone; she knows, now, that she is separate from him no matter what she wants. Her "How can I make you—" amounts almost to "If only I could make you—if only there were some way to make you—but there is no way."

He responds not to what she says but to what she does, to "She was opening the door wider." He threatens, as a child would threaten: "If—you—do!" He sounds like a giant child, or a child being a giant or an ogre. The "If—you—do!" uses as its principle of being the exaggerated slowness and heaviness, the *willedness* of his nature. (Much about him reminds me of Yeats's famous definition: "Rhetoric is the will trying to do the work of the imagination"; "Home Burial" might be called the story of a marriage between the will and the imagination.) The dashes Frost inserts between the words slow down the words to the point where the slowedness or heaviness itself, as pure force and menace, is what is communicated. Then the man says, trying desperately—feebly—to keep her within reach of that force or menace: "Where do you mean to go? First tell me that. / I'll follow and bring you back by force. I *will!*—" The last sentences of each of her previous speeches (her despairing emotional "Oh, I won't, I won't!" and her despairing spiritual "How can I make you—") are almost the exact opposite of the "I *will!*" with which he ends the poem. It is appropriate that "force," "I," and *"will"* are his last three words: his proverbial, town-meeting understanding has failed, just as his blankly imploring humility has failed; so that he has to resort to the only thing he has left, the will or force that seems almost like the mass or inertia of a physical body. We say that someone "throws his weight around," and in the end there is nothing left for him to do but throw his weight around. Appropriately, his last line is one more rhetorical announcement of what he is going to do: he will follow and bring her back by force; and, appropriately, he ends the poem with one more repetition—he repeats: "I *will!*"

FOCUS: READING REVIEW

1. According to Jarrell, what is Frost's poem about?
2. Jarrell constructs portraits for the two speakers in Frost's poem. What qualities does he give to each? What elements in the poem develop these characteristics?
3. What psychological interpretation does the author bring to the characters in Frost's poem?

FOCUS: AUTHOR'S STRATEGIES

1. How does Jarrell draw his reader into Frost's poem and conduct him through it?
2. What aspects of Jarrell's language enhance the reader's understanding of the events Frost's poem dramatizes?

FOCUS: DISCUSSION AND WRITING

1. Jarrell emphasizes the connotations of Frost's language. Do the associations Jarrell ascribes to the words correspond to your own? In what ways do you respond differently?
2. In "Criticism, Visible and Invisible," Frye says that criticism establishes "contexts for the works being studied." What contexts does Jarrell establish? Explain how these bring the reader closer to Frost's poem.

Lady Macbeth

A. C. Bradley

A. C. Bradley (1851–1935), is often regarded as one of the greatest English critics of Shakespeare. Bradley received his education from Balliol College at Oxford University, and served as a professor of literature and history at University College, Liverpool, as professor of English language and literature at Glasgow University, and as a professor of poetry at Oxford. His book Shakespearean Tragedy, *from which this selection is taken, assesses the achievement of* King Lear, Hamlet, Macbeth, *and* Othello *through analysis and interpretation of character and plot interrelationships. Bradley's "Lady Macbeth" shows how Shakespeare created a strong though flawed character who deteriorates as the play progresses. The strength of Bradley's study lies in his descriptive power.*

To regard *Macbeth* as a play, like the love-tragedies, in which there are two central characters of equal importance is certainly a mistake. But Shakespeare himself is in a measure responsible for it, because the first half of *Macbeth* is greater than the second, and in the first half Lady Macbeth not only appears more than in the second but exerts the ultimate deciding influence on the action. In the opening Act at least,

Lady Macbeth is the most commanding and perhaps awe-inspiring figure that Shakespeare drew. She knows her husband's weakness and she sets herself without a doubt or conflict to counteract this weakness. To her there is not separation between will and deed; and, as the deed falls in part to her, she is sure it will be done. By personal appeals, through the admiration she extorts from Macbeth, and through sheer force of will, she impels him to kill Duncan. Her eyes are fixed upon the crown and the means to it; she does not attend to the consequences.

In the earlier scenes of the play Lady Macbeth seems invincible—also inhuman. Yet if the Lady Macbeth of these scenes were really inhuman, the Lady Macbeth of the sleep-walking scene would be an impossibility. If we look below the surface, there is evidence enough in the earlier scenes of preparation for the later. In the opening scenes she is deliberately counteracting the 'human kindness' of her husband. Besides she shows some signs of feminine weakness and human feeling. When she remarks of Duncan "Had he not resembled / My father as he slept, I had done 't" suggests that she could never have done the murder if her husband had failed. Further the greatness of Lady Macbeth lies almost wholly in courage and force of will [and not in intellect.] The limitations of her mind appear most in the point where she is most strongly contrasted with Macbeth—in her comparative dullness of imagination. In this lack of imagination she does not fully conceive of the cruelty of murder nor does she foresee the inward consequences. When the murder has been done, the discovery of its hideousness comes to Lady Macbeth with a shock and her nature begins to sink. At last her nature, not her will, gives way.

To regard *Macbeth* as a play, like the love-tragedies *Romeo and Juliet* and *Antony and Cleopatra,* in which there are two central characters of equal importance, is certainly a mistake. But Shakespeare himself is in a measure responsible for it, because the first half of *Macbeth* is greater than the second, and in the first half Lady Macbeth not only appears more than in the second but exerts the ultimate deciding influence on the action. And, in the opening Act at least, Lady Macbeth is the most commanding and perhaps the most awe-inspiring figure that Shakespeare drew. Sharing, as we have seen, certain traits with her husband, she is at once clearly distinguished from him by an inflexibility of will, which appears to hold imagination, feeling, and conscience completely in check. To her the prophecy of things that will be becomes instantaneously the determination that they shall be:

Glamis thou art, and Cawdor, and shalt be
What thou art promised.

She knows her husband's weakness, how he scruples 'to catch the nearest way' to the object he desires; and she sets herself without a trace of doubt or conflict to counteract this weakness. To her there is no separation between will and deed; and, as the deed falls in part to her, she is sure it will be done:

> The raven himself is hoarse
> That croaks the fatal entrance of Duncan
> Under my battlements.

On the moment of Macbeth's rejoining her, after braving infinite dangers and winning infinite praise, without a syllable on these subjects or a word of affection, she goes straight to her purpose and permits him to speak of nothing else. She takes the superior position and assumes the direction of affairs,—appears to assume it even more than she really can, that she may spur him on. She animates him by picturing the deed as heroic, 'this night's *great* business,' or 'our *great* quell,' while she ignores its cruelty and faithlessness. She bears down his faint resistance by presenting him with a prepared scheme which may remove from him the terror and danger of deliberation. She rouses him with a taunt no man can bear, and least of all a soldier,—the word 'coward.' She appeals even to his love for her:

> from this time
> Such I account thy love;

—such, that is, as the protestations of a drunkard. Her reasonings are mere sophisms;[1] they could persuade no man. It is not by them, it is by personal appeals, through the admiration she extorts from him, and through sheer force of will, that she impels him to the deed. Her eyes are fixed upon the crown and the means to it; she does not attend to the consequences. Her plan of laying the guilt upon the chamberlains is invented on the spur of the moment, and simply to satisfy her husband. Her true mind is heard in the ringing cry with which she answers his question, 'Will it not be received ... that they have done it?'

> Who dares receive it other?

And this is repeated in the sleep-walking scene: 'What need we fear who knows it, when none can call our power to account?' Her passionate courage sweeps him off his feet. His decision is taken in a moment of enthusiasm:

> Bring forth men-children only;
> For thy undaunted mettle should compose
> Nothing but males.

And even when passion has quite died away her will remains supreme. In presence of overwhelming horror and danger, in the murder scene and the banquet scene, her self-control is perfect. When the truth of what she has done dawns on her, no word of complaint, scarely a word of her own suffering, not a single word of her own as apart from his, escapes her when others are by. She helps him, but never asks his help. She leans on nothing but herself. And from the beginning to the end—though she makes once or twice a slip in acting her part—her will never fails her. Its grasp upon her nature may destroy her, but it is never relaxed. We are sure that she never betrayed her husband or herself by a word or even a look, save in sleep. However appalling she may be, she is sublime.

In the earlier scenes of the play this aspect of Lady Macbeth's character is far the most prominent. And if she seems invincible she seems also inhuman. We find no trace of pity for the kind old king; no consciousness of the treachery and base-ness of the murder; no sense of the value of the lives of the wretched men on whom the guilt is to be laid; no shrinking even from the condemnation or hatred of the world. Yet if the Lady Macbeth of these scenes were really utterly inhuman, or a 'fiend-like' queen,' as Malcolm calls her, the Lady Macbeth of the sleep-walking scene would be an impossibility. The one woman could never become the other. And in fact, if we look below the surface, there is evidence enough in the earlier scenes of preparation for the later. I do not mean that Lady Macbeth was naturally humane. There is nothing in the play to show this, and several passages subsequent to the murder-scene supply proof to the contrary. One is that where she exclaims, on being informed of Duncan's murder,

> Woe, alas!
> What, in our house?

This mistake in acting shows that she does not even know what the natural feeling in such circumstances would be; and Banquo's curt answer, 'Too cruel anywhere,' is almost a reproof of her insensibility. But, admitting this, we have in the first place to remember, in imagining the opening scenes, that she is deliberately bent on counteracting the 'human kindness' of her husband, and also that she is evi-dently not merely inflexibly determined but in a condition of abnormal excita-bility. That exaltation in the project which is so entirely lacking in Macbeth is strongly marked in her. When she tries to help him by representing their enter-prise as heroic, she is deceiving herself as much as him. Their attainment of the crown presents itself to her, perhaps has long presented itself, as something so glorious, and she has fixed her will upon it so completely, that for the time she sees the enterprise in no other light than that of its greatness. When she solilo-quises,

> Yet do I fear thy nature:
> It is too full o' the milk of human kindness
> To catch the nearest way: thou wouldst be great;
> Art not without ambition, but without
> The illness should attend it; what thou wouldst highly,
> That wouldst thou holily,

one sees that 'ambition' and 'great' and 'highly' and even 'illness' are to her simply terms of praise, and 'holily' and 'human kindness' simply terms of blame. Moral distinctions do not in this exaltation exist for her; or rather they are inverted: 'good' means to her the crown and whatever is required to obtain it, 'evil' whatever stands in the way of its attainment. This attitude of mind is evident even when she is alone, though it becomes still more pronounced when she has to work upon her husband. And it persists until her end is attained. But, without being exactly forced, it betrays a strain which could not long endure.

Besides this, in these earlier scenes the traces of feminine weakness and human feeling, which account for her later failure, are not absent. Her will, it is clear, was exerted to overpower not only her husband's resistance but some resistance in herself. Imagine Goneril[2] uttering the famous words,

> Had he not resembled
> My father as he slept, I had done 't.

They are spoken, I think, without any sentiment—impatiently, as though she regretted her weakness—but it was there. And in reality, quite apart from this recollection of her father, she could never have done the murder if her husband had failed. She had to nerve herself with wine to give her 'boldness' enough to go through her minor part. That appalling invocation to the spirits of evil, to unsex her and fill her from the crown to the toe topfull of direst cruelty, tells the same tale of determination to crush the inward protest. Goneril had no need of such a prayer. In the utterance of the frightful lines,

> I have given suck, and know
> How tender 'tis to love the babe that milks me:
> I would, while it was smiling in my face,
> Have pluck'd my nipple from his boneless gums,
> And dash'd the brains out, had I so sworn as you
> Have done to this,

her voice should doubtless rise until it reaches, in 'dash'd the brains out,' an almost hysterical scream. These lines show unmistakably that strained exaltation which, as soon as the end is reached, vanishes, never to return.

The greatness of Lady Macbeth lies almost wholly in courage and force of will. It is an error to regard her as remarkable on the intellectual side. In acting a part she shows immense self-control, but not much skill. Whatever may be thought of the plan of attributing the murder of Duncan to the chamberlains, to lay their bloody daggers on their pillows, as if they were determined to advertise their guilt, was a mistake which can be accounted for only by the excitement of the moment. But the limitations of her mind appear most in the point where she is most strongly contrasted with Macbeth,—in her comparative dullness of imagination. I say 'comparative,' for she sometimes uses highly poetic language, as indeed does everyone in Shakespeare who has any greatness of soul. Nor is she perhaps less imaginative than the majority of his heroines. But as compared with her husband she has little imagination. It is not *simply* that she suppresses what she has. To her, things remain at the most terrible moment precisely what they were at the calmest, plain facts which stand in a given relation to a certain deed, not visions which tremble and flicker in the light of other worlds. The probability that the old king will sleep soundly after his long journey to Inverness is to her simply a fortunate circumstance; but one can fancy the shoot of horror across Macbeth's face as she mentions it. She uses familiar and prosaic illustrations, like

> Letting 'I dare not' wait upon 'I would,'
> Like the poor cat i' the adage,

(the cat who wanted fish but did not like to wet her feet); or,

> We fail?
> But screw your courage to the sticking-place,
> And we'll not fail;

or,

> Was the hope drunk
> Wherein you dress'd yourself? hath it slept since?
> And wakes it now, to look so green and pale
> At what it did so freely?

The Witches are practically nothing to her. She feels no sympathy in Nature with her guilty purpose, and would never bid the earth not hear her steps, which way they walk. The noises before the murder, and during it, are heard by her as simple facts, and are referred to their true sources. The knocking has no mystery for her: it comes from 'the south entry.' She calculates on the drunkenness of the grooms, compares the different effects of wine on herself and on them, and listens to their snoring. To her the blood upon her husband's hands suggests only the taunt,

> My hands are of your colour, but I shame
> To wear a heart so white;

and the blood to her is merely 'this filthy witness,'—words impossible to her husband, to whom it suggested something quite other than sensuous disgust or practical danger. The literalism of her mind appears fully in two contemptuous speeches where she dismisses his imaginings; in the murder scene:

> Infirm of purpose!
> Give me the daggers! The sleeping and the dead
> Are but as pictures: 'tis the eye of childhood
> That fears a painted devil;

and in the banquet scene:

> O these flaws and starts,
> Impostors to true fear, would well become
> A woman's story at a winter's fire,
> Authorised by her grandam. Shame itself!
> Why do you make such faces? When all's done,
> You look but on a stool.

Even in the awful scene where her imagination breaks loose in sleep she uses no such images as Macbeth's. It is the direct appeal of the facts to sense that has fastened on her memory. The ghastly realism of 'Yet who would have thought the old man to have had so much blood in him?' or 'Here's the smell of the blood still,' is wholly unlike him. Her most poetical words, 'All the perfumes of Arabia will not sweeten this little hand,' are equally unlike his words about great Neptune's ocean. Hers, like some of her other speeches, are the more moving, from their greater simplicity and because they seem to tell of that self-restraint in suffering which is so totally lacking in him; but there is in them comparatively little of imagination. If we consider most of the passages to which I have referred, we shall find that the quality which moves our admiration is courage or force of will.

This want of imagination, though it helps to make Lady Macbeth strong for immediate action, is fatal to her. If she does not feel beforehand the cruelty of Duncan's murder, this is mainly because she hardly imagines the act, or at most imagines its outward show, 'the motion of a muscle this way or that.' Nor does she in the least foresee those inward consequences which reveal themselves immediately in her husband, and less quickly in herself. It is often said that she understands him well. Had she done so, she never would have urged him on. She knows that he is given to strange fancies; but, not realising what they spring from, she has no idea either that they may gain such power as to ruin the scheme, or that, while they mean present weakness, they mean also perception of the future. At one point in the murder scene the force of his imagination impresses her, and for a moment she is startled; a light threatens to break on her:

> These deeds must not be thought
> After these ways: so, it will make us mad,

she says, with a sudden and great seriousness. And when he goes panting on, 'Methought I heard a voice cry, "Sleep no more," ' . . . she breaks in, 'What do you mean?' half-doubting whether this was not a real voice that he heard. Then, almost directly, she recovers herself, convinced of the vanity of his fancy. Nor does she understand herself any better than him. She never suspects that these deeds *must* be thought after these ways; that her facile realism,

> A little water clears us of this deed,

will one day be answered by herself, 'Will these hands ne'er be clean?' or that the fatal commonplace, 'What's done is done,' will make way for her last despairing sentence, 'What's done cannot be undone.'

Hence the development of her character—perhaps it would be more strictly accurate to say, the change in her state of mind—is both inevitable, and the opposite of the development we traced in Macbeth. When the murder has been done, the discovery of its hideousness, first reflected in the faces of her guests, comes to Lady Macbeth with the shock of a sudden disclosure, and at once her nature begins to sink. The first intimation of the change is given when, in the scene of the discovery, she faints. When next we see her, Queen of Scotland, the glory of her dream has faded. She enters, disillusioned, and weary with want of sleep: she has thrown away everything and gained nothing:

> Nought's had, all's spent,
> Where our desire is got without content:
> 'Tis safer to be that which we destroy
> Than by destruction dwell in doubtful joy.

Henceforth she has no initiative: the stem of her being seems to be cut through. Her husband, physically the stronger, maddened by pangs he had foreseen, but still flaming with life, comes into the foreground, and she retires. Her will remains, and she does her best to help him; but he rarely needs her help. Her chief anxiety appears to be that he should not betray his misery. He plans the murder of Banquo without her knowledge (not in order to spare her, I think, for he never shows love of this quality, but merely because he does not need her now); and even when she is told vaguely of his intention she appears but little interested. In the sudden emergency of the banquet scene she makes a prodigious and magnificent effort; her strength, and with it her ascendancy, returns, and she saves her husband at least from an open disclosure. But after this she takes no part whatever in the action. We only know from her shuddering words in the sleep-walking scene, 'The Thane of Fife had a wife: where is she now?' that she has even learned of her husband's worst crime; and in all the horrors of his tyranny over Scotland she has, so far as we hear, no part. Disillusionment and despair prey upon her more and more. That she should seek any relief in speech, or should ask for sympathy, would seem to her mere weakness, and would be to Macbeth's defiant fury an irritation. Thinking of the change in him, we imagine the bond between them slackened, and Lady Macbeth left much alone. She sinks slowly downward. She cannot bear darkness, and has light by her continually: 'tis her command. At last her nature, not her will, gives way. The secrets of the past find vent in a disorder of sleep, the beginning perhaps of madness. What the doctor fears is clear. He reports to her husband no great physical mischief, but bids her attendant to remove from her all means by which she could harm herself, and to keep eyes on her constantly. It is in vain. Her death is announced by a cry from her women so sudden and direful that it would thrill her husband with horror if he were any longer capable of fear. In the last words of the play Malcolm tells us it is believed in the hostile army that she died by her own hand. And (not to speak of the indications just referred to) it is in accordance with her character that even in her weakest hour she should cut short by one determined stroke the agony of her life.

The sinking of Lady Macbeth's nature, and the marked change in her demeanour to her husband, are most strikingly shown in the conclusion of the banquet scene; and from this point pathos is mingled with awe. The guests are gone. She is completely exhausted, and answers Macbeth in listless, submissive words which seem to come with difficulty. How strange sounds the reply 'Did you send to him, sir?' to his imperious question about Macduff! And when he goes on, 'waxing desperate in imagination,' to speak of new deeds of blood, she seems to sicken at the thought, and there is a deep pathos in that answer which tells at once of her care for him and of the misery she herself has silently endured,

You lack the season of all natures, sleep.

We begin to think of her now less as the awful instigator of murder than as a woman with much that is grand in her, and much that is piteous. Strange and almost ludicrous as the statement may sound, she is, up to her light, a perfect wife. She gives her husband the best she has; and the fact that she never uses to him the terms of affection which, up to this point in the play, he employs to her, is certainly no indication of want of love. She urges, appeals, reproaches, for a practical end, but she never recriminates. The harshness of her taunts is free from mere personal feeling, and also from any deep or more than momentary contempt. She despises what she thinks the weakness which stands in the way of her husband's ambition; but she does not despise *him*. She evidently admires him and thinks him a great man, for whom the throne is the proper place. Her commanding attitude in the moments of his hesitation or fear is probably confined to them. If we consider the peculiar circumstances of the earlier scenes and the banquet scene, and if we examine the language of the wife and husband at other times, we shall come, I think, to the conclusion that their habitual relations are better represented by the later scenes than by the earlier, though naturally they are not truly represented by either. Her ambition for her husband and herself (there was no distinction to her mind) proved fatal to him, far more so than the prophecies of the Witches; but even when she pushed him into murder she believed she was helping him to do what he merely lacked the nerve to attempt; and her part in the crime was so much less open-eyed than his, that, if the impossible and undramatic task of estimating degrees of culpability were forced on us, we should surely have to assign the larger share to Macbeth.

'Lady Macbeth,' says Dr. Johnson, 'is merely detested'; and for a long time critics generally spoke of her as though she were Malcolm's 'fiend-like queen.' In natural reaction we tend to insist, as I have been doing, on the other and less obvious side; and in the criticism of the last century there is even a tendency to sentimentalise the character. But it can hardly be doubted that Shakespeare meant the predominant impression to be one of awe, grandeur, and horror, and that he never meant this impression to be lost, however it might be modified, as Lady Macbeth's activity diminishes and her misery increases. I cannot believe that, when she said of Banquo and Fleance,

> But in them nature's copy's not eterne,

she meant only that they would some day die; or that she felt any surprise when Macbeth replied;

> There's comfort yet: they are assailable;

though I am sure no light came into her eyes when he added those dreadful words, 'Then be thou jocund.' She was listless. She herself would not have moved a finger against Banquo. But she thought his death, and his son's death, might ease her husband's mind, and she suggested the murders indifferently and without remorse. The sleep-walking scene, again, inspires pity, but its main effect is one of awe. There is great horror in the references to blood, but it cannot be said that there is more than horror; and Campbell was surely right when, in alluding to Mrs. Jameson's analysis, he insisted that in Lady Macbeth's misery there is no trace of contrition. Doubtless she would have given the world to undo what she had done; and the thought of it killed her; but, regarding her from the tragic point of view, we may truly say she was too great to repent.

Notes

¹ A sophism provides a clever and plausible but fallacious argument.
² Goneril is Lear's evil daughter in *King Lear.*

FOCUS: READING REVIEW

1. As Bradley describes Lady Macbeth he repeatedly uses the word "will." What does this come to mean? What significance does it have?
2. Bradley suggests that a tension exists between Lady Macbeth's *sheer* will and her sleep-walking scene. What exists below the surface that prepares for the sleepwalking scene? What is her weakness?
3. What does Bradley mean by the "comparative dullness of imagination" in reference to Lady Macbeth?
4. What change in Lady Macbeth does Bradley describe? What elements of the play illustrate this change?

FOCUS: AUTHOR'S STRATEGIES

1. Bradley's purpose is creating for his audience a better understanding of the play. Explain how he uses analysis to achieve this.
2. This essay counters earlier critical interpretations of Lady Macbeth. What are these views? How does Bradley's argument refute these?

FOCUS: DISCUSSION AND WRITING

In "Against Interpretation" Sontag addresses the difficulty that lies in seeing literature as mimetic. To what degree does Bradley assume that literature is mimetic? Cite passages to support your response.

Leonardo da Vinci

Walter Pater

Walter Pater (1839–1894) is often recognized for defining criticism as a prose genre. While at King's School in Canterbury, he read John Ruskin's study, Modern Painters, *which stirred his interest in both art and aesthetics. He attended Queen's College, Oxford, but left to travel to Italy where he immersed himself in Italian Renaissance art. Upon returning to England, he became associated with a coterie of poets and painters and wrote extensively on the arts for many of the influential journals. Pater's study of da Vinci, from* Studies in the History of the Renaissance, *provides a marked contrast to Gombrich's essay "Harmony Attained." Pater's emotionally colored descriptions of da Vinci's paintings draw on stories about the painter's life—his restlessness, his perfectionism, his depression, his love for women. While both Gombrich and Pater inspire appreciation for the master's work, each elicits his reader's response in a different way.*

By a certain mystery in his work, and something enigmatical beyond the usual measure of great men, Da Vinci fascinates, or perhaps half repels. His life is one of sudden revolts, with intervals in which he works not at all. His life has three divisions—thirty years at Florence, nearly twenty years at Milan, then nineteen years of wandering, till he sinks to rest under the protection of Francis the First. [In Florence, Da Vinci was apprenticed to Verrocchio where he surpassed the master. Here he learned the love of beautiful toys (details) and perfected the Florentine style of miniature painting], with patient putting of each leaf upon trees and each flower in the grass. [The perfection of that style awoke in Leonardo a seed of discontent and he plunged into the study of nature. This fascination with the performance of natural magic] confirmed in him two ideas: the smiling of women and the motion of water.

[In 1483 he was called to Milan.] It was a life of brilliant sins and exquisite amusements. There he plunged into the study not only of nature but of human personality. The drawings of this period reflect this. [There too he acquired students, and it is through their works that we come very near to Leonardo's genius.] Though he handles sacred subjects continually, he is the most profane of painters. *The Last Supper,* painted in oil on a refectory wall by a man refusing to work except at the moment of invention, was another effort to lift a given subject out of the range of its traditional associations.

The remaining years of Leonardo's life are more or less years of wandering. Perhaps necessity kept his spirit excited; the next four years are one prolonged rapture of ecstasy of invention. His work was less with the saints than the living women of Florence. In the houses of Florence he saw Lisa, the third wife of Francesco del Giocondo. *La Gioconda* is, in the truest sense, Leonardo's masterpiece. From childhood we see this image defining itself on the fabric of his dreams, and but for express historical testimony, we might fancy that this was but his ideal lady. The presence is expressive of what in the ways of a thousand years men had come to desire. Hers is the head upon which all "the ends of the world are come," and the eyelids are a little weary. It is a beauty wrought out from within upon the flesh. Certainly Lady Lisa might stand as the embodiment of the old fancy, the symbol of the modern idea.

In Vasari's life of Leonardo da Vinci as we now read it there are some variations from the first edition. There, the painter who has fixed the outward type of Christ for succeeding centuries was a bold speculator, holding lightly by other men's beliefs, setting philosophy above Christianity. Words of his, trenchant enough to justify this impression, are not recorded, and would have been out of keeping with a genius of which one characteristic is the tendency to lose itself in a refined and graceful mystery. The suspicion was but the time-honoured mode in which the world stamps its appreciation of one who has thoughts for himself alone, his high indifference, his intolerance of the common forms of things; and in the second edition the image was changed into something fainter and more conventional. But it is still by a certain mystery in his work, and something enigmatical beyond the usual measure of great men, that he fascinates, or perhaps half repels. His life is one of sudden revolts, with intervals in which he works not at all, or apart from the main scope of his work. By a strange fortune the pictures on which his more popular fame rested disappeared early from the world, like the *Battle of the Standard;* or are mixed obscurely with the product of meaner hands, like the *Last Supper.* His type of beauty is so exotic that it fascinates a larger number than it delights, and seems more than that of any other artist to reflect ideas and views and some scheme of the world within; so that he seemed to his contemporaries to be the possessor of some unsanctified and secret wisdom; as to Michelet and others to have anticipated modern ideas. He trifles with his genius, and crowds all his chief work into a few tormented years of later life; yet he is so possessed by his genius that he passes unmoved through the most tragic events, overwhelming his country and friends, like one who comes across them by chance on some secret errand.

His *legend,* as the French say, with the anecdotes which every one remembers, is one of the most brilliant chapters of Vasari. Later writers merely copied it, until, in 1804, Carlo Amoretti applied to it a criticism which left hardly a date fixed, and not one of those anecdotes untouched. The various questions thus raised have since that time become, one after another, subjects of special study, and mere antiquarianism has in this direction little more to do. For others remain the editing of the thirteen books of his manuscripts, and the separation by technical criticism of what in his reputed works is really his, from what is only half his, or the work of his pupils. But a lover of strange souls may still analyse for himself the impression made on him by those works, and try to reach through it a definition of the chief elements of Leonardo's genius. The *legend,* as corrected and enlarged by its critics, may now and then intervene to support the results of this analysis.

His life has three divisions—thirty years at Florence, nearly twenty years at Milan, then nineteen years of wandering, till he sinks to rest under the protection of Francis the First at the *Château de Clou.* The dishonour of illegitimacy hangs over his birth. Piero Antonio, his father was of a noble Florentine house, of Vinci in the Val d' Arno, and Leonardo, brought up delicately among the true children of that house, was the love-child of his youth, with the keen, puissant nature such children often have. We see him in his boyhood fascinating all men by his beauty, improvising music and songs, buying the caged birds and setting them free, as he walked the streets of Florence, fond of odd bright dresses and spirited horses.

From his earliest years he designed many objects, and constructed models in relief, of which Vasari mentions some of women smiling. His father, pondering over this promise in the child, took him to the workshop of Andrea del Verrocchio, then the most famous artist in Florence. Beautiful objects lay about there—reliquaries, pyxes, silver images for the pope's chapel at Rome, strange fancy-work of the middle age, keeping odd company with fragments of antiquity, then but lately discovered. Another student Leonardo may have seen there—a lad into whose soul the level light and aërial illusions of Italian sunsets had passed, in after days famous as Perugino. Verrocchio was an artist of the earlier Florentine type, carver, painter, and worker in metals, in one; designer, not of pictures only, but of all things for sacred or household use, drinking-vessels, ambries, instruments of music, making them all fair to look upon, filling the common ways of life with the reflexion of some far-off brightness; and years of patience had refined his hand till his work was now sought after from distant places.

It happened that Verrocchio was employed by the brethren of Vallombrosa to paint the Baptism of Christ, and Leonardo was allowed to finish an angel in the left-hand corner. It was one of those moments in which the progress of a great thing—here, that of the art of Italy—presses hard on the happiness of an individual, through whose discouragement and decrease, humanity, in more fortunate persons, comes a step nearer to its final success.

For beneath the cheerful exterior of the mere well-paid craftsman, chasing brooches for the copes of *Santa Maria Novella,* or twisting metal screens for the tombs of the Medici, lay the ambitious desire to expand the destiny of Italian art by a larger knowledge and insight into things, a purpose in art not unlike Leonardo's still unconscious purpose; and often, in the modelling of drapery, or of a lifted arm, or of hair cast back from the face, there came to him something of the freer manner and richer humanity of a later age. But in this *Baptism* the pupil had surpassed the master; and Verrocchio turned away as one stunned, and as if his sweet earlier work must thereafter be distasteful to him, from the bright animated angel of Leonardo's hand.

The angel may still be seen in Florence, a space of sunlight in the cold, laboured old picture; but the legend is true only in sentiment, for painting had always been the art by which Verrocchio set least store. And as in a sense he anticipates Leonardo, so to the last Leonardo recalls the studio of Verrocchio, in the love of beautiful toys, such as the vessel of water for a mirror, and lovely needle-work about the implicated hands in the *Modesty and Vanity*, and of reliefs, like those cameos which in the *Virgin of the Balances* hang all around the girdle of Saint Michael, and of bright variegated stones, such as the agates in the *Saint Anne*, and in a hieratic preciseness and grace, as of a sanctuary swept and garnished. Amid all the cunning and intricacy of his Lombard manner this never left him. Much of it there must have been in that lost picture of *Paradise*, which he prepared as a cartoon for tapestry, to be woven in the looms of Flanders. It was the perfection of the older Florentine style of miniature-painting, with patient putting of each leaf upon the trees and each flower in the grass, where the first man and woman were standing.

And because it was the perfection of that style, it awoke in Leonardo some seed of discontent which lay in the secret places of his nature. For the way to perfection is through a series of disgusts; and this picture—all that he had done so far in his life at Florence—was after all in the old slight manner. His art, if it was to be something in the world, must be weighted with more of the meaning of nature and purpose of humanity. Nature was "the true mistress of higher intelligences." He plunged, then, into the study of nature. And in doing this he followed the manner of the older students; he brooded over the hidden virtues of plants and crystals, the lines traced by the stars as they moved in the sky, over the correspondences which exist between the different orders of living things, through which, to eyes opened, they interpret each other; and for years he seemed to those about him as one listening to a voice, silent for other men.

He learned here the art of going deep, of tracking the sources of expression to their subtlest retreats, the power of an intimate presence in the things he handled. He did not at once or entirely desert his art; only he was no longer the cheerful, objective painter, through whose soul, as through clear glass, the bright figures of Florentine life, only made a little mellower and more pensive by the transit, passed on to the white wall. He wasted many days in curious tricks of design, seeming to lose himself in the spinning of intricate devices of line and colour. He was smitten with a love of the impossible—the perforation of mountains, changing the course of rivers, raising great buildings, such as the church of *San Giovanni*, in the air; all those feats for the performance of which natural magic professed to have the key.

Later writers, indeed, see in these efforts an anticipation of modern mechanics; in him they were rather dreams, thrown off by the overwrought and labouring brain. Two ideas were especially confirmed in him, as reflexes of things that had touched his brain in childhood beyond the depth of other impressions—the smiling of women and the motion of great waters.

And in such studies some interfusion of the extremes of beauty and terror shaped itself, as an image that might be seen and touched, in the mind of this gracious youth, so fixed that for the rest of his life it never left him. As if catching glimpses of it in the strange eyes or hair of chance people, he would follow such about the streets of Florence till the sun went down, of whom many sketches of his remain. Some of these are full of a curious beauty, that remote beauty which may be apprehended only by those who have sought it carefully; who, starting with acknowledged types of beauty, have refined as far upon these, as these refine upon the world of common forms. But mingled inextricably with this there is an element of mockery also; so that, whether in sorrow or scorn, he caricatures Dante even. Legions of grotesques sweep under his hand; for has not nature too her grotesques—the rent rock, the distorting lights of evening on lonely roads, the unveiled structure of man in the embryo, or the skeleton?

All these swarming fancies unite in the *Medusa* of the *Uffizii*. Vasari's story of an earlier Medusa, painted on a wooden shield, is perhaps an invention; and yet, properly told, has more of the air of truth about it than anything else in the whole legend. For its real subject is not the serious work of a man, but the experiment of a child. The lizards and glow-worms and other strange small creatures which haunt an Italian vineyard being before one the whole picture of a child's life in a Tuscan dwelling—half castle, half farm—and are as true to nature as the pretended astonishment of the father for whom the boy has prepared a surprise. It was not in play that he painted that other Medusa, the one great picture which he left behind him in Florence. The subject has been treated in various ways; Leonardo alone cuts to its centre; he.alone realises it as the head of a corpse, exercising its powers through all the circumstances of death. What may be called the fascination of corruption penetrates in every touch its exquisitely finished beauty. About the dainty lines of the cheek the bat flits unheeded. The delicate snakes seem literally strangling each other in terrified struggle to escape from the Medusa brain. The hue which violent death always brings with it is in the features; features singularly massive and grand, as we catch them inverted, in a dexterous foreshortening, crown foremost, like a great calm stone against which the wave of serpents breaks.

The science of that age was all divination, clairvoyance, unsubjected to our exact modern formulas, seeking in an instant of vision to concentrate a thousand experiences. Later writers, thinking only of the well-ordered treatise on painting which a Frenchman, Raffaelle du Fresne, a hundred years afterwards, compiled from Leonardo's bewildered manuscripts, written strangely, as his manner was, from right to left, have imagined a rigid order in his inquiries. But this rigid order would have been little in accordance with the restlessness of his character; and if we think of him as the mere reasoner who subjects design to anatomy, and composition to mathematical rules, we shall hardly have that impression which those around Leonardo received from him. Poring over his crucibles, making experiments with colour, trying, by a strange variation of the alchemist's dream, to discover the secret, not of an elixir to make man's natural life immortal, but of giving immortality to the subtlest and most delicate effects of painting, he seemed to them rather the sorcerer or the magician, possessed of curious secrets and a hidden knowledge, living in a world of which he alone possessed the key. What his philosophy seems to have been most like is that of Paracelsus or Cardan; and much of the spirit of the older alchemy still hangs about it, with its confidence in short cuts and odd byways to knowledge. To him philosophy was to be something giving strange swiftness and double sight, divining the sources of springs beneath the earth or of expression beneath the human countenance, clairvoyant of occult gifts in common or uncommon things, in the reed at the brook-side, or the star which draws near to us but once in a century. How, in this way, the clear purpose was overclouded, the fine chaser's hand perplexed, we but dimly see; the mystery which at no point quite lifts from Leonardo's life is deepest here. But it is certain that at one period of his life he had almost ceased to be an artist.

The year 1483—the year of the birth of Raphael and the thirty-first of Leonardo's life—is fixed as the date of his visit to Milan by the letter in which he recommends himself to Ludovico Sforza, and offers to tell him, for a price, strange secrets in the art of war. It was that Sforza who murdered his young nephew by slow poison, yet was so susceptible of religious impressions that he blended mere earthly passion with a sort of religious sentimentalism, and who took for his device the mulberry-tree—symbol, in its long delay and sudden yielding of flowers and fruit together, of a wisdom which economises all forces for an opportunity of sudden and sure effect. The fame of Leonardo had gone before him, and he was to model a colossal statue of Francesco, the first Duke of Milan. As for Leonardo himself, he came not as an artist at all, or careful of the fame of one; but as a player on the harp, a strange harp of silver of his own construction, shaped in some curious likeness to a horse's skull. The capricious spirit of Ludovico was susceptible also to the power of music, and Leonardo's nature had a kind of spell in it. Fascination is always the word descriptive of him. No portrait of his youth remains; but all tends to make us believe that up to this time some charm of voice and aspect, strong enough to balance the disadvantage of his birth, had played about him. His physical strength was great; it was said that he could bend a horseshoe like a coil of lead.

The *Duomo*,[1] work of artists from beyond the Alps, so fantastic to the eye of a Florentine used to the mellow, unbroken surfaces of Giotto and Arnolfo, was then in all its freshness; and below, in the streets of Milan, moved a people as fantastic, changeful, and dreamlike. To Leonardo least of all men could there be anything poisonous in the exotic flowers of sentiment which grew there. It was a life of brilliant sins and exquisite amusements: Leonardo became a celebrated designer of pageants; and it suited the quality of his genius, composed, in almost equal parts, of curiosity and the desire of beauty, to take things as they came.

Curiosity and the desire of beauty—these are two elementary forces in Leonardo's genius; curiosity often in conflict with the desire of beauty, but generating, in union with it, a type of subtle and curious grace.

The movement of the fifteenth century was twofold; partly the Renaissance, partly also the coming of what is called the "modern spirit," with its realism, its appeal to experience. It comprehended a return to antiquity, and a return to nature. Raphael represents the return to antiquity, and Leonardo the return to nature. In this return to nature, he was seeking to satisfy a boundless curiosity by her perpetual surprises, a microscopic sense of finish by her *finesse*, or delicacy of operation, that *subtilitas naturae* which Bacon notices. So we find him often in intimate relations with men of science,—with Fra Luca Paccioli the mathematician, and the anatomist Marc Antonio della Torre. His observations and experiments fill thirteen volumes of manuscript; and those who can judge describe him as anticpating long before, by rapid intuition, the later ideas of science. He explained the obscure light of the unilluminated part of the moon, knew that the sea had once covered the mountains which contain shells, and of the gathering of the equatorial waters above the polar.

He who thus penetrated into the most secret parts of nature preferred always the more to the less remote, what, seeming exceptional, was an instance of law more refined, the construction about things of a peculiar atmosphere and mixed lights. He paints flowers with such curious felicity that different writers have attributed to him a fondness for particular flowers, as Clement the cyclamen, and Rio the jasmin; while, at Venice, there is a stray leaf from his portfolio dotted all over with studies of violets and the wild rose. In him first appears the taste for what is *bizarre* or *recherche* in landscape; hollow places full of the green shadow of bituminous rocks, ridged reefs of trap-rock which cut the water into quaint sheets of light,—their exact antitype is in our own western seas; all the solemn effects of moving water. You may follow it springing from its distant source among the rocks on the heath of the *Madonna of the Balances*, passing, as a little fall, into the treacherous calm of the *Madonna of the Lake*, as a goodly river next, below the cliffs of the *Madonna of the Rocks*, washing the white walls of its distant villages, stealing out in a network of divided streams in *La Gioconda* to the seashore of the *Saint Anne*—that delicate place, where the wind passes like the hand of some fine etcher over the surface, and the untorn shells are lying thick upon the sand, and the tops of the rocks, to which the waves never rise, are green with grass, grown fine as hair. It is the landscape, not of dreams or of fancy, but of places far withdrawn, and hours selected from a thousand with a miracle of *finesse*. Through Leonardo's strange veil of sight things reach him so; in no ordinary night or day, but as in faint light of eclipse, or in some brief interval of falling rain at daybreak, or through deep water.

And not into nature only; but he plunged also into human personality, and became above all a painter of portraits; faces of a modelling more skilful than has been seen before or since, embodied with a reality which almost amounts to illusion, on the dark air. To take a character as it was, and delicately sound its stops, suited one so curious in observation, curious in invention. He painted thus the portraits of Ludovico's mistresses, Lucretia Crivelli and Cecilia Galerani the poetess, of Ludovico himself, and the Duchess Beatrice. The portrait of Cecilia Galerani is lost, but that of Lucretia Crivelli has been identified with *La Belle Feronière* of the Louvre, and Ludovico's pale, anxious face still remains in the Ambrosian library. Opposite is the portrait of Beatrice d'Este, in whom Leonardo seems to have caught some presentiment of early death, painting her precise and grave, full of the refinement of the dead, in sad earth-coloured raiment, set with pale stones.

Sometimes this curiosity came in conflict with the desire of beauty; it tended to make him go too far below that outside of things in which art really begins and ends. This struggle between the reason and its ideas, and the senses, the desire of beauty, is the key to Leonardo's life at Milan—his restlessness, his endless retouchings, his odd experiments with colour. How much must he leave unfinished, how much recommence! His problem was the transmutation of ideas into images. What he had attained so far had been the mastery of that earlier Florentine style, with its naive and limited sensousness. Now he was to entertain in this narrow medium those divinations of a humanity too wide for it, that larger vision of the opening world, which is only not too much for the great, irregular art of Shakespeare; and everywhere the effort is visible in the work of his hands. This agitation, this perpetual delay, give him an air of weariness and *ennui*.[2] To others he seems to be aiming at an impossible effect, to do something that art, that painting, can never do. Often the expression of physical beauty at this or that point seems strained and marred in the effort, as in those heavy German foreheads—too heavy and German for perfect beauty.

For there was a touch of Germany in that genius which, as Goethe[3] said, had "thought itself weary"—*müde sich gedacht*. What an anticipation of modern Germany, for instance, in that debate on the question whether sculpture or painting is the nobler art! But there is this difference between him and the German, that, with all that curious science, the German would have thought nothing more was needed. The name of Goethe himself reminds one how great for the artist may be the danger of overmuch science; how Goethe, who, in the *Elective Affinities* and the first part of *Faust*, does transmute ideas into images, who wrought many such transmutations, did not invariably find the spellword, and in the second part of *Faust* presents us with a mass of science which has almost no artistic character at all. But Leonardo will never work till the happy moment comes—that moment of *bien-être*,[4] which to imaginative men is a moment of invention. On this he waits with a perfect patience; other moments are but a preparation, or after-taste of it. Few men distinguish between them as jealously as he. Hence so many flaws even in the choicest work. But for Leonardo the distinction is absolute, and, in the moment of *bien-être*, the alchemy complete: the idea is stricken into colour and imagery: a cloudy mysticism is refined to a subdued and graceful mystery, and painting pleases the eye while it satisfies the soul.

This curious beauty is seen above all in his drawings, and in these chiefly in the abstract grace of the bounding lines. Let us take some of these drawings, and pause over them awhile; and, first, óne of those at Florence—the heads of a woman and a little child, set side by side, but each in its own separate frame. First of all, there is much pathos in the reappearance, in the fuller curves of the face of the child, of the sharper, more chastened lines of the worn and older face, which leaves no doubt that the heads are those of a little child and its mother. A feeling for maternity is indeed always characteristic of Leonardo; and this feeling is further indicated here by the half-humorous pathos of the diminutive, rounded shoulders of the child. You may note a like pathetic power in drawings of a young man, seated in a stooping posture, his face in his hands, as in sorrow; of a slave sitting in an uneasy inclined attitude, in some brief interval of rest; of a small Madonna and Child, peeping sideways in half-reassured terror, as a mighty griffin with batlike wings, one of Leonardo's finest *inventions*, descends suddenly from the air to snatch up a great wild beast wandering near them. But note in these, as that which especially belongs to art, the contour of the young man's hair, the poise of the slave's arm above his head, and the curves of the head of the child, following the little skull within, thin and fine as some sea-shell worn by the wind.

Take again another head, still more full of sentiment, but of a different kind, a little drawing in red chalk which every one will remember who has examined at all carefully the drawings by old masters at the Louvre. It is a face of doubtful sex, set in the shadow of its own hair, the cheek-line in high light against it, with something voluptuous and full in the eyelids and the lips. Another drawing might pass for the same face in childhood, with parched and feverish lips, but much sweetness in the loose, short-waisted childish dress, with necklace and *bulla,* and in the daintily bound hair. We might, take the thread of suggestion which these two drawings offer, when thus set side by side, and, following it through the drawings at Florence, Venice, and Milan, construct a sort of series, illustrating better than anything else Leonardo's type of womanly beauty. Daughters of Herodias, with their fantastic head-dresses knotted and folded so strangely to leave the dainty oval of the face disengaged, they are not of the Christian family, or of Raphael's. They are the clairvoyants, through whom, as through delicate instruments, one becomes aware of the subtler forces of nature, and the modes of their action, all that is magnetic in it, all those finer conditions wherein material things rise to that subtlety of operation which constitutes them spiritual, where only the final nerve and the keener touch can follow. It is as if in certain significant examples we actually saw those forces at their work on human flesh. Nervous, electric, faint always with some inexplicable faintness, these people seem to be subject to exceptional conditions, to feel powers at work in the common air unfelt by others, to become, as it were, the receptacle of them, and pass them on to us in a chain of secret influences.

But among the more youthful heads there is one at Florence which Love chooses for its own—the head of a young man, which may well be the likeness of Andrea Salaino, beloved of Leonardo for his curled and waving hair—*belli capelli ricci e inanellati*—and afterwards his favourite pupil and servant. Of all the interests in living men and women which may have filled his life at Milan, this attachment alone is recorded. And in return Salaino identified himself so entirely with Leonardo, that the picture of *Saint Anne*, in the Louvre, has been attributed to him. It illustrates Leonardo's usual choice of pupils, men of some natural charm of person or intercourse like Salaino, or men of birth and princely habits of life like Francesco Melzi—men with just enough genius to be capable of initiation into his secret, for the sake of which they were ready to efface their own individuality. Among them, retiring often to the villa of the Melzi at *Carnonica al Vaprio*, he worked at his fugitive manuscripts and sketches, working for the present hour, and for a few only, perhaps chiefly for himself. Other artists have been as careless of present or future applause, in self-forgetfulness, or because they set moral or political ends above the ends of art; but in him this solitary culture of beauty seems to have hung upon a kind of self-love, and a carelessness in the work of art of all but art itself. One of the secret places of a unique temperament he brought strange blossoms and fruits hitherto unknown; and for him, the novel impression conveyed, the exquisite effect woven, counted as an end in itself—a perfect end.

And these pupils of his acquired his manner so thoroughly, that though the number of Leonardo's authentic works is very small indeed, there is a multitude of other men's pictures through which we undoubtedly see him, and come very near to his genius. Sometimes, as in the little picture of the *Madonna of the Balances*, in which, from the bosom of His mother, Christ weighs the pebbles of the brook against the sins of men, we have a hand, rough enough by contrast, working upon some fine hint or sketch of his. Sometimes, as in the subjects of the *Daughter of Herodias* and the *Head of John the Baptist*, the lost originals have been re-echoed and varied upon again and again by Luini and others. At other times the original remains, but has been a mere theme or motive, a type of which the accessories might be modified or changed; and these variations have but brought out the more the purpose, or expression of the original. It is so with the so-called *Saint John the Baptist* of the Louvre—one of the few naked figures Leonardo painted—whose delicate brown flesh and woman's hair no one would go out into the wilderness to seek, and whose treacherous smile would have us understand something far beyond the outward gesture or circumstance. But the long, reedlike cross in the hand, which suggests Saint John the Baptist, becomes faint in a copy at the Ambrosian Library, and disappears altogether in another version, in the *Palazzo Rosso* at Genoa. Returning from the latter to the original, we are no longer surprised by Saint John's strange likeness to the *Bacchus* which hangs near it, and which set Theophile Gautier thinking of Heine's notion of decayed gods, who, to maintain themselves, after the fall of paganism, took employment in the new religion. We recognise one of those symbolical inventions in which the ostensible subject is used, not as matter for definite pictorial realisation, but as the starting-point of a train of sentiment, subtle and vague as a piece of music. No one ever ruled over the mere *subject* in hand more entirely than Leonardo, or bent it more dexterously to purely artistic ends. And so it comes to pass that though he handles sacred subjects continually, he is the most profane of painters; the given person or subject, Saint John in the Desert, or the Virgin on the knees of Saint Anne, is often merely the pretext for a kind of work which carries one altogether beyond the range of its conventional associations.

About the *Last Supper*, its decay and restorations, a whole literature has risen up, Goethe's pensive sketch of its sad fortunes being perhaps the best. The death in childbirth of the Duchess Beatrice was followed in Ludovico by one of those paroxysms of religious feeling which in him wer constitutional. The low, gloomy Dominican church of *Saint Mary of the Graces* had been the favourite oratory of Beatrice. She had spent her last days there, full of sinister presentiments; at last it had been almost necessary to remove her from it by force; and now it was here that mass was said a hundred times a day for her repose. On the damp wall of the refectory, oozing with mineral salts, Leonardo painted the *Last Supper*. Effective anecdotes were told about it, his retouchings and delays. They show him refusing to work except at the moment of invention, scornful of any one who supposed that art could be a work of mere industry and rule, often coming the whole length of Milan to give a single touch. He painted it, not in fresco, where all must be *impromptu* but in oils, the new method which he had been one of the first to welcome, because it allowed of so many afterthoughts, so refined a working out of perfection. It turned out that on a plastered wall no process could have been less durable. Within fifty years it had fallen into decay. And now we have to turn back to Leonardo's own studies, above all to one drawing of the central head at the *Brera*, which, in a union of tenderness and severity in the face-lines, reminds one of the monumental work of Mino da Fiesole, to trace it as it was.

Here was another effort to lift a given subject out of the range of its traditional associations. Strange, after all the mystic developments of the middle age, was the effort to see the Eucharist, not as the pale Host of the altar, but as one taking leave of his friends. Five years afterwards the young Raphael, at Florence, painted it with sweet and solemn effect in the refectory of Saint Onofrio; but still with all the mystical unreality of the school of Perugino. Vasari pretends that the central head was never finished. But finished or unfinished, or owing part of its effect to a mellowing decay, the head of Jesus does not consummate the sentiment of the whole company—hosts through which you see the wall, faint as the shadows of the leaves upon the wall on autumn afternoons. This figure is but the faintest, the most spectral of them all.

The *Last Supper* was finished in 1497; in 1498 the French entered Milan, and whether or not the Gascon bowmen used it as a mark for their arrows, the model of Francesco Sforza certainly did not survive. What, in that age, such work was capable of being—of what nobility, amid what racy truthfulness to fact—we may judge from the bronze statue of Bartolomeo Colleoni on horseback, modelled by Leonardo's master, Verrocchio (he died of grief, it was said, because, the mould accidentally failing, he was unable to complete it), still standing in the *piazza* of Saint John and Saint Paul at Venice. Some traces of the thing may remain in certain of Leonardo's drawings, and perhaps also, by a singular circumstance, in a far-off town of France. For Ludovico became a prisoner, and ended his days at Loches in Touraine. After many years of captivity in the dungeons below, where all seems sick with barbarous feudal memories, he was allowed at last, it is said, to breathe fresher air for awhile in one of the rooms of the great tower still shown, its walls covered with strange painted arabesques, ascribed by tradition to his hand, amused a little, in this way, through the tedious years. In those vast helmets and human faces and pieces of armour, among which, in great letters, the motto *Infelix Sum* is woven in and out, it is perhaps not too fanciful to see the fruit of a wistful after-dreaming over Leonardo's sundry experiments on the armed figure of the great duke, which had occupied the two so much during the days of their good fortune at Milan.

The remaining years of Leonardo's life are more or less years of wandering. From his brilliant life at court he had saved nothing, and he returned to Florence a poor man. Perhaps necessity kept his spirit excited: the next four years are one prolonged rapture or ecstasy of invention. He painted now the pictures of the Louvre, his most authentic works, which came there straight from the cabinet of Francis the First, at Fontainebleau. One picture of his, the *Saint Anne*—not the *Saint Anne* of the Louvre, but a simple cartoon, now in London—revived for a moment a sort of appreciation more common in an earlier time, when good pictures had still seemed miraculous. For two days a crowd of people of all qualities passed in naive excitement through the chamber where it hung, and gave Leonardo a taste of the "triumph" of Cimabue. But his work was less with the saints than with the living women of Florence. For he lived still in the polished society that he loved, and in the houses of Florence, left perhaps a little subject to light thoughts by the death of Savonarola—the latest gossip (1869) is of an undraped Mona Lisa, found in some out-of-the-way corner of the late *Orleans* collection—he saw Ginevra di Benci, and Lisa, the young third wife of Francesco del Giocondo. As we have seen him using incidents of sacred story, not for their own sake, or as mere subjects for pictorial realisation, but as a cryptic language for fancies all his own, so now he found a vent for his thought in taking one of these languid women, and raising her, as Leda or Pomona, as Modesty or Vanity, to the seventh heaven of symbolical expression.

La Gioconda is, in the truest sense, Leonardo's masterpiece, the revealing instance of his mode of thought and work. In suggestiveness, only the *Melancholia* of Durer is comparable to it; and no crude symbolism disturbs the effect of its subdued and graceful mystery. We all know the face and hands of the figure, set in its marble chair, in that circle of fantastic rocks, as in some faint light under sea. Perhaps of all ancient pictures time has chilled it least. As often happens with works in which invention seems to reach its limit, there is an element in it given to, not invented by, the master. In that inestimable folio of drawings, once in the possession of Vasari, were certain designs by Verrocchio, faces of such impressive beauty that Leonardo in his boyhood copied them many times. It is hard not to connect with these designs of the elder, by-past master, as with its germinal principle, the unfathomable smile, always with a touch of something sinister in it, which plays over all Leonardo's work. Besides, the picture is a portrait. From childhood we see this image defining itself on the fabric of his dreams; and but for express historical testimony, we might fancy that this was but his ideal lady, embodied and beheld at last. What was the relationship of a living Florentine to this creature of his thought? By what strange affinities had the dream and the person grown up thus apart, and yet so closely together? Present from the first incorporeally in Leonardo's brain, dimly traced in the designs of Verrocchio, she is found present at last in *Il Giocondo*'s house. That there is much of mere portraiture in the picture is attested by the legend that by artificial means, the presence of mimes and flute-players, that subtle expression was protracted on the face. Again, was it in four years and by renewed labour never really completed, or in four months and as by stroke of magic, that the image was projected?

The presence that rose thus so strangely beside the waters, is expressive of what in the ways of a thousand years men had come to desire. Hers is the head upon which all "the ends of the world are come," and the eyelids are a little weary. It is a beauty wrought out from within upon the flesh, the deposit, little cell by cell, of strange thoughts and fantastic reveries and exquisite passions. Set it for a moment beside one of those white Greek goddesses or beautiful women of antiquity, and how would they be troubled by this beauty, into which the soul with all its maladies has passed! All the thoughts and experience of the world have etched and moulded there, in that which they have of power to refine and make expressive the outward form, the animalism of Greece, the lust of Rome, the mysticism of the middle age with its spiritual ambition and imaginative loves, the return of the Pagan world, the sins of the Borgias. She is older than the rocks among which she sits; like the vampire, she has been dead many times, and learned the secrets of the grave; and has been a diver in deep seas, and keeps their fallen day about her; and trafficked for strange webs with Eastern merchants; and, as Leda, was the mother of Helen of Troy, and, as Saint Anne, the mother of Mary; and all this has been to her but as the sound of lyres and flutes, and lives only in the delicacy with which it has moulded the changing lineaments, and tinged the eyelids and the hands. The fancy of a perpetual life, sweeping together ten thousand experiences, is an old one; and modern philosophy has conceived the idea of humanity as wrought upon by, and summing up in itself, all modes of thought and life. Certainly Lady Lisa might stand as the embodiment of the old fancy, the symbol of the modern idea.

Notes

[1] *Duomo* is an Italian cathedral. Milan's *duomo* is the third largest in Europe, after St. Peter's in Rome and Seville's cathedral.

[2] *Ennui*: "boredom" in French.

³ Goethe: (1749–1832), the great German poet, novelist, and playwright, is best known for his dramatic verse masterpiece *Faust*.

⁴ *bien-être*: "well-being" in French.

FOCUS: READING REVIEW

1. What does the picture of da Vinci's youth have on the character of the artist Pater is creating?
2. What personality emerges for da Vinci from Pater's biographical sketch? How is this personality created?
3. What significance does Pater find in da Vinci's interest in nature? How does this affect his painting?
4. Pater says that Goethe "reminds one how great for the artist may be the danger of overmuch science." What does this mean? What does it illustrate about da Vinci?
5. What concrete details does Pater provide about the *Mona Lisa?* What in his description creates his own image of her?

FOCUS: AUTHOR'S STRATEGIES

1. Pater's own philosophy is stated in "the way to perfection is through a series of disgusts." How does he shape the biographical material to illustrate his own perspective?
2. In his description of Leonardo's drawings, Pater's language, as much as the paintings themselves, creates the mood. How does his language operate here?

FOCUS: DISCUSSION AND WRITING

What does Pater's study suggest about the creative experience? What does it reveal about criticism?

HARMONY ATTAINED
E. H. Gombrich

In his 1972 study The Story of Art, *Gombrich relates art history in terms of the "culture of the arts," a period's conventions, and the artists' own experiments and innovations. This study repudiates the idea that art has evolved to a better and better imitation of reality and suggests instead that each culture has valued a different way of representing experience. This selection on da Vinci describes the social environment that enabled the Italian Renaissance artists to achieve their artistic triumphs and, more particularly, how da Vinci's own nature studies and experimentation with his medium led to his renowned works, the* Last Supper *and the* Mona Lisa. *Information on Gombrich appears in the headnote to his essay "Conditions of Illusion" in chapter 10.*

The beginning of the sixteenth century, the *Cinquecento*, is the most famous period of Italian art, one of the greatest periods of all time. We can try to see what the conditions were which made this sudden efflorescence of genius possible. The pride of the cities was a great incentive to the masters to outdo each other. [The Renaissance discoveries] brought the Italian artist to mathematics to study the laws of perspective and to anatomy to study the build of the human body. The love of fame on the patrons' part, which made them seek immortality in buildings, tombs, and painting, placed a premium on the talents of great artists. In no sphere was the effect of this change so marked as in architecture.

Leonardo da Vinci (1452–1519), the oldest of these famous masters, was born in a Tuscan village. He was apprenticed to a leading Florentine workshop, [where he learned his craft]. In the case of any other gifted boy, this training would have been sufficient to make a respectable artist. But Leonardo was more than a gifted boy. He was a genius. He thought that the artist's business was to explore the visible world with greater intensity and accuracy [than his predecessors]. He thought that by placing it on scientific foundations he could transform his beloved art of painting from a humble craft into an honored and gentlemanly pursuit. It is possible that this view often affected Leonardo's relationship with his patrons. We know that Leonardo often failed to carry out his commissions. By a singular misfortune, the few works which Leonardo did complete have come to us in a very bad state of preservation. When we look at what remains of the famous wall-painting of the 'Last Supper' we must imagine how it may have appeared to the monks for whom it was painted. There was nothing in this work that resembled older representations of the same theme. There was drama in it, and excitement. Far beyond such technical matters as composition and draftsmanship, we must admire Leonardo's deep insight into the behavior and reactions of man, and the power of imagination which enabled him to put the scene before our eyes.

There is another work of Leonardo's which is perhaps even more famous than 'The Last Supper'. It is the portrait of a Florentine lady whose name was Lisa. 'Mona Lisa'. What strikes us first is the amazing degree to which Lisa looks alive. Leonardo certainly knew how he achieved this effect, and by what means. The painter must leave the beholder something to guess. If the outlines are not quite so firmly drawn, if the form is left a little vague, stiffness will be avoided. This is Leonardo's famous invention which the Italians call *'sfumato'*—the blurred outline and mellowed colours that allow one form to merge with another and always leave something to our imagination. Leonardo has used this with the corners of the mouth and the corners of the eyes—the place where expression mainly rests—in the 'Mona Lisa'.

The beginning of the sixteenth century, the *Cinquecento*, is the most famous period of Italian art, one of the greatest periods of all time. This was the time of Leonardo da Vinci and Michelangelo, of Raphael and Titian, of Correggio and Giorgione, of Durer and Holbein in the North, and of many other famous masters.

One may well ask why it was that all these great masters were born in the same period, but such questions are more easily asked than answered. One cannot explain the existence of genius. It is better to enjoy it. What we have to say, therefore, can never be a full explanation of the great period which is called the High Renaissance, but we can try to see what the conditions were which made this sudden efflorescence of genius possible.

We have seen the beginning of these conditions far back in the time of Giotto,[1] whose fame was so great that the Commune of Florence was proud of him and anxious to have the steeple of their cathedral designed by that widely renowned master. This pride of the cities, which vied with each other in securing the services of the greatest artists to beautify their buildings and to create works of lasting fame, was a great incentive to the masters to outdo each other—an incentive which did not exist to the same extent in the feudal countries of the north, whose cities had much less independence and local pride. Then came the period of the great discoveries, when Italian artists turned to mathematics to study the laws of perspective, and to anatomy to study the build of the human body. Through these discoveries, the artist's horizon widened. He was no longer a craftsman among craftsmen, ready to carry out commissions for shoes, or cupboards, or paintings as the case may be. He was a master in his own right, who could not achieve fame and glory without exploring the mysteries of nature and probing into the secret laws of the universe. It was natural that the leading artists who had these ambitions felt aggrieved at their social status. This was still the same as it had been at the time of ancient Greece, when the snobs might have accepted a poet who worked with his brain, but never an artist who worked with his hands. Here was another challenge for the artists to meet, another spur which urged them on towards yet greater achievements that would compel the surrounding world to accept them, not only as respectable heads of prosperous workshops, but as men of unique and precious gifts. It was a difficult struggle, which was not immediately successful. Social snobbery and prejudice were strong forces, and there were many who would gladly have invited to their tables a scholar who spoke Latin, and knew the right turn of phrase for every occasion, but would have hesitated to extend a similar privilege to a painter or a sculptor. It was again the love of fame on the part of the patrons which helped the artists to break down such prejudices. There were many small courts in Italy which were badly in need of honour and prestige. To erect magnificent buildings, to commission splendid tombs, to order great cycles of frescoes, or dedicate a painting for the high altar of a famous church, was considered a sure way of perpetuating one's name and securing a worthy monument to one's earthly existence. As there were many centres competing for the services of the most renowned masters, the masters in turn could dictate their terms. In earlier times it was the prince who bestowed his favours on the artist. Now it almost came to pass that the roles were reversed, and that the artist granted a favour to a rich prince or potentate by accepting a commission from him. Thus it came about that the artists could frequently choose the kind of commission which they liked, and that they no longer needed to accommodate their works to the whims and fancies of their employers. Whether or not this new power was an unmixed blessing for art in the long run is difficult to decide. But at first, at any rate, it had the effect of a liberation which released a tremendous amount of pent-up energy. At last, the artist was free.

In no sphere was the effect of this change so marked as in architecture. Since the time of Brunelleschi, the architect had had to have some of the knowledge of a classical scholar. He had to know the rules of the ancient 'orders', of the right proportions and measurements of the Doric, Ionic and Corinthian[2] columns and entablatures. He had to measure ancient ruins, and pore over the manuscripts of classical writers like Vitruvius who had codified the conventions of the Greek and Roman architects, and whose works contained many difficult and obscure passages, which challenged the ingenuity of Renaissance scholars. In no other field was the conflict between the requirements of the patrons and the ideals of the artists more apparent than in this field of architecture. What these learned masters really longed to do was to build temples and triumphal arches—what they were asked to do was to build city palaces and churches. We have seen how a compromise was reached in this fundamental conflict by artists such as Alberti, who wedded the ancient 'orders' to the modern city palace. But the true aspiration of the Renaissance architect was still to design a building irrespective of its use; simply for the beauty of its proportions, the spaciousness of its interior and the imposing grandeur of its ensemble. They craved for a perfect symmetry and regularity such as they could not achieve while concentrating on the practical requirements of an ordinary building. It was a memorable moment when one of them found a mighty patron willing to sacrifice tradition and expediency for the sake of the fame he would acquire by erecting a stately structure that would outshine the seven wonders of the world. Only in this way can we understand the decision of Pope Julius II in 1506 to pull down the venerable Basilica of St. Peter which stood at the place where, according to the legend, St. Peter lay buried and to have it built anew in a manner which defied the ago-old traditions of church buildings and the usages of Divine service. The man to whom he entrusted this task was Donato Bramante (1444–1514), an ardent champion of the new style. One of the few of his buildings which have survived intact shows how far Bramante had gone in absorbing the ideas and standards of classical architecture without becoming a slavish imitator. It is a chapel, or 'little temple' as he called it, which should have been surrounded by a cloister in the same style. It is a little pavilion, a round building on steps, crowned by a cupola and ringed round by a colonnade of the Doric order. The balustrade on top of the cornice adds a light and graceful touch to the whole building, and the small structure of the actual chapel and the decorative colonnade are held in a harmony as perfect as that in any temple of classical antiquity.

To this master, then, the Pope had given the task to design the new church of St. Peter, and it was understood that this should become a true marvel of Christendom. Bramante was determined to disregard the Western tradition of a thousand years, according to which a church of this kind should be an oblong hall with the worshippers looking eastwards towards the main altar where Mass is read.

In his craving for that regularity and harmony that alone could be worthy of the place, he designed a circular church with a ring of chapels evenly arranged round a gigantic central hall. This hall was to be crowned by a huge cupola resting on colossal arches. Bramante hoped, it was said, to combine the effects of the largest ancient buildings, whose towering ruins still impressed the visitor to Rome, with that of the Pantheon. For one brief moment, admiration for the art of the ancients and ambition to create something unheard of overruled considerations of expediency and time-honoured traditions. But Bramante's plan for St. Peter's was not destined to be carried out. The enormous building swallowed up so much money that, in trying to raise sufficient funds, the Pope precipitated the crisis which led to the Reformation. It was the practice of selling indulgences[3] against contributions for the building of that church that led Luther in Germany to his first public protest. Even within the Catholic Church, opposition to Bramante's plan increased, and by the time the building had progressed sufficiently, the idea of a circular church was abandoned. St. Peter's, as we know it today, has little in common with the original plan, except its gigantic dimensions.

The spirit of bold enterprise which made Bramante's plan for St. Peter's possible is characteristic of the period of the High Renaissance, the period round about 1500 which produced so many of the world's greatest artists. To these men nothing seemed impossible, and that may be the reason why they did sometimes achieve the apparently impossible. Once more, it was Florence which gave birth to some of the leading minds of that great epoch. Since the days of Giotto round about 1300, and of Masaccio round about 1400, Florentine artists cultivated their tradition with special pride, and their excellence was recognized by all people of taste. We shall see that nearly all the greatest artists grew out of such a firmly established tradition, and that is why we should not forget the humbler masters in whose workshops they learned the elements of their craft.

Leonardo da Vinci (1452–1519), the oldest of these famous masters, was born in a Tuscan village. He was apprenticed to a leading Florentine workshop, that of the painter and sculptor Andrea del Verrocchio (1435–88). Verrocchio's fame was very great, so great indeed that the city of Venice commissioned from him the monument to Bartolomeo Colleoni, one of their generals to whom they owed gratitude for a number of charities he had founded rather than for any particular deed of military prowess. The equestrian statue which Verrocchio made shows that he was a worthy heir to the tradition of Donatello.[4] We see how minutely he studied the anatomy of the horse, and how clearly he observed the position of the muscles and veins. But most admirable of all is the posture of the horseman, who seems to be riding ahead of his troops with an expression of bold defiance. Later times have made us so familiar with these riders of bronze that have come to people our towns and cities, representing more or less worthy emperors, kings, princes and generals, that it may take us some time to realize the greatness and simplicity of Verrocchio's work. It lies in the clear outline which his group presents from nearly all aspects, and in the concentrated energy which seems to animate the man in armour and his mount.

In a workshop capable of producing such masterpieces, the young Leonardo could certainly learn many things. He would be introduced into the technical secrets of foundry-work and other metalwork, he would learn to prepare pictures and statues carefully by making studies from the nude and from draped models. He would learn to study plants and curious animals for inclusion in his pictures, and he would receive a thorough grounding in the optics of perspective, and in the use of colours. In the case of any other gifted boy, this training would have been sufficient to make a respectable artist, and many good painters and sculptors did in fact emerge from Verrocchio's prosperous workshop. But Leonardo was more than a gifted boy. He was a genius whose powerful mind will always remain an object of wonder and admiration to ordinary mortals. We know something of the range and productivity of Leonardo's mind because his pupils and admirers carefully preserved for us his sketches and notebooks, thousands of pages covered with writings and drawings, with excerpts from books Leonardo read, and drafts for books he intended to write. The more one reads of these papers, the less can one understand how one human being could have excelled in all these different fields of research and made important contributions to nearly all of them. Perhaps one of the reasons is that Leonardo was a Florentine artist and not a trained scholar. He thought that the artist's business was to explore the visible world just as his predecessors had done, only more thoroughly and with greater intensity and accuracy. He was not interested in the bookish knowledge of the scholars. Like Shakespeare, he probably had 'little Latin and less Greek'. At a time when the learned men at the universities relied on the authority of the admired ancient writers, Leonardo, the painter, would trust nothing but his own eyes. Whenever he came across a problem, he did not consult the authorities but tried an experiment to solve it. There was nothing in nature which did not arouse his curiosity and challenge his ingenuity. He explored the secrets of the human body by dissecting more than thirty corpses. He was one of the first to probe into the mysteries of the growth of the child in the womb; he investigated the laws of waves and currents; he spent years in observing and analysing the flight of insects and birds, which was to help him to devise a flying machine which he was sure would one day become a reality. The forms of rocks and clouds, the effect of the atmosphere on the colour of distant objects, the laws governing the growth of trees and plants, the harmony of sounds, all these were the objects of his ceaseless research, which was to be the foundation of his art. His contemporaries looked upon Leonardo as a strange and rather uncanny being. Princes and generals wanted to use this astonishing wizard as a military engineer for the building of fortifications and canals, of novel weapons and devices. In times of peace, he would entertain them with mechanical

toys of his own invention, and with the designing of new effects for stage performances and pageantries. He was admired as a great artist, and sought after as a
splendid musician, but, for all that, few people can have had an inkling of the
importance of his ideas or the extent of his knowledge. The reason is that Leonardo never published his writings, and that very few can even have known of
their existence. He was left-handed, and had taken to writing from right to left so
that his notes can only be read in a mirror. It is possible that he was afraid of
divulging his discoveries for fear that his opinions would be found heretical. Thus
we find in his writings the five words 'The sun does not move', which show that
Leonardo anticipated the theories of Copernicus which were later to bring Galileo
into trouble. But it is also possible that he undertook his researches and experiments simply because of his insatiable curiosity, and that, once he had solved a
problem for himself, he was apt to lose interest because there were so many other
mysteries still to be explored. Most of all, it is likely that Leonardo himself had no
ambition to be considered a scientist. All this exploration of nature was to him
first and foremost a means of gaining knowledge of the visible world, such as he
would need for his art. He thought that by placing it on scientific foundations he
could transform his beloved art of painting from a humble craft into an honoured
and gentlemanly pursuit. To us, this preoccupation with the social rank of artists
may be difficult to understand, but we have seen what importance it had for the
men of the period. Perhaps if we remember Shakespeare's *Midsummer Night's
Dream* and the rôles he assigns to Snug the joiner, Bottom the weaver, and Snout
the tinker,[5] we can understand the background of this struggle. Aristotle had codified the snobbishness of classical antiquity in distinguishing between certain arts
that were compatible with a 'liberal education' (the so-called Liberal Arts such as
rhetorics, grammar, philosophy and dialectic) and pursuits that involved working
with the hands, which were 'manual' and therefore 'menial', and thus below the
dignity of a gentleman. It was the ambition of such men as Leonardo to show that
painting was a Liberal Art, and that the manual labour involved in it was no more
essential than was the labour of writing in poetry. It is possible that this view often
affected Leonardo's relationship with his patrons. Perhaps he did not want to be
considered the owner of a shop where anyone could commission a picture. At any
rate, we know that Leonardo often failed to carry out his commissions. He would
start on a painting and leave it unfinished, despite the urgent requests of the patron. Moreover, he obviously insisted that it was he himself who had to decide
when a work of his was to be considered finished, and he refused to let it go out of
his hands unless he was satisfied with it. It is not surprising, therefore, that few of
Leonardo's works were ever completed, and that his contemporaries regretted the
way in which this outstanding genius seemed to fritter away his time, moving
restlessly from Florence to Milan, from Milan to Florence and to the service of the
notorious adventurer Cesare Borgia, then to Rome, and finally to the court of
King Francis I in France, where he died in the year 1519, more admired than
understood.

By a singular misfortune, the few works which Leonardo did complete in his mature years have come down to us in a very bad state of preservation. Thus when we look at what remains of Leonardo's famous wall-painting of the 'Last Supper' we must try to imagine how it may have appeared to the monks for whom it was painted. The painting covers one wall of an oblong hall that was used as a dining-room by the monks of the monastery of Santa Maria delle Grazie in Milan. One must visualize what it was like when the painting was uncovered, and when, side by side with the long tables of the monks, there appeared the table of Christ and his apostles. Never before had the sacred episode appeared so close and so lifelike. It was as if another hall had been added to theirs, in which the Last Supper had assumed tangible form. How clear the light fell on to the table, and how it added roundness and solidity to the figures. Perhaps the monks were first struck by the truth to nature with which all details were portrayed, the dishes on the table-cloth, and the folds of the draperies. Then, as now, works of art were often judged by laymen according to their degree of lifelikeness. But that can only have been the first reaction. Once they had sufficiently admired this extraordinary illusion of reality, the monks would turn to the way in which Leonardo had presented the biblical story. There was nothing in this work that resembled older representations of the same theme. In these traditional versions, the apostles were seen sitting quietly at the table in a row—only Judas being segregated from the rest—while Christ was calmly dispensing the Sacrament. The new picture was very different from any of these paintings. There was drama in it, and excitement. Leonardo, like Giotto before him, had gone back to the text of the Scriptures, and had striven to visualize what it must have been like when Christ said, ' "Verily I say unto you, that one of you shall betray me", and they were exceeding sorrowful and began every one of them to say unto him "Lord, is it I?" ' (Matthew xxvi. 21–2). The gospel of St. John adds that 'Now there was leaning on Jesus' bosom one of his disciples, whom Jesus loved. Simon Peter therefore beckoned to him that he should ask who it should be of whom he spake' (John xiii. 23–4). It is this questioning and beckoning that brings movement into the scene. Christ has just spoken the tragic words, and those on his side shrink back in terror as they hear the revelation. Some seem to protest their love and innocence, others gravely to dispute whom the Lord may have meant, others again seem to look to Him for an explanation of what He has said. St. Peter, most impetuous of all, rushes towards St. John, who sits to the right of Jesus. As he whispers something into St. John's ear, he inadvertently pushes Judas forward. Judas is not segregated from the rest, and yet he seems isolated. He alone does not gesticulate and question. He bends forward and looks up in suspicion or anger, a dramatic contrast to the figure of Christ sitting calm and resigned amidst this surging turmoil. One wonders how long it took the first spectators to realize the consummate art by which all this dramatic movement was controlled. Despite the excitement which Christ's words have caused, there is nothing chaotic in the picture. The twelve apostles seem to fall quite naturally into four groups of three, linked to each other by gestures and movements. There is so much order in this variety, and so much variety in this order, that one can never quite exhaust the harmonious interplay of movement and answering movement. Perhaps we can only fully appreciate Leonardo's achievement in this composition if we think back to the problem in the description of Pollaiuolo's 'St. Sebastian'. We remember how the artists of that generation had struggled to combine the demands of realism with that of design. We remember how rigid and artificial Pollaiuolo's solution of this problem looked to us. Leonardo, who was little younger that Pollaiuolo, had solved it with apparent ease. If one forgets for a moment what the scene represents, one can still enjoy the beautiful pattern formed by the figures. The composition seems to have that effortless balance and harmony which it had in Gothic paintings, and which artists like Rogier van der Weyden and Botticelli, each in his own way, had tried to recapture for art. But Leonardo did not find it necessary to sacrifice correctness of drawing, or accuracy of observation, to the demands of a satisfying outline. If one forgets the beauty of the composition, one suddenly feels confronted with a piece of reality as convincing and striking as any we saw in the works of Masaccio or Donatello. And even this achievement hardly touches upon the true greatness of the work. For, beyond such technical matters as composition and draughtsmanship, we must admire Leonardo's deep insight into the behaviour and reactions of man, and the power of imagination which enabled him to put the scene before our eyes. An eye-witness tells us that he often saw Leonardo at work on the 'Last Supper'. He would get on to the scaffolding and stand there for a whole day, just thinking, without painting a single stroke. It is the result of this thought that he has bequeathed to us, and, even in its ruined state, 'The Last Supper' remains one of the great miracles wrought by human genius.

There is another work of Leonardo's which is perhaps even more famous than 'The Last Supper'. It is the portrait of a Florentine lady whose name was Lisa, 'Mona Lisa'. A fame as great as that of Leonardo's 'Mona Lisa' is not an unmixed blessing for a work of art. We become so used to seeing it on picture postcards, and even advertisements, that we find it difficult to see it with fresh eyes as the painting of a real man portraying a real person of flesh and blood. But it is worth while to forget what we know, or believe we know, about the picture, and to look at it as if we were the first people ever to set eyes on it. What strikes us first is the amazing degree to which Lisa looks alive. She really seems to look at us and to have a mind of her own. Like a living being, she seems to change before our eyes and to look a little different every time we come back to her. Even in photographs of the picture we experience this strange effect, but in front of the original in the Paris Louvre it is almost uncanny. Sometimes she seems to mock at us, and then again we seem to catch something like sadness in her smile. All this sounds rather mysterious, and so it is; that is the effect of every great work of art. Nevertheless, Leonardo certainly knew how he achieved this effect, and by what means. That great observer of nature knew more about the way we use our eyes than anybody who had ever lived before him. He had clearly seen a problem which the conquest of nature had posed to the artists—a problem no less intricate than the one of combining correct drawing with a harmonious composition. The great works of the Italian Quattrocento masters who followed the lead given by Masaccio have one thing in common: their figures looked somewhat hard and harsh, almost wooden. The strange thing is that it clearly is not lack of patience or lack of knowledge that is responsible for this effect. No one could be more patient in his imitation of nature than Van Eyck;[6] no one could know more about correct drawing and perspective than Mantegna.[7] And yet, for all the grandeur and impressiveness of their representations of nature, their figures look more like statues than living beings. The reason may be that the more conscientiously we copy a figure line by line and detail by detail, the less we can imagine that it ever really moved and breathed. It looks as if the painter had suddenly cast a spell over it, and forced it to stand stock-still for evermore, like the people in 'The Sleeping Beauty'. Artists had tried various ways out of this difficulty. Botticelli,[8] for instance, had tried to emphasize in his pictures the waving hair and the fluttering garments of his figures, to make them look less rigid in outline. But only Leonardo found the true solution to the problem. The painter must leave the beholder something to guess. If the outlines are not quite so firmly drawn, if the form is left a little vague, as though disappearing into a shadow, this impression of dryness and stiffness will be avoided. This is Leonardo's famous invention which the Italians call 'sfu-mato'—the blurred outline and mellowed colours that allow one form to merge with another and always leave something to our imagination. If we now return to the 'Mona Lisa', we may understand something of its mysterious effect. We see that Leonardo has used the means of his 'sfumato' with the utmost deliberation. Everyone who has ever tried to draw or scribble a face knows that what we call its expression rests mainly in two features: the corners of the mouth, and the corners of the eyes. Now it is precisely these parts which Leonardo has left deliberately indistinct, by letting them merge into soft shadow. That is why we are never quite certain in what mood Mona Lisa is really looking at us. Her expression always seems just to elude us. It is not only vagueness, of course, which produces this effect. There is much more behind it. Leonardo has done a very daring thing, which perhaps only a painter of his consummate mastership could risk. If we look carefully at the picture, we see that the two sides do not quite match. This is most obvious in the fantastic dream landscape in the background. The horizon on the left side seems to lie much lower than the one on the right. Consequently, when we focus the left side of the picutre, the woman looks somehow taller or more erect than if we focus the right side. And her face, too, seems to change with this change of position, because, even here, the two sides do not quite match. But with all these sophisticated tricks, Leonardo might have produced a clever piece of jugglery rather than a great work of art, had he not known exactly how far he could go, and had he not counterbalanced his daring deviation from nature by an almost miraculous rendering of the living flesh. Look at the way in which he modelled the hand, or the sleeves with their minute folds. Leonardo could be as painstaking as any of his forerunners in the patient observation of nature. Only he was no longer merely the faithful servant of nature. Long ago, in the distant past, people had looked at portraits with awe, because they had thought that in preserving the likeness the artist could somehow preserve the soul of the person he portrayed. Now the great scientist, Leonardo, had made some of the dreams and fears of these first image-makers come true. He knew the spell which would infuse life into the colours spread by his magic brush.

Notes

[1] Giotto (1266–1377), a Florentine painter, determined the course of European painting by breaking Byzantine formulas and creating figures with mass.

[2] Doric, Ionic, and Corinthian describe three columns found in ancient Greek architecture. The Doric column has no base; it has twenty flutes and is topped by a simple capital (or cap). The Ionic column is slenderer than Doric; it has twenty-four flutes and its capital is spreading and scroll-shaped. The Corinthian column is similar to the Ionic but is more slender. Its top is circular and decorated by layered leaves resembling artichokes.

[3] Indulgences were written forgivenesses of sin signed by the Pope.

[4] Donatello (1386?–1466) was a Florentine sculptor viewed as one of Renaissance art's great innovators.

[5] Smug, Bottom, and Snout are Shakespeare's common laborers tormented and rendered ridiculous by fairies in *A Midsummer Night's Dream.*

[6] Jan Van Eyck (1370–1426), a Flemish painter, played a crucial role in perfecting the medium of oil. His interest in texture representing such material substances as laces or jewels influenced the Flemish School.

[7] Andrea Mantegna (1431–1506), an Italian painter of the Paduan School, was one of Northern Italy's most celebrated artists whose work evidenced his interest in Greek and Roman art.

[8] Sandro Botticelli (1444–1510), the Florentine painter who was a Medici family favorite, was a master of rhythmic line and color.

FOCUS: READING REVIEW

1. What circumstances in Renaissance life raised the status of artists from artisans to masters?
2. What about Bramante's plan for St. Peter's in Rome reflects Renaissance reliance on classical models? What characterized the "spirit" of the High Renaissance?
3. What is remarkable about Verrocchio's equestrian statue? Why does Gombrich include this example in his discussion of da Vinci?
4. What kind of research did da Vinci do and why?
5. Why does so little remain of da Vinci's art?
6. How does da Vinci's *Last Supper* differ from earlier paintings done on the same subject?
7. Explain the artistic technique da Vinci discovered which gives the *Mona Lisa* an impression of reality.

FOCUS: AUTHOR'S STRATEGIES

1. For what audience is Gombrich writing? How do his explanations and definitions indicate this?
2. The author develops this essay through different kinds of analysis—causal analysis, spatial analysis, and analysis of artistic technique. Explain how he uses these by referring to specific sections of the essay.

FOCUS: DISCUSSION AND WRITING

1. What does Gombrich's treatment of the Renaissance suggest about the evolution of art?
2. Based on this selection, what criteria does Gombrich apply to judge greatness in an artist or a work of art?
3. Explain to what degree Gombrich's discussion of the circumstances of da Vinci's life increases your appreciation of his art.

From *The Pleasures of Listening to Music*
Aaron Copland

Aaron Copland (b. 1900), the recognized American composer, has written several books on music and taught music composition at Harvard. Among his best known musical scores are Appalachian Spring *(1944), which won a Pulitzer Prize,* Billy the Kid *(1938), and* Rodeo *(1942). Copland's music uses classical structures, asymmetrical rhythms, and folk melodies. His books on music include* What We Listen For in Music *(1939),* Music and Imagination *(1952), and* Copland on Music *(1960), from which this selection is taken. "The Pleasures of Listening to Music," which was delivered in the Distinguished Lecture Series at the University of New Hampshire in 1959, performs one of writing's most difficult tasks—describing music. It is often difficult to imagine unfamiliar music from reading a description, but Copland's metaphors and images draw us near to the experience he describes.*

Our musical instinct is one of the prime puzzles of consciousness. The physical nature of sound has been thoroughly explored; but the phenomenon of music as an expressive, communicative agency remains as inexplicable as ever it was. Meaningful music demands one's undivided attention. When serious music is listened to in this way, music gives pleasure simultaneously on the lowest and highest levels of apprehension. Our love of music is bound up with its forward motion; nonetheless it is precisely the creation of that sense of flow, its interrelation with and resultant effect upon formal structure that calls forth high intellectual capacities of a composer, and offers keen pleasures for listening. Musical flow is largely the result of musical rhythm. Tone color is another basic element in music that may be enjoyed on various levels of perception. An infinitude of possible color combinations is available when instruments are mixed, especially when combined in that wonderful contraption, the symphony orchestra. Part of the pleasure of being sensitive to the use of color in music is to note in what way a composer's personality traits are revealed in his tonal color schemes. Thus far I have been dealing with generalities. Now I wish to concentrate on the music of a few composers. Verdi can be commonplace at times, but his saving grace is a burning sincerity. The musician who came closest to composing without human flaw was Johann Sebastian Bach. Never since that time has music so successfully fused contrapuntal skill with harmonic logic. Those interested in studying the relationship between a composer and his work should turn especially to the life and work of Ludwig van Beethoven. His finest works are the enactment of a triumph.

Perhaps I had better begin by explaining that I think of myself as a composer of music and not as a writer about music. This distinction may not seem important to you, especially when I admit to having published several books on the subject. But to me the distinction is paramount because I know that if I were a writer I would be bubbling over with word-ideas about the art I practice, instead of which my mind—and not my mind only but my whole physical being—vibrates to the stimulus of sound waves produced by instruments sounding alone or together. Why this is so I cannot tell you, but I can assure you it is so. Remembering then that I am primarily a composer and not a writer, I shall examine my subject mostly from the composer's standpoint in order to share with others, in so far as that is possible, the varied pleasures to be derived from experiencing music as an art.

That music gives pleasure is axiomatic. Because that is so, the pleasures of music as a subject for discussion may seem to some of you a rather elementary dish to place before so knowing an audience. But I think you will agree that the source of that pleasure, our musical instinct, is not at all emementary; it is, in fact, one of the prime puzzles of consciousness. Why is it that sound waves, when they strike the ear, cause "volleys of nerve impulses to flow up into the brain," resulting in a pleasurable sensation? More than that, why is it that we are able to make sense out of these "volleys of nerve signals" so that we emerge from engulfment in the orderly presentation of sound stimuli as if we had lived through a simulacrum[1] of life, the instinctive life of the emotions? And why, when safely seated and merely listening, should our hearts beat faster, our temperature rise, our toes start tapping, our minds start racing after the music, hoping it will go one way and watching it go another, deceived and disgruntled when we are unconvinced, elated and grateful when we acquiesce?

We have a part answer, I suppose, in that the physical nature of sound has been thoroughly explored; but the phenomenon of music as an expressive, communicative agency remains as inexplicable as ever it was. We musicians don't ask for much. All we want is to have one investigator tell us why this young fellow seated in Row A is firmly held by the musical sounds he hears while his girl friend gets little or nothing out of them, or vice versa. Think how many millions of useless practice hours might have been saved if some alert professor of genetics had developed a test for musical sensibility. The fascination of music for some human beings was curiously illustrated for me once during a visit I made to the showrooms of a manufacturer of electronic organs. As part of my tour I was taken to see the practice room. There, to my surprise, I found not one but eight aspiring organists, all busily practicing simultaneously on eight organs. More surprising still was the fact that not a sound was audible, for each of the eight performers was listening through earphones to his individual instrument. It was an uncanny sight, even for a fellow musician, to watch these grown men mesmerized, as it were, by a silent and invisible genie. On that day I fully realized how mesmerized we earminded creatures must seem to our less musically inclined friends.

If music has impact for the mere listener, it follows that it will have much greater impact for those who sing it or play it themselves with some degree of proficiency. Any educated person in Elizabethan times was expected to be able to read musical notation and take his or her part in a madrigal-sing. Passive listeners, numbered in the millions, are a comparatively recent innovation. Even in my own youth, loving music meant that you either made it yourself or were forced out of the house to go hear it where it was being made, at considerable cost and some inconvenience. Nowadays all that has changed. Music has become so very accessible it is almost impossible to avoid it. Perhaps you don't mind cashing a check at the local bank to the strains of a Brahms symphony, but I do. Actually, I think I spend as much time avoiding great works as others spend in seeking them out. The reason is simple: meaningful music demands one's undivided attention, and I can give it that only when I am in a receptive mood, and feel the need for it. The use of music as a kind of ambrosia to titillate the aural senses while one's conscious mind is otherwise occupied is the abomination of every composer who takes his work seriously.

Thus, the music I have reference to in this article is designed for your undistracted attention. It is, in fact, usually labeled "serious" music in contradistinction to light or popular music. How this term "serious" came into being no one seems to know, but all of us are agreed as to its inadequacy. It just doesn't cover enough cases. Very often our "serious" music *is* serious, sometimes deadly serious, but it can also be witty, humorous, sarcastic, sardonic, grotesque and a great many other things besides. It is, indeed, the emotional range covered that makes it "serious" and, in part, influences our judgment as to the artistic stature of any extended composition.

Everyone is aware that so-called serious music has made great strides in general public acceptance in recent years, but the term itself still connotes something forbidding and hermetic[2] to the mass audience. They attribute to the professional musician a kind of Masonic initiation into secrets that are forever hidden from the outsider. Nothing could be more misleading. We all listen to music, professionals and non-professionals alike, in the same sort of way—in a dumb sort of way, really, because simple or sophisticated music attracts all of us, in the first instance, on the primordial level of sheer rhythmic and sonic appeal. Musicians are flattered, no doubt, by the deferential attitude of the layman in regard to what he imagines to be our secret understanding of music. But in all honesty we musicians know that in the main we listen basically as others do, because music hits us with an immediacy that we recognize in the reactions of the most simple-minded of music listeners.

It is part of my thesis that music, unlike the other arts, with the possible exception of dancing, gives pleasure simultaneously on the lowest and highest levels of apprehension. All of us, for example, can understand and feel the joy of being carried forward by the flow of music. Our love of music is bound up with its forward motion; nonetheless it is precisely the creation of that sense of flow, its interrelation with and resultant effect upon formal structure, that calls forth high intellectual capacities of a composer, and offers keen pleasures for listening minds. Music's incessant movement forward exerts a double and contradictory fascination: on the one hand it appears to be immobilizing time itself by filling out a specific temporal space, while generating at the same moment the sensation of flowing past us with all the pressure and sparkle of a great river. To stop the flow of music would be like the stopping of time itself, incredible and inconceivable. Only a catastrophe of some sort produces such a break in the musical discourse during a public performance. Musicians are, of course, hardened to such interruptions during rehearsal periods, but they don't relish them. The public, at such times, look on, unbelieving. I have seen this demonstrated each summer at Tanglewood during the open rehearsals of the Boston Symphony Orchestra. Large audiences gather each week, I am convinced, for the sole pleasure of living through that awe-full moment when the conductor abruptly stops the music. Something went wrong; no one seems to know what or why, but it stopped the music's flow, and a shock of recognition runs through the entire crowd. That is what they came for, though they may not realize it—that, and the pleasure of hearing the music's flow resumed, which lights up the public countenance with a kind of all's-right-with-the-world assurance. Clearly, audience enjoyment is inherent in the magnetic forward pull of the music; but to the more enlightened listener this time-filling, forward drive has fullest meaning only when accompanied by some conception as to where it is heading, what musical-psychological elements are helping to move it to its destination, and what formal architectural satisfactions will have been achieved on its arriving there.

Musical flow is largely the result of musical rhythm, and the rhythmic factor in music is certainly a key element that has simultaneous attraction on more than one level. To some African tribes rhythm *is* music; they have nothing more. But what rhythm it is! Listening to it casually, one might never get beyond the earsplitting poundings, but actually a trained musician's ear is needed to disengage its polyrhythmic intricacies. Minds that conceive such rhythms have their own sophistication; it seems inexact and even unfair to call them primitive. By comparison our own instinct for rhythmic play seems only mild in interest—needing reinvigoration from time to time.

It was because the ebb of rhythmic invention was comparatively low in late-nineteenth-century European music that Stravinsky[3] was able to apply what I once termed "a rhythmic hypodermic" to Western music. His shocker of 1913, *The Rite of Spring,* a veritable rhythmic monstrosity to its first hearers, has now become a standard item of the concert repertory. This indicates the progress that has been made in the comprehension and enjoyment of rhythmic complexities that nonplused our grandfathers. And the end is by no means in sight. Younger composers have taken us to the very limit of what the human hand can perform and have gone even beyond what the human ear can grasp in rhythmic differentiation. Sad to say, there is a limit, dictated by what nature has supplied us with in the way of listening equipment. But within those limits there are large areas of rhythmic life still to be explored, rhythmic forms never dreamed of by composers of the march or the mazurka.

In so saying I do not mean to minimize the rhythmic ingenuities of past eras. The wonderfully subtle rhythms of the anonymous composers of the late fourteenth century, only recently deciphered; the delicate shadings of oriental rhythms; the carefully contrived speech-based rhythms of the composers of Tudor England; and, bringing things closer to home, the improvised wildness of jazz-inspired rhythms—all these and many more must be rated, certainly, as prime musical pleasures.

Tone color is another basic element in music that may be enjoyed on various levels of perception from the most naïve to the most cultivated. Even children have no difficulty in recognizing the difference between the tonal profile of a flute and a trombone. The color of certain instruments holds an especial attraction for certain people. I myself have always had a weakness for the sound of eight French horns playing in unison. Their rich, golden, legendary sonority transports me. Some present-day European composers seem to be having a belated love affair with the vibraphone. An infinitude of possible color combinations is available when instruments are mixed, especially when combined in that wonderful contraption, the orchestra of symphonic proportions. The art of orchestration, needless to say, holds endless fascination for the practicing composer, being part science and part inspired guesswork.

As a composer I get great pleasure from cooking up tonal combinations. Over the years I have noted that no element of the composer's art mystifies the layman more than this ability to conceive mixed instrumental colors. But remember that before we mix them we hear them in terms of their component parts. If you examine an orchestral score you will note that composers place their instruments on the page in family groups: in reading from top to bottom it is customary to list the woodwinds, the brass, the percussion, and the strings, in that order. Modern orchestral practice often juxtaposes these families one against the other so that their personalities, as families, remain recognizable and distinct. This principle may also be applied to the voice of the single instrument, whose pure color sonority thereby remains clearly identifiable as such. Orchestral know-how consists in keeping the instruments out of each other's way, so spacing them that they avoid repeating what some other instrument is already doing, at least in the same register, thereby exploiting to the fullest extent the specific color value contributed by each separate instrument or grouped instrumental family.

In modern orchestration clarity and definition of sonorous image are usually the goal. There exists, however, another kind of orchestral magic dependent on a certain ambiguity of effect. Not to be able to identify immediately how a particular color combination is arrived at adds to its attractiveness. I like to be intrigued by unusual sounds that force me to exclaim: Now I wonder how the composer did that?

From what I have said about the art of orchestration you may have gained the notion that it is nothing more than a delightful game, played for the amusement of the composer. That is, of course, not true. Color in music, as in painting, is meaningful only when it serves the expressive idea; it is the expressive idea that dictates to the composer the choice of his orchestral scheme.

Part of the pleasure in being sensitive to the use of color in music is to note what way a composer's personality traits are revealed through his tonal color schemes. During the period of the French impressionism, for example, the composers Debussy and Ravel[4] were thought to be very similar in personality. An examination of their orchestral scores would have shown that Debussy, at his most characteristic, sought for a spraylike iridescence, a delicate and sensuous sonority such as had never before been heard, while Ravel, using a similar palette, sought a refinement and precision, a gemlike brilliance that reflects the more objective nature of his musical personality.

Color ideals change for composers as their personalities change. A striking example is again that of Igor Stravinsky, who, beginning with the stabbing reds and purples of his early ballet scores, has in the past decade arrived at an ascetic grayness of tone that positively chills the listener by its austerity. For contrast we may turn to a Richard Strauss[5] orchestral score, masterfully handled in its own way, but overrich in the piling-on of sonorities, like a German meal that is too filling for comfort. The natural and easy handling of orchestral forces by a whole school of contemporary American composers would indicate some inborn affinity between American personality traits and symphonic language. No layman can hope to penetrate all the subtleties that go into an orchestral page of any complexity, but here again it is not necessary to be able to analyze the color spectrum of a score in order to bask in its effulgence.

Thus far I have been dealing with the generalities of musical pleasure. Now I wish to concentrate on the music of a few composers in order to show how musical values are differentiated. The late Serge Koussevitzky, conductor of the Boston Symphony, never tired of telling performers that if it weren't for composers they would literally have nothing to play or sing. He was stressing what is too often taken for granted and, therefore, lost sight of, namely, that in our Western world music speaks with a composer's voice and half the pleasure we get comes from the fact that we are listening to a particular voice making an individual statement at a specific moment in history. Unless you take off from there, you are certain to miss one of the principal attractions of musical art—contact with a strong and absorbing personality.

It matters greatly, therefore, who it is we are about to listen to in the concert hall or opera house. And yet I get the impression that to the lay music-lover music is music and musical events are attended with little or no concern as to what musical fare is to be offered. Not so with the professional, to whom it matters a great deal whether he is about to listen to the music of Monteverdi or Massenet, to J.S. or to J.C. Bach.[6] Isn't it true that everything we, as listeners, know about a particular composer and his music prepares us in some measure to empathize with his special mentality? To me Chopin[7] is one thing, Scarlatti quite another. I could never confuse them, could you? Well, whether you could or not, my point remains the same: there are as many ways for music to be enjoyable as there are composers.

One can even get a certain perverse pleasure out of hating the work of a particular composer. I, for instance, happen to be rubbed the wrong way by one of today's composer-idols, Serge Rachmaninoff.[8] The prospect of having to sit through one of his extended symphonies or piano concertos tends, quite frankly, to depress me. All those notes, think I, and to what end? To me Rachmaninoff's characteristic tone is one of self-pity and self-indulgence tinged with a definite melancholia. As a fellow human being I can sympathize with an artist whose distempers produced such music, but as a listener my stomach won't take it. I grant you his technical adroitness, but even here the technique adopted by the composer was old-fashioned in his own day. I also grant his ability to write long and singing melodic lines, but when these are embroidered with figuration, the musical substance is watered down, emptied of significance. Well, as André Gide[9] used to say, I didn't have to tell you this, and I know it will not make you happy to hear it. Actually it should be of little concern to you whether I find Rachmaninoff digestible. All I am trying to say is that music strikes us in as many different ways as there are composers, and anything less than a strong reaction, pro or con, is not worth bothering about.

By contrast, let me point to that perennially popular favorite among composers, Giuseppe Verdi.[10] Quite apart from his music, I get pleasure merely thinking about the man himself. If honesty and forthrightness ever sparked an artist, then Verdi is a prime example. What a pleasure it is to make contact with him through his letters, to knock against the hard core of his peasant personality. One comes away refreshed, and with renewed confidence in the sturdy non-neurotic character of at least one musical master.

When I was a student it was considered not good form to mention Verdi's name in symphonic company, and quite out of the question to name Verdi in the same sentence with that formidable dragon of the opera house, Richard Wagner.[11] What the musical elite found difficult to forgive in Verdi's case was his triteness, his ordinariness. Yes, Verdi is trite and ordinary at times, just as Wagner is long-winded and boring at times. There is a lesson to be learned here: the way in which we are gradually able to accommodate our minds to the obvious weaknesses in a creative artist's output. Musical history teaches us that at first contact the academicisms of Brahms,[12] the *longueurs* of Schubert,[13] the portentousness of Mahler[14] were considered insupportable by their early listeners—but in all such cases later generations have managed to put up with the failings of men of genius for the sake of other qualities that outweigh them.

Verdi can be commonplace at times, as everyone knows, but his saving grace is a burning sincerity that carries all before it. There is no bluff here, no guile. On whatever level he composed a no-nonsense quality comes across; all is directly stated, cleanly written with no notes wasted, and marvelously effective. In the end we willingly concede that Verdi's musical materials need not be especially choice in order to be acceptable. And, naturally enough, when the musical materials *are* choice and inspired, they profit doubly from being set off against the homely virtues of his more workaday pages.

Verdi's creative life lasted for more than half a century, advancing steadily in musical interest and sophistication. So prolonged a capacity for development has few parallels in musical annals. There is a special joy in following the milestones of a career that began so modestly and obscurely, leading gradually to the world renown of *Traviata* and *Aida,* and then, to the general astonishment of the musical community, continuing on in the eighth decade of his life to the crowning achievements of *Otello* and *Falstaff.*

If one were asked to name one musician who came closest to composing without human flaw I suppose general concensus would choose Johann Sebastian Bach. Only a very few musical giants have earned universal admiration that surrounds the figure of this eighteenth-century German master. America should love Bach, for he is the greatest, as we would say—or, if not the greatest, he has few rivals and no peers. What is it, then, that makes his finest scores so profoundly moving? I have puzzled over that question for a very long time, but have come to doubt whether it is possible for anyone to reach a completely satisfactory answer. One thing is certain; we will never explain Bach's supremacy by the singling out of any one element in his work. Rather it was a combination of perfections, each of which was applied to the common practice of his day; added together, they produced the mature perfection of the completed *oeuvre.*

Bach's genius cannot possibly be deduced from the circumstances of his routine musical existence. All his life long he wrote music for the requirements of the jobs he held. His melodies were often borrowed from liturgical sources, his orchestral textures limited by the forces at his disposal, and his forms, in the main, were similar to those of other composers of his time, whose works, incidentally, he had closely studied. To his more up-to-date composer sons Father Bach was, first of all, a famous instrumental performer, and only secondarily a solid craftsman-creator of the old school, whose compositions were little known abroad for the simple reason that few of them were published in his lifetime. None of these oft-repeated facts explains the universal hold his best music has come to have on later generations.

What strikes me most markedly about Bach's work is the marvelous rightness of it. It is the rightness not merely of a single individual but of a whole musical epoch. Bach came at the peak point of a long historical development; his was the heritage of many generations of composing artisans. Never since that time has music so successfully fused contrapuntal skill with harmonic logic.[15] This amalgam of melodies and chords—of independent lines conceived linear-fashion within a mold of basic harmonies conceived vertically—provided Bach with the necessary framework for his massive edifice. Within that edifice is the summation of an entire period, with all the grandeur, nobility, and inner depth that one creative soul could bring to it. It is hopeless, I fear, to attempt to probe further into why his music creates the impression of spiritual wholeness, the sense of his communing with the deepest vision. We would only find ourselves groping for words, words than can never hope to encompass the intangible greatness of music, least of all the intangible in Bach's greatness.

Those who are interested in studying the interrelationship between a composer and his work would do better to turn to the century that followed Bach's, and especially to the life and work of Ludwig van Beethoven.[16] The English critic, Wilfred Mellers, had this to say abut Beethoven, recently: "It is the essence of the personality of Beethoven, both as man and as artist, that he should invite discussion in other than musical terms." Mellers meant that such a discussion would involve us, with no trouble at all, in a consideration of the rights of man, free will, Napoleon and the French Revolution, and other allied subjects. We shall never know in exactly what way the ferment of historical events affected Beethoven's thinking, but it is certain that music such as his would have been inconceivable in the early nineteenth century without serious concern for the revolutionary temper of his time and the ability to translate that concern into the original and unprecedented musical thought of his own work.

Beethoven brought three startling innovations to music: first, he altered our very conception of the art by emphasizing the psychological element implicit in the language of sounds. Because of him, music lost a certain innocence but gained instead a new dimension in psychological depth. Secondly, his own stormy and explosive temperament was, in part, responsible for a "dramatization of the whole art of music." The rumbling bass tremolandos, the sudden accents in unexpected places, the hitherto-unheard-of rhythmic insistence and sharp dynamic contrasts—all these were externalizations of an inner drama that gave his music theatrical impact. Both these elements—the psychological orientation and the instinct for drama—are inextricably linked in my mind with his third and possibly most original achievement: the creation of musical forms dynamically conceived on a scale never before attempted and of an inevitability that is irresistible. Especially the sense of inevitability is remarkable in Beethoven. Notes are not words, they are not under the control of verifiable logic, and because of that composers in every age have struggled to overcome that handicap by producing a directional effect convincing to the listeners. No composer has ever solved the problem more brilliantly than Beethoven; nothing quite so inevitable had ever before been created in the language of sounds.

One doesn't need much historical perspective to realize what a shocking experience Beethoven's music must have been for his first listeners. Even today, given the nature of his music, there are times when I simply do not understand how this man's art was "sold" to the big musical public. Obviously he must be saying something that everyone wants to hear. And yet if one listens freshly and closely the odds against accceptance are equally obvious. As sheer sound there is little that is luscious about his music—it gives off a comparatively "dry" sonority. He never seems to flatter an audience, never to know or care what they might like. His themes are not particularly joyous or memorable; they are more likely to be expressively apt than beautifully contoured. His general manner is gruff and unceremonious, as if the matter under discussion were much too important to be broached in urbane or diplomatic terms. He adopts a peremptory and hortatory[17] tone, the assumption being, especially in his most forceful work, that you have no choice but to listen. And that is precisely what happens: you listen. Above and beyond every other consideration Beethoven has one quality to a remarkable degree: he is enormously compelling.

What is it he is so compelling about? How can one not be compelled and not be moved by the moral fervor and conviction of such a man? His finest works are the enactment of a triumph—a triumph of affirmation in the face of the human condition. Beethoven is one of the great yea-sayers among creative artists; it is exhilarating to share his clear-eyed contemplation of the tragic sum of life. His music summons forth our better nature; in purely musical terms Beethoven seems to be exhorting us to Be Noble, Be Strong, Be Great in Heart, yes, and Be Compassionate. These ethical precepts we subsume from the music, but it is the music itself—the nine symphonies, the sixteen string quartets, the thirty-two piano sonatas—that holds us, and holds us in much the same way each time we return to it. The core of Beethoven's music seems indestructible; the ephemera of sound seem to have little to do with its strangely immutable substance.

What a contrast it is to turn from the starkness of Beethoven to the very different world of a composer like Palestrina.[18] Palestrina's music is heard more rarely than that of the German master; possibly because of that it seems more special and remote. In Palestrina's time it was choral music that held the center of the stage, and many composers lived their lives, as did Palestrina, attached to the service of the Church. Without knowing the details of his life story, and from the evidence of the music alone, it is clear that the purity and serenity of his work reflects a profound inner peace. Whatever the stress and strain of daily living in sixteenth-century Rome may have been, his music breathes quietly in some place apart. Everything about it conduces to the contemplative life: the sweetness of the modal harmonies, the stepwise motion of the melodic phrases, the consummate ease in the handling of vocal polyphony. His music looks white upon the page and sounds "white" in the voices. Its homogeneity of style, composed, as much of it was, for ecclesiastical devotions, gives it a pervading mood of impassivity and other-worldliness. Such music, when it is merely routine, can be pale and dull. But at its best Palestrina's masses and motets create an ethereal loveliness that only the world of tones can embody.

My concern here with composers of the first rank like Bach and Beethoven and Palestrina is not meant to suggest that only the greatest names and the greatest masterpieces are worth your attention. Musical art, as we hear it in our day, suffers if anything from an overdose of masterworks, an obsessive fixation on the glories of the past. This narrows the range of our musical experience and tends to suffocate interest in the present. It blots out many an excellent composer whose work was less than perfect. I cannot agree, for instance, with Albert Schweitzer,[19] who once remarked that "of all arts music is that in which perfection is a *sine qua non,*[20] and that the predecessors of Bach were foredoomed to comparative oblivion because their works were not mature." It may be carping to say so, but the fact is that we tire of everything, even of perfection. It would be truer to point out, it seems to me, that the forerunners of Bach have an awkward charm and simple grace that not even he could match, just because of his mature perfection. Delacroix[21] had something of my idea when he complained in his journal about Racine[22] being too perfect: that "that perfection and the absence of breaks and incongruities deprive him of the spice one finds in works full of beauties and defects at the same time."

Notes

[1] simulacrum: a vague representation or simulation.

[2] hermetic: magical.

[3] Igor Stravinsky (1882–1971) was a U.S. composer born in Russia.

[4] Claude Debussy (1862–1918) and Maurice Ravel (1875–1937) were French early modern composers. Debussy was an influential experimenter in harmony and musical texture, Ravel a master of form and interpretation.

[5] Richard Strauss (1864–1949), the great German contemporary of Debussy and Ravel, conducted the Berlin Philharmonic and wrote the operas *Der Rosenkavalier, Salome,* and *Electra.*

[6] Claudio Monteverdi (Italy, 1567–1643), Jules Massenet (France 1842–1912), Johann Sebastian Bach (Germany, 1685–1750), and Johann Christian Bach (Germany, 1735–1782) were all composers.

[7] Frederic Chopin (1810–1849) was a Polish composer and pianist who lived in France after 1831. His music with its contrasts and disciplined emotion is said to have revolutionized piano music.

[8] Serge Rachmaninoff (1873–1943), a Russian contemporary of Ravel and Debussy, was both a pianist and a composer who worked in traditionally romantic forms to create piano and orchestral works that have become staples of popular concert programs.

[9] André Gide (1869–1951) was a French novelist and critic.

[10] Giuseppe Verdi (Italy, 1813–1901) became a leading figure in the European world of music with the appearance of the opera *Rigoletto* in 1851. Among his most famous operas are *Otello* (1877), *Falstaff* (1893), and *Aida* (1871).

[11] Richard Wagner (Germany, 1813–1883) composed powerful operas on themes from German folklore. Best known is his *Ring* trilogy.

[12] Johannes Brahms (1833–1897) was a German Romantic symphony composer.

[13] Franz Schubert (German, 1797–1828) developed the Romantic German art song. He also wrote at least eight symphonies, fifteen string quartets, and many choral works. *Lonqueurs* are tedious passages.

[14] Gustav Mahler (Austria, 1860–1911), a brooding, driving man who was often depressed, wrote symphonic music that was ambitious, "dark" in mood, and, in his own day, generally unpopular. In recent years Mahler has developed a considerable following.

[15] Counterpoint adds a related but independent melody or melodies to a basic melody according to fixed rules of harmony. Harmony is the simultaneous sounding of two tones that complement each other rather than create dissonance.

[16] Ludwig van Beethoven (Germany 1770–1827) wrote music in every established form, but his lack of convention expanded the limits of these forms.

[17] hortatory: giving good advice or encouraging.

[18] Giovanni Perluigi, called Palestrina (1525?–1594), an Italian composer, met the Catholic church's need for reformed church music following the Protestant Reformation.

[19] Albert Schweitzer (1875–1965) was an Alsatian medical missionary, theologian, and musician in Africa.

[20] *sine quo non:* (Latin) an essential condition.

[21] Eugéne Delacroix (1798–1863) was the major painter of the Romantic movement in France.

[22] Jean Racine (1639–1699), a famous French dramatist, incorporated dramatic principles from the Classics into his plays.

FOCUS: READING REVIEW

1. What does meaningful music require? What kind of music is an abomination to a serious composer?
2. Explain what Copland means when he says that "music, unlike the other arts, with the exception of dancing, gives pleasure simultaneously on the lowest and highest levels of apprehension."
3. What is tone color and how is it created?
4. Of what importance are composers in appreciating music?
5. Why does Copland value Verdi?
6. What does Copland mean by the "rightness" of Bach's work?
7. What are the revolutionary features of Beethoven's work?

FOCUS: AUTHOR'S STRATEGIES

1. What attitudes toward music does Copland anticipate in his audience? How does he direct his discussion toward these attitudes?
2. To describe tonal color schemes Copland uses visual imagery—"spraylike iridescence," and "ascetic grayness of tone." What do you imagine the music would be like for each of these?

FOCUS: **DISCUSSION AND WRITING**

Select a composer whose music Copland describes, and after researching his life and times, explain how this knowledge increases your appreciation of his music.

Escape to Islip
Tom Wolfe

Tom Wolfe (b. 1931) is probably best known for The Right Stuff, *his study of the American astronauts who participated in the first moon landing. His writing combines a professional journalist's respect for fact with a creative writer's imagination to create studies of American life filled with wit and insight. Wolfe received his Ph.D. in American Studies from Yale University and has worked as a reporter for the* Springfield Union, *the* Washington Post, *and the* New York Herald Tribune. *He has received two Washington News Guild Awards and the 1980 Columbia Journalism Award. His books include* The Kandy-Kolored Tangerine-Flake Streamline Baby *(1965),* The Electric Kool-Aid Acid Test *(1968),* Radical Chic and Mau-Mauing the Flack Catcher *(1970), and* From Bauhaus to Our House *(1981), from which this selection is taken. "Escape to Islip" identifies European worker housing of the 1920s as the source of American high-rise architecture. His descriptions of high rises combine with observations on public response to these designs to demonstrate the chasm lying between the artist and the society for which he creates.*

Here we come upon one of the ironies of American life in the twentieth century. After all, this has been *the American century.* In short, this has been America's period of full-blooded, go-to-hell, belly-rubbing wahoo-yahoo youthful rampage—and what architecture has she to show for it? An architecture whose tenets prohibit every manifestation of exuberance, power, empire, grandeur, or even high spirits and playfulness, as the height of bad taste. The reigning architectural style in this, the very Babylon of capitalism, became worker housing, as developed by a handful of architects amid the rubble of Europe in the early 1920s. It was made to serve every purpose, except housing for workers. The workers managed to avoid public housing and headed out instead to the suburbs. The only people left trapped in worker housing in America today are those who don't work at all and are on welfare and, of course, the urban rich who live in places such as the Olympic Tower on Fifth Avenue in New York. Since the 1950s the term "luxury highrise" has come to denote a certain type of apartment house that is in fact nothing else but the worker housing of Frankfurt and Berlin, with units stacked up thirty, forty, fifty stories high, to be rented or sold to the bourgeoisie. Every respected instrument of architectural opinion and cultivated taste told the urban dwellers of America that this was *living.* The terms *glass box* and *repetitious,* first uttered as terms of opprobrium, became badges of honor. For American architects what did it matter if they said you were imitating Mies van der Rohe or Gropius or Corbu? The single greatest monument of the architecture of the Dutch and German compounds was the Seagram Building on Park Avenue. Mies' vision of ultimate nonbourgeois purity was a building composed of nothing but steel beams and glass, with concrete slabs creating the ceilings and floor, but American building codes and the need for draperies created compromises which became more decorative than functional. This architecture justified itself by saying that no craftsmen existed to build other styles and that other styles were more expensive. In fact, it put craftsmen out of work and replaced quality with flimsy, cheap construction. Not even the bottom dogs, those on welfare, trapped in the projects, have embraced this architecture [as the examples of the Pruitt-Igoe and the Oriental Gardens projects illustrate.]

Here we come upon one of the ironies of American life in the twentieth century. After all, this has been *the American century*, in the same way that the seventeenth might be regarded as the British century. This is the century in which America, the young giant, became the mightiest nation on earth, devising the means to obliterate the planet with a single device but also the means to escape to the stars and explore the rest of the universe. This is the century in which she became the richest nation in all of history, with a wealth that reached down to every level of the population. The energies and animal appetites and idle pleasures of even the working classes—the very term now seemed antique—became enormous, lurid, creamy, preposterous. The American family car was a 425-horsepower, twenty-two-foot-long Buick Electra with tail fins in back and two black rubber breasts on the bumper in front. The American liquor-store deliveryman's or cargo humper's vacation was two weeks in Barbados with his third wife or his new cookie. The American industrial convention was a gin-blind rout at a municipal coliseum the size of all Rome, featuring vans in the parking lot stocked with hookers on flokati rugs for the exclusive use of registered members of the association. The way Americans lived made the rest of mankind stare with envy or disgust but always with awe. In short, this has been America's period of full-blooded, go-to-hell, belly-rubbing wahoo-yahoo youthful rampage—and what architecture has she to show for it? An architecture whose tenets prohibit every manifestation of exuberance, power, empire, grandeur, or even high spirits and playfulness, as the height of bad taste.

We brace for a barbaric yawp over the roofs of the world—and hear a cough at a concert.

In short, the reigning architectural style in this, the very Babylon of capitalism, became worker housing. Worker housing, as developed by a handful of architects, inside the compounds, amid the rubble of Europe in the early 1920s, was now pitched up high and wide, in the form of Ivy League art-gallery annexes, museums for art patrons, apartments for the rich, corporate headquarters, city halls, country estates. It was made to serve every purpose, in fact, except housing for workers.

It was not that worker housing was never built for workers. In the 1950s and early 1960s the federal government helped finance the American version of the Dutch and German Siedlungen[1] of the 1920s. Here they were called public housing projects. But somehow the workers, intellectually undeveloped as they were, managed to avoid public housing. They called it, simply, "the projects," and they avoided it as if it had a smell. The workers—if by workers we mean people who have jobs—headed out instead to the suburbs. They ended up in places like Islip, Long Island, and the San Fernando Valley of Los Angeles, and they bought houses with pitched roofs and shingles and clapboard siding, with no structure expressed if there was any way around it, with gaslight-style front-porch lamps and mailboxes set up on lengths of stiffened chain that seemed to defy gravity—the more cute and antiquey touches, the better—and they loaded these houses with "drapes" such as baffled all description and wall-to-wall carpet you could lose a shoe in, and they put barbecue pits and fishponds with concrete cherubs urinating into them on the lawn out back, and they parked the Buick Electras out front and had Evinrude cruisers up on tow trailers in the carport just beyond the breezeway.

As for the honest sculptural objects designed for worker-housing interiors, such as Mies' and Breuer's chairs, the proles either ignored them or held them in contempt because they were patently uncomfortable. This furniture is today a symbol of wealth and privilege, attuned chiefly to the tastes of the businessmen's wives who graze daily at the D & D Building, the major interior-decoration bazaar in New York. Mies' most famous piece of furniture design, the Barcelona chair, retails today for $3,465 and is available only through decorators. The high price is due in no small part to the chair's worker-housing honest nonbourgeois materials: stainless steel and leather. Today the leather can be ordered only in black or shades of brown. In the early 1970s, it seems, certain bourgeois elements were having them made in the most appalling variations . . . zebra skin, Holstein skin, ocelot skin, and *pretty fabrics.*

The only people left trapped in worker housing in America today are those who don't work at all and are on welfare—these are the sole inhabitants of "the projects"—and, of course, the urban rich who live in places such as the Olympic Tower on Fifth Avenue in New York. Since the 1950s the term "luxury highrise" has come to denote a certain type of apartment house that is in fact nothing else but the Siedlungen of Frankfurt and Berlin, with units stacked up thirty, forty, fifty stories high, to be rented or sold to the bourgeoisie. Which is to say, pure nonbourgeois housing for the bourgeoisie only. Sometimes the towers are of steel, concrete, and glass; sometimes of glass, steel, and small glazed white or beige bricks. Always the ceilings are low, often under eight feet, the hallways are narrow, the rooms are narrow, even when they're long, the bedrooms are small (Le Corbusier[2] was always in favor of that), the walls are thin, the doorways and windows have no casings, the joints have no moldings, the walls have no baseboards, and the windows don't open, although small vents or jalousies may be provided. The construction is invariably cheap in the pejorative as well as the literal sense.

That builders could present these boxes in the 1950s, without a twitch of the nostril, as luxury, and that well-educated men and women could accept them, without a blink, as luxury—here is objective testimony, from those too dim for irony, to the aesthetic sway of the compound aesthetic, of the Silver Prince and his colonial legions, in America following the Second World War.

Every respected instrument of architectural opinion and cultivated taste, from *Domus* to *House & Garden*, told the urban dwellers of America that this was *living*. This was the good taste of today; this was modern, and soon the International Style became known simply as modern architecture. Every Sunday, in its design section, *The New York Times Magazine* ran a picture of the same sort of apartment. I began to think of it as *that apartment*. The walls were always pure white and free of moldings, casings, baseboards, and all the rest. In the living room there were about 17,000 watts' worth of R-40 spotlights encased in white canisters suspended from the ceiling in what is known as track lighting. There was always a set of bentwood chairs, blessed by Le Corbusier, which no one ever sat in because they caught you in the small of the back like a karate chop. The dining-room table was a smooth slab of blond wood (no ogee edges, no beading on the legs), around which was a set of the S-shaped, tubular steel, cane-bottomed chairs that Mies van der Rohe had designed—the second most famous chair designed in the twentieth century, his own Barcelona chair being first, but also one of the five most disastrously designed, so that by the time the main course arrived, at least one guest had pitched face forward into the lobster bisque. Somewhere nearby was a palm or a dracena fragrans or some other huge tropical plant, because all the furniture was so lean and clean and bare and spare that without some prodigious piece of frondose Victoriana from the nursery the place looked absolutely empty. The photographer always managed to place the plant in the foreground, so that the stark scene beyond was something one peered at through an arabesque of equatorial greenery. (And *that apartment* is still with us, every Sunday.)

So what if you were living in a building that looked like a factory and felt like a factory, and paying top dollar for it? Every modern building of quality looked like a factory. That was *the look of today*. You only had to think of Mies' campus for the Illinois Institute of Technology, most of which had gone up in the 1940s. The main classroom building looked like a shoe factory. The chapel looked like a power plant. The power plant itself, also designed by Mies, looked rather more spiritual (as Charles Jencks would point out), thanks to its chimney, which reached heavenward at least. The school of architecture building had black steel trusses rising up through the roof on either side of the main entrance, after the manner of a Los Angeles car wash. All four were glass and steel boxes. The truth was, this was inescapable. The compound style, with its *nonbourgeois* taboos, had so reduced the options of the true believer that every building, the beach house no less than the skyscraper, was bound to have the same general look.

And so what? The terms *glass box* and *repetitious*, first offered as terms of opprobrium, became badges of honor. Mies had many American imitators, Philip Johnson, I. M. Pei, and Gordon Bunshaft being the most famous and the most blatant. And the most unashamed. Snipers would say that every one of Philip Johnson's buildings was an imitation of Mies van der Rohe. And Johnson would open his eyes wide and put on his marvelous smile of mock innocence and reply, "I have always been delighted to be called Mies van der Johnson." Bunshaft had designed Lever House, corporate headquarters for the Lever Brothers soap and detergent company, on Park Avenue. The building was such a success that it became the prototype for the American glass box, and Bunshaft and his firm, Skidmore, Owings & Merrill, did many variations on this same design. To the charge that glass boxes were all he designed, Bunshaft liked to crack: "Yes, and I'm going to keep on doing them until I do one I like."

For a hierophant[3] of the compound, confidence came easy! What did it matter if they said you were imitating Mies or Gropius or Corbu or any of the rest? It was like accusing a Christian of imitating Jesus Christ.

Mies' star had risen steadily since his arrival in the United States in 1938, due in no small part to the influence of Philip Johnson. Johnson had chosen Mies as one of the four great modernists in his "International Style" piece in 1932. He then helped arrange his emigration to America and his extraordinary job at the Armour Institute. In 1947, after most of Mies' campus buildings were underway, Johnson published the first book on his work. Mies was pushing sixty, but thanks to Johnson he had a glorious new career in America. With or without Johnson, however, Mies knew his way around in an era of art compounds. He had been director of architecture for the Novembergruppe back in 1919; he had founded the group's magazine, *G* (which stood for *Gestaltung*, meaning "creative force"); he had become a skilled propagandist with a flair for aphorisms. His most famous was "Less is more," to which he added: "My architecture is almost nothing." His idea was to combine the usual worker-housing elements in ways that were austere and elegant at the same time, along the lines of what today is called "minimalism." Mies himself was anything but austere. He was a big, beefy but handsome individual who smoked expensive cigars. Full coronas, they were. He looked rather like a Ruhr industrialist. He was also an affable soul, so much so that even Frank Lloyd Wright liked him. He was the one white god Wright could abide.

In 1958, the greatest single monument to the architecture of the Dutch and German compounds went up on Park Avenue, across the street from Lever House. This was the Seagram Building, designed by Mies himself, with Philip Johnson as his assistant. The Seagram Building was worker housing, utterly nonbourgeois, pitched up thirty-eight stories on Park Avenue for the firm that manufactured a rye whiskey called Four Roses. In keeping with the color of the American whiskey bottle, the glass for this greatest of all boxes of glass and steel was tinted brownish amber. When it came to the exposed steel—well, since brownish steel didn't exist, except in a state of rust, bronze was chosen. Wasn't this adding a *color*, like poor Bruno Taut? No, bronze was bronze; that was the way it came, right out of the foundry. As for the glass, all glass ended up with a tint of some sort, usually greenish. Tinting it brown was only a machine-made tint control. Right? (Besides, this was *Mies*.) Exposing the metal had presented a problem. Mies' vision of ultimate nonbourgeois purity was a building composed of nothing but steel beams and glass, with concrete slabs creating the ceilings and floors. But now that he was in the United States, he ran into American building and fire codes. Steel was terrific for tall buildings because it could withstand great lateral stresses as well as support great weights. Its weakness was that the heat of a fire could cause steel to buckle. American codes required that structural steel members be encased in concrete or some other fireproof material. That slowed Mies up for only a little while. He had already worked it out in Chicago, in his Lake Shore apartment buildings. What you did was enclose the steel members in concrete, as required, and then reveal them, *express* them, by sticking vertical wide-flange beams on the outside of the concrete, as if to say: "Look! Here's what's inside." But sticking things on the outside of buildings . . . Wasn't that exactly what was known, in another era, as applied decoration? Was there any way you could call such a thing *functional*? No problem. At the heart of functional, as everyone knew, was not *function* but the spiritual quality known as *nonbourgeois*. And what could be more nonbourgeois than an unadorned wide-flange beam, straight out of the mitts of a construction worker?

The one remaining problem was window coverings: shades, blinds, curtains, whatever. Mies would have preferred that the great windows of plate glass have no coverings at all. Unless you could compel everyone in a building to have the same color ones (white or beige, naturally) and raise them and lower them or open and shut them at the same time and to the same degree, they always ruined the purity of the design of the exterior. In the Seagram Building, Mies came as close as man was likely to come to realizing that ideal. The tenant could only have white blinds or shades, and there were only three intervals where they would stay put: open, closed, and halfway. At any other point, they just kept sliding.

No intellectually undeveloped impulses, please. By now this had become a standard attitude among compound architects in America. They policed the impulses of clients and tenants alike. Even after the building was up and the contract fulfilled, they would return. The imitators of Le Corbusier—and there were many—would build expensive country houses in wooded glades patterned on Corbu's Villa Savoye, with strict instructions that the bedrooms, being on the upper floor and visible only to the birds, have no curtains whatsoever. Tired of waking up at 5 a.m. every morning to the light of the summer sun, the owners would add white curtains. But the soul engineer would inevitably return and rip the offending rags down . . . and throw out those sweet little puff 'n' clutter Thai-silk throw pillows in the living room while he was at it.

In the great corporate towers, the office workers shoved filing cabinets, desks, wastepaper baskets, potted plants, up against the floor-to-ceiling sheets of glass, anything to build a barrier against the panicked feeling that they were about to pitch headlong into the streets below. Above these jerry-built walls they strung up makeshift curtains that looked like laundry lines from the slums of Naples, anything to keep out that brain-boiling, poached-eye sunlight that came blazing in every afternoon ... And by night the custodial staff, the Miesling police, under strictest orders, invaded and pulled down these pathetic barricades thrown up against the pure vision of the white gods and the Silver Prince. Eventually, everyone gave up and learned, like the haute bourgeoisie above him, to take it like a man.

They even learned to accept the Mieslings' two great pieces of circular reasoning. To those philistines who were still so gauche as to say that the new architecture lacked the richness of detail of the old Beaux-Arts[4] architecture, the plasterwork, the metalwork, the masonry, and so on, the Mieslings would say with considerable condescension: "Fine. You produce the craftsmen who can do that kind of work, and then we'll talk to you about it. They don't exist anymore." True enough. But why? Henry Hope Reed tells of riding across West Fifty-third Street in New York in the 1940s in a car with some employees of E. F. Caldwell & Co., a firm that specialized in bronze work and electrical fixtures. As the car passed the Museum of Modern Art building, the men began shaking their fists at it and shouting: "That goddamn place is destroying us! Those bastards are killing us!" In the palmy days of Beaux-Arts architecture, Caldwell had employed a thousand bronzeurs, marble workers, model makers, and designers. Now the company was sliding into insolvency, along with many similar firms. It was not that craftsmanship was dying. Rather, the International Style was finishing off the demand for it, particularly in commercial construction. By the same token, to those who complained that International Style buildings were cramped, had flimsy walls inside as well as out, and, in general, looked cheap, the knowing response was: "These days it's too expensive to build in any other style." But it was not *too* expensive, merely *more* expensive. The critical point was what people would or would not put up with aesthetically. It was possible to build in styles even cheaper than the International Style. For example, England began to experiment with schools and public housing constructed like airplane hangars, out of corrugated metal tethered by guy wires. Their architects also said: "These days it's too expensive to build in any other style." Perhaps one day soon everyone (*tout le monde*) would learn to take this, too, like a man.

The Selection Committee stood by at all times, to aid in the process. The day of the monarch such as Ludwig II of Bavaria, or the business autocrat such as Herbert F. Johnson of Johnson Wax, who personally selected architects for great public buildings was over. Governments and corporations now turned to the selection committee. And the selection committee typically included at least one prestigious architect, who, being prestigious, was of course a product of the compounds. And as the baffling and forbidding plans came in, from other compound architects, the various directors and executive officers on the committee turned, nonplussed, to the architect, and he assured them: "These days it's too expensive to build in any other style." And: "Fine. You produce the craftsmen, and then we'll talk to you about it." And the circle closed once and for all. And the mightiest of the mighty learned to take it like a man.

Not even the bottom dogs, those on welfare, trapped in the projects, have taken it so supinely. The lumpenproles have fought it out with the legions of the Silver Prince, and they have won a battle or two. In 1955 a vast worker-housing project called Pruitt-Igoe was opened in St. Louis. The design, by Minoru Yamasaki, architect of the World Trade Center, won an award from the American Institute of Architects. Yamasaki designed it classically Corbu, fulfilling the master's vision of highrise hives of steel, glass, and concrete separated by open spaces of green lawn. The workers of St. Louis, of course, were in no danger of getting caught in Pruitt-Igoe. They had already decamped for suburbs such as Spanish Lake and Crestwood. Pruitt-Igoe filled up mainly with recent migrants from the rural South. They moved from areas of America where the population density was fifteen to twenty folks per square mile, where one rarely got more than ten feet off the ground except by climbing a tree, into Pruitt-Igoe's fourteen-story blocks.

On each floor there were covered walkways, in keeping with Corbu's idea of "streets in the air." Since there was no other place in the project in which to *sin* in public, whatever might ordinarily have taken place in bars, brothels, social clubs, pool halls, amusement arcades, general stores, corncribs, rutabaga patches, hayricks, barn stalls, now took place in the streets in the air. Corbu's boulevards made Hogarth's Gin Lane[5] look like the oceanside street of dreams in Southampton, New York. Respectable folk pulled out, even if it meant living in cracks in the sidewalks. Millions of dollars and scores of commission meetings and task-force projects were expended in a last-ditch attempt to make Pruitt-Igoe habitable. In 1971, the final task force called a general meeting of everyone still living in the project. They asked the residents for their suggestions. It was a historic moment for two reasons. One, for the first time in the fifty-year history of worker housing, someone had finally asked the client for his two cents' worth. Two, the chant. The chant began immediately: "Blow it . . . *up!* Blow it . . . *up!* Blow it . . . *up!* Blow it . . . *up!* Blow it . . . *up!*" The next day the task force thought it over. The poor buggers were right. It was the only solution. In July of 1972, the city blew up the three central blocks of Pruitt-Igoe with dynamite.

That part of the worker-housing saga has not ended. It has just begun. At almost the same time that Pruitt-Igoe went down, the Oriental Gardens project went up in New Haven, the model city of urban renewal in America. The architect was one of America's most prestigious compound architects, Paul Rudolph, dean of the Yale School of Architecture. The federal government's Department of Housing and Urban Development, which was paying for the project, hailed Rudolph's daring design as the vision of the housing projects of the future. The Oriental Gardens were made of clusters of prefabricated modules. You would never end up with more disadvantaged people than you bargained for. You could keep adding modules and clustering the poor yobboes up until they reached Bridgeport. The problem was that the modules didn't fit together too well. In through the cracks came the cold and the rain. Out the doors, the ones that still opened, went whatever respectable folks had gone in in the first place. By September of 1980 there were only seventeen tenants left. Early in 1981, HUD itself set about demolishing it.

Other American monuments to 1920s Middle European worker housing began falling down of their own accord. These were huge sports arenas and convention centers, such as the Hartford Civic Center coliseum, which had flat roofs. The snow was too much for them—but they collapsed piously, paying homage on the way down to the dictum that pitched roofs were bourgeois.

Notes

[1] Dutch and German Siedlungen of the 1920s were worker housing.

[2] Le Corbusier (1887–1965), a French architect, influenced twentieth-century international design by proposing the "vertical city."

[3] A hierophant teaches great religious mysteries.

[4] Beaux-Arts architecture, characterized by craftsmanship and decoration, emerged in France in the nineteenth century from the École des Beaux-Arts.

[5] William Hogarth's (1697–1764) *Gin Lane* attacks alcohol and prostitution by satirically depicting degenerates.

FOCUS: READING REVIEW

1. What is the relation between American architecture in the midtwentieth century and worker housing?
2. What was the actual worker housing of midcentury United States?
3. What is a "luxury highrise"? What are its characteristics? Who lives in them?
4. How did Mies van der Rohe adapt the international style to American codes in the Seagram building in New York?
5. What does the confrontation over window coverings between builders and inhabitants suggest about "modern" architecture?
6. What is the relation between modern architecture and Beaux-Arts craftsmen?
7. What do the examples of Pruitt-Igoe and Oriental Gardens tell about the efficacy of international design architecture for nonbourgeois housing? What problems exist?

FOCUS: AUTHOR'S STRATEGIES

1. The writer's tone reveals both the persona and some of the essay's purpose. What is the tone? What creates it? What does this tell you about the persona and the purpose?
2. For what audience is Wolfe writing? What does the use of words like "prole" and "bourgeois" suggest about the audience? What other references do you find to social class? What do these tell you?

FOCUS: DISCUSSION AND WRITING

1. What do the concrete details in Wolfe's description of "*that apartment's*" furnishings suggest about the people who live in them?

2. On what grounds does Wolfe object to "modern" architecture? What are his implicit criteria for this evaluation? Using these criteria, describe and evaluate a building in your community (either modern or traditional).

The Getty
Joan Didion

Joan Didion (b. 1934) worked as a New York journalist even before she graduated from the University of California, Berkeley, with a degree in English. She has worked as associate editor for Vogue *and as a contributing editor for* National Review *and* Saturday Evening Post. *Her fiction writing includes several screenplays and four novels:* Run River *(1963),* Play It As It Lays *(1970),* The Book of Common Prayer *(1978), and* Democracy *(1981). Her essays on contemporary culture, which have appeared in numerous magazines, are collected in* Slouching Towards Bethlehem *(1968) and* The White Album *(1979). In "The Getty," from* The White Album, *Didion examines criticisms of the J.P. Getty Museum in Malibu, California, and finds, as she surveys the collection and the building that houses it, that the criticisms derive from the distance between the modern critical temperament and the collection's antiquities.*

Mysteriously and rather giddily splendid, the seventeen-million-dollar villa built by the late J. Paul Getty to house his antiquities and paintings and furniture manages to strike a peculiar nerve in almost everyone who sees it. From the beginning, the Getty was said to be vulgar. The Getty seems to stir up social discomforts at levels not easily plumbed. To mention the museum to the more enlightened is to invite a kind of nervous derision, as if the place were an affront to good taste. The collection itself is usually referred to as "that kind of thing," which translates to "not our kind of thing." The Getty collection is in certain ways unremittingly reproachful, and quite inaccessible to generations trained in the conviction that a museum is meant to be fun, with Calder mobiles and Barcelona chairs. In short the Getty is a monument to "fine art," in the old-fashioned didactic sense. At a time when all our public convictions remain rooted in a kind of knocked-down romanticism, when the celebration of natural man's capacity for moving onward and upward has become a kind of official tic, the Getty presents us with an illustrated lesson in classical doubt. The Getty's founder may or may not have had some such statement in mind, but his idea of the place seems to have been this: here was a museum built not for those elitist critics but for "the public." As a matter of fact large numbers of people who do not ordinarily visit museums like the Getty a great deal. On the whole "the critics" distrust great wealth, but "the public" does not.

The place might have been commissioned by The Magic Christian. Mysteriously and rather giddily splendid, hidden in a grove of sycamores just above the Pacific

Coast Highway in Malibu, a commemoration of high culture so immediately productive of crowds and jammed traffic that it can now be approached by appoint-
ment only, the seventeen-million-dollar villa built by the late J. Paul Getty to
house his antiquities and paintings and furniture manages to strike a peculiar
nerve in almost everyone who sees it. From the beginning, the Getty was said to be
vulgar. The Getty was said to be "Disney." The Getty was even said to be Jewish,
if I did not misread the subtext in "like a Beverly Hills nouveau-riche dining
room" (*Los Angeles Times,* January 6, 1974) and "gussied up like a Bel-Air
dining room" (*New York Times,* May 28, 1974).

The Getty seems to stir up social discomforts at levels not easily plumbed. To
mention this museum in the more enlightened of those very dining rooms it is said
to resemble is to invite a kind of nervous derision, as if the place were a local hoax,
a perverse and deliberate affront to the understated good taste and general class of
everyone at the table. The Getty's intricately patterned marble floors and walls are
"garish." The Getty's illusionistic portico murals are "back lot." The entire
building, an informed improvisation on a villa buried by mud from Vesuvius in 79
A.D. and seen again only dimly during some eighteenth-century tunneling around
Herculaneum, is ritually dismissed as "inauthentic," although what "authentic"
could mean in this context is hard to say.

Something about the place embarrasses people. The collection itself is usually
referred to as "that kind of thing," as in "not even the best of that kind of thing,"
or "absolutely top-drawer if you like that kind of thing," both of which translate
"not our kind of thing." The Getty's damask-lined galleries of Renaissance and
Baroque paintings are distinctly that kind of thing, there being little in the modern
temperament that responds immediately to popes and libertine babies, and so are
the Getty's rather unrelenting arrangements of French furniture. A Louis XV
writing table tends to please the modern eye only if it has been demystified by a
glass of field flowers and some silver-framed snapshots, as in a Horst photograph
for *Vogue.* Even the Getty's famous antiquities are pretty much that kind of thing,
evoking as they do not their own period but the eighteenth- and nineteenth-century rage for antiquities. The sight of a Greek head depresses many people, strikes
an unliberated chord, reminds them of books in their grandmother's parlor and of
all they were supposed to learn and never did. This note of "learning" pervades the
entire Getty collection. Even the handful of Impressionists acquired by Getty
were recently removed from the public galleries, put away as irrelevant. The
Getty collection is in certain ways unremittingly reproachful, and quite inaccessible to generations trained in the conviction that a museum is meant to be fun,
with Calder mobiles and Barcelona chairs.

In short the Getty is a monument to "fine art," in the old-fashioned didactic
sense, which is part of the problem people have with it. The place resists contemporary notions about what art is or should be or ever was. A museum is now
supposed to kindle the untrained imagination, but this museum does not. A museum is now supposed to set the natural child in each of us free, but this museum
does not. This was art acquired to teach a lesson, and there is also a lesson in the

building which houses it: the Getty tells us that the past was perhaps different from the way we like to perceive it. Ancient marbles were not always attractively faded and worn. Ancient marbles once appeared just as they appear here: as strident, opulent evidence of imperial power and acquisition. Ancient murals were not always bleached and mellowed and "tasteful." Ancient murals once looked as they do here: as if dreamed by a Mafia don. Ancient fountains once worked, and drowned out that very silence we have come to expect and want from the past. Ancient bronze once gleamed ostentatiously. The old world was once discomfitingly new, or even nouveau, as people like to say about the Getty. (I have never been sure what the word "nouveau" can possibly mean in America, implying as it does that the speaker is gazing down six hundred years of rolled lawns.) At a time when all our public conventions remain rooted in a kind of knocked-down romanticism, when the celebration of natural man's capacity for moving onward and upward has become a kind of official tic, the Getty presents us with an illustrated lesson in classical doubt. The Getty advises us that not much changes. The Getty tells us that we were never any better than we are and will never be any better than we were, and in so doing makes a profoundly unpopular political statement.

The Getty's founder may or may not have had some such statement in mind. In a way he seems to have wanted only to do something no one else could or would do. In his posthumous book, *As I See It,* he advises us that he never wanted "one of those concrete-bunker-type structures that are the fad among museum architects." He refused to pay for any "tinted-glass-and-stainless-steel monstrosity." He assures us that he was "neither shaken nor surprised" when his villa was finished and "certain critics sniffed." He had "calculated the risks." He knew that he was flouting the "doctrinaire and elitist" views he believed endemic in "many Art World (or should I say Artsy-Craftsy?) quarters."

Doctrinaire and elitist. Artsy-craftsy. On the surface the Getty would appear to have been a case of he-knew-what-he-liked-and-he-built-it, a tax dodge from the rather louche world of the international rich, and yet the use of that word "elitist" strikes an interesting note. The man who built himself the Getty never saw it, although it opened a year and a half before his death. He seems to have liked the planning of it. He personally approved every paint sample. He is said to have taken immense pleasure in every letter received from anyone who visited the museum and liked it (such letters were immediately forwarded to him by the museum staff), but the idea of the place seems to have been enough, and the idea was this: here was a museum built not for those elitist critics but for "the public." Here was a museum that would be forever supported by its founder alone, a museum that need never depend on any city or state or federal funding, a place forever "open to the public and free of all charges."

As a matter of fact large numbers of people who do not ordinarily visit museums like the Getty a great deal, just as its founder knew they would. There is one of those peculiar social secrets at work here. On the whole "the critics" distrust great wealth, but "the public" does not. On the whole "the critics" subscribe to the romantic view of man's possibilities, but "the public" does not. In the end the Getty stands above the Pacific Coast Highway as one of those odd monuments, a palpable contract between the very rich and the people who distrust them least.

FOCUS: READING REVIEW

1. What are some of the responses to the Getty? What features of the museum elicit these responses?
2. In what ways is the Getty collection reproachful?
3. What are contemporary notions about what art should be? How do these notions come into conflict with the Getty?
4. Didion suggests that the Getty presents a lesson in "classical doubt." How does the context define this term? How does this compare with the critics' "romantic view of man's possibilities"?

FOCUS: AUTHOR'S STRATEGIES

1. For what audience is "The Getty" written? What is Didion's attitude toward this audience? What specific statements in the essay indicate her attitude?
2. The author shapes her essay in response to comments about the Getty. What are these comments? How does she respond to them?

FOCUS: DISCUSSION AND WRITING

1. In this essay Didion is a critic. Whom does she criticize? On what grounds?
2. What should be the purpose of an art museum? Describe your ideal art museum and explain the relationship between the building and the collection.

Underground Man
Pauline Kael

Pauline Kael (b. 1919) began reviewing movies in the 1950s as film critic for the New Yorker, The New Republic, *and* McCall's. *Kael majored in philosophy at the University of California, Berkeley. Her reviews, which are quick to ridicule pretentiousness or preachiness, reflect her interest in the sociology of the movies. Her essays are collected in* I Lost It at the Movies *(1965),* Kiss Kiss Bang Bang *(1968),* Going Steady *(1970), and* Deeper into Movies *(1973). "Underground Man," a* New Yorker *review of Martin Scorsese's 1976 film* Taxi Driver, *examines not only the acting and directing that make this a powerful film but also the way the film presents the alienation and resulting violence of the central character, Travis Bickle.*

Taxi Driver is the fevered story of an outsider in New York—a man who can't find any point of entry into human society. Travis Bickle (Robert De Niro), the protagonist of Martin Scorsese's new film, from a script by Paul Schrader, can't find a life. Travis becomes sick with loneliness and frustration, and then, like a commando preparing for a raid, he purifies his body and goes into training to kill. This picture, more ferocious than Scorsese's volatile *Mean Streets*, is a two character study—Travis versus New York. Scorsese may just be naturally an Expressionist, but his Expressionism isn't anything like the German; he uses documentary locations, but he pushes discordant elements to their limits and the cinematographer gives the street life a seamy, rich pulpiness. Scorsese handles the cast immaculately. As a director, Scorsese has the occasional arbitrariness and preening of a runaway talent, but the Bernard Herrmann score is a much bigger problem. Some actors are said to be empty vessels, but that's not what appears to be happening here with De Niro. De Niro's performance has something of the undistanced intensity that Brando's had in *Last Tango*—bottled up, impacted energy and emotion, with a blood-splattering release. The violence in this movie is so threatening precisely because it's cathartic for Travis.

Taxi Driver is the fevered story of an outsider in New York—a man who can't find any point of entry into human society. Travis Bickle (Robert De Niro), the protagonist of Martin Scorsese's new film, from a script by Paul Schrader, can't find a life. He's an ex-Marine from the Midwest who takes a job driving a cab nights, because he can't sleep anyway, and he is surrounded by the night world of the uprooted—whores, pimps, transients. Schrader, who grew up in Michigan, in the Christian Reformed Church, a zealous Calvinist splinter (he didn't see a movie until he was seventeen), has created a protagonist who is an ascetic not by choice but out of fear. And Scorsese with his sultry moodiness and his appetite for the pulp sensationalism of forties movies, is just the director to define an American underground man's resentment. Travis wants to conform, but he can't find a group pattern to conform to. So he sits and drives in the stupefied languor of anomie. He hates New York with a Biblical fury; it gives off the stench of Hell, and its filth and smut obsess him. He manages to get a date with Betsy (Cybill Shepherd), a political campaigner whose blondness and white clothes represent purity to him, but he is so out of touch that he inadvertently offends her and she won't have anything more to do with him. When he fumblingly asks advice from Wizard (Peter Boyle), an older cabdriver, and indicates the pressure building up in him, Wizard doesn't know what he's talking about. Travis becomes sick with loneliness and frustration; and then, like a commando preparing for a raid, he purifies his body and goes into training to kill. *Taxi Driver* is a movie in heat, a raw, tabloid version of *Notes from Underground,* and we stay with the protagonist's hatreds all the way.

This picture is more ferocious than Scorsese's volatile, allusive *Mean Streets. Taxi Driver* has a relentless movement: Travis has got to find relief. It's a two-character study—Travis versus New York. As Scorsese has designed the film, the city never lets you off the hook. There's no grace, no compassion in the artificially lighted atmosphere. The neon reds, the vapors that shoot up from the streets, the dilapidation all get to you the way they get to Travis. He is desperately sick, but he's the only one who tries to save a twelve-and-a-half-year-old hooker, Iris (Jodie Foster); the argument he invokes is that she belongs with her family and in school—the secure values from his own past that are of no help to him now. Some mechanism of adaptation is missing in Travis; the details aren't filled in—just the indications of a strict religious background, and a scar on his back, suggesting a combat wound. The city world presses in on him, yet it's also remote, because Travis is so disaffected that he isn't always quite there. We perceive the city as he does, and it's so scummy and malign we get the feel of his alienation.

Scorsese may just naturally be an Expressionist; his asthmatic bedridden childhood in a Sicilian-American home in Little Italy propelled him toward a fix on the violently exciting movies he saw. Physically and intellectually, he's a speed demon, a dervish. Even in *Alice Doesn't Live Here Anymore* he found a rationale for restless, whirlwind movement. But Scorsese is also the most carnal of directors—movement is ecstatic for him—and that side of him didn't come out in *Alice.* This new movie gives him a chance for the full Expressionist use of the city which he was denied in *Mean Streets,* because it was set in New York but was made on a minuscule budget in Southern California, with only seven shooting days in New York itself. Scorsese's Expressionism isn't anything like the exaggerated sets of the German directors; he uses documentary locations, but he pushes discordant elements to their limits, and the cinematographer, Michael Chapman, gives the street life a seamy, rich pulpiness. When Travis is taunted by a pimp, Sport (Harvey Keitel), the pimp is so eager for action that he can't stand still; the hipster, with his rhythmic jiggling, makes an eerily hostile contrast to the paralyzed, dumbfounded Travis. Scorsese gets the quality of trance in a scene like this; the whole movie has a sense of vertigo. Scorsese's New York is the big city of the thrillers he feasted his imagination on—but at a later stage of decay. This New York is a voluptuous enemy. The street vapors become ghostly; Sport the pimp is always in movement.

No other film has ever dramatized urban indifference so powerfully; at first, here, it's horrifyingly funny, and then just horrifying. When Travis attempts to date Betsy, he's very seductive; we can see why she's tantalized. They're talking across a huge gap, and still they're connecting (though the wires are all crossed). It's a zinger of a scene: an educated, socially conscious woman dating a lumpen lost soul who uses one of the oldest pitches in the book—he tells her that he knows she is a lonely person. Travis means it; the gruesome comedy in the scene is how intensely he means it—because his own life is utterly empty. Throughout the movie, Travis talks to people on a different level from the level they take him on. He's so closed off he's otherworldly; he engages in so few conversations that slang words like "moonlighting" pass right over him—the spoken language is foreign to him. His responses are sometimes so blocked that he seems wiped out; at other times he's animal fast. This man is burning in misery, and his inflamed, brimming eyes are the focal point of the compositions. Robert De Niro is in almost every frame: thin-faced, as handsome as Robert Taylor one moment and cagey, ferrety, like Cagney, the next—and not just looking at the people he's talking to but spying on them. As Travis, De Niro has none of the peasant courtliness of his Vito Corleone in *The Godfather, Part II.* Vito held himself in proudly, in control of his violence; he was a leader. Travis is dangerous in a different, cumulative way. His tense face folds in a yokel's grin and he looks almost an idiot. Or he sits in his room vacantly watching the bright-eyed young faces on the TV and with his foot he slowly rocks the set back and then over. The exacerbation of his desire for vengeance shows in his numbness, yet part of the horror implicit in this movie is how easily he passes. The anonymity of the city soaks up one more invisible man; he could be legion.

Scorsese handles the cast immaculately. Harvey Keitel's pimp is slimy, all right, yet his malicious, mischievous eyes and his jumpiness are oddly winning. Jodie Foster, who was exactly Iris's age when she played the part, is an unusually physical child actress and seems to have felt out her line readings—her words are convincingly hers. Cybill Shepherd has never been better: you don't see her trying to act. She may actually be doing her least acting here, yet she doesn't have that schoolgirl model's blankness; her face is expressive and womanly. There's a suggestion that Betsy's life hasn't gone according to her expectations—a faint air of defeat. The comedian Albert Brooks brings a note of quibbling, plump pomposity to the role of her political co-worker, and Leonard Harris, formerly the WCBS-TV arts critic, has a professionally earnest manner as Palatine, their candidate. Peter Boyle's role is small, but he was right to want to be in this film, and he does slobby wonders with his scenes as the gently thick Wizard, adjusted to the filth that Travis is coiled up to fight; Boyle gives the film a special New York-hack ambience, and, as the cabby Doughboy, Harry Northup has a bland face and Southern drawl that suggest another kind of rootlessness. Scorsese himself is sitting on the sidewalk when Travis first sees Betsy, and then he returns to play a glitteringly morbid role as one of Travis's fares—a man who wants Travis to share his rancid glee in what the Magnum he intends to shoot his faithless wife with will do to her. As an actor, he sizzles; he has such concentrated energy that this sequence burns a small hole in the screen.

As a director, Scorsese has the occasional arbitrariness and preening of a runaway talent; sometimes a shot calls attention to itself, because it serves no visible purpose. One can pass over a lingering closeup of a street musician, but when Travis is talking to Betsy on a pay phone in an office building and the camera moves away from him to the blank hallway, it's an Antonioni pirouette. The Bernard Herrmann score is a much bigger problem; the composer finished recording it on December 23rd, the day before he died, and so it's a double pity that it isn't better. It's clear why Scorsese wanted Herrmann: his specialty was expressing psychological disorder through dissonant, wrought-up music. But this movie, with its suppressed sex and suppressed violence, is already pitched so high that it doesn't need ominous percussion, snake rattles, and rippling scales. These musical nudges belong back with the rampaging thrillers that *Taxi Driver* transcends.

Scorsese got something out of his asthma: he knows how to make us experience the terror of suffocation.

Some actors are said to be empty vessels who are filled by the roles they play, but that's not what appears to be happening here with De Niro. He's gone the other way. He's used his emptiness—he's reached down into his own anomie. Only Brando has done this kind of plunging, and De Niro's performance has something of the undistanced intensity that Brando's had in *Last Tango*. In its own way, this movie, too, has an erotic aura. There is practically no sex in it, but no sex can be as disturbing as sex. And that's what it's about: the absence of sex—bottled-up, impacted energy and emotion, with a blood-splattering release. The fact that we experience Travis's need for an explosion viscerally, and that the explosion itself has the quality of consummation, makes *Taxi Driver* one of the few truly modern horror films.

Anyone who goes to the movie houses that loners frequent knows that they identify with the perpetrators of crimes, even the most horrible crimes, and that they aren't satisfied unless there's a whopping climax. In his essay "The White Negro," Norman Mailer suggested that when a killer takes his revenge on the institutions that he feels are oppressing him his eruption of violence can have a positive effect on him. The most shocking aspect of *Taxi Driver* is that it takes this very element, which has generally been exploited for popular appeal, and puts it in the center of the viewer's consciousness. Violence is Travis's only means of expressing himself. He has not been able to hurdle the barriers to being seen and felt. When he blasts through, it's his only way of telling the city that he's there. And, given his ascetic loneliness, it's the only real orgasm he can have.

The violence in this movie is so threatening precisely because it's cathartic for Travis. I imagine that some people who are angered by the film will say that it advocates violence as a cure for frustration. But to acknowledge that when a psychopath's blood boils over he may cool down is not the same as justifying the eruption. This film doesn't operate on the level of moral judgment of what Travis does. Rather, by drawing us into its vortex it makes us understand the psychic discharge of the quiet boys who go berserk. And it's a real slap in the face for us when we see Travis at the end looking pacified. He's got the rage out of his system—for the moment, at least—and he's back at work, picking up passengers in front of the St. Regis. It's not that he's cured but that the city is crazier than he is.

[February 9, 1976]

Notes

[1] *Notes from Underground* is the title of Dostoevski's novel that chronicles the central character's alienation.

[2] The Expressionist movement in film began in Germany after World War I. Expressionist films were characterized by their interest in the dark side of human experience—the

fantastic and the irrational—and by high contrast between dark and light, oblique filming angles, and distorted backgrounds.

FOCUS: READING REVIEW

1. Kael begins her critique of *Taxi Driver* by describing the film's central character, Travis Bickle, as someone who cannot fit in. What are some of the character's characteristics that she uses to support her contentions?
2. Kael states that Travis "has got to find relief." Why? How does he accomplish this?
3. Kael says that the film dramatizes "urban indifference." What in the film creates this picture?
4. What role does violence play in this film?

FOCUS: AUTHOR'S STRATEGIES

1. Besides focusing on the creation of Travis Bickle's character, what other aspects of the film does Kael discuss in her analysis?
2. What is the author's purpose in this essay? What in her analysis and language indicate this?

FOCUS: DISCUSSION AND WRITING

1. Ultimately, does Kael approve or disapprove of *Taxi Driver?* What assumptions about film's place in society form her judgment?
2. Kael says that the violence in *Taxi Driver* is so threatening because it is cathartic. Consider a film you have recently seen which is violent. Explain the role violence plays in the film in relation to the character committing the violence. Using your evidence, argue whether or not cinematic violence threatens the audience.

Chapter *12*
Critical Responses to Art and Literature

Does criticism really take us closer to art's imaginative experience? The essays in this chapter challenge this assumption. Susan Sontag's "Against Interpretation" finds that critical interpretation buries art beneath layers of subjective responses. The only criticism which, she believes, can bring us closer to a work is a consideration of artistic form. While Sontag appeals for greater objectivity in art criticism, Steinberg demonstrates how art studies ultimately rely upon and engage in valuation, a subjective response. Steinberg finds in this subjectivity the greatest part of artistic pleasure.

Against Interpretation
Susan Sontag

Susan Sontag (b. 1933), a writer, philosopher, and filmmaker, graduated from the University of Chicago and received M.A.'s in English and philosophy from Harvard. She has taught at Sarah Lawrence, Rutgers, and Columbia, and contributed short stores, reviews, essays, and articles to Atlantic Monthly, American Review, Nation, Harper's, and several other periodicals. "Against Interpretation" examines both the assumptions that un-

derlie art criticism and the predominant critical practice of assigning meaning to art content interpretation. To correct the "stifling" effect that interpretation has on art, Sontag advocates that criticism focus on form.

Although the earliest experience of art must have been magical, the earliest theory of art proposed that art was mimesis, an imitation of reality. Mimetic theory challenges art to justify itself. For Plato, art is neither particularly useful (the painting of a bed is no good to sleep on), nor, in the strict sense, true. [For Aristotle, art's value lay in its own therapy.] With this focus on artistic content, artistic form becomes separated off and subordinate. Whatever it may have been in the past, the idea of content is today mainly a hindrance. What the overemphasis on the idea of content entails is the perennial, never consummated project of *interpretation.* Interpretation originated when scientific emphasis on reality broke the power of myth and ancient religious texts needed to be reconciled to "modern" demands. Interpretation in our times, however, is more complex. It digs "behind" the text with an overt contempt for appearances. This interpretation is the revenge of intellect upon art which makes art manageable, conformable. Interpretation does not, of course, always prevail. In fact, a great deal of today's art may be understood as motivated by a flight from interpretation, particularly modern painting. Ideally, it is possible to elude the interpreter in another way, by making works of art whose surface is so unified and lean that the work can be . . . just what it is. It does happen in films.

What kind of criticism, of commentary on the arts, is desirable today? What is needed, first, is more attention to form in art. What is needed is a descriptive vocabulary for forms. Equally valuable would be acts of criticism which would supply a really accurate description of the appearance of a work of art. *Transparence* is the highest, most liberating value in art—and in criticism—today. Transparence means experiencing the luminousness of the thing in itself, of things being what they are.

The earliest experience of art must have been that it was incantatory, magical; art was an instrument of ritual. (Cf. the paintings in the caves at Lascaux, Altamira, Niaux, La Pasiega, etc.) The earliest *theory* of art, that of the Greek philosophers, proposed that art was mimesis, imitation of reality.

It is at this point that the peculiar question of the *value* of art arose. For the mimetic theory, by its very terms, challenges art to justify itself.

Plato, who proposed the theory, seems to have done so in order to rule that the value of art is dubious. Since he considered ordinary material things as themselves mimetic objects, imitations of transcendent forms or structures, even the best painting of a bed would be only an "imitation of an imitation." For Plato, art is neither particularly useful (the painting of a bed is no good to sleep on), nor, in the strict sense, true. And Aristotle's arguments in defense of art do not really challenge Plato's view that all art is an elaborate *trompe l'oeil,*[1] and therefore a lie. But he does dispute Plato's idea that art is useless. Lie or no, art has a certain value according to Aristotle because it is a form of therapy. Art is useful, after all,

Aristotle counters, medicinally useful in that it arouses and purges dangerous emotions.

In Plato and Aristotle, the mimetic theory of art goes hand in hand with the assumption that art is always figurative. But advocates of the mimetic theory need not close their eyes to decorative and abstract art. The fallacy that art is necessarily a "realism" can be modified or scrapped without ever moving outside the problems delimited by the mimetic theory.

The fact is, all Western consciousness of and reflection upon art have remained within the confines staked out by the Greek theory of art as mimesis or representation. It is through this theory that art as such—above and beyond given works of art—becomes problematic, in need of defense. And it is the defense of art which gives birth to the odd vision by which something we have learned to call "form" is separated off from something we have learned to call "content," and to the well-intentioned move which makes content essential and form accessory.

Even in modern times, when most artists and critics have discarded the theory of art as representation of an outer reality in favor of the theory of art as subjective expression, the main feature of the mimetic theory persists. Whether we conceive of the work of art on the model of a picture (art as a picture of reality) or on the model of a statement (art as the statement of the artist), content still comes first. The content may have changed. It may now be less figurative, less lucidly realistic. But it is still assumed that a work of art *is* its content. Or, as it's usually put today, that a work of art by definition *says* something. ("What X is saying is . . . ," "What X is trying to say is . . . ," "What X said is . . . " etc., etc.)

2

None of us can ever retrieve that innocence before all theory when art knew no need to justify itself, when one did not ask of a work of art what it *said* because one knew (or thought one knew) what it *did*. From now to the end of consciousness, we are stuck with the task of defending art. We can only quarrel with one or another means of defense. Indeed, we have an obligation to overthrow any means of defending and justifying art which becomes particularly obtuse or onerous or insensitive to contemporary needs and practice.

This is the case, today, with the very idea of content itself. Whatever it may have been in the past, the idea of content is today mainly a hindrance, a nuisance, a subtle or not so subtle philistinism.

Though the actual developments in many arts may seem to be leading us away from the idea that a work of art is primarily its content, the idea still exerts an extraordinary hegemony.[2] I want to suggest that this is because the idea is now perpetuated in the guise of a certain way of encountering works of art thoroughly ingrained among most people who take any of the arts seriously. What the over-emphasis on the idea of content entails is the perennial, never consummated project of *interpretation*. And, conversely, it is the habit of approaching works of art in order to *interpret* them that sustains the fancy that there really is such a thing as the content of a work of art.

3

Of course, I don't mean interpretation in the broadest sense, the sense in which Nietzsche (rightly) says, "There are no facts, only interpretations." By interpretation, I mean here a conscious act of the mind which illustrates a certain code, certain "rules" of interpretation.

Directed to art, interpretation means plucking a set of elements (the X, the Y, the Z, and so forth) from the whole work. The task of interpretation is virtually one of translation. The interpreter says, "Look, don't you see that X is really—or, really means—A? That Y is really B? That Z is really C?

What situation could prompt this curious project for transforming a text? History gives us the materials for an answer. Interpretation first appears in the culture of late classical antiquity, when the power and credibility of myth had been broken by the "realistic" view of the world introduced by scientific enlightenment. Once the question that haunts post-mythic consciousness[3]—that of the *seemliness* of religious symbols—had been asked, the ancient texts were, in their pristine form, no longer acceptable. Then interpretation was summoned, to reconcile the ancient texts to "modern" demands. Thus, the Stoics,[4] to accord with their view that the gods had to be moral, allegorized away the rude features of Zeus and his boisterous clan in Homer's epics. What Homer really designated by the adultery of Zeus with Leto, they explained, was the union between power and wisdom. In the same vein, Philo of Alexandria interpreted the literal historical narratives of the Hebrew Bible as spiritual paradigms. The story of the exodus from Egypt, the wandering in the desert for forty years, and the entry into the promised land, said Philo, was really an allegory of the individual soul's emancipation, tribulations, and final deliverance. Interpretation thus presupposes a discrepancy between the clear meaning of the text and the demands of (later) readers. It seeks to resolve that discrepancy. The situation is that for some reason a text has become unacceptable; yet it cannot be discarded. Interpretation is a radical strategy for conserving an old text, which is thought too precious to repudiate, by revamping it. The interpreter, without actually erasing or rewriting the text, *is* altering it. But he can't admit to doing this. He claims to be only making it intelligible, by disclosing its true meaning. However far the interpreters alter the text (another notorious example is the Rabbinic and Christian "spiritual" interpretations of the clearly erotic Song of Songs), they must claim to be reading off a sense that is already there.

Interpretation in our time, however, is even more complex. For the contemporary zeal for the project of interpretation is often prompted not by piety toward the troublesome text (which may conceal an aggression), but by an open aggressiveness, an overt contempt for appearances. The old style of interpretation was insistent, but respectful; it erected another meaning on top of the literal one. The modern style of interpretation excavates, and as it excavates, destroys; it digs "behind" the text, to find a sub-text which is the true one. The most celebrated and influential modern doctrines, those of Marx and Freud, actually amount to elaborate systems of hermeneutics,[5] aggressive and impious theories of interpretation. All observable phenomena are bracketed, in Freud's phrase, as *manifest content.* This manifest content must be probed and pushed aside to find the true meaning—the *latent content*—beneath. For Marx, social events like revolutions and wars; for Freud, the events of individual lives (like neurotic symptoms and slips of the tongue) as well as texts (like a dream or a work of art)—are all treated as occasions for interpretation. According to Marx and Freud, these events only *seem* to be intelligible. Actually, they have no meaning without interpretation. To understand *is* to interpret. And to interpret is to restate the phenomenon, in effect to find an equivalent for it.

Thus, interpretation is not (as most people assume) an absolute value, a gesture of mind situated in some timeless realm of capabilities. Interpretation must itself be evaluated, within a historical view of human consciousness. In some cultural contexts, interpretation is a liberating act. It is a means of revising, of transvaluing, of escaping the dead past. In other cultural contexts, it is reactionary, impertinent, cowardly, stifling.

4

Today is such a time, when the project of interpretation is largely reactionary, stifling. Like the fumes of the automobile and of heavy industry which befoul the urban atmosphere, the effusion of interpretations of art today poisons our sensibilities. In a culture whose already classical dilemma is the hypertrophy[6] of the intellect at the expense of energy and sensual capability, interpretation is the revenge of the intellect upon art.

Even more. It is the revenge of the intellect upon the world. To interpret is to impoverish, to deplete the world—in order to set up a shadow world of "meanings." It is to turn *the* world into *this* world. ("This world"! As if there were any other.)

The world, our world, is depleted, impoverished enough. Away with all duplicates of it, until we again experience more immediately what we have.

5

In most modern instances, interpretation amounts to the philistine[7] refusal to leave the work of art alone. Real art has the capacity to make us nervous. By reducing the work of art to its content and then interpreting *that,* one tames the work of art. Interpretation makes art manageable, comformable.

This philistinism of interpretation is more rife in literature than in any other art. For decades now, literary critics have understood it to be their task to translate the elements of the poem or play or novel or story into something else. Sometimes a writer will be so uneasy before the naked power of his art that he will install within the work itself—albeit with a little shyness, a touch of the good taste of irony—the clear and explicit interpretation of it. Thomas Mann[8] is an example of such an overcooperative author. In the case of more stubborn authors, the critic is only too happy to perform the job.

The work of Kafka,[9] for example, has been subjected to a mass ravishment by no less than three armies of interpreters. Those who read Kafka as a social allegory see case studies of the frustrations and insanity of modern bureaucracy and its ultimate issuance in the totalitarian state. Those who read Kafka as a psychoanalytic allegory see desperate revelations of Kafka's fear of his father, his castration anxieties, his sense of his own impotence, his thralldom to his dreams. Those who read Kafka as a religious allegory explain that K. in *The Castle* is trying to gain access to heaven, that Joseph K. in *The Trial* is being judged by the inexorable and mysterious justice of God. . . . Another oeuvre that has attracted interpreters like leeches is that of Samuel Beckett.[10] Beckett's delicate dramas of the withdrawn consciousness—pared down to essentials, cut off, often represented as physically immobilized—are read as a statement about modern man's alienation from meaning or from God, or as an allegory of psychopathology.

Proust, Joyce, Faulkner, Rilke, Lawrence, Gide . . . one could go on citing author after author; the list is endless of those around whom thick encrustations of interpretation have taken hold. But it should be noted that interpretation is not simply the compliment that mediocrity pays to genius. It is, indeed, *the* modern way of understanding something, and is applied to works of every quality. Thus, in the notes that Elia Kazan[11] published on his production of *A Streetcar Named Desire,* it becomes clear that, in order to direct the play, Kazan had to discover that Stanley Kowalski represented the sensual and vengeful barbarism that was engulfing our culture, while Blanche Du Bois was Western civilization, poetry, delicate apparel, dim lighting, refined feelings and all, though a little the worse for wear to be sure. Tennessee Williams' forceful psychological melodrama now became intelligible: it was *about* something, about the decline of Western civilization. Apparently, were it to go on being a play about a handsome brute named Stanley Kowalski and a faded mangy belle named Blanche Du Bois, it would not be manageable.

6

It doesn't matter whether artists intend, or don't intend, for their works to be interpreted. Perhaps Tennessee Williams thinks *Streetcar* is about what Kazan thinks it to be about. It may be that Cocteau[12] in *The Blood of a Poet* and in *Orpheus* wanted the elaborate readings which have been given these films, in terms of Freudian symbolism and social critique. But the merit of these works certainly lies elsewhere than in their "meanings." Indeed, it is precisely to the extent that Williams' plays and Cocteau's films do suggest these portentous meanings that they are defective, false, contrived, lacking in conviction.

From interviews, it appears that Resnais[13] and Robbe-Grillet[14] consciously designed *Last Year at Marienbad* to accommodate a multiplicity of equally plausible interpretations. But the temptation to interpret *Marienbad* should be resisted. What matters in *Marienbad* is the pure, untranslatable, sensuous immediacy of some of its images, and its rigorous if narrow solutions to certain problems of cinematic form.

Again, Ingmar Bergman[15] may have meant the tank rumbling down the empty night street in *The Silence* as a phallic symbol. But if he did, it was a foolish thought. ("Never trust the teller, trust the tale," said Lawrence.) Taken as a brute object, as an immediate sensory equivalent for the mysterious abrupt armored happenings going on inside the hotel, that sequence with the tank is the most striking moment in the film. Those who reach for a Freudian interpretation of the tank are only expressing their lack of response to what is there on the screen.

It is always the case that interpretation of this type indicates a dissatisfaction (conscious or unconscious) with the work, a wish to replace it by something else.

Interpretation, based on the highly dubious theory that a work of art is composed of items of content, violates art. It makes art into an article for use, for arrangement into a mental scheme of categories.

7

Interpretation does not, of course, always prevail. In fact, a great deal of today's art may be understood as motivated by a flight from interpretation. To avoid interpretation, art may become parody. Or it may become abstract. Or it may become ("merely") decorative. Or it may become non-art.

The flight from interpretation seems particularly a feature of modern painting. Abstract painting is the attempt to have, in the ordinary sense, no content; since there is no content, there can be no interpretation. Pop Art works by the opposite means to the same result; using a content so blatant, so "what it is," it, too, ends by being uninterpretable.

A great deal of modern poetry as well, starting from the great experiments of French poetry (including the movement that is misleadingly called Symbolism) to put silence into poems and to reinstate the *magic* of the word, has escaped from the rough grip of interpretation. The most recent revolution in contemporary taste in poetry—the revolution that has deposed Eliot[16] and elevated Pound[17]—represents a turning away from content in poetry in the old sense, an impatience with what made modern poetry prey to the zeal of interpreters.

I am speaking mainly of the situation in America, of course. Interpretation runs rampant here in those arts with a feeble and negligible avant-garde: fiction and the drama. Most American novelists and playwrights are really either journalists or gentlemen sociologists and psychologists. They are writing the literary equivalent of program music. And so rudimentary, uninspired, and stagnant has been the sense of what might be done with *form* in fiction and drama that even when the content isn't simply information, news, it is still peculiarly visible, handier, more exposed. To the extent that novels and plays (in America), unlike poetry and painting and music, don't reflect any interesting concern with changes in their form, these arts remain prone to assault by interpretation.

But programmatic avant-gardism—which has meant, mostly, experiments with form at the expense of content—is not the only defense against the infestation of art by interpretations. At least, I hope not. For this would be to commit art to being perpetually on the run. (It also perpetuates the very distinction between form and content which is, ultimately, an illusion.) Ideally, it is possible to elude the interpreters in another way, by making works of art whose surface is so unified and clean, whose momentum is so rapid, whose address is so direct that the work can be . . . just what it is. Is this possible now? It does happen in films, I believe. This is why cinema is the most alive, the most exciting, the most important of all art forms right now. Perhaps the way one tells how alive a particular art form is, is by the latitude it gives for making mistakes in it, and still being good. For example, a few of the films of Bergman—though crammed with lame messages about the modern spirit, thereby inviting interpretations—still triumph over the pretentious intentions of their director. In *Winter Light* and *The Silence*, the beauty and visual sophistication of the images subvert before our eyes the callow pseudo-intellectuality of the story and some of the dialogue. (The most remarkable instance of this sort of discrepancy is the work of D. W. Griffith.)[18] In good films, there is always a directness that entirely frees us from the itch to interpret. Many old Hollywood films, like those of Cukor, Walsh, Hawks, and countless other directors, have this liberating anti-symbolic quality, no less than the best work of the new European directors, like Truffaut's *Shoot the Piano Player* and *Jules and Jim*, Godard's *Breathless* and *Vivre Sa Vie*, Antonioni's *L'Avventura*, and Olmi's *The Fiances*.

The fact that films have not been overrun by interpreters is in part due simply to the newness of cinema as an art. It also owes to the happy accident that films for such a long time were just movies; in other words, that they were understood to be part of mass, as opposed to high, culture, and were left alone by most people with minds. Then, too, there is always something other than content in the cinema to grab hold of, for those who want to analyze. For the cinema, unlike the novel, possesses a vocabulary of forms—the explicit, complex, and discussable technology of camera movements, cutting, and composition of the frame that goes into the making of a film.

8

What kind of criticism, of commentary on the arts, is desirable today? For I am not saying that works of art are ineffable,[19] that they cannot be described or paraphrased. They can be. The question is how. What would criticism look like that would serve the work of art, not usurp its place?

What is needed, first, is more attention to form in art. If excessive stress on *content* provokes the arrogance of interpretation, more extended and more thorough descriptions of *form* would silence. What is needed is a vocabulary—a descriptive, rather than prescriptive, vocabulary—for forms.[20] The best criticism, and it is uncommon, is of this sort that dissolves considerations of content into those of form. On film, drama, and painting respectively, I can think of Erwin Panofsky's essay, "Style and Medium in the Motion Pictures," Northrop Frye's essay "A Conspectus of Dramatic Genres," Pierre Francastel's essay "The Destruction of a Plastic Space." Roland Barthes' book *On Racine* and his two essays on Robbe-Grillet are examples of formal analysis applied to the work of a single author. (The best essays in Erich Auerbach's *Mimesis*, like "The Scar of Odysseus," are also of this type.) An example of formal analysis applied simultaneously to genre and author is Walter Benjamin's essay, "The Story Teller: Reflections on the Works of Nicolai Leskov."

Equally valuable would be acts of criticism which would supply a really accurate, sharp, loving description of the appearance of a work of art. This seems even harder to do than formal analysis. Some of Manny Farber's film criticism, Dorothy Van Ghent's essay "The Dickens World: A View from Todgers'," Randall Jarrell's essay on Walt Whitman are among the rare examples of what I mean. These are essays which reveal the sensuous surface of art without mucking about in it.

9

Transparence is the highest, most liberating value in art—and in criticism—today. Transparence means experiencing the luminousness of the thing in itself, of things being what they are. This is the greatness of, for example, the films of Bresson[21] and Ozu[22] and Renoir's *The Rules of the Game*.

Once upon a time (say, for Dante), it must have been a revolutionary and creative move to design works of art so that they might be experienced on several levels. Now it is not. It reinforces the principle of redundancy that is the principal affliction of modern life.

Once upon a time (a time when high art was scarce), it must have been a revolutionary and creative move to interpret works of art. Now it is not. What we decidedly do not need now is further to assimilate Art into Thought, or (worse yet) Art into Culture.

Interpretation takes the sensory experience of the work of art for granted, and proceeds from there. This cannot be taken for granted, now. Think of the sheer multiplication of works of art available to every one of us, superadded to the conflicting tastes and odors and sights of the urban environment that bombard our senses. Ours is a culture based on excess, on overproduction; the result is a steady loss of sharpness in our sensory experience. All the conditions of modern life—its material plenitude, its sheer crowdedness—conjoin to dull our sensory faculties. And it is in the light of the condition of our senses, our capacities (rather than those of another age), that the task of the critic must be assessed.

What is important now is to recover our senses. We must learn to *see* more, to *hear* more, to *feel* more.

Our task is not to find the maximum amount of content in a work of art, much less to squeeze more content out of the work than is already there. Our task is to cut back content so that we can see the thing at all.

The aim of all commentary on art now should be to make works of art—and, by analogy, our own experience—more, rather than less, real to us. The function of criticism should be to show *how it is what it is*, even *that it is what it is*, rather than to show *what it means*.

10

In place of a hermeneutics we need an erotics of art.

Notes

[1] *Trompe l'oeil* (literally a trick of the eye) is a painting that creates such a strong illustration of reality that the viewer at first sight doubts whether the thing depicted is real or a representation.

[2] hegemony: leadership, authority or influence.

[3] "post-mythic consciousness" describes the modern way of seeing experience in terms of natural causation rather than mythic or religious causes.

[4] Stoics were disciples of the Greek philosopher Zeno (308 B.C.), who taught that men should be free from passion, unmoved by joy and grief, and submit without complaint to the divine will and unavoidable necessity by which all things are governed. In modern times this term has been used to describe people unaffected by passion and capable of maintaining austere indifference to joy, grief, pleasure, or pain.

[5] hermeneutics: the practice of interpretation.

[6] hypertrophy: an excessive increase in size.

[7] A philistine is a person regarded as smugly narrow and conventional in his or her views or tasks, lacking in or indifferent to aesthetic and cultural values.

[8] Thomas Mann (1875–1955), a German novelist, wrote the esteemed *Magic Mountain.*

[9] Franz Kafka (1883–1924), an Austrian-Czech writer, viewed with some cynicism the human condition in the modern world in his works, including *Metamorphosis.*

[10] Samuel Beckett (b. 1906), an Irish poet, novelist, and playwright, wrote in France, mostly in French. His plays were highly experimental.

[11] Elia Kazan (b. 1909) is a U.S. stage and film director, actor, writer, and producer who was born in Turkey. His films of the fifties, *Streetcar Named Desire* (1951), *On the Waterfront* (1954), and *East of Eden* (1955), made an impact on the American cinema.

[12] Jean Cocteau (1889–1963), a French avant-garde film director and screenwriter, made the well-known films *La Belle et Le Bete (Beauty and the Beast)* and *Orphee (Orpheus).*

[13] Alain Resnais (b. 1922), a French film director, is best known for *Hiroshima Mon Amour* and *Nuit et Brouillard (Night and Fog),* about concentration camps.

[14] Alain Robbe-Grillet (b. 1922), a French novelist, scriptwriter, and film director, repudiates objective reality and conventional narrative conventions to create a world of ambiguous relationships and sexual fantasy.

[15] Ingmar Bergman (b. 1918), a Swedish film director, significantly influenced filmmakers by the symbolism and despair in early films like *The Seventh Seal* (1957), *Wild Strawberries* (1952), and *The Virgin Spring* (1960). His more recent films, while highly personal, reflect his interest in psychosexual themes and powerful visual imagery.

[16] T.S. Eliot (1888–1965) was a British poet and critic born in the United States whose poetry, particularly *The Wasteland,* influenced the twentieth century. His critical essay "Tradition and the Individual Talent" appears in this volume.

[17] Ezra Pound (1885–1972), an American poet, participated in a literary coterie in England during World War I and the years following that gave him tremendous influence over other poets. He influenced Eliot's final form of *The Wasteland* and many of the writers whose work appeared in *The Dial.* He is best known for his poem *The Cantos.*

[18] D.W. Griffith (1875–1948), an American film director, is one of the most significant figures in film history because of his tremendous technical innovations in camera movement, dramatic lighting, directing actors, and narrative technique. His best-known film is the 1915 full-length film about the Civil War and Reconstruction *Birth of a Nation.*

[19] ineffable: too overwhelming to be expressed or described in words.

[20] One of the difficulties is that our idea of form is spatial (the Greek metaphors for form are all derived from notions of space). That is why we have a more ready vocabulary of forms for the spatial than for the temporal arts. The exception among the temporal arts, of course, is the drama; perhaps this is because the drama is a narrative (i.e., temporal) form that extends itself visually and pictorially, upon a stage. . . . What we don't have yet is a poetics of the novel, any clear notion of the forms of narration. Perhaps film criticism will be the occasion of a breakthrough here, since films are primarily a visual form, yet they are also a subdivision of literature. [Sontag]

[21] Robert Bresson (b. 1907) is a French film director.

[22] Yasujiro Ozu (1903–1963), a Japanese filmmaker, is regarded by the Japanese as their most traditional and most Japanese director.

FOCUS: READING REVIEW

1. What is Plato's view of art?
2. What are content and form in art?
3. How does Sontag define interpretation?
4. What distinction does Sontag make between the old style of interpretation and interpretation in our own time?
5. On what grounds does Sontag object to interpretation?
6. In her discussion of Kafka what approaches to literature does Sontag suggest exist?
7. In what ways does Sontag say today's art is motivated by a "flight from interpretation"?
8. What is programmatic avant-gardism? What is the problem with it?
9. What kind of criticism does Sontag advocate? Why does she feel it is necessary?

FOCUS: AUTHOR'S STRATEGIES

1. What does Sontag's essay seek to achieve?
2. To achieve her purpose, what audience would Sontag's essay have to reach? Is this the same audience that her definitions and assumptions suggest she is writing for? Why or why not?

FOCUS: DISCUSSION AND WRITING

1. Explain how a study of form might increase the sensual immediacy of art.
2. For what does Sontag appeal when she asks for an "erotics" of art? How does this compare with Frye's critical goal?

Objectivity and the Shrinking Self
Leo Steinberg

Leo Steinberg (b. 1920) is Benjamin Franklin Professor and University Professor of Art at the University of Pennsylvania. An expert on Renaissance art, he has written Michelangelo's Last Paintings *(1975),* Borromini's San Carballe Quattro Fontane: A Study of Multiple Form and Architectural Symposium *(1977), and contributed to* Art Bulletin, ARTnews, Art Quarterly, Art in America, Critical Inquiry, *and* Daedalus. *This selection, which appeared in* Other Criteria *(1972), was written in response to a letter inviting him to attend a conference on "The Condition of the Humanities." Steinberg responds here to the demand for objectivity which has permeated critical studies in all areas of twentieth-century art. While Steinberg admits that objectivity can increase our knowledge of art's contexts, he argues that enthusiasm and judgment derive ultimately from subjectivity. His letter suggests that overreliance on "scientism" can perhaps deprive art of its special place in human experience.*

[In the area of art history two conditions exist.] There is far more good work coming out than I get to read. On the other hand, the bulk of what is now being published, especially by young scholars, seems tedious beyond endurance without being exactly bad. Two questions suggest themselves: first, whether this new professionalism should usurp the whole field; and, second, why it should be the work of young scholars and recent graduates that turns out to be especially tame. [The design and implementation of the freshman art history course at the City University of New York illustrates the problem.] It seems that we are trying to sell art history to our freshmen for its pioneer spirit; whereas a pioneer spirit characterizes neither the condition nor even the aspiration of institutionalized art history at this moment. The great immigrant European scholars who taught most of us what to teach could afford to lay every stress on objective historical discipline because their humanism was bred in the bone. What the field needed when they were entering it was the corrective of a more rigorous scientism than had ever before been applied to art. And it is because they succeeded that the correctives we need are no longer the same. Can objectivity be made too much of? Though we all hope to reach objectively valid conclusions, this purpose is not served by disguising the subjectivity of interest, method, and personal history which in fact conditions our work. The finest among modern art historians seem at times somewhat confused in assessing the historical significance of subjectivity. An example from John Shearman's *Mannerism* illustrates this. He dismisses the work of European Expressionists who restored Mannerism's reputation by saying Mannerist art can stand on its own when it was subjective interest that revived Mannerism. With the disdain of subjectivity goes the demand that value judgments be eliminated from serious investigations of art since they cannot be objectified. The artistic universe is so thoroughly value-structured that the objectivity claims, were they taken seriously, would amount to mere cant. Art is cherished, or it does not survive. To say it in other words, the record of past valuations is integrally part of art history, and that record is meaningless without present revaluation. Further part of this valuation and revaluation relies on the subjective ability of experts to make distinctions between styles and individual differences in arts. Even within one artist divergent styles could wreck havoc on objectivity claims. The objects of our attention differ from those of the sciences and social sciences because they are remarkable feats, never repeated. And any exclusive scientism in our discipline has the negative side effect of screening out forces of unpredictable relevance that continually feed into the art of the past as well as the present.

October 1967

Dear James Ackerman,

I am putting down some of the thoughts that occur to me as I ponder your proposed topic, "The Condition of the Humanities." The word "condition" is not mine; in fact, it embarrasses me. Not only does it suggest a pathological state, but it implies that the speaker comes armed with diagnosis and cure; and I want to make no such claims. I will even confess that my field (the study of Renaissance and Baroque art) appears to me sometimes to be in a fairly interesting condition. There is far more good work coming out than I get to read. On the other hand, the bulk of what is now being published, especially by young scholars, seems tedious beyond endurance without being exactly bad; it is all based on A-papers—the sound, unimpeachable output of academic art history. And if this output leaves some of us disappointed, the fault probably lies in our own obsolete expectations. It is *retardataire*[1] to demand traditional humanistic rewards from art historical studies whose concern is the kind of data that should only be scanned, processed, and indexed for convenient retrieval.

Two questions suggest themselves: first, whether this new professionalism should unsurp the whole field; and, second, why it should be the work of young scholars and recent graduates that turns out to be especially tame and conventional. Presumably, our discipline is not now attracting, or holding on to, those younger people who might approach problems with imagination and courage. We prefer on the whole to nurture the other kind. We introduce them to the technology of research and teach them the proper set of questions to ask with respect to art.

A few years ago the new Graduate Center of the City University of New York undertook to redesign some of the university's undergraduate freshman courses. Those of us who were charged with the art historical end of the project began by asking what one should show and tell a group of incoming college freshmen, most of whom might never again be exposed to a formal presentation of art. Our answer in part called for breaking up the regular lecture sequence with talks by young scholars. But we would invite only those who had once asked a new question, evolved a way of pursuing it, and come up with a novel insight. It was part of the plan that this new insight contrast with the traditional interpretation which the student would have found in his book. We wanted the irony; the textbook itself was to be put in a new, somewhat dimmer light. What we were hoping to celebrate was a marriage of art scholarship and adventure.

We got off to a splendid start. Our first guest speaker unfolded a revolutionary interpretation of one of the key monuments of Western art, and the students could be seen holding their breaths in the excitement of seeing it done. The speaker indeed had met all but one of our requirements—that of youth. Her opening remark explained that the first fertile question that had started her on the track of discovery occurred to her during a seminar she took in Hamburg in 1928. Two more guest speakers followed, both passing forty, and then that part of the project collapsed. During scores of professional talks delivered at the annual national conferences of art historians, we listened for new questions asked by young scholars—and gave up at last. It seems that we were trying to sell art history to our freshmen for its pioneer spirit; whereas a pioneer spirit characterizes neither the condition nor even the aspiration of institutionalized art history at this moment.

Institutions cannot, of course, teach people to ask new questions or make them imaginative beyond their gifts. But they do cheer and check. They create a climate of encouragement or disapproval for one set of qualities or another. And to a large extent they predetermine who shall survive the rigors of the environment they create. The value structure of our great graduate schools is familiar. They may still reserve first place for the genius, but lacking genius, they promote the methodical archivist, while the leaper with the unproved hypothesis is encouraged to seek his fortune elsewhere.

The great immigrant European scholars who taught most of us what to teach could afford to lay every stress on objective historical discipline because their humanism was bred in the bone. What the field needed when they were entering it was the corrective of a more rigorous scientism than had ever before been applied to art. And it is because they succeeded that the correctives we need are no longer the same.

Can objectivity be made too much of? When I was a student, a great art historian advised me never to tell my readers or listeners how I came to a problem, or by what steps I proceeded, but to come clean with my findings. His advice has remained so much alive with me that it has urged me ever since to pursue the opposite course. I admire the art historian who lets the ground of his private involvement show. Though we all hope to reach objectively valid conclusions, this purpose is not served by disguising the subjectivity of interest, method, and personal history which in fact conditions our work.

Recently, in a public talk, I heard a senior scholar demonstrate that an important sixteenth-century fresco gained new dimensions of meaning by being referred to an actual site in Rome. Later, in private, he described the circumstances of the first observation that eventually led to his findings. He had climbed a steep Roman hill, had stopped to recover his breath, and turned around with his eyes open. But the ensuing epiphany was censored out of his formal talk, leaving the objective evidence to stand alone. And yet, in this case, the subjective experience pointed to an overwhelmingly important objective fact—namely, that the meaning newly found in the picture had been always accessible, and not only to research scholars, but to every footloose pilgrim in Rome. I suspect that if this excellent scholar had found his own experience of hill-climbing and revelation anticipated in some old traveler's diary, he would have cited it as objective evidence.

The finest among modern art historians seem at times somewhat confused in assessing the historical significance of subjectivity in our field. Let me cite another example taken, as all my examples are, from work that is truly exemplary: John Shearman's *Mannerism*.[2] Its second paragraph introduces the author's methodological credo as follows:

> The contradictions in contemporary meanings for the word "Mannerism" are to a great extent due to the fact that most of them are too contemporary and not sufficiently historical. In the attempt to rescue sixteenth-century art from the ill repute that much of it enjoyed in the nineteenth century, it has been endowed with virtues peculiar to our time—especially the virtues of aggression, anxiety and instability. They are so inappropriate to the works in question that some pretty odd results are bound to follow. . . . My conviction is that Mannerist art is capable of standing on its own feet.

It can and ought to be appreciated or rejected on its *own* terms, and according to its *own* virtues, not ours.

Can one quarrel with such a program? Yes, on one point; because Shearman's historical sense fails to apply itself to his immediate parent generation. His "conviction that Mannerist art is capable of standing on its own feet" is itself unhistorical, unrelated to Mannerism's known afterlife, during which it suffered ridicule and eclipse. Whatever feet of its own it may have had, Mannerism proved incapable of standing on them. A handful of early twentieth-century scholars at last restored it to consideration and admiration, apparently by endowing it with a wrong set of virtues. Mannerism was rehabilitated in a passionate recognition of kinship by men who were experiencing modern European Expressionism.[3] The inappropriateness of the virtues they projected upon this sixteenth-century art sprang from their felt affinity with another age of anxiety. And it was this subjective intuition of kinship that lent motive, energy, and excitement to their explorations. In the end, their subjectivity constitutes nothing less than the historical precondition for the rediscovery of the subject. Therefore it seems both ungenerous and unhistorical to dismiss as mere error and hindrance the subjective projections of these earlier discoverers. An error which discovers a continent is at least as valuable as any later correction.

With the disdain of subjectivity goes the demand that value judgments be eliminated from serious investigations of art since they cannot be objectified. Needless to say, much of the work art historians do is well done only in the objective mood, as in the physical examination of monuments, the searching of archives and texts, or tracing the provenance[4] of an altarpiece by identifying its local saints. No one doubts that value judgments would be a frivolous interference in this sort of work. The point about the general disdain of such judgments is that it tends to bar or belittle any work that is not of this sort. It is not that objectivity is ever misplaced; but that the restriction to objective criteria simply rules out certain interests. Since objective criteria are the given criteria, we are faced with a bid to confine research to the filling out of preformed questionnaires. In protecting art history from subjective judgments, we proscribe the unpredictable question into which value and personality may surely enter, but which pertains to art because of art's protean nature. Our probity in always excluding the speaker resembles, even as it inverts, the piety which in the Middle Ages always included God—as in the equation 2 + 2 (God willing) = 4.

The artistic universe is so thoroughly value-structured that the objectivity claims, were they to be taken seriously, would amount to mere cant. We still operate with the primitive categories "good" "mediocre," and "best." And we constantly make "objective" conclusions flow from the application of these categories, as when we decide that a certain medieval manuscript is of sufficiently superlative quality to be localized in an imperial scriptorium.

A refusal to suspend value judgments may be realistic in its own way. It reminds one that the world of art works is not self-existent, like the animal kingdom, but that the objects of our enquiry depend for their sheer existence on admiration. Art is cherished, or it does not survive. A succession of value judgments, embodied in acts of neglect or preservation, largely determines what we receive from the past. And it is esthetic judgment that largely structures the world of artistic forms at their inception: It was the *best* artists who got the big royal commissions; the *best* architects who came to St. Peter's. Whenever this sureness of valuation breaks down, as in the nineteenth century—when the knighthood bypasses Turner to settle on Sir Edwin Landseer[5]—then the failure to choose what we now regard as the greater value becomes itself the material of history.

To say it in other words, the record of past valuations is integrally part of art history, and that record is meaningless without present revaluation. We know it as an "objective fact" that in the Rome of 1510 the *best* artists enjoyed the greatest acclaim; that in the Paris of 1870 the *best* were passed up;[6] that at the time only the *best* critics knew it; and that the artistic consciousness of our own century rests largely on the universal acknowledgment of those former *misjudgments*. We review and judge all past opinions with more of our own, the process being simply the life and afterlife of all art. If Manet[7] did not seem greater to us than Léon Gérôme,[8] then a history of nineteenth-century painting in France would not even be possible; only an incomplete index of paintings produced.

The professional plea to suspend value judgments is neither wholly honest nor practical, and the pretense that this has ever been done is not realistic. This is self-evident if one considers recent phases of art that have yet to become history, or better still if one thinks of the whole phenomenon of film, in which, at this moment, an entire history of art can be seen foreshortened. The process of structuring the field by constant evaluation has of course been going on steadily, while the historian had his back turned. When he finally turns to confront it, the material he receives will have been qualitatively structured already. He may modify that structure over and over, but he will never unstructure it.

Similarly, in the study of older art forms, we can insulate our discipline against subjective judgments only because we safely enjoy a rich and unrepudiated inheritance of such judgments. "Objectivity" leaves it to others to say why the matter in hand is being studied at all. But who are these others? This is precisely the present challenge to every humanistic curriculum.

An eminent scholar teaching in one of the great universities of Western Europe describes a new low of irreverence attained by his students. "Raphael[9] stinks," they declare. Here then is an occasion to reconsider why Raphael should be in. But how? To what objective data do you appeal? Can his inclusion in the curriculum be justified without admiration, on objective grounds alone, by expounding the power and wealth of his patrons, his fame, his innovations and influence—that is to say, without again choosing him, without passionate reaffirmation of his genius today?

In the light of these considerations, the one-sided professional caution against value judgments and subjectivity in scholarship seems like a strangely perverse assimilation of a humanistic field to alien standards.

I remember a conversation I had with Mr. Philip Pouncey some years ago in the Print Room of the British Museum. Mr. Pouncey is universally recognized as the surest eye in the field of Italian drawings. He was criticizing the normal process of art history education which, he thought, hitched cart to horse in wrong order. Students were taught Raphael before they had learned to tell in a given drawing what made it a Raphael rather than a work of Perino or Giulio. Would it not be wiser, he asked, to start students off with the simple elements of connoisseurship? Should not this be the foundation of all other studies, since it can hardly make sense to study an artist's style, development, or iconography before you have learned how to distinguish the object of your studies? Mr. Pouncey was of course recommending his own kind of connoisseurship as preparation for all other studies in the field. He was doing it with that offhand air that well-bred Englishmen use to deprecate their own skills. It was the merest ABC he was talking about, the trivial but necessary exordium[10] to more ambitious and sophisticated pursuits.

Obviously, Mr. Pouncey deserved better than to have me agree. I therefore suggested that one introductory course in connoisseurship would not produce connoisseurship enough. The sort of perceptiveness in attribution which he had in mind was—as he knew perfectly well—not an elementary attainment, like that of any army recruit who has a course in aircraft recognition behind him. It was rather an ultimate virtuosity, compounded of many gifts and long practice. At this point, the great attributionist, warming to the subject but hushing his voice, confessed that this must indeed be the case, for he had felt again and again how his own sensitivity to distinct drawing styles could be blunted by an absence of even one or two weeks during vacations; how any interruption of his continuous exposure to Italian Renaissance drawings would make him feel—I am quoting his very words—"as if some vital power had departed from me."

It is conceivable that a Linnaeus,[11] or any scientific taxonomist, would describe his ability to differentiate within his field in the language of magic?

Of the late Richard Offner it was said (by Panofsky,[12] summarizing the achievements of "Three Decades of Art History in the United States") that he "developed connoisseurship in the field of the Italian Primitives into the closest possible approximation to an exact science." How close is that? Offner had summoned all his resources to distinguish between non-Giotto and Giotto.[13] Inconclusively: for in the end, it is not scientific exactitude which determines the issue, but an idea about human freedom. The question is how far Giotto, or any trecento artist, or any artist at all, can move willfully from one style to another. No criteria that science lends answer that sort of question.

The question also involves our ideas about the self-consciousness of the creative process. That artists can work in diverse styles simultaneously is a fairly recent discovery. For an older scholar, a stylistic divergence within, say, a Titian[14] altarpiece would have been evidence of interference by studio hands, of incompleteness or of later rework, restoration, etc. Whereas we may read this same variable as evidence that Titian chose to distinguish donors from saints by rendering the adoration of the former in a stiff archaic manner.

Phenomena of stylistic simultaneity are now being reported from every art historical area; and, no doubt, every responsible scholar feels that he finds them in the given evidence. But it seems to me that it is the *style* of mid-twentieth-century scholarship to be finding this evidence, or rather, to interpret the data in terms of simultaneity.

Now, by a curious coincidence, simultaneity of divergent styles—to an extent never dreamt of before—is the outstanding trait of the most powerful artistic *oeuvre* of our century—that of Picasso.[15] Irrelevant? It does indeed sound preposterous to suggest that the question of what Titian could or could not have painted depends, in some remote sense, on the Picasso experience. Such a suggestion would make havoc of our objectivity claims! And yet, if a historian studying an earlier age were to discover in it a formal correspondence between its creative output and its own scholarly methodology, he would surely point to that correspondence as a significant symptom of period character.

The objects of our attention differ from the concerns of physical science in being existential human creations; and they differ from the concerns of social science because (in the cases that interest us the most) they are remarkable feats, never repeated. We do not expect them to demonstrate regularities; to the extent that works of art are subjectively structured by personalities formed in the total experience of both art and life, no one orthodox method at any one time can comprehend them. And any exclusive scientism in our discipline has the negative side effect of screening out forces of unpredictable relevance that continually feed into the art of the past as well as the present. The attempts to cope with more private or more freely metaphorical and evasive aspects of art become professionally suspect. They tend to be left to art writers, popularizers, critics, psychologists—that is, to men who have neither the habits nor the responsibilities of the historian's hard-won methodology, so that their contributions to the literature of art serve to confirm the discredit of the whole enterprise.

Notes

[1] *retardataire:* out of date

[2] *Mannerism* is the name now given to the style prevalent in Italian art from about 1520 to 1590. Prior to the twentieth century, the art from between the death of Raphael and the rise of Carracci and Caravaggio was regarded as decadent. Twentieth-century reevaluation has recognized that the style now identified as mannerist is characterized by painters deriving their conceptions not from nature but from intellectual conceptions modified by aesthetic considerations and by the study of other artworks.

[3] Modern European Expressionism, whose hallmarks are distortion, fragmented communication, and violent overstressed emotion, began in Germany between 1910 and 1924.

[4] provenance: origins

[5] Joseph Turner (1775–1851), an English Romantic landscape artist, pioneered the study of light, color, and atmosphere. Sir Edwin Henry Landseer (1802–1873), also a landscape painter, was inferior to Turner, even though he enjoyed a good reputation for some time.

⁶ In Paris in the 1870s the new Impressionist movement, which revolutionized painting, met with critical disapprobation.

⁷ Edouard Manet (1832–1883), a French painter, led the Impressionist movement. Manet's credo was "only one thing is real, paint what you see the very first time."

⁸ Léon Gérôme (1824–1904) was a contemporary of the Impressionists whose work remained traditional.

⁹ Raphael (1483–1520), an Italian Florentine painter, shares with Michelangelo and da Vinci the reputation as the three greatest and most representative artists of the High Renaissance.

¹⁰ exordium: an introduction to a discourse.

¹¹ Carolus Linnaeus (1707–1778), a Swedish botanist, was the first to state the principles for defining species and genera for biological classification.

¹² Erwin Panofsky is an art historian whose work during the first half of the twentieth century significantly influenced later art history studies.

¹³ Giotto (1266–1337) was an Italian Florentine painter whose ambition to depict men and objects realistically with mass and dimension marks him as the first modern painter.

¹⁴ Titian (1477–1576), an Italian Venetian painter, is considered the eminent representative of the Venetian Baroque style, remarkable for its ample nudes, late-afternoon sensual landscapes, and langorous flesh.

¹⁵ Pablo Picasso (1881–1973), born in Spain, was perhaps the best-known modern painter. He painted in several twentieth-century styles: neoclassicism, primitivism, and cubism.

FOCUS: READING REVIEW

1. Steinberg identifies the concern of art historical studies with "the kind of data that should only be scanned, processed, and indexed for convenient retrieval." To what kind of information does he refer? How does this differ from his own "humanistic expectations"?

2. The author says he would like to "sell art history for its pioneer spirit." How might art history have a pioneer spirit?

3. The author uses "scientism" to refer to objective art historical studies. What is it? Why was this approach introduced? What would be the alternative?

4. How does the example of mannerism's reputation illustrate the relation of objectivity and subjectivity in art historical studies?

5. In what ways are art historical studies value structured?

6. How are records of past valuations integrally part of art history?

7. How does the object of the art historian's attention differ from that of the physical or social scientist's?

FOCUS: AUTHOR'S STRATEGIES

1. This selection was written as a letter. What is the stated purpose? What other ends does it accomplish?

2. Although the tone is fairly formal, the author presents a clear persona. What is it? What in the essay reveals it?

FOCUS: DISCUSSION AND WRITING

1. Explain how art studies can be objective. Do you agree that subjectivity is important? Why?
2. Define scientism, and argue for or against the necessity of scientism as a way of approaching knowledge.

TOPICS: **Further Research, Synthesis, and Writing in the Arts and Literature**

1. Frye advances the view that literary studies can be objective. Select an essay on literature. Identify the kind of evidence used in the study. Is the treatment subjective or objective? Write an essay in which you advance a thesis on the value of objectivity for literature studies based on the evidence from your investigation.

2. What value does knowledge of an artist's life lend to a discussion of his or her art? Find good color reproductions of da Vinci's *Mona Lisa* and *Last Supper;* then reconsider Pater's and Gombrich's essays. Write an essay in which you explain how knowledge of an artist's life does or does not increase understanding of art based on these paintings and the essays about them.

3. Writing about film requires concise, vivid description and careful analytical abilities. Consider these elements in Kael's essay. Using this as a model, write a review for your college newspaper of a recent film.

4. As Didion's essay suggests, the environment in which we view art affects our response to the art. Visit an art gallery or museum. Before you go make a list of environmental features you will look for—light, color, space, decor. Carefully observe these elements separate from the art collection, and then consider the art in relation to the environment. Write an essay in which you describe and evaluate the relationship between art and environment in that gallery. You may write this as a review for a local publication, or you may write it as a study recommending changes.

5. Read Shakespeare's *Macbeth* carefully. Then find two other views of Lady Macbeth besides Bradley's. Compare and contrast the three views, being careful to note the kinds of arguments the writers construct and the kinds of evidence they use to support their arguments. Write an essay assessing the importance of Lady Macbeth in Shakespeare's play. You may offer your own interpretation, argue in favor of one of the other writer's positions, or offer a synthesis of the various views.

6. Frye, Booth, Sontag, and Steinberg all address the question of subjectivity and objectivity in the relationship between the student of art and art itself. Write an essay on the value of objectivity or subjectivity, relying on the essays here for evidence.

7. Implicit in nearly every essay in the art and literature chapters is the idea that knowledge about an artwork enriches the reader/viewer/listener's experience. Prepare for a research project on a particular work of art by establishing categories of knowledge related to art—the artist's life, his other work, the art movement and country in which the artist worked, the political environment, and so forth. Select a novel, poem, play, painting, sculpture, musical composition, film, or building, and research all the categories of related knowledge you have identified. Write a paper in which you explain this background and analyze its influence on the artist. Include a discussion of how this knowledge increases your understanding of the art object.

Subject Index

Index of Names and Titles